HISTORY OF THEOLOGY

III
The Renaissance

HISTORY OF THEOLOGY

III
The Renaissance

Edited by
Giulio D'Onofrio

Translated by
Matthew J. O'Connell

A Michael Glazier Book
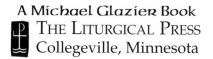
THE LITURGICAL PRESS
Collegeville, Minnesota

A Michael Glazier Book published by The Liturgical Press

Cover design by David Manahan, O.S.B.

This book was originally published in Italian under the title *Storia della Teologia, III, Età della Rinascita* © 1995 by EDIZIONI PIEMME Spa (Via del Carmine 5, 15033 Casale Monferrato (AL), Italy. All rights reserved.

1	2	3	4	5	6	7	8

Library of Congress Cataloging-in-Publication Data

Storia della teologia. English.
   History of theology / edited by Angelo Di Berardino and Basil
Studer ; translated by Matthew J. O'Connell.
      p.   cm.
   Includes bibliographical references and index.
   Contents: I. The patristic period.
   ISBN 0-8146-5915-2
   ISBN 0-8146-5917-9 (vol. III)
    1. Theology, Doctrinal—History. 2. Catholic Church—Doctrines—
History. I. Di Berardino, Angelo.   II. Studer, Basil, 1925–
III. Title.
BT21.2.S7613   1996
230'.09—DC20   96-42160
                                                CIP

Contents

A Note on Proper Names of Persons

This book contains a great many names of theologians and philosophers, Italian, Spanish, French, German, and others. The Italian text gives the first names of all of them in an Italian form. I have given them all English first names. Names of rulers, painters, architects, and so on, especially in the Chronological Tables, are given in the form customary in history books. Thus: Lawrence Valla, but Lorenzo de'Medici; Peter Pomponazzi, but Piero della Francesca. [Tr.]

Introduction

Giulio D'Onofrio

In the triumph of theology as depicted by Raphael Sanzio in his fresco in the Stanze della Segnatura, the glorification of the eucharistic mystery by both the triumphant and the militant churches dissolves into a contrast between the harmonious council of saints who are contemplating the majesty of Christ in the upper half of the picture and the lively discussion going on among the doctors who, in the lower half, are carrying on a spirited debate around the Most Holy Sacrament exposed on the altar. The name, *Debate About the Sacrament,* which quickly became the popular title of the work, corresponds, therefore, only partially to what the painter intended to celebrate. But the humanists of the Curia, who were advising the painter from Urbino in his plans for the cycle of pictures in the Stanze Vaticane, were perhaps not unaware of how suitable the image of a debate was in depicting the lack of agreement between doctrines and opinions that still marked the discussion of theology in the West at the beginning of the sixteenth century, despite the continual calls for theological harmony that had been repeated throughout Christendom for more than a century and a half.[1]

In fact, what we see in the history of theological thought during the period from the convocation of the Council of Constance to the first meetings of the Council of Trent cannot but show the intellectual uneasiness that was bemoaned by the leaders of religious thought, irritated as they were by the open contradiction between the many conciliar undertakings aimed at peace in the Church and the perpetuation of divisions.[2] If we start with Petrarch's appeal to the pope, that the Holy See should return and give the Roman tradition its proper central place,[3] and if we review the writings and speeches of authors "who were" active at Constance (1414–18), Basel (from 1431 on), the reunion Council of Ferrara-Florence-Rome (1438–45), and down to the convocation of

1

the Fifth Lateran Council (1512–17), we find that the theme which inspired the thinking and activity of all who were devoted to the healing of Christian society was the exhortation to the restoration of unity. They meant the restoration of the now lost *unanimitas* (oneness of mind) that, from Augustine on, had been the support and the very reason for the existence of medieval Christendom and that, beginning with the tragic events of the schism, seemed condemned to disappear in a continual alternation of ruptures and laborious but sensitive recoveries of balance, until the final, irreversible blow was inflicted by the Protestant Reformation. And while the irremediable opposition between conciliarism and papal theocracy went on and on, the lack of politico-ecclesiastical unity placed a heavy burden on the work of the theologians, who were from time to time given the task of finding arguments in defense of the irreconcilable doctrinal positions which the conflicting sides were maintaining.

From the beginning of the fifteenth century on, the realization of the inability to resolve the crisis that was fragmenting the unity of Christendom found expression in an urgent call for a renewal of the methods, themes, and purposes of theological thought. The call was issued from many quarters and paralleled the widespread and frequent exhortations to reform of the Church, as well as the incipient challenge of the first humanists to the degradation of letters and the Scholastic monopoly of education. The tainted root of the religious ruptures in the Christian world lay, in fact, in the pulsing heart of the official theology, that is, in the university faculties, which were being scourged by a division of schools in a debate back and forth on methods and doctrines.[4]

But despite the common desire to heal the situation of dissension among the theologians and despite the series of empty formal proclamations that unity had been restored at conciliar meetings, divisions and reasons for debate keep multiplying throughout the fifteenth century. And then in 1517, only a few months after the close of the Lateran Council, which proclaimed for the umpteenth time that the kingdoms of Europe were united in a crusade against the Turks, when we see Martin Luther publishing his ninety-five theses, thereby initiating the definitive religious division of modern Christendom, we have almost the impression of being present at the end of a process begun a hundred years earlier with the condemnation of Huss and Jerome of Prague and the severance of the Bohemian church at the assembly in Constance, although this council supposedly had for its purpose to restore unity. Even the very basis of Luther's theological thinking, namely, the principle of a total separation of opposites (of the divine from the human, the particular from the universal, completely unmerited redemption from merits obtained by works), was in the final analysis nothing but a conscious acceptance of the irremediable rupture in the theoretical axis that should have linked human being and God, Creator and creature, as intended by a long tradition of theologians in Western Christendom, from John Scotus Eriugena to Nicholas of Cusa.[5]

It is fitting, then, that we should ask whether and in what measure the Renaissance plan for the reform of theology, while it admittedly did not lead to the reunification of Christendom as initially desired, did go beyond the mere criticism of Scholastic science that was the starting point for the theologians of the fifteenth century and the first half of the sixteenth, and achieve a fruitful renewal of perspectives, methods, and tools for reflection on the faith.

It is possible to show, from various angles, numerous points of contact between the crisis with which the Middle Ages ended and which seemed to continue through the hundred and fifty years of the Renaissance period, even while a way out of it was being sought, and that other, distant crisis that had rent the unity of the Roman world of late antiquity a thousand years before. At that earlier time, too, the breakdown of a sound ideological and administrative system into a fragmented jumble of peoples and cultures had in fact revealed, under the surface of a world in agony, the slow genesis of a new universe in which the civil community sought to win new life by trust in the cohesive power and ethical message of the Christian religion. At the end of the Middle Ages, however, the situation was inverted, since what was now on the point of dying was the civilization that had been born under the Carolingians with the creation of Europe's Christian cultural and political identity.

This development was attested, consciously or not, by many men of letters during the fifteenth and sixteenth centuries, men moved by a sincere interest in the monuments, testimonies, and historical works of the Roman imperial decline, in which they saw another example of a laborious effort to revive a broken system that was trying to achieve a rebirth. But this same perspective can be seen as confirming and clarifying the renewed interest of the Renaissance theologians in the works of the Fathers of the Church, who had been direct observers of the serious crisis of the Roman world and had evaluated this precisely from the standpoint of a theology of history. For the humanists the patristic sources were no longer simply *auctoritates* (authorities) to be regularly cited in support of the technical divisions of the *quaestiones* (questions) under discussion. They were also evidences of another way of thinking that followed freer and more fruitful criteria than those rigidly fixed by medieval Aristotelean rationalism.

This new relationship with the patristic model was one of the basic innovations in theological thought in the Renaissance period as compared with the Middle Ages. Even though in the light of studies done in recent decades it is no longer permissible to reduce Scholastic theology exclusively to a heightened kind of rationalistic formalism,[6] there is no denying that in their activity the *magistri* (masters of theology) of the later Middle Ages set a greater value on methodology as compared with the content of sacred doctrine. By contrast, the humanists' search for new room in which to move and a new, freer, and more expansive approach in their meditation on sacred Scripture led to a triumphal return to the way of discoursing on the faith that had been proper to the patristic age and, later, to the early Middle Ages. Thus, just as the formal perfection of the classical writers was rediscovered behind the barbarization of the Latin language that had occurred amid the imperfections and shabbiness of the medieval Gothic world, so too the discovery was made that the emphasis on dialectics in Scholastic theological science had been preceded, in the works of the Fathers, by a more direct and effective approach of the human mind to the truths of the faith and, consequently, by a better cognitive representation of divine truth to human beings.[7] The Fathers, therefore, together with a few leading theologians of the early Middle Ages such as Boethius and Anselm, became the classics of humanist theology.

Medieval Scholastic wisdom had not been free of classicism, this last being understood as the knowledge and use of the formal and speculative models of the past. Proof of this is the simple fact that while the methodical and planned use of an ancient model of thought, the Aristotelean, was the main cause of methodological immobilism for the majority of the *magistri,* it also provided the thirteenth and fourteenth centuries with its main intellectual food. But even in this area, perhaps more than in others, it is advisable to distinguish between medieval classicism and Renaissance classicism.

Down to the fourteenth century inclusive, the use of the works of antiquity was limited to the search for ideas, materials, and tools that were to be integrated into a system of knowledge and reflection that was already firmly established. Even the best known and widely read classics such as Virgil and Cicero, once purged of elements inherent in the pagan religious spirit, were accepted by the Middle Ages as though they were contemporary interlocutors, and their authors were mentally represented, even in their external garb and attitudes, as men of that time and not of antiquity.

In the humanistic renewal, on the other hand, love of the classics took on a new and hitherto unknown dimension: the history of philosophical and theological antiquity (that is, to generalize somewhat, Aristotle and Augustine) was now investigated precisely as the history of the past and relieved of modernizing encrustations. In theology, the most important result of this new kind of approach was the discovery that it was possible to apply philological criticism to the earliest expressions of Christian wisdom. In addition to the manuscripts of the poets and writers of antiquity, those of the Fathers, too, were searched out, collected, collated, and corrected; even the writing desk of the theologians was often transformed into a laboratory in which studies of the original texts of the patristic sources were carried on.[8] In a further step, the same method was extended even to biblical revelation.

One result was that not infrequently the philological work was combined with popularization. The theologian-philologists, who were concerned to recover the original, pure form of patristic texts and of the Scriptures behind the mistaken readings introduced by commentaries, translations, and corruptions of the manuscript tradition, also felt responsible for making these originals accessible to the widest possible public. And within the complicated process whereby the laity became involved—a process begun with the spread of the *Devotio moderna* and then marked by successive and more widespread manifestations of popular religious feeling such as the epic deeds of Joan of Arc, the devotion of the Bianchi, and the Piagnoni movement, down to the evangelical movements resulting from the preaching of the Reformation—a fundamental part was played by that very important and sensitive instrument, the vernacular tongue. This was used first of all in translating the sacred Scriptures and the writings of the Fathers and then, even more directly, in composing the works of the new theology.

Precisely in this expansion of the beneficiaries of the theological patrimony, hitherto strictly reserved to a few specialists who were authorized to practice and absorb it, there lurked, however, some very risky outcomes that might not only favor but also bring discredit on the projected rebirth of studies. Above all, there was the danger that philology might claim to reduce to human dimensions the sacred untouchableness of the authority of Scripture and the dignity of traditional doctrine by showing the latter to be a detrimental anthropomorphization of the sacred. Such an outcome would be no less perilous than the domination of logic in the Scholastic *magistri* had been. The danger can be glimpsed, for example, when doubts began to emerge about the authenticity of fundamental pillars of religious wisdom, such as the writings in the Corpus Areopagiticum, or of ecclesiastical tradition, such as the Donation of Constantine. There was also the danger that the use of the vernaculars in theology could have as a consequence a renewed impossibility of maintaining doctrinal uniformity among the various nationalities. The abandonment of Latin and the ability it gave the wise to communicate with one another could also lead to new difficulties in communication among all parties and to doctrinal obstinacies as cultures and traditions became more differentiated. An example was the denunciation uttered by John Huss, before the pyre was lit that silenced him forever, against judges who by their own admission were unable to read what he had written in the Czech language for his faithful.

In order to prevent these dangers, it was necessary that the application of the philological method to theological wisdom never forget that it was a means, and never presume to make itself the goal of the interpreter's task. This meant that despite their taste for linguistic forms, theologians must never forget that their task was to show, from the documents of revelation and the earliest and most authoritative meditations on them, the priceless self-manifestation in history of that uniquely true word, the Word of God, which no human language can ever pronounce but from which all true words in the multitude of human languages derive their partial truth.

One of the main aims, then, that inspired the work of the Renaissance theologians was best expressed in the formula of Erasmus of Rotterdam: "Theology is not possible apart from philology." The aim seems to have been to reconnect the understanding of the faith as far as possible with the irre-placeable depths of the scriptural message, and this precisely in order to free it of enslavement to a scientific rationality, that of Aristotelean Scholasticism, which was only one of the countless forms in which the divine Logos takes flesh and is circulated through creation. As a result of this deliverance, there would be access to all the other possible ways of knowing the suprasensible, all of them useful for bringing human beings to the truth but all of them al-ways erroneous when they claim to replace the truth. And in fact, thanks to the philological approach, humanity was shown other ways, besides dialectics, of approaching the truth; these could open up a variety of paths on which the foundations of theology could just as well be laid. Theology is not one kind of thinking among others, nor is it a science limited to a narrow and specific field of study; it cannot have just a single method or a single kind of exact proof. In all of its highest manifestations, theological thought is always a human meditation on revelation and can be carried on with all available tools and in all the forms which God has put at the mind's disposition for knowing the created world and seeing the Creator present in it.

The lively Renaissance discussions of the possibility of proving the soul's immortality or of defining in metaphysical formulas the ineffable change that takes place in the eucharistic consecration are sufficiently clear evidence of how doubt about the licitness of demonstrating the dogmas of faith could be liberating for theology; theology was thereby urged to reflect on its own lim-itations and therefore also on its own real competence and possibilities. For the theologians of the Renaissance, this meant going back and making their own the moderately skeptical attitude which Augustine saw as basic to the "true philosophy" available to Christians, that is, the wisdom that does not at-tempt by its own powers to ascertain the inmost depths of a truth that is of its nature hidden but has been made known to human beings through revelation.[9]

The revival of philosophical skepticism during the fifteenth to the seven-teenth centuries had its origin in the rediscovery of Sextus Empiricus and spread from the Florence of Savonarola and John Francis Pico to France and ultimately to Montaigne.[10] But in some of its aspects it resulted naturally from the critical maturation of the initial distancing of the early-fifteenth-century humanists from the dogmatism and mental rigidity of the Scholastics. We do not know whether Montaigne had read the *Examen vanitatis doctrinae gen-tium* of John Francis Pico, although the author saw to its circulation in France and dedicated a copy to Lefèvre d'Étaples. But it was certainly from the pre-ceding generation of French humanists that Montaigne acquired his special interest in the *Liber creaturarum* of Raymund Sibiuda (or Sabunde), in which he claims to have found a stimulus to and suggestions for developing a method of acquiring truth that was based solely on direct observation of na-ture and did not involve grammar or logic or any other liberal art or even any dependence on Scripture.[11] The attitude, therefore, of doubt that was widespread in the theological world of the Renaissance was clearly not a radical "skepticism" or an end in itself, but rather a moderate "probabilism" that had for its purpose to limit the presumptuousness of the *magistri* and open the way to enrichments coming from other ways of knowing besides the rationalistic method given such a privileged place in the schools. Montaigne himself expressly admits that Sibiuda's methods make the reader "want the dogmas to be true." This basing of theological study more on the hope of truth than on the presumption of acquiring certainty through rational methods cannot help but remind us of the similar renunciation of radically rational methods of demonstration that led Pietro Pomponazzi to attribute to the human soul, and to the theologian who reflects on the nature of the soul, a "desire" for immortality.

A concrete application of this theological probabilism inspired the acquisition of Christian learning through a broad use of the contribution of the patristic sources, such as we see in a little work, significantly entitled *De vera philosophia,* of Adrian Castellesi. But an even more explicit example of how the methodical adoption of the probabilistic outlook could lead to the rediscovery of a unified Christian wisdom, in which the disagreements of the theologians were overcome and reconciled, can be found in a passage of Thomas More. Responding to the observation that the holy Doctors sometimes disagree, the author says that the reason for their possible differences is the limits of the human cognoscitive intellect, in even the holiest and best prepared of thinkers. Therefore scholars who tackle the pages of the Fathers and Doctors with an honest awareness of the natural deficiencies of language and writings, but at the same time with a careful philological method that guarantees the restoration of the true meaning of the words, can easily find unity through the gift of the divine Spirit. For this Spirit leads the wise by different ways to knowledge of the faith, but this diversity does not mean that they are less "of one mind" in regard to the truth.[12]

To sum up, theological probabilism bids us consider all the conquests of the rational mind, and therefore all the conclusions formulated by the scientific disciplines such as logic, mathematics, and metaphysics, but also those reached by speculative theology, to be always and everywhere simply likely or probable, that is, true only to the extent that they imperfectly represent a truth unknowable in itself and guaranteed only by faith. Consequently, every science is true only in the sphere and within the limits proper to it. Theology, insofar as it is the "queen of the sciences" (as the Scholastic taught), has the task of confirming the (probable) results reached by the lesser sciences, and this within the higher, inclusive, and adaptive framework that only a wisdom based on the certainty of the faith is able to develop.

Such is the outlook that we find, for example, toward the end of the Renaissance period, in what Lutheran Andreas Osiander says in his famous *Praefatio ad lectorem* to Nicholas Copernicus' *De revolutionibus orbium caelestium.* He proposes to regard heliocentrism as a hypothesis that is mathematically correct (and therefore probable) but not necessarily true; for while the astronomer is satisfied with the reliability of his calculations, and the philosopher seeks to acquire probability, "neither of the two, however, reaches or teaches the understanding of any certainty, unless it is revealed to them by God."[13]

By establishing for itself the boundaries not to be crossed, instead of insisting on the certainties it reaches, the new theology bids thinkers consider the entire history of human understanding as a common journey toward the recovery—to be definitively completed only in the state of beatitude—of the original harmony between natural knowledge and dialogue with God, that is, of the accord, which all theologians seek, between reason and faith. All the truly wise human beings, of every age and civilization, can therefore be recognized, in the light of this universal "concordism," as both prophets and persons of learning, provided that modern theologians do not lose sight of the limits of their teaching, especially at the point when they are trying to track down, gather up, and put together the fruits of this teaching in a comprehensive synthesis which, the more inclusive it is, shows all the more clearly the harmony between the parts and the whole.

Concordism is an evolving theme that accompanies all the phases of the history of Renaissance thought. From Albertino Mussato and Boccaccio to the *De laboribus Herculis* of Salutati, it takes its first steps by rehabilitating pagan poetry, which expresses, in imaginative form, truths that rational theology is not successful in grasping.[14] The theme is expanded in the debate on the agreement between Plato and Aristotle.[15] It reaches maturity in the celebration of the *pia philosophia* (devout philosophy) by Marsilius Ficino, John Pico, and Giles of Viterbo, who bring into a single synthesis the ancient insights of the *prisci theologi* (earliest theologians) and the subtle arguments of the *magistri moderni* (modern masters). Finally, the theme leads to the idea of the *perennis philosophia* (perennial philosophy) of Augustine Steuco.

The task of providing internal justification for this eclectic, faith-regulated synthesis of the humanists is, significantly, entrusted by many Renaissance writers and in particular by Marsilius Ficino, to Platonic speculation, the "true philosophy" that comes from the same divine source as "true religion." The Platonists' exhortation to recognize the divine nature of truth is in fact the presupposition that justifies the admission of the human mind's inability to reach and represent the ultimate reality of things by means either of the imagination or of concepts.[16] Conversely, the principle of the Aristotelean science of cognition—that knowledge must be reducible to a conformity of the mind to the nature of things through the interior formulation of a formal definition of the object—is utterly unusable for the purposes of the theologian, since it claims to reduce the divine object to the finite dimensions of the human subject.

Platonism thus introduced into Renaissance thought an inversion of the gnoseological perspective that was dominant in Scholastic speculation and thereby also a different conception of knowledge, one based on a tripartite hierarchical ordering of the soul's faculties. At the lowest level is the corporeal and image-producing knowledge proper to the senses; it is limited to individuals and their accidental manifestations. At an intermediate level is rational, discursive, and demonstrative knowledge *(ratio* or *dianoia),* which fixes the concepts resulting from abstraction by subjecting them to the rules of logic, and which proceeds by way of successive definitions and deductions. Finally, beyond reasoning, there is intellectual knowledge *(intellectus* or *nous),* which introduces the mind to an unmediated contemplation of what is true: a direct and comprehensive vision that is completely separated from the senses but also, for that reason, cannot be fixed or expressed, since it cannot be subjected to the reductive conditions of logical definition. This doctrine, which originated in the thought of the ancient Neoplatonists, is the same as that which, after being passed on to the Alexandrian Fathers and Augustine, inspired the theologico-philosophical reflection of the late patristic period and the early Middle Ages, from Boethius to John Scotus Eriugena and Anselm (that is, until it was replaced by the later prevailing Aristotelean epistemology). It was, however, also kept alive in some isolated parts of more recent Scholastic wisdom, for example, in the Pseudo-Dionysian tradition, in the Albertinism of Cologne, and in Lullism.

The humanists of the Renaissance, on their journey back to the wisdom of the ancient philosophers and the Fathers of the Church, found in the fruitful dynamics of this tripartite gnoseology a useful tool by which the theological mind was given new and superior ways of correctly approaching the truth. Dianoetic reason was, in fact, incapable of directly grasping the perfection of the divine, but it showed its usefulness when it was applied to explaining and clarifying the unmediated and ineffable contents of the noetic intellect's unified intuition, which could not otherwise be known in a distinct way or communicated in intelligible language. Reason was thereby exhorted to acknowledge its inferiority and subordination to the *nous* and to exercise, in relation to *nous,* the same function that Scholastic theology called upon it to exercise in relation to the faith, that is, to explain and clarify the content of a knowledge which it could never be able to gain by its own unaided powers. Here we have the reason why all the conclusions developed by the masters of speculative theology were only probable: all were imperfect attempts at a dianoetic-rational explanation and organization of dogma, but none of them was true, except to the extent that it allowed itself to be led by noetic-intellectual intuition, which operates on a higher plane, to a harmony with the true understanding of the faith, in which all disagreements can be reconciled. The concordist synthesis that nourished Renaissance thought represented, then, a comprehensive effort on the part of theologians to use the results of human philosophical and theological wisdom in the restoration, as far as this is possible, of the higher oneness of truth as grasped by noetic intuition and by faith.

This reversal of the epistemological and gnoseological parameters current in Scholasticism restored the same philosophical perspective that, at the beginning of the Middle Ages, had guided Boethius in his *Consolatio philosophiae,* as he did away, by means of a noetic intuition of the freedom of cosmic providence, with the seeming inevitability of fate. It is especially significant, therefore, that we find an explicit return to this same perspective in the *Consolatio theologiae* which John Gerson wrote while in exile after the close of the Council of Constance and which by its very title was set over against Boethius' work, as though claiming to replace it.[17] Gerson calls upon theology as a consolation for the schismatic wounds that have been opened up in Christendom. His starting point is precisely the observation that an autonomous philosophy, especially when it claims to impose its own rules on theological learning, has led only to the formulation of one-sided and prejudicial hypotheses about God; these in turn have caused error every time that pseudo-theologians have taken up one or the other and regarded them as irrefutable positions.[18]

Reinterpreting Boethius, Gerson urges acceptance of the fact that true theology, which is on a higher level than philosophy (springing as the latter does from *ratio*), must identify itself with noetic knowledge. As to the mysteries of the truth, "many astrologers, physicians, and philosophers have had a good deal to say, with the last-named differing and contradicting one another; so too have many poets, practicioners of magic, false prophets, and idolaters." But theology, from its higher vantage point, "first accepts from all these speakers what they have said that is probable, while rejecting everything that is improbable; it brings such truths together and combines them into a unity, thereby making available as much of the truth as is possible for human beings under the conditions of earthly life and of a nature corrupted by sin."[19] This "intellectual operation" leads human beings to the same cognoscitive level as the angels even if it must then necessarily fall back on dianoetic tools in order to express its contents,[20] "understanding pure and simple, without movement or discourse" must always be the common aspiration of all true theologians during this earthly life.[21]

As Cassirer's studies have shown, the reversal of cognitive relationships between subject and object found one of its most effective expressions in the work of Nicholas of Cusa.[22] Here the significance and limitations of the contribution of dianoetic reason to the logical formulation of the contents of the faith as intuited by the intellect are outlined with a technical precision never before achieved. In Nicholas' thinking, the idea that all philosophies (and all philosophical theologies) can be brought together in the higher unity of noetic knowledge is extended to the acknowledgment that even the various religions of history have been attempts by natural reason to approach the divine and that all of them can therefore be welcomed as bearers of partial truths, provided that these truths can be assimilated to the one true intellectual theology, the

Christian, which seeks harmony between the human intelligence and the eternal truth in the divine mind, that is, the Word. Only in this way will it be possible to bring about in the minds of Christians the same *concordantia catholica* or universal harmony (this is the title of one of his most important works) that reigns everywhere in creation thanks to the *coincidentia oppositorum* ("synthesis of opposites") which by the divine will exists in the cosmic harmony.[23]

The form that such a final reunification of the religious universe might take is described by Nicholas, with a splendid combination of speculative wisdom and poetic imagination, in a short work entitled *De pace fidei*.[24] The author introduces, in dialogue form, the story of a vision that occurred in a well-defined condition of *intellectualis altitudo* (elevation of intellect). At a heavenly council, which is as it were the response of authentic theology to the failures of earthly ecclesiastical assemblies in search of unity, wise men from the most diverse cultural, philosophical, and confessional backgrounds are united around God in everlasting peace. One after the other enters into dialogue with the Word/divine Intellect, and all are brought to understand how much partial truth they possess in their respective doctrinal positions and, furthermore, the degree to which it is possible for their minds, still immersed in multiplicity and contradiction, to return to unity, by modeling themselves on the exemplar, the divine suprarationality. Thus both the Greek and the Italian, who are the ambassadors of the philosophical learning of antiquity, admit that each of them participates only partially and in diverse ways in true wisdom, which in itself is undivided and unchangeable. The Indian, lover of mathematico-geometric study, is urged to contemplate the perfect harmony that the intellect discovers in the accord of unity and trinity in the divine Persons, while the Jewish and Islamic monotheists acknowledge the greater fruitfulness of this dynamic identity as compared with the immobility of a unity that can produce nothing other than itself. Toward the end of the work the Bohemian Hussite agrees with the substance of Pauline teaching on the Eucharist, and the English Lollard accepts the truth of the other sacraments, while from on high all are given permission to preserve their differences in ceremonial, since conformity is made impossible by the diversity of their cultures and traditions. In this way, the harmony of all religions in a single faith is sanctioned in the heaven of suprarationality and, with it, the harmony of all theologies in a single truth.[25]

Cusa wrote this ideal celebration of religious unity and peace at a time when the memory of the recent fall of Constantinople was still very painful. A few years later, humanist Aeneas Silvius Piccolomini, a tireless promotor of Catholic peace who had become pope with the name of Pius II, gave Nicholas the task of opposing the oppression by the Turks, thus putting him in open contradiction to the religious concordism which he proclaimed in his *De pace fidei*. Nicholas was to do this both by means of a theological refutation of

Islam that led to the writing of his *Cribratio Alcorani* and, on the practical side, by preaching a crusade and making preparations for it.[26] A short time afterward, however, Nicholas' ideal of universal harmony inspired the same pope to write a letter to the Turkish sultan, Muhammad II. Unlike other such documents composed in the West during this period, all of which were enlivened by the condemnation and demonization of the adversary, in this exceptional testimony (perhaps never actually sent to the addressee) Piccolomini again proposes the approach of dialogue with the Muhammedans (an approach advocated, quite some time ago, even if without any great effect on historical events, by Lullism). He offers the sultan the seemingly quite absurd invitation to convert to the Christian faith, along with all of his people, and in this way restore peace in the world.[27]

Like his theological thought, Piccolomini's life and political activity were constantly inspired by the anxious desire to restore the fragile unity of the Catholic world. He explicitly assigns the responsibility for movement in the opposite direction to the presumptuous and subversive theology of the schools. "Among errors against the faith is there any that did not come from the theologians? Who introduced the Arian madness that separated the Greeks from the Church? Who led the Bohemians astray, if not the theologians?"[28] He also regards it as necessary to locate the guarantee of peace in the power of a doctrinal authority that rises above all partialities and ideologies. In his youth he embraced the conciliarist thesis of Basel, under the illusion that only a theocratic republic could ensure peace, including theological and religious peace, among the peoples. But once he had ascended the papal throne, he came to the conviction that the preservation of religion and of Christian ethical principles must be entrusted to the unifying power of an absolute monarchy. This would exercise the needed control over the interpretation of the faith and would thereby make it possible for theologians to find in the restored absoluteness of dogma the basis for the spiritual reunification which the masters of theology and the conciliar assemblies were no longer able to secure.[29]

It was, therefore, also in obedience to this fundamental inspiration that, as head of a recently reunified Roman Church, Piccolomini was anxious to give a role and an identity once again to the empire, the second universal authority, which God had established to support and defend the political and cultural unity of the Middle Ages. Thus the anomalous invitation to the sultan of Turks to take peaceful possession, with the forces of Christ, of the entire civilization which he was now attempting to destroy with the bloody weapons of conquest, was only one element, perhaps the most extreme but for that very reason one of the most significant, in the pope's anxious desire to overcome divisions and restore the lost unity. "All Christians will revere you and make you judge in their quarrels. . . . As a result, universal peace would come about, the Christian people throughout the world would rejoice, and there would be a return to the age of Augustus and to the times which the poets call the golden age." In the pope's wishful thinking, however, it was not either reason of state or political advantage that were to be the real motive of the sultan's conversion: rather it was theological argument, along the lines indicated in Nicholas' dialogue on ecumenism, that was to lead to the realization of universal unity. As soon as Muhammad II would yield his will and make the decisive act of faith, Christian theologians would be in a position to show him and his very numerous subjects the ultimate reasonableness of the truth brought by Christ, that authentic wisdom which every human being from time immemorial has desired and sought. Constantine, Clovis, Charlemagne, and Stephen of Hungary are invoked as precedents, showing how the sultan, too, can become the founder of a renewed city of God by restoring theological unity: "Like them, you too will surely be most renowned, if, as a wise man, you join us in worshiping the one Christ."

About sixty years later, Charles of Habsburg was crowned emperor at Aachen, in the suggestive Carolingian setting in which the glory of the first Charles, the creator of medieval concord *(unanimitas)* was revived. But the political, religious, and cultural venture of Charles V, with its universalist aim, was soon halted by the impossible task of imposing peace along with the faith in a world too thoroughly divided by the one-sided perspectives created by the interests of persons and nations. When, in 1555, against the will and efforts of the Holy See, the Peace of Augsburg accepted that there was no political remedy for the ideological division, Nicholas of Cusa's and Pius II's dream of unity faded away for good.

Witnesses to this development were the Christian heretics of the sixteenth-century diaspora, the Reformed preachers and theologians, the majority of them of Italian birth, who were unwilling to fit into any of the new Protestant ecclesiastical structures and were consequently tormented by a double intolerance, that of both the Catholics and the Calvinists. Elements of the Cusan ecumenical ideal appear in their work: the invitation to let reason play its moderating role, along with the plea for tolerance, but not any longer any desire for religious unification, which these men can henceforth see only as violence and as an attack on the dignity and freedom of individuals in their direct relationship with God. Since intolerance was a result of the certainty of possessing the truth, the extreme recourse to authority seemed to Pius II to be the only way of obtaining peace. But in the personal tragedy of the first "Churchless Christians" of the sixteenth century, this recourse showed rather how factiousness had its origin in the absurd assumption that it is possible to combat dissent without replacing it with the spontaneous concord of truth. For this reason, at the very time when the nascent Protestant churches were beginning to develop new methodological tools with which to reinforce their own special theological science (we need think only of Melanchthon and his *loci communes*), the heretics who dissented from both Catholicism and Protestantism proved themselves true heirs of Renaissance thought by invoking, against the authority principle, dubitative and probabilistic reason, which preferred likelihood to all presumptions of truth, even when these were very carefully (but always unilaterally) delimited. This attitude was amply documented in, for example, the *De arte dubitandi* of Sebastian Castellione, the *De orbis concordia* of William Postel, and the *De Christi efficacitate* of Francis Pucci of Florence, who explicitly acknowledges his links with the philosophical and theological concordism of Ficino, Pico, and Steuco.[30]

But at the very moment when Calvinism was justifying its split with Catholicism by a definitive and radical belittling of theological rationalism, there was obviously a danger that the pursuit of a probabilistic approach to the understanding of the faith along the lines of Renaissance concordism would overly weaken the capacity of Christian theology to put up a united resistance against Protestant divisiveness. How serious this danger might be became clear from the successive failures of all attempts made by reform-minded Catholic theologians, such as Sadoleto, Contarini, More, and Pole, to dialogue with the Protestants. It can also be seen in the negative outcome of the discussions that enlivened the repeated meetings between the parties, meetings which Charles V encouraged as a way of restoring the broken religious unity (down to the failure of the Colloquy of Ratisbon in 1541 and, with it, of the last hopes of the more conciliatory Catholics). The lack of agreement on the principles guiding research and on the criteria for certainty in interpretation was increasingly causing a dangerous reemergence of theological disagreements that henceforth became rigidified into divergent and opposing orthodoxies.

The danger can be seen, above all, in the uselessness of the development, by Catholics who were moderate adherents of the demand for reform, of doctrinal hypotheses that should have favored reunification but instead, because they lacked internal coherence at the level of theological demonstration, collapsed before criticism from both sides. Let one example suffice: the "double justification" theory which Gaspar Contarini laboriously developed and defended as a means of mediating between the two sides; it did not achieve its purpose and was abandoned by both Catholics and Reformers, perhaps precisely for the reason that, instead of being produced by a rigorous method of demonstration and persuasion that would have made it unassailable, it sprang from good sense and an intuitive perception of the possibilities of finding the "peace of the faith" beneath the differences and by an application of moderate reasonableness.[31]

In response to the irritation caused by the new struggle over the interpretation of dogma, the more radical and less conciliatory theology of restoration (with the Jesuits as its main spokesmen) was spurred to find within itself a rigorous scientific structure in order to safeguard its own unassailability and, consequently, its own effectiveness. This led to the revival, this time victorious and definitive, of a cognoscitive understanding, through causes, of the meaning of revelation, a meaning then projected on to the objective data of faith; this was an understanding purified of the gnoseological attenuations of the Platonic subjectivism so extolled by many theologians of the Renaissance. All this meant a triumphal return to theological Aristoteleanism in its most perfect form, the one developed by Thomas Aquinas. But that is another story, one that would lead to a new and quite different maturation of Catholic theological thought.

In conclusion, the image of a balance sheet showing the failure of the alleged Renaissance revolution in theology seems to be confirmed. This result could have already been foreseen, even before the lacerating explosion of Protestantism, when the Fifth Lateran Council—in the final moments of which Gianfrancesco Pico himself, the apostle of Late Renaissance moderate probabilism, would lament the betrayal of the aims of ecclesiastical reform that had been the initial motive of the movement—issued a decree on the obligation of philosophers to demonstrate the immortality of the soul in accordance with sacred Scripture. The methodological principle which the prelates signing this decree felt could not be abandoned was one that was fundamental to Aristotelean-Thomistic logic and epistemology: the absolute univocity of truth, which cannot be distorted by any imbalance between truths demonstrated by reason and truths accepted by faith: "And since truth cannot contradict truth, we define that every statement contrary to the enlightened truth of the faith is totally false."[32]

But even if it be true that Renaissance theology ends in a result that seems completely at odds with the premises with which it started, it would be a mistake not to acknowledge the important function which fifteenth- and sixteenth-century speculation had in the history of Christian theological method. This function was to have traveled, under the impulse of a noble curiosity, new ways along which to move theological reflection out of the dialectical immobilism and doctrinal contradictions caused by the predominance of rationality as a tool over the very purposes it should have served. The results of this period of intense research, though they did not come together in a comprehensive and commanding system of thought, were neither few nor unimportant for the future of Christian theology.

Above all, there was the recovery, alongside the first principles of Aristotelean logic, of another principle indispensable for reaching a true understanding of the faith: the principle that the ultimate goal of every theological activity should be nothing else than to see God in the simplicity of God's self-manifestation. And in fact the introduction of this elementary but essential premise into the vast sea of varied late medieval Scholastic allegiances served as a seed for a rebirth of Christian wisdom and ensured new and safe developments of it. It is true that the resulting call to Scripture and nature as the two privileged sources in which to perceive God's self-manifestation to human beings encountered, in the radicalism of the Reformers and the enthusiasm of the pantheists respectively, the dangerous boundaries beyond which orthodoxy could be compromised. But in contrast to the abstract deductions of the *magistri,* it also promoted the recovery, within the Catholic tradition, of these two essential factors (Scripture and nature) in the human approach to the divine; these had predominated in the patristic tradition but at this period were in danger of being obscured if not of being lost beyond recovery.

A second fundamental contribution of Renaissance theology was the introduction, in the form of theological probabilism, of the methodology of doubt. As used in Renaissance theology in order to strengthen reason by showing the limits it must not transgress, this tool gave concrete form at the level of study to the constant reminder of the negation aspect proper to a theology inspired by Pseudo-Dionysius. This theology was very attractive to the sensibilities of many writers of this period, from Denis the Carthusian to Marsilius Ficino, from John Colet to William Grocyn. It is not out of place here to remind the reader that the method of doubt was destined to play a fundamental role in the Cartesian revolution in philosophy and in the decisive effects which the latter had even on the theological thinking of the seventeenth century.

In addition, the discounting of claims to a cognoscitive systematization of religious realities and the resultant focusing of interest on reflection on the subject and its interior life produced an effective opening to the practical side of theology. From Gerson to Thomas More and Erasmus, but also in the ethical integralism of Italian humanists such as Valla and Callimachus Esperiens and, by way of these, in the Italian heretics of the sixteenth century, theologians responded to the economic and social imbalances that were troubling Christian society at the beginning of the modern age. They did so by entrusting to reason, which was being disparaged at the theoretical level, the task of finding in the faith norms that would teach human beings how to submit action to the control of the operative unity of soul and body, a unity restored to its rightful place in the Renaissance celebration of the *dignitas hominis* (dignity of the human person).[33]

To summarize: when we construct the theological history of the Renaissance period, we enter, as it were, into a vast, busy research laboratory in which experiments are carried on and countless results produced, for over a century and a half, by a complex and ambitious project for renewing the tools and methods to be used in bringing the search for the truth back to the main path. It was a spacious workshop of thought in which the imitation of masters and the continual proposal and checking of techniques and materials produced a great deal that was exaggerated and idiosyncratic (occasional works lacking homogeneity, rarely didactic in origin, most often in the form of letters, sermons, learned collections of notes, or unsystematic encyclopedias) and few masterpieces. At the same time, however, this workshop laid down important and unrenouncible premises, both positive and negative, for the future development of philosophical and theological thought in the modern age.

CHAPTER 1

The Theology of Italian Humanism in the Early Fifteenth Century

Cesare Vasoli

1. The "Question" About the Fifteenth Century: "Continuity" or "Rupture"?

Even a short essay on the theological ideas developed and expressed by the first generations of humanists raises many preliminary questions of a historiographical and methodological kind; these questions are always unavoidable when dealing with cultural events in the decades of the late fourteenth century and the first thirty years of the fifteenth. Thus we would have to take a position in the long-lasting dispute, still far from over, about such fundamental historiographical concepts as "renaissance," "humanism," and "humane letters"; these are still the subject of controversies that have reappeared as part of the growing debate over the characteristics of "modernity." It would be necessary, next, to dwell with special emphasis on the question, likewise still open, of the relations of "continuity" and "rupture" linking the intellectual experiences of the first humanists with the millennial medieval tradition, its methods, and its sources.[1]

Then we would still have to ask whether these decades saw the emergence of a new and different course for Western culture or whether, on the contrary, as maintained by some scholars who are especially hostile to humanistic thought, there occurred a kind of speculative regression which (they claim) led to the eclipse of the classical metaphysical and theological tradition; the interruption of advances, already extensive, on the road leading to a "new logic" and a "new science" (a road barred, they say, by the priority given to renewed rhetorical and merely literary influences); and finally, the triumph of an inferior intellectual model that was henceforth incapable of understanding the reasonings of "true" philosophy and a solid "magisterial" theology.

But that is not all, for problems of this kind, whatever their resolution, require an investigation of the underlying historical causes that led, in the period under consideration, to the emergence of intellectual tendencies and attitudes at odds among themselves and to the end of the system of unified, "corporative" knowledge so typical of the medieval university and its kindred institutions. Nor is it possible to avoid an analysis of the particular "national" or "regional" characteristics that marked experiences and traditions often destined to collide in bitter polemics, or to deal also with subjects of exceptional importance, such as the character and nature of language and the relations between language and every form and expression of knowledge.

It is obvious that such questions as these would require analyses and investigations much more comprehensive than are possible within the limits of a discussion of the very specific themes and arguments of theological discourse. I think, however, that even a study limited to particular authors, traditions, and intellectual environments cannot be excused from clarifying at least some essential traits of the historical situation in which the humanist experience was born, became established, and spread abroad, and from identifying the characteristics that distinguished it from and often opposed it, in an intensely polemical way, to the culture of the "schools," with their methods and language.

Admittedly, even these characteristics are not to be schematized in an absolute way, so as to assume a radical "rupture" and to transform an obvious and real antagonism into a kind of utterly irreconcilable conflict. We know, in fact, that while the rejection of Scholastic learning was generally clear and decisive and moved at times from criticism of the "modern" philosophers and theologians to a critique of the very origins of the medieval traditions, there were not lacking authors and works that made their own the ideas and doctrines taught by the *magistri* or even proposed them once again, but always in the light of new spiritual needs and of a clearer and more lucid awareness of their origins and their connection with the gospel message itself. Nor do the many examples and proofs of this that the supporters of "continuity" often cite have to be given here for us to recognize that in the late fourteenth and early fifteenth centuries, alongside attitudes that called into question traditions which were among the most ancient and best accredited, there were still operative at a deep level ethical teachings, religious and mystical experiences, theological problematics, exegetical methods, and forms of preaching that we can regard as typically medieval.

The presence of these can be seen in the Franco-Burgundian, English, and German cultures but also in Italian intellectual circles and institutions, even those of the central and northern parts of the country. Moreover, it is now a commonplace that the period of the humanist "renaissance" was also the "autumn" of the Middle Ages;[2] it was a time that produced outstanding examples of Scholastic theology and was already debating, with growing intensity, the very subjects that would emerge very strongly at the center of the religious crisis of the sixteenth century. The austere piety of the "beguinages" or the "Observantine Congregations" of the more important religious orders, but also the extreme offshoots of the great medieval penitential movements or the renewed millenniarist expectations, would inspire not only popular religiosity but also the spirituality of educated people.

We know, then, that there are not lacking historians who are quite ready to reduce the thinking of the first generations of humanists to a mere literary exercise while leaving to the ideas enfleshed in the works and teaching of the *magistri* the task of bearing witness to immutable truths supposedly exempt from the wear and tear of time and history. But such notions, often supported by a brilliant display of scholarship, cannot successfully deny an important fact that is now firmly embedded in the historical consciousness, namely, that this very period saw the crisis, in many ways irreversible, of the institutional and ideological unity of Western Christendom, shattered as this was by events, conflicts, and profound transformations of the social, political, and cultural orders; by wounds increasingly inflicted on the ecclesial order; and by an ever-growing religious restlessness at all levels of the society of the time.

In the sphere of theoretical discourse, this assessment of the situation already finds confirmation in the common awareness of the distance separating reality from human linguistic tools. This distance can be seen in the progressively formalistic emphasis in the nominalistic procedures of late Scholasticism and in the resolute humanistic reassertion, based on analysis of grammatical and rhetorical ways, of the "persuasive" and "argumentative" character of language.

But the assessment takes on a rather more explicit and clear historical importance if we reflect on the particular situations of every kind (cultural, first of all, but also social and political) that, as early as about the second half of the fourteenth century, made possible, in central and northern Italy, the formation of a new intellectual and educational model that became increasingly different from the principles and methods in control in official institutions. The success, first in Italy and then throughout Europe, of humanist teaching and culture was not, in fact, connected solely with the internal difficulties of the corporative system of intellectual learning and its language, which were accessible only to a restricted public of *magistri,* but rather with the emergence of new social and political demands, with the intellectual rise of the middle classes in the cities, and with the rise of institutions requiring the development of varied activities and professions. It is difficult, therefore, to understand the attitude of the humanists toward the intellectual life of their time unless we bear in mind that their culture took shape in a historical environment which, at the moment, was more favorable to the development of a learning henceforth unconnected with the traditional figure of the "cleric" and which aimed at subjecting to an increasingly coherent and sharp critique the certainly magnificent inheritance of knowledge and teaching that had been developed in the Scholastic world. Meanwhile, the humanists were offering new answers to real problems raised by profound historical changes.

2. The Crisis of Universalism

All this means that at the source of the most characteristic traits of humanist culture there was in fact a widespread crisis throughout a large section of Western society. This society was being devastated by bitter dynastic and feudal conflicts, peasant revolts, rebellions of the underclasses in the cities, and the terrible social and economic consequences of the great plague, but also by the emergence of forms of civil and political organization that were irreducible to the ancient hierarchies and the universalist myths of the past. It is understandable that this crisis struck harder at the emblematic institutions of medieval Europe that had for centuries embodied the idea, which was both religious and political, of the sacral unity of the *Respublica christiana*.

At the very beginning of the fourteenth century the Church had experienced in the pontificate of Boniface VIII a high point of its power but also of political humiliation. Now it was compelled to submit to the burdensome control of the French monarchy, until at last, in 1378, it would plunge into the dramatic rupture of the Great Schism that would be drawn out and worsen until the precarious solution reached at the Council of Constance (1418). But the clash between papal authority and the views of the conciliarists would soon break out anew at the Council of Basel (1431–49), at the beginning of a new period of violent divisions and ecclesial struggles that would give increasing relevance to the attack on the corruption and decadence of ecclesial institutions and the ecclesial hierarchy, to the call for a complete reform of head and members, and to the renewal of apocalyptic preaching on the coming of the Antichrist.

The empire, reduced now in fact to "an empty name without any subjects," had likewise lost its ancient sacral prestige as the supreme institution and authority in Christendom; the ups and downs of the "long interregnum" and then the weakness of the sovereigns who succeeded one another from 1273 on did not restrain and even increased the feudal chaos which broke up the "Teutonic nation." Struggles between princes and minor vassals, between lay lords and their ecclesiastical "superiors," between free cities and clerical authorities, but also among the Church "potentates" themselves plagued a large part of German society, while the dramatic, intolerable misery of the peasants increased as did the malaise of the minor military nobility (the *Rittertum*) who lacked land and wealth.

Nor was this all, for in the more distant lands of the empire, in Bohemia, the Hussite revolt combined a rebellion against the German aristocracy and the economic and political control of the Roman Church with the proposal of radical theological doctrines and a call for no less drastic reforms of ecclesial institutions. This was the first manifestation of the fermenting revolts that would become increasingly serious throughout the fifteenth century.

But even the most solid political institutions of late medieval Europe—the French and English monarchies—passed through a lengthy period of hard trials and bitter disputes, a period marked by the alternating successes and failures of the Hundred Years' War, by the weakening of their power, the renewed predominance of the feudal upper aristocracy, and serious rendings of the fragile social fabric. Again in France and England, there were frequent violent uprisings of the peasants (the *jacquéries*), as well as successive rebellions by the mercantile classes in the cities, which wanted new privileges and immunities, and sudden tremors in the poorest groups of urban society.

To sum up: in the larger countries of the West (those in which Scholastic culture had its most prestigious institutions), the great political and social changes that were at the origin of "modern" Europe led to upheavals and conflicts that weighed seriously on the development of the intellectual life and at times (as can be seen in the vicissitiudes of the University of Paris during the civil war between the Burgundians and their opponents, the followers of Bernard of Armagnac) even caused a lengthy decline in teaching and speculation. On the other hand, in central and northern Italy, though under very diverse political and institutional forms and amid internal and external struggles that continued through a great part of the fifteenth century, the most obvious political phenomenon was the formation of a powerful middle-class patriciate of mercantile and financial origin that acquired a growing influence or control in government and in the administration of the political institutions that emerged as the communes developed. Even where, as in Florence, the clash between the various classes or groups was more severe (we need think only of the rebellion of the Ciompi, in many ways a decisive episode of Florentine history), the second half of the fourteenth century ended with the henceforth solidly established hegemony of a limited oligarchy that controlled the economic and political life of the city.

Elsewhere, the development of stable "upper class" regimes did not keep this patriciate from sharing to a notable degree in the exercise of power. It is true, of course, that even the patrician oligarchies did not break down the corporative structures that marked the organization of the cities, nor did they do away with the obvious vestiges of feudalism that were still present in many aspects of civil and political institutions. Nevertheless, as these groups of bankers, big merchants, and entrepreneurs were transformed into ruling classes in the true and proper sense, they also developed a culture of their own that was naturally unconnected with the Scholastic system of learning; they also developed ethical and political concepts that would soon find their fullest expression in the teaching of the humanists.

Moreover, their manner of living and practicing the Christian religion could no longer find satisfaction in the complex theological thinking of the schools, in their bold dialectic, and in their increasingly "technical" language that frequently left its traces even in preaching and in the forms of everyday piety as taught by the *magistri*. Even in this area the needs of the new ruling classes were met rather by the new way of learning proposed by other intellectuals who were opposed to the Scholastic traditions and routine, that is, by the teachers of the *studia humanitatis* (humane studies), the representatives of a culture that started precisely with a critique of Scholastic learning and language and went on to denounce the decline and critical state of all the most important religious and human institutions; to pronounce an extremely negative judgment on the long centuries of "barbarism" that had polluted and muddied all traditions; and to set forth the myth of a renewal that would restore these traditions to their original perfection.

3. Francis Petrarch

Whether they were notaries, jurists, chancellors of republics, secretaries of lords, or teachers in the public schools of grammar and rhetoric that emerged in the major civic centers, the "humanists" (as they were to be called, with a name that clearly distinguished them from the practicioners of the *studia divinitatis* and the other disciplines, the law and medicine typical of the schools) were, in fact, a new kind of intellectual. They combined an enthusiastic study of classical poetry and eloquence and a diligent reading of Cicero, Seneca, and the ancient historians with a direct experience of political events and an intense and heartfelt participation in the expectation of a profound change in intellectual, ethical, and religious life. They looked for a new age that would bring the birth of a human race worthy of its divine sonship and educated by letters to an inner understanding of its earthly and supernatural destiny.

These men were immersed in the historical events of late-fourteenth-century Italy and were sometimes actors in these events by reason of their functions and of important political choices and decisions. As such, their thinking moved between a constant appeal to the great examples of the ancient civilizations, which were proposed as an indispensable model for human transformation, and the search for a learning that would be useful in civic life, as well as the commitment to a simple and sincere religious life that would be based on the teaching of the Gospel and be reserved toward a "disputational" theology and its "subtleties." Nor should we find surprising their resolute and often clearly polemical indifference to the prominent theological, metaphysical, and scientific interests of the Scholastic tradition, which they regarded as the last and most dangerous expression of "barbarism."

All this explains why the master to whom they looked for their common inspiration was certainly not one of the more recent *magistri,* whether William of Ockham or Duns Scotus, John Buridan or John of Jandun, nor even one of the greatest philosophers and theologians of the thirteenth century, such as Thomas Aquinas or Albert the Great, but a famous man of letters and poet, Francis Petrarch, who was regarded as the foremost writer in the rebirth of the *studia humanitatis.*

As a matter of fact, even the humanist attitude to theology, with its return to the patristic tradition (often polemically contrasted with the tiresome "modern" theologians) and its strong emphasis on some characteristic Augustinian themes, was deeply influenced by the teaching and spirituality of Petrarch. Thus some of his well-known attacks were the source of the condemnation of Scholastic prolixity, the rejection of a learning such as that of the physicians and the natural philosophers that was regarded as ignorant of the most profound truths about the human being, and the renewed attack on Averroan ungodliness. This last was in reality rather a pretext for opposing the renewed "wisdom" learned through lengthy conversation with the "great minds" of antiquity to the "obscure" and "vain" learning of the schools.

Francis Petrarch (1304–74), who likewise belonged by origin to the class of notaries and schoolmen and who, like many future humanists, was trained in literary and juridical studies, was indeed the central and dominant personality in the profound cultural renewal that took shape with increasing intensity around the middle of the fourteenth century. In fact, no one could match him in expressing the desire for a "rebirth" that was at once intellectual, civil, and religious; the new ideal of a learning based on the quest of wisdom and on discourse that was pure, effective, and persuasive; the aversion to methods and ways of thinking that were judged entirely opposed to "true" human and divine wisdom. It was he who denounced a widespread state of decline to which he opposed a nostalgia for ancient virtue; his was the myth of a long-past perfection that had to be regained through a difficult labor of research and "restoration"; and his a knowledge, ever broader, more extensive, and sure, of a great cultural inheritance that had been forgotten or no longer understood.

But this refined man of letters and poet, this patient philologist[3] who sought out and annotated the codices and testimonials of antiquity, conceived of the rebirth of the *studia humanitatis* as not simply a return to a philosophy of the human being that was solidly grounded in the teaching of the classics. For him this was also the only way to put an end to the corruption of all forms of human life and experience and to achieve the spiritual and political resurrection of "poor Italy"; the rebirth of ancient "civic" virtue; the recovery of a pure Latin that had been ravaged by so many "barbarians"; and the "reform" of the Church of Christ, once this was delivered from the "shameful ruin" represented by the Avignon See. From the well-known letter to John Colonna, written from the Campidoglio on March 15, 1337, to the attacks in his *Sine nomine,* from the famous verses of the song *Italia mia,* which dates from around 1345, to the letter of 1347 to Cola di Rienzo,[4] Petrarch called without ceasing for this rebirth that was both spiritual and political and for peace and concord in human society as a condition required for the purification of Christianity.

It is certainly in this perspective that we must interpret his meeting with Cola di Rienzo and his deeply felt participation in an event whose utopian character and more hidden political aims historians have made clear, but, as seen in the words of this Roman notary and in the symbols he evokes, seems so revelatory of the spiritual tension in the early humanist period. It is enough to recall the letter which Cola wrote from Avignon at the end of January 1343 in which the charming interweaving of classical images and memories gives new power to the millenniarist themes that had for two centuries fed the mystical expectation of the spirituals; in which, too, certainty about the "rebirth" of the "Roman people," "surrounded and regenerated by every virtue," is combined with the hope of a new coming of the Holy Church of the apostles as it rose from its ruins.

It is true that once the false hopes connected with the brief appearance of Cola had collapsed, Petrarch set all his hope on the establishment of an ideal community of wise souls who, following the example of the ancients, would discover the most indispensable "renewal" in the hidden truth of poetry, in ethical reflection, and in profound meditation on the gospel message. Not only, however, did he oppose his never-surrendered nostalgia for the perfection of antiquity to the "base" standard of his own time, but he also took the ancient gospel metaphor that described the pagan era before the incarnation of Christ as an "age of darkness," and he applied it to the crowning decadence of recent centuries that had drowned all traditions.

As a result, in Petrarch's writings the contrast between the two cultures—that of the schools, which was connected with a false and distorted image of the past, and that which was dedicated to the noble pursuit of the *studia humanitatis*—was transformed into a definitive conflict that found clear expression in the image of a difficult and stubborn "war" against every kind of barbarism. But the poet did not place any hopes on the learned men of his day, for he regarded them as alien to his program of renewal, far removed from his love of antiquity, and indifferent to the call to an interior life that could put an end to the errors of human beings and guide them back from their dispersion and darkness to self-conquest and self-education.

Also well-known—and often cited even if misunderstood—is the sorrowful passage in the *Rerum memorandorum libri,*[5] in which Petrarch seems to look upon his own labors as a solitary and final testimony to authentic civilized behavior at the point of transition between two eras. On the one hand, there were those centuries in which the loss of so many treasures of the ancient world had not prevented at least the survival of the memory of ancient greatness and ancient humanity. On the other, an age still darker and more barbarous, in which the last vestiges of any wisdom had disappeared due to the empty curiosity of philosophers intent on the study of the physical world, the sophistical dialectic that was triumphant in the schools, and the arid theology of *magistri* who were increasingly removed from the words of the gospel.

Over against this dark prospect the poet sets his celebration of the humanities, understood as a lofty spiritual exercise that better enables us to recover ourselves and that leads us, by means of a purer knowledge of our souls, to control of our passions, harmony of conscience, and an intimate experience of the divine, such as was not often to be obtained through the teachings of the theologians. Thus, in the conversation which the soul is always carrying on with itself and in which it finds the deepest explanation for its communion with all other human beings, a daily familiarity with the unchanging testimonials to truth and the "beautiful and salvific study" of poetry are joined to silent meditation on one's own destiny and on the task to which the Christian duty of charity calls us.

For while it is possible to reach charity and holiness even without any education, it is no less true that "learning has not kept anyone from holiness" and that the "devout" piety of the man of letters is always superior to the piety of those who, being unlearned, do not possess "the finest light" and cannot reach the highest point of their ascent. Nor does the withdrawal of the soul into solitude, which is, according to the teaching of Augustine, the necessary way for Christians, mean rejecting the way of "salvation" which the wisdom of the ancients, of Cicero and Plato, opens up to us in the search for truth by bringing us ever closer to an understanding of the very words of God.

In this sense the conflict between love of the ancients and Christian faith, between vocation in the world and persistent mystical tension, which some historians have considered to be the insuperable barrier in Petrarch's attitude to history, seems to be already resolved in the ideal encounter between revelation and human inquiry, these being experiences that are not opposed but converge in shedding light on the human drama and destiny. Not even the Christian awareness of the destructive power of time, of the wretchedness and frailty of our nature, of the weakness of the soul that is too often overcome by empty desires and earthly cares, can in fact deny the value of a training that teaches its students to understand the true meaning of things and to free themselves from the "deceitfulness" of the world so as better to understand the divine "reason" *(ratio)* and grasp the inner harmony present in the wonderful order that governs all things. Above all, whether in society or in solitude, whether in daily conversation with other people or in hidden contemplation within one's own soul, the shared reading of Cicero and Augustine, Plato and the Fathers, reveals a single, unchanging "humanity" that is as certain of its own insuperable limits and its own limitless misery and nobility as it is sure that natural and earthly "virtue" is not opposed to the Christian duty of charity, which in fact it even helps strengthen.

This is why on several occasions, but most explicitly in one of the *Seniles* (XV, 6), addressed to Louis Marsili, a young hermit,[6] Petrarch advises him to follow his own nature, as "if he were God," and to regard this "as lord and master" over all things without paying heed to those who would turn theologians away from the study of letters. Such folk are unaware that without that knowledge neither Lactantius nor Augustine would have been able to combat the "superstitions" of the pagans or erect the spiritual edifice of the *civitas Dei*. It is true, of course, that all the sciences obey and serve the "science of God," the supreme Cause on which all things depend. But true theologians should follow the teaching of Augustine and, like him, aim to acquire all knowledge and study whatever the mind can grasp and the memory retain, while always remembering that the sole purpose of theology and philosophy is to attain to true wisdom, which is Christ "the Son of God."

This authentic theology, which Petrarch identifies with a profound participation in the divine Word, has nothing in common with the deceptive knowledge that in fact turns human beings away from God and the world or with a "teaching of the masters" that sets a steep wall of words and abstruse concepts between them and the truth. On the contrary, this authentic theology confirms the fact that even for Christians the experience and certainty of faith are achieved in concrete "virtuous activity," in the performance of those duties which all are called upon to carry out during their "earthly exile" by participating in the joint civic activity that is so pleasing even to the supreme ruler of the universal order.

It is quite true that beyond this life and this world human beings have another destiny and another happiness in comparison with which even earthly virtue and earthly glory fade into nothingness, sinking into that unknown abyss before which all human wisdom is reduced to confusion. But the enthusiastic reader of Augustine (who with death constantly in mind was always seeking salvation from this most painful of human sufferings) also knows that the best preparation for the hope of immortality is precisely the service rendered to our fellows, activity that strengthens the bond uniting all in an everlasting participation in good both human and divine.

Petrarch can, therefore, celebrate both Cicero and Augustine as masters of the meditation that always leads us back to God without therefore denying the "city of this world," the active community in which Christian "virtue," too, can and ought to be developed. The certainty of being thus able to reconcile gospel truth and the truth of the "authentic" philosophers is even his defense against acedia, the unsatisfied restlessness, the uncertainty that makes him hesitate between, on the one hand, love of "glory" and worldly fame and, on the other, the awareness of his transiency, for which he can find comfort only in a longing for an eternity beyond all earthly expectations. While his lengthy conversation with Augustine warns him against the emptiness of a life wholly taken up with time and of the fame that seems to come only after death and to vanish like a dream, he is saved from horror of the end by the realization that the passing life of time finds its meaning in the simplicity of faith and the expectation of an immortality that does not destroy but even confirms the noble "measure" of a life.

Threatened as they are by a future whose hidden expiration they do not know, human beings find their only possible peace and serenity in fleeing from the jumble and banality of everyday life and resolving their interior crisis through a resolute contemplation of their own death. Or, in the words of a passage in the *Secretum* that was extraordinarily effective and always present to the minds of the humanists in their religious reflection:

> Especially during the nights, when the mind, wearied by the cares of the day, recollects itself somewhat, I arrange this body of mine after the manner of the dying and thus I imagine the hour of my death. My mind is able to conjure up something fearful, so that at times I am passing through the final agony and seem to see the infernal kingdom and all those evils . . . and I am so deeply shaken by this vision that I rise up terrified and trembling.[7]

Only in this way, in fact, is it possible to understand how the "power" and "glory" of life must find the way to eternity beyond time, without on that account rejecting the strength and help given by familiarity with poetry and human wisdom. The "spirit" that speaks in the silence of our souls and exhorts us to return to our true "homeland" does not dissipate the memory of those wise men and women who have taught us to listen to it.

4. The Studia Humanitatis *Versus the Schools*

The philosophical wisdom of which Petrarch speaks is therefore a way to and entry into a religious experience that in turn gives rise to a discourse on the divine that is quite different and remote from the one being carried on, at this same period, in the theological schools and colleges, with their logical procedures and the exegetical tools developed by two centuries of theoretical labor. And it is quite understandable that with his eye on the perennial sapiential enlightenment which ancients and Christians had in common, he should be opposed to the teachings of the Scholastics and should condemn with particular harshness their most recent results, which he identified with the "sophisms" of the "modern" logicians, with the attitude of those Aristotelean physicists and physicians who regarded nature as a system of principles and absolute laws, and above all, with the "godlessness" of the Averroists, which he considered to negate the human hope of immortality. In his *De sui ipsius et multorum ignorantia* and his *Invectiva in medicum*[8] (which we may not put on the same trivial level as so many university disputations of the time), the condemnation of an exclusively "physical" knowledge that risks polluting even our knowledge of *res divinae* is clear and explicit:

Who could give the name of human being to those who, even though they see the movements of the heavens so finely ordered, the mechanisms of the stars so well arranged, and everything so wonderfully connected and bound together, would say that reason is not at work in them, and would claim that chance governs these things which human minds, however gifted, can certainly not create?

They do not admit that this "harmony" is governed by a divine mind, the same mind that reveals itself in the hidden recesses of the soul and expresses itself in the soul's "power." Against "the foolish people who think they can clutch the heavens in their fists" and lock themselves up in the most absurd errors, Petrarch sets the contemplation of the perfection and order of the world, which is a mirror of a providence unrecognized by those who think that material events yield the only understanding of the world: "I ask myself," he writes, "of what use is it to know a great deal about the wild beasts, the birds, the fishes, and the snakes while being ignorant of and not concerned to know the nature of human beings, why we are born, whence we come, and whither we are going?"[9]

Elsewhere, while denying that the empirical and always uncertain knowledge of physicians can properly be included in a "collection" of "bizarre" experiences, he does say that the most hidden "secrets of God," which Christians humbly accept in faith, cannot be even distantly touched on by those who proceed on the assumption that they possess all knowledge. Harsher still, however, is his attack on the Averroists. This is the name he gives to all the most radical proponents of Aristotelean "naturalism," which is forever incapable of understanding that the human person is not reducible to merely natural processes and that the "soul" has a further freedom and a further destiny. Even in the final period of his life Petrarch urges Marsili to take up and continue this battle that is so necessary in order to free philosophy from the worst kind of untruth and from an error that can destroy both human wisdom and faith. This is why in his defense of human autonomy and of the providence that governs the world he harks back to Plato, who, together with his favorite author, Cicero, can teach a philosophy utterly different from that which is still in control in the official institutions of learning.

Now, there is no doubt that Petrarch's knowledge of the works of Plato was limited to the dialogues which the medieval doctors had also known and admired: the *Phaedo,* the *Timaeus,* and perhaps the *Meno,* the only ones available in Latin translation. He was unable to derive great profit from his relations with the Basilian monk Barlaam as far as knowledge of the Greek language and Greek "wisdom" was concerned. It is also true that his rebellion against the *"magistri,"* the "physicists," the "dialecticians," and even the theologians, who were by now entirely dominated by a "corrupt" philosophy, never reached the point of attacking the philosophical authority of Aristotle (whom Petrarch, like the other humanists of the first generations, regarded as a supremely wise and eloquent man but a victim of his false followers who had made him "hard" and "thorny"). But by choosing Plato as his philosophical model, Petrarch pointed out another path which the philosophical and theological culture of humanism would follow in the next century with decisive results: a broader view of the records of ancient "wisdom" and an ever more extensive and more direct knowledge of the culture that had provided food even for the early expressions of Christian "doctrine" and which, in the person of Plato, had been the inspiration of the authentic patristic "sources."

The fame and fortune of Petrarch immediately became extraordinarily widespread and far reaching; it will not be necessary here to recall the many testimonies in proof of this statement. But the circle that best understood his teaching even in its religious aspect was the small group of his Florentine friends and followers, who were thus linked to the rise and spread of the new culture. As early as 1360 John Boccaccio, in his *De genealogiis deorum gentilium,*[10] had renewed Petrarch's defense of ancient poetry, and in a debate with those philosophies and theologians who disapproved of the study of letters he had defended the sublime "truths" hidden even under the veil of pagan myth and fable. During these same years two young men of quite different origin and intellectual formation turned back to the ancients: to Cicero, Virgil, Seneca, and the other very great models of ancient eloquence and poetry. The two were Coluccio Salutati and a monastic hermit, Louis Marsili, to whom, it is said, Petrarch himself had entrusted the task of eradicating the godlessness of Averroes and his followers.

Marsili (d. 1394) was a learned theologian who had completed his studies in Paris at the most illustrious university in Christendom; he was a student of philosophy but also an enthusiastic reader of the ancients. He had then joined the brotherhood of humanists who used to gather in the Augustinian convent of Santo Spirito under the leadership of Salutati. To this last-named humanist, who became chancellor of the Republic of Florence, Marsili was especially close in the time of the difficult conflict between Florence and the pope (War of the Eight Saints, 1374–78), when, in his role as theologian for the city, he defended its rights and prerogatives against the claims of the Roman Curia.

His memory, however, depends solely on the praise of friends and contemporaries, on a small group of letters harshly attacking the corruption of the Avignon church, and on a commentary on Petrarch's poem *All'Italia*. Rather more important, however, than the few evidences that remain to us seems to have been his teaching, which was conducted not only in his convent and from his chair in the Florentine Studium (house of studies) but also at meetings of his humanist friends and in their discussions, which took place either at Santo Spirito or in the suburban villa of the Alberti family. In these settings, the friar-theologian, an enthusiastic reader of Augustine and Cicero, used to discuss religious and philosophical subjects not only with Salutati and his young disciples but with a public made up of middle- and lower-class people, among whom there were even some women.

Such associations on the part of a theologian who was also a "religious under rule" were regarded as rather unseemly by Angelo Torini, a man of stern religious outlook, who was especially close to John of Celle[11] and his "spiritual coterie." In fact, however, even in these free and "informal" discussions the interests of these cultivated men were in subjects and authors of purely theological relevance; the subjects were treated without any kind of "magisterial" formalism, and there was a growing emphasis on criticism of Scholastic education, which was accused of having misunderstood not only the teachings of the ancients but even those of the Fathers. Above all, concepts and ideas that had long been the exclusive inheritance of the group of *magistri* were taken up in discussions that included the direct participation of persons who had no familiarity with Scholastic "science," as, for example, Nicholas Niccoli, a former merchant; Palla Strozzi, a rich and powerful burgher; and Robert de'Rossi and James Angeli, two young humanists.

5. The Defenders of the Schools and Traditional Learning

The increasingly harsh attacks on the culture of the schools (which did not prevent courteous discussion with important "physicists" and physicians such as Biagio Pelacani and Marsilio da Santa Sofia) were not, of course, sympathetically received by other participants in learned disputes, the convinced defenders of traditional science and of a learning on which the philosophical, theological, and poetic experience of the greatest of Florentine intellectuals, Dante Alighieri, had been based. Thus the attack on the "moderns," which, however, Salutati toned down in his prudent defense of the spiritual value of literature and poetry, elicited a response from musician and mathematician Francis Landino in a poem in praise of William of Ockham.[12]

This poem was a harsh indictment of the arrogance of the ill-equipped "school teachers" *(grammatici)* who dared to condemn without knowing them the penetrating teachings of the Scholastics and their profound understanding of "human" and "divine" knowledge. These people (Landino wrote, putting his words on the lips of Ockham) were simply "idle fellows," driven by envy and their own ignorance, able only to slander the real sciences and to describe them with the most insulting names, accusing all who cultivated them—"dialecticians," philosophers, and theologians—of being useless and harmful sophists and using a "barbaric" language. Yet the wisdom of these people consisted solely of a few empty, "timid" words, always spoken carelessly, showing that their constant appeal to Cicero concealed a very faulty, unlearned, and confused discourse which Landino judged to be full of errors, grammatical mistakes, and solecisms, as well as of absurd and irrational expressions.

In a like manner, Cino Rinuccini in his *Invectiva contro a cierti calunnia-tori di Dante e di Messer Francesco Petrarca e di Messer Giovanni Boccaccio*[13] condemned the impertinence of the "new sophists," fanatical admirers of the "ancients" (the reference was especially to Nicholas Niccoli), whom he regarded as "a pack of twitterers who, to seem very scholarly in the eyes of the common people, talk loudly in public about how many diphthongs the ancients had and why only two are used today; and which grammar is better, that of the time of the comic writer Terence or that of the epic poet Virgil." But such disputes, immediately branded as "daydreaming and a waste of time," certainly did not authorize these "scholars" to deal with logic and rhetoric and, still less, to reject en bloc the higher doctrines, that is, arithmetic, music, astrology, and even "subtle natural philosophy," "delightful astronomy," "excellent moral philosophy," "the holy precepts of the laws," and finally, even "true and holy theology."

Rinuccini (who must have been thinking of such attitudes on the part of Petrarch himself and his most ardent admirers) also censured those who even maintained that "Plato is a greater philosopher than Aristotle" and in the area of ethics cited only Cicero, while paying scant heed to Aristotle's *Ethics.* Above all, however, Rinuccini found utterly scandalous certain opinions current among the young humanists, who according to him were capable of having higher regard for "Varro and his books on the pagan gods" than for the Fathers and Doctors, and of claiming that "those gods were truer than this one," while never mentioning and venerating "the miracles of our saints." Thus, while exhorting these "rash fellows" to meditate more fully on the writings of Paul and Augustine in order to learn what "the true faith" is and in what "lofty theology" consists, he expressed very serious doubts about their Christian faith and denounced the shameless effrontery that led them to regard Dante as a "shoemaker's poet" simply because of his firm acceptance of the solid learning of the schools.

As is clear, the polemical portrait of the young humanists as drawn by Rinuccini went beyond any literary disagreement and decisively contrasted their culture with the traditional system of learning at the apex of which was the "science of things divine" and its sacred "authorities." No less harsh was the reaction of religious circles that cultivated an intense and sincere piety and cherished proposals for reform but regarded as extremely dangerous the return to the poetry, myths, philosophy, and moral code of the ancients, all of which were incompatible with the sincere profession of the Christian faith. I have already referred to Torini and his open rebuke of Marsili for his associations and his teaching; this rebuke implied a no less explicit condemnation of the cult of "pagan" poetry and, in general, of an excessive love of the *studia humanitatis,* which were now in a position to challenge the primacy of the *studia divinitatis* and to set up a new and excessively "lay" and "secular" conception of the intellectual task.

But the reaction of this devout man, who was greatly venerated in Florence for his "holy life," was not an isolated response but rather a manifestation of a fear widely shared by those who identified "divine learning" with the theology of the *magistri* and still more with the education given in the Studia of the religious orders or in monastic settings. The dispute in around 1396 between Salutati himself and one of the most well-known and important religious of his time, Dominican theologian and future cardinal John Dominici,[14] shows how widespread these concerns were and how they involved even persons of great intelligence, men well trained in Scholastic studies and not insensitive to some aspects of even the humanists' experience. I shall return later to this very revealing episode in a debate that certainly had a considerable influence in defining some character traits of the new humanist religious spirit. For the moment, the point to be emphasized is how the attitude of Marsili (whom a piece of fiction, *Il Paradiso degli Alberti,*[15] shows us intent on explaining allegorically the story of Circe, who is taken as a symbol of the evil actions that transform human beings into beasts) was in radical contrast with the rigid piety of men like Torini, who in his little treatise *Della miseria dell'umana condizione*[16] shows himself a convinced follower of the traditional "contempt for the world."

6. Coluccio Salutati

Despite all this, protests and attacks were unable, then or later, to keep the "new" studies from becoming increasingly popular. Nor did they keep a new generation of young intellectuals from turning to these studies, men who no longer felt at home with the learning of the schools but were looking for a new conception of ethics and were especially receptive to the religious teaching of Petrarch and Marsili. At times they even carried their attack to the point of a complete rejection of any experience not solidly based on the wisdom and eloquence of the ancients.

Their common teacher was Ser Coluccio Salutati (1331–1496), chancellor of the Republic of Florence from 1375 on. He was a learned notary whose youthful study of rhetoric had soon brought him to Petrarch and to the practice of a wise philosophy that had for its aim (as he wrote in 1374, on the occasion of the poet's death) "to control all the passions," "expel all the vices," and be "queen and mother of all the sciences."[17] And since human beings have no more effective ties with one another than those established by language, he always identified this wisdom with the lofty educational role of literature and the persuasive power of eloquence, which, in virtue of "the fire of mutual charity," is capable of delivering human beings from moral corruption and awakening in them the primitive power of reason.

It is not surprising, then, that the most effective and constant themes of his meditation and teaching were the preeminence of the will and its freedom; the primacy of "active" virtue, which, as Petrarch had already said, is constantly exercised in the "civic life" of human communities; and the call to a religious life lived in the inner sanctuary of the person's conscience. In the first of his moral treatises, *De saeculo et religione* (1381),[18] which was written to strengthen his friend Nicholas of Lapo di Uzzano in his call to the cloistered life, even Salutati undoubtedly seems to make his own ideas long rooted in medieval Christian culture when he speaks of the world as "the devil's battle-field," "the training ground of temptation," and "the machine shop of the wicked and the factory of the vices" and denounces the emptiness and even the horror of this "hell of the living," in which no happiness is possible because everything is suffering and pain, transiency and death, misery, iniquity, and corruption.

In the first book, when sketching the usual picture of the endless unhappiness of the present world, the humanist makes use, with well-practiced eloquence, of the commonplaces customary in a great deal of theological and devotional literature. He then goes on to celebrate the only sure way of salvation, the difficult but virtuous way of the cloistered life, which can lead human beings "beyond the ravines of the world to the delightful fields of paradise" by increasing "merit" and lessening human "sin" in the "bond of charity" that joins and binds us to God.

Now, as Garin has effectively shown, even this exaltation of the virtues of "religious" did not in fact imply, for Salutati, a rejection and denial of the world or a renunciation of the struggle which every Christian and even every human being is called upon to undergo during their stay on earth. Nor did the awareness of the sin and evil that constantly lie in wait for human activity and of the suffering that constantly disturbs our life mean that religious life should be regarded as a snug refuge from the dangers and travails imposed on those who accept the teaching of the Gospel. On the contrary, this was the strongest and highest motive for facing in mutual love the hard duty imposed by virtue and winning, in the "arena" in which God has placed us, at least the hope of future peace. "The world is the way for mortals, the guide and track of our pilgrimage," Salutati wrote. He again advised his readers to accept the "testing" that can win us the "highest merit" by fighting always "for justice, truth, integrity." Even the seeming peace of the cloister is marked, then, by the struggle shared by every Christian soul: the quest, carried on interiorly and in active love of the neighbor, for the most perfect relationship with the divine that human beings can achieve during their mortal journey.

Consequently, when Pellegrino Zambeccari was hoping to find in the solitude of the cloister a liberation from the cares of the world, Salutati reminded him that "to flee from people, to avoid seeing what is unpleasant, and to withdraw to a cloister or hermitage is not in fact the best way to salvation." For only those who are able to "enter into themselves" and recover self-mastery in the silence of their conscience, even amid the tumult of political events or the cares of family life, acquire a more worthy claim to charity. Indeed, in Salutati's view, "service" to family, friends, and city was the best way to follow the teachings of Christ; he was sure that "active holiness gives edification to many because it is evident to many, and it leads many along in the ascent to heaven because it gives them an example." A flight from the world should never deceive us into thinking that we are "justified"; in fact, it often represents a falling back "from heaven to earth," unlike the active and fruitful work that always pleases God in his care for human beings and the bonds between them and the community they form.[19]

It has been very well said that "when faced with the choice between Martha and Mary, Leah and Rachel, Salutati did not hesitate."[20] He said that in our life "Leah comes before Rachel" and that persons cannot be regarded as true followers of Christ if they ignore the sufferings of their neighbor, do not suffer at the loss of their own, and do not participate enthusiastically or sorrowfully in the destiny of their own civil community. The decision to show charity to all who suffer is not only in keeping with the precepts of true and active evangelical piety; it is also the best answer to the call of the Father, who calls human beings to enjoy his eternal kingdom.

It is therefore quite understandable that, for the same reasons, Salutati assigns a very high value to the married state; this is a duty to which human beings are called by God himself by reason of their obligations toward family, country, and the human community. The virginal state can be the privilege of only a few, because otherwise families, cities, and kingdoms would disappear, and the world itself would be reduced to a dark, abandoned ruin. Nor can Salutati agree that it is a sign of a lower state for Christians to participate in the continuity of life and contribute to the preservation of the "mystical body" made up of the human multitude and its institutions (he is here touching on a theme destined to have a long life in humanist literature). In any case—and this is a point he repeats in his *De verecundia* (1390), which was written in response to the courteous questions put to him by a Florentine physician, Anthony Baruffaldi[21]—it is, of course, not external circumstances that determine the value and motivation for our moral life but always and only the conscience, which "not only sees what we have done . . . but . . . bears witness to our intentions, is present to our thoughts, and accompanies our actions." Nothing and no one can escape its secret yet relentless judgment; in our conversation with ourselves all fictions are set aside, and the evidence of our sin accuses us constantly.

In this appeal to the supreme ethical and religious foundation that is the conscience, Salutati is the faithful disciple of Petrarch, whose deeply Augustinian vein of thought he continues. But in his persevering assertion of the primacy of the will and human activity, which is so focused on the building up of "civil" and historical life, he does not ignore the dramatic philosophical and theological problem that constantly arises when the theme of freedom and choice becomes central.

In his *De fato, fortuna et casu*,[22] begun in 1396 and completed in 1399, the elderly chancellor looks for an answer that will resolve all the contradictions and antinomies posed by the conflict between freedom and inevitable necessity that seems to preside over every human activity and by the relationship between freedom and divine grace that is so central in Christian thought. And characteristically it is to the figure of Socrates, the humanists' ideal philosopher, that Salutati entrusts the celebration of the most heroic kind of virtue, that which freely chooses death in order to remain faithful to a moral calling. Salutati extols the decision of this man—who deserved to be born a Christian and who "died for the sake of perfect justice and of truth"—to surrender the easy freedom of a life which he could have preserved but only by renouncing the higher and truer freedom that consists in the complete consistency of a "guiltless" conscience. That is why Socrates decides not to flee, as he could have, in response to the laws that denied his teaching. He transforms the violence of his enemies into a personal acceptance of a fate in which he decides the true meaning of life:

> I have lived without guilt, and without guilt I shall die. I have always taught that to despise death is supreme wisdom and supreme virtue. I must now confirm in action what I have maintained in discussion; it is, however, stupid to hurl oneself into dangers, and it is virtuous not to go looking for them and even to flee them when they arise. But, even though it is possible to flee, let us die gloriously if it so pleases the gods, if the magistrates have so decided, if it pleases the people. Let us avenge ourselves on judges who love power and not right, and when they compel us to die and use death as a threat, let us show, by freely remaining and dying, that they are unable either to compel us or frighten us.[23]

It is easy to see in these words a return to a classic attitude of the Stoics that had attracted not a few Christian consciences. But Salutati is well aware that for Christians such a freedom (and the "power" it expresses) does not mean salvation, because no one can be saved by "works," and that divine grace, which is absolute and sovereign and given out of "kindness" and not out of "justice," is a gift of God working through faith. The echo of the theological discussions and controversies, which in these years (and still more in the following decades) already confirm the central place of the perennial dialectic of freedom and grace, is certainly present in these pages which savor of Augustine. And yet the common teaching that faith is a completely unmerited gift does not mean either that human activity is vain and useless or that the "charity" by which human beings give themselves to God is not at the same time God's gift to them. On the contrary, this humanist does not doubt that grace will never be lacking in human activity provided "we take care to order the will according to the standard of right reason." There is in fact no question of an absurd attempt to impose on God a kind of exchange in which human beings may expect an agreed-upon reward that God cannot refuse; there is rather an infinite love that establishes a correspondence between the "good will" of human beings and the salvific freedom promised by Christ. God alone, in his absolute power, can be the guarantor of this bond that transcends every rational norm and is celebrated in the divine acceptance of action done in spontaneous "devotion."

These are the deeper reasons for the preeminent place that Salutati assigns to the will in comparison with the intellect, which is the will's "light" but also its "instrument"; the possible Scotist overtones of this outlook have often pointed out. It is not surprising that he opposes every form of determinism and, in particular, the astrological doctrines of Cecco d'Ascoli. It is more important, however, to register his rejection of the difficult dialectical formulas and complicated logical devices of Scholastic theology, to which he opposes the essential simplicity of an experience that is always seen within the inner tension between time and eternity. With Augustine and Petrarch in mind, Coluccio emphasizes the antithesis between the changeless present of the divine eternity, in which there is no past or future, and the entirely temporal measure of human life, which is a continuum that is constantly consuming itself and breaking down into succession and multiplicity. At the same time, however, he sees in our awareness of our finitude and its limitations the root of an unconquerable aspiration to eternity that no human doctrine or formula can explain and that nevertheless is the very measure of true knowledge and the foundation of the act of love in which faith consists. But this faith is not a blind surrender of reason to the darkness of a mystical clinging to God; rather it is a slow and difficult conquest that is achieved only with the precious help of the *studia humanitatis,* these being understood as a continual renewal and rediscovery of the person's own original spiritual nature.

This carefully thought out defense of humanistic studies thus reflects the keenest intellectual predilections of the humanist chancellor, a lover of the arts that "by helping human communities" are also an ethical guide for individuals. That a humanistic education should be the source of wisdom and, in particular, of the sure training of human wills for mutual harmony is repeated in the discussion carried on in *De nobilitate legum et medicinae* (1400).[24]

This little work was written in response to physician Bernard of Ser Pistorio, who had published a short treatise extolling the superiority of the medical profession. But Salutati's work goes well beyond its polemical purpose because it takes a stand on the opposition between knowledge of the human will and action (and of the "civil" and "divine" norms that should dictate it) and a learning that centers only on the natural world and is limited to understanding of its phenomena. Laws "whose principles are within us, being naturally dictated by the mind with such certainty that they cannot be evaded, without it being necessary to look for them outside," are in fact far superior to those disciplines that take phenomena external to human nature as their field of study and have no solid and evident foundation. The reason is, Salutati writes, that "the goal of speculation is learning whose object is truth. The purpose of the laws is to direct human actions. Their subject, therefore, is the good; not just any good, however, but that most divine good which is the common good." Whereas the principles of medicine, developed as they are out of experience, are uncertain and deceptive and can at best help to physical well-being, the knowledge of the laws, on the other hand, and the learning stored up by the memory of history and by "the persuasiveness of eloquence" are a true cause of the common "health." Or, as Salutati says in his closing peroration, which is put on the lips of the medical art:

> As I reflected within myself on the mystical body that is made up of the human multitude, the families, regions, cities, nations, kingdoms, and the empire, which is the kingdom of kingdoms, and on how laws order, regulate, and preserve everything, I saw that . . . the true health of human societies depends not on the art of medicine but on spiritual harmony. . . . All these bodies that make up human society, and the human race as a whole, are beyond the reach of our attention and, being cemented together as it were by laws, are preserved, increased, and nourished.[25]

The deepest motifs of Petrarch's polemical writings emerge again in these pages, but enriched by a new intellectual outlook that has come to maturity through the practical experience of a magistrate's office and of political life, and this in a society of active and industrious burghers. But the claims of the historical and linguistic dimensions of all cultural experience, even that which is directly connected with understanding of the divine word, is even more clearly expressed in Salutati's reflections on history in various passages of his *Epistolario* and most especially in the letters he exchanged with John Fernández de Heredia, a Spanish nobleman, in 1392.[26]

History, he wrote, is the sole light capable of illumining the ceaseless whirl of things human and "shedding light on the changeable destiny that controls all events past and future"; it is the only source of knowledge that, far more than any philosophical sect, can teach how "to exercise correct judgment" and safeguard "the principles and laws" of human communities. Therefore, while others were devoting themselves to empty Scholastic disputes and seeking to prove abstruse and impenetrable doctrines "by means of painstaking but inexplicable arguments," this humanist was urging that people seek in the teaching of history the way that best enables them to grasp truth, which is always manifested to human beings within time. Nor did he fail to say that even the sacred Scripture and the theological science derived from it would, if cut off from every element of history, become arid narratives incapable of touching and moving souls and of being transformed into life-giving doctrines.

The letters to Heredia are among the most important testimonies to the connection that Salutati meant to set up between knowledge of literature and the testimony of history. I think, however, that the importance he assigned to humanistic studies as the basis of a renewed education and human formation (including the science of things divine) is made even more explicit in another letter, written in 1396 in response to polemical allusions in the *Lucula noctis* of John Dominici (1347–1419).[27]

This Dominican master, of whom I shall speak further on, had in fact criticized the "voluntarism" and primacy of action that were so characteristic of Salutati's moral thinking and had brought up their veiled departure from the theses of St. Thomas. Above all, he had clearly voiced his downright aversion to the secular cult of eloquence and his serious suspicions of the humanists' enthusiasm for the poetry and alleged wisdom of the ancients. He regarded as "trifling" and "useless" the grammatical, rhetorical, and literary discussions in which the chancellor engaged with his friends and disciples; he not only rejected the humanities program that would make the classics the basis of a new educational model, but he also denied its compatibility with the teaching of the Gospel and with Christian ethics. His condemnation was even more drastic: the arts, he said, alienate the soul in every way from the "science of things divine" and must therefore be expelled from the city of the faithful, of which they cannot be worthy guests.

In his reply Salutati did not restrict himself to defending the great "civic" and ethical value of ancient poetry but went on to point out that the study of literature provided a method for obtaining a deeper understanding of the divine word itself. Grammar was not at all a matter of barren and useless curiosity and of empty and useless questions; on the contrary, it was the tool that made it possible to grasp, at its source, the authentic meaning of any thought and the way in which the latter fixed itself in forms and according to the laws of expression. Convinced that only by understanding the "primary intention" of the "word" was it possible to grasp its direct reference to things, Salutati conceived of grammar as an analysis that could rise from mere linguistic "custom" to the essential foundations of language in the indissoluble bond between language and humanness. For this reason the study of etymology, although immature and rudimental, was already able to take on a new and critical dimension as it attempted to retrieve the thought process that showed the true "filiation of 'words.'"

But Salutati went even further when he demonstrated the indissoluble bond between the study of the humanities and the study of divinity, between grammar and theological interpretation: "Literary studies are connected and theological studies are connected, so that it is impossible to have a true and complete knowledge of one of these areas apart from the other." Moreover, sacred Scripture, too, is rich in "mystical" meanings and "manifold mysteries," as is the wisdom hidden in the poetry of the ancients. The humanist did not neglect to emphasize the point that while sacred science does indeed consist in the deepest possible understanding of the divine word, its process of interpretation must begin with a complete understanding of the text and with the grammatical study of the languages and expressions in which the meaning is communicated.

I shall not dwell further on this theme, since this might lead to prolonging Salutati's ideas beyond their real historical horizon in the direction of future developments in philosophy and biblical criticism. On the other hand, it is not out of place to point out how, in the way Salutati pointed out, the study of literature became the only avenue, in every area of knowledge, to the realities which nominalist criticism had so sharply separated from the "formalized" universe of words and signs. This was the reason that led Salutati in another well-known letter, this one to Peter degli Alboini, a keen practicioner of the "logic of the moderns," to emphasize the sapiential value of words and their roots, which are always poetical and irreducible to the "sophistic" dialectic of the "British barbarians." Later on, toward the end of his life, he once again included in his vast work on the ancient tales, *De laboribus Herculis*,[28] a defense of the hidden but intelligible truth that always manifests itself in the allusive form of myth. It is as if he wanted to celebrate in the figure of the ancient hero his idea of the human person as victorious over all "monsters" and all forms of "barbarism."

The *De laboribus* (in which so many motifs and themes of medieval culture made their appearance) was the definitive seal on Salutati's long career as teacher of the humanities. But it was not only his writings that contributed to the success of the *studia humanitatis* in the culture and education of the new century; it was also, and no less, his unwearying labors as collector and glosser of ancient texts, as arbiter in the early literary and philological disputes, and as motivator of new studies and researches. It is indeed not possible to say anything here about the library he managed to put together, which was fairly extensive for his times, or about some of his contributions to the reconstruction of some textual and scholarly traditions.

Moreover, anyone studying the history of theology cannot overlook Salutati's contribution to the revival of studies of the Greek language and of the teaching of Greek in the great Scholastic institutions of the West. He himself, admittedly, never really learned Greek and had only some basic elements of it; it is also a fact that even before Coluccio's lengthy stay in Florence the Byzantine monk Leontius Pilatus had already given public lectures on Greek in Florence and that these were received with great interest by the friends and followers of Petrarch. And yet the chancellor, who condemned the roughness, grammatical defects, and lack of fidelity in the medieval translations of Greek texts, must be given the credit for establishing the first regular chair for the Greek language at the Studium of Florence; he had the learned Byzantine Manuel Chrysoloras (1350–1415) appointed to the chair.[29] Chrysoloras began his teaching in February of 1397 and immediately attracted the young representatives of a new generation of humanists, such as Leonard Bruni and Peter Paul Vergerio.

Thus began a new phase of humanist culture, one no longer directed solely to the reconquest of the Latin classics but henceforth open to the world of Hellenism, to the knowledge of its poets, orators, and philosophers, and to even its Christian theologians, whose deep roots in Platonism and links to the most important speculative discussions of the ancients were soon realized. Soon, in the first thirty years of the new century, the rediscovery of Greek wisdom, known now in its own language and in its historical stature, would be interwoven with the many political and ecclesial arguments that called for a last attempt to reunify Western and "Oriental" Christianity.

7. Leonard Bruni

Coluccio Salutati died in 1406, after having been for more than thirty years the dominant figure in early Florentine humanism. Twenty years later, in 1427, one of Salutati's young disciples, Leonard Bruni (1370?–1444), took the chancellor's chair, thereby assuring, in fact, the primacy of the "new" culture. It was in the school of Chrysoloras that Bruni began his career as expert in and popularizer of the Greek philosophers as seen from the humanist standpoint.

This is not the place, of course, to speak of his work as a translator—especially of some works of Plato *(Phaedo, Gorgias, Phaedrus, Apologia, Crito, Letters,* and part of the *Symposium)* and Aristotle *(Nicomachean Ethics,* works on political economy, *Politics)*—as a historian, and as a politician who played no small part in events in Florence in his time. Nor can I spend too much time on the attacks that greeted his version of the *Ethics* (1417), especially the dispute that arose between him and the learned Spanish jurist and theologian Alphonsus García of Cartagena, who rose up to defend the medieval translations of Aristotle's writings and to challenge the linguistic, stylistic, and philosophical norms adopted and defended by the humanist.

In the preface to his own version Bruni had in fact criticized the most current Latin translation of the *Ethics* (the so-called *textus recognitus*—formed in the workshop of William of Moerbecke—of Grosseteste's translation), claiming that its author was a person completely ignorant of Greek and that due to his lack of skill in the language he had turned one of the most eloquent philosophers of antiquity into a "barbarian" by misunderstanding his teachings and obscuring his real ideas. Then, in his *De recta interpretatione,*[30] written at the beginning of the twenties, Bruni had tried to establish the new "canons" of the humanist method of translation; a translation had to be based on a complete knowledge of the two languages, be marked by stylistic qualities of a superior kind, and in particular, had to show the translator's ability to "reflect" fully the most subtle nuances of thought and language.

But it was precisely these criteria that García challenged; in his view philosophical, like theological, truth was utterly indifferent to the linguistic vehicle by which it was transmitted. In fact, faithful to his teaching as a *magister* formed in the Scholastic discipline and methods, he wrote expressly: "Since, then, Aristotle himself did not base argument on authority but authority on argument, we must think that Aristotle said whatever is according to reason, and we should judge that whatever our Latin translation conveys with true understanding is what was written in the Greek." As a good Thomist, he did not miss the opportunity to insist, against the humanist exaltation of Cicero as teacher of the wisdom and eloquence of antiquity, that the Roman "orator" could not be placed on the same level as Aristotle, a true "man of learning" in ethics, and that in any case, mastery of the supreme disciplines, such as philosophy and theology, should be completed separated from mastery of teachings about "preaching and rhetoric."

I shall not delay on the further development of this controversy, which is so instructive for anyone desirous of understanding the essential reasons for the long conflict between Scholastic education and humanist education. It must be said, however, that it was Bruni who contributed to establishing as central some of the themes of this conflict. He did so in a short youthful work, *Dialogi ad Petrum Paulum Istrum;*[31] there is still disagreement about the date of the work and about its more immediate purpose, but in any case it remains an extremely important piece of evidence for the ongoing quarrel between two different conceptions of learning.

Bruni showed great literary skill in choosing as the principal figure of his dialogues Salutati's most enthusiastic disciple, Nicholas Niccoli. The latter had changed from merchant to humanist and had carried the attack on "Scholastic" culture far beyond the prudent limits observed by his teacher. He had included in his condemnation of the *moderni* even the "three crowns" of Florence, Dante, Petrarch, and Boccaccio, accusing them of being too far removed from the perfection of the classic writers.

In Bruni's work the entire opening discourse of Niccoli is devoted, in fact, not only to a glorification of the philosophers, rhetors, poets, and grammarians of antiquity but to the condemnation of an age and a culture that had lost the true meaning of wisdom by reducing philosophy, which Cicero had brought from Greece to Rome and nourished with "his golden stream of eloquence," to a barren exercise of sophisms and empty syllogisms. Mindful of Petrarch's attacks on the "Scottish and British barbarians," the humanist set up a contrast between, on the one side, the splendor of antiquity, its philosophical freedom, and the "eloquent" purity of its teachings and, on the other, the barbarousness of those *magistri* who had preferred to the precious writings of

Cicero and Seneca the uncouth "barbarity" of Cassiodorus and other authors whom no even moderately learned man would dare read nowadays.

But his harshest attack was on the language of the schools, said to be made up of "harsh, silly, and inharmonious" words, and on the privileged place given to the authority of Aristotle, who had even been turned into an "oracle" by ignorant men unable to realize that the writings and ideas which they attributed to Aristotle did not in fact reflect his authentic thought but were the result of a monstrous corruption of it. Here Bruni was tackling the same subject which we saw to be dominant in his dispute with García: the "incorrectness" and "infidelity" of the medieval translations of the Greek text or of the Arabic, which, in his judgment, had completely distorted the tradition of ancient wisdom. It was enough to point out that whereas Cicero had always spoken of Aristotle as a writer who "pursued eloquence," the translations of Aristotle used in the schools contained the most barbarous expressions and the worst language ever written.

This is not all: the concluding peroration echoes even more harshly the attack on the philosophy that had now become the tool of the theology of the *magistri* but that Bruni regarded as incapable of understanding its own arguments and of being the basis for any knowledge whatsoever. Once again, his immediate target is certainly the logical doctrines that are "muddied by British sophisms" and by the work of teachers who show even by their barbarous names ("Farabrich, Buser, Ockham") that they are soldiers in the army of Rhadmanthys. But despite the intervention of Salutati, who defends the "three crowns" and especially Dante, Niccoli's indictment seems to allow no limits: the opposition between the ancients and the moderns is extended to an attack on Dante and even the "fathers" of humanism, Petrarch and Boccaccio, because of their excessive links to the teachings of the "barbarians" and their still unclassical Latinity.

It is true, of course, that at the end of the second dialogue, when Niccoli is asked to respond to his own attack, he ends his discourse by extolling the "three crowns" as worthy to stand beside Virgil and Cicero. Nor is it necessary to remind the reader that in his *Lives* of Dante and Petrarch,[32] which are written in the vernacular, Bruni not only shows his admiration for the two greatest Florentine poets but even sees in Dante the perfect example of the "civic-minded man," who does not shut himself up in solitary learning and even takes part in the affairs of his city and fellow citizens. At the same time, however, even the rejection of the extreme applications of Niccoli's attack on the moderns does not imply a withdrawal from the polemical arguments for the rejection of Scholastic culture. While Salutati's reply and Niccoli's second discourse seem to react positively to the defenders of the Florentine "tradition" by accepting Dante, Petrarch, and Boccaccio into the list of the new classics, they do not seem ready to soften their rejection of methods and a language henceforth identified with "barbarism."

This attitude does not change even in a work of Bruni written quite a bit later, the *De studiis et litteris,*[33] which he composed between 1423 and 1426 for an educated gentlewoman named Baptist Malatesta. Here again the rejection of a learning such as that of the schools, which is held to be incapable of providing a true ethical formation and a truly "human" doctrine, is accompanied by a defense of an active, diligent wisdom that makes no claim to resolve the greatest speculative problems but does aim to be a guide to a virtuous life marked by the "civic" virtues. The writer asserts once again the perfect accord between the *studia humanitatis* and Christian "truth," between the teaching of the great "ancients" and the word of God as conveyed by the Scriptures and the teaching of the Fathers.

In short, in Bruni's view not only can there not be any opposition between "liberal" studies and the Christian faith; in addition, he writes off as mere pretexts the fears of those pretended "believers" (elsewhere called "hypocrites") who regard the study of the "pagan" poets and philosophers as extremely dangerous and the excessive cultivation of poetic elegance and oratorical "eloquence" as unbecoming to Christian austerity. On the contrary, only minds that are attuned to harmony and beauty can better rein in the passions, truly understand the divine message, and ascend from the truths hidden under the "veil" of ancient poetry and "fables" to the wisdom which God has communicated to Christians. "The wisest human beings of antiquity taught that the poets are divinely inspired; therefore they called them prophets, because they speak out of an interior exaltation and divine inspiration." Thus speaks Bruni in a passage of the *De studiis* in which the defense of literature and poetry becomes an impassioned sign-posting of the only path that can lead to the complete formation of a human being who is no less "devout" than learned.

But Bruni is well aware that the educational power of literature must always be combined with real experience of "things," with "real" information that is utterly necessary if "literary skill" is not to be barren and empty. On the other hand, even the knowledge of "things," whether human or divine, becomes "a dark blind alley" when it lacks the lucidity and harmony bestowed by exact and elegant expression; even the highest truths are betrayed by language that is "uncouth" and "unskilled."

For this reason in another of his writings, the *Isagogicon moralis disciplinae ad Galeottum Ricasolanum* (1424),[34] a successful introduction to the ethical teachings of Aristotle, Leonardo presents his own conception of moral knowledge considered in its highest end, the "common good"; because of this end moral knowledge is more valuable than "natural science," for while this last is certainly "sublime and excellent" it is less useful for life and for the virtue, both individual and "civic," of human beings. Nor is it surprising that he does not restrict himself to finding in the *Ethics* and *Politics* of Aristotle the surest norms for personal behavior and for the "government" of states but also aims to lay a foundation for the common idea of an "honorable happiness," which consists in the close accord between virtue and happiness, a point on which there is agreement among all the main philosophical schools of antiquity, from the Peripatetics to the Stoics, from the Platonists even to the Epicureans. This claim is also a sign of the new attitude of the humanists to the philosophical doctrines of antiquity, the authors and works of which were becoming increasingly better known, while their *concordia discors* (discordant concord or harmony) was already beginning to be reassessed in relation to the authority of Aristotle.

8. Poggio Bracciolini

Bruni's critical outlook and interest in "philology" are the traits that most closely link him to Poggio Bracciolini (1380–1459), another of the major representatives of the second generation of Florentine humanists. Bracciolini's reputation is linked especially to his fortunate discoveries of ancient texts (among the most important the *De rerum natura* of Lucretius, which was so influential in the fifteenth-century revival of Epicurus; a complete copy of Quintilian's *Institutiones oratoriae;* and the *Astronomicon* of Manilius), to his extensive body of letters, and to his brilliant use of humor and satire in his *Facetiae*.[35] He also had a keen and liberal mind, was well aware of the deeper significance of the humanist movement, was alert to the new ethical and religious demands on the society in which he was living, and was able to tackle, with irony as one of his tools, subjects that were especially topical in the theological debates and the ecclesiology of the time.

In his *De varietate fortunae* (1443), for example, he developed with great literary effectiveness the motif, so often recurring in humanist literature, of the conflict between "virtue" and "luck," that is, between the blind inevitability of chance and the human will and desire that are bent on their own fulfillment but are also always caught by the unforeseen and unforeseeable changes that events bring. In his *De infelicitate principum* (1443) and his *De miseria humanae conditionis* (1454) he emphasized even more the darkness in the picture of human history, which is dominated by the violence of the natural world and that of wars and invasions and by the continual rise and fall of the "wheel of fortune."

But the writer's perhaps most personal thoughts were set down in the *Contra hypocritas* (1447–48), an ironic and sarcastic condemnation of the "pauperism" of the various "Observantine Congregations" belonging to the monastic and mendicant orders. These groups are presented as congregations of "uncouth hypocrites," parasites who go about hunting for food in the name of religion but without toiling and working and meanwhile preaching poverty and contempt for material goods to others. On the other hand, Bracciolini had earlier defended in his *De avaritia* (1428–29) a temperate desire for wealth and a zeal for human works that look for a reward of labor even in the present world. Recognizing the social necessity of wealth ("which is to the state as nerves are to the body"), he regarded as "supremely useful" in civic life those persons who in pursuit of their desire became the real "basis and foundation" of society. To the ascetic ideals so prevalent in the pontificate of Eugene IV, he opposed the desolate picture of a city "populated by useless mere semblances of people," deprived of "splendor . . . beauty . . . adornment," and "half asleep" in "sluggish" speculation.

Even the traditional commendation of the wise as persons satisfied with their knowledge and proud of their virtue seemed to him reprehensible. As he wrote in his *De nobilitate* (1440), philosophers who remain shut "in a library, unknown even to themselves" had no claim to real merit in comparison with their neighbors and no right to aspire to renown.

9. Lawrence Valla: Philology and Theological Method

The humanist, however, who left the most profound mark on the history of theological ideas during the first part of the fifteenth century was Lawrence Valla (1407–57), whose exceptional contribution to the beginnings of philology and modern historical criticism hardly needs mention.

A Roman by birth, he began his humanistic studies early, under the guidance of Giovanni Aurispa, and at that time also established his first relations with Florentine circles. Decisive for him, however, were the years (1429–31) that he spent, first at Piacenza, then at Pavia, for it was then, in the course of fierce debates with the representatives of the Scholastic tradition and especially the jurists, that he conceived some of his key works and composed the first version of his *De voluptate*.[36] This work later became his *De vero bono* (1433–49),[37] by way of a radical revision and the substitution of friends from his Pavian period for the original participants in the dialogue: Bruni, Panormita, and Niccoli.

The dialogue (composed, perhaps, as a polemical answer to the *De felicitate* of the well-known canonist Francis Zabarella) is a fundamental document in the "Epicurean renaissance," an event that played so important a part in the philosophical culture of the century. It is also and above all a clear and uncompromising celebration of the goodness and fruitfulness of nature, which is seen as a "minister" of God that bears the imprint of the perfection of its maker. It is precisely on this explicit reaffirmation of the laws and values of nature that Valla bases his attack on every form of ascetic morality and in particular on the ethical attitude of the Stoics, who condemn and reject the most natural impulses and desires.

To these and all the philosophers who follow them in this error that is destructive of human desires and needs, Valla opposes his defense of *voluptas*, of "pleasure" understood as an "honorable" enjoyment and measured by the happiness, present and future, that is the real aim and reason of all our activity and the goal to which all the sciences and arts, technological discoveries, toilsome labor, and refined artistic creation are directed. The "barren" virtue so dear to the Stoics that they wanted all the blessings and pleasures of life to be sacrificed to it is therefore false and hypocritical, useless and unattainable for any human creature. True, active, "natural" virtue, on the other hand, is the behavior of those who are able to discern the right order of pleasures and to attain to a rational and peaceful ethical balance without sacrificing anything of their real nature.

This kind of virtue, which is capable of accepting with heartfelt confidence the joys to which nature itself has predisposed us, is therefore not something alien or opposed to the norms of a sound moral discipline. Valla is, in fact, always concerned to distinguish between a rational and informed acceptance of the *bonum naturae* (the good that is nature itself) and a distressing and exhausting search for a disordered and unsatisfactory pleasure that in reality brings only suffering and interior disorder. True *voluptas,* on the contrary, should be the free enjoyment of a life that is accepted in its totality and in complete agreement with the perfect work of a divinity who seems to have ordered everything so as to give joy to his favorite creatures. Nor is it surprising that while giving Epicurus credit for this doctrine, Valla regards it as in no way opposed to the teaching of the Gospel, which also teaches "happiness" and leads from the "joy" of earthly life to the everlasting blessedness of the life to come.

This is why Valla so decisively rejects any "contamination" by the ascetic teachings of Stoicism, which, especially in the work of Boethius (target of an attack that really should be aimed at Augustine), has radically perverted and corrupted the religious and ethical truth of Christianity. As a result, in this dialogue the praises of nature which Panormita mingles with an unrestrained and unprejudiced commendation of all the pleasures nature provides is followed, in the words of Niccoli, by a call to the highest and supreme happiness that awaits every Christian but that does not do away with or forbid the joys of life. The good desired by Christ's faithful is undoubtedly "the ladder by which we ascend to that blessedness which the soul, stripped of its mortal members, enjoys in the presence of the Father of all things from which the soul came." But this good is always also *voluptas;* so too the love and vision are an ineffable "pleasure" with which, admittedly, no other can be compared but which nonetheless does not differ, except in its supreme perfection, from the honorable delights of this life.

We would, then, not be giving God the honor and love due him if, due to a mistaken ascetical rigorism that is utterly alien to Christian truth, we were to reject the goods which he himself created and the beauty and joy which he is constantly and generously giving us through the wonderful richness and harmony of nature. To love God means, in fact, to love all the things of which he is the creator and origin. Indeed, only this love, so superior to the abstract and captious arguments of the "dialecticians" and theologians of the schools, is truly an "enjoyment" of God and the bond of charity and reciprocal unitive virtue that identifies human beings with the Creator and his work.

These ideas, which were substantially maintained, though in more cautious language, in the *De vero bono,* aroused bitter reactions, and not only among theologians and moralists with the closest ties to the tradition. But Valla further clarified his ethical and religious outlook in another writing, the *De libero arbitrio,*[38] which was completed in 1439, perhaps shortly after the *De vero bono.* Some scholars have contrasted this little work with the teachings in the *De voluptate* and have thought it to be a shrewd device of the humanist to conceal his heterodox views; in fact, however, the book is a consistent and natural development of the earlier work. For in fact the never-ceasing attack on a theological learning that aspires to attain by reason to the knowledge of the divine mysteries is accompanied by a firm summons back to the true and ancient roots of Christian truth; this finds clear expression in the concluding appeal to faith and the love which faith generates.

Renouncing an empty science that "renders" its possessors "stupid," Valla asserts the impossibility for any mind, human or angelic, of entering into the inaccessible secret of a will that is presumed to be absolute, into the mysterious "ways" that strengthen believers in their piety and faith while others are hardened in sin. The insistently drawn contrast between "humble" belief and the rash propositions of the philosophers who "debate everything, raising their faces to heaven and trying to climb up to it and . . . break into it" never means, however, a rejection of the "human" rights of reason, which are always recognized in the sphere of worldly knowledge. Conscious as he is that the instruments of natural reason cannot be used for understanding the divine mysteries, Valla makes a firm distinction between the acceptance of the faith and a submission to entirely human authorities, such as the theological teachings of the masters. The attack on the "presumptuous" Scholastics thus becomes a criticism of "modern" theology which confuses Aristotelean syllogisms with scriptural revelation and thereby separates itself from the enlightened wisdom of the Fathers.

We are dealing here with conclusions that are entirely in keeping with the humanistic formation of this Roman teacher and that, not many decades later, will supply more innovative and reforming tendencies with valuable tools of criticism. But if we want to understand more fully the part played by Valla's works, even before the middle of the century, we must immediately attend to the fact that the ethical and theological reflections in these writings are inseparable from the refined philological analysis that seeks to get beyond all the deviations and corruptions, inevitable in the transmission of any tradition whatsoever, to the original "form" and "language."

The entire literary activity of this humanist during his lengthy stay at the court of Alfonso of Aragon, at a time of bitter conflict between the new sovereign of the kingdom of Naples and the Roman See, was in fact dominated by a ceaseless criticism of all those, whether philosophers or theologians, who lacked any concrete knowledge of linguistic methods and practices and were therefore unable to assess the real meaning of a concept, to understand the origin and meaning of a doctrine, and to grasp its theoretical implications. Accepting as they did authorities that were beyond discussion and acknowledging traditions as authentic despite ignorance of their true basis, these philosophers and theologians were unable to apply to their own learning the "sieve," or close examination, on which the soundness of any knowledge whatsoever depends.

Nor did they understand that language, which is the medium of every kind of communication and every transmission of culture, is subject to a process of alienation that not only separates it from the reality signified but crystallizes it into forms that are increasingly deprived of concrete meaning and increasingly distant from their original "intentions" and are often also betrayed by their passage through different tongues or "jargons." In Valla's opinion this was the main reason for the most tenacious errors, the most insuperable misunderstandings, the most absolute and unquestioned dogmas. It was also, however, the source of the habit of accepting without any discussion any and every opinion, teaching, or belief that had on its side the apparent backing of some hallowed authority, the witness of continuity with the distant past, or the deceptive support of time. In particular, the theologians made the divine word obscure and uncertain by relying on a text of the Vulgate that often was clearly corrupt, by mingling with the science of things divine metaphysical disputes or dialectical subtleties that were wholly alien to it, and by accepting words and expressions that were poorly understood and, still worse, badly translated from their original linguistic setting.

Errors such as these could be eliminated only by tracing all doctrinal questions and conflicts back to their real historical causes, that is, through an accurate linguistic and philological knowledge that made it possible to understand meanings and reasons too often forgotten or ignored. Above all, it had to be recognized that it is impossible to be real philosophers, jurists, logicians, or theologians without first of all being good philologists. The reason for this is that the study of words enables us to reconstruct the process followed by all thinking: from its initial formation, through the various phases of its development and transmission, down to its most recent results. It is clear that any authority subjected to such a "check" ceases to be an authority and becomes the object of an analysis on which its concrete value and certainty depends.

But if theologians, like logicians, jurists, or philosophers, were to accomplish this task, they had to be able to set aside all the preestablished interpretations or exegeses that interpose themselves like screens between the original meaning of a concept or text and the way it is presently understood. But this presupposed the establishment of a true "grammatical" and "rhetorical" science that would precede all the others as their foundation and would make it possible to recover a pure, simple, and fundamental language as the vehicle for expressing limpid and accurate thinking. For Valla, then, the humanist recovery of classical Latinity and the return to the Greek sources of the common "wisdom" were indispensable presuppositions for a radical and integral renewal of all the forms of knowledge; this claim was extended, of course, even to the "sacred" disciplines, which needed to be rescued from the damage done to them by a lengthy period of "barbarism." The restoration of its dignity, power, and expressiveness to the "Latin language" *(sermo latinus)* would bring an understanding of the way in which there had come down to us not only the most important experiences of ancient learning (these would reveal to us their true features) but also the divine "word," cleansed at last of the many human stains that obscured it.

The most complete examples of this method as consistently applied to the analysis of philosophical and even theological discourse are two works which Valla planned and reworked over a long period, beginning perhaps in 1433, and both of which had a decisive influence on the most critical developments of humanist culture; the two works are his *Elegantiae latinae linguae*[39] and his *Dialectica.*[40]

Behind the superficial veil of grammatical and rhetorical analysis in the first of these two works, it was in fact fundamental concepts of metaphysical and theological vocabulary that were being analyzed and discussed (for example: person, faith, mystery, suffrage) and restored to their linguistic "functions" in a setting marked by full awareness of the particular syntactical and semantic structures peculiar to the language of Scripture but also and especially to the language of theology.

In the *Dialectica,* the appeal to "customary usage," or in other words, the "consensus of educated people," is the critical argument that is constantly used, in the various editions of the work,[41] in conducting a radical philologico-philosophical analysis of speculative theology and its sources, and in recovering the language of the Bible and the Fathers. In fact, in the first book some very important philosophical and theological terms are analyzed from both the grammatical and the semantic points of view, with reference to the treatment not only of metaphysical, ethical, and psychological questions but also of explicitly theological questions.

It is, of course, not possible here to follow Valla into, for example, the details of a study aimed at reducing the "transcendental" terms (being, something, true, good, one) to the single term "thing" *(res),* which is considered to be the most universal and concrete, or in his demonstration of the substantial identity of such terms as "to be" *(esse),* essence *(essentia),* and being *(ens).* It is to be noted, however, that by analyzing the word *res,* as compared with its Greek equivalent *pragma,* Valla is able to bring out the multiplicity and wealth of meanings that the Latin word conveys and to recognize that substance *(substantia),* quality *(qualitas),* and action *(actio)* are, according to correct rhetorical teaching, simply predicates of *res.* But this means that beings such as "God" and "human being" cannot be referred to by the term substance, since the reality of each is an indivisible whole made up of its concrete nature and its proper characteristics and activities. In fact, to distinguish substance from accident means, in this case, denying a fundamental unity which Valla designates by the term *consubstantia.* Consequently, the use of the term "quality" should be reserved for signifying the "acts" that qualify a thing, person, or event, when these are considered in their concrete aspects or in their ethical or political implications.

Appealing to the rhetorical teaching on *qualitas* that had already been set forth by Quintilian in the context of oratory, Valla is thus able to develop his criticism of Boethius' definition of "person," as given in the latter's *Contra Eutychen,* which had such an influence on Scholastic theological teaching: "In Latin, 'person' *(persona)* signifies a quality of the soul or body or condition, although Boethius, with a great lack of skill, wants to argue that it is the substance."[42] And in fact Valla holds that Boethius had attributed to "person" a meaning and a "definition" completely opposed to the common use of that word in the Latin language and, more specifically, to its reception in the language and rhetoric of law. It is a term that, strictly understood, can be predicated only of human beings in accordance with their nature as rational beings; it can be used only analogically when it is applied to the divinity. The reason is that the "person" is constituted by the special functions which individuals exercise in their social relationships, by the way in which they exercise them, and by the specific characteristics which ensue from their behavior, as well as by even their physical constitution and by the set of conditions, relations, and connections which determine their identity over against various institutions and other "comparable" things.

The theologians, following Boethius, could certainly object that this reduction of the "person" to a "quality" turns it into something "accidental," which may even be "lacking" without thereby destroying the "reality" of the individual. Nor does Valla overlook the consequences which such an objection may have for the use of the concept of "person" in the development of trinitarian dogma. In the first version of the *Dialectica* and, for that matter, in the *Elegantiae,* he nonetheless maintains that the word "person" can, in its strict sense, be applied only to human beings and not to "animals," much less to God; but the now-established use of the word in theological language makes it necessary to determine as accurately as possible the semantic field occupied by the various terms in their original and correct meaning: "The *persons,* which the Greeks call *hypostases,* that is, *substances,* and the ancient Latins *naturae,* are simply qualities of the divine substance."

It is not surprising, then, that while rejecting the equivocal use of the concept of substance with its two meanings of "essence" and "subsistence" (which he finds not only in Boethius but in Augustine), Valla proposes his own different exegesis of the dogma of the Trinity. As we shall see, this exegesis had a direct bearing on the great theological disputes of the age.

> Some maintain that as in the sun there is a substance in the proper sense, so in God, the Father is the "substance" and the Son is, as it were, the "light" and the Holy Spirit is as it were the "burning heat." But if this be true, then, as the Father is "substance," will the Son be "quality" and the Holy Spirit "action?" Not so. In fact, each of the three is "substance," each "quality," and each "action." But the "substance" is one and therefore common to all, while the "quality" and the "action" are proper to each individually. I refer to "substance" understood in our manner, since the "substance" which I call "consubstance" cannot be common to the three, unless the person that is included under the name substance is also to be common to the three. While I distinguish, better than the philosophers do, between the substance and the "person" in God (the term person here being a metaphorical transfer of the "person" in the human being), I call it also "quality," and do so, I maintain, in no less proper a way than those who speak of three "persons," three "natures," three "substances." I do not mean that the Father, the Son, and the Holy Spirit are only "qualities," although they are distinct from each other "by their quality." What we may call "vibration" is the Father, who is in the proper sense the life, power, and eternity of God, as "vibration" explains the same aspects of the sun. The "light" is the Son, who is the wisdom of God, born of that power, just as we discover in the sun the "vibration" that shakes the solar body and, in a way, generates and produces light. The "burning heat" is the Holy Spirit, who is God's love, just as we know that in the sun there is a heat that is not generated but appears, spreads out, and issues forth. To "vibrate, produce, and emit" is the action of the Father; to "shine," that of the Son; to "burn," that of the Holy Spirit. None of the three is prior to the others, but all three are simultaneously, and in their one substance are, as it were, God the sun; each of the three will be the sun, that is, God: the Father, the "vibrating sun," the Son, the "radiant sun," the Holy Spirit, the "burning sun."[43]

What we have here is a linguistic and philological analysis, and for some time now scholars have correctly pointed out its direct connection with the debate on the Trinity between Catholic and Orthodox theologians that was central in the Council of Ferrara-Florence (1438–39).[44] It has also been noticed that Valla's criticism was made public at a time of serious conflict between the king of Aragon and the Roman See. The fact is, however, that by rejecting the Scholastic language and terminology Valla brought to light the linguistico-semantic difficulties originating in an erroneous transposition of Greek terms into Latin as well as in the use of Aristotle's speculative vocabulary in the sphere of Christian theology.

Terms such as *essentia, substantia, persona (ousia, hypostasis, prosôpon),* or *principium (aitia)* did not correspond fully in the two languages. This had hindered the Latin and Byzantine theologians in understanding each other's points of view precisely because the words had taken on a different meaning in the two patristic traditions and, in addition, could have different meanings depending on whether they were used with an abstract or a concrete reference.

The uncritical acceptance of Aristotelean concepts (which were in themselves obscure and equivocal) was, to Valla's mind, the primary cause of a lack of understanding that had with time become the cause of division and condemnation, as theological language, distancing itself ever more from the words of Scripture, had modeled itself on the vocabulary of Aristotle's logic and metaphysics, even though these were fundamentally alien to it. The questions of terminology that were raised by the debate over the *Filioque* (which will be dealt with in detail later in this book) showed how at the origin of these lengthy and bitter theological disputes there were misunderstandings due to the specific words used and how these misunderstandings rendered dogmatic differences insuperable and prevented recognition even of definite, real points of agreement. It is not surprising that, with his eye on the discussions conducted in Florence in March 1439, Valla should write: "Every question of this kind that the philosophers and theologians twist into knots in their debates is a matter solely of words. But it seems to me that, once this is realized, it is pointless to wear oneself out in discourses and captious disagreements about words, especially when these are not based on any solid authority."[45]

Valla's discussion of terminology and his linguistico-theological criticisms provided, at least in their ultimate conclusions, an objective support for the arguments which Mark Eugenicus developed on this subject against the Latin theologians as he reasserted concepts and teachings typical of the Eastern "doctrine." Nor is it surprising that in the inquisitorial trial of 1444 the accusation of heresy should be leveled at him, based on the claim that he had cast doubt on the authenticity of the Apostles' Creed and, above all, that "in writing about the Holy Spirit . . . he had denied the teaching of the Church." In his *Apologia,*[46] which was sent to Eugene IV, Valla defended both his interpretation of the concept of *voluptas* and his criticism of the vocabulary of Aristotelean logic and metaphysics, while at the same time he reasserted his own philological arguments on the historical tradition regarding the Apostles' Creed.

In regard to the specific point at issue in the discussion of the Trinity, he stated that his intervention had been inspired by the intention of providing the Latin theologians with a more precise and solid argument, which would also enable them to deal without misunderstanding or prejudice with their Byzantine colleagues, whose language and arguments they needed to understand. It was, however, characteristic of him that he should raise the question, as a matter of philology, of the legitimacy of adding the *Filioque* to the

Nicene-Constantinopolitan Creed, this being the definitive profession of faith of the universal Church, and that in his debate (1444) with the Franciscan Anthony of Bitonto he should have denied the apostolic origin of the Apostles' Creed, the actual composition of which he claimed to have shown, without trusting in any legend.

Philology thus became a key element in the work of theology, the sources of which needed to be reconstructed and analyzed with great critical rigor, by eliminating all external interventions affecting the purity of their transmission and seeking to reestablish their original "language" and "truth." This explains why Valla shared with other humanists of the time the demand that the traditional Vulgate version of the biblical text be completely revised by directly relating it to the original "form" of the Old and New Testaments.

It is also a well-known fact that humanist philologists and scholars were much concerned to collect ancient codices of the Scriptures (John Aurispa, Ciriacus of Ancona, Nicholas Perotti) and that they widely deplored the "corruptions" introduced into the word of God by the ignorance or carelessness of copyists. In any case it was Valla who first undertook a critical revision of the scriptural text in its Latin form, starting this project in the first version of his *Collatio Novi Testamenti*[47] (in the second version it became *Adnotationes* and was published under this title by Erasmus of Rotterdam in 1505) and in the very important *Epistola dedicatoria* to Nicholas V, which was prefixed to the *Collatio*. With regard to the historical significance and importance of this exceptional philological project, P. Camporeale has rightly said that it marks "a line of division between a before and an after in the history of biblical exegesis, a line lasting from the end of the fourteenth century to the beginning of the sixteenth, that is, from Nicholas of Lyra to Erasmus."[48]

In Valla's view, then, a theologian must first of all be a philologist of the divine word and must proceed to theoretical development only after having ascertained the correct sacred text, which has inevitably been exposed to all the causes of contamination and distortion that affect humanly transmitted documents. Even the sacred Scriptures, therefore, must be subjected to an assessment by all the tools of philology and linguistics that are needed for a sure and adequate reading of the text. Like the pagan authors and any other document whatsoever (we may think of Valla's *De falso credita et ementita Constantini donatione,*[49] in which he proves that a document on which papal claims to political sovereignty over the entire West were based was in fact counterfeit), even the Bible, which contains the word of God, calls for an investigation capable of establishing the authenticity of an authority that is essential for human salvation.

Consequently, even before subjecting the Vulgate tradition to his criticism Valla seeks to establish with as much certainty as possible both the text of the Latin translation and the Greek text regarded as "original." The search for and collation of codices is therefore the starting point of an investigation that becomes a first attempt at "a retranslation of the New Testament"; the attempt is based on critical reflection on the structural differences between the Greek and Latin languages, differences that had in fact influenced the entire development of theological discourse. But in bringing out the many inaccuracies and flaws of the Vulgate, Valla was setting himself an even more ambitious task: to show theologians that if they were to provide a true interpretation of the word of God they must go back to its Greek "source" while also observing all the "precepts of the art of grammar," which are essential for their task. His criticism of Augustine and Thomas Aquinas as "exegetes" is based precisely on their lack of an adequate literary and philological education and a real capacity to understand texts. Men who had spoken a language that was "awkward" and "muddled" and whose knowledge was therefore no less uncertain had developed an exegesis and a theology that, in Valla's eyes, were too far removed from the right methodology for a "science of things divine."

10. The Roman Academy

I shall not dwell further on these aspects of Valla's work, which are in so many ways at the origin of modern biblical criticism and were to have a deep influence on sixteenth-century culture, especially by way of the controversial writings and exegesis of Erasmus. But I must call attention to the fact that the critical attitudes and philological work of this humanist were to have even more radical results in connection with his defense of Epicurus and with his own teaching on pleasure, a teaching so filled with anti-Augustinian motifs. In fact, the spread of Valla's writings and ideas played a part in the intellectual formation of some of the humanists who met at the Roman Academy, right in the capital of Catholicism, and who cultivated attitudes and ideas entirely hostile to Christian theological traditions.

The most typical representative of this circle was Pomponius Laetus (1428–97).[50] This man was, first and foremost, a learned and enthusiastic student of the humanities and the classical civilizations, which, like the young Niccoli, he regarded as the perfect model of a "humanness" set free of its old ethical and religious ties and restored to its full autonomy so that it could satisfy its own desires and enjoy its own earthly *voluptas*. But Leto and his disciples—among whom I shall mention the well-known Bartholomew Platina (1421–81) and the Tuscan humanist Philip Bonaccorsi (better known under the name of Callimachus Esperiens) (1437-96)[51]—would not be limited simply to venerating and reviving the traditions and memories of ancient Rome and to celebrating its festivals and rituals in accord with models made sacrosanct by the works of the ancients. Rather, their "Epicurean" sympathies, their rejection of current morality, and their open and mocking attacks on every form of asceticism seem to have taken definite shape in some ideas that would for a long time feed a hidden antireligious and anti-Christian polemics.

According to the information available in Roman diplomatic circles in 1468, when the principal representatives of the Academy were imprisoned for allegedly hatching a plot against Pope Paul II, these men had even asserted that the soul is destined to perish along with the body, that the sole purpose of life is to seek knowledge, and that all religious beliefs and institutions are only superstitions and clever "impostures." Their hostility to every form of faith was supposedly pushed to the point of making their own a typical theme that cropped up constantly in medieval manifestations of unbelief in both Christian and non-Christian societies: that Moses, Christ, and Muhammad were "impostors" and "seducers" of peoples and that "through diligence and malice" they had imposed their own ethical and political "laws" on uneducated and ignorant men and women.

The condemnations with which the persons guilty of the imagined plot were threatened and the flight of those most endangered put an end to this brief affair of the Roman "dandies," who were immediately accused of "atheism." After a not very lengthy period of imprisonment Pomponio Leto resumed his activity as philologist, scholar, and teacher of the humanities. Platina, who was already in a Roman prison, hastened to write a *De falso et vero bono,* an explicit retraction that made use of the most characteristic commonplaces of the Stoic-Platonic ethical tradition in condemning the "ill-fated" teachings of Epicurus, to which he opposed undeniable Christian truth. Callimachus Esperiens, after various adventures, took refuge in distant Poland, where he became a quite important political figure; he continued to cultivate a covert Epicureanism, which led him later on into a debate with Marsilius Ficino on the intrinsic contradictions in the Platonic idea of the immortality of the soul and of the soul's relationship with the body as well as on the ambiguous doctrine of the "spirit."

In subsequent years and decades the renewed success of Epicurean ideas, due, among other things, to the rapid spread of the Latin translation of Diogenes Laertius' *Vitae philosophorum,* helped sustain and continue a covert attack, often expressed in masked and allusive ways, that had by now passed from criticism of the theology of the masters to an attack on the very principles of Christian doctrine.

11. Ambrose Traversari

The humanist who produced the Latin translation of the *Vitae philosophorum* and thereby made possible the wide circulation of a book that expounded in detail the physical and ethical ideas of Epicurus was a devout Camaldolese monk, Ambrose Traversari (1386–1439),[52] who was long active in the monastery of Santa Maria degli Angeli in Florence. This was a favorite meeting place of the third generation of Florentine humanists, those who received their training during the first two decades of the fifteenth century. Ambrogio himself, in his extensive correspondence, provides rather important testimonies regarding the intellectual environment in this monastery, which had a scriptorium and produced splendid illuminated codices. The memory of ancient monastic experience and of Basil's teaching had never died out here, nor had the close connection with the thinking of the great teachers of Christianity in the East been broken; this connection was still attested by some characteristic elements of monastic and eremitical life, by the visits of monks of Greek or other Eastern origin, and by the hospitality given to some well-educated Byzantines.

More than this, the Camaldolese Order had its "geographical" center in the territory that sloped down from the Tuscan-Romagnese Apennines toward the Adriatic along roads that dropped down to the Marches, the Adriatic, and the cities of the Veneto, or in other words, the territory most influenced by Byzantium and as far as Venice, where the Camaldolese had long played a preeminent role in the religious life of the city.

It is easy to understand why the younger humanists who had, even by the end of the fourteenth century, devoted themselves to acquiring a knowledge of Greek literature under the guidance of Chrysoloras were attracted to a religious institution that could best answer their deepest intellectual needs by reason of the fundamentally "patristic" nature of its culture, its distance from the "disputational" and "dialectical" theology of the schools, and its appeal to a spiritual tradition born of "Greek" Christianity.

But the reason for Traversari's influence on the Florentine humanists born at the end of the fourteenth century and the beginning of the new century becomes even more intelligible if we recall that between 1400 and 1405 some of the best representatives of the generation that had been formed by Salutati (James Angeli, Bracciolini, and Bruni) left Florence for the Roman Curia; their continual shifting of residence, especially during the time of the Council of Constance, made possible the great period of discovery of manuscripts. It is true that about ten years later Bruni returned to Florence for good and began his work as "civil" historian of the republic and an increasingly intense activity as translator of the ancient philosophers, this last being closely connected with his thinking as theoretician of humanist culture and education.

In the first two decades of the fifteenth century, however, and even later, the most stable point of reference for the new Florentine culture was Niccoli, who quickly became an associate of the young Camaldolese monk. He also became a diligent frequenter of the informal discussions held at Santa Maria degli Angeli, where a scientist like Paul of Pozo Toscanelli found himself in the company not only of refined men of letters such as Carlo Marsuppini but also of notaries and jurists such as Ser Ugolino Peruzzi, possessor of an extensive library; enthusiastic bibliophiles such as Palla Strozzi; and even shrewd bankers and politicians, among them Cosimo de'Medici and his brother Lorenzo.

But the humanists' appeal to the past, their intention of getting back to the purity of the "beginnings" in language as in literature, in philosophy as in the "restoration" of religious life and institutions, certainly had no less deep an attraction for those religious men, to whose number Traversari belonged, who in difficult times of decadence and crisis in the Church and in monasticism were looking to the Scriptures and the teachings of the Fathers as to the only "star" that could guide Christianity to its own renewal. To this end, these men took the tools, methods, and linguistic and historical skills used by the humanists and put these at the service of the study and recovery of another aspect of *graecitas,* the Christian aspect, which had been one in its original tradition before this unity was broken by a separation that was equally deadly for the life of the two churches, the Eastern and the Western.

These reflections are enough to show why Traversari devoted himself to translating into Latin an extensive collection of patristic texts and why, even when he had become an important and influential churchman, he continued this patient and difficult labor. He was sustained in it by his humanistic enthusiasm for every new discovery and by his never abandoned search for manuscripts, information, and documents that could give a better knowledge of Christian origins and of the teachings of the early trustees of a divine "truth" that had been expounded also by wise and learned experts in the ancient literatures and philosophies.

His letters[53] and his *Hodoeporicon,*[54] a diary of the journeys undertaken during his missions as general of the order and as papal diplomat, provide us with information about the libraries or the otherwise unknown "deposits" of books that he visited and the searches devoted to recovering texts and authors of every kind (from the *De musica* of Ptolemy to the "large volume" that contained a good many Aristotelean and pseudo-Aristotelean writings, from Origen to Archimedes, from Eusebius to Galen, from Apollonius of Rhodes to Julius Firmicus and Julian). They also show us that the Greece to which he was looking was above all a Christian land, whose return to the unity of the Church was expected to bring not only salvation from the imminent Turkish threat but also the end of a lengthy "age of troubles" for the Western Church as well as the renewal which so many prophetic traditions linked with the restoration of the "one sheepfold."

The return to the Greek Fathers and theologians—Athanasius, Basil, John Climacus, John Chrysostom, Ephraem and John Moschus, Origen and Dionysius the Areopagite (Traversari's favorite)—meant in fact the recovery of a way of understanding and living the word, the intense spirituality of which the West did not adequately know and appreciate precisely because it was ignorant of the authentic language of these writers and could not penetrate to their genuine inspiration. In addition, Traversari, a sincere champion of *pax christiana* and a man who dedicated so much of his life to reconciliation with Byzantium, knew that it was not possible to renew the often attempted but never really cultivated dialogue with the Eastern Christian world unless the West first understood its culture. This was a culture that also had deep roots in an intellectual history far richer and more complex than that with which Western theologians were familiar. New philological and textual discoveries by the humanists were at last making that history increasingly intelligible.

In this light, even the care which Traversari devoted, often amid great difficulty and with scrupulous effort, to turning the *Vitae philosophorum* into Latin, was not the incidental activity it is made to seem in overly hagiographical presentations of his work as a humanist. The reason is that this book described the more important undertakings and teachings of Greek philosophical wisdom, which was so different from the image that late medieval culture had of it. This wisdom was connected with the cult of the "Philosopher" par excellence and was, in many of its aspects, foreign to the teachings and languages on which even the theoretical development of Eastern theologies was based.

It is true, of course, that in Traversari's eyes the wisdom of the ancient poets and philosophers had been radically elevated and transfigured by the light of the Gospel message that had inspired the Fathers and made available to them an absolute and eternal truth. At the same time, however, the Greek language and Greek learning had provided the first human means of interpreting revelation and developing the dogmatic and theoretical form it needed. And it is certainly significant that during almost the same years in which Bruni was implementing his extraordinary program of translations, the Camaldolese monk was providing a valuable body of translations of Greek patristic theological and spiritual works. These were often connected with the history of monasticism and were accompanied by other texts that could serve as excellent tools in the still desired meeting with the easterners.

Moreover, it was again Traversari who maintained close relations and friendships with the patrician humanists of Venice, Francis and the elder Ermalaus Barbaro and Leonard Giustiniani. These men also shared Traversari's spiritual aspirations, and they were very influential in establishing important intellectual, diplomatic, and political contacts between the representatives of the two Christendoms in the years preceding and preparing for the Council of Ferrara-Florence and the final attempt to restore the unity of the Church. We know that Traversari's intense and enthusiastic participation in the work of this council, during which he was the most direct intermediary between the Latin and the Eastern theologians, was also the closing event of his life, the fulfillment of a plan he had always had in mind in his work as searcher for manuscripts and as translator and admirer of the teaching of the Fathers.

12. The Pedagogy of the Humanists and Theology

Even during the first half of the century humanist traditions and their influence on the intellectual life of the age, on the order of studies and the system of learning (and therefore also on theological education), were the source of a pedagogical and scholastic renewal that would provide some basic models for educational methods and institutions unconnected with or even alternative to those of the Studia or medieval schools. I shall speak of this point here, of course, only insofar as these methods and institutions had a relation to theological studies and learning.

I must recall, then, how the Istrian humanist Peter Paul Vergerio of Capodistria (1370–1444), who had studied in Padua and then in Bologna and Florence, where he had been a student of Chrysoloras, proposed in his *De ingenuis moribus et liberalibus adolescentiae studiis* (1400–2)[55] a program of instruction based on the humanities, which he regarded as the only subjects that "befit a free human being" and form the person for civic life. The "constitutive" disciplines were, therefore, eloquence, moral philosophy, and history, this last being the beginning of all learning. But the essential formation thus given, which was common to all, had to be completed by the study of poetry, music, drawing, and in addition, the mathematical sciences, astronomy, the natural sciences, law, and metaphysics, following an encyclopedic and hierarchic order that culminated, of course, in theology; the learning of theology was made clearer and surer by the acquisition of a complete "literary" and "liberal" education.

When Gasparino Barzizza (ca. 1360–Milan, 1431) opened a school of the humanities at Padua in 1408, it was immediately attended by young Venetian patricians who were dissatisfied with the instruction given in the Studium. He also included, beyond the study of the literary disciplines, an introduction to the "higher" disciplines, of which theology was, of course, one.

The decisive factor, however, in the birth of a new kind of school that reflected the humanists' intellectual "reform" was the work of Guarino Guarini of Verona (1374–1460).[56] He too had been trained by Chrysoloras, who inspired him with the idea of a complete and harmonious formation of the person and who wanted his school to be a place of free comradeship in which teachers and students collaborated in a common search for knowledge and in the achievement of a perfect ethical balance. Especially after 1436, when Guarini moved to Ferrara, where he was entrusted with the education of Lionel d'Este, he organized his school into three courses (elementary, grammatical, rhetorical) according to a logical and systematic progression which he regarded as in keeping with the natural development of the students' abilities.

It must be noted, however, that the grammatical course began with the reading of Priscian, Cicero's letters, and passages of Virgil; it also included a "historical" section preparatory to the study of Valerius Maximus and Justin and then of Statius, Ovid's *Fasti,* Seneca, Terence, and Juvenal, and of the Latin geographers and the writers who tackled a variety of subjects. The high point of the instruction came in the rhetorical course with the reading of Cicero, Quintilian, and the *Rhetorica ad Herennium,* before passing on to the more difficult introduction to texts of Plato and Aristotle. It would be a mistake, however, to think that Guarini's program was limited to the study of skills in speaking and to a literary and oratorical training. Knowledge of the classical languages was meant, in fact, to open the way to a critical understanding, based on the direct interpretation of texts, of the philosophical and scientific doctrines of antiquity and to the knowledge of authors and works, the understanding of which was regarded as indispensable if the student were truly to profit from divinity studies.

A sincere and deep religious inspiration combined with a personal vocation to asceticism and an admiration for the devotional experience of Bernardine of Siena also directed the educational work of the other great humanist "teacher," Vittorino de'Rambaldoni da Feltre (1287–1446), and especially his school in Mantua (the "Zoiosa"). Here Vittorino educated not only the young Gonzaga princes but various young men of the bourgeoisie, or the common people, who had an aptitude for studies. Vittorino's disciples— Sassuolo da Prata, Francis Prendilacqua, and Bartholomew Sacchi, known as Il Platina—have left records of his educational methods and of the moral attraction exerted by this man who, though he left no written work, became a kind of symbol of the humanist educational reform.[57]

On the one hand, these records enable us to reconstruct Vittorino's Scholastic programs, which were based on a distinction between an introductory course on grammar, a course in oratory, and a more advanced instruction in the mathematical disciplines. On the other hand, they show that the ultimate goal was a solid ethical and religious education but one that was free of any Scholastic formalism and of the "trickeries" and "sophisms" of the modern theologians. Vittorino certainly intended that after his students had thoroughly studied the disciplines of the trivium and quadrivium, they should devote themselves for a time to the study of philosophy (and therefore read Plato and Aristotle in the original language). He maintained that these bodies of knowledge ought to be possessed by all who wanted subsequently to acquire the professional knowledge officially imparted in the faculties of law, medicine, or theology. But the records and documents of Vittorino's school show that the properly human formation of the students took place in the propaideutic courses. They show, too, that the mastery of the languages, oratorical techniques, and teachings of the ancients was to be combined with a strict but not coercive moral and religious education, to be acquired from the books of the "sages" and from the divine testimony of the Scriptures.

BIBLIOGRAPHY

Francis Petrarch (Arezzo, 1304–Arquà, 1374)

EDITIONS

Opera latina. Basel, 1554, 1581.

Prose latine. Ed. G. Martellotti and others. Naples-Milan, 1955. With an Italian translation. This work includes *Secretum*, ed. Carrara (21–215); *De vita solitaria*, ed. Martellotti (285–91); *De ocio religioso,* ed. Ricci (592–603); *De remediis utriusque fortunae,* ed. in part by Ricci (605–45); *De sui ipsius et multorum ignorantia,* ed. Ricci (710–67).

Epistolae de rebus familiaribus et variae. Ed. G. Fracassetti. 3 vols. Florence, 1859–70.

Rerum senilium libri. Trans. G. Fracassetti. 2 vols. Florence, 1869–70.

Sine nomine. Ed. P. Piur. Halle, 1925.

Familiarium rerum libri XXIV. Ed. V. Rossi and U. Bosco. Florence, 1931–42.

Invectivarum contra medicum quendam libri IV. Ed. P. G. Ricci. Rome, 1950; updated ed., 1978.

Rerum memorandarum libri. Ed. G. Billanovich (Florence, 1943–45).

BIBLIOGRAPHIES

Ferrazzi, G. I. *Bibliografia petrarchesca.* Bassano, 1887.

Calvi, E. *Bibliografia analitica petrarchesca, 1877–1904.* Rome, 1904.

Calcaterra, C. "Il Petrarca e il petrarchismo." *Questioni e correnti di storia letteraria.* Milan, 1949. Pp. 166–73.

Bosco, U. "Francesco Petrarca." *Letteratura italiana* I. *Maggiori* 2 (Milan, 1956) 111–83.

STUDIES

Nolhac, P. de. *Pétrarque et l'humanisme.* Paris, 1907.

Burdach, K. *Reformation, Renaissance, Humanismus.* Berlin-Halle, 1918.

Aus Petrarcas ältesten deutschen Schülerkreise. Texte und Untersuchungen. Ed. K. Burdach and R. Kienasts. Berlin-Halle, 1929.

Rossi, V. *Studi sul Petrarca.* Florence, 1930.

Petrarcas Briefwechsel mit deutschen Zeitgenossen. Ed. P. Piur and K. Burdach. Berlin-Halle, 1933.

Sapegno, N. "Il Petrarca e l'umanesimo." *Annali della Cattedra petrarchesca* 8 (1938) 97–114.

Martellotti, G. "Linee di sviluppo dell'umanesimo patrarchesco." *Studi petrarcheschi* 2 (1949) 51–80.

Billanovich, G. *Petrarca letterato. Lo scrittoio del Petrarca.* Rome, 1947.

Withfield, J. H. *Petrarca e il Rinascimento.* Bari, 1949.

Kristeller, P. O. "Il Petrarca, l'umanesimo e la scolastica a Venezia." *La civiltà veneziana del Trecento.* Florence, 1956. Pp. 147–48. Now in Kristeller. *Studies in*

Renaissance Thought and Letters. Rome, 1985. Pp. 217–38.

Wilkens, E. H. *Studies in the Life and Work of Petrarch.* Cambridge, Mass., 1955.

_____. *Petrarch's Correspondence.* Padua, 1960.

_____. *Life of Petrarch.* Chicago, 1961.

Bosco, U. *Petrarca.* Bari, 1961[3].

Petrarca e il petrarchismo. Atti del III congresso dell'Associazione internazionale per gli studi delle lingua e della letteratura italiana. Bologna, 1961.

Quaglio, A. E. *Francesco Patrarca.* Milan, 1967.

Tripet, A. *Pétrarque ou la connaissance de soi.* Geneva, 1967.

Baron, H. *From Petrarch to Leonardo Bruni.* Chicago, 1968.

Rico, F. *Vida y obra de Petrarca.* Chapel Hill, 1975.

Francesco Petrarca Six Centuries Later: A Symposium. Chicago, 1975.

Francesco Petrarca. Atti del Convegno internazionale promosso dall'Accademia dei Lincei. Rome, 1976.

Wilkins, E. H. *Studies on Petrarch and Boccaccio.* Padua, 1978.

Dotti, U. *Petrarca e la scoperta della coscienza moderna.* Milan, 1978.

Billanovich, G. *La tradizione del testo di Livio e le origini dell'Umanesimo.* Padua, 1981.

Martellotti, G. *Scritti petrarcheschi.* Padua, 1983.

Foster, K. *Petrarch: Poet and Humanist.* Edinburgh, 1984.

Branca, V. "Petrarca, Francesco." *Dizionario critico della letteratura italiana* 3 (Turin, 1986[2]) 419–32. Extensive bibliographical information.

Fubini, R. *Umanesimo e secolarizzazione da Petrarca a Valla.* Rome, 1990. See the index.

Codici latini del Petrarca nelle biblioteche fiorentine. Catalogo della Mostra (19 maggio–30 giugno, 1991). Ed. M. Feo. Florence: Biblioteca Medicea Laurenziana, 1991.

Quillen, C. E. "A Tradition Invented: Petrarch, Augustine, and the Language of Humanism." *JHistIdeas* 53 (1992) 179–207 (especially on the *Invectivae contra medicum quendam*).

Louis Marsili (Florence, 1342–94)

EDITIONS

Lettere, ed. O. Morini. Naples, 1978.

Commento a una canzone di Francesco Petrarca. Bologna, 1863; reprinted: Bologna, 1986.

John of Celle and Louis Marsili. *Lettere.* Ed. F. Giambonini. 2 vols. Florence, 1991.

STUDIES

Secolo, F. del. *Un teologo dell'ultimo Trecento. Luigi Marsili.* Trani, 1898.

Casari, C. *Notizie intorno a Luigi Marsili.* Lovere, 1900.

Bellandi, S. *Luigi Marsili degli Agostiniani, apostolo e anima del rinascimento letterario in Firenze (1343–1394).* Florence, 1911.

Mariani, U. *Petrarca e gli Agostiniani*. Rome, 1946. Pp. 66–96.
Vasoli, C. "La *Regola per ben confessarsi* di Luigi Marsili." Idem. *Studi sulla cultura del Rinascimento*. Maduria, 1968. Pp. 40–47.

Coluccio Salutati (Stignano, 1331–Florence, 1406)

EDITIONS

Epistolario. Ed. F. Novati. 4 vols. Rome, 1891–1905.
De nobilitate legum et medicinae. De verecundia. Ed. E. Garin. Florence, 1947. With Italian translation.
De laboribus Herculis. Ed. B. L. Ullmann. Zurich, 1951.
De saeculo et religione. Ed. B. L. Ullmann. Florence, 1957.
De fato et fortuna. Ed. C. Bianca. Florence, 1985.

STUDIES

Novati, F. *La giovinezza di Coluccio Salutati (1331–1351)*. Turin, 1888.
Walser, E. "Coluccio Salutati der Typus eines Humanisten der italienischen Frührenaissance." Idem. *Gesammelte Studien*. Berlin, 1916.
Martin, A. von. *Mittelalterliche Welt und Lebensanschauungen im Spiegel der Schriften Coluccio Salutati's*. Berlin, 1916.
————. *Coluccio Salutati und das humanistische Lebensideal*. Berlin, 1916.
Borghi, L. "La dottrina morale di Coluccio Salutati." *Annali della R. Scuola Normale Superiore di Pisa,* Ser. 2, 3 (1934) 75–112.
————. "La concezione umanistica di Coluccio Salutati." Ibid., 460–72.
Gasperetti, L. "Il *De fato, fortuna et casu* di Coluccio Salutati." *La Rinascita* 4 (1941) 555–82.
Garin, E. *I trattati morali di Coluccio Salutati*. Florence, 1944.
Sciacca, G. M. *La visione della vita nell'umanesimo di Coluccio Salutati*. Palermo, 1954.
Ruegg, W. "Entstehung, Quellen und Ziel von Salutati's *De fato et fortuna*." *Rinascimento* 5 (1954) 143–50.
Garin, E. "A proposito di Coluccio Salutati." Idem, *L'età nuova*. Naples, 1969. Pp. 167–78.
O'Donnell, J. R. "Coluccio Salutati on the Poet-Teacher." *Mediaeval Studies* 22 (1960) 240–56.
Bonnell, R. A. "An Early Humanistic View of the Active and Contemplative Life (Coluccio Salutati)." *Italica* 43 (1966) 225–39.
Kessler, E. *Das Problem des frühen Humanismus. Seine philosophische Bedeutung bei Coluccio Salutati*. Munich, 1968.
Luttrel, A. "Coluccio Salutati's Letter to Juan Fernández de Heredia." *Italia medievale e umanistica* 13 (1970) 235–43.
Petrucci, A. *Coluccio Salutati*. Rome, 1972.
De Rosa, D. *Coluccio Salutati: il cancelliere e il pensatore politico*. Florence, 1980.
Atti del Convegno su Coluccio Salutati (Buggiano Castello, giugno 1980). Buggiano, 1981.

Lombardo, P. A. "'Vita activa' versus 'vita contemplativa' in Petrarch and Salutati." *Italica* 59 (1982) 83–92.

Witt, R. G. *Hercules at the Crossroads: The Life, Works, and Thought of Coluccio Salutati.* Durham, 1983.

Kahn, V. "Coluccio Salutati on the Active and Contemplative Life." *Arbeit, Musse, Meditation, Betrachtungen.* Zurich, 1985.

Michel, A. "La mythologie et ses interprétations de l'Antiquité à la Renaissance: le *De laboribus Herculis* de Salutati." *Les mythes poétiques.* Paris, 1985.

Trinkaus, Ch. "Coluccio Salutati's Critique of Astrology in the Context of His Natural Philosophy." *Speculum* 65 (1989) 46–68.

Fubini, R. *Umanesimo e secolarizzazione da Petrarca a Valla.* Rome, 1990. See the index.

Di Cesare, D. "La poesia come poiesis politica in Coluccio Salutati." *Historia Philosophiae Medii Aevi,* ed. B. Mojsisch and O. Pluta. Amsterdam, 1991. I, 193–210.

Leonard Bruni (Arezzo, 1370?–Florence, 1444)

EDITIONS

Humanistisch-philosophische Schriften. Ed. H. Baron. Leipzig-Berlin, 1928. Reprinted: Wiesbaden, 1969.

Epistolarum libri VIII. Ed. L. Mehus. Florence, 1741.

Dialogi ad Petrum Istrum. Ed. in E. Garin. *Prosatori latini del Quattrocento.* Milan-Naples, 1952. Pp. 39–99. With references to earlier editions.

STUDIES

Tocco, F. "L'*Isagogicon moralis disciplinae* di Leonardo Bruni Aretino." *ArchGeschPhil* 6 (1892) 157–69.

Freudenthal, I. "Leonardo Bruni als Philosoph." *Neues Jahrbuch für das klassische Altertum* 27 (1911) 48–66.

Beck, F. "Studien zu Leonardo Bruni." *Abhandlungen zur mittleren und neueren Geschichte* 36 (1912) 1–83.

Birkenmajer, A. *Der Streit des Alonso von Cartagena mit Leonardo Bruni Aretino.* BGPM 20, 5. Münster, 1922.

Baron, H. "Das Erwecken des historischen Denkens im Humanismus des Quattrocento." *Historische Zeitschrift* 147 (1932) 5–20.

David, M. *La prima "institutio" umanistica femminile. "De studiis et litteris" di Leonardo Bruni Aretino.* Turin, 1935.

Baron, H. "Lo sfondo storico del Rinascimento fiorentino." *La Rinascita* 1 (1938) 50–72.

Franceschi, E. "Leonardo Bruni e il *vetus interpres* dell'*Etica a Nicomaco.*" *Medioevo e Rinascimento. Studi in onore di Bruno Nardi.* Florence, 1955. I, 297–319.

Aurigemma, M. "Leonardo Bruni." *Letteratura italiana. I Minori.* Milan, 1959. I, 405–25.

Garin, E. "I Cancellieri della republica fiorentina." Idem. *La cultura filosofica del Rinascimento italiano*. Florence, 1961. Pp. 21–42.

Baron, H. *From Petrarch to Leonardo Bruni*. Chicago, 1968.

Siegel, J. J. *Rhetoric and Philosophy in Renaissance Humanism*. Princeton, 1968. See the index.

Garin, E. *Dal Rinascimento all'Illuminismo*. Pisa, 1970. Pp. 21–42.

Vasoli, C. "Bruni, Leonardo." *DBI* 14 (Rome, 1972) 618–33. With bibliography.

Gerl, H. B. "Die philosophische Bedeutung des *Ornatus* bei Leonardo Bruni. Zum Problem der Vermittlung von *Scientia rerum* und *Litterae*." *TijdFil* 39 (1977) 421–34.

_____. *Philosophie und Philologie: Leonardo Brunis Übertragung der Nikomachischen Ethik in ihren philosophischen Prämissen*. Munich, 1981.

Fubini, R. "L'ebraismo nei riflessi della cultura umanistica: Leonardo Bruni, Giannozzo Manetti, Annio da Viterbo." *Medioevo e Rinascimento* 2 (1988) 283–324.

Osmond De Martino, P. "'The Idea of Constantinople': A Prolegomenon to Further Study." *Historical Reflections/Réflexions historiques* 15 (1988) 323–26.

Vasoli, G. "Leonardo Bruni alla luce delle più recenti ricerche." *Atti e memorie della Accademia Petrarca di lettere, arti e scienze*, N.S. 50 (1988) 4–26.

Garin, E. "Leonardo Bruni: politica e cultura." Idem. *Umanisti, artisti, scienziati. Studi sul Rinascimento italiano*. Rome, 1989. Pp. 35–47.

Leonardo Bruni Cancelliere della Repubblica di Firenze. Convegno di studi (Firenze, 27–29 ottobre 1987). Ed. P. Viti. Istituto Nazionale di Studi sul Rinascimento, Atti di Convegni, 18. Florence, 1990.

Fubini, R. *Umanesimo e secolarizzazione da Petrarca a Valla*. Rome, 1990. See the index.

Hankins, J. "The Latin Poetry of Leonardo Bruni." *Humanistica Lovaniensia* 39 (1990) 1–39.

Per il censimento dei codici dell'epistolario di Leonardo Bruni. Seminario internazionale di Studi (Firenze, 30 ottobre 1987). Ed. L. Gualdo Roa and P. Viti. Rome, 1991.

Poggio Bracciolini (Terranova Bracciolini, 1380–Florence, 1459)

EDITIONS

Opera. Strasbourg, 1515; Basel, 1538. Reprinted, with other texts and writings published in various places, in *Opera omnia*. Ed. R. Fubini. Turin, 1964–69.

Lettere. Ed. E. Hart. 3 vols. Florence, 1984–87.

STUDIES

Walser, E. *Poggius Florentinus. Leben und Werke*. Leipzig, 1914.

Rubinstein, N. "Poggio Bracciolini cancelliere e storico di Firenze." *Atti e memorie dell'Accademia Petrarca di lettere, arti e scienze*, N.S. 37 (1958–64) 215–39.

Tateo, F. "Poggio Bracciolini e la dialoghistica del Quattrocento." Idem. *Tradizione et realtà dell'Umanesimo italiano*. Bari, 1967. Pp. 223–78.

Fubini, R. "Un'orazione di Poggio Bracciolini sui vizi del clero scritta al tempo del Concilio di Costanza." *GSLI* 162 (1965) 24–33.

Bigi, E., and A. Petrucci, "Bracciolini, Poggio." *DBI* 13 (Rome, 1971) 640–46.

Fubini, R. *Introduzione alla lettura del "Contra Hypocritas."* Turin, n.d. (1971).

Oppel, J. W. "Poggio, San Bernardino of Siena and the Dialogue *On Avarice.*" *Renaissance Quarterly* 30 (1977) 564–87.

Goldbrunner, H. "Poggius' Dialog über die Habsucht. Bemerkungen zu einer neuen Untersuchung." *Quellen und Forschungen aus italienischen Archiven und Bibliotheken* 59 (1979) 436–52.

Cesarini Martinelli. L. "Note sulla polemica Poggio-Valla e sulla fortuna delle *Elegantiae.*" *Interpres* 3 (1980) 29–79.

Poggio Bracciolini 1380–1980. Nel VI centenario della nascita. Florence, 1982.

Fubini, R. "Poggio Bracciolini e S. Bernardino: temi e motivi di una polemica." *Atti del Convegno storico Bernardiniano, in occasione del sesto centenario della nascita di S. Bernardino di Siena (L'Aquila, 7–9 maggio 1980).* Teramo, 1982. Pp. 155–88.

Vasoli, C. *Imagini umanistiche.* Naples, 1983. Pp. 149ff.

Garin, E. *Umanisti, artisti, scienziati. Studi sul Rinascimento italiano.* Rome, 1989. Pp. 49–73.

Fubini, R. *Umanesimo e secolarizzazione da Petrarca a Valla.* Rome, 1990. See the index.

Guidi, R. "Sottintesi e allusioni tra Poggio e il Sarteano a proposito di una polemica mancata" [on the Franciscan Observantines]. *AFH* 83/1–2 (1990) 118–61.

Lawrence Valla (Rome, 1407–57)

EDITIONS

Opera. Basel, 1540 and 1543. Photostatic reprint, together with other more recent editions of writings by Valla, ed. E. Garin. Turin, 1962.

Elegantiae latinae linguae. Rome, 1471.

De voluptate ac vero bono declamationes ac disputationes in libros tres contractae. Paris, 1512.

Opuscula tria. Ed. J. Vahlen, in *Sitzungsberichte der Wiener Akademie, philos.-histor. Klasse* 61 (1868) 6–67; 357–444, and 62 (1869) 93–159. Reprinted separately: Vienna, 1869.

De falso credita e ementita Constantini donatione. Ed. B. C. Coleman. New Haven, 1922. Ed. W. Schwan. Leipzig, 1928.

De libero arbitrio. Ed. M. Anfossi. Florence, 1934.

Collatio Novi Testamenti. Ed. A. Perosa. Florence, 1970.

De vero falsoque bono. Ed. M. De Panizza Lorch. Bari, 1970.

Defensio quaestionum in philosophia. Ed. G. Zippel. *Italia medioevale e umanistica* 13 (1970) 82–94.

Repastinatio dialectice et philosophie. Ed. G. Zippel. 2 vols. Padua, 1982.

Epistolae. Ed. O. Besomi and M. Regoliosi. Padua, 1984.

De professione religiosorum. Ed. M. R. Cortesi. Padua, 1987.

STUDIES

Gabotto, F. *Lorenzo Valla e l'epicureismo del Quattrocento*. Milan-Turin, 1889.

Mancini, G. *Vita di Lorenzo Valla*. Florence, 1891.

Barozzi, L., and R. Sabbadini. *Studi sul Panormita e sul Valla*. Florence, 1981.

Wolf, M. von. *Lorenzo Valla*. Vienna, 1893.

Schwan, W. *Lorenzo Valla*. Berlin, 1893.

Freudenthal, J. "Lorenzo Valla als Philosoph." *Neue Jahrbücher für das klassiche Altertum* 27 (1909) 224–36.

Meier, E. *Die Willensfreiheit bei Lorenzo Valla und Pietro Pomponazzi*. Bonn, 1914.

Corsano, A. "Note sul *De voluptate* dell Valla." Idem. *Studi sul Rinascimento*. Bari, 1949. Pp. 7–35.

Radetti, G. "Nota bibliographica sulla filosofia del Valla." *Umanesimo e Machiavellismo*. Pp.127–35. = *ArchFil* 5 (1949).

Antonazzi, G. "Lorenzo Valla e la donazione di Costantino nel secolo XV." *RSCI* 4 (1950) 186–234.

Gaeta, F. *Lorenzo Valla. Filologia e storia nell'Umanesimo italiano*. Naples, 1955.

Radetti, G. "La religione di Lorenzo Valla." *Medioevo e Rinascimento. Studi in onore di Bruno Nardi*. Florence, 1955. II, 595–620.

Vasoli, C. "Le *Dialecticae disputationes* del Valla e la critica umanistica della logica aristotelica." *RCSF* 12 (1957) 412–34; 13 (1958) 27–46.

Mesnard, P. "Une application curieuse de l'humanisme à la théologie: l'Éloge de Saint Thomas par Laurent Valla." *Revue thomiste* 56 (1955) 159–76.

Zippel, G. "Note sulla redazione della *Dialectica* di Lorenzo Valla." *Archivio storico per le provincie parmensi,* Ser. 4, 9 (1957) 301–15.

_____. "La *Defensio quaestionum in philosophia* di Lorenzo Valla e un noto processo dell'Inquisizione napoletana." *Bulletino dell'Istituto storico italiano per il Medio Evo e Archivio Muratoriano* 62 (1957) 319–47.

Gray, H. H. "Valla's *Encomium of Saint Thomas Aquinas* and the Humanist Conception of Christian Antiquity." *Essays in History and Literature*. Chicago, 1965. Pp. 37–52.

Caserta, E. "Il problema religioso nel *De voluptate* della Valla e nell'*Aegidius* del Pontano." *Italica* 43 (1966) 240–52 and 260–62.

Anderson, M. W. "Lorenzo Valla (1407–1457): Renaissance Critic and Biblical Theologian." *Concordia Theological Monthly* 39 (1968) 10–27.

Vasoli, C. *La dialettica e la retorica dell'Umanesimo. 'Invenzione' e 'methodo' nella cultura del XIV e XV secolo*. Milan, 1968. Pp. 28–77, and see the index.

Fois, M. *Il pensiero cristiano di Lorenzo Valla ned quadro storico-culturale del suo tempo*. Rome, 1969.

Trinkaus, Ch. *In Our Image and Likeness: Humanity and Divinity in Italian Humanist Thought*. London, 1970. See the index.

Camporeale, S. I. *Lorenzo Valla. Umanesimo e teologia*. Florence, 1972.

_____. "Da Lorenzo Valla a Tommaso Moro." *MemDom* 90 (1973) 9–102.

Fabris, G. "Teologia e paolinismo in Lorenzo Valla." *Studium* 69 (1973) 671–83.

Janik, L. G. "Lorenzo Valla: The Primacy of Rhetoric and the Demoralisation of History." *History and Theory* 123 (1973) 389–404.

Gerl, H. B. *Rhetorik als Philosophie. Lorenzo Valla*. Munich, 1974.

Setz, W. *Lorenzo Vallas Schrift gegen die Konstantinische Schenkung: zur Interpretation und Wirkungsgeschichte.* Tübingen, 1975.

Jardine, L. "Humanism and the Sixteenth-Century Cambridge Arts Course." *History of Education* 6 (1975) 16–31.

Fubini, R. "Intendimenti umanistici e riferimenti patristici dal Petrarca al Valla." *GSLI* 151 (1974) 520–78.

_____. "Note su Lorenzo Valla e la composizione del *De voluptate*," *I classici nel Medioevo e nel Umanesimo.* Genoa, 1975. Pp. 11–57.

Bentley, J. H. "Biblical Philology and Christian Humanism: Lorenzo Valla and Erasmus as Scholars of the Gospel." *Sixteenth Century Journal* 8 (1977) 8–28.

Camporeale, S. I. "Senso della morte e amore della vita nel Rinascimento. Susone, Valla, Erasmo e 'il problema della salvezza.'" *MemDom* 94–95 (1977–78) 439–50.

Cappello, G. "Umanesimo e Scolastica; il Valla, gli umanisti e Tommaso d'Aquino." *RivFilNeo* 69 (1977) 423–42.

Fois, M. "Ancora su Lorenzo Valla. Chiarimenti e repliche." *RSCI* 31 (1977) 183–203.

Jardine, L. "Lorenzo Valla and the Intellectual Origins of Humanistic Dialectic." *JHistPhil* 15 (1977) 143–64.

De Caprio, V. "Retorica e ideologia nella *Declamatio* di Lorenzo Valla sulla donazione di Costantino." *Paragone-Letteratura* 29 (1978) 36–56.

Panizza, L. A. "Lorenzo Valla's *De vero falsoque bono,* Lactantius and Practical Scepticism." *JWarCourt* 41 (1978) 76–107.

Marsh, D. "Grammar, Method, and Polemic in Lorenzo Valla's *Elegantiae.*" *Rinascimento,* Ser. 2, 19 (1979) 91–116.

Kessler, E. "Freiheit des Willens in Valla's *De libero arbitrio.*" *Acta Conventus neo-latini Turonensis* (IIIᵉ Congrès international d'études néo-latines; Tours, Université Fr. Rabelais, 6–10 septembre 1976). Ed. J.-C. Margolin. 2 vols. De Pétrarche à Descartes 38. Paris, 1980. II, 637–47.

Panizza Lorch, M. "Valla and Virgil." Ibid., I, 163–73.

Marx, B. "Zur Verbreitung von Lorenzo Valla's Werken; Aspekte und Probleme." *Wolfenbüttler Renaissance Mitteilungen* 4 (1980) 29–31.

Jardine, L. "Dialectic or Dialectical Rhetoric? A. Nifo's Criticism of Lorenzo Valla." *RCSF* 36 (1981) 253–70.

Bellone, E. "Appunti sull'*Encomiun Sancti Thomas* di Lorenzo Valla." *Bulletin du Centre d'Études Franco-Italien* 10 (1982) 5–23.

Chomarat, J. "Aspects de la conscience européenne chez Valla et Erasme." *La conscience européenne au XVe et au XVIe siècles.* Paris, 1982. Pp. 64–74.

Gerl, H. B. "Abstraktion und Gemeinsinn: Zur Frage des Paradigmenwechsel von der Scholastik zum Humanismus in der Argumentationstheorie Lorenzo Valls." *TijdFil* 44 (1982) 269–89.

Panizza Lorch, M. "'Mors omnia vincit improba': l'uomo e la morte nel *De voluptate.*" *Miscellanea di studi in onore di Vittore Branca.* Florence, 1983. III, 177–91.

Kahn, V. "The Rhetoric of Faith and the Use of Usage in Lorenzo Valla's *De libero arbitrio.*" *Journal of Mediaeval and Renaissance Studies* 13 (1983) 91–109.

Struever, N. "Lorenzo Valla: Humanist Rhetoric and the Critique of Classical Languages of Morality." *Renaissance Eloquence: Studies in the Theory and Practice of Renaissance Rhetoric.* Berkeley, 1983. Pp. 191–206.

Antonazzi, G. *Lorenzo Valla e la polemica sulla donazione di Costantino.* Rome, 1985.

Camporeale, S. I. "Lorenzo Valla: *Repastinatio* liber primus: retorica e linguaggio." *Renaissance Studies in Honor of Craig Hugh Smyth.* Florence, 1985. I, 261–79.

Pugliese, O. "The Rhetoric of Deviation in Lorenzo Valla's *The Profession of Religious.*" *Renaissance and Reformation/Renaissance et Réforme* 9 (1985) 263–74.

Lorenzo Valla e l'Umanesimo italiano. Atti del convegno internazionale di studi umanistici; Parma, 18–19 ottobre 1984. Ed. O. Besomi and M. Regoliosi. Medioevo e Umanesimo 59. Padua, 1986.

Fubini, R. "Ricerche sul*De voluptate* di Lorenzo Valla." *Medioevo e Rinascimento* 1 (1987) 189–239.

Struever, N. "Lorenzo Valla's Grammar of Subject and Object: An Ethical Inquiry." *I Tatti Studies* 2 (1987) 239–67.

Camporeale, S. I. "Lorenzo Valla e il *De falso credita donatione.* Retorica, libertà ed ecclesiologia nel '400." *Immagine e parola, Retorica filologica, Retorica predicatoria: Valla e Savonarola.* Pistoia, 1988. = *MemDom* 19 (1988) 192–293.

———. "Per una rilettura del *De falso credita donatione* di L. Valla." *Ambrogio Traversari nel VI centenario della nascità.* Convegno internazionale di Studi; Camaldoli-Firenze, 15–19 settembre 1986. Ed. G. C. Garfagnini. Florence, 1988. Pp. 95–103.

Monfasani, J. "Bessarion, Valla, Agricola, and Erasmus." *Rinascimento,* Ser. 2, 28 (1988) 319–20.

Garin, E. *Umanisti, artisti, scienziati. Studi sul Rinascimento italiano.* Rome, 1989. Pp. 75–89.

Boba, I. "La *Donatio Constantini* e l' 'oratio' del Valla a confronto." *Angelicum* 67 (1990) 215–39.

Camporeale. S. I. "Lorenzo Valla: The Transcending of Philosophy through Rhetoric." *Romance Notes* 30 (1990) 269–84.

Fubini, R. *Umanesimo e secolarizzazione da Petrarca a Valla.* Rome, 1990. See the index.

———. "Lorenzo Valla tra il Concilio di Basilea e quello di Firenze, e il processo dell'Inquisizione." *Conciliarismo, Stati nazionali, inizi del Umanesimo.* Atti del XXV Convegno storico internazionale; Todi, 9–12 ottobre 1988. Spoleto, 1990. Pp. 287–318.

Cesarini Martinelli, L. "Lorenzo Valla e le arti." *Sapere e/è potere. Discipline, Dispute e Professioni nell'Università medievale e moderna: il caso bolognese a confronto.* Atti del 4° Convegno (Istituto per la Storia di Bologna, 13–15 aprile 1989). Ed. L. Avellini and others. Bologna, 1991. III, 117–49.

Gavinelli, S. "Teorie grammaticali nelle *Elegantiae* e la tradizione scolastica del tardo umanesimo." *Rinascimento,* Ser. 2, 31 (1991) 155–81.

Laffranchi, M. "Il rinnovamento della filosofia nella *Dialectica* di Lorenzo Valla." *RivFilNeo* 84 (1992) 13–60.

Regoliosi, M. "Lorenzo Valla e la concezione della storia." *La storiografia umanistica.* Atti del Convegno internazionale di Studi (Messina, 22–25 ottobre 1987). Messina, 1992. I, 459–71.

(Julius) Pomponius Laetus (Diana, 1428–Rome, 1497)

STUDIES

Carini, I. "La *Difesa* di Pomponio Leto pubblicata e illustrata." *Miscellanea per nozze Cian Sappa - Flondinet*. Bergamo, 1894.

Torre, A. Della. *Paolo Marsi da Pescina*. Rocca San Casciano, 1903.

Zabughin, V. *Giulio Pomponio Leto. Saggio critico*. 2 vols. I: Rome, 1909. II: Grottaferra, 1910–12.

Garin, E. "La letteratura degli umanisti." *Il Quattrocento e l'Ariosto*. Milan, 1967. Pp. 142–58.

Palmerio, R. J. "The Roman Academy, the Catacombs, and the Conspiracy of 1468." *ArchHistPont* 18 (1980) 117–55.

Medioli Masotti, P. "L'Accademia Romana e la congiura del 1468." With an appendix by A. Campana. *Italia medioevale e umanistica* 25 (1982) 189–204.

————. "Callimaco, L'Accademia Romana e la congiura del 1468." *Callimaco Esperiente poeta e politico del '400*. Convegno internazionale di Studi (San Gimignano, 18–20 ottobre 1985). Florence, 1987. Pp. 169–79.

Philip Bonaccorsi (or Buonaccorsi) (Callimachus Esperiens) (San Gimignano, 1437–Krakow, 1496)

EDITIONS

Epistolae (on philosophy, to Ficino and Pico), in R. Zeissberg, "Kleinere Geschichtsquellen im Mittelalter." *Archiv für österreichische Geschichte* 55 (1877) 41–94.

Libellus de daemonibus, in P. O. Kristeller. *Supplementum ficinianum*. Florence, 1937. II, 225–28.

Quaestio de peccato, in E. Garin, *La cultura filosofica del Rinascimento italiano*. Florence, 1961, 1979². Pp. 280–86.

Praefatio in somniarum Leonis Tusci philosophi. Ed. A. Kempfl, in *Odrodzenie i Reformatia w Polsce* 12 (1967) 179–90.

STUDIES

Kieszkowsky, B. "Filippo Buonaccorsi detto Callimaco e le correnti filosofiche del Rinascimento." *GCSF* 15 (1934) 281–94.

Radetti, G. "Demoni e sogni nella critica di Callimaco Esperiente al Ficino." *Umanesimo ed esoterismo*. Ed. E. Castelli. Padua, 1960. Pp. 111–21. = *ArchFil* 30 (1960).

Zathey, G. "Quelques recherches sur l'humaniste Kallimach." Ibid., 123–39.

Kempfl, A. "Une polémique méconnue de Callimaque à propos de Marsilio Ficino." *Archives internationales d'histoire des sciences* 17 (1964) 263–72.

Radetti, G. "L'epicureismo di Callimaco Esperiente nella biografia di Gregorio di Sanok." *Atti del covegno italo-ungherese di studi rinascimentali (1964)*. = *Ungheria d'oggi* 5 (1965) 46–53.

_____. "Il problema del peccato in Giovanni Pico della Mirandola e in Filippo Buonaccorsi detto Callimaco Esperiente." *L'opera e il pensiero di Giovanni Pico della Mirandola nella storia del'umanesimo*. Convegno internazionale, Mirandola, 15–18 settembre 1963. Florence, 1965. II, 103–17.

Zathey, C. "Le milieu de Callimaque Esperiens e de Pic." Ibid., II, 119–47.

Paparelli, G. *Callimaco Esperiente (Filippo Buonaccorsi)*. Salerno, 1971.

Caccamo, D. "Buonaccorsi, Filippo (Callimachus Experiens)." *DBI* 15 (Rome, 1872) 78–83. With a bibliography.

Callimaco Esperiente poeta e politico del '400. Convegno internazionale di studi; San Gemignano, 18–20 ottobre 1985. Florence, 1987.

Bartholomew Sacchi, known as Platina (Piadena, 1421–Rome, 1481)

Editions

Opera omnia. Venice, 1511; Cologne, 1519; Paris, 1530.

Liber de vita Christi ac omnium pontificum (Opus in vitas summorum pontificum). Ed. G. Gaida, in *Rerum Italicarum scriptores* III/1, 1913–32.

De principe. Ed. G. Ferraù (Messina, 1979). See also below, in the bibliography on Vittorino da Feltre.

Studies

Caregaro Negrin, N. "Il *De felicitate* di Francesco Zabarella e due trattati sul bene e la delicità del secolo XV," *Classici e Neolatini* (1906) 288ff.

Zabughin, V. *Giulio Pomponio Leto. Saggio critico* I. Rome, 1909. Passim.

Garin, E. *Filosofi italiani del Quattrocento*. Florence, 1942. Pp. 263–73. With a selection of passages.

Kölmel, W. "Machiavelli und der Machiavellismus. Mit einem Exkursus zu Platinas Schrift *De principe*." *Historisches Jahrbuch* (1969) 372–408.

Milham, M. E. "Platina and His Correspondent." *Acta conventus neo-latini Bononensis/Proceedings of the Fourth International Congress of Neo-Latin Studies*. Bologna, August 26 to September 1, 1979. Ed. R. J. Schoeck. Binghamton, 1985. Pp. 144–48. = Medieval and Renaissance Texts and Studies 37.

Bartolomeo Sacchi il Platina (Piadena 1421–Rome 1481). Atti del Convegno internazionale di Studi per il V Centenario (Cremona, 14–15 novembre 1981). Medioevo e Umanesimo 62. Ed. A. Campana and P. Medioli Masotti. Padua, 1986.

Milham, M. E. "Platina and Papal Politics." *Du manscrit à la table*. Ed. C. Lambert. Montreal, 1992. Pp. 81–84. = Études médiévales.

Ambrose Traversari (Bagno di Romagna, 1386–Florence, 1439)

Editions

Epistolae. Ed. L. Mehus (Florence, 1749).

Hodoeporicum. In A. Dini Traversari, *Ambrogio Traversari e i suoi tempi* (Florence, 1912) 111–39.

STUDIES

Dini Traversari, A. *Ambrogio Traversari e i suoi tempi*. Florence, 1912.
Mioni, E. "Le *Vitae Patrum* nella tradizione di Ambrogio Traversari." *Aevum* 24 (1950) 319–33.
Décarreaux, J. "Un moine helléniste et diplomate: Ambroise Traversari." *Revue des études italiennes* 3 (1957) 101–43.
Geanakoplos, D. J. *Byzantine East and Latin West: Two Worlds of Christendom in the Middle Ages*. New York-Evanston, 1966. See the index.
Mercati, G. *Ultimi contributi alla storia degli umanisti* I. *Traversariana*. Vatican City, 1973².
Cherubini Baldelli, S. "I manoscritti della Biblioteca Fiorentina degli Angeli." *La Bibiofilia* 74–75 (1972–73) 9–47.
Stinger, Ch. L. *Humanism and the Church Fathers: Ambrogio Traversari (1368–1439) and Christian Antiquity in the Italian Renaissance*. Albany, 1977.
Castelli, P. "*Lux Italiae*. Ambrogio Traversari monaco camaldolese. Idee e immagini nel Quattrocento fiorentino." *Atti e memorie dell'Accademia toscana di scienze e lettere La Columbaria*, N.S. 47 (1982) 39–90.
Gain, B. "Ambrogio Traversari monaco camaldolese (1386–1439). Lecteur et traducteur de Saint Basile." *Rivista di storia e letteratura religiosa* 21 (1985) 56–76.
Somigli, C., and Bargellini, T. *Ambrogio Traversari monaco camaldolese*. Bologna, 1986.
Ambrogio Traversari nel VI Centenario della nascita. Convegno internazionale di studi (Camaldoli-Firenze, 15–18 settembre 1986). Ed. G. C. Garfagnini. Florence, 1988.

On Traversari's activity during the Council of Ferrara-Florence:
Gill, J. *The Council of Florence*. Cambridge, 1959. See the index.
_____. *Personalities of the Council of Florence*. Oxford, 1964.
Décarreaux, J. *Les Grecs au Concile de l'Union, Ferrare-Florence 1438–1439*. Paris, 1970.

Peter Paul Vergerio (Capodistria, 1370–Buda, 1444)

EDITIONS

De ingenuis moribus et liberalibus adolescentiae studiis. Ed. A. Gnesotto, in *Atti e memorie della R. Accadamia de Scienze, Lettere e Arti di Padova* 34 (1918) 75–156; to be completed by *Vergeriana*, ibid., 37 (1920–21).
Epistolae. Ed. L. Smith (Rome, 1934).

STUDIES

Ziliotto, B. *La cultura letteraria di Trieste e dell'Istria* I. Trieste, 1912. Pp. 37–85.
Bischoff, C. *Studien zu Pier Paolo Vergerio dem älteren*. Berlin, 1909.
Calò, G. "La genesi del primo trattato pedagogico dell'umanesimo."
_____. *Dall'umanesimo alla scuola del lavoro*. Florence, 1940. I, 37–66.
Robey, D. "Humanism and Education in the Early Quattrocento: *De ingenuis moribus* of Pier Paolo Vergerio." *BibHumRen* 42 (1980) 27–58.

McManaman, J. M. "Innovation in Early Humanistic Rhetoric: The Oratory of Pier Paolo Vergerion the Elder." *Rinascimento,* Ser. 2, 22 (1982) 3–32.

Guarino Guarini (Guarino Veronese) (Verona, 1384–Ferrara, 1460)

EDITIONS

Epistolae. Ed. R. Sabbadini (Venice, 1915–18; reprinted: Turin, 1967).

STUDIES

Sabbadini, R. *Vita di Guarino Veronese* (Genoa, 1891).
_____. *La scuola e gli studi di Guarino Guarini Veronese.* Catania, 1896. Reprinted: Turin, 1964.
_____. *Il metodo degli umanisti.* Florence, 1920.
Bertoni, G. *Guarino da Verona tra letterati e cortigiani a Ferrara (1429–1460).* Geneva, 1921.
Garin, E. "Motivi della cultura ferrarese nel Rinascimento." Idem. *La cultura filosofica del Rinascimento italiano.* Florence, 1961. Pp. 402–31, and in idem, *Ritratti di umanisti.* Florence, 1967. Pp. 69–106.
Colombo, C. "Some New Additions to the Correspondence of Guarino da Verona." *Italia medioevale e umanistica* 8 (1965) 341–50.
_____. "Giunta all'epistolario di Guarino da Verona. Altri inediti guariniani." Ibid., 14 (1971) 485–86.
Piana, C. "L'evoluzione degli studi nell'Osservanza francescana nella prima metà del '400 e la polemica tra Guarino da Verona e fra Giovanni da Prato a Ferrara (1450)." *Analecta Pomposiana* 7 (1982) 249–89.
Weiss, R. "Guarino Veronese." *Dizionario critico della letteratura italiana* 2 (Turin, 1986²) 459–60. With bibliography.
Pade, M. "Guarino and Caesar at the Court of the Este." *La Corte di Ferrara e il suo mecenatismo (1441–1598).* Atti del convegno internazionale (maggio 1987). Ed. M. Pade and others. Copenhagen, 1990. Pp. 71–91.

Vittorino da Feltre (Vittorino de'Rambaldoni) (Feltre, 1378–Mantua, 1446)

For testimonies concerning his activity and his school, see E. Garin, *L'Umanesimo.* I classici della pedagogia italana 3. Florence, 1958. Pp. 504–718. With editions of the pedagogical writings of Sassolo da Prato, Francesco di Castiglione, Francesco Prendilacqua, and Bartolomeo Platina, and with pertinent bibliography.

STUDIES

Woodward, W. H. *Vittorino da Feltre and Other Humanist Educators.* Cambridge, 1897.
Pesenti, G. "Vittorina da Feltre e gli inizi della scuola di greco in Italia." *Athenaeum* 2 (1924) 241–60; 3 (1925) 1–16.

Gambaro, A. *Vittorino da Feltre.* Turin, 1946.

Vittorino da Feltre. Pubblicazione commemorativa del V centenario della morte. Brescia, 1947. With analytic bibliography by G. Avanzo on pp. 87–103.

Bozio Boz, P. *Vittorino da Feltre.* Albi, 1947.

Nardi, B. *Contributo alla biografia di Vittorino da Feltre.* Padua, 1958. Also in *Bollettino del Museo civico di Padova* 45 (1956) 1–31.

Faccioli, E. "Vittorino da Feltre e la sua scuola." *Mantova - Le Lettere* 2 (Mantua 1962) 5–52.

Signorini, R. *In traccia del Magister Pelicanus.* Mantua, 1979.

Vittorino e la sua scuola. Umanesimo, pedagogia, arti. Florence, 1981.

Chambers, D. S. "An Unknown Letter by Vittorino da Feltre." *JWarCourt* 52 (1989) 219–21.

Marchand, J.-J. "La concezione antiuniversitaria delle arti negli elogi e nelle vite di Vittorino da Feltre." *Sapere e/è potere. Disciplina, Dispute e Professioni nell'Università medievale e moderna: il caso bolognese a confronto.* Atti del 4° Convegno (Istituto per la storia di Bologna, 13–15 aprile 1989). Ed. L. Avellini, A. Cristiani, and A. De Benedictis. Bologna, 1991. I, 67–84.

CHAPTER 2

Italian Scholasticism and Ecclesiastical Culture in the Fifteenth Century: Continuity and Innovation

Cesare Vasoli

1. Meeting and Opposition of Two Cultures

The culture of the Italian humanists of the first half of the fifteenth century remained largely unconnected with the development of theory in the
Scholastic centers. It did, however, tackle problems that were obviously theological in nature; these problems also impacted on such religious ideas as
were more widespread in intellectual and social circles that were already capable of taking up, in an increasingly autonomous way, the discussion of the
most important themes of the Christian religious tradition. On the other hand,
in the great schools of Europe, including those of Italy, the methods used and
the procedures followed in theological discourse were still focused on the
problems raised by the great masters of the fourteenth century; the early fifteenth century saw the final results of Ockhamist teaching, the wide diffusion
of Scotist theses, and the development of a system of doctrines that were inspired by the work of Thomas Aquinas and were soon transformed into what
became known as "Thomism."

As I shall try to show in the following pages, Italy saw a confrontation between two different conceptions of culture, the humanist and the Scholastic,
which often met and intertwined but at times were bitterly opposed, and this
in the same circles and the same cities. Two types of intellectuals, different in

origin and training, in studies and interests, set forth, even for theological discourse, conceptions and methods that differed profoundly from each other and were inspired by different ways of understanding the gospel message and the activity of those called upon to interpret this message to "the faithful people."

On the one side, Scholastic theology still retained the close connection with the "Peripatetic" philosophical tradition that had been established during the thirteenth century and was still maintained in substance even by the "modern" theologians. The Scholastics thought of their teaching as the lofty intellectual product of a group of "clerics," the *magistri* (masters of theology), to whom it belonged by right to deal with the science of things divine.

On the other side were the humanists who, as we saw in the preceding chapter, appealed to authors and texts with which the masters were only partly familiar; the humanists asserted the value of the humanities even for the study of theology, defended the rhetorical and persuasive devices so necessary for teaching the faith, and above all, aimed to free the discussion of the great religious themes from the language and "techniques" of the school and to recast it in a form that would make it accessible to a new audience consisting of scholars and artists, merchants and politicians, artisans and skilled workers. This explains why, following the example of Dante in his *Convivio,* the humanists soon began using the vernacular in discussing subjects that concerned not only popular piety or traditional apologetics but also dogmas and theological "mysteries."

In order to appreciate better the different horizons of the two cultures, we must look at the authorities, that is, the texts, to which the Scholastics continued to give a central role in their work of exegesis and of dogmatic development and discussion. The humanists and the *magistri* had this in common, of course, that they read the Fathers of the Church; in fact, the vicissitudes of the Council of Ferrara-Florence and the enthusiastic study by the humanists of all the testimonies to "Greek wisdom" furthered the interest in the Fathers of the "East," who were regarded as closer to the apostolic origins. Augustine, Jerome, and the other "ancient Doctors" of the Latin Church likewise remained constant points of reference in a discourse which, however, on the part of the humanists, was not lacking in criticisms of details and in decisive discussions of points of philology.

At the same time, however, in the Scholastic culture the authors who had been given priority during the last two centuries were still the fundamental ones: Aristotle (in the Latin translations of the twelfth and thirteenth centuries), Averroes, and Avicenna; and obviously, along with these, the greater "Western" masters: Thomas Aquinas and John Duns Scotus, with their immediate followers; also Henry of Ghent and Giles of Rome, and, in the Franciscan houses of study, the other major theologians of the order, from Bonaventure of Bagnoreggio to Matthew of Acquasparta. Above all, there was the profound and quite widespread influence of William of Ockham and those authors who had continued in the new course taken by "modern" Scholasticism: John Buridan and "Suisset" (Swineshead). For a good part of this century the works of these men still influenced the activity of the "physicists" and the logicians of the universities and houses of study and were not without an impact even on theological discussion. In fact, in Italy perhaps more than elsewhere, nominalist doctrines and British "sophistries" coexisted with speculative attitudes and theological argumentations of Thomist or Scotist origin. Meanwhile, the presence of an Averroist tradition that was already well rooted in Italian Scholastic culture rendered even more complicated and problematic the doctrinal context of the work of the theologians themselves.[1]

It is true that, especially in the exegesis of the *De anima,* a subject so often in dispute between the "physicists" and the theologians, the Averroist solution exerted an attraction that drew even *magistri* who, in other areas of their theoretical work, moved in quite different directions. But the acceptance of some theses of the "Commentator" in the purely philosophical sphere did not mean that those who accepted them followed his guidance in everything or accepted all his teachings; still less did it mean that they were not open also to the new spiritual demands raised by the humanists with their appeal to the ancient tradition of the Fathers, a tradition given new vigor and rendered more relevant by the return of the "ancient philosophers" and by a discussion that ended up appropriating some of the most sensitive themes in the historical development of dogma and even in the "institutional" history of the Church.

2. The Problem of the Human Soul in the Theological Thought of Paul of Venice

The most famous representative of Italian Scholastic culture in the early fifteenth century was a master who was an Augustinian Hermit, Paul Nicoletti of Udine (Paul of Venice, 1372–1429). To a sure knowledge of Averroist doctrine, which he had gotten by way of Siger of Brabant, he joined a great skill as a "modern" logician who was bent on defining in the most rigorous possible way the meaning and values of terms and their operations.[2] This aspect of his teaching, which Bochenski sees as a typical forerunner of modern formal logic,[3] is of interest to us here only from the viewpoint of Scholastic "method" and the training of theologians, many of whom developed their own logical tools as a result of reading his *Logica parva,* which by the end of the century became the obligatory textbook for instruction in logic at the University of Padua.

It is more important that we look here at some themes in his commentary on the *De anima* and in his *Summa naturalium* (1408) that have greater relevance to theological problems, inasmuch as they have to do with the debate over the immortality of the soul.[4]

In his commentary Paul intends (1) to determine and analyze the concrete solution which Aristotle proposes in the *De anima* and which is not always in agreement with that defended by Averroes; (2) to discuss contrary theses and to offer his own point of view, in relation both to Aristotle and to Averroist exegesis. Consequently, in a "question" *(quaestio)* of Book III he proceeds to discuss the opinions of Plato, Alexander of Aphrodisias, and the "modern" philosophers before asking whether the Stagirite really maintained the "unicity" of the human intellect. He concludes by saying he is convinced that this thesis is really founded on the principles of Aristotle's philosophy and that the Averroist interpretation is faithful and valid. In the next *quaestio,* this opinion is confirmed. However, Paul offers four arguments against Aristotle and four against Averroes, concluding at last that "according to the faith" the human intellect is "plural," in accordance with the "plurality" of individuals in the "human species."

As we see, two solutions are offered here as a result of strictly following the rules of Scholastic dialectic: the first is developed according to the canons of "natural philosophy" (as espoused by the great Aristotle and his most faithful interpreter); the second, on the contrary, aims to show that the "unicity" of the human soul is a controverted opinion on which no probative argument can be based, since it can be met by objections of significant weight based both on pure reason and on the truth of the faith. Now, as has been pointed out again recently,[5] the thesis on the "unicity" of the soul reappears in other passages of the commentary but always as a doctrine of "natural philosophy." We know, too, that in his *Summa naturalium* Paul states the Averroist solution and gives his assent, in substance, to the teaching of Siger of Brabant. He is well aware that the solution proposed by the philosopher of Brabant is not the one that can be attributed to Averroes; but Siger, too, maintains that the possible intellect, while being the form of the human composite, is one and the same for all human beings, as authentic Aristotelean teaching certainly professes.

Despite all this, although Paul regards the "unicity" of the intellect as a teaching common to Aristotle and Averroes, in his commentary he stresses the point that the two philosophers have different opinions on the relation between this intellect and human individuals, since for Averroes, unlike Aristotle, the intellect is not the substantial form of the human person. Paul's discussion of the opinions proposed by Giles of Rome and John of Jandun, both of which are rejected, leads him then to accept the Thomist position that the "substantial form" is the principle that locates the individual in its species. Now the human being would not be different from the animals if the intellect that determines its rationality and specific difference were not its substantial form; in such a situation, intellection would be the action only of the intellect and not of the human being. The human composite is therefore made up of the body and its "substantial form," namely, the intellectual soul or "intellect"; these two parts of the being are, respectively, "mover" and "moved."

But how can Paul reconcile the identification of the human intellect as "substantial form" of the individual with the Averroist theme of the "oneness" of the intellect? Kuksewicz, who has produced an especially perspicacious study of the commentary on the *De anima,* has noted that the Augustinian writer appeals to two concepts that are typical of the Averroist tradition: the "inhering form" and the "informing form" (introduced by Thomas Wilton). On the basis of these, Paul asserts that the intellect is a "substantial form" separate from the body as far as inherence goes but bound to it as "informing." Thus the same intellect can inform various human bodies, so that at the birth of each individual it begins to inform it without thereby ceasing to inform other bodies.[6]

Not only that: every living body has multiple forms, which are ordered among themselves in a kind of hierarchy. Thus animals possess two souls, one "vegetative," which is "partial," and the other "sensitive," which is "total." But the case of the human being is more complex: it possesses two "partial" souls (the "vegetative" and the "sensitive") and has two others that are "total": the "cogitative" and the "intellective." The first of these two can be generated and is subject to corruption, while the second is eternal; the first is "inhering," while the second is an "informing form." This view is confirmed even by the logical definition of the human being as "rational animal," which seems to presuppose the existence of two different souls, each of which gives the being one of its two "qualifications."

However, only one of the two "total" souls is truly an "act," namely, the intellective soul, which is united to a potential being, namely, the "cogitative" soul. The latter (which is an "inhering form") gives the human being its material existence and all the operations and functions proper to a human being, except for those of the intellect. To the "cogitative" soul is joined the "intellective" soul, thereby forming a higher, "specific" being: the human person, a "rational animal." It is clear that we are dealing here with an explanation that is consistently maintained at every point on the level of natural philosophy. But Paul has no doubt that it ought also be accepted at the level of faith, in accordance with the revealed truth that asserts the plurality of individual human intellects.

In regard to the relation between the agent intellect and the possible intellect with its specific nature, the thought of Paul of Venice has other particularly interesting aspects. In his commentary on the *De anima* and in his *Summa* he discusses the opinion of Avicenna and Alghazali, who regard the two intellects as two distinct substances (the "possible intellect," which is identified with the form of the human being, and the "agent intellect," regarded as the intelligence of the tenth celestial sphere). However, he also criticizes the thesis of Thomas Aquinas and of the master of his own order, Giles of Rome, who consider these two intellects to be two "accidents" of the human soul. Paul dismisses all these opinions, just as he refutes the doctrine, attributed to Wyclif, that holds the "possible intellect," the "agent intellect," and the "will" to be three "powers" of a single substance, with an emphasis on the analogy with the three persons of the Trinity.

Paul's own conclusion is a different one, which he regards as completely conformed to that of Aristotle and undoubtedly different from that of Averroes: the "possible intellect" is a "faculty" of the intellective soul, whereas the "agent intellect" is a separated substance identical with God. It does not follow from this, however, that perfect beatitude can consist (as Averroes would have it) in the union of the "possible intellect" with the divine intellect, since such blessedness can be reached only in reaching the supernatural destiny of the human person. This point shows how constantly watchful the Hermit was to exclude all aspects of Averroism that might seem heterodox and to follow, instead, those teachings of Siger that seemed more reconcilable with theological truth.

Such an outlook on Paul's part has led Kuksewicz to maintain that in this Augustinian Hermit's conception of the matter two perspectives coexist: an Aristotelico-Averroist that is substantially accepted in the framework of natural philosophy and another inspired by faith, and that the author seeks a possible convergence of the two. As an interpreter of Aristotle, Paul accepts, as the authentic teaching of the Philosopher, the thesis of the oneness of the "possible intellect," this being a separated substance and single for the entire human species. But there is another theory that admits the plurality of possible intellects, each of them united to a human being as its "informing form." Even according to this second doctrine, the structure of the human being is unchanged, constituted as it is by a plurality of forms in a hierarchy at the top of which is the intellect, which is "a total form in act," while the "agent intellect," identical with God, does not in fact enter into the composition of the human soul.

The question remains, of course, which of these two different theories of the soul was accepted as his own by this philosopher who was also a "religious" and who, even in his ambiguousness, must have had constantly in mind the harsh attacks of the theologians on Averroist "godlessness."[7]

In any case, it is significant that in the commentary on the *De anima* Paul should appeal to the reflections of another "Averroist," John of Jandun, when he says that God is the final cause of what is moved but that this causality is remote and "mediated" in its efficacy, since the "primary" causes are the souls proper to each celestial sphere, in connection with the soul of the first sphere. He does, of course, regard it as an error, and also contrary to the thought of Aristotle, to deny all "efficiency" to God; but the passage leads us to think that Paul had in mind a causality exercised via the intelligences. It is not an accident that in a passage of his commentary on the *De coelo* in which he discusses the question of whether, inside or outside the world, there can be any infinite power that preserves the world in its eternal duration, his answer is entirely negative, on the grounds that such a power can never exist within a "material" being such as the world is, while it makes no sense to speak of time or space outside of the world. The eternal motion of the universe is due to the individual, mover intelligences, both "informing" and "inhering," which, though possessing only a finite power, are nonetheless "sustained" by an "applied intelligence" that is identified with God, who moves them through an endless time.[8]

3. Gaetano of Thiene

Gaetano of Thiene (1387–1465) was a secular master, a disciple of Paul of Venice at the University of Padua and his successor in the chair of logic and natural philosophy there.[9] Gaetano was known especially for his commentaries on the *Sophismata* of Heytebury (the "Entisber" so harshly condemned by the humanists), whose procedures he also used in a *Tractatus de intentione et remissione formarum* and in his *Tractatus de reactione*.

Our interest here, however, is rather in another work, the *Commentaria in tres libros Aristotelis de anima,* which was composed around 1443 and to which was added a *Quaestio de perpetuitate intellectus.*[10] In his work as interpreter, Gaetano, too, was a strict follower of the text of Aristotle; but while he always had the Averroist thesis in mind, he also made use of other authors, Albert the Great and Giles of Rome, whose closeness to his personal *dubitationes* he not infrequently emphasized. He had no doubt that the *De anima* belongs among the "physical books" of Aristotle and deals solely with natural philosophy. At the same time, however, he did not fail to point out that the *De anima* treats of the loftiest *(praestantior)* subject of that science and that the soul has an intrinsic higher "nobility." In fact, the doctrine on the soul is useful even in treating of the "divine" philosophy (metaphysics), precisely because its object is "substances removed from matter," immaterial realities that can only be thought by the intellect, which itself is "intelligent" and "immaterial."[11]

Following the Aristotelean definition, Gaetano considers the soul to be the form or act of a physical, organized body which has "life in potency"; he therefore asserts that the soul is "one" in each "substance" and, precisely because it is "indivisible," is "entire in the entire body" and in "each of its parts." On the other hand, the soul is essentially immaterial and is also the "informing and inhering form" of "each human being." As a philosopher, Gaetano is not unaware of the entirely different conception maintained by Averroes (which he distinguishes clearly from that of Siger, regarding the latter as an impossible effort to "mediate" between the teaching of the Commentator and that of Christian theologians); in fact, he stresses the point that Averroes supposes a single soul for all human bodies, as their "close and nearby" form.

In the *Quaestio,* the problem of the immortality of the soul is then taken up in a more organized and systematic way. Gaetano distinguishes three different kinds of "forms": (1) a form that informs matter and is "educed" from the potency of matter; (2) a form that is entirely free of matter, does not inform any matter, is not drawn from the potency of matter, and "cannot be generated" or "corrupted"; and (3) a form halfway between the first two, in that it informs matter but is not drawn from the potency of matter. The human soul belongs to this third kind. But if we are to understand fully the nature of the soul, we must clearly distinguish the various meanings of the term "intellect," according as we are dealing with the "intellectual soul" (whose operation consists in "understanding discursively"), the "agent intellect" and the "possible intellect" (two "natural potencies"), the "intellect in act" (which is the act of understanding) or the "habitual intellect" (the "proximate potency" for understanding). On the basis of these distinctions it can be concluded that the intellectual soul is produced by a divine creative act and infused into matter as its "informing form."

The Averroists would certainly object that since the soul is "incorruptible," it also "cannot be produced" and therefore cannot be created. But Gaetano distinguishes "natural generation" from that "simple action of the first cause" which theologians call "creation" and which is peculiar to the soul. On the other hand, the "intellect in act" and the "habitual intellect" can be produced and corrupted, because that is the nature of every "habit" or "act" produced in the soul after its union with the body.

The final conclusion is obvious: the human soul with its natural potencies, the intellect and the will, is incorruptible, that is, immortal; consequently, the personal immortality of the soul of every human being is likewise assured. We are dealing (says Gaetano) with a teaching that is identical with what the Christian faith teaches, but it is possible to maintain it on the basis of philosophical arguments, provided that reason is able to transcend the limits of natural philosophy and understand that the human soul is not generated by a particular "agent" or drawn from the potency of matter but immediately created by God.

In dealing with divine causality and infinity Gaetano's approach is complex and not easily defined. In his commentary of the *Physica*[12] he discusses the Averroist theory of the two movers of the heavens, one proper to each heaven and cause of its successive movements, and the other common to all the heavens, which tend toward it as to their proper end. He therefore proposes two problems: Does this second mover have a finite or an infinite "power," or, in any case, an infinite potency that is intensive or final. Now, according to Averroes, the divine perfection is finite; and John of Jandun agrees with this interpretation of the text of Aristotle. But the teacher from Thiene reminds his readers that others distinguish God from the first mover and consider him to possess infinite power, because he has the ability to produce an infinitely perfect effect, even though he has not yet actually done so. It seems, then, that in substance, Gaetano accepts as entirely reasonable the concept of God infinite in perfection, and that he approximates the Thomist solution, according to which God causes movement not only as an end but also as an "agent."

As we can see, Gaetano's general approach is that of a Scholastic who, while accepting many Averroist solutions in the interpretation of Aristotelean "physics" distances himself from them when dealing with problems and themes that could lead to heterodox conclusions. In these cases, though very cautiously and not without ambiguity, he suggests conceptual distinctions that make possible a rational confirmation of doctrines "of faith."[13]

4. Augustine Favaroni

Gaetano of Thiene was a simple *magister* who, unlike his own teacher, Paul of Venice, did not belong to a religious order, whereas Augustine Favaroni (1360–1443), a theologian, was a Hermit of St. Augustine.[14] Augustine was first a student, then a bachelor and a master in the Augustinian houses of higher studies (the Studia) in Bologna and Florence. He was prior general of the order from 1419 to 1431 and then archbishop of Nazareth. Various theological writings have survived; only a few have been published, the rest are in manuscript. Especially important are his *Commentarius in Apochalypsim beati Joannis Apostoli,* in four books, and his commentary on the *Sentences* of Peter Lombard; to these should be added his commentaries or *Expositiones* of the Pauline letters and his commentaries on the *Ethica* and the *Metaphysica* of Aristotle.

These works make clear Favaroni's mental outlook: although he sometimes seems to follow methods typical of nominalism, he is, in general, rather mistrustful of the Scholastic tradition, in contrast with his limitless confidence in the teachings of the Fathers and Doctors, especially Augustine, Gregory the Great, Gregory of Nazianzus, John Damascene, Basil, Athanasius, Origen, and Bede. Anselm of Aosta, Bernard of Clairvaux, and the Victorines are numbered among the "more traditional Doctors" and contrasted with the masters of the thirteenth and fourteenth centuries and Favaroni's contemporaries. These positions (and the fact that he also cites Cicero, Virgil, Pliny, Horace, and often even Seneca) have led scholars to assume some "affinity" with the humanists, an assumption strengthened by, among other things, his stay in such a spirited intellectual center as the Convent of Santo Spirito in Florence. But two recent students of his works, Fathers Ciolini and Friemel, have rightly emphasized the genuinely Scholastic character of his writings and modes of arguing, which, moreover, are devoted to subjects that are entirely typical of traditional theological discourse and developed by methods wholly those of the "masters."

The most important aspect of his work from a historical point of view is the christological teachings which he develops extensively in his two major works. In fact, as early as his commentary on the *Sentences,* when discussing the union of the human nature with the Word, Favaroni seems to tend toward the doctrine that this nature is God, but by reason of the person *(personaliter),* not by its own nature *(naturaliter).* However, he does not agree that in Christ there are two "natures," two "supposits," and only one "person," which is not distinct from the Word; in fact, in order to avoid any accusation that he is close to the Nestorian heresy, he maintains that in Christ there are two distinct "natures" but a single "supposit" and a single "person," identical with the person of the Word. But despite this subtle distinction, the Council of Basel, at its twenty-second session (July 15, 1435), condemned seven of his christological propositions, taken from the *Commentarius in Apochalypsim;* the reason was that they were regarded as akin to the teaching of John Huss, which had already been "condemned" at the Council of Constance.[15]

The first of these propositions: "The human nature in Christ is really Christ," seemed both to the official spokesman *(relator),* John of Torquemada, and to the council fathers to be completely indistinguishable from the Hussite thesis: "The two natures, the divinity and the humanity, are one Christ, who is the head of his spouse." The decree claimed that the Augustinian theologian meant to say that the "divinity" and the "humanity" together made up the person of Christ, and that just as Christ is his "divinity," so also he is his "humanity."

Admittedly, Favaroni was moved by reasons of a purely theoretical and logical kind, unlike Huss, whose starting point was his "ecclesiological" presupposition, the purpose of which was to lead to the position that according to his "divinity" Christ is the "external head" of the Church and according to his "humanity," the "internal head" (thereby making it impossible for the pope to be in any sense a "head of the Church"). In fact, after laying down the principle that the human "nature" is the "person" of the Word, Favaroni deduced from it that this nature is the Word, precisely in virtue of the identity of personality. Just as in the Trinity "generator" and "generated" are not two "gods" because they have the identical "nature," so too, in the incarnation, the Word is Christ, and the human "nature" is Christ; consequently, there are not two "Christs," but a single Christ by reason of the identity of "person."

It has seemed to Favaroni's recent historians, too, that in avoiding the Nestorian heresy he ended up falling into the Hussite heresy. But it is a fact that in his reasoning this theologian insistently appealed to passages of Augustine and Anselm of Aosta, which he regarded as completely favorable to his thesis. Furthermore, he appealed to these same authors and also to Hugo of St. Victor in saying that the "hypostatic union" consists in the fact that the "intimate cause" *(ratio suppositalis)* of the Word (which determines the divine "nature") also determines the human "nature," without being really distinct from it and thereby making it share in the Word's personality, with the result that the human "nature" of Christ is a "person" and, specifically, the "person" of the Word.

In addition, Favaroni maintained that in the divine being the "person" is not distinct from the "nature" and that the "person" of the Word is therefore not really distinct from the divine "nature." But then, if the human "nature" is not distinct from the "person" of the Word, it will be only rationally, and not really, distinct from the divine "nature." It is not surprising, then, that the council fathers should have also condemned the following propositions, which sounded especially suspect: "The intimate cause that determines the human nature in Christ is not really distinguished from the nature that is determined"; "The human nature in Christ is . . . really the person who assumes." Nor is it surprising that the fathers should have thought these especially close to those of the Hussites.

Favaroni did not, of course, mean by these propositions that the human "nature," considered in its specific concept, is God and that therefore the attributes of the divinity belong to it. In fact, in his reasoning he emphasized the point that even after the hypostatic union this "nature" remains temporal, finite, and "passible," a "creature" and not the "creator." And yet his identification of the "nature" with the "person" of the Word led him, always on the basis of the "authorities" dear to him, to propose these further conclusions: "The human nature assumed by the Word in a personal union is truly God, natural and proper"; "The Word is a person, and the man assumed is a person, but they are one person, not two."[16]

The other, most typical, christological theses of Favaroni go on to maintain doctrines that flow directly from the principles so consistently held. Namely: In his created will, Christ loves the created "nature" that is united to the "person" of the Word just as much as he does the divine "nature"; just as the three "persons" in God are equally lovable, so are the two "natures" in Christ, the human and the divine, "on account of the common person"; and the soul of Christ sees God with the same intensity and clarity as God sees himself.

In summary, we are dealing with conceptions that must have seemed suspect for these further reasons: their emphasis on the clear "humanization" of the "person" of Christ; and, on the other hand, the explicit statement that the created mind, like that of Christ, when elevated to the vision of God, is thereby made more perfect than it already was by reason of its own intrinsic perfection. Nor could people have found very pleasing the Augustinian's admonition to the theologians of his day, who seemed to him too inclined to limit the power of the divine intellect and will, thus adopting the errors of the Beghards. In Favaroni's view the soul of Christ, inasmuch as it is divine, received an infinite knowledge and an infinite love, so that he loves the human "nature" and the "elect" with an infinite love. Finally, since he identified charity with the Holy Spirit, it was not difficult for him to say that acts proceeding from this divine principle are infinite and that the Spirit reveals himself in Christ in the entirety of his infinite power.

When summoned to justify himself before the council, Favaroni refused to appear; later on, he appealed to the pope against the sentence (which, moreover, was in no way prejudicial to him personally), but he did not obtain its withdrawal. He tenaciously rejected the identification of his teachings with those of Huss, whose ecclesiology and attack on the papacy he did not share. In fact, his treatise *De principatu Papae*[17] follows the main line of the theologico-political writings of Giles of Rome, Augustine of Ancona (Augustinus Triumphus), and James of Viterbo, when he asserts that every authority, including that of the emperor, is completely subordinate to the authoritative power of the pope, which, by natural law, is "preceptive" and "preponderant" precisely because it has as its purpose the "speculative" or "theological happiness" of human beings and all other ends are subordinate to this one. This explains why Favaroni engages in a detailed refutation of Dante's *De monarchia* and of the distinction between the "two ends," which he rejects with particular polemical vigor.[18]

5. John Dominici's Defense of Theological Traditionalism

The teachings of these Augustinian masters and of Gaetano of Thiene were, in any case, deeply influenced by the methods and modes of thought of the so-called *via nova* ("new way"), which showed itself with special clarity in the way in which books on logic from the school of Paul of Venice were composed. At the same time, however, Italy still had a solid tradition of the *via antiqua* ("old way"), which was in the hands especially of the schools and theologians of the two major mendicant orders, the Dominicans and the Friars Minor.

Fidelity to the great masters of their philosophical and theological past marked the work of these professors, who were in almost every case engaged in teaching in the schools of their respective orders. They did not, however, limit themselves to explaining and glossing the teachings of Thomas Aquinas or John Duns Scotus but took their part in a complex labor aimed as a complete theoretical organization of doctrinal "systems." This labor did not exclude efforts to "reconcile" various authors (e.g., Thomas Aquinas and Albert the Great) and the absorption of fourteenth-century developments of Thomism and Scotism. Nor, for that matter, did the Dominican and Franciscan theologians ever remain completely untouched by the "novelties" of humanistic culture, with which they entertained relations often polemical but at times also marked by a friendly understanding.

I have already had occasion, when speaking of Coluccio Salutati, to mention the debate, characterized by open but cordial disagreement, between Salutati and a Dominican religious, the future Cardinal John Dominici (1357–1419).[19] I must now speak at greater length of this friar who entered the order at a very young age and soon became a fervent advocate of the Observance and a close collaborator of Raymond of Capua, the confessor and spiritual guide of Catherine of Siena. Dominici was reader in theology at Venice in the Dominican Studium of Santi Giovanni e Paolo (1387), then vicar general of all the reformed convents of Italy and founder (in Venice) of the women's convent of Corpus Christi, where he was also spiritual director.

In 1399, during the Bianchi movement, he initiated a similar movement, but this displeased the Venetian government, which exiled him from the city. In the years that followed, he lived mainly in Florence (in Fiesole he founded the reformed convent of San Domenico), carried on his debate with Salutati, and undertook difficult diplomatic missions for the Signoria of Florence before becoming archbishop of Ragusa and a cardinal during the papacy of Gregory XII. He always remained loyal to this pontiff, even during the events associated with the Council of Constance, at which time he carried out various missions for this pope in Hungary and Poland. He was confirmed in his position as cardinal by Martin V after the abdication of Gregory; he died at Buda in 1419 while on another mission.

These facts are enough to show that Dominici's life was mainly that of a religious dedicated to preaching, spiritual activity, and high ecclesiastical charges rather than of a speculative thinker engaged in difficult theological enterprises. The writings he has left us—from the *Libro d'amor di carità* (1392–94)[20] to the *Trattato delle dieci quistioni* (1404),[21] from the *Lucula noctis* (1405)[22] to the *Regola del governo di cura familiare* (1420),[23] from the *Lettere spirituali*[24] to the *Tractatus de proprio: an liceat fratribus ordinis Praedicatorm in communi vel particulari possessiones habere* (1401–3)— show us that this religious had broad intellectual interests, a not inconsiderable knowledge of theology, and also a special awareness of the needs of the new social groups that had emerged as a result of the economic and political transformations of the late period of the communes.[25]

On the other hand, he was rather suspicious of the humanists' enthusiasm for the poetry and wisdom of the pagans, for he regarded these as a real danger to the faith, even though he acknowledged the inevitable necessity of a carefully supervised study of the ancient writings. It was also symptomatic of his outlook that, as a Thomist, he harshly criticized the primacy of the will and activity that was so often defended in the writings of Salutati.[26] But his judgment of the "natural" sciences was no less negative, since he regarded all of them as uncertain because based on the confused weakness of the senses and on a human philosophy that is always no more than "opinion" and uses methods which he regarded as suspect and contradictory.

In fact, his reflections (inspired by Thomas Aquinas but also by Augustine, Bernard of Clairvaux, Bonaventure, the Victorines, and above all, the constant reading of the Scriptures) are a tireless exaltation of charity, which he regards as the true center of the Christian spiritual life and the complete foundation of the universal order. The will must, of course, be always guided by the intellect and "is barren if not united to its spouse, the intellect." Yet Oechslin, one of his most careful commentators, is right when he insists that although Dominici fears the consequences of "an absolute voluntarism," he attributes rather extensive powers and functions to the will in connection with the centrality of charity.[27]

Charity must permeate every human action and thought, whether the subject is the "word," meditation on the mysteries of the faith, the meaning of miracles, almsgiving, or even martyrdom. It is the highest of all the virtues, including even faith and hope. In fact, it is through the action of charity that our material and fleshly language is able, by an angelic intervention, to reach our interior spirit and inflame it with love of God. Even the union of the soul with the body (of which it is the "form," as taught by Thomist Aristoteleanism) could not take place without the intervention of charity. It is quite true that the soul is "most noble" because of its "likeness" to God, but for this very reason it is difficult to understand how the soul could be united to a "nature" which is as different from it as the "flesh" is and which is so radically and despicably indigent. Only a love far higher than any natural love or "appetite" can bring about the wonderful bond between these two natures that are so "abhorrent" to each other and thereby establish a unity that has love as its substance. Even this is not enough: in Dominici's view charity is also the bond that unites and makes perfect the entire created order; it is manifested in the beauty of creatures and in the gifts given even to lower natures. Therefore, no gift or perfection in this world has meaning unless it participates, through charity, in the divine being.

Such a theology of charity could not avoid discussing a subject that had already been taken up in the preceding century and had provided material for an interesting debate: the "nature" of this virtue. Dominici was aware, of course, of the controversy that had opposed the Thomists to the followers of the teaching of Peter Lombard. The latter had identified charity with the Holy Spirit, who is poured out into the human will, whereas the Thomists, following the teaching of their master, regarded it as a faculty of the mind.

The solution offered by the Florentine Dominican is obviously an effort to reconcile these two quite divergent positions: Dominici claims that God himself "heats" the human spirit without the mediation of any creature and that this heat deeply transforms it. As a result, the "act" or "habit" of charity, although in itself an "accident" of the mind, can receive this heat and participate in it. In short, according to Dominici, the Thomist theologians are correct in saying that charity is an "accident of the mind," but so is Lombard when he says that charity is, "in essence," God himself. The reason is that it is always God who generates this habit or act.

Moreover, the ultimate end to which every soul must move is union with God, and only the love that is charity can lead to that end. To attain to the end, however, we must always "seek" Christ, the supreme, divine Mediator, whom we find in the Scriptures, in the sacrament of the Eucharist, in prayer, and even in creatures. In addition, it is impossible to be united with God unless we accept and welcome his will without qualification, struggling against our own will, continually resisting our passions, accepting every evil and every good, and never asking and desiring anything but this union, which is always imperfect in the present life but to which he himself has nonetheless called us.

6. The Practical Theology of Antoninus Pierozzi

Dominici was the first teacher of a young Florentine, Antoninus Pierozzi (1389–1459),[28] whose precocious Dominican vocation he fostered. Thus began a long life as religious, high Church dignitary, and theologian that ended with his elevation to the altars. After becoming a Dominican novice in 1406, Antoninus spent a great part of his life in Observantine convents in Cortona, Fiesole, Foligno, Naples, and Rome before becoming vicar general of the Observance in Italy (1437) and thus prior of the new convent of San Marco, which came into existence through the generosity of Cosimo de'Medici. In 1436 Eugene IV appointed him archbishop of Florence, and the Dominican led the diocese until his death; he was its guiding light by the sincere piety that inspired his every action but also by his firmness in dealing with the mighty of his day. We know, for example, that despite his personal friendship with Cosimo, he did not hesitate to condemn strongly those political measures and practices of his that were in the main harmful to the institutions and "liberties" of the republic.

His basic theoretical work is the *Summa theologiae,* or *Summa moralis,*[29] composed between 1440 and 1459. This rather spacious but systematic treatment of the most important subjects of moral theology is based on Thomist teaching but also deploys a vast array of "authorities," drawn from the Fathers (Augustine, Ambrose, Jerome, Gregory, John Chrysostom, Basil) and medieval authors (Isidore, Anselm of Aosta, Bernard of Clairvaux, and, then, among more recent writers, Albert the Great, Peter of Palude, Innocent V, Vincent of Beauvais, Bonaventure, Alexander of Hales, Nicholas of Lyra, Bartholomew of Brescia, Richard of Peñafort, Peter of Ancarano, and Lawrence Ridolfi); the vast extent of his learning and reading is evident.

There is no doubt that Pierozzi's *Summa* was the first attempt at an organized development of a true and proper ethical "anthropology," which starts with the theories of Thomistic "psychology" and moves to an analysis of the various forms of sin and an exposition of the basic principles of truly Christian "behavior." The entire first part is devoted to an extensive analysis of the concept of "law" ("in itself" and in its various specifications: "eternal," "natural," "Mosaic," "evangelical," "customary," "canonical," "civil," "privileges") and the problems and casuistry that follow from it.

But this is not the most interesting and original "material" in Antoninus' lengthy doctrinal exposition; these adjectives apply rather to the second part of the work, which is devoted to an analysis of the capital sins, "vows," and "restitutions." Here, using a rich supply of cases furnished him by other masters and by canonists, the theologian gives a very complex and developed picture of fifteenth-century ethical and economic practice, and this in close connection with the character of the most typical activities of contemporary society and its financial and commercial development.

As has been often pointed out, Antoninus is not successful in formulating an organized teaching on "economic ethics," nor is his work marked by an especially mild or an especially stern attitude toward all the activities that suggested usury, a sin which he connected with avarice and, in line with tradition, condemned in principle. Nor does there seem to be anything new about his claim that wealth, commerce, and all the activities connected with it (such as banking or money exchange) must be placed at the service of the human person and its ethical and supernatural ends. Consistently with these presuppositions, he denies that money can be, of itself, "productive" (following a doctrine common to Aristotle and Thomas Aquinas) and that it is, consequently, licit to profit from dealing in it.

On the other hand, he looks at the various economic practices followed in the concrete conduct of business and at the necessity of these, with special attention to those that may conceal speculative practices similar to "usury": sales for future delivery, sales of *census,* interest charged by lending institutions or state banks, contracts to provide pasture, bank deposits, and the various kinds of "exchange" ("by hand," "by letter," "barren"). While his outlook is often based substantially on Thomist theses, he does not fail to advert to the increasing pressure of economic realities that were demanding recognition of the special value of money to merchants and bankers; he does not deny these agents the right to make their capital bear fruit and to derive a moderate profit from it.[30]

In accepting these concessions Antoninus admittedly voices all the reservations dictated by a conscience that tolerates rather than consents but that is always ready to make distinctions, case by case. For example, he allows the buying of a bad debt at a low price because of the high risk connected with it. He also says it is licit to gamble on the fluctuation of exchange rates in two different places, provided the operation is carried on "by letter," since a negative outcome for the gambler is not excluded. However, he resolutely condemns "barren" exchanges, which he regards as loans of a usurious kind. He is even more strongly opposed to interest produced by a deposit in a bank, although he acknowledges that the lender can receive at least a part of the profit he would have obtained had he invested his money in commercial activities.

Less interesting but not without some noteworthy topics are the third and fourth parts of the work, which deal with the Church, the sacraments, and the various states of Christian life, as well as with the cardinal virtues and the gifts of the Holy Spirit. Scholars have been particularly attentive to the section on "Temporal Lords," in which Antoninus discusses the various relationships among the sovereigns of the West and also the struggle against the Turks in the light of the now imminent fall of Constantinople. It would be easy to point out other important passages of the *Summa,* from those having to do with councils (and showing the Dominican's inclination to full recognition of papal supremacy) to the extensive development of a complete teaching on Mariology, from the mention of the "Bianchi movement" to renewed reflections on "divine punishment," these being related to that tragic episode of Church history in the years spanning the change of the centuries.

Antoninus' *Summa* had a wide readership, as can be seen from the series of printings between 1477 and 1515. No less successful was another of his writings, the *Chronicon,*[31] which was likewise composed during the last twenty years of his life, while he was working on his *Summa*. With the extensive help of medieval sources but also of some contemporary writers (Minerbetti and Poggio Bracciolini), the *Chronicon* aims at a complete history of the world, following the eight ages from the creation of Adam to the contemporary world. The work is heavily influenced by theological ideas and the device of "examples," which are given in the frequently recurring and lengthy biographical excursuses. In short, the work is not much different in character from analogous medieval historical narratives, although the abandonment of the traditional annals format has led some scholars to see in this work, despite its obvious compilatory character, some influence of humanistic culture, with which Archbishop Antoninus did have documented connections.

There are other treatises that are faithful to the tradition and essentially intended, like the *Summa,* for the preparation and instruction of preachers and confessors: for example, a *Confessionale* in three parts *(Defecerunt; Curam illius habe* [in the vernacular: *Medicina dell'anima*], and *Omnium mortalium cura* [in the vernacular: *Specchio di coscienza*]; all three of which found a place in the *Summa); De ornatu mulierum*; *Libretto della dottrina per i putti piccoli e giovanetti; Opera a ben vivere;* and *Trialogus super enarrationem evangelicam de duobus discipulis euntibus in Emmaus*. These works fill out the historical picture of a theologian who was at once faithful to the doctrinal inspiration of his order and, at the same time, had an eye for the social and political reality in which his life was lived and for the changed values that were henceforth predominant.

7. The Concordist Tendencies of Dominicans Anthony de Carlenis and John Gatto

Antoninus' theological thinking was eminently of a practical kind, devoted to dealing with the concrete ethical problems that were connected with the exercise of the more typical pastoral ministries. Quite different was the prevailing trend among the other more important Italian Dominican masters of the period. These men devoted themselves chiefly to the systematic development of the philosophical and theological teachings of Thomism and to their defense against their Franciscan colleagues, who were followers of Scotism and often engaged in very lively disputes over its most distinctive positions in the science of God.

The first of the Dominicans to be mentioned was a Neapolitan contemporary of Antoninus, Anthony de Carlenis (1386–1449),[32] who was already a mature man when he entered the order and had taught rhetoric at the University of Bologna and held other offices. We do not have much information about his life, but we know that from 1439 to 1442 he taught as a bachelor in the Dominican Studium of Bologna. It is also likely that he attended the Council of Ferrara-Florence, perhaps in the retinue of his provincial, John of Montenero, whose interventions in the debates with the Byzantine theologians I shall mention further on. Reason for thinking that de Carlenis attended this council is his *Quaestio,* to which Di Agresti in particular has called attention, in which he deals with the problem of the *Filioque* and, as to be expected, defends the teaching of the Latin theologians.[33]

Later on, in 1449, after having been a professor at the well-known Neapolitan Studium of S. Domenico Maggiore, de Carlenis became archbishop of Amalfi, an office which he held to the end of his life. He left behind him a solid reputation as a teacher and a scholar who devoted himself to explaining the principal theses of the Angelic Doctor in the form of both metaphysical meditation and theological reflection.

His interests can be seen in his three unpublished collections of *Quaestiones (Quaestiones in libros XII Metaphysicorum; Quaestiones in libros I et II Analyticorum posteriorum Aristotelis;* and *Quaestiones in IV libros Sententiarum);* in these there is a consistent application of Thomist methods and concepts, in direct disagreement not only with the teachings of John Duns Scotus and his followers (Francis of Meyronnes and Anthony Andreae) but also with those of "more recent masters," which the Dominican knows and discusses in a competent manner. In particular he focuses his analysis and detailed treatment on the major themes of the doctrine of being, at the point where metaphysics and theology meet, and maintains and defends the principle of the analogy of being, which he regards as the key to any understanding of the supreme principles of being. And yet, despite his fidelity to Thomism, his writings seem to show an inclination to evaluate positively the possible convergences with other teachings and to reduce to mere differences of language such oppositions as he thinks easily reconcilable, provided proper account is taken of the deeper affinity brought to light by an "unprejudiced" analysis.

If we think about it, this attitude (for which he was later sternly rebuked by Dominic of Flanders, a stricter and more rigid Thomist) is not much different from that of another, younger Dominican master from the south, John Gatto (1420–84).[34] His contemporaries judged him to a man of especially penetrating intelligence and learned in the most varied disciplines: a theologian but also a jurist and an astronomer. In addition to all this he was well versed in the "three languages." It is said—with what degree of truth we do not know—that he journeyed to Greece and stayed there several years in order to perfect his knowledge of a language so important for biblical and theological studies. His activity as teacher took him chiefly to Bologna, Florence, and Ferrara; the "disputation" which he conducted in Rome, during a general chapter of the order and in the presence of Nicholas V and Bessarion, was said to have been memorable. Similar demonstrations of an uncommon talent and culture favored his rapid ecclesiastical career, which culminated in 1472 with his election to the See of Cefalù and, in 1477, to the archiepiscopal See of Catania.

This Dominican's time as archbishop was not, however, a happy one, since he became involved in the conflict between Ferdinand II and Sixtus IV and was forced to abandon his see, to which he was unable to return before his death.

It is not these details that interest us here so much as Gatto's membership in the circle of scholars often known as the "Academy of the Cardinal [Bessarion] of Nicaea." Other members, in addition, of course, to Bessarion himself, were some of the most illustrious representatives of the humanist culture of the age: from Nicholas Perotti to Theodore of Gaza, from Andronicus Callistus to Domitius Calderini and Pomponius Leto. The special closeness of the Dominican to the Byzantine cardinal is confirmed by an explicit reference in Bessarion's *In calumniatorem Platonis,* where he is described as "a professor of theology and our close friend."

Now, although a Dominican, Gatto was also interested in the teaching of Scotus as interpreted in a concordist manner, for he was firmly convinced that the two greatest masters of Western theology were in agreement on all essential points in the discipline of theology. It is therefore understandable that he could influence Bessarion to make shrewd use of Thomist and Scotus theses in his work so as to deny the natural convergence between the "philosophy" of Aristotle and Christian "truth." I cannot enter here in the details of a discussion aimed at demonstrating, with the help of theological texts, the profound contrast between the false image of a Christianized Aristotle that was proposed by George of Trebizond, and the real character of a philosophy that was completely alien, and at times directly opposed, to the principles of faith and to fundamental dogmas. We must still consider, however, that while citations from the writings of Thomas are more numerous and are very skillfully used to bring out the profound differences between Aquinas and the Philosopher (whom Bessarion admired), the works of Scotus, too, play a by no means secondary role in this important polemic.

In particular, Bessarion appeals to the teachings of the English Franciscan to clinch the point that the philosophy of Aristotle does not accept divine omnipotence, denies all contingency, and postulates only the eternal existence of the world. Scotist theses are also used when Bessarion wants to challenge the "Peripatetics'" inability to conceive of the "true" immortality of the soul and its "separated" nature as well as their serious error in regarding the soul rather as an "instrument." In all cases, moreover (the question is of "formalities" or the doctrine of "thisness" *[haecceitas]*); differences between Thomas and Scotus are depicted rather as being different forms of a common theological language that is, in any case, irreducible to the speculative horizon of the greatest "pagan" philosophers.[35]

8. Dominicans Faithful to Thomism; The Synthesis of Dominic of Flanders; The Debate over the Immaculate Conception

Unlike Gatto, other contemporary Dominican theologians maintained a rather strict fidelity to Thomas; concerning these men, however, we have less extensive and detailed information.

Of Peter of Bergamo (+ 1492)[36] we know only that he was a professor of theology in the Dominican Studium in Bologna and that Paul Barbo was one of his students there. The most important thing we know about Peter is his effort to develop a general "overview" of the works of Thomas Aquinas by means of the "tabular" system so often used by the fifteenth- and sixteenth-century theologians in organizing and systematically arranging all the basic concepts and passages of the various authoritative sources *(auctores)*. Peter's *Tabula,* usually known as the *Tabula aurea,* was published at Bologna in 1475 and enjoyed notable success, due above all to its "methodical" form, which made it a useful tool especially for confessors, preachers, and more generally, for anyone desiring to tackle metaphysical and theological problems, even in their practical aspect.

Peter divided his work into two distinct parts. The first, entitled *Index universalis in omnia opera D. Thomae de Aquino,* was conceived as a subject index that would allow easier access to the fundamental themes of Thomist philosophy and theology. The second part was a more doctrinal digest and was intended to show the agreement of Thomist texts with one another, including those texts which adversaries claimed were contradictory. This part bore the title of *Concordantia locorum doctoris Angelici quae sibi invicem adversari videntur,* the very wording of which shows how the effort to show an overriding harmony within the many works and extensive thought of Aquinas was increasingly made by these late disciples who were aiming to construct an all-inclusive Thomism as a definitive answer to all the problems of metaphysics and theology.

This was the course also followed by Paul Barbo of Soncino (+ 1494),[37] who had been a student in the Dominican Studium of Bologna and was later a professor there and who was also a master at Milan, Ferrara, and Siena. He had dealings with John and John Francis Pico, who knew his reputation as a careful and rigorous interpreter of Thomist teaching. He was a very prolific author, both of philosophical works—*Elegantissima expositio in artem veterem Aristotelis in quaestionibus; Metaphysicales quaestiones* (partly reissued as *Quaestiones metaphysicales super divinam sapientiam Aristotelis*); *Quaestiones in VIII libros physicorum, in logicam Aristotelis* (collected and reorganized by James Rossetti in 1587); *Commentaria in X Aristotelis praedicamenta; Commentaria in quinque Porphyrii praedicabilia*—and of a *Divinum Epitoma quaestionum in IV libros Sententiarum a principe Thomistarum Ioanne Capreolo Tolosano disputatarum,*[38] a work that shows how extensive and deep, even in Italy, was the influence of the French theologian [Capreolus], who so skillfully organized the main points of Thomist teaching into a systematic form.

Paul's works, almost all of them published at the end of the fifteenth century and during the early decades of the sixteenth and frequently reprinted (some of them right into the seventeenth century), confirm his outstanding powers of exposition. He was an accurate reader of Thomas and sought to present and analyze the Angelic Doctor's fundamental themes with great subtlety and acumen and to explain his most complex and controverted passages, which were constantly used for the sake of their exegesis of Aristotle. In fact, Paul's often stated and emphatically repeated opinion was that Aristotelean philosophy had found in Aquinas its most "legitimate" and sure interpreter, the only one capable of freeing it from the distortions of less "faithful" commentators (meaning Averroes, Alexander of Aphrodisias, and Themistius).

Always concerned, as he was, with defending the thought of his great teacher from every kind of "corruption," Paul did not hesitate to edit Aquinas' writings himself; thus in 1488, he published *S. Thomas Aquinatis opuscula XLIX*[39] in a considerably corrected version. He was also alert to other, more recent expressions of Dominican spirituality: in that same year he published the *Sermones de sanctis* of Vincent Ferrer[40] and appended to these a letter to the order's vicar general for the provinces of Lombardy, which is of interest for understanding how the editor rated the work of his Spanish confrere.

Barbo's reputation was not limited to the schools of Italy; it was also echoed in no small measure in the Dominican Studia "beyond the mountains," where one work in particular was widely used: the *Tabula titulorum quaestionum magistri Pauli Soncinatis super Metaphysicam,* which was published shortly after his death.[41]

However, the most representative master of the "Italian" tradition of fifteenth-century Thomism was a foreign professor who became a Dominican and a theologian after a career as teacher of philosophy that had begun and continued for several years at the most important center of studies in Western Christendom, the University of Flanders. The man was Dominic of Flanders. The researches of Meersseman,[42] Schikowski,[43] and Mahieu[44] have greatly contributed to our knowledge of the events of the life of this quite cultivated and subtle "Scholastic" and of his activity as teacher and exegete. We still do not know the exact date and place of his birth, which probably took place in modern French Flanders. We can, however, suppose that he was born around 1425 and that, to judge by information found in his works, he studied at Paris under the guidance of a Thomist master with "Albertist" sympathies, John Versor, whose writings on logic, natural philosophy, and metaphysics Dominic often cites. Dominic's "secular" name was, in all probability, Balduin Lottin; and since no such name occurs in Denifle's *Cartularium* (which stops at 1472), we may suppose that he completed his studies in Paris and obtained the title of *magister* between 1453 and 1461, in which year he already belonged to the Dominicans.

One fact, however, is certain: in 1461 Dominic was a friar at Bologna in the convent of San Domenico, one of the most active centers of the Dominican Observance and the location of one of the major Studia, in which various of his confreres from Flanders, Brabant, and Holland were studying and teaching.

Dominic spent the years from 1462 and 1470 in the study of theology and perhaps also in teaching it, if it be true that, according to information given in a codex, he composed the first six books of his *Summa divinae philosophiae* before 1468. It is probable that during the latter year he also composed his *Quaestiones sex principiorum,* his commentary on the *Physica,* and his *Tractatus de modibus.* In 1472 he was certainly *magister sacrae paginae* ("master of the sacred page" = Scripture; that is, master of theology) and was teaching at the Studium in Pisa, having been called there (it is said) by Lorenzo the Magnificent himself, who in any case paid for the preparation of the ornate copy of the first six books of the *Summa* that is now kept in the Biblioteca Laurenziana. Another evidence of his connection with Florentine circles is the dedication to Nicholas Martelli of his commentary on the *Analytics,* composed in 1472, after he had been professor of philosophy and logic in the Florentine Studium for the 1471–72 school year. After moving to the Bologna Studium in 1474–75, he returned briefly to Pisa in 1475; but the next year found him again in Bologna, where he remained until October, when he became regent of the Dominican Studium in Florence. He still held this office on July 16, 1479, the day of his death.

Dominic of Flanders' career was evidently that of a brilliant master who alternated teaching in the schools of the order with teaching in other university institutions of the time, thanks to his indisputable reputation as an excellent authority on the texts of Aristotle and the teachings of Thomas; he proved himself a faithful interpreter of these last, although he did not forget his initial formation, which had set a special value on the teaching of Albert. His reputation seems to be confirmed by the lengthy list of his works that has come down to us; it includes writings on logic, metaphysics, physics, and moral philosophy, as well as a commentary on the *Propositiones de causis Proculi*, some *Quodlibeta,* and a *Tractatus brevis de ordine divinarum personarum.*

Of these many writings the only ones we now have are the *Quaestiones* on the *Posterior Analytics,* the *Expositio super fallacias,* the *Tractatus brevis de suppositionibus,* the *Quaestiones* on the *De anima,* and, most important, the *Summa divinae philosophiae,* a very extensive, systematic commentary on the *Metaphysics* that has been preserved in several manuscripts, was printed in Venice in 1499, and was still being reprinted well into the seventeenth century.[45]

The *Summa* is divided into "questions" and "articles," following the example of Thomas, and in a meticulous, clear, and concise way explains the teachings of Aristotle, but always in line chiefly with the teachings of the Angelic Doctor. It is clear, however, that Dominic intends his work primarily for the preparation of future theologians, for whom instruction in metaphysics has a fundamental importance and value. As a result, this is a commentary in which the theological perspective is always present, just as the didactic intention plays a controlling role; this intention finds clear expression in the way that the author furnishes, for every "question," accurate and clearly stated solutions, while also systematically discussing opinions alien or opposed to Thomist teaching, which is regarded as the only truly accurate and "scientific" doctrine.

Dominic had no sympathy for the sophistic methods and excessive dialectical virtuosity of the "modern" masters, whose useless subtleties he rejected, just as he attacked the authors of "speculative grammars" and, in general, the excessive use of logical methods that render obscure and uncertain even the clearest of teachings. Nonetheless, while he makes strong attacks on the Averroists and Alexandrinists, the "Buridanists," the "big-headed grammarians," and the "young syllogizers," the most constant object of his criticism is the Scotists and, in particular, Anthony Andreae, Francis of Meyronnes, John of Marbres (the "Canon"), and those masters whom he regarded as already moving toward nominalism, such as Burley and Bonet. Nor, as was already mentioned, does he fail to pass a severe judgment on those Thomists whom he thinks too accommodating to "alien" doctrines, especially de Carlenis, who is often called "a false Thomist" or "a Thomist in name but not in fact."

Despite all this, it would be a mistake to think that Dominic of Flanders blindly accepted all Thomist teachings and that he had no original views or positions and was not open to various doctrinal influences. As a matter of fact, his vast philosophical and theological learning enabled him to cite and make appropriate use of many authors, from the Fathers to modern philosophers such as Paul of Venice and Gaetano of Thiene, from the *Liber de causis* and

Pseudo-Dionysius to Avicebron, Avicenna, Alghazali, and of course, Averroes. He is also familiar with the interpretations given by Alexander of Aphrodisias and Themistius; he cites the *Timaeus* of Plato and does not overlook Euclid. To say nothing, then, of the very numerous Thomist masters whom he frequently mentions, he also shows his familiarity with Giles of Rome, Hervé Nédellec, Capreolus, his old teacher John Versor, and Dominic Dominici.

At the same time, however, after Thomas the author he most cites and uses is certainly Albert the Great, all of whose most important writings he cites; his intention is clearly to reconcile some of the two authors' opinions. It is typical of him that while he always strives to deny any contradiction within the thought of Thomas and interprets passages so as to harmonize them with one another, he not infrequently brings to mind the quite different solutions of Albert, for which he shows a great deal of understanding and has at times a real "inclination."

In his lengthy commentary on Aristotle Dominic does not conceal the obvious contrasts between the "letter" of the Philosopher and the solutions proposed by Thomas, these being regarded as "true" and "certain" in their specifically doctrinal meaning. Nor does he conceal the different interpretations of these solutions that have been given by various disciples and followers of Thomas, who often disagree in their exegesis of the master. Dominic chooses from among these with great freedom, while often offering lively criticism of those he regards as farfetched or hardly faithful to the "spirit" of Aquinas, just as, on other occasions, he distances himself from attitudes common to other Thomists and tries to gain a deeper understanding and resolution of the more serious doctrinal oppositions.

In particular, when he takes up the important subject of the analogy of being, he discusses the Scotist concept of "univocity" with exceptional openness and the intention of identifying an essential point of agreement between the two doctrines. He always remains, indeed, a very firm supporter of analogy; and it is not an accident that to his harsh attack on the particular interpretation of univocity given by Anthony Andreae, he adds a no less firm critique of de Carlenis as being a Thomist whose principles are not too "solid." In the end, however, he asks whether the difference between the two masters is really substantial or whether, on the contrary, the difference between Thomists and Scotists on this point is simply a matter of words and without any real foundation ("thus there will be no difference between the Scotists and us, except in words, and no disagreement on the reality").

Meersseman has rightly described Dominic of Flanders as one of the most important "codifiers of the Thomist synthesis," and has emphasized the role of the Italian Scholastics in this complex and difficult undertaking. It will be helpful here to add that the dispute between Thomists and Scotists was made even more complicated and difficult by the lengthy dispute over the Immaculate

Conception. Many of the Italian Dominicans and Franciscans, massed in opposing ranks, took part in this dispute.

Among the Thomist theologians who were most involved in this debate was Vincent Bandelli (1435–1506),[46] a person of considerable prominence in his order. He was teaching as a bachelor at the Bologna Studium as early as 1478 and soon distinguished himself by his special abilities in dialectics; thus in 1484, at Rome and in the presence of Innocent VIII, he conducted a solemn disputation that won him the immediate grant of the title of Master. He was an inquisitor at Bologna in 1490 and twice vicar general of the Province of Lombardy (1484 and 1493); in 1500 he became vicar general of the order and, in that same year, prior general. In this position he championed a reform of the Dominicans that had as its leading ideas the return to the order's more authentic apostolic ideals, the priority of studies, and a strict fidelity to Thomist teaching.

As a strict and determined Thomist, Bandelli sided resolutely against the Marian "privilege" of the Immaculate Conception, which seems to him utterly opposed to the teaching of Aquinas. There is no doubt that his intervention was quickened by a bull issued in 1465 by Sixtus IV (a document which many Dominicans regarded as entirely "partisan"), in which the pontiff forbade anyone to call "wicked" or "heretical" those which believed in this "privilege."[47] As is well-known, other Dominican theologians, among them John of Torquemada and John of Monzón, reacted in a very firm manner. And Bandelli himself published a *Libellus recollectorius de veritate conceptionis Beatae Mariae Virginis* (Milan, 1475), in which he asserted in the most explicit way that it was "wicked" and "rash" to maintain the exemption of the Virgin from conception in original sin. He even added: "The Virgin Mary was not only capable of sinning but in fact sinned."

When, in 1476, Sixtus IV approved the Office of the Immaculate Virgin that had been composed by Leonard of Nogarola, a Franciscan, Bandelli spoke out again with a counter-office, in which it was said that sanctification of Mary took place "after the infusion of the soul." The increasingly fiery controversy continued during the following years and became one of the many contrasts in theology, discipline, and ecclesiology that divided the two orders. Thus at Bologna, in 1481, Bandelli published his *Tractatus de singulari puritate et praerogativa conceptionis Salvatoris nostri Iesu Christi;* this was later expanded into the *Liber ducentorum et sexaginta sanctorum, virginem Mariam in originali peccato fore conceptum dicentium, dicta continens,* published at Lübeck around 1485.

The theses defended in the three works of Bandelli are substantially the same, although the polemical motives differ. In the *Libellus,* where he starts from the doctrine of "primitive" justice and original sin, the theologian states unhesitatingly that it is "impious" to want to exempt the Virgin from the common law of conception in sin and that those who maintain the exception are subverting the foundations of the faith and setting themselves against the orthodox decrees and norms of the Church. Bandelli insisted that the acceptance of the doctrine of the Immaculate Conception would imply several things: an unjust decision of God in not exempting Mary from the common law of death; a limitation on the uniqueness and universality of Christ's mediation; and a substantial assimilation of Mary to her Son, at least from the viewpoint of "purity."

In the *Tractatus* his attitude is more cautious, for he falls back on the distinction between "physical conception" and conception according to the spirit, according to which Mary was created by God; consequently, he admits that the "adversaries" have some justification. Nevertheless, as later in the *Liber,* he lists a lengthy series of patristic, theological, and canonical authorities (among them, seventy-two Dominican writers, thirty-two Franciscans, and thirty-two from other orders) who agree in maintaining the doctrine of Mary's conception in sin. To these he adds Scripture passages and theological arguments. He concludes that it is not in fact permissible to affirm Mary's exemption from original sin, and he distinguishes Mary's sanctification from her conception, even if only for an imperceptible moment of time ("an imperceptibly short delay"). In 1475 or, more probably, in 1477, Bandelli debated publicly on the subject with John Sansone, general of the Franciscans.

Bandelli's conclusions did not alter the papal decrees already issued nor did they influence the pope's future decisions. In 1482, in the bull *Grave nimis,* Sixtus IV declared false and erroneous the statements of those who, like the Dominican, meant to limit the scope of the Church's festive celebration to the "spiritual" and "sanctificatory" conception of the Virgin. Then, in 1483, in a new issue of the same bull, the pope condemned those who regarded the celebration of the Office of the Immaculate Conception as sinful.

9. Tensions in the Dominican Order: The Debate over Savonarola

Another serious disagreement, one that, this time, divided Dominican theologians among themselves and led to oppositions destined to last well beyond the limits of the century, was the one that during the 'nineties opposed the followers and adversaries of Friar Jerome Savonarola. I shall speak further on about this major protagonist in the tensions and spiritual crisis of his age. In the present context, I shall limit myself to recalling one of his more pugnacious critics, his Florentine confrere John Caroli (1428/29–1503).[48]

John belonged to the important middle-class family of the Berlinghieri (the patronymic "Caroli" took the place of his surname). After entering the Cistercians as a very young boy, he passed over to the Dominicans, in the convent of S. Maria Novella in Florence, in 1442. It was in his own city and in this convent that he spent his entire life (except for a fairly short period of forced residence in the Dominican house of S. Romano in Lucca). Here he served three times as prior and in other offices of the order, among which is to be mentioned especially the office of "regent" of the conventual Studium. Beginning in 1455 he was also reader in the *Sentences* and the Scriptures at the University of Florence; he was accepted as a *magister* of the University in 1456 and later, in 1469, became dean of the theological faculty.

His work, *Liber dierum lucensium,* which he wrote during his exile in Lucca, is an interesting testimony to the spiritual and disciplinary oppositions and conflicts in Florentine religious circles. His *Vitae nonnullorum fratrum Beatae Mariae Novellae* is a biographical source often used by Dominican historians. His *De exemplis sacrae scripturae,* which is also known as *De virtutibus et vitiis et de moribus bonorum et malorum* (published anonymously in Paris 1478), is directly connected with his roles as teacher and as master of preachers and confessors. On the other hand, his various "spiritual" writings, which he composed for monks and devout persons, especially during the last years of his life, are rather illuminating expressions of a religious spirit founded on meditation on the Scriptures: *Esposizione sopra gli inni di S. Giovanni Battista; Esposizione sopra gli inni penitenziali; Esposizione sopra gli inni del Corpo di Cristo; Ufficio del miracolo del corpo di Cristo e sue significazioni spirituali; Oratio de iubilei divinitate.* In these writings he takes the occasion at times to condemn philosophical doctrines that denied the immortality of the individual soul, and he set over against these the conceptions of the Thomists.

We are told that beginning in 1495 Caroli, who was a friend of the humanists and had close ties with Landino in particular, became closely involved in the attack on Savonarola. The reason for the attack was both the supposed infractions of discipline by the San Marco friar and his followers and the challenge to the liceity and truthfulness of his prophecies. Caroli's first intervention was a piece of writing that took as its starting point the Pauline verse "No one serving as a soldier gets involved in civilian affairs" (2 Tim 2:4 NIV) and claimed that no "religious" could fill civic offices and take part in civic disputes. Then, when the friars of San Marco refused to join their confreres from the other convents, whom they considered "deformed" in forming the Tuscan-Romagnolan Congregation desired by Alexander VI (on this occasion Savonarola even wrote an *Apologeticum fratrum Sancti Marci*), Caroli responded with a refutation of the reasons given for not obeying the papal order.

He then intensified his attack by adducing disciplinary and theological arguments in answer, first, to a writing by an unknown follower of Friar Jerome, and then, in his *Contro la lamentazione della falsa sposa di Cristo e lamentazione dello sposo* (1497), to Savonarola's own *Lamentum sponsae Christi.* Finally, in 1498, Caroli launched a new attack in his *Esposizione del salmo 25: Iudica me, Domine,* in which he dealt directly with the preaching of the San Marco friar (and in particular with his Septuagesima and Sexagesima sermons on Exodus), refuting his prophecies with an appeal to Thomist teachings.

It is not surprising that in the same spirit he should have written a *Libellus* against John Nesi, the author of *Oraculum de novo secolo,* who combined a long-standing love of Ficino and a warm admiration for Pico with a newfound enthusiasm for Savonarola. Nor that after Savonarola's tragic end he should have fully justified the papal condemnation and the actions of the Florentine religious and political authorities who, in his judgment, had defended the Church against disorder and heresy.[49] Finally, in his *Super quibusdam conclusionibus Joannis Pici Mirandulani principis* he proved a stern critic of Pico, whose dangerous appeal to the Cabala and "obscure" tendencies to esotericism he rejected.

10. The Carmelites and Thomism: Baptist Spagnoli

The spread of Thomist doctrines throughout the theological world of the fifteenth century in Italy was due to the presence of skilled and renowned masters, the large number of Dominican Studia, and the attraction which these had even for "secular" masters and lay philosophers. But this spread did not fail to elicit some typical reactions as well. Among these, it will be opportune to mention here the work of a humanist, poet, and theologian belonging to the Carmelite Order: the *Opus aureum in Thomistas* of Baptist Spagnoli of Mantua (1447–1516).[50]

Having received an authentically humanist formation (he had been a pupil of Gregory Tifernate and George Merula at Mantua and later a student in Padua), Spagnoli had entered the order in 1463, after his first experiments as a poet and precocious "orator." He continued, moreover, to devote himself to poetry and sacred oratory for the rest of his life, as is attested by his abundant outpouring of sacred verse, religious and spiritual writings, apologetic works, and operettas on moral subjects. In these he gave voice to an austere and sincere piety, inspired to some extent by the model products of the *Devotio moderna;* with this he combined a humanist's mastery of literary and rhetorical tools and a keenly perceptive "imitation" of the classics that won him a reputation as a "Christian Virgil." But Spagnoli, who was destined for a brilliant career in the order, culminating in his appointment as general in 1513, was also a theologian and regent in the Carmelite Studia of Bologna and Mantua. In addition to his *De potentia,* a work inspired by his meditation on the Scriptures and his experience of life at the courts of princes, he wrote, around 1392, an *Opus aureum,* the original title of which was *Apologia pro fratre Petro Nebulario.*[51]

This last work was occasioned by the violent attack of some Thomists, in 1391, on a fellow Carmelite and close friend of Spagnoli, Peter Gavassetti of Novellara, also known as Peter Nebulario. The occasion of the attack was a Lenten sermon preached in Mantua, which had given him the opportunity to extol, among the glories of that city, its possession of a relic of the real blood of Christ and its veneration for this. As we shall see below when I deal with this subject at greater length in connection with a writing of Francis Della Rovere (Sixtus IV),[52] the discussion both of the authenticity of such relics and of the union of the person of the Word with the blood shed by Christ during his passion had been going on for quite some time. It had reached a special intensity in 1362, when James of the Marches,[53] a famous Franciscan preacher, and James of Brescia, Dominican inquisitor for Lombardy, had bitterly attacked each other. At that time their opposition had threatened to turn into a conflict between the two orders, and Pius II was persuaded to issue a formal ban on any discussion of the subject. But minds were not appeased, and from time to time this disagreement burst forth again on quite different occasions.

At this time, then, Spagnoli initially limited himself, in defense of his confrere, to a short treatise on the blood of Christ. But he then changed and expanded the part devoted to Thomism, that is, the second part of the *Apologia,* turning it into a substantial autonomous document. The *Opus aureum* was written with the humanist elegance typical of its author and enriched with continual references not only to Thomist texts but to Aristotle, Cicero, Seneca, and the Fathers, especially Augustine, as well as references to recent or contemporary authors such as Petrarch, Ficino, and Pico.

In this new form, however, the work had for its purpose to challenge the supposed superiority of Thomist teachings and their identification with orthodox truth. Spagnoli says that from the very beginning of his studies he had been struck by the intransigence of the Thomists who, even in questions having nothing to do with the truths of faith, condemn whoever does not agree with their teachings. Moreover, they are quick to attack their adversaries verbally, whether these be the more important Scotists or the greatest of the Carmelite masters, John Bacon (Baconthorpe). Spagnoli acknowledges, of course, the outstanding wisdom of Thomas Aquinas, his extraordinary piety and holiness, and the very great value of his thought. He thinks, however, that the Thomists have become accustomed to reading only Thomas' and their own works and that this habit has left them ignorant of the ideas of others, which they reject without knowing them. Yet this is a rather dangerous attitude, since it impoverishes the Church and its capacity for intellectual development.

Moreover, very learned men have challenged some conceptions and ideas of Thomas, even while respecting his lofty genius. It is a fact, too, that since the earliest times the philosophers have freely argued among themselves and maintained opposing and divergent views, so that Christian philosophy now has, by common consent, three very great teachers: Thomas Aquinas, Henry of Ghent, and John Duns Scotus, whose ideas differ on many points. This is entirely as it should be, because, the Carmelite repeats, every philosopher and theologian has different abilities and speculative tendencies, which are ordained by God himself through the variety of astral influences.

On the other hand, Spagnoli has no doubt that, like all the sciences, the doctrine of the faith is built up slowly over time, in accordance with what God himself intends to reveal to us on each occasion. Nor can it be said, as the Thomists maintain, that the teaching of their master, approved as it is by the Church, must be seen as absolute truth beyond challenge. For historical experience shows that opinions maintained by holy Doctors and teachers and approved have later been regarded as untrue. It is certain that only the canonical books are completely without falsity, but this is precisely because they are the "word of God" and not of human beings. The Thomists ought, therefore, to show at least a greater humility and acknowledge that not Thomas alone but the other Doctors regarded as "sound" by the Church are to be praised and that, provided it is not prejudicial to divine truth, the disagreement between various opinions does not lessen but increases the value and power of the faith.

11. Scotism and the School of Padua

This calm discussion by Spagnoli the humanist testified to the freedom of opinion shown also by other Carmelite theologians of that century, such as James Alberti (+ 1426), Agnello de Augustinis (+ 1438), and John of Paraga or of Florence (+ 1435). His work ended, moreover, with a call for moderation and tolerance. But the Thomists were opposed, even in Italy, by well-trained Scotist masters, who sometimes derived new formulations for their teachings from the contemporary renaissance of Platonism and were encouraged especially by the ascent to the papal throne of a Franciscan who had been a Scotist theologian and philosopher, Francis Della Rovere, who took the name of Sixtus IV.

The center for formation in and the spread of Scotism in Italy was undoubtedly the Franciscan Studium, which was located near the basilica and convent of San Antonio in Padua and was known as the Santo.[54] It was here that those Franciscans were trained and acquired their master's degree who later also taught in the University of Padua when a special chair of Scotism *(in via Scoti)* was established to match the chair of Thomism *(in via Thomae)* held by the Dominicans. It was also from Padua that the Scotists, not a few in number, came who taught in the various Studia of the order or in the Italian universities of the middle and late sixteenth century. I am referring here, of course, only to the more celebrated and better studied of these men; among these Francis Della Rovere (1414–84)[55] occupies a very special place. I shall limit myself here to recalling only his long career as a teacher at Padua (where he was already regent of the Studium of the Santo in 1444–45 and, at the same time, full professor in the chair of philosophy at the university, in competition with Gaetano of Thiene); Bologna; Florence (regent of the Studium at Santa Croce in 1450); Perugia (1451–57 and again in 1458–60); Siena (1457–58); and the Roman Sapienza, where he did his final teaching before becoming a cardinal.

The list of manuscripts which he used in his teaching or which he donated make quite clear his doctrinal partialities, for in this list we find the names of truly typical authors, from Scotus to Francis of Meyronnes, from Burley to Gaetano of Thiene, from Paul of Venice to John of Jandun, from Marbres to Biaggio Pelacani, James of Forlì, and John of Casale. His own theological ideas, which showed a clear leaning to the "moderns" but were always expounded with a great deal of moderation and prudence, are documented in a few writings that were printed when he was already pope but had been written in earlier years.

The first of these is the short treatise *De sanguine Christi*,[56] which originated in a theological debate in which he had participated in 1462, on occasion of the clash between James of the Marches and James of Brescia. It must be said that the question at issue was not unimportant in light of the complete divergence of opinions between the theologians of the two schools. The divergence had come to light a century earlier when the debate over the liceity of giving latreic veneration to the relics of the blood of Christ had already pitted a Franciscan theologian, Francis Bagnuli, against Nicholas Rosell, Dominican inquisitor of Aragon.[57]

Without going into the lesser details of the dispute, I shall say only that the Thomist theologians maintained that the body of Christ preserved its identity thanks to its direct link to the Word; the Scotists, on the other hand, relying on their theory of the plurality of substantial forms, maintained that the body of Christ remained identical in its corporeal form. In the particular case of the blood shed during the passion, the Dominicans were convinced that it was reassumed by Christ at his ascension and that it had, of course, retained its connection with the divinity of the Word. The Franciscans claimed, however, that this shed blood was no longer subsumed under the form of corporeity and could therefore no longer be connected with the divinity.

James of the Marches had reasserted this teaching in his Lenten sermon of 1462, thereby eliciting an immediate reaction from the Dominican inquisitor, who had appealed to a papal decree of 1352 (though this had not been proposed in a way that met the conditions for an ex-cathedra statement) and proceeded against him with a demand that he retract. There was a strong outcry because of the personality of the famous preacher, and in a short time the dispute had involved various friars and even the faithful. Pius II forbade any public discussion of the subject, but he called the theologians of the two sides together to see whether they could reach an agreement. Among the Franciscans summoned, in addition to the celebrated Parisian Scotist William of Vaurillon, was Della Rovere, whose position is set down in the little treatise.

In a dedication to Pius II, Della Rovere writes that his aim is to settle a quarrel which had now become a "seedbed of major scandal." In keeping with an attitude which he always adopted, he says that while the two masters, Thomas and Scotus, may seem to disagree, they can in fact be harmonized "in a single opinion."

But the Franciscan theologian then goes on immediately to an analysis of trinitarian terms *(persona, suppositum, individuum, singulare)* and of the concepts of incommunicability and negation, and comes to these conclusions: (1) the human nature united to the divine Word in the hypostatic union does not have a "person" of its own, because it is communicated in act to a "supposit" (the divine Word) of a different nature, whereas a true "human person" is constituted only by its own individual character, which cannot be communicated to another; (2) the "relation" proper to the hypostatic union is, however, based on a "human person" that is assumed in its concrete individual reality and, on the other hand, on the particular and special "person" of the Word, which is distinct from the other trinitarian "persons" who have not become "incarnate"; the same argument applies to the question of the blood of Christ and its union with the Word.

The divine Word has, then, assumed an "individual" and "singular" human person and, with this, the blood that was conceived along with the "person" of Christ. Nevertheless, in this assumption some things were assumed directly *(principaliter)* and others less directly *(minus principaliter),* the latter including the blood, which, as Aristotle, Avicenna, and Thomas himself teach, is not part of the "human being" but rather of "human nature" in general. It seems clear, therefore, that the divine Word only "co-assumed" the blood, with the result that as long as this blood was united to the body of Christ it was not separated from the divinity, but when it was shed and scattered, it was "probably" separated from the divinity. Della Rovere regards it as entirely permissible to maintain that it was neither necessary nor appropriate for Christ at his resurrection to "reassume" all the blood shed during the passion.

I shall not here follow this theologian as he discusses the medical doctrines invoked to confirm his opinions, although these doctrines are of interest because they show how, in the Scholastic theological culture of the time, the science of things divine often had philosophico-scientific arguments interwoven into it.[58] It is more important to observe how, in his awareness of the problems of every kind that would be raised by a rejection of the popular cult of such relics, Della Rovere thinks it right that the Church should "tolerate" a "pious practice" not forbidden by divine laws. But this tolerance does not mean that the theoretical outlook of the Scotists is not entirely legitimate and that one is not free to assert the separation from the divinity of the blood shed by Christ and not reassumed at the resurrection.

Della Rovere's other writings are no less interesting. In *De potentia Dei,*[59] composed after he had become a cardinal (on September 18, 1467), the author says that his intention is to refute the arguments raised by some theologians against the "infinite" and "unlimited" power of God. Recalling, therefore, the classical distinction between "ordered power" *(potentia ordinata)* and "absolute power" *(potentia absoluta),* he forcefully asserts that God acts through an intellect and will which are not subject to any law; his power is therefore both "law" and the "rightness of the law," that is, the first cause and the primordial norm that cannot be altered by any prior power. For this Scotist theologian, the admission that the divine intellect regulates the divine will in a determinative way would mean a revival of the dangers of some typical heresies formerly condemned by Peter Lombard.

Not only that: God is infinitely superior to any earthly ruler, such as the emperor or even the pope, who likewise are not subject to the laws they enact. He is therefore not subject either to human laws (which would be entirely unworthy of his majesty) or to the natural laws he has established. As a sovereign who is absolutely "unbound by laws," God is the sole foundation of every law and can change, suspend, or abrogate these by an utterly free decision. Della Rovere does not deny, of course, that even God cannot accept evil "insofar as it is against his law," because not even he can cause a will to act worthily and unworthily at the same time; this would be a clear and implicit contradiction. At the same time, however, in virtue of his absolute power he could establish a law quite different from that which he has already established, and such a law would be in any event just, because established by his will. Just as earthly rulers could, if they wished, establish laws rewarding those who offend them, so God could accept or even prescribe blasphemy or any other sin, which would thereby immediately cease to be a sin. It does not seem appropriate, of course, that God should accept such acts, but "mortals" have no way of proving this, since his will could, can, and will be able to ordain things differently from the laws hitherto in force.

This, Della Rovere acknowledges, is a conclusion which his adversaries reject, arguing that God acts according to his own will and therefore cannot do what he cannot will, such as accepting an evil of which he disapproves and, in particular, so serious a sin as blasphemy, which is clearly an act of infidelity and rebellion. But the theologian's reply is categorical: the justice of the law as God has established it is certainly beyond doubt; but if he were to legislate the precept of blasphemy, then such an action would likewise be just, would not contradict the common good, and would be completely conformed to his will. Anyone saying otherwise would even be acting against God and the order of justice, which demands of us first and foremost unqualified obedience to the divine will. In fact, as he insists against the Thomists, a law is unjust only when he is not pleased with it or has not accepted it or has not established it by his own power. For the same reason, God, the first and free cause of grace, can give eternal life even to one who does not possess the "habit" of grace, since grace is only a secondary and occasional cause. In short, the divine power cannot be limited in any way in its absolute and infinite majesty, which transcends every order whatsoever, every norm, and every consideration our minds can offer.

The *De potentia Dei* can also shed light on the attitude which Della Rovere adopted in another major theoretical debate of his time: the dispute over contingent futures. This episode, which is so important for the history of fifteenth-century theology, will be discussed elsewhere;[60] I shall limit myself here to recalling that the Franciscan's intervention came in 1470, when he was already a cardinal, and at the request of his colleague, Bessarion, to whom he was especially close.[61] Moreover, he accepted and acknowledged as valid the accusations made by van Zömeren against Peter of Rivo, although he immediately added that were these accusations to be submitted to the judgment of the Church, Peter would have to be declared innocent.

It is also typical of the man that he regarded as "harsh" and "impious" some statements of the same van Zömeren that seemed to regard the authority of Scripture as entirely superior to that of the pope and the Church; van Zömeren failed to take into account that as far as human beings are concerned, only the ecclesiastical magisterium can explain and clarify the very meaning of the revelation. Consequently, as far as the substance of the problem was concerned, Della Rovere set forth the solution already given by Scotus. In his judgment this solution safeguarded at once the absolute freedom of God, the contingency of his action, and the perfection of his foreknowledge. He also regarded this solution as identical with that of Thomas Aquinas, in keeping with the "agreement of the Doctors," which he himself always looked for in his own teaching.

A man very close in his teaching to Della Rovere was another Scotist master, the Bosnian Franciscan Juraj Dragisic[62] (ca. 1450 to 1520), better known by the name of George Benignus Salviati, which he adopted during his stay in Florence. I shall not dwell here on the varied and rather complex events of this writer's life. After having studied at the major Italian schools of his order (and especially at Padua), he is supposed to have attended the great universities of Paris and Oxford before beginning an ecclesiastical career that ended with his appointment as archbishop of Nazareth. Nor shall I even describe the details of events in which he found himself involved: from the dispute over contingent futures to the Savonarola affair, from his part in the reworking and circulation of one of the most widespread prophecies of his time, the *Apochalypsis nova,*[63] to his belated intervention in the controversy surrounding Reuchlin.

It is certain that while still very young, in about 1471–72, he had regular connections with Bessarion's circle and supposedly defended the cardinal against the *Adnotationes* of George of Trebizond, a work subsequently lost. He also intervened in the disagreement between Peter of Rivo and van Zömeren in the form of a treatise *De libertate et immutabilitate Dei,*[64] which reached conclusions close to those of Della Rovere and was inspired by "pure" Scotist teaching. Later on, at the court of Urbino where he was the teacher of the young Guidubaldo, he wrote a *De animae regni principe,*[65] in which his adherence to Scotist voluntarism finds expression in a celebration of the primacy of the will, on which, in the final analysis, even the supreme beatitude of contemplation depends. It is certain, however, that some of his most interesting and most typical writings were composed or conceived during his stay in Florence (1486–94), when he was one of the "family" of Lorenzo the Magnificent and had direct connections with Ficino, Pico, and Nesi.

During these years in Florence and in a debate with the Hungarian Dominican, John de Mirabilibus, he maintained, in the presence of Lorenzo and the intellectuals of his court, that if Adam had not sinned, humanity could not have enjoyed divine grace and, moreover, that it was not heretical to maintain that God was the cause of sin (1489).[66] Of even greater interest is the little treatise *(In opus septem quaestionum)* which he wrote, in around 1489, as a commentary of a theological sonnet of Lorenzo.[67] Here he reasserted the dependence of everything that exists or has existed on the absolute will of God; he also claimed once again that even sin is caused, in a certain sense, by God. But the discussion quickly went on to include problems connected with the relationship between free will and grace and in particular the following familiar doctrinal standbys: (1) whether human beings, independently of divine grace, can accomplish works that merit the reward of everlasting life, or whether grace is absolutely necessary; (2) whether God wills absolutely that human beings participate in this grace, or whether he wills it only conditionally, limiting this participation to those who are already "disposed" or "inclined"; (3) what disposition or inclination or conversion is to be regarded as necessary in those who "accept" grace; (4) whether grace precedes the disposition.[68]

The solutions which Benignus gives are always inspired by Scotist teaching, but this is interpreted with the obvious intention of "harmonizing" "true" and "Catholic" theological opinions and of reasserting the genuine views of the great teacher of his order in a way that frees them of the distortions introduced by "false" followers.

I would say, however, that some of Salviati's most typical spiritual concerns find expression in another short work, *In opus de natura angelica,* which was written after 1488.[69] In this little treatise he discussed the incorporeal nature of the angels, their role as "messengers" of prophetic revelations, as well as their creation (and their own ability or inability to create), their immortality, and their formal structure. The Franciscan also asks whether the angels know themselves by means of their own essence; whether they have "innate" in them the "species" of the divine essence; and whether they know all things through a single intellectual habit and not by means of several or more "species."

Later on, Benignus was forced to leave Florence because of his close connections with the fugitive Piero de'Medici (1494), and he took refuge at Ragusa (Dubrovnik). Even here he did not fail to take part in the bitter dispute that had developed over the prophetic preaching of Jerome Savonarola and, in general, over his religious and political activity. In 1497 Benigno published his *Propheticae solutiones,*[70] which was a staunch defense of the Dominican, the truthfulness of his "predictions," and the holiness of his life and teaching, which was entirely authentic and orthodox. Then, while still in exile at Ragusa, he had his most important and most ambitious work published in Florence in 1499: the large volume entitled *De natura angelica.*[71]

The themes already mentioned in connection with the preceding shorter work on the subject are developed here to a far greater extent and with significant emphasis on the theological problems that had always interested the author: providence and foreknowledge, prophetic knowledge, and angelic inspiration. In the first book, the Franciscan takes up the problems raised by the special nature of angelic intellects; in the second, he speaks of the way in which the angels understand God and share in divine and human knowledge as well as in knowledge of the future; in the third book he moves on to a lengthy excursus on the distinction between will, nature, and intellect and to the question of what the freedom of the will means; in the fourth book, he analyzes the various theological and philosophical doctrines having to do with the first cause of the angels, whom he himself considers to have been created directly by God and to be sharers, in a way, in the work of creation. The fifth book is then devoted to the original state of the angels and to the question of whether or not they merited their blessedness. The sixth book is a lengthy discussion (in which some typical passages of the *Apochalypsis nova* are already cited) of the nature of the "first sin," the lot of the "wicked angels," and the possibility or impossibility of the latter being "disposed for grace." The seventh book develops a teaching on the movement of the angels, while the eighth explains the various degrees of their hierarchies and, above all, their relations with human beings and their role as transmitters of prophetic truths.

In the following years, Benignus, now living in Rome, was involved, as I noted earlier, in the spread of the *Apochalypsis nova,* gaudy traces of which are to be seen in the writings which he published later on: from the *Apologeticon seu defensorium* (written in 1511 to defend Francis Maria Della Rovere against the accusation of having murdered Cardinal Alidosi) to the *Vexillum christianae victoriae* (dedicated, after 1515, to Francis I) and the *Virginis Matris theoremata,*[72] which expresses the eschatological, prophetic, and esoteric interests of the Bosnian Franciscan. But his career as a theologian ended only still later with two works that show him taking part in the lengthy controversy over Reuchlin (one of whose judges he was): his *Defensio*[73] of the German humanist, and his preface to one of the classics of "Christian cabala," the *Opus . . . de arcanis catholicae veritatis*[74] by the Apulian Franciscan Peter Galatino, who was likewise a defender of Reuchlin and, like Benignus, a firm believer in the prophecy about the angelic pope and in the coming of a general reform of Christianity.

A good deal less complicated and closer to the usual pattern of a career as a *magister* was the life of Franciscan Anthony Trombetta (1436–1517).[75] He entered the order at a very young age in the convent of the Santo in Padua; it was there, too, that he did his studies, which were marked by a complete acceptance of the teachings of Scotus. He was also a student in the theological faculty of the University of Padua and received his degree there in 1467. He became regent of the school of metaphysics in the Santo Studium, which was the center of lively discussions involving all the more important Scholastic authors; in 1471 he was a professor of theology at the university and meanwhile saw to the printing of Scotus' commentary on the first Book of the Sentences. In 1476 or 1477 he took the Scotist chair of metaphysics, over against the Thomist chair, held at that time by Francis Securo of Nardò. For several years he was a courteous opponent of Nardò, but then the Thomist chair was given to a young Dominican, Thomas de Vio, a more determined and polemically minded man.

Trombetta was regarded as one of the major interpreters of Scotist metaphysics and theology and a professor of high merit. He published his own works only at a relatively late date, during the nineties. In 1490 he published his commentary on the *De coelo et mundo* in Venice, and in 1493 his *Opus doctrinae scotisticae Patavii in thomistas discussum* (this included a treatise on contingent futures; forty-six *Quaestiones metaphysicales;* and a commentary on the treatise of Anthony Sirrect on "formalities").[76] In 1497 he finished his *De animarum humanarum plurificatione,* in opposition to the Averroists of Padua, and sent it to Peter Barozzi, bishop of Padua (and author of a decree excommunicating those professors who proposed, outside the university, the thesis of the unicity of the intellect without adding the reasons, based on the faith, for which the thesis must be rejected, as well as the contrary arguments given by orthodox philosophers and theologians).[77]

In 1498, at the end of his third term as provincial prior, Trombetta found himself in a rather difficult situation that ended with his acquittal, but only after a short period of imprisonment. He was then able to continue teaching at Padua, whither various students followed him, including several Venetian patricians. In fact, around 1501, he was called upon to pass judgment on a work, entitled *Ricordo,* of Gabriel Biondo, a spiritualist mystic whose teachings had spread even to Venice, especially in the convents of women and other feminine circles of the patriciate. Trombetta issued a nonnegative judgment of the little book, which he evaluated chiefly with an eye on the anti-Savonarola polemic apparently being carried on by Biondo but also on some calls for reform which he himself shared.[78]

Trombetta continued to teach for a good many years, until the tragic days of the war of the Cambrai League (1509), which had a serious impact on the University of Padua. Then, in 1511, after being appointed bishop of Urbino, he had to leave his city for Rome, where he was involved in the work of the Fifth Lateran Council. He was a member of the commission for the preservation of the faith, to which was entrusted the composition of the decree condemning doctrines that maintained the unity or mortality of the soul.[79] The decree ordered that not only those who denied the immortality of the soul but those as well who cast doubt on it even from the viewpoint of natural philosophy were to be considered heretics. It also set down strict norms for the discussion of pagan philosophical concepts, such as the idea of the eternity of the world and the mortality or unicity of the soul, that were contrary to the faith, and it obliged teachers to answer the arguments of these pagan philosophers and to reassert the truths of the faith in response to them.

We do not know what part Trombetta played in the drawing up of this decree. In any case, it did not meet with approval from Thomas de Vio (Cajetan), who at that time was already rather doubtful that a purely rational proof of the immortality of the soul was possible. But in a work written in 1497 the Franciscan had already appealed to Aristotle and Thomas Aquinas in providing his rational proof of the immortality of the soul, a proof based chiefly on the principle that in the activity of intellection the human soul performs a completely special operation which, according to Aristotelean teaching, confirms its full separability from the body and therefore its incorruptibility as well. Then, in 1499, he enthusiastically approved the self-criticism of Vernia *(Contra perversam Averroys opinionem de unitate intellectus et de animae foelicitae),* who repented of his past Averroist outlook and chose to heed the stern warnings of Barozzi.[80]

A. Poppi's studies have clearly shown that in discussing the causality at work in being and motion Trombetta was following the Scotist solution; he criticized Thomist teaching, which "made God alone the efficient cause of the existence of beings," and he asserted instead a "coordination" of the absolute Cause and secondary causes "in bestowing existence." Later on, in a treatise published at Venice in 1513 and dedicated to Leo X (the *Quaestio de efficientia primi principii quod est Deus et de eius infinitate intensiva),*[81] he repeated the arguments traditional in Paduan Scotism and affirmed a divine causality that is not only final but also "efficient" in the movement of the heavens. His intention was to demonstrate, against the theses of the Averroists, that divine perfection by its nature requires that God possess it in its fullest possible extension, that is, in an infinite degree. Therefore the perfection of being, which God possesses with an absolute fullness, must also be intensively infinite.

Trombetta was certainly one of the most important representatives of the Scotist tradition in fifteenth-century Italian Scholasticism. But we ought not forget another master, Francis Licheto or Lichitto (d. 1520), who is well known for his bitter controversy with Augustine Nifo *(Theoremata disputata contra Augustinum Suessanum)*[82] and for his long years of teaching and his service in high offices of the order, culminating in 1518 with his election as general. As a master in various Franciscan houses of study, from Brescia to Naples and the Isola del Garda (where he taught classes in metaphysics and theology that were attended by many students), he was a faithful Scotist, much influenced by the teachings of Peter Tatareto, which he explained in his commentary on Scotus' commentary on the *Sentences* and in his commentary on the *Quaestiones quodlibetales;* he accepted, among other things, their debated interpretation of the concept of the "hypostatic" union.[83]

On the other hand, like Trombetta, he, too, was especially involved in the dispute over the immortality of the soul; in this debate he took a position very close to that of his own teachers. That is, he maintained that it is impossible to demonstrate by reason the preexistence of the soul and its separation from the body and that it is therefore impossible to prove the soul's immortality. In his commentary on Scotus' *Quodlibet* IX, he takes the immaterial nature of "intellection" as evident, but he rejects the Thomist doctrine of the soul as "a form that has an existence of its own" and insists that it is not possible to conclude from reason alone that its existence does not also depend on matter.[84] This was a thesis not accepted by other Franciscan masters such as John of Ferrara (d. 1492), who in his *Liber de coelesti vita et de animarum immortalitate* holds that the immortality of the soul is "naturally known," thus adhering to the theses of the Thomists.

12. The Franciscan Order: Preaching and Theology

Some of the greatest preachers of the century belonged to the Franciscan Order and its Observantine branch; their names are very well known and they range from Bernardine of Siena to Albert of Sarteano, James of the Marches, and John of Capistrano. In the present setting I shall speak of these very important representatives of fifteenth-century Italian religious life only in connection with the theological ideas expressed in their preaching; I shall not dwell on the details of their activity or on their ascetical or mystical experiences.

Consequently, in speaking of Bernardine of Siena of the Albizzeschi family (1380–1444), I shall limit myself to recalling his special devotion to the name of Jesus (represented by the three letters JHS, which were surrounded by rays of the sun), a devotion that was the subject of a lengthy controversy and bitter accusations. I mention also his profound links with the tradition of purest Franciscan spirituality, from Bonaventure to Peter John Olivi and to the *Arbor vitae crucifixae Jesu* of Ubertino of Casale; in relation to the latter, however, Bernardine played down his fiery millenniarism and evident Joachimite emphases and celebrated instead the radical need of love, charity, humility, and poverty, which was in his view the true meaning of Christian life.[85]

Although as a preacher he wanted to address not the learned but the people and lowly folk, Bernardine had a solid and rich knowledge of theology, which he always used for purposes of instruction and spiritual admonition. Consequently he avoided the great speculative problems; he never discussed reform of the Church, or the powers of pope and emperor, or questions of metaphysics and dogmatic theology. Instead, his aim was always to shed light on questions or matters related to everyday moral and religious life, from cursing to private or political hatreds, from love of neighbor to love of family and spouse, from the duties proper to the various states and conditions of society to the nature and purpose of all the works of mercy, from economic practices bordering on usury to sexual deviations such as sodomy, which he confronts and discusses without fear of giving rise to scandal or accusations.

At every point in his preaching the basic and dominant characteristic is his profoundly christological inspiration, which finds its full expression in the call to put Christ always at the center of religious experience and to make him the first and essential motive of Christian life, which is and ought to be an imitation of the Master. It is precisely this that also explains his devotion to the Name of Jesus; the purpose of this devotion was certainly not to encourage a superstitious veneration but to remind the people in their devotional life of their essential faith in Christ and to strengthen them in this faith. Bernardine always links this faith in Christ with a fervent devotion to Mary.[86]

It is the special character of Bernardine's preaching that has naturally led scholars to emphasize, above all, those aspects that seem more closely bound up with the peculiarities of his time and the traits of the society in which he worked.[87] It is understandable that they have given special prominence to his economic and social ideas, which admittedly reveal a detailed knowledge of the most varied aspects of the mercantile and financial activity of the age and of the relationship between this activity and the essential principles of Christian ethics. Bernardine is quite strong when it comes to the strict observance of theological teaching on usury, but he also has a keen understanding of the most typical characteristics of economic reality in his world; he grasps the peculiar nature of financial capital insofar as it is money intended for commercial activities, and he accepts, in substance, the henceforth acknowledged concepts of "lost profit" and "diminution of capital," from which is derived the possibility of an "honest" gain.

But these ideas, expressed especially in his *Tractatus de contractibus et usuris* (which extends through fourteen sermons of his Lenten series, *De evangelio aeterno*), do not alter in the slightest his ideal of Christian life and renewal. In response to the growing spiritual restlessness of his age, he describes this ideal as consisting in complete poverty, unqualified humility, charity toward all, and love for Christ, which means fervent adherence to his teaching, his sufferings, and his redemptive work.

Another preacher, one especially close to Bernardine, was Albert Berdini of Sarteano (1385–1450), who before entering the Observance had followed the humanistic courses of Guarino in Florence and always remained the friend and correspondent of many humanists (such as Nicholas Niccoli, Guarino himself, Bracciolini, Francis Barbaro, and Traversari).[88] Like them, he always extolled the "true knowledge" that serves not only in understanding the "great ancients" but also, and above all, in grasping the truth of the sacred writings.

Himself a learned and eloquent speaker and a man able to put the fruits of his humanistic education and associations at the service of his work of teaching and the apostolate, Albert had no doubt about the greatness of the Christian heroes who far outstripped those of antiquity and whose deeds were worth much more than the splendid eloquence of Cicero and Demosthenes. True enough, in 1433, when asked by Cosimo de'Medici, he did not hesitate to travel to Naples in order to acquire Greek and Latin codices for the library of the influential banker and politician. But his own polished discourses were used, first and foremost, to preach peace; to restore peaceful coexistence in cities divided by bitter partisan hatreds; to condemn pomp and usury, the rarity with which the Christian duty of charity was observed, and the departure of the society of his day from the authentic norms of Christian life; and to call for a return to the love of Christ as the way to the humility and poverty required for final salvation. Thus, when Bracciolini in his *Contra hypocritas* harshly attacked the members of the Observance except for Bernardine and Albert himself, this humanist friar replied with an asperity not usual for him, even though he had no desire to break the bonds of friendship that bound him to the world of the learned, the men who in fact admired his eloquence.

It was precisely Albert's qualities of moderation and culture that explained why he played so important a part, first, in persuading the court of Byzantium to accept the council proclaimed by Eugene IV and to reject the invitation of the fathers at Basel, and then in winning the acceptance by the Copts, the Jacobites, and the Ethiopians of the restored unity.[89] Later on, in 1443, along with James of the Marches, he was one of the very eloquent preachers chosen to urge the new crusade against the Turks. Albert was an outstanding personality as a popular preacher and as a man who was open to the new culture and who shared the tastes and language of the humanists. In short, he was a typical representative of a new way of living the gospel tradition and sharing the intense expectations of a renewal that would extend to the life and experience of the Church.

In the preceding pages I have several times mentioned the name of James of the Marches (Dominic Gangali, 1394–1476)[90] and the dispute over the blood of Christ, which he reopened in 1462. In the present context I must again recall that this preacher from the Observance had entered the Franciscan Order as an older man, after having completed his legal studies and acquired a quite good secular education. Also well known was his zeal as a fervent follower of Franciscan ideals; this led him to preach unwearyingly for many years, not only in the larger cities of Italy but also in Hungary, Dalmatia, Slovenia, Croatia, Bosnia, and Poland; everywhere he spread Bernardine's devotion to the Name of Jesus. Even his opposition to the latreutic veneration paid to the relics of the blood of Christ can be interpreted as a reaction to a kind of devotion that seemed to derogate from the absolute worship due to the Godhead.[91]

The other most famous preacher from the Franciscan Observance, John of Capistrano (1386–1456), had originally been a lawyer and even a judge at Perugia from 1413 to 1415.[92] In his many writings on dogmatic and moral theology and on canon law he showed not only his vast knowledge of Scripture but also his competence in the Fathers and his extensive knowledge of the Scholastic writers, of whom he said that Thomas Aquinas was his favorite. In his case, too, it is not possible here to dwell on his preaching activity in so many places of Italy and Europe or on his participation in the crusade against the Turks which was led by John Hunyadi and culminated in the battle of Belgrade (1456).

In the present context we must recall rather that he was a resolute defender of Bernardine when the saint was accused, in 1320, of propagating, in the form of veneration of the Name, a superstitious and sacrilegious practice that bordered on magic; and that on several occasions he served as inquisitor, especially in the case of the Fraticelli. Like Bernardine, but with greater inflexibility and a lesser feeling for economic realities, he fought usury, which was radically condemned in his *De cupiditate,* the fruit of Lenten sermons preached at Verona in 1438. But he was also an intransigent adversary of the Jews, against whom he repeated the most ill-omened traditional accusations, just as he maintained the necessity of very strict sumptuary laws. But he was always a faithful observer of Franciscan poverty and, like Bernardine, was averse to all ecclesiastical honors and positions of authority apart from the leadership of the Observance and the defense of its rights within the order.[93]

Another preacher from the Franciscan Observance was John of Prato, concerning whom we have little information but whom we do know to have enjoyed a noteworthy reputation around the middle of the century. In all likelihood he is to be identified with the friar who was commissioned in 1445 to deal with the still unresolved matter of the difficult relations between the Conventuals and the Observants and who in 1455 was among those whom Callistus III sent out to preach the crusade against the Turks. He was the author of *Conciones quadragesimales* and *Conciones de tempore,* but he is remembered more for his exchange of letters with Guarino of Verona;[94] these were occasioned by a cycle of sermons that he preached in Ferrara in 1450.

In the course of these sermons the Franciscan had condemned the reading of the pagan poets and in particular of "lascivious" Terence, on whom Guarino was commenting to his students just at that time. The humanist of Verona responded with a lengthy and learned letter, in which he did not restrict himself to defending Terence (reminding the preacher of the praises Jerome had heaped on the poet), but he also cited many testimonies of the Fathers and Doctors in favor of the reading and study of the classics. In particular, he sought to show that Virgil, the only ancient poet whom the preacher had not condemned, was in fact not more chaste than the other ancient poets. John answered in turn in a letter that has come down to us only in mutilated form; he repeated his judgment on Terence as an author who should not be set before the young, especially during Lent; and while expressing his personal esteem for this teacher of Albert of Sarteano, he repeated his judgment of Virgil, an author praised by Augustine.

13. Jerome Savonarola

But the most celebrated preacher of the final decades of the fifteenth century was Jerome Savonarola, a Dominican from Ferrara (1452–98). As a religious with a calling to be a prophet, he gave deeper expression to the great spiritual crisis of his age and renewed in his strikingly eloquent preaching the long-standing expectation of a radical reform of the Church and the coming of a new age of Christian history.

There is an extraordinarily rich and complex literature about the man and the events of his life that ended so tragically on the scaffold and pyre in the Piazza della Signoria and about the character, sources, origins, and very extensive influence of his prophetic preaching. This literature has taken on a markedly controversial tone and continues even today to offer ever new and different interpretations that are very much influenced also by events and disputes in the contemporary Church.[95]

It is obviously outside the scope of the present study to deal with his proclamation of the "quick and ever quicker" coming of a time of punishment and penance for the Church and sinful Christianity; the need for a reform of Christian society "in head and members" that would bring it back to its pure origins; the eschatological expectation of the coming of the "last days" and the fulfillment of the gospel promises. Nor may I dwell on the nature of his piety, which was so intense, so simple, and so averse to any excessive complication or doctrinal subtlety, such as could well arise in the spiritual experience of a man of studies.

In fact, after entering the order when no longer young, he had followed the regular course of studies and had himself been a master and reader of Scripture in the Dominican houses of study. It is more important to observe how the program for an integral recovery of "true" Christian spirituality (which required a rigorous purification of morals and called for a detachment from "false" pagan wisdom) and the mystical and ascetical call that inspired him could attract even some of the more important intellectuals of his time, such as Ficino himself (who, for a while at least, was far from being hostile to the friar of San Marco), various "fellow Platonists," and, above all, John Pico and his young nephew, John Francis.

The fact is that Savonarola wanted the basis of his preaching to be always and only a pure adoration of God and Christ, an adoration to be lived "in spirit and in truth," and in addition, the certainty that after a period of "God's anger" the authentic faithful were to share in the building of the "new Jerusalem," the city of "God's kingdom" that would at last be purified of all sin. For this reason the Dominican (who claimed he had never read the prophecies of Bridget of Sweden or even those of Ferreri or "Abbot Joachim") referred always and exclusively to the biblical "prophecies," these being interpreted, however, as is evident from the context of his sermons, in keeping with the long prophetic and millenniarist tradition of the preceding four centuries.

In his view, moreover, Christian life constantly required the mission of the prophet, who is the humble mouthpiece of divine truth and speaks in a state of complete ignorance that makes him truly an instrument of God. A prophet is a seer who speaks of things completely beyond natural knowledge, future realities that are communicated to him solely by divine choice, and above all, future contingents that are dependent on free human wills but always fit into the unconditioned and mysterious plan of God. The prophet, then, has received a supernatural gift, and his utterances bring peace and eternal salvation to all believers. Moreover, because he speaks in God's name, he can demand that everyone—common folk and gentlepersons, clerics and laity, and the mighty of the world and the Church—listen to him so that the Christian people may have divine guidance and enlightenment.

This explains why Savonarola so very resolutely opposed those who claimed that the prophetic age had ended long ago and that the prohibition against prophesying, which Innocent III had imposed on some "corrupt and wicked" laypersons, was binding on the entire Church and, in particular, on those who felt called to make known the divine will and divine truth. Fra Jerome, who had such wonderful visions and mystical illuminations and was certain that he heard "heavenly words," did not doubt that his prophecies were the work of God's mercy, a final warning before the day of wrath and inexorable punishment. Resistance, therefore, to anyone trying to keep him from making them known to all the faithful "brothers and sisters" was not only a right but a duty laid on him as a priest and a man of God.

I shall not speak here of the predominant themes of Savonarola's prophecies or their development in the course of time, a development closely linked to the events of Italy's history during that period. Nor shall I speak of his prediction of the coming of a "new Cyrus," that seemed to be fulfilled in the Italian adventures of Charles VIII[96] and in the onset of a lengthy period of wars and misfortunes.

I must rather point out that as a philosopher and theologian, Savonarola was a faithful follower of Thomist (but also, at times, of Albertist) teachings, as has been shown by the recent edition of his *Compendium philosophiae naturalis* and *Compendium philosophiae moralis,* in which the original structure of these works has been restored.[97] These works admittedly reflect Scholastic teaching and have no originality of their own. It is noteworthy, however, that in outlining the essential foundations of his ethico-political teaching the friar is concerned to show that every kind of state must aim at the full achievement of the natural virtues and perfections of human beings, but for the purpose of thereby predisposing them for the enjoyment of supernatural beatitude, and while substantially subordinating every strictly political norm to the ultimate religious goal. It is also noteworthy that, in complete accord with Thomist teaching, he regards a monarchy "inspired by love" and utterly opposed to tyrannicide as the best form of government.

Moreover, when Savonarola published his *Trattato circa il reggimento e governo della città di Firenze* in 1498,[98] he did not depart from these principles but solemnly declared that a good government promotes the common good and that its primary task is to foster and promote the continual effort of each citizen who is trying to exercise the natural virtues and those proper to a Christian and thereby to carry out his duties to God and neighbor. Nevertheless, in sketching his plan for the constitutional reform of Florence, he was not completely utopian but looked rather to the mixed kind of government which other political writers likewise thought they saw in the institutional structure of Venice. He also wanted the common people to share in the government of the republic via the "Major Council" while at the same time allowing many essential powers to remain in the hands of a moderate and enlightened oligarchy. More than that, he continued faithful to his Thomist formation when he asserted that the presence of monarchical institutional forms would make such a political order a truly balanced one, although he concluded that given the political situation in Florence it was not possible to introduce these forms and that the only solution was to establish fully a "civil regime."

Evidence of Savonarola's Thomism is also to be found in his other theoretical writings, such as the *Opus perutile de divisione, ordine ac utilitate omnium scientiarum* (an attempt at a general classification—traditional in character—of the sciences, with grammar as "falling short" of, and theology as "transcending," what is understood by "science"); the *Compendium logicae;*[99] the *Logicales quaestiones centum;*[100] and the *Aristotelis pene omnia opera et Platonis abbreviata.*

Most importantly, some scholars have emphasized the "structural" affinity between the *Summa contra gentes* and one of Savonarola's most famous works, the *Triumphus crucis,*[101] which was devoted to a radical critique of the theology of the philosophers and poets as being full of errors and obscurities, in contrast to the light and sovereign truth of Christian revelation. The fact that Savonarola did not accept in the slightest degree the *docta religio* (learned religion) of Fico with its esoteric myth of a *prisca theologia* (primitive/very early theology) or Landino's and Pico's exegesis of the *theologia poetica* (poetic theology) is confirmed by his *Apologeticus,*[102] written in 1491 in response to the *Carmen de Christiana religione ac vitae monasticae foelicitate* and to the introductory letter of the Platonic and Ficinian philosopher, Ugolino Verino, who had become a fiery "Piagnone."

In the *Apologeticus,* after having, in the first two books, outlined the same general classification of the sciences that was mentioned above, the Dominican contrasted Ficino's passion for poetry with Plato's radical condemnation of it in his *Republic.* He also asked whether on the day of the Last Judgment the philosopher would not rise up to condemn the culpable blindness of Christians in regard to the falsity and immorality of the pagan poets. Not a few pages of the *Trattato contra li astrologi,*[103] written in 1497, also seem to be directed against Ficino; in them he repeats and makes widely known the radical refutation of judicial astrology that had already been made by Pico. It is quite understandable that Savonarola should emphasize with special severity the condemnation of those aspects of "erroneous" astrological science that he regarded as especially opposed to the revealed truth about "free will" and as a direct attack on the absolute omnipotence of God.

14. Political Theology: Roderick Sánchez de Arévalo and John of Torquemada

A history of Scholastic theology in fifteenth-century Italy must make at least some reference to the extensive theologico-political literature that was produced especially in Roman curial circles. Among the authors who played a part in the great debate about the relative superiority of council or pope (a debate begun at the Council of Constance and continued in the stormy events of the Council of Basel and the renewal of the "little schism"), mention must be made of Cardinal Francis Zabarella, a well-known canonist but also author of important philosophical and theological works (1360–1417). In his *De schismate,* he attributed the fullness of authority to the Church alone and in particular to its representative body, an ecumenical council, while, in line with the fundamental doctrines of the conciliarist tradition, he asserted that the pope's authority was only that of the "first" among the "ministers" of the Church. A pope could therefore be judged and deposed by a council and did not have authority to issue norms binding the whole of Christendom unless he had the consent of at least the cardinals.

Similar theses were sanctioned by the Council of Constance in its decrees confirming the superiority of council over popes; the latter were deprived of the right to transfer or close councils without their explicit consent. This led to a remarkable renewal also of discussions about the relationship between the spiritual authority of the pope and the temporal authority of princes. Among the most important works produced by this debate mention should be made of the *Monarchia seu tractatus de potestate imperatoris et papae* of canonist Anthony Roselli (1380–1466). While defending the primacy of the pope over councils, he defended the complete autonomy of the temporal power and attacked *Unam sanctam* in particular. But even more numerous were authors who lined up to maintain the primacy of papal authority, such as Peter del Monte, humanist and protonotary apostolic *(De summi pontificis origine et potestate)*, Bishop Peter of Brescia (d. 1457) *(De potestate summi pontificis)*, and Dominic Dominici or Domenichi, theologian and bishop of Venice *(De potestate papae*, 1455/58).

The most important of the theologico-political writers were, however, two theologians and jurists who were Spanish in origin and formation but lived for a long time in Italy and in the Roman Curia: Roderick Sánchez de Arévalo (1405–70) and John of Torquemada (1388–1468). The former, after having been several times the ambassador of Juan II of Castile at the principal courts of Europe, became secretary of Pius II, while also a bishop and high-ranking dignitary of the Curia.[104] This friend of Bessarion and other Roman humanists was the author of many works, some in the vernacular, others in Latin, in which the influence of humanist pedagogical ideas is evident. In his *De arte, disciplina et modo alendi et erudiendi filios* (1453),[105] the main sources of which are Plutarch and Jerome, he endeavors to show the superiority of Christian ethics over pagan ethics, but he acknowledges that education must promote the free development of adolescents and support this through the exercise of the natural and evangelical virtues. In his *Vergel de los principes* (1456/57) his aim is to direct the favorite activities of future sovereigns (arms, hunting, and music) toward the development of the virtues such men would need for their future tasks.[106] Again, in his *Tractatus ad quendam venerandum religiosum cartusianum* (1461/64) he discusses the spiritual importance of the presence of religious at the courts of princes, where their duty is to give the example of a reformed Christian life and of obedience to the supreme authority of the Church and the pope. Nor does he fail to disagree, in his *De pace et bello* (1468),[107] with the pacifist ideas set forth by humanist Bartholomew Platina, whose friendly and lenient guardian Sánchez was during the young man's imprisonment in Castel Sant'Angelo.

Sánchez' best known works are the *Speculum vitae humanae* (1467/68),[108] a lengthy treatise devoted to the study of the various states of life (laity, clerics, and monks) and their particular advantages and drawbacks (but in this work he also takes up the theme of "the reformation of the Church in head and members"); and, above all, the *Liber de monarchia orbis* (1467). In the latter, no less than in the *Defensorium Ecclesiae* (1466), Sánchez champions the idea of a universal monarchy entrusted to the pope, to whom he attributes a full and complete authority over all human beings and all countries.[109] All authority, whether spiritual or temporal, belongs by full right to the Roman pontiff, who has not only the power but also the duty to resolve and decide all conflicts that can arise between the various temporal sovereigns. Moreover, as one sensitive to the new historical institutions of his age, the Spanish bishop denies that the emperor can extend his authority beyond the German-speaking lands, and he acknowledges the full sovereignty of the monarchies of France and the Iberian countries. Finally, he proclaims the principle of the complete sovereignty and majesty of the pope in another work, *De paupertate Christi et apostolorum* (1466), which he wrote to refute the teaching of the Fraticelli, to defend the need the Church hierarchies have to "own property," and to launch a sharp attack on the teachings of Marsilius of Padua.[110]

Some of Roderick Sánchez' most characteristic views were criticized by Torquemada,[111] a Dominican cardinal, who at the Council of Constance had already strongly defended the superiority of papal authority over that of the council fathers. As a papal theologian at the councils of Basel and Ferrara-Florence,[112] he had shared with his fellow countrymen a clear opposition to conciliarist theories, as he showed in some of his interventions *(Contra decreta concilii Constantiensis; Tractatus contra avisamentum quoddam Basileensium quod non licet appellare a conciliis ad papam).*

Thus, in his *Tractatus notabilis de potestate papae et concilii generalis auctoritate* and in his *Flores sententiarum Divi Thomae de potestate papae,*[113] relying heavily on Thomist texts, Torquemada defends a hierarchic and unitary conception of the Church, all of whose authority is to be located in a "supreme hierarch," from whom it spreads down to the lower degrees of authority in the ecclesial society. In replying to the defenders of conciliarist theses, whom he regards as tools of the devil for dividing the Church, he claims that apart from cases of obvious heresy the pope cannot be subject to or bound by any conciliar decree, although he is subject to the precepts of divine and natural law. The pontiff is subject only to the supreme majesty of Christ and therefore cannot be subject to any human law, just as none of his acts and decrees can be annulled. Even in the case of a pope who lives a scandalous life it is the duty of the Christian people to be patient, pray, and admonish him. The extreme step that can be taken is to call a council that will convey its protests to him but that cannot depose him if it wishes not to exceed its authority.

This teaching Torquemada repeats and develops in an organized way in his *Summa de Ecclesia* (1448/49),[114] which he dedicated to Nicholas V. Taking as his starting point the parallelism set up in the Pseudo-Dionysian writings between the heavenly hierarchy and the angelic hierarchy, he conceives of the Church as a perfect society that is necessary for the attainment of the supernatural ends of the human person and is organized on the principle of the strictest obedience to the pope and the college of cardinals, these two being the successors of Peter and the "apostolic college," respectively. At the same time, however, still with Thomas as his authority, Torquemada recognizes the separation of the temporal power from the spiritual and asserts that the pope cannot claim the authority of a "master of the entire world," or usurp the jurisdiction of kings and emperors, or exercise authority and functions that belong to princes "of the world." The pontiff does, indeed, have the authority and duty of intervening in the temporal order when this is required by the carrying out of his mission and his role as supreme pastor of Christ's faithful. But this intervention (which Torquemada makes very easy and far-reaching) springs not from a specific jurisdictional authority but only from a derivative authority founded in the universality of the pope's spiritual authority.

The teachings of this Dominican theologian had a very great influence on the history of theologico-political ideas during the subsequent centuries; they were the source of inspiration for the theoreticians of the indirect power of the Roman pontiff as they formulated a conception that was destined to be for a long time a firm line of defense for the right of ecclesiastical intervention in the temporal order.

Despite all this, Torquemada was one of the last of the most determined defenders of the universal authority of the empire; he defended its prerogatives and powers against Sánchez de Arévalo in his *Opusculum ad honorem Romani imperii et dominorum Romanorum* (1468), which extols the ancient medieval myth of a supreme temporal hierarchy that perfectly parallels and mirrors the supreme spiritual hierarchy.

BIBLIOGRAPHY

Paul of Venice (Paul Nicoletti) (Udine, 1372–Padua, 1429)

EDITIONS

Summa naturalium or *Summa totius philosophiae naturalis.* Milan and Venice, 1496; Venice, 1502; reprinted: Hildesheim, 1970.
Summulae logicales. Venice, 1472; reprinted: Hildesheim, 1970.
Super librum de anima. Venice, 1481.
Super I Sententiarum Johannis de Ripa lecturae abreviatio. Prologus. Ed. F. Ruello. Florence, 1980.

BIBLIOGRAPHY

Perreiah, A. *Paul of Venice: A Bibliographical Guide.* Bowling Green, 1986.

STUDIES

Rossi, G. *Alcune ricerche su Paolo Veneto.* Turin, 1904.
Momigliano, T. F. *Paolo Veneto e le correnti del pensiero religioso e filosofico del suo tempo.* Turin, 1907.
Gentile, G. "Intorno alla biografia di Paolo Veneto." Idem. *Studi sul Rinascimento.* Florence, 1936²; 1968³. Pp. 98–108.
Nardi, B. *Sigieri di Brabante nel pensiero del Rinascimento italiano.* Rome, 1945. Pp. 115–32.
Duhem, P. *Le système du monde* X. Paris, 1959. Pp. 377–439.

Nardi, B. "Paolo Veneto e l'averroismo padovano." Idem. *Saggi sull aristotelismo padovano dal secolo XIV al XVI.* Florence, 1958. Pp. 75–93, and see the index.

Napoli, G. Di. *L'immortalità dell'anima nel Rinascimento.* Turin, 1963. See the index.

Risse, W. "Averrosimo e alessandrinismo nella logica del Rinascimento." *Filosofia* 15 (1964) 15–30.

Poppi, A. *Causalità e infinità nella scuola padovana dal 1480 al 1513.* Padua, 1966. See the index.

Perreiah, A. "A Biographical Introduction to Paul of Venice." *Augustiniana* 17 (1967) 450–61.

Crescini, A. *Il problema metodologico alle origini della scienza moderna.* Rome, 1972. Passim.

Ruello, F. "Paul de Venise, théologie 'averroiste'?" *Multiple Averroès.* Actes du Colloque (Paris, 1976). Paris, 1978. Pp. 257–73.

Aristotelismo veneto e scienza moderna. Atti del 25° Anno Accademico del Centro per la storia della tradizione aristotelica nel Veneto. Ed. L. Olivieri. 2 vols. Padua, 1983. See the index.

Bottin, F. "Logica e filosofia naturale nelle opere di Paolo Veneto." *Scienza e filosofia all'Università di Padova nel Quattrocento.* Ed. A. Poppi. Centro per la storia dell'Università di Padova 1. Padua, 1983. Pp. 85–124.

Kessler, E. "The Intellective Soul." *The Cambridge History of Renaissance Philosophy,* Ed. Ch. B. Schmitt and others. Cambridge, 1988. Pp. 485–534.

On the relationship between theology and logic in Paul of Venice, and for the pertinent bibliography, see Vol. II of the present work, part 6, chapter 6.

Gaetano of Thiene (Gaeta, 1387–Padua, 1465)

EDITIONS

Commentaria in tres libros Aristotelis de anima. Padua, 1475.
Commentaria in libros Methereorum. Padua, 1476.
Recollectae super octo libros Physicorum Aristotelis. Vicenza, 1487.
Expositio in quattuor Aristotelis libros de coelo et mundo. Padua, 1480.
Quaestio de perpetuitate intellectus. Padua, 1483.

STUDIES

Sartori, A. D. *Gaetano di Thiene filosofo averroista nell Studio di Padova.* Rome, 1938.

Valsanzibio, S. da. *Vita e dottrina di Gaetano di Thiene filosofo nello Studio di Padova.* Padua, 1949.

Clagett, M. *Giovanni Marliani and Late Medieval Physics.* New York, 1941. Passim.

Bertola, E. "La Quaestione del 'senso agente' in Gaetano di Thiene." Idem. *Saggi e studi di filosofia medioevale.* Padua, 1961. Pp. 53–69.

Randall, J. H. *The School of Padua and the Emergence of Modern Science.* Padua, 1961. Passim.

Bottin, F. "Gaetano di Thiene e i 'calculatores.'" *Scienza e filosofia all'Università di Padova nel Quattrocento.* Ed. A. Poppi. Centro per la storia dell'Università di Padova 1. Padua, 1983. Pp. 125–34.

Bernardinello, S. "Sulla biblioteca di Gaetano da Thiene, lettore allo studio e canonico della cattedrale di Padova." *Viridiarum floridum. Studi di storia veneta offerti dagli allievi a Paolo Sambin.* Medioevo e Umanesimo 54. Padua, 1984. Pp. 337–53. See also the studies listed under Paul of Venice by Nardi, *Saggi sull'aristotelismo padovano;* De Napoli, *L'immortalità dell'anima;* Poppi, *Causalità e infinità;* Crescini, *Il problema metodologico;* Kessler, "The Intellective Soul"; and *Aristotelismo veneto e scienza moderna.*

On the relationship of Gaetano of Thiene to Averroism see also in the present history Vol. II, part 6, chapter 9, section 3.

Augustine Favaroni (Rome, 1360–Prato, 1443)

WORKS

Commentarius in apocalipsim beati Joanni Apostoli.
De sacramento unitatis Christi et Ecclesiae suae.
Contra quosdam errores haereticorum.
Defensorium sacramenti unitatis Christi et Ecclesiae.
De Christo integro.
De Christo capite Ecclesiae, et eius inclito principatu.
De principatu Papae et potestate summi pontificatus.
De caritate Christi erga electos et de eius infinito amore.
Lectura super epistulam B. Pauli ad Hebraeos.
Super Sententias libri quattuor.
Liber circa quaestionem num divinitas Christo ab anima et corpore fuerit separata post mortem.
De sacerdotio Christi et electorum.
De libero arbitrio.
De peccato per originem tracto.
De perfecta iusticia militentibus Ecclesiae in praesenti.
De meritis Christi.
Comentum super I Ethicorum Aristotelis.
Expositio super epistulam B. Pauli ad Romanos.
Lectura supra epistulam B. Pauli ad Galatas.
Expositio in epistulam B. Pauli ad Ephesios.
Expositio in epistolam B. Pauli ad Colossenses.
Comentarium in epistolas B. Pauli ad Philippenses.
Expositio super epistolam primam B. Pauli ad Corinthios.
Introductiones quadragesimales: formula de creatione Adae et Evae et eorum lapsu.
Expositio in psalmum "Miserere mei Deus."

For information on the manuscripts containing these works see the studies of Ciolini and Friemel listed below.

EDITIONS

Diaz, G. "Un tratado inédito sobre el sacerdocio de Augustín Favaroni (d. 1443)." *La Ciudad de Dios* 173 (1960) 584–637.

Da sacramento unitatis Christi et ecclesiae suae, De Christo integro. Ed. A. Piolanti. Vatican City, 1971.

Diaz, G. "Un tratado inédito sobre la santidad de la Iglesia de Agustín Favaroni (d. 1443)." *La Ciudad de Dios* 187 (1974) 258–313.

_____. *Comentario inédito de Agustín Favaroni a la Carta de San Paulo a los Filippenses*. Idem. *Estudio sobre la Baja Edad Media*. El Escorial, 1977.

Eckermann, W. *Opera inedita historiam XXII sessionis concilii Basiliensis respicientia: Augustini de Roma OESA Contra quosdam errores haereticorum, et Defensorium sacramenti unitatis Christi et ecclesiae, atque Henrici Kalteisen OP Propositiones in condemnatione libelli Augustini de Roma*. Rome, 1978.

Diaz, G. "Tratado inédito *De principatu Papae* de Agustín Favaroni OSA (d. 1443). *Analecta Augustiniana* 53 (1990) 95–192.

STUDIES

Müller, A. V. "Agostino Favaroni (+ 1443) Generale OESA, Arcivescovo di Nazareth e la teologia di Lutero." *Bilychnis* 3 (1914) 373–87.

Ciolino, G. *Agostino da Roma (Favaroni, + 1443) e la sua cristologia*. Florence, 1944.

Friemel, D. S. *Die theologische Prinzipienlehre des Augustinus Favaroni von Rom OESA (+ 1443)*. Würzburg, 1950.

Toner, N. "The Doctrine of Original Sin and Justification According to Augustine of Rome." *Augustiniana* 7 (1957) 100–17.

Zumkeller, A. "Die Augustinereremiten in der Auseinandersetzung mit Wyclif und Hus, ihre Beteiligung an den Konzilien von Konstanz und Basel." *Analecta Augustiniana* 28 (1965) 5–56.

Vallone, A. "Favarone de'Favaroni e il suo trattato inedito *De principatu Papae*." *Studi storici in onore di Gabriele Pepe*. Bari, 1969. Pp. 499–507.

_____. *Di alcuni aspetti del pensiero politico del XIV secolo*. Manduria, 1970. Pp. 177–86.

_____. *Antidantismo politico del XIV secolo*. Naples, 1973. Pp. 107–20.

Eckermann, W. "Zur Hermeneutik theologischer Aussagen. Überlegungen Heinrich Kalteisens OP auf dem Basler Konzil zu Propositionen des Augustinus Favaroni von Rom OESA." *Augustiniana* 25 (1975) 24–42.

Pispisa, E. "Il *De primatu papae* di Augustinus Favaroni von Rom OESA." Idem, *Dante nel pensiero e nella esegesi dei secoli XIV e XV*. Florence, 1975. Pp. 375–84.

Eckermann, W. "Augustinus Favaroni von Rom und Johannes Wyclif. Der Ansatz ihrer Lehre über die Kirche." *Scientia Augustiniana*. Ed. C. P. Meyer and W. Eckermann. Würzburg, 1975. Pp. 323–48.

Walsh, K. "Pastoral Involvement, Rural Seclusion, and the Search for an Observant Identity: The Reform Congregation of Monte Ortone." *Analecta Augustiniana* 52 (1989) 257–97.

Other information on the sources and other bibliography in W. Eckermann, "Augustinus Favaroni," *TRE* IV (Berlin–New York, 1979) 739–42. In press: D. Gionta, "Favaroni," *DBI*.

John Dominici (Florence, 1356?–Buda, 1419)

EDITIONS

Regola del governo di cura familiare. Ed. D. Salvi. Florence, 1860. Ed. P. Bargellini. Florence, 1927.
Il libro di amor di carità. Ed. A. Ceruti. Bologna, 1889.
Lucula noctis. Ed. R. Coulon. Paris, 1908. Ed. E. Hunt. Notre Dame, 1940; 1960[2].
Trattato delle dieci quistioni. Ed. A. Levasti. Florence, 1947.
Da Prati, P. *Linguaggio e poesia di Giovanni Dominici nel "De conceptione Beatae Virginis."* Naples, 1965.
Lettere spirituali. Ed. M. T. Casella and G. Pozzi. Fribourg, 1969.
Casella, M. T. "Una nuova predica del Dominici." *Miscellanea G. G. Meersseman.* Padua, 1960. Pp. 369–96.
A letter to Boccaccio in G. Billanovich, "Pietro Piccolo da Monteforte tra il Petrarca e il Boccaccio," in *Medioevo e Rinascimento. Studi in onore di Bruna Nardi* (Florence, 1955) I, 1–76.

BIBLIOGRAPHY

A very extensive but not always accurate bibliography in *MemDom,* N.S. 1 (1970) 201–35.

STUDIES

Sauerland, H. V. "Kardinal Johannes Dominici und sein Verhalten zu den kirchlichen Unionsbestrebungen während der Jahre 1406–1415." *Zeitschrift für Kirchengeschichte* 9 (1887–88) 242ff.
Roesler, A. *Kardinal Johannes Dominici OP, ein Reformatorenbild aus der Zeit des grossen Schismas.* Freiburg i. B., 1893.
_____. *Kardinal Johannes Dominicis Erziehungslehre und die übrigen pädagogischen Leistungen Italiens im XV. Jahrhundert.* Freiburg i. B., 1894.
Ferretti, L. *La chiesa e il convento de S. Domenico di Fiesole.* Florence, 1901.
Galletti, A. "Prediche inedite di Giovanni Dominici." *Miscellanea di studi critici pubblicati in onore di Guido Mazzoni.* Florence, 1907. I, 253–78.
Peter, A. *Studien über den Kardinal Johannes Dominici.* Freiburg i. B., 1911.
Santamaria, L. "Il concetto di cultura e di educazione nel beato Giovanni Dominici." *MemDom,* N.S. 1 (1930) 14–27, 97–106, 340–52, 392–400, 481–515.
Orlandi, S. *Necrologio di Santa Maria Novella* II. Florence, 1955. Pp. 77–108.
The Council of Constance: The Unification of the Church. New York–London, 1961. See the index.
Garin, E. *La cultura filosofica del Rinascimento italiano.* Florence, 1961. Pp. 224–25.
Di Agresti, G. "Considerazioni intorno a due scritti del beato Giovanni Dominici." *MemDom,* N.S. 32 (1962) 5–125.
Ullman, B. L. *The Humanism of Coluccio Salutati.* Padua, 1963. See the index.
Cracco, G. "Banchini, Giovanni di Domenico (Giovanni Dominici, Banchelli Giovanni)." *DBI* 5 (Rome, 1963) 657–64.

Da Prati, F. *Giovanni Dominici e l'umanesimo*. Naples, 1965.

Bertucci, S. M. "Dominici, Giovanni." *BibSanct* 4 (Rome, 1967) cols. 748–56.

Trinkaus, C. *In Our Image and Likeness*. Chicago, 1970. See the index.

Sbriziolo, L. "Note su Giovanni Dominici." *RSCI* 24 (1970) 4–30; 29 (1975) 7–35.

Giovanni Dominici (+ 1419) = MemDom, N.S. 1 (1970).

Öchslin, R.-L. "Jean Dominici (bienheureux)." *DSp* 8 (Paris, 1972) 7–35.

Petrocchi, G. *Storia della spiritualità italiana* I. *Il Duecento, il Trecento e il Quattrocento*. Rome, 1978. See the index.

Cracco, G. "Des saints aux sanctuaires: hypothèses d'une évolution en terre vénitienne." *Faire croire. Modalité de la diffusion et de la réception des messages religieux du XIIᵉ au XVᵉ siècle*. Table ronde organisée par l'École française de Rome (Rome, 22–23 giugno 1979). Ed. A. Vauchez. Rome, 1981. Pp. 279–97.

Denley, P. "Giovanni Dominici's Opposition to Humanism." *Studies in Church History* 7 (1981) 103–14.

Mésionat, G. *"Poëtica theologica": la "Lucula noctis" di Giovanni Dominici e le dispute letterarie tra '300 e '400*. Rome, 1984.

Dobrowolski, P. T. "Piety and Death in Venice: A Reading of the Fifteenth-century 'Chronicle' and the 'Necrology of Corpus Domini.'" *BIstStorArchMur* 92 (1985–86) 295–324.

Ronconi, G. "Dominici, Giovanni." *Dizionario critico della letteratura italiana* II. Turin, 1986². Pp. 169–75.

Cracco, G. "Giovanni Dominici e un nuovo tipo di religiosità." *Conciliarismo, Stati nazionali, inizi dell'Umanesimo*. Atti del XXV Convegno storico internazionale (Todi, 9–12 ottobre 1988). Spoleto, 1990. Pp. 1–20.

Lesnick, D. R. "Civic Preaching in the Early Renaissance. Giovanni Dominici's Florentine Sermons." *Christianity and the Renaissance: Image and Religious Imagination in the Quattrocento*. Ed. T. Verdon and J. Henderson. Syracuse, 1990. Pp. 208–25.

Antoninus of Florence (Antoninus Pierozzi) (Florence, 1389–1459)

WORKS AND EDITIONS

Summa theologiae, or *Summa moralis*. Venice, 1477, and subsequently Venice, 1479, 1480, 1481, 1571, 1582; Spira, 1477; Basel, 1502, 1511; Verona, 1740; Florence, 1741 (but some parts of the *Summa* were published separately).

Chronicon, in *Opera omnia*. Venice, 1474–79; then: Nuremberg, 1484; Basel, 1491; Lyons 1517, 1525, 1527, 1581–87 (and see R. Morçay, *Chroniques de S. Antonin: fragments originaux du XXII 1387–1459* [Paris, 1913]).

For the very numerous editions of the lesser works *(Confessionale* or *Summula confessionis; Cura illius habe = Medicina dell'anima; Omnis mortalium cura = Specchio di coscienza),* which became parts of the *Summa,* see R. Morçay, "Antonin, saint," *DHGE* 3 (Paris, 1924) cols. 858–60, especially 858; see this same article for the editions of the *De ornatu mulierum,* (= *Summa* II, t. IV, c. V) and the *Libretto della dottrina cristiana per i putti piccoli e giovanetti*.

Opera a ben vivere. Ed. F. Palermo. Florence, 1858.

Regola di vita cristiana. Ed. F. Palermo. Florence, 1866.

Trialogus super enarrationem evangelicam de duobus discipulis euntibus ad Emmaus. Ed. T. Corsetto. Florence, 1989.

Unpublished sermons for Lent are preserved in mss.: Florence, Biblioteca Nazionale, Conventi soppressi, A. 8. 1750, and Florence, Biblioteca Riccardiana, 308.

STUDIES

Mandonnet, P. "Antonin (Saint)." *DTC* 1 (Paris, 1903). Cols. 1450–54.

Morçay, R. *Saint Antonin fondateur du couvent de Saint-Marc, archevêque de Florence.* Tours-Paris, 1914.

Tinagli, C. *S. Antonino Pierozzi.* Florence, 1923.

Senesi, E. "S. Antonino e l'umanesimo." *La Rinascita* 3 (1940) 105–16.

_____. *La vita di S. Antonino arcivescovo di Firenze.* Florence, 1941.

Calzolai, C. C. *S. Antonino Pierozzi domenicano arcivescovo di Firenze.* Florence, 1959.

S. Antonino = MemDom 76 (1959) fasc. 2–3.

S. Antonino O.P. maestro di vita spirituale = Rivista di ascetica e mistica (1959).

Calzolai, C. C. *Frate Antonino Pierozzi del Domenicani, arcivescovo di Firenze.* Padua-Rome-Naples, 1961.

_____. *Bibliografia antoniniana.* Vatican City, 1961.

Orlandi, S. *S. Antonino. La sua famiglia, I primi cinque anni di episcopatu. Studi bibliografici.* 2 vols. Florence, 1959–60 (1961).

D'Addario, A. "Antonino Pierrozi, santo." *DBI* 3 (Rome, 1961) 524–32. The section on "Opere e dottrina" is by an anonymous writer.

Di Agresti, G. "Antonino Pierozzi." *BibSanct* 2 (Rome, 1962) cols. 88–104.

Vereecke, L. "Medicine et morale chez saint Antonin de Florence (+ 1459)." *Sciences ecclésiastiques* 15 (1963) 153–72.

Creytens, R. "Les *Consilia* de S. Antonin de Florence." *AFP* 39 (1967) 263–342.

Donelly, J. P. "Marriage from Renaissance to Reformation: Two Florentine Moralists." *Studies in Medieval Culture* 11 (1977) 161–71.

Paravy, P. "Le traité de la visite pastorale de François Du Puy, officiel du diocèse de Grenoble (fin XVe siècle). Lecture et influence de la *Summa theologiae moralis* de saint Antonin de Florence." *Horizons marins, itinéraires spirituels (V^e–XVIIIe siècles).* Ed. H. Dubois and others. Paris, 1987. I, 213–33.

Rouse, R. H., and M. A. Rouse. "St. Antoninus of Florence on Manuscript Production." *Litterae Medii Aevi. Festschrift für Johannes Autenrieth zu ihrem 65. Geburtstag.* Ed. M. Borgolte and H. Spilling. Sigmaringen, 1988. Pp. 255–63.

Howard, P. "'Non parum laborat formica ad colligendum unde vivat': Oral Discourse as the Context of the *Summa theologica* of St. Antoninus of Florence." *AFP* 59 (1989) 89–148.

Izbicki, Th. M. "Pyres of Vanities: Mendicant Preaching on the Vanity of Women and Its Lay Audience." *De Ore Domini: Preacher and Word in the Middle Ages.* Ed. Th. L. Amos and others. Kalamazoo, 1989. Pp. 211–34.

STUDIES ON THE ECONOMIC, HISTORICAL, AND JURIDICAL THOUGHT OF ST. ANTONINUS

Jarrett, B. *S. Antonino and Medieval Economics.* London, 1914.

Walker, J. B. *The "Chronicles" of Saint Antonino: A Study in Historiography.* Washington, D.C., 1933.

Dalle Molle, L. *Il contratto di cambio nei moralisti dal secolo XIII al secolo XVIII.* Rome, 1954. See the index.

Barbieri, G. "Le forze del lavoro e della produzione nelle *Summa* di sant'Antonino." *Economia e storia* 7 (1960) 10–36.

Veraja, A. F. *Le origini della controversia teologica sul contratto di censo.* Rome, 1960. See the index.

Brezzi, P. "Gli scritti storici e l'azione politica di Sant'Antonino." Idem. *Studi di storia cristiana ed ecclesiastica. Età moderna e contemporanea.* Naples, 1967. Pp. 67–84.

Roover, R. de. *San Bernardino da Siena and Sant'Antonino of Florence: The Two Great Economic Thinkers of the Middle Ages.* Boston, 1967.

Spicciani, A. "S. Antonino, S. Bernardino e Pier Giovanni Olivi nel pensiero economico medievale." *Economia e storia* 19 (1972) 315–41.

_____. "Note su Sant'Antonino economista." *Economia e storia* 22 (1975) 171–92.

McDonough, E. "Canon Law in Pastoral Perspective: Principles for the Application of Law According to Antoninus of Florence." *Dissertation Abstracts International. A. The Humanities and Social Sciences* 43 (1983) 192.

Anthony de Carlenis (Naples, before 1386–Amalfi, 1460)

WORKS

Quaestiones in libros XII Metaphysicorum. Cambridge mss.: Jesus College Library 17; Florence, Biblioteca Nazionale, Conventi soppressi, 1136; Naples, Biblioteca Nazionale, VIII G 75; Biblioteca Apostolica Vaticana, Vat. lat. 5987.

Quaestiones in IV libros Sententiarum. Milan mss.: Biblioteca Trivulziana, 1682, ff. 1–117; Oxford, Bodleian Library, Canon. misc. 573, ff. 172–377; Rome, Biblioteca Casanatense, 1025; Biblioteca Apostolica Vaticana, Reg. lat, 592, ff. 105–224v (Books I–III only).

STUDIES

Meersseman, "Antonio de Carlenis OP, Erzbischof von Amalfi." *AFP* 3 (1933) 81–131. With bibliography to that point.

_____. "Ergänzung zu den Schriften des Antonius Carleni von Neapel." Ibid., 5 (1935) 357–63.

Käppeli, Th. *Scriptores Ordinis Praedicatorum Medii Aevi* I. Rome, 1970. P. 109.

Di Agresti, D. "Carleni, Antonio." *DBI* 20 (Rome, 1977) 135–36.

Peter of Bergamo (Bergamo, 1400–Bologna, 1482)

EDITIONS

Tabula super omnia opera S. Thomae (Tabula aurea). Bologna, 1476; Basel, 1478.
Ethimologia id est concordantia conclusionum in quibus Divus Thomas videtur sibimet contradicere (or *Concordantiae textuum discordantium Divi Thomae Aquinatis*). Venice, 1476; Cologna, 1480; reprinted: Florence, 1982. A critical edition of the *Tabula aurea* is planned, with T. Stierli as editor.

STUDIES

Kriutwagen, B. *S. Thomae de Aquino Summa opusculorum.* Kain, 1924. Pp. 82–90.
Bonetti, A. "Pietro da Bergamo, la *Tabula aura* e la sua tomba in Piacenza." *Bolletino storico piacentino* 56 (1961) 127–28.
Colosio, I. "La *Tabula aura* di Pietro da Bergamo." *Divus Thomas* (Piacenza) 64 (1961) 119–32.
Piana, C. *Ricerche sulle università di Bologna e Parma.* Quaracchi, 1963. Pp. 112–14.
––––––. "Il suddiaconato di Fra' Girolamo Savonarola." *Rinascimento,* Ser. 2, 6 (1966) 287–94. See 288 in particular.
Käppeli, Th. *Scriptores Ordinis Praedicatorum Medii Aevi* III. Rome, 1980. P. 219.

Paul Barbo (of Soncino) (Soncino, ?–Cremona, 1494)

EDITIONS

Divinum epitoma quaestionum in IV libros Sententiarum a principe Thomistarum Ioanne Capreolo Tolosano disputatarum. Pavia, 1522; Lyons, 1528 and 1580; Salamanca, 1580.
Elegantissima dispositio in artem veterem Aristotelis in quaestionibus. Venice, 1499.
Tabula titulorum questionum super Metaphysicam. Venice, 1498.
Quaestiones metaphysicales super divinam sapientiam Aristotelis. Venice, 1502, 1526, 1576, 1580; Lyons, 1579; Mainz, 1622.
Quaestiones in VIII libros Metaphysicorum, in logicam Aristotelis correctae et dispositae. Venice, 1587.
Barbo also published, in a considerably corrected edition, *S. Thomas Aquinatis opuscula XLIX* (Milan, 1488) and Vincent Ferrer's *Sermones de sanctis* (Milan, 1488).

STUDIES

Grabmann, M. *Mittelalterliches Geistesleben.* I. Munich, 1926. Pp. 390–400. II. Munich, 1936; reprinted: Munich, 1956. Pp. 100 and 483. III. Munich, 1956. Pp. 390–400.
Mandonnet, P. *DTC* 2 (Paris, 1932). Col. 387.

Vilde, V. de. *DHGE* 6 (Paris, 1932). Cols. 663–64.
Vasoli, C. "Barbo, Paolo." *DBI* 5 (Rome, 1964) 256–57.

Dominic of Flanders (Beaudoiin or Balduin Lottin) (Merris or Merville, ca. 1425–Florence, 1481)

EDITIONS

In XII libros Metaphysicae Aristotelis secundum expositionem Angelici Doctoris lucidissimae quaestiones. Venice, 1499; Cologne, 1521; Venice, 1565; reprinted: New York–Frankfurt a. M., 1967.
Quaestiones et adnotationes in tres libros De anima cum commentariis sancti Thomae in eosdem. Venice, 1503.
Quaestiones quodlibetales. Venice, 1500.
Summa divinae philosophiae. Venice, 1565; reprinted: New York–Frankfurt a. M., 1967.

STUDIES

Meersseman, G. G. "Een Vlaamsch Wijsger: Dominicus van Vlanderen." *Thomistisch Tijdschrift voor Katholiek Kulturleven* 1 (1930) 385–400.
_____. "Het geestelijk en wijsgeerig midden van Dominicus van Vlanderen." Ibid., 590–92.
Schikowski, U. "Dominicus de Flandria: sein Leben, sein Schriften, seine Bedeutung." *AFP* 10 (1940) 169–221.
Mahieu, L. *Dominique de Flandres et sa métaphysique.* Paris, 1942.
Markowski, M. "Definicje substancji w Kommentarzu do Metafisyhi Dominica za Flandrii." *Studia mediewistyczne* 1 (1964) 19–52.
Käppeli, Th. *Scriptores Ordinis Praedicatorum Medii Aevi* I. Rome, 1970. Pp. 315–18.
Verde, A. "Dominico di Fiandria, intransigente tomista non gradito nello Studio fiorentino." *MemDom*, N.S. 7 (1976) 301–21.
Krause, F. "Klassifizierung der Wissenschaften nach Dominikus von Flandern." *Studia mediewistyczne* 27 (1990) 41–52.

Vincent Bandello (Castelnuovo Scrivia 1435–Altomonte, 1506)

EDITIONS

Libellus recollectorius de veritate conceptionis Beatae Virginis Mariae. Milan, 1475.
Tractatus de singulari puritate et praerogativa conceptionis Salvatoris nostri Iesu Christi. Bologna, 1481.
Liber ducentorum et sexaginta sanctorum, Virginem Mariam in originali peccato fore conceptam dicentium, dicta continens. Lübeck, ca. 1485.

STUDIES

Masi, E. *Matteo Bandello*. Bologna, 1900.

Mortier, D. A. *Histoire des Maîtres Généraux de l'Ordre des Frères Prêcheurs* V. Paris, 1911. Pp. 66–127.

Almeida, S. de. "Chronica Ordinis Praedicatorum." *Analecta Ordinis Fratrum Praedicatorum* 43 (1935) 115–20.

Monumenta Ordinis Fratrum Praedicatorum historica. Rome, 1947. Pp. 63, 162, 172.

Duval, A. "La dévotion mariale dans l'Ordre des Frères Prêcheurs." *Maria* 2 (1952) 760–810.

Ferrua, A. "Bandelli, Vincenzo." *DBI* 5 (Rome, 1963) 666–67.

John Caroli (John de Carlo Berlinghieri (Florence, 1428–1503)

MANUSCRIPTS

The works of Caroli are preserved in these manuscripts: Florence, Archivio di S. Maria Novella, VII.C.4. — Florence, Biblioteca Nazionale, Conventi soppressi, A.3.495; A.7.908; B.4.7; C.8.277–79; D.9.278–79; F.4.17; G.4.276; Conventi soppressi da reordinare, 129 (F.50); Magl. II.4.67; XXXVI.9.70; XXXVIII.10.124; XL.9.46. — Florence, Biblioteca Medicea Laurenziana, codd. 20, 260, 361, 571, and plut. LXXXIX, inf. 1. — Biblioteca Apostolica Vaticana, Vat. lat. 5878, 6329, 8088.

STUDIES

Orlandi, S. *La biblioteca di S. Maria Novella in Firenze dal secolo XIV al secolo XIX*. Florence, 1952. See the index.

————. *Necrologia di S. Maria Novella* I. Florence, 1955. Pp. 203–5. II, 353–80.

Garin, E. *La cultura filosofica del Rinascimento italiano*. Florence, 1962. Pp. 224–26.

Marchetti, V. "Caroli, Giovanni." *DBI* 20 (Rome, 1977) 523–26.

Camporeale, S. I. "Giovanni Caroli, 1460–1480: Death, Memory, and Transformation." *Life and Death in Fifteenth Century Florence*. Durham-London, 1989. Pp. 16–27.

————. "Giovanni Caroli O.P. and the *Liber dierum lucensium* (Humanism and the Religious Crisis of the Late Quattrocento)." *Christianity and the Renaissance: Image and Religious Imagination in the Quattrocento*. Ed. T. Verdon and J. Henderson. Syracuse, 1990. Pp. 445–66.

Baptist Spagnoli (Mantua, 1477–1516)

EDITIONS

Opera omnia. Bologna, 1502; Paris, 1507; Antwerp, 1576.

De calamitatibuis temporum libri tres. Ed. P. Wessels. *Analecta Ordinis Carmelitarum* 4 (1917) 19–93.

STUDIES

Fanucchi, I. *Della vita del Beato Battista Spagnolo detto il Mantovano*. Lucca, 1887.

Gabotto, F. "Un poeta santificato, schizzo di Battista Spagnoli da Mantova." *Archivio veneto,* Ser. 16, 1 (1892) 3–19.

Caioli, P. *Il Beato Battista Spagnoli e la sua opera*. Rome, 1917.

Zabughin, V. "Un Beato poeta." *Analecta Ordinis Carmelitarum* 4 (1917) 125–57.

Benvenuto, P. *Beato Battista Spagnoli detto il Mantovano, notizie storico-bibliografiche*. Padua, 1919.

Santolla, A. *Il Mantovano riformatore e le sue egloghe*. Rome, 1926.

Saint-Paul, A. de. "Baptiste de Mantoue (le bienheureux)." *DTC* 9 (Paris, 1927). Cols. 1918–23.

Enrique del Sagrado Corazón. "La mariología de Juan Bautista Spagnoli 'El mantuano.'" *El Monte Carmelo* 48 (1947) 329–55.

Vincente de la Eucaristía, Juan. "El mejor humanista christiano pretridentino." *Revista de Espiritualidad* 6 (1947) 48–70.

_____. "Libamentum aesthetico-marianum ex B. Baptistae Mantuani operibus." *Analecta Ordinis Carmelitarum Discalceatorum* 20 (1948) 205–59.

Lokkers, A. "Baptista Mantuanus asceta et mysticus." *Analecta Ordinis Carmelitarum* 3 (1948) 193–98.

Russel, P. "Baptist of Mantua, Fifteenth Century Humanist." Ibid., 216–37.

Saggi, L. *La congregazione mantovana dei Carmelitani sino all morte del Beato Battista Spagnoli (1516)*. Rome, 1954.

Bolisani, E. "Battista Spanoli scolaro a Padova." *Padova* 2 (1956) 20–29.

Sewell, B. *Blessed Baptist of Mantua, Carmelite and Humanist (1447–1516)*. Rome, 1960.

Coccia, E. *Le edizioni delle opere del Mantovano*. Rome, 1960.

_____. "Spagnoli, Battista, detto il Mantovano." *BibSanct* 11 (Rome, 1968). Cols. 1340–42.

Simeon de la Sagrada Familia. "Doctrina y devoción del Beato Bautista Mantuano a San José." *Estudios Josefinos* 28 (1974) 159–76.

Marmier, J. "Un poète au Carmel: Nicolas Didier, traducteur de la *Parthénice Mariane* (1613)." *Annales de Bretagne* 79 (1972) 525–49.

Rosa, R. "Tomismo e antitomismo in Battista Spagnoli Mantovano (1447–1516)." *MemDom,* N.S. 7 (1976) 227–64.

Trümphy, H. *Die "Fasti" des Baptista Mantuanus von 1516 als volkskundliche Quelle*. Nieuwkoop, 1979.

Echard, G. "The *Eclogues* of Baptista Mantuanus: A Medieval and Humanist Synthesis." *Latomus* 45 (1986) 837–47.

Francis Della Rovere (Sixtus V, Pope) (Celle Ligure, 1414–Rome, 1484)

EDITIONS

De sanguine Christi; De potentia Dei. Rome, after August 10, 1471.
De futuris contingentibus. Rome, 1473.

Report sent to Bessarion and published in L. Baudry, *La querelle des futurs contingents (Louvain 1465–1475). Textes inédits* (Paris, 1950) 113–25.

STUDIES

Brotto, G., and G. Zonto. *La Facoltà teologica di Padova.* Parte prima (secoli XIV–XVI). Padua, 1922. See the index.

Chenu, M.-D. "Sang du Christ." *DTC* 14 (Paris, 1939). Cols. 1094–97.

Teetaert, A. "Sixte IV." Ibid. Cols. 2200–1.

Bughetti B. "Francesco delle Rovere Ord. Min., lettore di filosofia, ministro generale e papa Sisto IV nelle sue relazioni con Perugia." *AFH* 36 (1943) 200–26.

Baudry, A. *La querelle des futurs contingents (Louvain 1465–1475). Textes inédits.* Paris, 1950. See the index.

Maier, A. "Alcuni autografi di Sisto IV." *RSCI* 7 (1953) 411–15.

Cortese, D. "Sisto IV Papa antoniano." *Il Santo* 12 (1972) 211–71.

————. "I teologi del Santo nel secolo XV." *Storia e cultura al Santo di Padova fra il XIII e il XX secolo.* Vicenza, 1976. Pp. 152–67.

Pusci, L. "Profilo di Francesco della Rovere, poi Sisto IV." Ibid., 279–88.

Poppi, A. "La teologia nell'università e nelle scuole." *Storia della cultura veneta, Dal primo Quattrocento al Concilio di Trento* III. Vicenza, 1981. Pp. 1–33. See pp. 28–29.

Cortese, D. "Francesco della Rovere e le *orationes* sull'Immacolata del vescovo di Padova Fantino Dandolo (1448)." *La tradizione scotista veneto-padovana.* Vol. II of *Regnum hominis et regnum Dei.* Acta quarti Congressi Scotistici Internationalis, Patavii, 24–29 Sept. 1976. Rome, 1978. Pp. 199–205.

Bianca, C. "Francesco della Rovere, un franscescano tra teologia e potere." *Un pontificato e une città. Sisto IV (1471–1484).* Atti del Convegno (Roma, 3–7 dicembre 1984). Ed. M. Miglio and others. Littera antiqua 5. Vatican City, 1986. Pp. 19–55.

Di Fonzo, L. "Sisto IV. Carriera scolastica e integrazioni biografiche." *Miscellanea francescana* 86 (1986) 1–491.

————. "Gli Studi Generali dei Frati Minori Conventuali nella due *Tabulae studiorum* dei Generali Della Rovere (1467) e Sansone (1488)." Ibid., 503–78.

Pusci, L. "Gli scritti e il pensiero di Francesco della Rovere dei Frati Minori Conventuali." Ibid., 493–502.

Roth, A. "Zur 'Reform' der päpstlichen Kapelle unter dem Pontifikat Sixtus IV (1471–1482)." *Zusammenhänge, Einflüsse, Wirkungen.* Kongressakten zum ersten Symposium des Mediävistenverbandes in Tübingen (1984). Ed. J. O. Fichte and others. Berlin, 1986. Pp. 168–95.

Ruysschaert, J. "La Bibliothèque Vaticane dans les dix premières années du pontificat de Sixte IV." *ArchHistPont* 24 (1986) 71–90.

Vasoli, C. "Sisto IV professore di teologia e teologo." *Atti e Memorie della Società Savonese di Storia Patria,* N.S. 24 (1988) 177–207. Reprinted in idem, *Tra 'maestri' umanisti e teologi. Studi quattrocenteschi.* Florence, 1981. Pp. 173–211.

Pfeiffer, H. W. "Gemalte Theologie in der sixtinischen Kapelle. I. Die Szenen des Alten und Neuen Testaments ausgeführt unter Sixtus IV." *ArchHistPont* 28 (1990) 99–159.

Eisman Lasaga, C. "Carta des condestable Iranzo al papa Sixto IV, defensor de la cristiandad y propulsor de las artes." *Boletín del Instituto de Estudios Giennenses* 37.11 (1991) 35–52.

George Benignus Salviati (Jurai Dragisi) (Srebenica 1445/50– Rome, 1520)

WORKS AND EDITIONS

In Francisci de libertate et immutabilitate Dei sententias: ms.: Biblioteca Apostolica Vaticana, Vat. lat. 1056.

In Fridericum de animae regni principe, in Z. C. Sojat. *De voluntate hominis eiusque praeeminentia et dominatione in anima secundum Georgium Gragisic (c. 1448–1520).* Rome, 1972. Pp. 129–224.

Ad Magnanimum Laurentium Petrifrancisci Medicen in opus de natura angelica, ms.: Florence, Biblioteca Medicea Laurenziana, plut. XVIII, 16.

Ad virum magnanimum Laurentium Petri Cosmi . . . opus septem quaestionum ab ipso propositarum, mss.: Florence, Biblioteca Riccardiana, 37 (M. II, 18) and Biblioteca Medicea Laurenziana, plut. LXXXIII, 8.

Dialectica nova. Florence, 1488.

Mirabilia septem et septuaginta in opusculo M. Nicolai de Mirabilibus reperta. Florence, n.d., but 1498.

Propheticae solutiones. Florence, 1497. Now in Garfagnini, "Giorgio Benigno Salviati e Girolamo Savonarola" (see Studies, below).

Opus de natura angelica. Florence, 1499.

Vexillum christianae victoriae, mss.: Milan, Biblioteca del Convento dei Cappuccini di S. Francesco, 16; Vienna, Nationalbibliothek, cod. palat. 4797; Paris, Bibliothèque Nationale, Bibl. Royale, III 439 (with the title *Contemplationes christianae*).

Contemplationes commendationum Virginis Gloriosae (or *Libellus de Virginis matris Assumptione*), mss.: Brussels, Bibliothèque Royale, 10783; Milan, Biblioteca Trivulziana, 453; Milan, Biblioteca del Convento dei Cappuccini di S, Francesco, 16; Milan, Biblioteca Ambrosiana, A. 30 sup.

Apologeticon seu defensorium ex divinis litteris aggressionis Francisci Mariae de Ruvere, ms.: Florence, Biblioteca Nazionale, cod. magl. XXX, 215.

Virginis Matris theoremata, ms.: Milan, Biblioteca Ambrosiana, A. 30 sup.

Defensio praestantissimi viri Joannis Reuchlin. (Cologne) 1517.

Preface for: Peter Galatino. *Opus toti christianae veritatis utile de archanis catholicae veritatis.* (Ortona a Mare) 1518.

STUDIES

Fabianich, D. *Storia dei Frati Minori dai primordi della loro costituzione in Dalmazia e Bosnia fino ai nostri giorni.* Zara, 1864. Pp. 241–43.

Jelénic, J. *Kultura i Bozanski Franjeci.* Sarajevo, 1912.

Papini, N. "Minoritae conventuales Lectores publici artium et scientiarum in Academiis, Universitatibus et Collegiis extra Ordinem." *Miscellanea Franciscana,* N.S. 33 (1933) 243–45.

Picotti, G. B. "Un episodio di politica ecclesiastica medicea." *Annali delle Università toscane,* N.S. 14 (1930) 86–202.

Harapin, J. T. "L'evoluzione della filosofia presso i Croati." *Croazia sacra.* Rome, 1943. Pp. 80–81.

Vanino, M. "Gli studi teologici presso i Croati." Ibid., 96.

Secret, F. "Umanisti dimenticati. Giorgius Benignus, il protetto di Bessarione." *GSLI* 137 (1960) 218–27.

Dionisotti, C. "Umanisti dimenticati?" *Italia medioevale e umanistica* 4 (1961). Pp. 287–321; see pp. 315–16.

Vasoli, C. "Notizie su Giorgio Benigno Salviati (Jurai Dragisic)." *Studi storici in onore di Gabriele Pepe.* Bari, 1969. Pp. 428–98.

_____. "Sul probabile autore di una 'profezia' politica cinquecentesca." *Il pensiero politico* 2 (1969) 464–72.

_____. "A proposito di Gabriele Biondo, Francesco Giorgio Veneto e Giorgio Benigno Salviati." *Rinascimento,* Ser. 2, 9 (1969) 325–30.

_____. "Ancora su Giorgio Benigno Salviati (Jurai Dragisic) e la 'profezia' dello pseudo-Amadeo." *Il pensiero politico* 3 (1970) 417–21.

Morisi, A. "*Apocalypsis nova.*" *Ricerche sull'origine e sulla formazione del testo dello pseudo-Amadeo.* Rome, 1970.

Gasnault, P. "Le manuscrit du *Vexillum christianae victoriae* de Giorgio Benigno Salviati." *Scriptorium* 26 (1972) 66–68.

Secret, F. "Rélations humanistes oubliées. I. Un élève oublié de Lefèvre d'Étaples: Johannes Aventinus; II. La dédicace du *Vexillum victoriae christianae* de Georgius Benignus de Salviatis à François Ier." *Studi francesi* 16 (1973) 295–98.

Vasoli, C. *Profezia e ragione, Studi sulla cultura del Cinquecento e del Seicento.* Naples, 1974. Pp. 15–127.

_____. *I miti e gli astri.* Naples, 1977. See the index.

_____. "Lo scotismo nella corrente platonica del Quattro/Cinquecento." *La tradizione scotista veneto-padovana.* Padua, 1979. Pp. 68–87.

_____. *Immagini umanistiche.* Naples, 1983. Pp. 231–36.

_____. "Un commento scotista a un sonetto del Magnifico: l'*Opus septem quaestionum* di Giorgio Benigno Salviati." *Tradizione classica e letteratura umanistica. Per Alessandro Perosa.* Rome, 1985. Pp. 533–75.

_____. "Giorgio Benigno Salviati, Pietro Galatino e l'edizione di Ortona, 1518 del *De archanis catholicae veritatis.*" *Cultura umanistica nel Meridione e la stampa in Abruzzo.* Atti del Convegno (12–14 novembre 1982). L'Aquila, 1984. Pp. 93–118.

_____. "L'*Apochalypsis nova:* Giorgio Benigno, Pietro Galatino e Guillaume Postel." *I Frati Minori tra '400 e '500.* Atti del XII Convegno internazionale (Assisi, 18–19 ottobre 1984). Assisi, 1986. Pp. 259–91.

_____. *Filosofia e religione nella cultura del Rinascimento.* Naples, 1988. See the index.

_____. "Giorgio Benigno Salviati e la tensione profetica di fine Quattrocento." *Rinascimento,* Ser. 2, 19 (1989). Pp. 53–78. Reprinted in idem, *Tra "maestri" umanistici e theologi. Studi quattrocenteschi.* Florence, 1991. Pp. 212–47.

Garfagnini, G. "Giorgio Benigno Salviati e Girolamo Savonarola. Note per una lettura delle *Propheticae solutiones.*" *Rinascimento,* Ser. 2, 29 (1989) 81–123.

Anthony Trombetta (Padua 1436–1517)

EDITIONS

Quaestiones Johannis Scoti super I Sententiarum. Venice, 1472.
In De caelo et mundo Aristotelis commentaria. Venice, 1493.
Quaestio de divina praescientia futurorum contingentium. Venice, 1493.
Quaestiones metaphysicales. Venice, 1493.
Sententia in tractatum formalitatum scotistarum. Venice, 1493.
Quaestio de animarum humanarum plurificatione. Venice, 1498.
Quaestio super articulos impositos domino Gabrieli sacerdoti. Venice, 1502.
Quaestio de efficientia primi principii quod est Deus et de eius infinitate intensiva.
   Venice, 1513.
De adulto non baptizato. Venice, 1514.

STUDIES

Brotto, G., and G. Zonta. *La facoltà teologica dell'Università di Padova.* Padua, 1922.
   Pp. 203–7.
Nardi, B. *Saggi sull'aristotelismo padovano dal secolo XIV al XVI.* Florence, 1958.
   See the index.
Poppi, A. "Lo scotista padovano Antonio Trombetta (1436–1517)." *Il Santo* 2 (1962)
   349–67.
_____. "L'antiaverroismo nella scolastica padovana del secolo XV." *Studia patavina*
   11 (1964) 102–24.
Di Napoli, G. *L'immortalità dell'anima nel Rinascimento.* Turin, 1963. See the index.
Poppi, A. *Causalità e infinità nella scuola padovana dal 1480 al 1513.* Padua, 1966.
   See the index.
Dionisotti, C. "Resoconto di una ricerca interrotta." *Annali della Scuola Normale
   Superiore di Pisa,* Ser. 2, 37 (1968) 259–69.
Mahoney, E. P. "Antonio Trombetta and Agostino Nifo on Averroes and Intelligible
   Species. A Philosophical Dispute at the University of Padua." *Storia e cultura al
   Santo di Padova fra il XIII e il XX secolo.* Vicenza, 1976. Pp. 485–538.
Bordin, A. "Profilo storico-spirituale della communità del Santo." Ibid., pp. 15–115;
   see 25, 42, 46, 49, 68, 70–71, 74, 77.
Rossetti, L. "Francescani del Santo docenti all'Università di Padova." Ibid., pp.
   169–207; see 180.
Marangon, P. "Lo studio di Aristotele nel convento del Santo (sec. XIII–XV)." Ibid.,
   pp. 209–44; see 214 and 220.
Poppi, A. "La tradizione biblica al Santo." Ibid., pp. 369–413; see 396–97.
Scapin, P. "La metafisica scotista a Padova dal XV al XVIII secolo." Ibid., 485–538;
   see 485–88 and 501–9.
Poppi, A. "La teologia nell' università e nelle scuole." *Storia della cultura veneta. Dal
   primo Quattrocento al Concilio di Trento* III. Vicenza, 1981. Pp. 1–33; see 17 and
   19–21.

Francis Licheto (Lichitto) (Brescia ?–Buda, 1520)

EDITIONS

Super primum Sententiarym clarissima comentaria. Naples, 1512.
Comentaria super secundum Sententiarum et super Quaestiones Quodlibetales. Salò, 1517.
Comentaria super primum et tertium Sententiarum. Brescia, 1518. The commentaries were reprinted together in Paris, 1519–20; Venice, 1520; Venice, 1589.

STUDIES

d''Alençon, E. "Lychet, François." *DTC* 9 (Paris, 1926). Cols. 1357–59.
Berengo Morte, A. "Fra' Francesco Lichetto e una scuola scotista nell'Isola di Garda." *Le Venezie francescane* 2 (1933) 123–25.
Di Napoli, G. *L'immortalità dell'anima nel Rinascimento.* Turin, 1963. Pp. 194 and 266.
Rulang, H. "Unterwegs zu Bañez und Molina. Lychetus und seine Diskussion mit Cajetanus über das göttliche Vorherwissen und Mitwirken." *TheolJb* 8 (1965) 364–89.

Bernardine of Siena (Bernardino degli Albizzeschi) (Massa Maritima, 1380–L'Aquila, 1444)

EDITIONS

Opera latina. Venice, 1591; Paris, 1635; Lyons, 1650; Venice, 1745. Critical edition: *Opera omnia* (9 vols. Quaracchi, 1950–65), and see D. Pacetti, *De sancti Bernardini Senensis operibua. Ratio criticae editionis* (Quaracchi, 1947).
Opere in lingua volgare. Ed. D. Pacetti. Florence, 1938. But see also *Le prediche volgari di S. Bernardino da Siena dette nella Piazza del Campo l'anno MCCCXXVII [sic!] ora primamente edite.* Ed. L. Bianchi. 3 vols. Siena, 1980–88. Reprinted in *Le prediche volgari.* Ed. P. Bargellini. Milan, 1936.
Quaresimale del 1424. Ed. C. Cannarozzi. 2 vols. Pistoia, 1934.
Quaresimale del 1425. Ed. C. Cannarozzi. 3 vols. Pistoia, 1940.

BIBLIOGRAPHIES

Facchinetti, V. "S. Bernardino da Siena." *Aevum* 5 (1931) 319–81.
Bertagna, M. "Rassegna bibliografica." *Bollettino di studi bernardiniani* 10 (1944–50) 175–204.
Schmidt, H. "Bernardin-Literatur, 1939–1949." *Franziskanische Studien* 32 (1950) 308–418.
Capezzali, W. "Rassegna di bibliografia bernardiniana nel VI centenario della nascita di s. Bernardino da Siena." *Bulletino della Deputazione abruzzese di storia patria* 70 (1980, but 1982) 201–25.

STUDIES

Thaureau-Dangin, P. *Un prédicateur populaire de l'Ialie de la Renaissance: saint Bernardin de Sienne (1380–1444)*. Paris, 1896.

Hefele, K. *Der hl. Bernardin von Siena und die franziskanische Wanderpredigt in Italien während des XV. Jahrhunderts*. Freiburg i. B., 1912.

Ferrers Howel, A. *St. Bernardin of Siena*. London, 1913.

Sticco, M. *Il pensiero di S. Bernardino da Siena*. Milan, 1924.

Scaramuzzi, D. *La dottrina del beato Giovanni Duns Scoto nella predicazione di Bernardino da Siena*. Florence, 1930.

S. Bernardina da Siena, Saggi e ricerche publicate nel quinto centenario della morte. Milan, 1945.

Sticco, M. *Pensiero e poesia in S. Bernardino da Siena*. Milan, 1945.

Di Fonzo, L. "La mariologia di S. Bernardino da Siena." *Miscellanea Franciscana* 47 (1947) 3–102.

Bertagna, M. *Christologia S. Bernardini Senensis*. Rome, 1949.

Trutenberger, A. *S. Bernardino da Siena, Considerazioni sullo sviluppo dell'etica cristiana nel primo Rinascimento*. Bern, 1951.

Piana, C. "I processi di canonizzazione sulla vita di S. Bernardino da Siena." *AFH* 44 (1951) 483–535.

Elmer, V. *St. Bernardin of Siena, Orator of Reform*. New York, 1953.

Concetti, I. *De christianae conscientiae notione et formatione secundum S. Bernardinum Senensem*. Rome, 1959.

Rinaldi, G. *L'attività commerciale nel pensiero di S. Bernardino da Siena*. Rome, 1959.

Pacetti, D. "L'*Expositio super Apocalypsim* di Matthia da Svezia." *AFH* 54 (1961) 273–302.

————. "Le postille autografe sopra l'Apocalisse di S. Bernardino da Siena recentemente scoperte nella Biblioteca Nazionale di Napoli." Ibid., 59 (1963) 40–70.

Korosak, B. "Bernardino da Siena." *BibSanct* 2 (Rome, 1963). Cols. 1294–1321.

Manselli, R. "Bernardino da Siena." *DBI* 9 (Rome, 1967) 215–26.

Roover, R. de. *San Bernardino da Siena and Sant'Antonino of Florence: The Two Great Economic Thinkers of the Middle Ages*. Boston, 1967.

Fioravanti Melli, G. "Bernardino da Siena. I quaresimali fiorentini del 1424–1425." *La rassegna delle letteratura italiana* 77 (1973) 565–84.

Arasse, D. "Iconographie et union spirituelle: la tablette de Saint Bernardin de Sienne." *Revue d'histoire de la spiritualité* 50 (1974) 433–56.

————. "*Fervebat pietate populus:* art, dévotion et société autour de la glorification de Saint Bernardin de Sienne." *Mélanges de l'École Française de Rome, Moyen âge, temps modernes* 89 (1976) 189–263.

Batazzi, F. "Le stimmate de S. Francesco nell'insegnamento di un grande maestro, S. Bernardino da Siena." *Studi francescani* 71 (1974) 177–97.

Bernardino predicatore nella società del suo tempo. Atti del XVI Convegno del Centro di studi sulla spiritualità medioevale (Todi, 9–12 ottobre 1975). Todi, 1976.

Delcorno, C. "L'*ars praedicandi* di Bernardino da Siena." *Lettere italiane* 32 (1980) 441–75.

Guidetti, A. "Le qualità morali dell'uomo politico in una predica popolare di S.

Bernardino da Siena." *La Civiltà Cattolica* 131 (1980) 236–48.

Arasse, D. "Andrea Biglia contre Saint Bernardin de Sienne. L'Humanisme et la fonction de l'image religieuse." *Acta Conventus neolatini Turonensis*. IIIᵉ Congrès international d'études néo-latines (Tours, Université Fr. Rabelais, 6–10 septembre 1976). Ed. J.-C. Margolin. De Pétrarque à Descartes 38. 2 vols. Paris, 1980. I, 413–37.

Vassallo, F. S. *Risposta dell'uomo a Dio. Studio di una teologia dinamica delle ispirazioni secondo S. Bernardino da Siena*. Naples, 1980.

Cenci, C. "Il Commento al vangelo di Luca di fra' Costantino da Orvieto O.P. fonte di S. Bernardino da Siena." *AFH* 74 (1981) 103–45.

Montanile, M. "S. Bernardino da Siena nel VI centenario della nascita (1380–1980)." *Cultura e scuola* 20 (1981) 252–57.

Rusconi, R. "Apocalittica ed ecatologia nella predicazione di Bernardino da Siena." *Studi medievali*, Ser. 3, 22 (1981) 85–128.

Atti del Convegno storico bernardiniano, in occasione del sesto centenario dalla nascita di S. Bernardino da Siena (L'Aquila, 7–8–9 maggio 1980). Teramo, 1982.

Atti del Simposio internazionale cateriniano-bernardiniano (Siena, 17–20 aprile 1980). Ed. D. Maffei and P. Nardi. Siena, 1982.

Bullettino della Deputazione abruzzese di storia patria 70 (1980, but 1982). A volume commemorating the sixth centenary of Bernardino's birth.

Bronzini, G. B. "La predicazione di Bernardino da Siena fra scrittura e oralità." *RSLR* 18 (182) 169–99.

Nicolosi, S. "Tensione escatologica e valori terreni in s. Bernardino da Siena." *Aquinas* 25 (1982) 118–42.

Origo, I. *Bernardino da Siena e il suo tempo*. Milan, 1982.

Jansen, P. "Un exemple de sainteté thaumaturgqique à la fin du Moyen Age. Les miracles de Saint Bernardin de Sienne." *Mélanges de l'École française de Rome. Moyen âge, temps modernes* 96 (1984) 129–51.

S. Bernardino da Sienna predicatore e pellegrino. Atti del Convegno Nazionale di Studi bernardiniani (Maiori, 20–22 giugno 1980). Ed. F. d'Episcopo. Galatina, 1985.

Mansolli, R. "Bernardina da Siena." *Dizionario critico della letteratura italiana*. Turin, 1986². Pp. 287–90.

Delcorno, C. "La diffrazione del testo omiletico. Osservazioni sulle doppie *reportationes* delle prediche bernardiniane." *Lettere italiane* 38 (1986) 455–77. Also in *Medioevo e Rinascimento* 3 (1989) 241–60.

Zanfarana, Z. *Da Gregorio VII a Bernardino da Siena* Perugia-Florence, 1987. See the index.

Szabó, T. "Un gioiello bernardiniano: il trattato *De vita christiana*. Studio critico sul testo autentico e definitivo." *Bonaventuriana. Miscellanea in onore Jacques Guy Bougerol O.F.M.* Ed. D. de Asis Chavero Blanco. 2 vols. Bibliotheca Pontificii Athenaei Antoniani 27–28. Rome, 1988. II, 729–62.

Guidi, R. L. "Columbini, Bernardino da Siena, Savonarola: Uomini e simulacri. II. Bernardino da Siena." *Benedictina* 36 (1989) 105–63.

Elm, K. "Tod, Todesbewältigung und Endzeit bei Bernhardin von Siena." *Conciliarismo, Stati nazionali, inizi dell'Umanesimo*. Atti del XXV Convegnmo storico inernazionale (Todi, 9–12 ottobre 1988). Spoleto, 1990. Pp. 79–96.

Zimdars-Swarts, S. L. "Joachimite Themes in the Sermons of St. Bernardino of Siena: Assessing the Stigmata of St. Francis." *Il Profetismo gioachimita tra Quattrocento e Cinquecento.* Atti del III Congresso Internazionale di Studi Gioachimiti (S. Giovanni in Fiore, 17–20 settembre 1989). Ed. G. L. Potestà. Pp. 47–59.

Albert of Sarteano (Albert Berdini) (Sarteano, 1385–Milan, 1450)

EDITIONS

Opera omnia. Ed. F. Harold. Rome, 1688.

STUDIES

Sabbadini, R. *La scuola e gli studi di Guarino Guarini Veronese.* Catania, 1896. Pp. 18, 139–43.

Neri, B. *La vita e i tempi di Alberto di Sarteano.* Quaracchi, 1902.

Cerulli, E. "L'Etiopia del secolo XV in nuovi documenti storici." *Africa italiana* 51 (1933) 58–80.

————. "Eugenio IV e gli Etiopi al Concilio di Firenze nel 1141." *Rendiconti della R. Accademia dei Lincei. Classe di scienze morali,* Ser. 6, 9 (1933) 346–68.

Biccellari, F. "Un francescano umanista. Il beato Alberto di S. Francesco a Fiesole." *Studi francescani* 10 (1938) 346–48.

Bughetti, B. "L'Archivio di S. Francesco a Fiesole." Ibid., pp. 60–86.

Biccellari, F. "Missioni del beato Alberto da Sarteano in Oriente per l'unione della Chiesa greca e il ristabilimento dell'Osservanza dell'Ordine francescano." Ibid., pp. 159–73.

Hofmann, G. "Copten und Aethiopien auf den Konzil von Florenz." *OCP* 8 (1942) 5–39.

Epistolae pontificiae ad Concilium Florentinum spectantes. Rome, 1940–46. See the index.

Dopcumenta Concilii florentini de unione Orientalium III. *De unione coptorum, Syrorum, Chaldaeorum Maronitarumque (4 feb. 1442–7 aug. 1445).* Textus et Documenta, Series theologica 22. Rome, 1951. See the index.

Pratesi, R. "Nuovi documenti sul b. Alberto da Sarteano (+ 1450)." *AFH* 53 (1960) 78–100.

Cerulli, E. "Berdini, Alberto (Alberto da Sarteano)." *DBI* 8 (Rome, 1966) 800–4.

James of the Marches (Dominic Gangali) (Monteprandone, 1394–Naples, 1476)

WORKS

Domenicale.
Quadragesimale.
Dialogus contra fraticellos.
Tractatus de sanguine Christi.

Sermones de festis, de sanctis.
Sermones praedicabiles.
Libri praedicationum.
Campus florum.

All these are from the author's library and preserved in the Communal Archive of Monteprandone; but listeners' notes *(reportationes)* of his sermons are preserved in various libraries.

EDITIONS

Dialogus contra fraticellos. Addita versione itala saeculi XV. Ed. D. Lasic. Falconara Marittima, 1975.
De sanguine Christi. Ed. D. Lasic. Falconara Marittima, 1976.
Sermones diminicales. Ed. R. Lioi. 3 vols. Falconara Marittima, 1978.

BIBLIOGRAPHIES

Somigli, T. *AFH* 17 (1924) 396–97.
Caselli, G. *Studi su S. Giacomo della Marca.* 2 vols. Ascoli Piceno-Offida, 1926. See vol. I.
Sgattoni, I. *Bolletino di studi bernardiniani* 4 (1939) 191–213.
Lioi, R. *Studi francescani* 3–4 (1944) 183–89.

STUDIES

Crivellucci, A. *I codici della libraria raccolta da Giacomo della Marca nel convento di. S. Maria delle Grazie presso Monteprandone.* Livorno, 1889.
Oliger, L. "De dialogo contra Fraticellos Sancti Jacobi de Marchia." *AFH* 4 (1911) 3–23.
Caselli, G. *Studi su S. Giacomo della Marca.* 2 vols. Ascoli Piceno-Offida, 1926.
Pacetti, D. "I *sermones dominicales* di S. Giacomo della Marca, in un codice autografo del convento francescano di Falconara." *Collectanea Franciscana* 11 (1941) 7–34 and 185–222.
_____. "Le prediche autografe di S. Giacomo della Marca." *AFH* 35 (1942) 296–327; 36 (1943) 75–97.
_____. "L'importanza dei *Sermones* di S. Giacomo della Marca." *Studi francescani* 14 (1942) 125–68.
Pagnani, G. "Alcuni codici della libreria di S. Giacomo della Marca recentemente scoperti." *AFH* 45 (1952) 171–92; 48 (1955) 131–46.
Pacetti, D. "I sermoni quaresimali di S. Giacomo della Marca contenuti nel cod. 184 della Biblioteca Angelica." *AFH* 46 (1953) 303–40.
_____. "Predica in onore di S. Bernardino da Siena recitata da S. Giacomo della Marca a Padova nel 1460." *Le Venezie francescane* 20 (1953) 18–50.
Lioi, R. "I *Sermones quadragesimales* di S. Giacomo della Marca in un codice della Biblioteca comunale di Foligno." *Annali del Pontificio Istituto Superiore Santa Chiara* 10 (1960) 37–137.

_____. "Un gruppo di *Sermones dominicales* di S. Giacomo della Marca nel cod. V. H. 270 della Biblioteca Nazionale di Napoli." *Studi francescani* 58 (1961) 3–61.

_____. "Il *Directorium juris* del francescano Pietro Quesnel nel sermoni domenicani di S. Giacomo della Marca." Ibid., 59 (1962) 213–69.

_____. "Alcuni aspetti della predicazione di S. Giacomo della Marca." *Annali del Pontificio Istituto Superiore Santa Chiara* 12 (1962) 99–132.

Candela, S. *San Giacomo della Marca.* Naples, 1962.

Lioi, R. "La devozione del nome di Gesù nella predicazione di S. Giacomo della Marca." *Cenacolo serafico* 1 (1963) 59–81.

_____. "Giacomo della Marca studioso di Dante." *Studi francescani* 61 (1964) 26–69.

_____. Giacomo della Marca." *BibSanct* 6 (Rome, 1965). Cols. 388–96.

Lasic, S. "Sermones S. Jacobi de Marchia in codd. Vat. lat. 778 et 7462 asservati." *AFH* 63 (1970) 475–565.

"Atti del I Convegno di Studi celebrato a Falconara Marittima il 28 dicembre 1967 e dedicato a problemi storiografici di S. Giacomo della Marca." *Picenum seraphicum* 6 (1969–70) 9–162.

Delcorno, C. "Due prediche volgari di Jacopo della Marca recitate a Padova nel 1460." *Atti dell'Istituto Veneto di Scienze, Lettere e Arti.* Cl. di scienza morali, letterarie e artistiche. 132 (1969–70) 135–205.

Dupré Theseider, E. "Sul dialogo contra i fraticelli di S. Giacomo della Marca." *Miscellanea G. G. Meersseman.* Padua, 1970. Pp. 577–611.

"Atti del II Convegno di studi celebrato a Falconara Marittima e dedicato a bibliografia e iconografia di S. Giacomo della Marca." *Picenum seraphicum* 7 (1970) 7–252.

"Atti del III Convegno di studi celebrato a Loreto il 28 dicembre 1970 e dedicato alla *libraria* di S. Giacomo della Marca." Ibid., 8 (1971) 7–219.

Candela, S. *S. Giacomo della Marca e Santa Maria la Nuova di Napoli.* Naples, 1972.

D'Andrea, F. G. *Il fondo di S. Giacomo della Marca nell'Archivio della Vice Postulazione della Provincia francescana del SS. Cuore di Gesù.* Naples, 1973.

Lasic, D. *De vita et operibus S. Jacobi de Marchia nel V centenario della morte.* Naples, 1976.

"Atti del l'VIII convegno di studi celebrato in Ascoli e Monteprandone il 1–2 maggio 1976 e dedicato a S. Giacomo e le Marche." *Picenum seraphicum* 13 (1976).

Gallucci, A. "Frate Giacomo della Marca bibliofilo e un episodio liibrario del 1450." *Miscellanea Augusto Campana.* Ed. R. Avesani and others. Medioevo e umanesimo 44–45. Padua, 1981. Pp. 313–54.

John of Capistrano (Capistrano, 1386–Hok, 1436)

EDITIONS

Most of his works are unpublished. Among them mention may be made of *Trattato de cupidtate, Speculum conscientiae, De papae et concilii auctoritate,* and *De iudicio universali.* But see A. Chiappini, *La produzione letteraria di S. Giovanni di Capistrano* (Gubbio, 1927), and the following:

Epistulae quaedam ineditae. Ed. S. Gaddoni. *AFH* 4 (1911) 97–121.

Sermo S. Johannis de Capistrano ineditus de S. Bernardino Senense. Ibid., 6 (1913) 76–90.

Bihl, M. "Duae epistolae S. Johannis a Capistrano altera ad Laodislaum regem, altera de victoria Belgradensi (1453–1456)." Ibid., 19 (1926) 63–75.

Lazzeri, S. "De epistola quadam inedita S. Johannis a Capistrano circa communionem paschalem." Ibid., 21 (1928) 269–84.

STUDIES

Voight, G. "Johannes von Capistrano, ein Heiliger der fünfzehnten Jahrhunderts." *Historische Zeitschrift von Sybel* 10 (1883) 398–475.

Kerval, L. *Saint Jean de Capistran, son siècle et son influence.* Bordeaux-Paris, 1887.

Jacob, E. *Johannes von Capistran. Das Leben und Wirken.* 3 vols. Breslau, 2903–14.

Festia, G. B. "Cinque lettere intorno alla vita ed alla morte di S. Giovanni da Capistrano." *Bollettino della R. Deputazione abruzzese di storia patria* 2 (1911) 1–58.

Masci, A. *Vita di S. Giovanni da Capestrano.* Naples, 1914.

Bölcskey. *Capestranoi Szent Jànnos Elète Es Kora.* 3 vols. Ezekésferhérvár, 1922–24.

Hofer, J. *Johannes von Capestrano.* Innsbruck, 1936.

"S. Giovanni da Capistrano nel V centenario della morte (1956)." *Bollettino della R. Deputazione abruzzese di storia patria.* Special vol. L'Aquila, 1956. Also in *Studi francescane* 53, nos. 3–4 (1956).

Nicolini, U. "S. Giovanni da Capestrano studente e giudice a Perugia." *AFH* 53 (1960) 39–77.

Luszczkil. *De sermonibus S. Johannis a Capistrano.* Rome, 1961.

Chiappini, A. "Giovanni da Capestrano." *BibSanct* 6 (Rome, 1965). Cols. 646–54.

Fochesato, L. *L'apostolo dell'Europa: S. Giovanni da Capestrano.* Grottaferrata, 1964.

Bonmann, O. "Die Persönlichkeit des Hl. Johannes Kapistran (1384–1845)." *Franciscan Studies* 43, no. 21 (1983) 205–17.

Cocci, N. *La devozione del Preziosissimo Sangue di nostro Signore Gesù Cristo: studio storico-teologico a proposito di un trattato inedito di S. Giovanni da Capestrano.* Albano Laziale, 1986. With edition of the work.

Muzzarelli, M. "*Contra mundanas vanitates et pompas.* Aspetti della lotta contro il lusso nell'Italia del XV secolo." *RSCI* 40 (1986) 371–90.

Zavalloni, R. "San Giovanni di Capestrano e la 'cultura francescana della pace.'" *Antonianum* 61 (1986) 520–39.

Murawiech, W. "Jan z Kapistrano. Kaznodzieja podrózujacy i reformator [John of Capistrano, Itinerant Preacher and Reformer]." *Studia Franciszkanski* 3 (1988) 273–94.

De Sandre Gasparini, G. "La parola e le opere. La predicazione di S. Giovanni da Capestrano a Verona." *Le Venezie francescane*, N.S. 6/1 (1989) 101–30. = Atti del II Convegno internazionale di studi francescani (Padova, 26–28 marzo 1987).

D'Elia, F. "Echi del profetismo gioachimita in Giovanni da Capestrano." *Il profetismo gioachimita tra Quattrocento e Cinquecento.* Atti del III Congresso Internazionale di Studi Gioachimiti (S. Giovanni in Fiore, 17–20 settembre 1989). Ed. G. L. Potestà. Genoa, 1991. Pp. 37–45.

Jerome Savonarola (Ferrara, 1452–Florence, 1498)

EDITIONS

(a) Philosophical Works
Compendium logicae. Pescia, 1492; Florence, 1497.
Compendium totius philosophiae tam naturalis quam moralis. Venice, 1534.
Apologeticus de ratione poeticae artis. Pescia, 1492; Venice, 1513.
Trattato contro li astrologi. Florence, after 1497; Venice, 1513.
All the preceding have now been critically edited in the National Edition: *Scritti filosofici.* Ed. G. C. Garfagnini and E. Garin. 2 vols. Rome, 1982–88.
Trattato circa il reggimento di Firenze. Florence, 1498. In the National Edition: *Prediche sopra Aggeo. Con il Trattato circa il reggimento e governo della città di Firenze.* Ed. L. Firpo. Rome, 1965.

(b) Theological Works
Dialogus cui titolus Solatium itineris mei nunc primum impressus. Venice, 1535, and in 1537 together with the *Expositione sopra il salmo "Miserere Mei Deus."* National Edition: ed. G. Cattin, Rome, 1978.
Compendio di rivelazione. Florence, 1495. Latin text: Florence, 1495; Paris, 1496; Ulm, 1496. National Edition: ed. A. Crucitti. Rome, 1974.
De simplicitate christianae vitae libri. Florence, 1496. National Edition: ed. M. Ferrara. Rome, 1961.
Triumphus crucis. Florence, 1497. National Edition: ed. M. Ferrara. Rome, 1961. Ed. A. Crucitti. Rome, 1974.
De veritate prophetica dyalogus. Florence, 1498; Venice, 1507. National Edition: together with the *Compendio di rivelazione.*
Confessionale pro instructione confessorum. Brescia, 1492(?).
Introductorium confessionis, with the *Epistola de humilitate.* Florence, 1500.

(c) Spiritual Writings
Del dispregio del mondo. Florence, 1862. Critical ed. in R. Ridolfi. *Studi savonaroliani.* Florence, 1935. Pp. 19–34 and 235–38.
Libro della vita viduale. Florence, 1492 and 1492–93.
Trattato del sacramento e misteri della messa and *Regola a tutti li religiosi molto utile.* Florence, 1491. Latin version of the *Regula* together with the *Oratio vel psalmus "Diligam te Domine"* and with the *Trialogus super evangelio* of Antoninus of Florence, Venice, 1495.
Operetta dell'amore di Jesù Christo. Florence, 1492.
Trattato dell'umilità. Florence, 1492, 1492–94, 1495.
Trattato in defensione e commendatione della orazione mentale. Florence, ca. 1492.
Trattato ovvero sermone della orazione. Florence, 1492 (twice).
Expositione del Pater noster. Florence, 1494, 1495.
Operetta sopra i dieci camandamenti di Dio. Florence, 1495, 1496(?).
Expositio Psalmi LXXVIII "Qui regis Israel" per modum orationis. Florence, 1496.
Del discreto e ordinato modo di vivere in religione. In *Epistole a diversi.* Florence, 1497(?).

Declarazione del mistero della croce. Florence, 1497–98.

Dieci regole da osservare al tempo delle grandi tribolazioni. In *Epistole alle suore del Terz'Ordine di S. Domenico.* Florence, 1497(?).

Expositio graduum S. Bonaventurae. Florence, 1498.

Regola del ben vivere. Florence, 1498. Also in *Operette.* Florence, 1499.

Expositio in psalmum "Miserere mei Deus." Ferrara, 1498; Reggio, 1499.

Expositio in psalmum XXX "In te domine speravi." Milan, ca. 1499; Magdeburg, ca. 1500; Augsburg, 1500.

All these works are now in the National Edition: *Tutte le opere spirituali.* Ed. M. Ferrara. 2 vols. Rome, 1976.

(d) Sermons

Cattin, G. *Il primo Savonarola. Poesie e prediche inedite del codice Borromei.* Florence, 1973.

Sermoni sopra il principio della Cantica et altri luoghi delle Sacre Scritture. Florence, 1973.

Sermones in primam divi Johannis epistolam. Venice, 1536. In the vernacular: Venice, 1547. National Edition: ed. A. F. Verde, Rome, 1989.

Prediche sopra il Genesi. Prediche sopra il Salmo "Quam bonus." Venice, 1528 and 1539.

Sermones quadragesimales super archam Noe. Venice, 1536.

Prediche sopra Aggeo. Venice, 1544. National Edition: ed. L. Firpo. Rome, 1965.

Predica della rinnovazione della Chiesa fatta il 13 gennaio 1494 (in Florentine reckoning: 1495). Florence, ca. 1495.

Predica fatta a di giugno 1994. Florence, 1498(?).

Prediche sopra i Salmi. Bologna, 1515; Venice, 1515. National Edition: ed. V. Romano. 2 vols. Rome, 1974.

Prediche sopra Amos. Florence, 1496–97. Later: *Sunto e registro delle predette sopra Amos e Zacharia.* Florence, 1948. National Edition: ed. P. Ghiglieri. 3 vols. Rome, 1972.

Prediche sopra Ruth e Michea. Florence, ca. 1499.

Prediche dell'arte di ben morire. Florence, 1946. This and the preceding are in the National Edition: ed. V. Romano. 2 vols. Rome, 1962.

Prediche sopra Ezzechiele. Bologna, 1515.

Predica fatta il venerdì santo l'anno 1497. Siena, 1553.

Predica fatta la mattina dell'Ascensione. Florence, 1497. This and the preceding are in the National Edition: ed. R. Ridolfi. 2 vols. Rome, 1955.

Prediche sopra l'Esodo (raccolte da ser Lorenzo Violo). Florence, 1505–8.

Prediche for February 11, 18, and 25 *a il sabbato dopo la secunda domenica di Quaresima.* Florence, 1498 (in separate booklets).

Lezione ovvero sermone fatto a molti sacerdoti religiosi e secolari in S. Marco. Florence, 1498. This and the preceding are in the National Edition: ed. P. G. Ricci. 2 vols. Rome, 1956.

Sermone fatto a' suoi fratelli nella vigilia di Pasqua di Natale. Florence, 1498.

Sermo in domino confido; Sermono in passione Domini; Sermo habitus terrae Prati in refectorium Fratrum . . . qui dicitur Triumphus fidei; Si quis diligit me. This and the preceding are in the National Edition: *Scritti vari e rari.* Ed. A. F. Verde. In preparation.

(e) Apologetic Writings

Proemium in apologeticum Fratrum Copngregationis S. Marci de Florentia. Florence, 1497.

Subscritione di fra Hieronimo sotto una lettera delli suoi figli che stanno a Prato. Florence, 1498. In R. Ridolfi. "Due documenti savonaroliani sopra la prova del fuoco." *La bibliofilia* 38 (1936) 234–42.

Esortazione fatta al popolo. . . . In *Prediche sopra l'esodo.* Florence, 1505–8, and in *Espozizione e prediche sopra l'Esodo.* Venice, 1515.

All the apologetic writings are collected in the National Edition: ed. V. Romano and A. F. Verde. Rome, 1984.

(f) Letters

Le lettere di Girolamo Savonarola. Ed. R. Ridolfi. Florence, 1936. Then in idem. *Studi savonaroliani.* Florence, 1935. And in idem. *Nuovi contributi.* Florence, 1936.

Polizzotto, L. "Una lettera inedita di Savonarola." *Rinascimento,* Ser. 2, 24 (1984) 181–89.

Lettere. Ed. R. Ridolfi and V. Romano. National Edition: Rome, 1984.

(g) Poetic Compositions

Poesie. Ed. M. Martelli. National Edition: Rome, 1986.

Further information on the editions of Savonarola's works and the codices containing them is given in A. F. Verde, "Savonarole (Jérôme)." *DSp* 14 (Paris, 1989). Cols. 370–87, and in the critical notes in the various volumes of the National Edition.

BIBLIOGRAPHIES

Ridolfi, R. *Bibliografia delle opere di Savolarola.* Florence, 1939.

Giovannuzzi, L. *Contributo alla bibliografia delle opere di Savonarola. Edizioni dei secoli XV e XVI.* Florence, 1935.

Avenzi, G. "La bibliografia savonaroliana. Saggio di un catalogo analitico (1719–1953)." *La bibliofilia* 55 (1953) 59–77.

Ferrara, M. *Nuova bibliografia savonaroliana.* Vaduz, 1981.

Schutte, A. J. *Printed Italian Vernacular Books 1465–1550: A Finding List.* Geneva, 1983. Pp. 329–52.

STUDIES

Bayonne, E. C. *Études sur Jérôme Savonarole d'après de nouveaux documents.* Paris, 1879.

Gherardi, A. *Nuovi documenti e studi intorno a Girolamo Savonarola.* Florence, 1887². Reprinted: Florence, 1972.

Lucas, H. *Fra Girolamo Savonarola. A Biographic Study.* London, 1895.

Villari, P. *La storia di fra' Girolamo Savonarola e de'suoi tempi.* 2 vols. Florence, 1898², 1930³.

Villari, P., and E. Casanova. *Scelta di prediche di fra' Girolamo Savonarola. Con nuovi documenti intorno alla sua vita.* Florence, 1898.

Schnitzer, J. *Quellen und Forschungen zur Geschichte Savonarolas.* 4 vols. Munich-Leipzig, 1902–10.

_____. *Savonarola Erzieher und Savonarola als Erzieher.* Berlin, 1913.

_____. *Savonarola im Streite mit seinem Orden and und seinem Kloster.* Munich, 1914.

_____. *Savonarola.* 2 vols. Munich, 1023–24.

_____. *Peter Delfin General des Camaldulensenordens (1444–1525). Ein Beitrag zur Geschichte der Kirchenreform, Alexander VI, und Savonarola.* Munich, 1926.

Ridolfi, R. *Studi savonaroliani.* Florence, 1935.

_____. *Opuscoli di storia letteraria e di erudizione.* Florence, 1942.

_____. "I processi di Savonarola." *La bibliofilia* 46 (1944) 3–41.

Semenkovsky-Kuril, N. *Savonarola Revolutionär, Ketzer oder Prophet?* Oltem, 1950.

Soranzo, G. *Il tempo di Alessandro VI Papa e di fra' Girolamo Savonarola.* Milan, 1950.

Ridolfi, R. *Vita di Girolamo Savonarola.* Rome, 1952; Florence, 1981[2].

Girardi, E. N. "L'*Apologetico* di Savonarola e il problema di une filosofia cristiana." *RivFilNeo* 45 (1952) 412–31.

Prete, S. "Savonarola apologeta: il *Triumphus crucis.*" *Studia Picena* 21 (1952) 1–51.

Taurisano, I. "Fra' Girolamo Savonarola (da Alessandro VI a Paolo VI)." *La bibliofilia* 55 (1953) 14–53.

Kruitwagen, B. "Le *Speculum exemplorum* (Deventer, 1481) dans les mains de Savonarole à Brescia." *Miscellanea Giovanni Mercati* IV. Vatican City, 1956. Pp. 209–44.

Klein, B. *Le procès de Savonarole.* Paris, 1957.

Gieraths, G. *Savonarola, Ketzer oder Heiliger.* Freiburg i. B., 1961.

Colosio, I. "La spiritualità di fra' Girolamo Savonarola studiata specialmente nelle sue prediche sopra Aggeo." *Rivista di ascetica e mistica* 11 (1966) 352–77.

Weinstein, D. *Savonarola and Florence. Prophecy and Patriotism in the Renaissance.* Princeton, 1968.

De Maio, R. *Savonarola e la curia romana.* Rome, 1969.

Gusberti, E. "Il Savonarola del Guicciardini." *Nuova Rivista Storica* 55 (1971) 21–89.

Ferrara, M. "Indagini savaroroliane." *MemDom,* N.S. 3 (1972) 127–45.

Crucitti, A. "Il *Compendium revelationum* del Savonarola: testo italiano e testo latino." *La bibliofilia* 74 (1972) 165–77.

Preiser, W. "Girolamo Savonarola als Staatsmann und politischer Denker." *Mitteilungen des Österreischen Staatsarchive* 25 (1972) 549–64.

Weinstein, D. "Macchiavelli and Savonarola." *Studies on Macchiavelli.* Florence, 1972. Pp. 251–64.

Chimienti, M. "La dottrina spirituale di Savonarola." *Théorie et pratiques politiques à la Renaissance.* XVIIIe Colloque international de Tours. Paris, 1977. Pp. 1–13.

Scaltriti, G. A. *L'ultimo Savonarola. Esame giuridico-teologico del carteggio (brevi e lettere) intercorso tra papa Alessandro VI e il frate Girolamo Savonarola.* Rome, 1976.

Steinberg, R. M. *Fra Girolamo Savonarola, Florentine Art, and Renaissance Historiography.* Athens, 1977.

Trexler, R. C. "Lorenzo de'Medici and Savonarola." *Renaissance Quarterly* 19 (1978) 111–23.

Uerga, A. *Savonarola, reformador y profeta.* Madrid, 1978.

Mazzone, U. *"El buon governo. Un progetto di rfiforma generale nella Firenze savonaroliana.* Florence, 1978.

Piper, E. *Savonarola: Umbriefe eines Politikers und Puritaners in Florenz der Medici.* Berlin, 1979.

Di Agresti, D. *Sviluppi del riforma monastica savonaroliana.* Florence, 1980.

Ridolfi, R. "Savonarola e gli studi." *La bibliofilia* 82 (1980) 183–87.

_____. "Il Savonarola e il Magnifico." Ibid., 83 (1981) 71–78.

Scaltriti, G. A. "La vita religiosa nel pensiero di Girolamo Savonarola." *Renovatio* 16 (1981) 183–87.

Zorzi Pugliese, O. "A Last Testimony by Savonarola and His Companions." *Renaissance Quarterly* 34 (1981) 1–10.

Firpo, M., and P. Simoncelli. "I processi inquisitoriali contro Savonarola (1558) e Carnesecchi (1566–1567): una proposta d'interpretazione." *Rivista di storia e letteratura religiosa* 18 (1982) 200–52.

Verde, A. F. "La Congregazione di S. Marco, il reale della predicazione savonaroliana." *MemDom,* N.S. 14 (1983) 151–237.

_____. "Dallo scrittoio savonaroliano di S. Marco." Ibid., 342–45.

Kent, F. W. "A Proposal by Savonarola for the Self-Reform of Florentine Women (March 1496)." Ibid., 335–41.

Hugede, N. *Savonarole et les Florentins.* Florence, 1984.

Verde, A. F. "Una miscellanea savonaroliana ritrovata." *La bibliofilia* 86 (1984) 68–72.

Gualtieri. A. "The Poetic of Asceticism: Savonarola's Poetry in the Light of His Theory of Art." *RSLR* 21 (1985) 77–113.

Fuhr, A. *Macchiavelli und Savonarola: Politische Rationalität und politische Prophetie.* Frankfurt a. M.-Bern-New York, 1985.

Meltzoff, S. *Botticelli, Signorelli, and Savonarola. "Theologia poetica" and Painting from Boccaccio to Politiziano.* Florence, 1987.

Verde, A. F. "Ser Lorenzo Violi 'secretario' di Savonarola." *MemDom,* N. S. 18 (1987) 381–98.

Garfagnini, G. C. "Savonarola e la profezia: tra mito e storia." *Studi medievali* 29 (1988) 173–201.

Giaconi, E. "Il volgarizzamento toscano dei *Sermoni sopra la prima lettera di S. Giovanni* di frate Girolamo Savonarola." *Immagine e parola. Retorica filologica, Retorica predicatoria: Valle e Savonarola.* Pistoia, 1988. Pp. 111–89. = *MemDom* 19 (1988).

Verde, A. F. "Le lezioni e i sermoni sull'*Apocalisse* di Girolamo Savonarola (1490). *Nova dicere et novo modo.*" Ibid., 5–109.

Garfagnini, G. C. "Ser Lorenzo Violi e le prediche del Savonarola." *Medioevo e Rinascimento* 3 (1989) 261–85.

Polizotto, L. "*Del Arte del ben morire.* The Piagnone Way of Death 1494–1545." *I Tatti Studies* 3 (1989) 27–87.

Weinstein, D. "Savonarola—Preacher and Patriot." *History Today* 39, no. 11 (1989) 30–36.

_____. "*The Art of Dying Well* and Popular Piety in the Preaching and Thought of Girolamo Savonarola." *Life and Death in Fifteenth-Century Florence.* Ed. M. Tetel and others. Duke Monographs in Medieval and Renaissance Studies 10. Durham, 1989. Pp. 88–104 and 213–16.

Guidi, R. L. "Columbini, Bernardino da Siena, Savonarola: Uomini e simulacri. III. Girolamo Savonarola." *Benedictina* 36 (1989) 349–439.

Leinardi, C. "Jérôme Savonarole et le statut de la prophétie dans l'Église." *Mélanges de l'École française de Rome. Moyen âge, temps modernes* 102 (1990) 589–96. = *Les textes prophétiques et le prophétie en Occident (XIIe–XVIe s.).* Table Ronde.

Morisi Guerra A. "Sulle orme di Savonarola: la riscoperta degli apologisti greci anti-pagani." *RSCI* 45, no. 1 (1991) 89–109.

Weinstein, D. "Hagiography, Demonology, Biography: Savonarola Studies Today." *Journal of Modern History* 63 (1991) 483–503.

Roderick Sánchez de Arévalo (Segovia, 1404–Rome, 1470)

EDITIONS

De arte, disciplina et modo alendi et erudiendi filios. Ed. in H. Keniston. "A Fifteenth-Century Treatise on Education." *Bulletin hispanique* 32 (1930) 193–217. The text: 204–17.

Vergel de los principes. Ed. F. de Uhagón. Madrid, 1900. Ed. M. Penna. Madrid, 1959.

Liber de paupertate Christi et apostolorum. Partially ed. in Toni (see Studies).

Speculum vitae humanae. Rome, 1468. Many later editions and translations.

Tractatus ad quendam venerandum religiosum cartusianum. Unpublished.

STUDIES

Butler, G. C. *Studies in Statecraft: Bishop Roderick and Renaissance Pacifism.* Cambridge, 1920.

López de Toro, J. "El primero tratado de pedagogía en España." *Boletín de la Universidad de Granada* 5 (1933) 259–76; 6 (1934) 153–75, 361–87.

Toni, T. "La realeza de Jesu Cristo en un tratado inédito del siglo XV." *Estudios eclesiásticos* 13 (1934) 369–98.

————. "Don Rodrigo Sánchez de Arévalo y uno de sus manoscritos inéditos." *Razon y Fe* 105 (1934) 356–73, 507–18.

————. *Don Rodrigo Sánchez de Arévalo. Su personalidad y actividades. El tratado "De pace et bello."* Madrid, 1935. = *Anuario de la historia del Derecho españõl* 12 (1935) 97–360.

Jedin, H. "Sánchez de Arévalo und die Konzilsfrage unter Paul II." *HistJb* 73 (1953) 95–119.

García y García, A. "Un opúsculo inédito de Rodrigo Sánchez: *De libera et irrefragabili auctoritate Romani Pontificis.*" *Salmanticensis* 4 (1957) 474–502.

Trame, R. H. *Rodrigo Sánchez de Arévalo: Spanish Diplomat and Champion of the Papacy.* Washington, D.C., 1958.

Rodríguez, J. "Autores espirituales españoles en la Edad Media." *Repertorio de historia de las ciencias eclesiásticas in España* 1 (1967) 303–4. With bibliography.

Laboa, J. M. *Rodrigo Sánchez de Arévalo alcaide de Sant'Angelo.* Madrid, 1973.

Santiago-Otero, H. "Rodrigo Sánchez de Arévalo. Discurso a Pio II con motivo de la conquista de Gibraltar (1462)." *Rivista española de Teología* 37 (1977) 153–58.

Isbicki, T. "A New Copy of Rodrigo Sánchez de Arévalo's Commentary on the Bull *Ezechielis* of Pope Pius II." Ibid., 41 (1981) 465–67.

Muñoz Delgado, V. "Las artes mecánicas y liberales en Rodrigo Sánchez de Arévalo (1404–1470), obispo de Zamora." *Studia Zamorensia* 4 (1983) 35–61.

For other bibliographical references (and information on nontheological works and their editions) see chapter 5 of the present volume and L. López Santidrían, "Sánchez de Arévalo (Rodrigo)," *DSp* 14 (Paris, 1989). Cols. 301–3.

John of Torquemada (Valladolid, 1388–Rome, 1468)

Editions

Declarationes revelationum S. Birgittae. Nuremberg, 1521 (together with the *Revelations* of St. Bridget); Rome, 1606, 1628; Munich, 1680; and in G. D. Mansi, *Sacrorum Conciliorum nova et amplissima collectio* 30. Cols. 550–90.

Repetitiones super quibusdam propositionibus Augustini de Roma [= Favaroni]. In Mansi, cols. 979–1034.

Tractatus de sacramento Eucharistiae. Delft, ca. 1480; Dillingen, 1558; Lyons, 1578.

Tractatus de veritate Conceptionis beatissimae Virginis. Rome, 1547; Oxford, 1868; Brussels, 1966.

Flores Sententiarum divi Thomae Aquinatis de auctoritate Summi Pontificis. Lyons, 1496; Venice, 1562; Florence, 1715; Naples, 1718.

Responsio pro parte Latinorum ad libellum a Graecis in Concilio Florentino exhibitum de purgatorio igne. Ed. L. Petit and G. Hofmann. *Concilium Florentinum* A. VIII, 2. Rome, 1969. Pp. 35–56.

Sermones duo de Eucharistia in Concilio Florentini habiti. Ed. G. Hofmann. Ibid., B VI. Rome, 1955. Pp. 236–38.

Responsio contra errores Basiliensium super potestate papae et concilii. Venice, 1563; Louvain, 1688; in J. T. Rocaberti, *Bibliotheca maxima pontificia* 13 (Rome, 1698). Cols. 576–609; and in Mansi, 30B, cols. 1941–48.

Apparatus super Decretum Florentinum unionis Graecorum. Venice 1561; ed. E. Candal. *Concilium Florentinum.* B. II. Rome, 1942.

Contra decreta Concilii Constantiniensis. Venice, 1563; Mansi 30, cols. 550–90.

Tractatus contra Madianitas et Ismaelitas. Ed. N. López Martínez and V. Proñao Gil. Burgos, 1957.

Aurea Decretorum sive nova compilatio Decreti. Ed. J. Fontanini. Rome, 1726.

Summa de Ecclesia. Rome, 1498; Lyons, 1495 and 1496; Salamanca, 1560; Venice, 1561.

Expositio in Decretum Gratiani. 6 vols. Lyons, 1519; Venice, 1524; Rome, 1555.

Tractatus contra principales errores Mahumeti. Brussels, 1475–80; Paris, 1494 and after 1500; Rome, 1606.

Expositio brevis et utilis super toto Psalterio. Rome, 1470; Mainz, 1474.

Tractatus contra Manicheos. Ed. D. Kanber. *Croatia sacra* 3 (1932) 27–93; ed. N. López Martínez and V. Proñao Gil. Burgos, 1958.

Collationes super Evangelia de tempore et de sanctis. Cologne, 1478; Nuremberg, 1478; Paris, 1508, 1510.

Meditationes (or *Contemplationes*). Rome, 1467; reprinted: Wiesbaden, 1968.

Libellus contra impugnantes paupertatem Christi et apostolorum. Unpublished. For the manuscripts in which the published and unpublished works are preserved see Th. Käppeli, *Scriptores Ordinis Praedicatorum Medii Aevi* 3 (Rome, 1980) 24–42.

STUDIES

Haller, J. *Concilium Basileense. Studien und Dokumente* 1–4. Basel, 1896–1903. See the index.

Garrastachu, J. M. "Los manuscritos del Cardinal Torquemada en la Biblioteca Vaticana." *Ciencia tomista* 41 (1930) 188–217, 291–322.

Beltrán de Heredia, V. "Colecció de documentos inéditos para illustrar la vida del Cardinal Juan de Torquemada." *AFP* 7 (1937) 210–55.

G. Hofmann. "Due discorsi del legato pontificio Giovanni de Torquemada nella dieta di Norimberga e nel congresso di Magonza." *MiscHistPont* 2 (Rome, 1940) 9–30.

Jedin, H. "Juan de Torquemada und das Imperium," *AFP* 12 (1942) 247–78.

Creytens, R. "Raphaël de Parnazio OP, auteur du *De potestate papae et concilii generalis* faussement attribué à Jean de Torquemada." Ibid., 13 (1943) 108–37.

Furlani, S. "Giovanni de Torquemada e il suo trattato contro i Bogomili." *Ricerche religiose* 18 (1947) 164–77.

Donati, C. "Meditationes Johannis de Turrecremata." *Studi di bibliografía e di argomento romano in memoria di L. di Gregori*. Rome, 1949. Pp. 99–128.

Stockmann, J. F. *Johannis de Turrecremata vita eiusque doctrina de corpore Christi mystico*. Bologna, 1951.

Binder, K. "Martino Gazati der Verfasser der Kardinal Juan de Torquemada zubeschriebenen *Centum quaestiones de ceto et auctoritate cardinalium*." *Angelicum* 28 (1951) 139–51.

————. "Kardinal Juan de Torquemada Verfasser der *Nova ordinatio decreti Gratiani*." *AFP* 22 (1952) 268–93.

————. "Il magistero del Sacro Palazzo Apostolico del cardinale di Torquemada." *MemDom* 71 (1954) 3–24.

Donati, L. "A Manuscript of *Meditationes Johannis de Turrecremata*." *Library Chronicle* 21 (1955) 51–60.

Binder, K. *Wesen und Eigenschaften der Kirche bei Kardinal Juan de Torquemada*. Innsbruck, 1955.

Alcántara, P. de. "La redención y el debito de María según Juan de Segovia y Juan de Torquemada." *RevEspTeol* 16 (1956) 3–51.

Massi, P. *Magistero infallibile del papa nella teologia di Giovanni di Torquemada*. Turin, 1957.

Donati, L. "I manoscritti delle *Meditationes Johannis de Turrecremata*." *Bullettino dell'Archivio paleografico italiano*, N.S. 2–3 (1956–57) 241–49.

Beltrán de Heredia, V. "Noticias y documentos para la biografía del Cardenal Juan de Torquemada." *AFP* 30 (1960) 53–148. Reprinted, along with the article of 1937 (above) in *Miscellanea Beltrán de Heredia*. Salamanca, 1972. I, 291–386.

Proñao Gil, V. "Doctrina de Juan de Torquemada sobre el concilio." *Burgense* 1 (1960) 45–71.

López Martínez, N. "El Cardinal Torquemada y la unidad de la Iglesia." Ibid., 45–71.

Undhagen, C.-G. "Une source du prologue (chap. 1) aux *Révélations* de S.te Brigitte par le Cardinal Juan de Torquemada." *Eranos. Acta philologica suecana* 58 (1960) 214–26.

Weigel, G. "Überlegungen zur Methodologie am Beispiel Johannes Torquemadas." *Gott im Welt. Festgabe für K. Rahner* I. Freiburg i. B., 1964. Pp. 392–404.

Binder, K. "Zum Schriftbeweis in der Kirchentheologie des Kardinals de Torquemada." *Wahrheit und Verkündigung. M. Schmaus zum 70. Geburtstag.* Paderborn, 1967. Pp. 511–50.

Horst, O. "Grenze der päpstlichen Autorität. Konziliäre Elemente in Ekklesiologie des Johannes Torquemada." *FZPT* 9 (1972) 361–80.

Binder, K. "Kardinal Torquemada O.P. über die Veranstaltung allgemeiner Konzilien." *Auftrag und Verwirkliching.* Vienna, 1974.

Donati, L. "Escorso sulle *Meditationes Johannis de Turcremata* (1476)." *La bibliofilia* 76 (1974) 1–34.

Izbicki, T. M. "Infallibility and the Erring Pope: Guido Terreni and Johannes de Turrecremata." *Law, Church, and Society: Essays in Honor of Stephen Kuttner.* Philadelphia, 1977. Pp. 97–111.

Tierney, B. "'Only Truth Has Authority': The Problem of 'Reception' in the Decretists and in Johannes de Turrecremata." Ibid., 69–96.

Molina Melia, A. "Juan Torquemada y la teoría de la podestad indirecta de la Iglesia en asuntos temporales." *Annales valentinos* 2 (1976–77) 45–78.

Isbicki, T. M. "Notes on the Manuscript Library of Cardinal Johannes de Turrecremata." *Scriptorium* 25 (1981) 306–11.

————. *Protector of the Faith, Cardinal Johannes de Turrecremata and the Defense of the Institutional Church.* Washington, D.C., 1981.

García y García, A. "Un nuevo estudio de Juan de Torquemada." *RevEspTeol* 43 (1983) 525–33.

Izbicki, T. M. "Papalist Reaction to the Council of Constance: Juan de Torquemada." *Church History* 55 (1986) 7–20.

Schmitt, C. "Le traité du Cardinal Jean de Torquemada sur la pauvreté évangélique." *AFP* 57 (1987) 103–44.

See also chapter 5 of the present volume.

CHAPTER 3

The Theology of Nicholas of Cusa

Graziella Federici Vescovini

1. Life and Works

Nicholas was born in the village of Cues (today Bernkastel-Kues) on the Moselle near Trier—whence the name "of Cusa"—between August 11, 1400, and August 1, 1401 (the indefiniteness is due to the variations of chronology before the reform of the calendar). His father was a prosperous boatman, Johannes Cryffts (or Krieffts or Kreves, which corresponds to the modern Krebs, meaning "crayfish" or "cancer"; whence the appellation "Nicholas Cancer"); his mother was Katerina Römer.

Due to the patronage of the count of Manderscheid he completed his early studies around 1413; we do not know where he did them, although an uncertain tradition has him as a student in one of the schools of the Brothers of the Common Life in Deventer. In 1416 he enrolled in the University of Heidelberg, where the Ockhamist tendency was dominant. A year later he transferred to Padua and enrolled in the Faculty of Law, from which he obtained the title of Doctor of Laws in 1423. In all likelihood he came in contact there with the philosophy, mathematics, and arts taught in Padua and sat under such masters as Prosdocimus de'Beldomani, a disciple of Biagio Pelacani of Parma, Paul of Venice, and others. The memory of the teaching of Peter of Abano and Marsilius was still alive at that time, and there were keen debates on scientific, mathematical, and astronomical subjects; these drew added intensity from the active exchanges between the masters of Padua and the university centers of Oxford and Paris.

In 1425 Nicholas enrolled in the University of Cologne in order to follow the courses in philosophy and theology of Eimeric of Kampen, who probably introduced him to the reading of Proclus, Pseudo-Dionysius, and the masters of the Albertist school, such as Berthold of Moosburg, Theodoric of Freiberg, and Eckhart. In 1426 he was engaged as secretary to Cardinal Orsini, who at that time was papal legate in Germany. After being ordained at Koblenz, Nicholas appeared at the Council of Basel in 1432; there he struck up friendships with important Italian churchmen and humanists. In 1433 he wrote his *De concordantia catholica,* in which he maintained positions favorable to the conciliarist theory, but he toned down the more conflictual aspects of that theory. In the following year he wrote his *De auctoritate praesidendi in concilio generali* on the thorny questions of the presidency of councils and the place to be assigned in them to papal legates.

He became increasingly convinced of the important role of the pope as reconciler and drew closer to the Roman Curia and Pope Eugene IV, with whom he warmly supported the transfer of the council to Ferrara in connection with the planned arrival of the Greek fathers. He was sent to Constantinople as papal legate in 1436 in order to invite the Eastern emperor and patriarch to take part in the council for the unification of the two Churches. During this journey, as he himself tells us, he received "as a gift from God," the intuition of the principle of "learned ignorance" *(docta ignorantia).* During 1436–37 he devoted himself to the study of astronomy in preparation for a reform of the calendar, a subject to which he devoted his *De reparatione kalendarii.*

In 1440, on the return journey from Constantinople, he wrote his *De docta ignorantia.* In Constantinople he had met Gemisthus Plethon, Bessarion, and other eminent Greek masters, and he brought back with him the *Theologia platonica* of Proclus, which he passed on to his friend Ambrose Traversari for translation. Between 1440 and 1447, he wrote, among other things, *De coniecturis* in two books that show a strong Neoplatonic influence; his *Dialogus de Deo abscondito* and the short theological works entitled *De quaerendo Deum, De filiatione Dei,* and *De dato Patris luminum;* then a series of short mathematical works, the successful little work of eschatological prevision entitled *Coniectura de ultimis diebus,* and the dialogues *De annuntiatione* and *De genesi.* During these same years he engaged in intense activity in the area of ecclesiastical politics, working on behalf of the pope, especially in Germany.

After having been appointed archbishop of Brabant and been made a cardinal in secret *(in petto),* in 1448 he received the open appointment as cardinal from the new pope, Nicholas V; he was assigned the church of St. Peter in Chains. Having been sent to Germany as apostolic legate, in the following year he wrote his *Apologia pro docta ignorantia* in which he defended himself against accusations of pantheism that were leveled against him by a theologian of Heidelberg and an Aristotelean, Johannes Wenck of Herrenberg, in a short work, *De ignota litteratura*. In 1449 he also wrote two successive short works entitled *De quadratura circuli*.

In 1450, a jubilee year, he returned to Rome for the reception of the cardinal's hat and was appointed prince-bishop of Brixen and papal legate for the preaching of the jubilee in Germany. In that same year he wrote his second major work, the dialogues of the *Idiota,* in four books (I–II, *De sapientia;* III, *De mente;* IV, *De staticis experimentis*). After many journeys as legate in Germany, Austria, the Rhineland, and the Low Countries, he settled down in his diocese of Brixen in 1452 and devoted himself to setting up a practical model of his own principles for the moral and disciplinary reform of the Church. He met with resistance, however, from the cathedral chapter and especially from the aristocratic nuns of Sonnenburg, whose abbess, Verena von Stuben, won the help of Sigismund, duke of Austria and count of the Tyrol, in challenging the bishop on the lands and rights which he was claiming. In 1453, despite the bitterness caused by this struggle, Nicholas managed to compose his *De visione Dei* and the *Complementum theologicum,* which were followed in the ensuing years by various works on mathematics.

In 1458, in order to put an end to the conflict with Sigismund, Pope Pius II asked Nicholas to return to Rome, where he appointed him his legate for the city. Nicholas wrote his *De mathematica perfectione,* his *De beryllo* (a precious stone that enables one to know invisible truths), and his *De possest* (that is, "the actual-potential"). In 1460 Nicholas returned to Brixen and renewed the struggle with the Duke, who forced him to take shelter in central Italy. After having written his *De cribratione Alkorani,* in which he compared Christianity and Islam, and his *De non-aliud,* he took up residence in Orvieto in 1462 and there collected the manuscripts of his works. In 1463 he composed his mature writings: the dialogue *De ludo globi,* the *De venatione sapientiae,* and the *Compendium,* in which he summed up and treated in greater depth the principal themes of his thought.

In 1464 he wrote his *De apice theoriae*. On August 11 of that year, while traveling from Rome to Ancona, to which he was going in order to gather soldiers for the crusade being prepared by Pius II, he died at Todi in the bishop's palace. His body was buried in the funerary monument in St. Peter in Chains, in Rome, but at his express wish his heart was preserved at Kues in the chapel of the hospital for the poor which he had established by means of a bequest in 1458. The hospital still contains his library, in which all his personal manuscripts are kept.

2. The Reform of Traditional Theology

While starting from a common experience of faith, theological thought at the end of the fourteenth century and in the first half of the fifteenth was using and transforming philosophical concepts inherited from the past, thereby creating speculative doctrines that varied according to the varying philosophical options, which in turn conditioned the structures and final forms of these doctrines.[1] The theology of Nicholas of Cusa is an example of the extraordinary wealth and fruitfulness of theological speculation after the proliferation of different schools at the end of the Middle Ages: Thomism, Scotism, Ockhamism, and the special type of Abertinism maintained, with its ramifications, by the German Dominicans. Aware as he was of this diversity among the schools of theology, Nicholas observed in his work *De filiatione Dei:* "One who is truthfully occupied with theology will find nothing, in all the variety of conjectures, which perturbs him" as he strains toward the one God.[2]

In his vast literary production, to which he was able to devote himself only in moments of rest from his intense engagement in the moral, political, and religious reform of the Church during a period as difficult as that of the Councils of Basel, Ferrara, and Florence,[3] Nicholas set up a constant tension between the word of God and the conceptual tools provided by the various doctrinal and philosophical traditions. But the search for a single and unified theological truth that lies beyond the factious perspectives of the schools suggested to him that he start with a radical criticism of the forms of the now traditional theology that had been developed in the medieval universities.[4] This is confirmed by his controversy with Scholastic theologian Johannes Wenck, who in his *De ignota litteratura* accused Nicholas of pantheism on the basis of the teachings in his *Learned Ignorance.*[5]

Nicholas' reply, in his *Defense of Learned Ignorance,* clearly attests to a different way of understanding theology and the philosophical approach to problems concerning God. There is an evident rejection of a series of basic logical, gnoseological, and metaphysical doctrines: the use of the notion of being in Aristotle for defining the divine substance; the concept of truth that is based on the principle of noncontradiction and the excluded third; the rejection of the theory of knowledge through abstraction and of knowledge through causes *(scire per causas);* the denial of the importance of the sensible phantasm for valid knowledge and the limitation of it to the rational sphere, which is inferior to the sphere of the intellect; the inadequacy of the Aristotelean principle that the process of motion cannot have a beginning and the consequent rethinking of the concept of infinity.

The mind is not moved to learn by a rational discourse that starts with data received from the senses; rather, it has within itself a lively intellectual power enabling it to rise up by entering into itself and developing its thought through similitudes and approximations.[6] Nicholas is therefore able to situate himself within the tradition of Christian thought that had been inspired by Augustine, from whom he takes the theme of the interiority of knowing: from within *(ab intra)* and not from outside *(ab extra).* God's revelation through the Word is internal to our minds and is not grasped in the medium of the external world.

The *Defense of Learned Ignorance,* with its harvest of citations from and references to Nicholas' preferred authors—among them Eckhart, whom he defends against accusations of pantheism[7]—also shows how he goes back, in an original way, to the Christian Neoplatonic tradition that runs from Pseudo-Dionysius to Albert the Great; how he is strongly influenced by the more mature results of Scotism and one kind of Lullism (all of these influences are still to be studied); and how he is also indebted to the teachings contained in the hermetic-Neoplatonic books on the twenty-four rules for theology, the *Liber XXIV philosophorum,* on which he draws so abundantly for his theological symbolism.[8]

In his writings Nicholas thus abandons the Scholastic procedures used in the medieval teaching of theology: the *quaestio* and the *disputatio* with their *determinatio magistralis* (solution by the teacher), which make clear Scholasticism's dread of contradiction and its methodological anxiety to ground everything in a truth of reason (a point that has been stressed by some scholars).[9] In this respect Nicholas already shows himself a modern theologian, a child of that renewed world that parades its own contradictions, whereas the medieval world had always tried to hide them. Scholastic theology, by and large, wanted to bring to expression the best possible situation and claimed to see the world with the eyes of God. Nicholas, too, would like to see the world as God sees it *(On the Vision of God),* but he knows that this is impossible because God is beyond our sight. We will continue always to see with our own eyes, although these are indeed privileged when compared with the eyes of other creatures, ours being *oculi mentis nostrae,* the eyes of the mind of the human person, who is the measure of the world and the link connecting creation and God.

Medieval culture had been unable to justify contradiction: contradiction could be tolerated at the empirical level, but theory was always being urged to resolve it. According to Thomas Aquinas (*Quaestio quodlibetalis* V, 2, 3), God cannot violate the logical principle according to which "this is" and "this is not" cannot be truthfully said of the same thing at the same time. Even in discussions of "the absolute power of God," at least down to Ockham, every answer stopped at the insurmountable limit posed by the principle of noncontradiction.

Nicholas pushes beyond this metaphysical, fundamentally Aristotelean vision of reality. He has a sense of the multidimensionality of the real and of its infinite perspectives, by reason of which everything can be brought into focus from different angles of vision (knowledge by conjecture), thus providing an inexhaustible fund of complementary pictures. But he also modifies the key principles of the Neoplatonic philosophies that are his starting point, such principles as the concepts of generation by emanation and of necessary manifestation; and the idea of the dynamic character of being or of the essence of form, in the proper and original sense. In doing so he gives these principles his own, original meaning. As a result of his development of them, Albert the

Great's teaching on imparticipable participation acquires a fruitful influence:[10] creatures participate in God without God being affected in the slightest by this participation, whether the latter be thought of simply as a disposition to receive or also as "the aptitude of matter for form" *(aptitudo materiae ad formam),* as Nicholas writes in his *Learned Ignorance,*[11] or in other words, according to their particular "contractions." The concept of "participation by contraction" is central to Nicholas' thought and refers only to creatures, because God is imparticipable.

As a result, Nicholas includes even evil—monsters, poisonous serpents, which he himself mentions—in the plan of creation, in this harmonious symphony[12] that we call the world, because monsters were not created by God but by our minds. For our minds are limited to the rational level of distinctions and are unable to discover the special kinds of proportion that are proper, at a level higher than reason, to the intellect, through the mathematical contraction of our intellectual powers.[13]

3. Learned Ignorance and Perfect Theology

A theology thus renewed and drawing on complex and little-known doctrinal currents is led to feed upon and draw new energy from the idea of knowledge through signs, symbols, and rough similarities, through enigmatic figures, through codes of transcendence. In this way, which leads beyond the universe of contradictions that this world is, there are revealed to us the one Absolute or identical oneness of truth (the Father), the proportion of equality (Son and Spirit), and therefore the Trinity, in a bond of inseparable identity that is God as One-Three, the object of perfect theology or true theology, as Nicholas writes. This is the theology of John, summed up in the verse "In the beginning was the Word."[14] It is a theology of the metahistorical Scriptures, based on the promise of salvation.

The One is the place where all possible determinations or attributes are completely identified; as such, it is none of these things in itself; it is such only for us, because it is the opposite of everything. Anyone who reads carefully all the writings of Nicholas cannot fail to see that his entire theological teaching is pervaded by the need to explain what he means by saying that God is the absolute identity of opposites, the opposite of the opposites, not because he is the root of these[15] but, on the contrary, because in him opposites or differences are nothing, since he is pure identity, equality, and proportion of equality, that is, he is infinite, incomprehensible, identical unity.

Thus the relation God-humanity-world undergoes a radical change in Nicholas' christology, because God, the imparticipable One, the Truth that is absolutely identical with itself, manifests himself spontaneously as light in his Word, the "word" *(verbum)* that "reverberates" the divinity; and because of our likeness to him we too can "reverberate" that same light as its finite and limited contractions. Nicholas' theology is therefore no longer theocentric but anthropocentric not because it substitutes the human being for God but because, by reason of the human person's likeness to the Word-Christ, it is conceived as the active center, the protagonist of the religious drama, of the creaturely effort to reach the divine in its loftiest, inaccessible mysteries, such as the death and resurrection of Christ, and in this way once again to discover the order and harmony of the world.

The method of theology can therefore no longer be a rational one using syllogisms, demonstrations, and refutations but will be a process using symbols and figures, in mirrors and enigmas, along the methodical way of learned ignorance. Learned ignorance is the synthesis of contraries or contradictories; it combines negative theology with positive theology in the assertion of an eminential theology of the absolute identity of opposites in God, beyond the oppositions, according to an interpretation—quite peculiar to and original with Nicholas—of the mystical theology of Dionysius, who in Nicholas' opinion is the greatest of all the theologians.

Nicholas thus radically alters the approach to the problems of theology, precisely because he changes the theory of human knowledge and the assessment of its importance in the economy of the universe. The human being is a microcosm, a "bond of the world" *(copula mundi),* precisely by reason of the fact that through Christ it is the restored image of God, the likeness of God *(similitudo Dei);* Nicholas' teaching is truly a christological humanism. And Christ is the privileged "code" *(cifra)*[16] of transcendence in a universe in which the whole is a system of signs, symbols, and enigmatic figures.[17] In earlier centuries, before Duns Scotus, as Cassirer has written, knowledge depended on reality and on the dignity of the ontological object (God); in the modern age, the truth of knowledge depends on the procedure or way by which it is obtained as well as on the level of certainty that is achieved. Nicholas systematizes in a radically new way the relations between philosophy and faith, theoretical arguments and scriptural texts, because when human beings start from the mathematical power of the created mind, insofar as it is a likeness of the divine mind of Christ, they can strive to reach, in the most diverse ways, the infinite One, the greatest and the least, which is imparticipable in itself but in which created things participate according to the modes of their freedom or potentiality, which is a gift from the Father of lights, and according to their particular contractions.[18]

The concept of "contraction" is central to Nicholas' theological speculation. He uses it within a general vision of a Neoplatonic kind of reality, which is divided into its degrees or regions, these being four: sense, soul, reason, and intelligence. By a contraction he understands a determination, a limitation, an individuation, of the higher order in the lower. He gives this theory of the contraction of the superior in the inferior in the work that followed upon *Learned Ignorance* and bore the title *On Conjectures (De conjecturis)* (1441–44). He later abandons this hierarchic vision of beings as ordered according to their quaternary contractions and develops, in the years around 1450, a doctrine of the privileged position of the human mind as a likeness of God; the mind contracts in itself all four contractions proper to knowledge that proceeds by conjecture: the sensible, the animate, the rational, and the intellectual. Creatures are therefore no longer the beings of Aristotle, understood as pure essences; they are something more and different, because understanding comes before being: each creature understands God according to its free participation, which comes from the attitude or disposition of the recipient to receive the gift of light. Creatures are therefore free wills, varied possibilities, depending on the conditions of their contracted natures or their individuations. They are also, therefore, according to Nicholas, varied, because contracted, that is, limited "assimilations" of the divine creation.[19]

Insofar as it is contracted, every creature is a kind of perspective on the whole, and when it rises to the contraction of intellectual vision, it possesses, though not in an eminent degree, the infinity of faces of the whole. This openness and expansion means that each part of the cosmos is related to the whole through proportion: a relative proportion indeed, that of the more and the less, but in any case a proportion and correspondence and therefore a harmony. The world is therefore revealed as a splendid harmonious beauty.[20]

For this reason, the ideas are no longer archetypical and stereotyped models of reality; the conceptual categories of Aristotle (time, motion, space, succession, instant, and so on) are unable to contain the living, concrete actions of reality. The ideas are numbers, tools which the human minds used for describing and understanding; they are not types immersed in things and abstractable from them.

In his *De mente* Nicholas uses some now famous expressions when he says that as God created real beings, so we, using minds made in his likeness, create the conceptual, mathematical entities of the world.[21] Our mind, therefore, behaves habitually like a geographer who draws a map of a world which he does not yet know. It is like a city with five gates, which are the five senses, through which ambassadors from all over the world enter in and tell us of how the world is arranged. It is by following the order contained in these reports that the geographer draws his map. And as a map is related to the real world, so the human being contemplates in himself, as geographer, the creator of the world; that is, "through his mind he contemplates the truth in the sign of the designated."[22]

Some years earlier in the *Dialogue on Genesis* Nicholas had said that the world is like a book written in obscure letters, as Greek letters are obscure to a German who does not know them; he can make them out only with great difficulty, without understanding their deeper meaning and while endeavoring in vain to grasp the mind or art of the writer. This art is a "quiddity" that will always elude him.[23] Only in our minds can we discover the art of the world's

Maker, even while being ignorant of it. The particular degree in which formed forms express and explain the existence of the Former which has placed them in being consists precisely in these forms being in their turn formative. The formed forms are centers of formation. Consequently, one of the characteristics of the forms is that they manifest the very process that formed them. In this sense, the form of the human mind is a contraction of the one who formed it, and by its dynamic connections it declares this. The human being is thus God's first collaborator in giving order and harmony to the world. A constant in Nicholas' thought is this idea of the collaboration and solidarity of forms, even in their contradictions and divisions, which, as he writes in *On the Peace of Faith,* can never be completely eliminated.[24]

Tremulous premonitions of a new world can be felt in Nicholas. The cosmos has splintered into facets representing countless possibilities, and the task of this man is tinged by a restlessness which will never leave him. The years of his maturity and old age were to be the ones most troubled and most deeply marked by all the religious and political tensions of the age, which he hoped that his wisdom might alleviate while realizing that he could not do away with them or avoid them entirely. But he never gave up appealing to the real ability human beings have for intervening positively in their world, because he held that our minds possess a treasure: the treasure contained in the mathematical and mechanical sciences of which it is master. Nicholas developed these ideas especially in Book IV *(Gli esperimenti di statica)* of the dialogues of *L'idiota.*[25]

4. Eminential Theology, or the Theology of the Absolute Identity of Opposites or Contradictories Beyond Themselves

What kind of theology is most in tune with Nicholas' thinking? What are human beings to do when they want to reach knowledge of a God who is conceived as a "hidden God" *(Deus absconditus),*[26] a God who, the more he reveals himself, the more he conceals himself, and the more he conceals himself, the more he reveals himself?

The descriptions of the nature of theological knowledge that can be found throughout the entire range of Nicholas' works, from *Learned Ignorance* (1440) to *The Summit of Wisdom* (1464) written shortly before his death, are always based first and foremost on a positive, speculative, and intellectual reinterpretation of the mystical theology of Dionysius. The latter's works are repeatedly cited in almost all of Nicholas' writings but especially in *On the Not-Other (De non-aliud),* in which mention is also made of the new Latin translation of Dionysius by Peter Balbo Pisano, bishop of Pisano, who died in 1479.[27]

But Nicholas does not seem to understand the mystical theology of Pseudo-Dionysius as an affective theology or a theology of the simple will that drowns in the light.[28] The conception of Dionysian theology that Nicholas develops reflects rather a very structured and complex philosophical meditation, on the basis of which it is reinterpreted as an eminential theology or theology of transcendence. The fundamental presupposition here is the absolute identity of contradictories in God, who is the opposition of opposites. In other words, God is defined as the absolute identity of origins, and this notion negates the logical principle of reason. But there is nothing radically negative about this teaching; it is not a mystical nullification of reason, even if it appeals not to the rational sphere but to the intellectual.

Nicholas is always concerned to save the absolute transcendence of the Creator in relation to creatures. In his view God is the negation of the world and its contradictions. At the same time, however, he acknowledges the value of creatures in all the variety they show in this earthly world, which he does not deny: "If you ask . . . why such a contrariety exists in the sensible world, you must say: because the opposites, placed side by side, shine forth all the more and there is for both only one knowledge."[29] But theology is opposed to knowledge of the world:[30] human beings enter the world in order to seek God, but they cannot find God by means of their abstract knowledge, which give them knowledge only of things in their individual distinctness. If we start from creatures in order to reach the Creator, Nicholas writes, we fall into the idolatry of the pagans, who began with the attributes of creatures and extended them to God, thereby mistaking the creature for the Creator.[31] Theology, on the contrary, is "the greatest and the least knowledge" because it is beyond every affirmation and every name, whether concrete or abstract, such as "deity," "entity," or "divinity." Thus the negations are true and the affirmations inadequate.[32]

Real theologians, such as Dionysius, but also Avicenna and Alghazali, worked out a negative theology that released and freed God from every name, whether singular or universal, and developed St. Paul's saying: "We know not what we are praying for." Knowledge, on the other hand, uses logic and the principle of noncontradiction. Human beings use these because logic is given to them by their nature.[33] Thus rational discourse moves between a starting point and an end point and describes as "contradictory" things opposed to each other. "These, then, are the opposed and disjunctive terms of discursive reason. In the realm of reason extremes are separate. . . . But in the realm of the intellect . . . we grasp by the mind's vision, and without reasoning, the coincidence of unity and plurality, of point and line, of center and circumference."[34] Thus Nicholas reaches the point of maintaining, not only in *Learned Ignorance* but also in the important work of 1453, *The Vision of God (De visione Dei)*, where he harks back to a conception he had already developed at length in his two books *On Conjectures (De coniecturis)* (1441–44), that God is beyond even the coincidence of contradictories, since he is the opposite, that is, the negation, of opposites.[35]

The great theologian Dionysius—whom "most all I admired," Nicholas wrote[36]—developed a concept of God that was not taken from creatures, which are the other, the different, the distinct, the more and less. These represent the world of the "other," which is that of diversity, wherein each thing is equal to itself and different from others. God, on the other hand, is beyond this diversity: he is the diversity of diversity and therefore the negation of the other and therefore the Non-Other. Knowledge of the Non-Other is nothing but a "learned ignorance." By this knowledge one can see with the eye of the mind the reality that Dionysius, too, was able to see:[37] that is, that God is the opposition of opposites without opposition. Prior to the opposites, nothing is opposed to opposition. Aristotle did not understand this truth, because reason cannot attain to that which is prior to reason; still less can all the techniques, the arts, and the sciences attain to it, since they are a product of reason. In order to strengthen his own meditation on the concept of God understood as Non-Other, Nicholas constantly develops—from the *Docta Ignorantia* to the *De non-aliud,* which dates from 1642—one of the twenty-four theological rules given in the *Liber XXIV philosophorum,* namely, proposition XIV, which says that "God is opposition without any mediation of being."[38]

5. The Theology of Transcendence, or the Passage Accomplished by Learned Ignorance

It is from this last idea that the teaching in eminential theology or the theology of transcendence flows, or in other words, the idea of the liberation of theological thought to move beyond affirmations, negations, and particular contractions.[39] This teaching is developed especially in the other very important work of Nicholas' maturity, *On the Vision of God (De visione Dei).* This work was composed in 1453 for the Benedictine monks of Tegernsee and also bore the title *The Icon.* Taking as his starting point a portrait of the face of Christ and from its especially penetrating gaze (the eye seemed to stare at the viewers and follow them persistently through all their movements and wherever they were), he seeks by means of this sensible image to lead the monks into the luminous darkness of paradise and help them overcome the barrier of the identity of opposites that separates us from God, who is beyond the barrier, in paradise, where all distinctions of essences, or all beings, are nothing.

In this work Nicholas aims to get beyond the knowledge of God in the form, and according to the method, shown in *Learned Ignorance.* There he had started from the concept of absolute truth which our mind possesses and which is identical with the concept of mathematical truth as unqualified accuracy. He had been forced, however, to admit that this absolute truth, which is grasped by our mind, is unattainable in itself, since for human beings the mathematical accuracy of truth is only that which is grasped within the realm of the world, of the more and less, that is, in the setting of the natural sciences, which describe only relative proportions and not absolute proportion (the Proportion of Equality).

In *The Vision of God,* on the other hand, he speaks of the vision of God who looks at us and, by looking at us, makes us be, because he is Light in the most intense degree. Taking over the image Plato uses in the *Republic* in connection with the idea of the Good, which is self-manifesting light, Nicholas says that God is both mirror and gaze, that he reveals himself spontaneously, and in this way, while remaining inaccessible in his essence and nature, he is the source of the being and knowledge of everything that is capable of seeing him. God's is the eye and mirror of light, in which all particular faces are reflected. Therefore every face capable of intuiting his face sees nothing other or different from itself, since each sees in him its own truth. The truth of the exemplar cannot be other or different, as the truth of the image is, for this is always amid diversity; and thus accidents are superimposed on the image because the latter is not the exemplar. As a result, human beings see only as a human being can.

However, the face of God can show itself more perfectly in frontal vision, which occurs when the eye of the human mind rises beyond all particular faces into an inmost, hidden silence, where there is neither knowledge nor concept of the face. In this darkness is found the power of the source of all powers, namely, the gift of the Father of lights, who through the Word gives, to all, the possibilities, that is, the virtues or freedom, to be itself in order to be him, so that God does not necessitate, but "waits to be chosen by me."[40] Through this gift of light, which is grace, we can make our way over the wall of paradise, which is the wall of the contradictions and is guarded by the spirit of reason.

The only concept suitable to the mind of God is eternity: all things exist only because God conceives them, but he conceives them in eternity. Things are not beings but "intentions" of the omnipotent will of God. When God is seen in paradise, surrounded by the wall of the identity of opposites, he is not seen either to complicate or to explain, and this either disjunctively or copulatively. Disjunction and copulation are the wall of the identity, beyond which God exists completely untied to anything that can be thought and expressed. Nicholas writes:

> Thus I come up against the absurdity of creating together with created being, but your creating is your being for us. To create and at the same time to be created is nothing else than to communicate your being to all things, that is, the Word, Jesus. To call into being the things that are not is to communicate being to nothingness. To call is to create; to communicate is to be created.[41]

Beyond this identity, which is Christ, is God: infinite, incommunicable, imparticipable.

In complete contrast to the earlier Scholastic theological tradition, Nicholas here develops two very important themes: one having to do with

God as object of truth, the other having to do with the creature understood as participation.

6. God Is Not Objective Substantial Truth

Unlike what was taught in medieval theological science, God is not, for Nicholas, objective substantial truth, because according to his conception of the theology of the transcending of the identity of opposites, he understands objective truth as the learning of pure truth in supereminence.[42] Philosophical truth, which is the truth proper to human beings, is simply a "mode" of God by which he communicates himself. Authentic objective truth is only the calming of every intellectual movement; it is the eternal rest in God. Nicholas writes therefore: "The truth is not God as He triumphs in Himself, but rather it is a mode of God, through which He can communicate himself in the eternal life of the intellect. . . . Therefore the truth alone is the intelligibility of everything intelligible." The absolute attributes of God, such as "being," "deity," "goodness," "truth," or even "virtue" and others are not names of God, who cannot be named, but they express the various intellectual modes of God himself.[43]

It is along these lines that Nicholas aims to modify and adapt to the Christian idea of transcendence the hierarchical teachings of the Neoplatonic emanationist philosophers, on whom he draws heavily: John Scotus Eriugena, Proclus, Avicenna, and Dionysius. God is not the One, but he is "the origin beyond the One and its measure, who in the One and in the mode of the One exhibits Himself as communicable." Thus we understand why God in himself cannot be known by any process of abstraction but only by the method that consists in transcending the contractions, that is, the limited and circumscribed participations in creatures, which are different by reason of their contractions. God can be attained only by going beyond, in freedom from the contractions which individual limitations express.

7. Participation as Contracted Reception of the Gift of Light

The concept of contraction is connected with the special way in which Nicholas understands participation in the creaturely being. This doctrine, as Haubst has brought out well,[44] is a personal, more deeply plumbed development of Albert the Great's idea of "participation," understood according to "the disposition of the recipient." Nicholas also calls it "the aptitude of matter" *(aptitudo materiae)*.

There are as many participations as there are dispositions of the recipient. The contractions of beings, which Nicholas arranges according to the Neoplatonic-Pythagorean four-step ladder of the sensible world, the soul, reason, and the intellect, as I noted above in connection with his work *On*

Conjectures,[45] represent the modes of their participation in the inaccessible and in itself imparticipable light of God, that is, insofar as they participate in this according to their distinct spheres of contraction. These contracted lights are nothing else but creatures taken as conjectures, that is, as approximate truths, distant from the absolute light.

The diversity of the contractions (that is, of the conditions of those receiving the light, or of the participations) are identified by Nicholas with the natural gift *(datum)* of light that is free will.[46] For this reason each creature participates in this light in a greater or lesser measure according to the four contractions mentioned and according to whether it raises itself to the intelligible sphere or remains in the sphere of the lowest contraction, the sensible. But the vision of God can be attained only through liberation from all four modes of contraction or limited participation. Thus creatures are beings only insofar as they participate in this contracted mode of the absolute unity to which they seek to be assimilated by freeing themselves from the contraction. Then the being will be capable of being brought back to the One in whom all things participate according to their measure.[47] By the act of creation all things accede to their proper being through their respective participations in that infinite power which is the One itself, "according to the mode in which one can participate variously in it. There is therefore nothing except the One, in which one cannot participate without the mode."[48] Conceived in this way, creation is an assimilation to the Creator through liberation from the contraction of creatures.[49] And creatures are better definable by means of this concept of assimilation than by that of being, which is the more common way.

It is therefore to be said that creation (or genesis) is this assimilation, through liberation, to the absolute being which is the One, the identical, which by identifying calls to itself the nothing that nonbeing is. Nonbeing emerges in the return to the absolute being, which is the identical, in the assimilation to it, that is, in becoming similar to the absolute identity.[50]

God therefore remains imparticipable in himself, because he is prior to the One itself, nor is he "the mode" of the One. Things, however, participate in him according to the mode of the One, and creaturely beings originate, specifically, according to how they participate in this unity, or, in other words, according to the gift of free will or of individual possibilities. This is confirmation that, according to Nicholas, creatures are substantially free wills, powers, or activities that are contractions within them of the various possibilities of knowing God. Creatures exist only insofar as they tend to become like, to "assimilate themselves to," the absolute divine intelligibility, which, as such, rests exclusively in the unattainable mind of God. For this reason, we will never comprehend God, since creatures are also the intentions, unknown to us, of their Author. The reason for the divine intention, Nicholas writes, is manifestation; in other words, God manifests his intention—which we would never know in itself—in creatures. It is, however, very difficult to ascend from the signs, which creatures are, to the intention of the Founding Intellect. It is in this context that he introduces the very fine example, already mentioned, of the world as a book written by God's hand in Greek letters of which a German is ignorant: the latter sees the signs but does not grasp the meaning, the essence or quiddity.[51]

It is also clear from all this that for Cusa, God, as objective truth, is not understood either entitatively or substantially but as the one who transcends all creaturely limitations or contractions. Nevertheless, he manifests himself and spontaneously communicates his light through the gift of grace, by means of the redemption wrought by Christ, in the word of the Word. He gives this light because he wants to be sought and found. The pagan philosophers presumed that they could find God by reason alone, without need of a revelation from God. But such knowledge has in fact been made possible only by the supernatural gift *(donum)* from the Father of lights, the gift, namely, of the grace of salvation in Christ: in each of us, through Christ, our exemplar, there appears the presence of a contracted power, like a millet seed or a mustard seed in a field, in which God has contracted all the potentialities of self-fulfillment.

8. Unfolding as Participation in Opposite Powers

Connected with the concept of contraction is that of unfolding, which in turn leads on to that of infolding.

In his *On Conjectures* Nicholas says that the entire activity of our intellect consists in a participation in the divine activity (which is omnipotence) in a variety of potential or contracted, that is, limited ways. Since the simple oneness of God is imparticipable, can creatures participate in it? This participation (he writes) must be regarded as a "power" subsisting in the unity of the substance. In this power the imparticipable oneness is identical with a participability, and the participation is the contraction of the One in the many. In the created world, therefore, we never grasp with absolute precision the identity of the One, but only his contracted presence.

The concept of unfolding is also used by Cusa as correlative with that of infolding. In response to the accusations of pantheism brought against him in connection with these concepts, Nicholas explains them in his work *Defense of Learned Ignorance,* in which he defends himself against the attacks of Johannes Wenck, an Aristotelean. According to Nicholas, the first principle of noncontradiction, which Wenck invoked, is first only in the realm of discursive reason but not in that of the intuitive intellect. Things exist in God only by infolding in an intuitive way, in that they unfold from him according to their contractions. This truth holds only for our intellect.[52] Cusa never asserted the identity of creatures with the Creator. He explains himself even better in his *Dialogue on Genesis:*

If . . . infinity or unattainability is unfolded in the maximum participation of the participating things in the greatest possible clarity, which the condition of the participating things permits, then accordingly the things participating in the entity itself are of opposing powers. However, since all entities are the same as themselves, these endeavor to effect the same; the warm endeavors to make warm, the cold to make cold. And since the warm calls the not-warm and the cold the not-cold, a battle arises and from this generation and corruption and all the like: temporality, fluidity, instability, and variety of motion,

which reason alone attains to, because it distinguishes and divides.[53]

In one of his most profound works, the third book, *De mente* (1450), of the dialogues entitled *Idiotae,* Nicholas clarifies even further this idea of unfolding by linking it to the measuring activity of our minds.

The concept of the unfolding of the human mind is here integrated with and explained by that of assimilation: "As God is the absolute entity that is the embrace of all beings, so our mind is the image of that infinite entity that embraces all the images." Therefore,

if you call this divine simplicity infinite mind, it is this that will be the exemplar of our mind. If you call the divine mind the totality of the truth of things, you will say that our mind is the totality of the assimilations of things and that it gives being to the totality of notions. The conception of the divine mind is the production of things. The conception of our mind is the notion of things. If the divine mind is absolute entity, its conception is the creation of beings, and the conception of our mind is the assimilation of beings.[54]

It was these well-known passages from the *De mente* of Nicholas that led Cassirer to see in him the founder of modern philosophy, inasmuch as he discovered the native functioning of the human intellect, of the unitary principle of knowledge that is constituted by the activity of the mind conceived as the measure *(mens = mensura)* of the surrounding world. The mind is understood as creating numbers and mathematical proportions. Nicholas grounds real beings in conceptual entities, the essence or quiddity of which is unknown to us because it resides in the inscrutable will of God. As a result, the mental mathematical world is the only really sound one for us, because we are its inventors. In Nicholas' works there is real exaltation of the human mind: "There is nothing more noble than the mind."[55] He arrives at this positive conception of human knowledge by developing his idea of christological humanism. As has already been said, the human mind, through Christ, its model, is a *similitudo Dei:* like the divine mind it is creative, but it creates conceptual entities, not real ones.

9. Theology That Is Mathematical or Symbolical Through Enigmas

The *Dialogi idiotae* or *(Dialogi sapientiae),* between an unlearned person *(idiota)* and a speaker *(orator),* mark an important turning point in Nicholas' theological speculation. This work, while leaving intact the idea of the imparticipability of the Truth as absolute precision, works out the theology of Word or of the message of salvation and thereby develops a positive conception both of knowledge and of the revelation of the absolute Truth. This Truth manifests itself as wisdom that cries in the world, in the marketplaces and squares, outside of books and the schools, because the seed of this wisdom (which is Christ) is within our mind and around us.

Our mind is, in fact, a likeness or image of God. But while the medieval thinkers understood this teaching in a static way by conceiving of the human being as an entified image of God, in Nicholas' thinking this teaching becomes dynamic by being related to the Neoplatonic concept, which he develops further, of form as dynamic. This idea is developed through reflection on the notion of knowledge through likeness-assimilation. Assimilation, or making like, is a dynamic process based on the fourfold power of the mind: sensible, animate, rational, intellectual. Thus by knowing, the mind makes itself like its substance, assimilating itself to the intelligibility of the Creator.

In the little work *On the Gift of the Father of Lights* this same concept is developed starting from the notion of assimilation on God's part, which is both opposed and complementary to assimilation on the creature's part. Assimilation in God is identification and, as I have already noted, it is creation in the sense that God, by identifying, calls to himself nothingness, that is, nonbeing. So then, since the identical is not multipliable, every identification consists in assimilation, or likeness, according to an incommensurable relationship. Assimilation in the creature is therefore the coincidence or identity of the descent of the identical into the nonidentical with the ascent of the nonidentical into the identical.[56]

Theology, therefore, says Nicholas in the tenth chapter of *La mente,*[57] is the science of God, but also of all things insofar as they are dynamically assimilated to God. It is, consequently, the science that "precedes" the science of any particular thing. In the *Dialogi idiotae,* which focuses on the relationship between the revelation of wisdom and the cognoscitive capacities of the human mind, after confirming, as he had done in *Learned Ignorance,* his idea of theology as a transcending and as eminence, Nicholas is in substance seeking to find a link between the doctrine of the knowledge of God by negation and a positive retrieval of theology, while always safeguarding the absolute transcendence of God and the thesis of the identity of opposites in God. Knowing well that precisely for this reason he has been accused of heresy, he writes in his *Defense of Learned Ignorance:* "Since control now is in the hands of the sect of the Aristoteleans, who believe that the identity of opposites is a heresy—whereas in fact the assertion of this identity is the beginning of the ascent to mystical theology—those who have been brought up in that insipid 'way' dismiss my way, which rejects Aristotle and seeks to go higher than he did."[58]

The way which Nicholas undertakes is that of the search for God *(De quaerendo Deo)*, or the way of salvation through the revelation of the light. It is an intellectual way that moves along a circular path. Nicholas, who constantly employs the metaphor of the circle in his theological symbology to the point of asserting that all theology follows a circle, starts with the idea that God the Father has given to everyone, along with his free gift of salvation, the possibility of reaching it, which possibility is sufficient for us to achieve salvation. The error of the ancient philosophers (Nicholas never wearies of repeating) is that they regarded God as necessity, whereas he is omnipotence, absolute power, the very power presupposed in everything that can exist.[59]

The theologians and philosophers, Nicholas writes, have tried to express the truth of God by introducing into it "modes," that is, structures of meaning; and the first of these modes is the One:

> The One is that which all theologians and philosophers endeavored to express in a variety of ways. . . . What Zeno, what Parmenides, what Plato, and whatever others have said concerning the truth is not in each case an other, but rather they all looked at the One and expressed it in various modes. Although these modes of expression appear contrary and incompatible with one another, they nonetheless strive for nothing other than in their own mode—the one affirmatively, the other negatively, still another doubtfully—to unfold the One that is unattainable beyond all contrariety. Indeed the one theology is the affirmative, which affirms everything concerning the One; the negative is that [same] one [theology], which denies everything concerning the One; the doubtful, which neither denies nor affirms; the disjunctive, which affirms the one, denies the other; and the copulative, which affirmatively connects the opposites or, negatively, rejects thoroughly the opposites.[60]

The *one* theology is the expression of the varying forms of theology of the ineffable One; but if we search for this ineffable One, it is because we already presuppose him. Thus he is not completely unknown to us; as Nicholas has already pointed out in *Learned Ignorance* and as he then confirms in later works in which he develops and reworks his own mathematical theology, the divine presupposition is the idea of mathematical truth, the notion of an absolute accuracy of truth, which is our mind's starting point when it proceeds by way of conjecture and tries to establish a proportion between this infinite origin and our understanding of the finite. But if this proportionality allows us to understand the mathematical truth of finite things precisely insofar as we can compare them with the One, then the same will allow us to draw near to God in his infinity. In other words, it will be possible, inversely, to start from the knowledge of what is known to us and to try to establish an unknown proportion, that is, a conjectural proportion between the finite and the unknown absolute accuracy.

Nicholas distinguishes two forms of mathematical knowledge: rational-sensible mathematics, which is the one that belongs among the sciences of

Boethius' quadrivium, and a symbolico-speculative mathematics that is founded on the power of imagination proper to the intellect, which expresses its proper objects symbolically and enables us to reach a conception of the Word as absolute accuracy, as the infinite in which the greatest and the least are identical. It is to this second kind of mathematics that Nicholas gives the task of achieving imaginative theological knowledge in which the proportional representability of God is glimpsed. It produces, in fact, the symbolico-theological figures in which it is possible, by the process of transcendence, to express the identity of the arc with the line, the circle with the polygon, the center with the circumference, and the Unity with the Trinity.

In 1453 Nicholas wrote the interesting little work *The Theological Complement,* in which he developed an idea that became a constant element of his thinking: that mathematics and its figures are the privileged, even if enigmatic, mirror of the divine, within which mathematical figures are symbols capable of expressing the incomprehensible identity in God of all the contrary figures, as in "shining propinquity."[61]

Symbols make it possible to move beyond likeness: spiritual realities, therefore, can be investigated only through symbols, which are unstable and mutable images of an inaccessible model. And among all symbols those of mathematics are privileged because they offer the images that are more stable than sensible symbols and more certain than any others.

God in fact creates the world by number, weight, and measure (Wis 11:21): number is therefore the symbolic exemplar of things and the reason that explains them. Mathematical entities are the most intelligible because their matter is not subject to any great change. As a discipline based on the concepts of accuracy and equality, it alone can express quiddities and it alone can embody in its forms the "theology of John," that is, the theology that, insofar as it is trinitarian, is perfect. The Father is equality and indivisibility prior to otherness; the Son is equal to the Father, or in other words, he is a proportion of equality, from which springs the Spirit, that is, the bond that is the identity of equality. For this reason, Nicholas says, "There is the origin of the origin; this is John's theology, which no philosopher has been able to recognize. The origin of the origin is the imparticipable origin that is the infinite, the eternity in which the origin of the origin exists." It is the absolute transcendence of the Father; but at the same time it is the uni-trinal origin, the eternal that is imparticipable in itself but is communicable in its creatures. Using the mathematical concepts of identity, equality, proportion of equality, and unity, Nicholas looks continually for a symbolico-speculative mathematical explanation of the Trinity, the God who is One and Three.[62]

With their idea of the Trinity, Christians have replaced the theology of the philosophers with that of John. "If you could see the origin of mathematics in its purity, you would see it to be uni-trinal. Our science, the true theological science, is in fact science through enigmas, which is infinitely superior to refutational science, to the syllogistic science of the Aristotelean sect."[63] The transcending power of mathematical figures can also be grasped through the deforming lens of the beryllus, a precious stone through which we can see the invisible in enigma and in a mirror.[64]

We read, in the little book whose full title is *The Theological Complement Represented in the Mathematical Complements,* that symbolical mathematics is a complement and an aid, because mathematical symbols make it possible to move beyond rational truths to the coincidence of opposites. Mathematical problems and the manner of dealing with them have a transcendent usefulness in theological figures, because when the figures of the circle, the triangle, rectitude, and circularity are applied to God, they complement what we can know, namely, that the differences among finite entities, between measure and measured, are equality or coincidence in God. In fact, opposition in God, in whom it is not nothing, can also be defined as the coincidence and equality of opposites. "We say that God, who is everything in everything, is the opposition of opposites. And that is nothing other than to say of Him, that He is the origin enfolding the absolute coincidence or the infinite equality."[65]

Mathematical theology is thus a circular theology in the sense that when a mathematician draws a polygon, in a wonderful way he contemplates the infinite exemplar of the circle, for when he traces a triangle, he does not see the sensible triangle but one free of all quantitative contractions; and thus he sees the circularity of the triangle, the square, the polygon in the infinite circle.[66] The absolute infinite cannot, in fact, be contracted by any reason; but the converse holds: that which is contracted—the triangle, the square, the polygon— can be "attracted" by the infinite and be freed from contraction in the infinite circle.[67] Theology is thus set within a circle, for this reason also, that all the names we attribute to God (such as angle, square, or goodness and justice) are confirmed each by the others circularly, so that in God supreme justice is also supreme truth, and vice versa.[68]

In short, the whole of theology can be compared, as I have said, to a "circle: in which all things are one through the infinite circulation of the absolute and imparticipable infinite:[69] the circle is the figure privileged by Nicholas because it includes all the figures, all the modes of speaking, all the names.

But the claim that theology is circular is also in perfect agreement with the principle of learned ignorance: we do not know how the infolding and unfolding of all things take place because their cause is the omnipotent will of God, whose mode we do not know. We know the images but not the mirror. And the images, which are creatures, are nothing in themselves, because they have being only through their dependence on that omnipotence. The contraction or limitation of creatures holds for the entire earthly universe, but it does not hold in the divine reality that is the Trinity. In the Trinity the unity is not contracted as the whole is contracted in its parts or as the universe is contracted in particular beings.[70] Not everything, then, coincides in God, but only the divine attributes coincide in God in whom there is the coincidence of unity and Trinity.[71] Circular theology is therefore unitive theology, because it is one. It is both the theology that denies and theology that affirms, and it is the single expression of the varied forms of theology of the ineffable One.

Mathematics, therefore, and not metaphysics, is the science closest to theology, insofar as it can be the latter's symbolical foundation. Nicholas writes that in the mathematical figures of our mind as in a living mirror, theological figures are seen "in shining propinquity," that is, through likeness and proximity. This is why Nicholas would write a number of short treatises on the squaring of the circle: in them he is looking for help in grasping theological truths.[72]

10. The Theology of the Supposition, or Sufficient Theology, or Theology of Discourse

In his *Defense of Learned Ignorance,* Nicholas writes: "A great many who boast of possessing the science of theology are blind." Almost all those who devote themselves to the study of theology turn to positive doctrines and their forms and believe that they are theologians when they are able to talk like those whom they have chosen as teachers. But the end of this science (Nicholas says) is hidden in God, and the science of this world is foolishness by comparison with it.[73] In his *On Conjectures* he likewise had harsh words to say about the direction taken by the "modern theologians," who (he wrote) subject God to the laws of their reason: "When we as rational human beings speak of God, we subject God to the laws of reason, to the point of affirming some things of God, denying others, and applying the opposites to him disjunctively. This is pretty much the direction taken by all the modern theologians who speak of God with the reason."[74]

But as I remarked earlier, it would be a mistake to attribute to Nicholas the intention of setting up in opposition to traditional theological science his own teaching on learned ignorance, that is, a theology that is profoundly negative or, more generally, mystical if not outright skeptical. Furthermore, his development of a mathematical theology showed the possibility of allowing for our mind a positive knowledge of God precisely because in seeking him as ineffable we presuppose him in some way. The mature Nicholas undertook, in his dialogues on the *Idiota,* the important task of creating and developing such a theology of the presupposition[75] or sufficient theology or theology of discourse *(theologia sermocinalis).*[76]

Those who search always presuppose that for which they search but do not presuppose the reason for their search. This is a profound mystery. All who seek knowledge suppose that knowledge is that by reason of which each wise person is wise.[77] Eternal wisdom may be tasted, therefore, in everything that carries its taste. Thus it cries out in the squares; it speaks in the book of the world that has been written by the hand of God and not in the books in libraries. It is loved in every lovable thing; it is the beauty in everything beautiful. But the most joyful life is that of the intellect, and the most joyous desire is intellectual desire. The fulfillment of this desire is the goal of knowledge; the desire consists in the desire of immortal life, in which desire there is already a foretaste of the eternal wisdom. But since nothing is desired that is completely unknown, in every desire of immortal life is hidden the immortality of life. This desire is like the iron that is drawn by the magnet, because in the iron there exists by nature a certain foretaste of the magnet: our magnet is Christ, who draws us, through himself, to the Father (according to an image which Nicholas takes from Albertus Magnus).

Along the same line, it can be said that every question *(quaestio)* about God supposed that which is asked *(quaesitum);* that is, in every question about God the very question presupposes God. In fact, God is signified in every signification of words, although he cannot signify himself. This theme of the theology of the presupposition is developed clearly and brilliantly especially in the second book, *La mente,* of the dialogues on the *Idiota:*

> *Idiota:* When I put to you the question whether God is, you tell me in answer what is presupposed, namely, that he is, because he is the entity presupposed in the question. Thus if someone asks what kind of being God is, you will answer that God is the absolute quiddity, because the question presupposes that there are quiddities. And so on in other questions. Nor is there any room for doubt. God is, in fact, the absolute presupposition of all things, in whatever way they are presupposed, just as in every effect the cause is presupposed. See, speaker, how easy the theological difficulty is.
> *Speaker:* This ease is indeed very great and astonishing.
> *Idiota:* I tell you even that God is infinite ease and that it never befits him to be infinite difficulty. . . .
> *Speaker:* If that which is presupposed in every question is, in theology, the answer to the question, then there is no real question about God, because in such questions the answer is the same as the question.
> *Idiot:* An accurate conclusion. And I add that since God is infinite rectitude and absolute necessity, no doubtful question has any place in him; rather in God every doubt is certainty. Therefore, every answer to a question about God is not a proper and precise reply since precision is only one and infinite, and it is God. Every answer participates in the absolute answer, which is infinitely precise. But what I was saying to you—that in theological questions the presupposition is the answer—must be understood in relation to the way the question was put. Realize, therefore, that this is enough, since it is not possible for either the question about God or the answer to the question to reach precision; according to the degree in which the question approximates precision, so in the same degree does the answer naming the presupposition. This is the sufficiency we receive from God, we who know that we cannot grasp the unattainable precision except in a

mode that participates in the mode of the absolute precision. And among these varied and manifold modes that participate in the unique mode of the precision, that of which we have already spoken comes closest to the absolute ease. And this is our sufficiency, in view of the fact that we cannot attain to another mode that would be both easier and truer.[78]

Nicholas does not mean to abandon the meanings and power of words; his intention is rather to go beyond them, in keeping with his particular doctrine on signs (as he will maintain in the late work, *Compendium*), and give positive effectiveness to all theological discourses:

> *Speaker:* As I understand it, you wish to say that in the theology of discourse, that is, the theology in which we recognize the validity of discourse about God and do not completely exclude the effectiveness of language, you have grounded the sufficiency of difficult truths in an ease in the way of forming truer statements about God.
>
> *Idiota:* You have grasped it. In fact, if I am to explain to you my concept of God, and if my discourse is to be of service to you, it must be such that its terms are meaningful in a way that can lead you to what is sought, thanks to the power of words known to both of us. God is what is being sought. Therefore the theology of discourse is that by which I endeavor to lead you to God, through the power of words, in the way that is easier for me and true.[79]

In this sense too, then, the Logos, who is the word *(sermo)* of God, is the connecting link between the absolute transcendence of God and the positivity of the secular world.

Theological discourse proves, in this way, to be possible precisely as discourse, although with all its natural contradictions, which Nicholas knows cannot be straightened out but which he invites us to surmount, in order to reconcile them by means of the mind and mathematical measure *(mensura)*. It is precisely in this way that he is able to bring to completion his plan for replacing theology as an objective science with a conception of theology as a different kind of cognoscitive approach—one that is conjectural and approximative through assimilation and likeness and no longer through abstraction and adequation—to the unattainable One in his trinitarian sameness or identity, which constitutes the Christian mystery.

BIBLIOGRAPHY

The first edition of the *Opera omnia* of Nicholas of Cusa was the Strasbourg edition of 1484. Roland Pallavicini had it reprinted in 1502, probably in Cortemaggiore. The third edition, Paris, 1514, edited by Lefèvre d'Étaples (reprinted: New York/Frankfurt a. M., 1962), was decidedly better. The fourth, Basel, 1565, was a reprint of the Paris edition, with the addition of some lesser mathematical writings (it is still the most complete edition).

The edition of the *Philosophische Schriften,* ed. A. Petzelt, Stuttgart, 1949, uses the text of volume I of the Basel edition, with references to the Paris edition. The Berlin, 1966, edition of the same, edited by P. P. Wilpert, uses the text of the Strasbourg edition.

Presently in progress is a critical edition of all the works by the Heidelberg Academy: Nicolai de Cusa, *Opera omnia,* iussu et auctoritate Academiae litterarum Heidelbergensis ad codicum fidem edita, Leipzig (to 1944), Hamburg (1950 to the present): Meier Publishing House. The same Academy is also publishing an *editio minor* in the Philosophische Bibliothek of the same publisher; at first this was only in German translation but now has a Latin text as well (which sometimes anticipates or corrects the text of the *editio maior*) and introductory studies and notes.

E. Zellinger had published a *Cusanus-Konkordanz,* Munich, 1950. Documents essential for a biography of Nicholas have been published in *Acta Cusana,* ed. E. Meuthen; 2 vols., Hamburg, 1976–83. See also (in order of publication):

Marx, J. *Geschichte des Armen-Hospitals zum heiligen Nikolaus zu Kues.* Trier, 1907. Reprinted by the Cusanus-Gesellschaft: Bernkastel-Kues, 1976.

Meuthen, *Die letzten Jahre des Nikolaus von Kues. Biographische Untersuchungen nach neuen Quellen.* Cologne-Opladen, 1958.

_____. "Neue Schlaglichter auf das Leben des Nikolaus von Kues." *MFCG* 4 (1964) 37–53.

_____. *Nikolaus von Kues (1401–1464). Skizze einer Biographie.* Münster, 1982³.

Laufner, R. "Eine Kurzbiographie des Nikolaus von Kues um 1550," *MFCG* 15 (1982) 81–85.

Übinger, J. "Kleinere Beiträge. Zur Lebensgeschichte des Nikolaus Cusanus." *HistJb* 14 (1983) 549–51.

Hallauer, H. J. "Das St. Andreas-Hispiz der Anima in Rom, Ein Beitrag zur Biographie des Nikolaus von Kues." *MFCG* 19 (1991) 25–52.

On Nicholas' Work

Das Werk des Nicolaus Cusanus. Eine bibliophile Einführung. Ed. G. Heinz-Mohr and W. P. Eckert. Cologne, 1963. Pp. 109–21.

On Nicholas' Library

Rotta, P. "La biblioteca del Cusano." *RivFilNeo* 21 (1927) 22–47.

Volkelt, P. "Der Bilderschmuck der Cusanus-Bibliothek." *MFCG* 4 (1964) 230–53.

Bianca, C. "La biblioteca romana di Niccolò Cusano." *Scrittura, Biblioteche e stampa a Rome nel Quattrocento.* Atti del 2º seminario della Scuola Vaticana di Paleografia, Diplomatica e Archivistica (6–8 maggio 1982). Littera Antiqua 3. Vatican City, 1983. Pp. 669–708.

The issues of the *Mitteilungen und Forschungen der Cusanus-Gesellschaft (MFCG)* systematically assemble the bibliography on Nicholas. See, in particular, the following surveys: 1 (1961) 95–126; 3 (1963) 223–37; 6 (1967) 178–202; 10 (1973) 207–34; 15 (1982) 121–47. For bibliography see also R. Kilbansky, in *Philosophy in Mid-Century,* ed. R. Klibansky (Florence, 1959) 88–94.

STUDIES (ALPHABETICALLY BY AUTHOR)

Nicolò da Cusa. Relazioni tenute al Convegno interuniversitario di Bressanone nel 1960. Florence, 1962.

Das Cusanus-Jubiläum. MFCG 4 (1964).

Cusano e Galileo. Archivio di filosofia, 1964.

Nicola de Cusa en el centenario de sua muerte (1464–1964). Madrid, 1967.

Nicolò Cusano agli inizi del mondo moderno. Atti del Congresso internazionale in occasione del V centenario della morte de N. C. (Bressanone, 6–10 settembre 1964). Facoltà di Magistero dell'Università di Padova 12. Florence, 1970.

Nikolaus von Kues als Promotor der Oekumene. MFCG 9 (1971).

Nikolaus von Kues. Einführung in sein philosophisches Denken. Ed. K. Jacobi. Freiburg-Munich, 1979.

Das Sehen Gottes nach Nikolaus von Kues. Akten des Symposions von Trier (vom. 25. bis 27. September 1986), Ed. R. Haubst. *MFCG* 18 (1989).

Nicholas of Cusa in Search of God and Wisdom. Essays in Honour of M. Watanabe. Ed. G. Christenson and T. M. Izbicki. Studies in the History of Christian Thought 45. Leiden–New York, 1991.

Concordia discors. Studi su Niccolò Cusano e l'umanesimo europeo offerti a G. Santinello. Ed. G. Piaia. Padua, 1993.

Alberigo, G. *Chiesa conciliare. Identità e significato del conciliarismo.* Brescia, 1981. Pp. 266–70 and 293–354.

Alvarez-Gómez, M. *Der verborgene Gegenwart des Unendlichen bei Nikolaus von Kues.* Munich-Salzburg, 1968.

_____. "Der Mensch als Schöpfer seiner Welt. Überlegungen zu *De coniecturis.*" *MFCG* 13 (1978) 160–66.

_____. "Zur Metaphysik der Macht bei Nikolaus von Kues." *MFCG* 14 (1980) 104–22.

Arduini, M. L. "*Ad hanc superadmirandam harmonicam pacem.* Riforma della Chiesa ed ecumenismo religioso nel pensiero di Nicolò Cusano: il *De pace fidei.*" *RivFilNeo* 72 (1980) 224–42.

Battaglia, F. *Il pensiero giuridico e politico di Nicolò Cusano.* Bologna, 1955.

_____. *Metafisica, religione e politica nel pensiero di Niccolò Cusano.* Bologna, 1965.

Baum, W. *Nicolaus Cusanus in Tirol. Das Wirken des Philosophen und Reformators als Fürstbischof von Brixen.* Bolzano, 1983.

Beierwaltes, W. "*Visio absoluta.* Reflexion als Grundzug des göttlichen Prinzips bei Nicolaus Cusanus." *Sitzungsberichte der Heidelberger Akademie der Wissenschaften,* Philos.-Hist. Klasse, 1978, no. 1, pp. 5–33.

_____. "Identität und Differenz. Zum Prinzip cusanischen Denkens." *Rheinisch-Westfälische Akademie der Wissenschaften* 1977. Pp. 5–42. Reprinted in idem, *Identität und Differenz.* Frankfurt a. M., 1980. Pp. 105–75.

_____. *Denken des Einen. Studien zur neplatonischen Philosophie und ihrer Wirkungsgeschichte.* Frankfurt a. M., 1985.

_____. "Eriugena und Cusanus." *Eriugena redivivus. Zur Wirkungsgeschichte seines Denkens im Mittelalter und im Übergang zur Neuzeit.* Vorträge des V. Intern. Eriugena-Colloquiums (Bad Homberg, 26.-30. August 1985). Heidelberg, 1987. Pp. 311–43.

Berti, E. "L'analogia dell'essere nella tradizione aristotelico-tomista." *Metafore dell'invisibile. Ricerche sull'analogia.* Ed. G. Santinello. Brescia, 1984.

Bett, H. *Nicholas of Cusa.* London, 1932.

Biecheler, J. E. *The Religious Language of Nicholas of Cusa.* Missoula, 1975.

_____. "Nicholas of Cusa and Muhammad: A Fifteenth-Century Encounter." *Downside Review* 101, no. 342 (1983) 50–59.

Bohnenstädt, E. *Kirche und Reich im Schrifttum des Nikolaus von Kues.* Heidelberg, 1939. = *Sitzungsberichte der Heidelberger Akademie der Wissenschaften,* 1988–89, no. 1.

Bonetti, A. *La ricerca metafisica nel pensiero di Nicolò Cusano.* Brescia, 1973.

Bormann, K. "Zur Frage nach der Seinserkenntnis in dem wahrscheinlich letzten philosophisch-theologischen Werk des Nikolaus von Kues, dem *Compendium.*" *ArchGeschPhil,* 1968, 181–88.

_____. "Die Koordinierung der Erkenntnisstufen *(descensus* und *ascensus)* bei Nikolaus von Kues." *MFCG* 11 (1975) 62–79.

_____. "'Übereinstimmung und Verschiedenheit der Menschen' (*De coniec.* II, 15)." *MFCG* 13 (1978) 88–104.

Borsche, T. "Entgrenzung des Naturbegriffs. Vollendung und Kritik des Platonismus bei Nikolaus von Kues." *Mensch und Natur im Mittelalter.* Ed. A. Zimmermann and A. Speer. Miscellanea Mediaevalia 21. Berlin, 1991. II, 562–71.

O'R. Boyle, M. "Cusanus at Sea: The Topicality of Illuminative Discourse." *Journal of Religion* 71 (1991) 160–201.

Bredow, G. von. "Der Gedanke der Singularitas in der Altersphilosophie des Nikolaus von Kues." *MFCG* 4 (1964) 375–83.

_____. "Die personale Existenz der Geistseele." *MFCG* 14 (1980) 123–45.

_____. "Nikolaus von Kues und die Alchemie. Ein Versuch." *MFCG* 17 (1986) 177–87.

Breidert, W., "Mathematik und symbolische Erkenntnis bei Nikolaus von Kues." *MFCG* 12 (1987) 116–26.

Breuning W. "Der Beitrag des Nikolaus von Kues zum Religionsgespräche der Gegenwart." *Trierer Theologische Zeitschrift,* 1964, 224–28.

Caminiti, F. N. "Nikolaus von Kues und Bonaventura." *MFCG* 4 (1964) 129–44.

Capitani, O. "Per il significato dell'attesa dell'età nuova in Niccolò da Cusa." *L'attesa dell'età nuova nella spiritualità del fine del Medioevo.* Convegno del Centro di Studi sulla Spiritualità medievale (Todi, Accademia Tudertina, 16–19 ottobre 1960). Todi, 1962. Pp. 197–216.

Casarella, P. "Neues zu den Quellen der cusanischen Mauersymbolik." *MFCG* 19 (1992) 273–86.

Cassirer, E. *Storia della filosofia moderna.* Turin, 1954². I, 39–96. Original: *Das Erkenntnisproblem in der Philosophie und Wissenschaft der neueren Zeit.* Berlin, 1906.

_____. *Individuum und Kosmos in der Philosophie der Renaissance.* Leipzig, 1927.

Christianson, G. "Cardinal Cesarini and Cusa's *Concordantia.*" *Church History* 54 (1985) 7–19.

Colomer Pons, E. *Nikolaus von Kues und Raimund Llull. Aus Handschriften der Kueser Bibliothek.* Berlin, 1961.

_____. "Individuo e cosmo in Nicolò Cusano e Giovanni Pico." *L'opera e il pensiero di Giovanni Pico della Mirandola nella storia dell'Umanesimo.* Convegno

Internazionale (Mirandola, 15–18 settembre 1963). II. Florence, 1965. Pp. 53–102.

————. "Nicolau de Cusa i el lul.lisme europeu quatrecentista." *Randa* 27 (1990) 71–85.

Coreth, E. "Nikolaus von Kues, ein Denker an der Zeitenwende." *Cusanus-Gedächtnisschrift*. Ed. N. Grass. Innsbruck-Munich, 1970. Pp. 3–16.

Cranz, F. F. "Saint Augustine and Nicholas of Cusa in the Tradition of Western Christian Thought." *Speculum* 28 (1953) 297–316.

————. "Cusanus, Luther, and the Mystical Tradition." *The Pursuit of Holiness in Late Medieval and Renaissance Religion*. Ed. C. Trinkaus and H. A. Oberman. Studies in Medieval and Reformation Thought 10. Leiden, 1974. Pp. 93–102.

D'Amico, C. "Nicolás de Cusa. *De mente:* La profondización de la doctrina del hombre-imagen." *Patristica et Mediaevalia* 12 (1991) 53–67.

Dangelmayr, S. *Gotteserkenntnis und Gottesbegriff in den philsophischen Schriften des Nikolaus von Kues*. Meisenheim a. G., 1969.

Decker, B. "Die Toleranzidee bei Nikolaus von Kues und in der Neuzeit." *Nicolò da Cusa* (see first entry in this bibliography). Pp. 197–216.

————. Nikolaus von Kues und der Friede unter der Religionen." *Humanismus, Mystik and Kunst in der Welt des Mittelalters*. Ed. J. Koch. Leiden-Cologne, 1953. Pp. 94–121.

Gandillac, M. de. *La philosophie de Nicolas de Cues*. Paris, 1942. Revised German edition: *Nikolaus von Kues*. Düsseldorf, 1953.

————. "Coexistence pacifique et véritable paix: Nicolai de Cusa *De pace fidei*." *Recherches de philosophie* 3–4 (1959) 405–7.

————. "Le *De concordantia catholica* de Nicolas de Cues." *RHE* 64 (1969) 418–23.

————. "Das Ziel der *una religione in varietate rituum*." *MFCG* 16 (1984) 192–213.

Doyon, J. "La christologie de Nicolas de Cusa." *Le Christ hier, aujourd'hui et demain*. Ed. R. Laflamme and M. Gervais. Quebec, 1976. Pp. 171–90.

Declow, D. F. "The Dynamics of Analogy in Nicholas of Cusa." *International Philosophical Quarterly* 21 (1981) 295–301.

————. "Anselm's *Proslogion* and Nicholas of Cusa's Wall of Paradise." *Downside Review* 100, no. 338 (1982) 22–30.

Dupré, L. "The Mystical Theology of Cusanus' *De visione Dei*." *Eros and Eris, Contributions to a Hermeneutical Phenomenology: Liber amicorum for Adrian Peperzak*. Ed. P. van Tongeren and others. Phaenomenologica 127. Dordrecht-Boston-London, 1992. Pp. 15–17.

Dupré. W. "Der Mensch als Mikrocosmos im Denken des Nikolaus von Cues." *MFCG* 13 (1978) 68–87.

————. "Menschsein und Mensch als Wahrheit im Werden." *MFCG* 16 (1984) 313–24.

————. "Nikolaus von Kues." *Millennium* 1 (1987) 27–37.

Durao, P. "O ecumenismo de Nicolau de Cusa." *Revista portuguesa de filosofia* 20 (1964) 385–500.

Federici Vescovini, G. "L'irenismo di Niccolò Cusano." *La tolleranza religiosa. Indagini storiche e riflessioni filosofiche*. Ed. M. Sina. Milan, 1991. Pp. 18–25.

————. "La 'dotta ignoranza' di Cusano e san Bonaventura." *Doctor Seraphiscus* 40–41 (1993–94) 49–68.

————. "Temi ermetico-neoplatonici de 'La dotta ignoranza' di Nicola Cusano." *Il neoplatonismo nel Rinascimento*. Atti del Convegno internazionale (Roma-

Firenze, 12–14 dicembre 1990). Ed. P. Prini. Rome, 1993. Pp. 117–32.

Flash. K. *Die Metaphysik des Einen bei Nikolaus von Kues, Problemgeschichtliche Stellung und systematische Bedeutung.* Leiden, 1973.

————. "Nikolaus von Kues und Pico della Mirandola." *MFCG* 14 (1980) 113–20.

Fräntzki, E. *Nikolaus von Kues und das Problem der absoluten Subjektivität.* Meisenheim a. G., 1972.

Garin, E. "Cusano e i Platonici italiani del Quattrocento." *Nicolò da Cusa* (first entry in this bibliography). Pp. 75–100. Also in idem. *L'età nuova. Ricerche di storia della cultura dal XII al XVI secolo.* Naples, 1969. Pp. 265–86.

————. "Ermolao Barbaro lettore di Cusano." *RCSF* 26 (1971) 79–80.

Hagemann, L. *Der Kur'an in Verständnis und Kritik bei Nikolaus von Kues. Beitrag zur Erhellung islamisch-christlicher Geschichte.* Frankfurt a. M., 1976.

Haubst, R. *Das Bild des Einen und Dreieinen Gottes in der Welt nach Nikolaus von Kues.* Trier, 1952.

————. "Zum Fortleben Alberts des Grosses, bei Heymeric von Kamp und Nikolaus von Kues." *Studia albertina.* Ed. B. Geyer, BGPTM, Supplbd. 4. Münster i. W., 1952. Pp. 420–70.

————. *Studien zu Nikolaus von Kues und Johannes Wenk aus Handschriften der Vatikanischen Bibliothek.* BGPTM 38.1. Münster i. W., 1955.

————. "Studien zu Nikolaus von Kues und Johannes Wenk. Neue Erörterung und Nachträge." *RömQ* 53 (1958) 81–88.

————. *Nikolaus von Kues und die moderne Wissenschaft.* Trier, 1963.

————. "Zusammenfassende Erwägungen (Zur Interpretation von *De coniecturis*)." *MFCG* 8 (1970) 192–98.

————. "Der Leitgedanke der *Repraesentatio* in der cusanischen Ekklesiologie." *MFCG* 9 (1971) 140–59.

————. "Theologie in der Philosophie. Philosophie in der Theologie des Nikolaus von Cusa." *MFCG* 11 (1973) 233–60.

————. "Das Werdenkönnen der Welt und die absolute Wirklichkeit Gottes." *Perspektiven der Philosophie* 16 (1990) 75–84.

————. "Albertus wie Cusanus ihm sah." *Albertus Magnus, doctor universalis (1290–1990).* Ed. G. Meer and A. Zimmermann. Mainz, 1980. Pp. 167–92.

————. "Das Neue in *De docta ignorantia*." *MFCG* 20 (1992) 27–53.

Haug, W. "Die Mauer des Paradieses. Zur *mystica theologia* des Nicolaus Cusanus in *De visione Dei*." *Theologische Zeitschrift* 45 (1989) 231–43.

————. "Das Kugelspiel des Nicolaus Cusanus und die Poetik der Renaissance." *Daphnis* 15 (1986) 357–74.

Heinz-Mohr, G. *Unitas christiana. Studium zur Gesellschaftslehre des Nikolaus von Kues.* Trier, 1968.

Hempel, H. *Nikolaus von Kues in seiner Beziehung zur bildenden Kunst.* Berlin, 1952.

Henningfeld, J. "La définition du langage chez S. Augustin et Nicolas de Cues." *Archives de philosophie* 54 (1991) 255–68.

Herbst, L. *Das organische Formprinzip im Weltbild des Nikolaus von Kues.* Berlin, 1940.

Herold, N. *Menschliche Perspektive und Wahrheit. Zur Deutung der Subjektivität in den philosophischen Schriften des Nikolaus von Kues.* Münster i. W., 1975.

————. "'Subjektivität' als Problem der Cusanus-Interpretation." *MFCG* 14 (1980) 146–66.

Hirschberger, J. "Das Prinzip der Inkommensurabilität bei Niholaus von Kues." *MFCG* 11 (1975) 39–61.

_____. "Die Stellung des Nikolaus von Kues in der Entwicklung der deutschen Philosophie." *Sitzungsberichte der wissenschaftlichen Gesellschaft an der J. W. Goethe-Universität a. M.* 15, 3 (1978) 119–37.

Hirt, P. "Vom Wesen der konjekturalen Logik nach Nicholaus von Kues." *MFCG* 8 (1970) 179–91.

Hoffmann, E. *Das Universum des Nikolaus von Kues.* Cusanus Studien. Heidelberg, 1929–30.

Hofman, J. E. "Mutmassungen über das früheste mathematische Wissen des Nikolaus von Kues." *MFCG* 5 (1965) 98–136.

Hopkins, J. *A Concise Introduction to the Philosophy of Nicholas of Cusa.* Minneapolis, 1980².

_____. *Nicolas of Cusa's Metaphysic of Contraction.* Minneapolis, 1983.

_____. *Nicolas of Cusa's Debate with John Wenck: A Translation and an Appraisal of De Ignota Literatura and Apologia Doctae Ignorantiae.* Minneapolis, 1984².

Hummel, C. *Nikolaus Cusanus.* Bern, 1961.

Imbach, R. "Einheit des Glaubens. Spuren des Cusanischen Dialogs *De pace fidei* bei Heymericus de Campo. *FZPT* 27 (1980) 5–23.

Izbicki, T. M. "Aszüge aus Schriften des Nikolaus von Kues im Rahmen der Geschichte des Basler Konzils. Untersuchung und Edition." *MFCG* 19 (1991) 117–35.

Iserloh, E. "Reform der Kirche bei Nikolaus von Kues." *MFCG* 4 (1964) 105ff.

Jacobi. K. *Die Methode der cusanischen Philosophie.* Freiburg-Munich, 1969.

Jacobi, M. *Die Weltgebäude Kardinals Nikolaus von Cues.* Berlin, 1904.

Jäger, A. *Der Streit Nikolaus von Cues mit dem Herzog von Österreich.* 2 vols. 1861. Reprinted: Frankfurt a. M. 1966–67.

Jaspers, K. *Nikolaus Cusanus.* Munich, 1964, 1968².

Kaiser, A. "Die Christologie des Nikolaus von Kues im Urteil Isaak August Dorners (1809–1894)." *MFCG* 19 (1991) 196–200.

Kalusa, Z. "Das *Centheologicon* des Heymericus de Campo und die darin enthaltenen Cusanus-Reminiszenzen: Hinweise und Materialen." *Traditio* 39 (1983) 457–77.

Kandler, K.-H. *"Theologia mystica - theologia facilis - theologia sermocinalis* bei Nikolaus von Kues." *Historia philosophiae medii aevi: Studien zur Geschichte der Philosophie des Mittelalters.* Ed. B. Mojsisch and O. Pluta. 2 vols. Amsterdam, 1991. I, 467–76.

Kiening, Ch. "*Gradus visionis.* Reflexion des Sehens in der cusanischen Philosophie." *MFCG* 19 (1991) 243–72.

Klibansky, R. "Copernic et Nicolas de Cues." *Léonard de Vinci et l'expérience scientifique au XVIe siècle.* Paris, 1953. Pp. 225–35.

Koch, J. *Die "ars coniecturalis" des Nikolaus von Kues.* Cologne-Opladen, 1956.

_____. "Der Sinn des zweiten Hauptwerkes de Nikolaus von Kues, *De coniecturis.*" Idem, *Kleine Schriften* Rome, 1973. I, 599–616.

_____. "Nikolaus von Cues und seine Umwelt. Untersuchungen zu Cusanus-Texte. IV. Briefe. Erste Sammlung." *Sitzungsberichte der Heidelberger Akademie der Wissenschaften,* 1944–1948, 2. Abh. Heidelberg, 1948. Pp. 45–78.

Königsberg, D. "Universality, the Universe, and Nicholas of Cusa's Untastable Foretaste of Wisdom." *European History Quarterly* 17 (1987) 1–33.

Kremer, K. "Erkennen bei Nikolaus von Kues. Apriorismus-Assimilation-Abstaktion."

MFCG 13 (1978) 23–57.

_____. "Die Hinführung *(manuductio)* von Polytheisten zum einen, von Juden und Muslimen zum dreieinen Gott." *MFCG* 16 (1984) 126–63.

_____. "Gott - in allen alles, in nichts nichts. Bedeutung und Herkunft dieser Lehre des Nikolaus von Kues." *MFCG* 17 (1986) 188–219.

_____. "Weisheit als Voraussetzung und Erfüllung der Sehnsucht des menschlichen Geistes." *MFCG* 20 (1992) 105–46.

Lenz, J. *Die docta ignorantia oder die mystische Gotteserkenntnis des Nikolaus Cusanus.* Würzburg, 1923.

Lentzen, W. *Den Glauben Christi teilen. Theologie und Verkundigung bei Nikolaus von Kues.* Stuttgart-Berlin-Cologne, 1991.

Lohr, Ch. "Die Exzerptensammlung des Nikolaus von Kues aus den Werken Ramon Lulls." *FZPT* 30 (1983) 373–84.

Lucentini, P. *Platonismo medievale. Contributi alla storia dell'eriugenismo.* Florence, 1980². Pp. 77–109 and 113–24 (edition of Nicholas' marginal notes in the *Clavis physicae* of Honorius of Autum and the *Periphyseon* of John Scotus Eriugena).

Lübke, A. *Nikolaus von Kues. Kirchenfürst zwischen Mittelalter und Neuzeit.* Munich, 1968.

Mannarino, L. "Visione intellettuale di Dio e fede universale: Cusano lettore di Eckhart." *Medioevo e Rinascimento* 2 (1988) 131–215.

Meier, S. "Von der Koinzidenz zur *Coincidentia oppositorum.* Um den philoso-phiehistorischnen Hintergrund des Cusanischen Koinzidenzgedankens." *Die Philosophie im 14. und 15. Jahrhundert. In memoriam K. Michalski.* Ed. O. Pluta. Amsterdam, 1988. Pp. 321–43.

Meinhardt, H. "Der christologische Impuls im Menschenbild des Nikolaus von Kues, Erwägungen eines Philosophen über den ersten christlichen Humanismus im drit-ten Buch von *De docta ignorantia.*" *MFCG* 13 (1978) 105–16.

Mennichen, P. *Nikolaus von Kues.* Leipzig, 1932.

Metzke, E. "Nikolaus von Kues und Hegel. Ein Beitrag zur Problem der philosophis-chen Theologie." *Kantstudien* 48 (1956–57) 216–34.

Meurers, J. "Nikolaus von Kues und die Entwicklung des astronomischen Weltbildes." *MFCG* 4 (1964) 395–417.

Meuthen, E. "Nikolaus von Kues in der Entscheidung zwischen Konxil und Papst." *MFCG* 9 (1971) 19–33.

_____. "Nikolaus von Kues und die Geschichte." *MFCG* 13 (1978) 234–52.

Miller, C. L. "Nicholas of Cusa's *The Vision of God*": An Introduction to the Medieval Mystics of Europe. Ed. P. E. Szarmach. Albany, 1984. Pp. 293–312.

Moffits Watts, P. *Nicholas Cusanus: A Fifteenth-Century Vision of Man.* Studies in the History of Christian Thought 30. Leiden, 1982.

Mojsisch, B. "'Nichts' und 'Negation.' Meister Eckhart und Nikolaus von Kues." *Historia philosophiae medii aevi. Studien zur Geschichte der Philosophie des Mittelalters.* Ed. B. Mojsisch and O. Pluta. 2 vols. Amsterdam, 1991. II, 675–93.

Morrissey, Th. E. "Cardinal Zabarella and Nicholas of Cusa: From Community Authority to Consent of the Community." *MFCG* 17 (1986) 157–76.

Morra, G. *Niccolò Cusano, la vita e la morte.* Bologna, 1966.

Nagel, F. *Nicolaus Cusanus und die Entstehung der exakten Wissenschaften.* Münster i. W., 1984.

Odie, S. "Über die Grundlagen der cusanischen Konjekturenlehre." *MFCG* 8 (1970) 147–78.

Otte, K. "Rechtfertigung aud Glauben als Religionsgrenzen übersteigende Kraft." *MFCG* 16 (1984) 333–42.

Pätzold, D. *Einheit und Andersheit. Die Bedeutung kategorialer Neubindungen in der Philosophie Nikolaus von Kues.* Cologne, 1981.

Pauli, H. "Freiheitsdenker und Gottsucher. Aus Leben und Gedankenwelt des Nikolaus von Kues." *Kurtrierisches Jahrbuch* 30 (1990) 77–98.

Pedersen, J. E. "The Unity of Religion and Universal Peace: Nicholas of Cusa and his *De pace fidei* (1453)." *War and Peace in the Middle Ages.* Ed. B. P. McGuire. Copenhagen, 1987. Pp. 195–215.

Pelikan, J. "Negative Theology and Positive Theology: A Study of Nicholas Cusanus' *De pace fidei.*" *Prudentia,* Suppl. 1981, Pp. 65–77.

Peters, A. "Zum christlichen Menschenbild: Freiheit, Erlösung und Rechtfertigung, Glaube und Werke." *MFCG* 16 (1984) 214–54.

Pindl-Büchl, Th. "Relació entre les epistemologies de Ramon Llull i Nicolau de Cusa." *Randa* 27 (1990) 87–98.

Platzcek, E. W. "El lulismo en las obras del Cardinal Nicola Krebs de Cusa." *RevEspTeol* 2 (1941) 731–65; 3 (1942) 237–324.

Posch, A. *Die "Concordantia catholica" des Nikolaus von Cues.* Paderborn, 1930.

Price, E. F. "Nicholas of Cusa's Idea of Wisdom." *Traditio* 13 (1954) 345–68.

Ranet, J. *Schöpfer und Geschöpf nach Kardinal Nikolaus von Cues.* Würzburg, 1924.

Reinhardt, K. "Islamische Wurzeln des cusanischen Mauersymbolik? Die 'Mauer des Paradieses' im 'Liber scalae Mahometi.'" *MFCG* 19 (1991) 287–91.

————. "Christus—'Wort und Weisheit Gottes.'" *MFCG* 20 (1992) 68–104.

Riccati, C. "Eriugena e Cusano: due concezioni del mondo come esplicazione della natura intellettuale." *Memorie dell'Accademia delle Scienze di Torino. II. Cl. di Scienze Morali, Storiche e Filologiche,* Ser. 5, 1 (1977) 85–87.

————. *"Processio" et "Explicatio." La doctrine de la création chez Jean Scot et Nicolas du Cues.* Naples, 1983. See review by W. Beierwaltes in *MFCG* 17 (1986) 272–77.

Ritter, J. *Docta ignorantia.* Leipzig, 1927.

Rogner, H. *Die Bewertung des Erkennens und das Sein in der Philosophie des Nikolaus von Kues.* Heidelberg, 1937.

Rombach, H. *Substanz, System, Struktur. Die Ontologie des Funktionalismus und der philosophische Hintergrund der modernen Wissenschaft.* 2 vols. Freiburg i. B.- Munich, 1965–66. I, 150–79 and 206–28.

Rössler, D. "Le concept de la nature chez Nicolas de Cuse: les origines chrétiennes du renouveau scientifique." *Etude de Lettres* 1 (1922) 59–66.

Rotta, P. *Il pensiero di Niccolò Cusano nei suoi rapporti storici.* Turin, 1911.

Saffar, L. "Sant'Anselmo, Cusano, Cantor: l'infinito attuale è contradditorio?" *ArchFil* 58 (1990) 459–69. = *L'argomento ontologico.* Ed. M. M. Olivetti.

Saitta, G. *Nicolò Cusano e l'umanesimo italiano, con altri saggi sul Rinascimento italiano.* Bologna, 1957.

Santinello, G. *Il pensiero di Niccolò Cusano nella sua prospettiva estetica.* Padua, 1958.

————. *Studi sull'umanesimo europeo. Cusano e Petrarca, Lefèvre, Erasmo, Colet, Moro.* Padua, 1969.

_____. *Introduzione a Niccolò Cusano*. Rome-Bari, 1971, 1987² (with updated bibliography).

_____. "Da Marsilio a Nicolò Cusano: insegnamenti da un trapasso storico." *Studia Patavina* 27 (1980) 296–99.

_____. "Nicolò Cusano e l'utopia dell'unità culturale e religiosa nel Quattrocento." *Ebraismo, ellenismo, cristianesimo*. Ed. M. M. Olivetti. Padua, 1985. I, 381–91. = *ArchFil* 53 (1985).

_____. "L'uomo *ad imaginem et similitudinem* nel Cusano." *Doctor Seraphicus* 37. 85–97.

_____. "Weisheit und Wissenschaft im cusanischen Verständnis. Ihre Einheit und Unterschiedenheit." *MFCG* 20 (1992) 57–67 and 97–104.

_____. "Il neoplatonismo di Nicolò Cusano." *Il neoplatonismo nel Rinascimento*. Atti del Convegno internazionale (Roma-Firenze, 12–15 dicembre 1990). Ed. P. Prini. Rome, 1993. Pp. 103–15.

Schnarr. H. *Modi essendi. Interpretationen zu den Schriften De docta ignorantia, De coniecturis und De venatione sapientiae*. Münster i. W., 1973.

Schneider, G. *Gott—das Nichtandere. Untersuchungen zum metaphysischen Grunde bei Nikolaus von Kues*. Münster i. W., 1970.

_____. *Die "Kosmische" Grösse Christi als Ermöglichung seiner universalen Heilswirksamkeit, an der Hand des kosmogenetischen Entwurfes Teilhard de Chardin und der Christologie des Nikolaus von Kues*. Münster i. W., 1979.

Schneider, S. "Cusanus als Wegbereiter der neuzeitlichen Wissenschaften." *MFCG* 20 (1992) 182–220 and 240–49.

Schulze, W. *Zahl, Proportion, Analogie. Eine Untersuchung zur Metaphysik und Wissenschaftshaltung des Nikolaus von Kues*. Münster i. W., 1978.

_____. *Harmonik und Theologie bei Nikolaus Cusanus*. Vienna, 1983.

Schwarz, W. *Das Problem der Seinsvermittlung bei Nikolaus von Kues*. Leiden, 1970.

Seidlmayer, M. "Nikolaus von Kues und der Humanismus." *Humanismus, Mystik und Kunst in der Welt des Mittelalters*. Ed. J. Koch. Leiden-Cologne, 1953. Pp. 1–38.

Senger, H. G. *Die Philosophie des Nikolaus von Kues vor dem Jahre 1440. Untersuchungen zur Entwicklung einer Philosophie in der Frühzeit des Nikolaus (1430–1440)*. BGPTM, N.F. 3. Münster i. W., 1971.

_____. "Griechisches und biblisch-patristisches Erbe im cusanischen Weisheitsbegriff." *MFCG* 20 (1992) 147–81.

Sieben, H. J. "Das Konzilstraktat des Nikolaus von Kues: *De concordantia catholica*." *Annuarium Historiae Conciliorum* 14 (1982) 171–226.

Sigmund, P. E. "Cusanus' *Concordantia*: A Re-Interpretation." *Political Studies* 10 (1962) 180–97.

_____. *Nicholas of Cusa and Medieval Political Thought*. Cambridge, Mass., 1963.

Stachel, G. "Schweigen vor Gott. Bemerkungen zur mystischen Theologie der Schrift *De visione Dei*." *MFCG* 14 (1980) 167–81.

Stallmach, J. "Zusammenfall der Gegensätze. Das Prinzip der Dialektik bei Nikolaus von Kues." *MFCG* 1 (1961) 52–75.

_____. "Der 'Zusammenfall der Gegensätze' und der unendliche Gott." *Nikolaus von Kues. Einführung in sein philosophisches Denken*. Ed. K. Jacobi. Freiburg-Munich, 1979. Pp. 56–73.

_____. "Geist als Einheit and Andersheit. Die Noologie des Cusanus in *De coniecturis* und *De quaerendo Deum.*" *MFCG* 11 (1975) 86–116.

_____. "Der Mensch zwischen Wissen und Nichtwissen. Beitrag zum Motiv der *Docta ignorantia* im Denken des Nikolaus von Kues." *MFCG* 13 (1978) 147–59.

_____. "Zum Charakter der cusanischen Metaphysik." *MFCG* 14 (1980) 87–103.

_____. "Einheit der Religionen—Friede unter den Religionen." *MFCG* 16 (1984) 61–81.

_____. "Nikolaus von Kues: 'Gottinnige Gottsuche.'" *MFCG* 19 (1991) 233–42.

Sullivan, D. D. "Apocalypse Tamed: Cusanus and the Traditions of Late Medieval Prophecy." *Journal of Medieval History* 9 (1983) 227–36.

Travaglini, C. "Metaproblematicità dell'essere nel pensiero di Nicolò Cusano." *Studia Patavina* 31 (1984) 93–113.

Valcke, L. "Il *De pace fidei*: Niccolò di Cusa ed Enea Silvio Piccolomini." *Pio II e la cultura del suo tempo.* Atti del I Convegno internazionale (1989). Ed. L. Rotondi Secchi Tatugi. Milan, 1991. Pp. 301–11.

Vansteenberghe, E. *Le cardinal Nicolas de Cues (1401-1464). L'action—la pensée.* Paris, 1920; reprinted: Frankfurt a. M., 1963.

_____. *Autour de la Docte Ignorance. Une controverse sur la théologie mystique.* BGPM 14/2–4. Münster i. W., 1915. Pp. 19–31.

Vasoli, C. "Il *De pace fidei* di Niccolò Cusano." Idem, *Studi sulla cultura del Rinascimento.* Manduria, 1968. Pp. 122–79.

_____. "De Nicholas de Cues et Jean Pic de la Mirandole à Jean Bodin. Trois colloques." *Jean Bodin.* Actes du Colloque interdisciplinaire d'Angers. Angers, 1985. Pp. 253ff.

Velthoven, T. van. *Gottesschau und menschliche Kreativität. Studien zur Erkenntnislehre des Nikolaus von Kues.* Leiden, 1977.

Wackerzapp, W. *Der Einfluss Meister Eckharts auf die ersten philosophischen Schriften des Nikolaus von Kues (1440–1450).* BGPTM 39/3. Münster i. W., 1962.

Watanabe, M. *The Political Ideas of Nicholas of Cusa (with Special Reference to His "De concordantia catholica").* Travaux d'Humanisme et Renaissance 58. Geneva, 1963.

_____. "Authority and Consent in Church Government: Panormitanus, Aeneas Sylvius, Cusanus." *Journal of the History of Ideas* 33 (1972) 217–36.

Weier, M. *Das Thema vom verborgenen Gott von Nicholaus von Kues zu Martin Luther.* Münster, 1967.

Wilpert, P. "Das Problem der *coincidentia oppositorum* in der Philosophie des Nikolaus von Kues." *Humanismus, Mystik und Kunst in der Welt des Mittelalters.* Ed. J. Koch, Leiden-Cologne, 1953. Pp. 39–55.

Winkler, N. "Koinzidenzdenken und Substanzbegriff bei Nikolaus von Kues im Spannungsfeld zwischen Platonismus und Aristotelismus. Präliminarien zu einer kritischen Rekonstruktion des Cusanischen Monismus." *Prima Philosophia* 4 (1991) 411–37.

Wyller, E. A. "Indentität und Kontradiktion. Ein Weg zu Cusanus' Unendlichkeitsidee." *MFCG* 15 (1982) 104–20.

CHAPTER 4

The Mature Stage of Humanist Theology in Italy

Cesare Vasoli

1. The Council of Ferrara-Florence and the Theological Confrontation Between Latins and Greeks

On July 6, 1439, in the cathedral of Florence amid a wondering and deeply moved throng, in the presence of Pope Eugene IV and the Eastern emperor as well as of ecclesiastical dignitaries of every order and rank and of the more important civic notables, the union of the Roman Catholic Church and the Orthodox Church was solemnly proclaimed, after four centuries of bitter controversies and stubborn conflicts.[1] In his pure prose Vespasian of Bisticci has left us a very lively description of this ceremony, which surpassed in pomp and splendor the opening of the council at Ferrara and which sanctioned the henceforth solidly established authority of the pope in relation to the fathers of Basel. Then, when the emperor and Orthodox dignitaries had departed, other confessions likewise gave their assent to the union, although in ways and forms that were often unclear: on November 22, the Armenians and then the Syrians, Copts, Ethiopians, and Chaldeans.

Two years had been spent in long and wearisome discussions that dealt with subtle doctrinal oppositions but, above all, had to tackle the difficult contrast between cultures and ecclesial traditions which were not only different but often quite remote from one another in language, customs, and traditions. Now Christian unity seemed to have been reestablished from the Balkan lands and the Danube to the distant communities of Asia Minor, from the Ukraine to fabled Ethiopia, from Russia to the wild mountains of Armenia. The ecumenical hope now seemed fulfilled that from the end of the fourteenth century to the first decades of the present century had inspired many religious persons who were convinced that the only way to the peace of Christendom and at the same time to a more effective defense against the impending Turkish peril was a return to a common accord on the evangelical faith. This was, then, the first phase of an even broader plan aimed at bringing about the joining of the three "religions of the Book," which a lengthy prophetic tradition had declared to be a necessary condition for the coming of the *Ecclesia spiritualis* (Church of the Spirit), reformed in body and spirit, on the eve of the *dies novissimi* (last days).

It is a fact, of course, that even over the splendid ceremonies in Florence dark shadows crowded and ever-deeper fears and worries lowered, both in the East and in the West. Shortly before, between May 6 and June 15, the fathers of the Council of Basel had overcome the last efforts at delay and had proclaimed as a truth of faith the superiority of a council over a pope. They had gone even further: they had declared that "Gabriel, formerly called Eugene IV," was "contumacious, disobedient to the precepts and orders of the universal Church," and they had deposed him, deprived him of the papacy and dismissed him from it and the Roman pontificate. By so doing they initiated a new schism in the West, one that was definitively ratified in November by the election of Amadeus VIII of Savoy as Antipope Felix V. The unity that had been laboriously restored with the East was thus broken again in the West, as though to prove how unstable, weak, and constantly threatened by new divisions was the seeming solidarity of an ecclesial society that not even the end of the Great Schism had set in motion toward the awaited reform.

It is true that the crisis begun at Basel did not have the same consequences as the tragic conflict started almost sixty years before by the election of Robert of Geneva, and that by their political skill the Roman pontiffs, and Nicholas V in particular, successfully isolated the rebellious fathers and, by means of a new compromise, put an end to this last attempt to hinder the establishment of the full papal supremacy. Nonetheless, new struggles, violent controversies, and an increasingly less controllable hostility and discontent would prevail in the life of the Church for over a decade, while spiritual uneasiness and restlessness increased at every level of Christian society, and the apocalyptic preaching of "regular" religious, hermits, and free itinerant preachers repeated the prophecy of imminent purgation and the condemnation of a corrupt hierarchy.

Nor was the news from the East to be any better in the immediately following years. In the Byzantine Church the antiunionist party became ever stronger, led now by Mark Eugenicus, now by George Scholarius. The pressure from the Turks became daily more uncontrollable, as was to be shown in the fall of 1440 by the military disaster at Varna, which was a clear advance announcement of the final destruction of Constantinople. Everywhere in the

East resentment of the Latins was more violent than before the fragile unification, and new obstacles were daily put in the way of the scattered and unconvincing attempts of the West to prevent the definitive disappearance of the last remains of the ancient empire and to transform into an effective institutional reality the compromise achieved so ambiguously during the stubborn and endless discussions in Ferrara and Florence.

In truth, the council that had apparently ended so triumphantly appeared rather to have exacerbated ancient and never-resolved doctrinal and institutional conflicts, which, now more than ever, were again dividing the two Christendoms. In fact, as Gill has accurately observed, in the eyes of not a few Eastern Christians "who remembered only their supposed oppression by the pope," the union established at Florence seemed to be precisely "a symbol of what ought not to have been done to heal the schism,"[2] that is, a purely political and hierarchical decision, alien to the traditions and culture of so very large a part of the ecclesial world and imposed by fear and an illusory hope of rescue.

Hardly a decade after the celebration in Santa Maria del Fiore, a quite different reality, consisting of mutual, irremediable misunderstandings and the tenacious defense of ancient traditions but also of a difficult balancing of authority and illusory hopes of an autonomous ability to survive the Turkish attack, gave the lie to the ecumenical enthusiasms of the council. In vain was the union, still opposed by so many, solemnly proclaimed and declared complete in Hagia Sophia on May 20, 1452, in the presence of the papal legate, Cardinal and Ruthenian Metropolitan Isidore of Kiev. A liturgical ceremony, however impressive and solemn, could certainly not halt the growing repudiation of a reconciliation which most of its supporters in both churches had regarded as a useful and necessary diplomatic maneuver, an expedient to shore up their own power or to avoid imminent catastrophe.

This is evidently not the place for analyzing the many and obvious political reasons that had had a decisive influence on the convocation of the council, even though this was so eagerly awaited by so many Christian souls and so desired by those who had hoped for the start of an authentic and profound spiritual rebirth. In any case, the studies done in recent years that have taken as their particular subject the internal and external history of this great event in the religious and civil history of the fifteenth century[3] have now made clear the problems and demands of every kind that surged together so tumultuously in the troubled course of the council. In this council sincere spiritual concerns and intense millenniarist expectations were interwoven with self-interested designs on power as well as with economic and financial interests, the reconstruction of which would require investigations much too alien from the nature of these pages.

It is certain that these harsh realities constantly made their oppressive weight felt in the course of the council's work, which was also conditioned by a military and political situation that became daily more calamitous for the Greeks. This explains why the attempt to overcome a diversity in traditions, language, method, and even the very way of conceiving the work of theology was finally lost from sight amid the ambiguous attitudes and formulas that were full of mental reservations and, above all, more calculated to conceal disagreement, which in fact remained deep-rooted, than to represent the attainment of a definitive degree of concord.

This appeared obvious from the very first skirmishes between the theologians of the two sides during the informal sessions, held in Ferrara starting in May 1438 while waiting for the actual public opening proper of the council's work. In fact, the Greeks refused to discuss any dogmatic questions in that setting and restricted themselves to listing the points of more important disagreement. These had to do with (1) the procession of the Holy Spirit, (2) Communion using leavened bread, (3) purgatory, (4) the place and prerogatives of the pope in the Church. Among these subjects, the first to be chosen by common accord was the problem of purgatory, concerning which important differences immediately manifested themselves. Catholic teaching was explained on June 4 by Cardinal Julian Cesarini[4] and then set down in a rather detailed document. In this it was said that repentant souls who died "in charity" "before having expiated by suitable penance for sins of commission and omission are purified after death by cleansing punishments" and may have these punishments alleviated "by the prayers of the faithful still alive." In addition, it was shown, with the aid of the Scriptures and the Fathers, that such an "intermediate state" of purgation existed and that in it the punishment of fire was applied.

The response of Byzantine Cardinal Bessarion,[5] which was read on June 14, declared that, on the contrary, the Greeks were in full agreement only on the final lot of the just and the reprobate, who are destined for paradise or hell. He immediately underscored the Greek disagreement with the Latins by pointing out that none of the Greek Fathers had ever spoken of a punishment by fire apart from the punishments of hell. He added that the teaching of the Latins was dangerous because it could come close to the heresy of Origen, which, by denying the eternity of the fires of hell, rendered the self-discipline of the faithful less severe.

Indeed, the Greeks too admitted the positive effects of the prayers of the faithful, but they maintained that the Latin Fathers had spoken less clearly of the doctrine of the temporary fire of purgatory, precisely because they were afraid of more serious errors; by acting in this way they also left uncertain a precise definition of the effects of the Church's prayers. And while the Latin document gave "divine justice" (which requires that every evil be expiated) as the theological reason for the necessity of purgatory, the metropolitan of Nicaea appealed by contrast to the infinite kindness of God who forgives all sins. He also insisted on the final equality in beatitude of all the "saved" in paradise who are completely "pure," and he objected that a soul deprived of its body, which is what those being "purified" are, could not be affected by a material element like fire.

Dominican theologian John of Torquemada[6] answered Bessarion's arguments while also asking that the Greeks explain their own positions and not limit themselves simply to criticizing the arguments of others. His question, essentially, was whether they believed that the souls of the just and the reprobate met their fate immediately after death or must wait for this until the final judgment; whether or not souls in an "intermediate" condition must be punished; and finally, whether this punishment consisted in a kind of imprisonment and darkness or ignorance, and whether, after having paid their debt, these souls went immediately to paradise.

On the other hand, Torquemada strongly denied that the Latin teaching had any connection with the heresy of Origen or that it persuaded the faithful to a less strict morality (if anything, this strictness was intensified by fear of the punishments of purgatory). He also peremptorily rejected Bessarion's criticisms of the Western Fathers and especially of Jerome and insisted that while repentance is possible only during this earthly life, punishment can be inflicted in both this and the other life; that the fire of purgatory is completely appropriate; and that the prayers of the Church have for their purpose precisely to alleviate these punishments. Firm in his defense of the exegetical methods followed by the Latin Fathers and Doctors, Torquemada also objected to Bessarion that the degree of blessedness could not depend on the degree of the purgation but only on each soul's degree of virtue and that, while spiritual substances cannot be affected by fire, God can arouse their "obediential" powers and habits so as to put them in a condition where they experience its effects.

This time, the Greeks entrusted their reply to Mark Eugenicus,[7] metropolitan of Ephesus and the Byzantine theologian who always showed himself most opposed to any compromise on dogma. According to Greek teaching (he said), the just and the wicked do not experience their definitive lot in the other world before the day of judgment. The former are with the angels, near to God or in the paradise from which Adam was expelled, and they enjoy the blessed vision of God and his light. The wicked are driven into hell but are not subjected to the punishment of fire. Supporting this doctrine with citations from Athanasius, Gregory of Nazianzus, and John Chrysostom, Eugenicus made it clear that he regarded the temporal punishment by fire as completely ineffective; this punishment could, in any case, consist only in an "imprisonment" of the soul in shame, remorse, and other like spiritual torments. As for the prayers of the Church, they are offered in the Eastern Church for all the dead, so that even the reprobate can profit by them (they are at least "comforted"), while those in the "intermediate state" have their hope strengthened. Not only that: even the blessed can become better in virtue of these prayers and can draw closer to the supreme beatitude, which they have not yet reached.

The Latins were not satisfied with this answer; many doubts were immediately proposed by Andrew Crysoberges, the Dominican bishop of Rhodes,[8] and then, it seems, put down in a further document that asked specific and detailed questions. Eugenicus replied by answering in writing the points that seemed to have been obscure in his presentation and that had elicited the more important objections. But in substance he repeated point by point the traditional teachings of the Greek Church without yielding on the essential points: the nonexistence of the temporal punishment of fire; the punishment of souls in the "intermediate state" (a state that consists solely of a sense of guilt and an uncertainty about one's destiny); the absence of any temporal punishment for sins already forgiven; the nature of the penance connected with the sacrament of confession, this penance serving only to help the penitent reach greater spiritual perfection and having no connection with any kind of temporal punishment. Obviously, the positions of the two sides remained quite far apart. If the conversations perhaps continued beyond July 17, the last date indicated in the conciliar documents, no agreement was reached, and the subject was tacitly put aside.

The discussion in Ferrara was officially and publicly renewed beginning on October 8 and lasting to the final session on December 13. The subject was the procession of the Holy Spirit. This was the truly central point of dogmatic disagreement, and, we shall see, it was the subject of most of the sessions in Florence. In Ferrara, however, it was debated especially from the viewpoint of the historical and disciplinary validity of the addition of the *Filioque* to the Creed in the Latin Church. The Latin speakers (Cardinal Cesarini; Andrew Chrysoberges; Ludovic of Pirano, bishop of Forli and a Franciscan;[9] John of Montenero, Dominican provincial of Lombardy;[10] Peter Perquerio, a Franciscan;[11] and John of San Toma, an Augustinian Hermit) and the Greek speakers (Eugenicus; Bessarion; Isidore, metropolitan of Kiev and the Russias;[12] George Gemistus Plethon, a lay philosopher;[13] Michael Balsamon, a "chartophylax"; and Theodore Xanthopoulus, the great "skeuophylax") thus found themselves dealing with the immediate historical question of the conflict between the two churches. Mark Eugenicus immediately attacked the addition of the *Filioque* as "illegitimate" and contrary to true Orthodox teaching.

The debate was thus formulated as a controversy over "legitimacy." Eugenicus himself, at the third session (October 16), set forth the documents that showed how the Creed had taken shape during the first four councils as well as the prescriptions forbidding any change in it (especially Canon VII of the third ecumenical Council of Ephesus, which was confirmed at the fourth Council of Chalcedon). Nor did he neglect to point out how all this was reaffirmed in connection with the "profession of faith" in the subsequent fifth, sixth, and seventh ecumenical councils.

The Latins, however, were already aiming as early as Ferrara at moving the discussion away from a legalistic dispute, although this was certainly based on the authority of the ecumenical councils and presented as a principle of absolute conformity with the foundations of the faith. Instead, they appealed in all their interventions to the argument of the inherent and coherent development of dogma and the legitimacy of theological method, which, while always remaining faithful to the principles of the oneness of faith and doctrine, made use of different methods and intellectual tools. On the other hand, they also appealed to the Western doctors of the postpatristic period and urged a reading of the texts and authorities that did not stop at the letter but looked for an effective doctrinal development. It was no accident that in their interventions the two Dominican theologians were, typically, already making extensive use of Aristotelean theories and vocabularies in accordance with the Scholastic method, which was now solidly exemplified by Thomistic teaching.

This was accepted and acknowledged as a clear sign of the cultural superiority of the Western theologians by one who, like Scolarius,[14] was a fervent admirer of Aristotle and Thomas and had a rather negative view of the education and intellectual abilities of the Orthodox clergy. But this approach elicited very negative reactions from the majority of the Byzantine theologians, whose theological training and mentality were profoundly different from those of their antagonists. It was highly significant that Eugenicus in particular, but many others as well, declared that they could not easily follow lines of theological argument which were set forth in a language alien to them and which they maintained were irrelevant to the "disciplinary" matter under discussion.

As a matter of fact, at the fourth and fifth sessions (October 20 and 25), Chrysoberges decided to approach the question of the *Filioque* in terms of a "development" of the principles of faith; the successive phases of this development were the Gospel, the Nicene Creed, the Constantinopolitan Creed, and the contested addition of words sanctioned by the Roman Church. The doctrine, he said, remained unchanged; there was simply a definitive "clarification" of a point in the Nicene Creed, which, though complete in its faith, was not yet so in its interpretation. Thus the Latin "variant" was not in fact an "addition" or "another article of faith" but simply an "unfolding" that had already been suggested by some of the Greek Fathers and unanimously proposed by the greatest Doctors of the Roman Church. It was a doctrinal and exegetical development that occurred within the data of revelation, without changing these but making them clearer and more explicit; consequently, it did not transgress the prohibitions set down by the councils.

Nor could the Church, given its historical tradition and its task of defending the faith against heresies, keep others or itself from proposing new doctrinal developments that are set forth in rigorous theoretical language; therefore, too, it could not keep from introducing into the Creed changes regarded as necessary in order to avoid dangerous ambiguities that were made all the more serious by peculiarities of the Latin language. Furthermore, the Roman

Church had the right and duty of ensuring that any development of dogma corresponded to the truth; the addition of the *Filioque* was therefore fully justified, being demanded by the special circumstances of Western Christianity.

In his reply (on November 1, sixth session) Bessarion sharply denied that the question could be dealt with under the rubric of an "internal development." Any new dogmatic definition implied, in fact, a new article of faith and therefore a change in the "principles" set down in the Scriptures and enunciated in the Nicene-Constantinopolitan Creed. Further, since this Creed was the common profession of faith of the universal Church, which believers uttered in the act of baptism, it was utterly necessary that its unqualified canonical integrity be preserved.

Despite being so ardent a supporter of union, the metropolitan recognized that the ancient Fathers had the full right to develop the data of faith in accurate dogmatic formulations and also to set these forth in "creedal" texts; but in the later centuries, while the Church retained the right to clarify and explain dogmas, it was forbidden to introduce variations or additions into the Creed of Christianity. It was precisely in order to avoid the surreptitious introduction of new dogmas that would render the profession of faith unsettled and therefore "changeable" that the Council of Ephesus forbade any addition or variation; it even abstained from introducing the word *theotokos,* "Mother of God," into it, though this would have been a useful and necessary action. Finally, Bessarion asked the Latins whether in their opinion the Ephesine prohibition referred to the Creed or to something else.

Bessarion's reply created an obvious difficulty for the Latins, who were reminded to avoid the discussion of dogma; the difficulty was increased by his insistence that according to Chrysoberges' own Aristotelean logic, the dogmatic development leading to the *Filioque* consisted in the passage from a premise already given (the procession of the Holy Spirit from the Father, as read in the Creed) to a conclusion (the procession of the Holy Spirit from the Son as well) by means of a third proposition: "Everything that belongs to the Father belongs also to the Son." At issue, in short, was an affirmation that was far from being "internal" to the articles of the Creed; it was, therefore, a dogmatic conclusion that was "added" to the articles of the universal profession of faith, a conclusion having nothing to do with any particular linguistic setting and therefore able simply to be transposed, in its own specific terms, from the one language to the other. In order, therefore, to bring out even more clearly the criteria to which the Greeks were appealing, Bessarion concluded in forceful terms: "Nothing is to be inserted into this text precisely because the divine creed is regarded by the Church as an expression in principle *(logos archês)* of the Christian faith."

Bessarion was no less categorical when it came to the authority of the Roman Church and its claim that the "addition" to the Creed was entirely legitimate. The Greeks (he said), while leaving untouched the rights and privileges, but also the limits, of that Church, denied such an authority not only to Rome but also to any church whatever and to any council, even an ecumenical one. The decrees of the fathers at Ephesus had, once and for all, denied "to the Church in its entirety" the authority to alter the profession of faith.

As can be seen, at this point the fathers of the council were back where they started, with the terms in which Eugenicus had raised the question. The answers given by Chrysoberges and later, at the seventh session (November 8), by Ludovic of Pirano, were unable to change the quite firm attitude of the Greeks. It was thus left to the juridical (and political) skill of Cardinal Cesarini to keep the council from being shipwrecked right at its start on this "preliminary" problem that seemed insuperable.

During the sessions that followed (November 11 and 18, December 4, 8, and 13), this former professor of canon law at Padua was involved in a continual dialectical confrontation with Eugenicus, who was constantly on guard to ask respect for the integrity of the Creed and for the Ephesine prohibition against "explaining, writing, and composing" any expression that would alter it. Cesarini therefore abandoned the way of theological discussion and "subtle and learned" discourses that only a few experts could understand and turned instead to the terrain of history and law that was rather more accessible even to "the laity and the uneducated."

He identified the lengthy controversy as having its real root where the Greeks had already located it: in Canon VII of Ephesus, that is, in a prohibition that was disciplinary in character and, like all laws, had to be interpreted according to the will of its legislators; he therefore referred to the particular contingent historical circumstances that controlled the work of that council as well as to the practice of the local churches of offering the faithful their own professions of faith as a way of explaining and completing the Nicene-Constantinopolitan Creed. The Ephesine prohibition, then, was not intended to prevent the explanation and clarification of the Creed; on the contrary, it struck at the composition of heterodox "professions of faith," the content of which, as in the case of Nestorius, clashed with what was said in the Creed. Moreover, just as the Creed of Constantinople already contained new expressions that did not change the true principles of the Nicene Creed, so it was licit to change some words in order that the meaning of the confession of faith might remain the same. The issue was therefore clear: if it is admitted that the addition of the *Filioque* was "true" and in full agreement with orthodoxy, then it should also be acknowledged that the addition was legitimate and that no law could prohibit it.

The debate with the Greeks continued to be rather tense, with its continual appeals to the opposition between the books produced by both sides (especially the *Contra Eunomium* of Basil) and the suspicions of Eugenicus, who regarded the texts brought by the Latins as having been interpolated. The majority of the Greeks, from Eugenicus to Scholarius, who later changed his opinion completely, were still convinced of the absolute legitimacy of their position. Bessarion, however, was compelled to acknowledge that Cesarini's argument had been accurate and convincing, to such a degree, in a word, as to raise doubts and uncertainties even in one who had until then been convinced as to the complete orthodoxy of the Oriental doctrines and the just basis of the schism.

In any case, however, many among the Greeks were now persuaded that the council ought by all means be brought to a close and its failure acknowledged without uselessly continuing the debates in Florence, to which city it was proposed that the council be transferred. Only the intervention of the emperor at a meeting of the Greek churchmen (January 2, 1439) managed to convince them that they could not abandon this ecumenical meeting of Christianity without at last facing the fundamental dogmatic question of the procession of the Holy Spirit, which had hitherto been discussed solely from the "disciplinary" viewpoint of the "addition" to the Creed. It is likely, however, that even more effective were the considerations of a political and economic nature, which the same sovereign brought up or hinted to the Byzantine ecclesiastics.

After the transfer to Florence, the discussion resumed on March 2, 1439, attention being turned now to the main themes of the respective trinitarian doctrines. It became immediately obvious not only that the partners in the dialogue spoke two entirely different languages but also that their theologies were hardly compatible or comparable in their foundations and methods.

As a matter of fact, two concepts of Greek origin—*ousia* and *hypostasis*—were fundamental to the Western theory of the Trinity. The first of these, however, had two possible meanings: the individual existing reality as such (Latin: *substantia*) but also the genus or species to which this individual belonged (this meaning corresponded to the Latin terms *essentia* or *natura*). *Hypostasis,* on the other hand, could signify an objectively existing reality (and therefore could be regarded as equivalent to *ousia*), but it could also signify the individual as numerically distinct from every other individual and, in the case of rational beings, the *persona*.

From the very beginnings, then, of trinitarian theology there had existed the doctrine that God is an *ousia* made up of three *hypostaseis*. Latin theology, however, found itself in the linguistic difficulties that were mentioned earlier when speaking of Lawrence Valla and the critique he set down in his *Dialectica* and *Elegantiae*.[15] The Latin authors had said that God is a "substance" *(substantia = ousia),* but in order to translate *hypostasis* (which was, in effect, identical with *substantia*), they had used the term *persona*. But the term corresponding to *persona,* namely, *prosôpon,* was unacceptable to the Greeks, since it suggested "appearance" rather than "reality." And, undoubtedly, the use of this term for the Son could have a heretical meaning.

Furthermore, in the theoretical development of dogma in the terms used by the Latins, the meaning of the words changed and became abstract.

Substantia kept its general meaning of "essence," while the quality by which a thing exists was signified by *subsistentia; natura* meant the set of essential qualities by which each thing is distinguished from others; *suppositum* signified all that to which individuality, *natura* and *subsistentia,* the characteristic properties, and the accidents could be attributed; *persona,* on the other hand, became the term identifying the objective reality, the *res naturae.*

I cannot dwell on the other difficulties of linguistic rendering that very greatly complicated relations between the two theologies, as, for example, the translation of the Greek *aitia* by *causa* (though it is closer in meaning to *principium*) and of the Greek *archê* (which is closer to *causa*) by *principium.* Nor can I dwell on the influence which typical habits of juridic discourse had on these choices. I must, however, emphasize the point that the Latin formula *(una substantia* and *tres personae)* and the Greek formula (one *ousia* and three *hypostaseis*) were the source of a lengthy and never-resolved theological discussion, which, from a doctrinal point of view, radically separated the Western and Eastern dogmatic traditions.

The Latins and Greeks were fully in agreement that the Father is the one from whom originate, as from a single "source," the Son "through generation" and the Holy Spirit "through procession." They were also in agreement on the generation of the Son from the Father. But there was and remained sharp disagreement, as was henceforth clear, when it came to the procession of the Holy Spirit. The Byzantine theologians, clinging strictly to the Scriptures, asserted that the Holy Spirit proceeded from the Father alone (although some Fathers had used the expression "proceeds from the Father through the Son"). The Latins maintained that the Spirit "proceeds from the Father and from the Son." This disagreement, which was already important and decisive from a purely dogmatic point of view, then became even more embittered because of the controversial linguistic rendering of the essential terms of trinitarian theology by the theologians of the two churches, and also by the questions of authority and tradition that had already emerged in the predominantly disciplinary treatment of the question of the addition of the *Filioque.*

Such were the terms in which the main dogmatic controversy of the council was presented. Behind this, of course, were hidden much more concrete causes of conflict that would emerge in dramatic fashion during the final days of the council's life. It goes without saying that we will not be able here to follow in detail the course of the discussions that began on March 2 and were conducted with great zeal and no less difficulty. It must be emphasized, however, that from the outset the two main spokesmen for the two parties, John of Montenero and Mark Eugenicus, were forced to deal with endless and subtle linguistic questions, just in an attempt to harmonize the interpretations of the patristic texts adduced as "proofs" of the sides' respective ideas.

Thus John claimed that the terms *essentia* and *esse* meant the same thing when applied to God, and therefore that the Holy Spirit proceeds from the

Father inasmuch as he derives his *esse* from him, but that he derives this *esse* also from the Son and therefore must also proceed from the Son. In response to Eugenicus' challenges, he then specified the distinction between Father and Son as meaning that the Father *is* the source, while the Son *is from* the source, even though they have everything in common including their *esse*. He explained, further, that the Father is the *persona* and the generating principle and that his *natura* is "the principle by which he generates the Son" and communicates himself to the Son. In God, of course, the nature and essence of the three persons is one and the same, but if one person is "from" the other, it is accurate to say that the one receives his existence and very person from the other. That is precisely what Basil and Epiphanius, the Fathers most cited in the course of the debate, meant to say when they said that the Holy Spirit has his being from the Son.

The explanation of the Latin doctrine disconcerted the Byzantine delegation. Eugenicus had to admit, in substance, that he was unable to follow the subtle and complex discourse of Montenero, since the latter's particular linguistic subtleties escaped him and therefore the discourse seemed to him full of contradictions. The Dominican then asked the official interpreter, Nicholas Sagundino, to translate into Greek the discourse he had given, which had aimed to show the complete congruence and coherence of the teaching being explained. Even Sagundino, however, could not easily find the corresponding Greek terms that would illumine the essential themes of the controversy. As a result, Chrysoberges had to intervene; he recognized, correctly, that the similarity of words created ambiguities and that "because of the ambiguity the two of you cannot agree on the theology common to both Latins and Greeks." He observed that when theologians speak of the "divine substance" they should be taken to mean that which is common to the Father, the Son, and the Holy Spirit, whereas the term "substance of the Father" can only refer to the "person" of the Father.

The ambiguity of the words used and the exegetical discussions of the passages from Basil and Epiphanius (these were checked against the manuscripts, but Eugenicus often questioned the authenticity of these) only served to accentuate the differences between the two theologians. That there was, moreover, a real difference in theory, which was difficult to get around, became clear when, at the sixth session (March 17), Eugenicus gave a complete exposition of Greek teaching, using arguments based on Scripture, on the Eastern Fathers, and on the conciliar documents already discussed at Ferrara.

The substance of his exposition was clear and unambiguous: it was not necessary, and it was even entirely false, to interpret the statement that the Holy Spirit proceeds from the Father as if it meant also a procession from the Son. The text from the Gospel of John (15:26) did not allow such an obvious forcing of its meaning; such an interpretation was in opposition to the true teaching of the Fathers and to the decrees of the councils, especially to those of the third ecumenical Council of Ephesus. After discussing the events and conclusions of that council and the limitations of the condemnation of Nestorius (which referred solely to his teaching on the incarnation of the Word), the controversy between Cyril and Theodoret, and the conclusions which the Fathers finally reached, Eugenicus concluded that the procession from the Father alone had become a dogma after Ephesus and that the Greek Church had been correct in holding to the truth taught by the Scriptures and the saints.

Montenero replied that the Latin Church had carefully avoided saying that there were two "causes" of the Holy Spirit. Its teaching was therefore to be understood in this very precise sense: the Father is the "principle" of the Son and the Holy Spirit, but the Son, who is identical with the Father in his nature, also receives from him the ability to produce the Holy Spirit, in regard to the nature which the Holy Spirit has in common with the Father; therefore, the Son, with the Father, is the "single" principle of the procession of the Spirit. The meeting ended with these words that seemed suddenly to open up a possibility of agreement. In fact, the Greeks, when brought together by the emperor, decided to propose as a basis for the agreement the letter of Maximus to Marinus, which seemed to express the same teaching. If the Latins had subscribed to it, the dogmatic union would have been immediately reached.

But the hope was short-lived. Montenero's reply to the arguments of Eugenicus (who was absent at the wish of the emperor, who wanted to put an end to the endless discourses of the theologians), and then the renewed discussion of the authenticity of the texts cited by the Latins, as well as the renewed contrast invoked between the "philosophical" and "dialectical" method of the Latins and the "scriptural" and "patristic" method of the Greeks—all these once again summoned up difficulties and contrasts that strengthened Eugenicus' unshakable opposition to any yielding on dogma.

On the other hand, the Greeks were now weary of the long months of disagreement, especially since they were under the pressure of the ever more catastrophic news coming from Constantinople, the financial difficulties caused them by their prolonged stay in Italy, and the necessity of somehow securing the military help of the West. Bessarion, Isidore of Kiev, and Scholarius were now convinced that even the Latins believed in a single "cause" of the Holy Spirit and that the phrases "from the Son" and "through the Son" had substantially the same meaning. Moreover, the Fathers and holy Doctors venerated in the East no less than in the West could not have erred, and their divergent expressions and words should be interpreted in the light of a "harmony" and a substantial identity of beliefs. This was the line along which the council should proceed in order to reach a common conviction of a doctrinal unity that transcended divergences caused by different languages, cultures, and traditions.

But by this time irreconcilable oppositions had arisen even among the Byzantine theologians. At a meeting on March 30 in the palace where the patriarch of Constantinople was staying, Isidore and Bessarion spoke in favor of union, while Eugenicus accused the Latins of heresy, and Dositheus of Monembasia[16] said that he would die rather than submit to the Latins. Nor was a subsequent meeting, held on March 31 in the presence of the emperor, able to get beyond the impasse reached by the conflict among the representatives themselves of the Orthodox Church. The next day, Dorotheus, metropolitan of Mytilene, and Bessarion proposed a formula that repeated in summary form the words of the letter of Maximus: the Holy Spirit proceeds substantially from the Father through the Son, who is generated in an ineffable way.

The Latin feast of Easter interrupted, for the moment, even private meetings. But on Friday of Easter week (April 3), after a further meeting, the Greeks, speaking through Eugenicus, Isidore, and Syropoulus, the "grand ecclesiarch,"[17] told the pope that they did not intend to continue the endless discussion and that it was now the task of the Latins to look for a different way of achieving the union. Pope Eugene answered by asking three preliminary questions: (1) whether the Greeks accepted the Latin proofs of the *Filioque;* (2) whether contrary texts from Scripture could be cited; and (3) whether there were texts of Scripture that showed the teaching of the Greeks to be better founded and more strictly orthodox. He suggested that each prelate of the two churches state his personal opinion under oath and that the opinion of the majority prevail. The emperor sent three representatives to the pope to object that this would mean the resumption of the useless and wearisome discussions and to threaten that if the pope's suggestion were followed he would immediately leave Florence. But he again proposed the trinitarian teaching of Maximus as the basis for union, despite the opposition of Eugenicus and Metropolitan Anthony of Heraclea.

The remainder of the month of April was spent in lengthy and unpredictable negotiations that involved the highest dignitaries of the two parties. Meanwhile, however, Bessarion was writing his *Oratio dogmatica,* which was completely in favor of the union; it aimed to show that all the Doctors, being inspired by the Holy Spirit, are always in agreement among themselves and that their opinions cannot be opposed and contradictory. For the Greeks (he wrote) only three solutions were left: (1) not to accept the *Filioque;* (2) to accept it; (3) to claim the utter falsity of the texts cited by the Latins. But the first was absurd and the third wrong; there remained, therefore, only the second, the rejection of which would have serious consequences for the spiritual and temporal "salvation" of the Greeks.

During these same days, Scholarius, too, in his address "On the necessity of bringing aid to Constantinople," warned his colleagues to give up the useless battle of words, in which the Latins were always victorious because of their dialectical and cultural superiority, and to think instead of the fate of their fatherland. In any case, the complete harmony that had now been shown to exist in the words of the saints was the best confirmation of the need of reaching an agreement that would guarantee the Greeks the preservation of their Creed.

I shall not dwell on the further negotiations, the documents presented by both sides, the ever sharper divisions between the Byzantine prelates and the lay representatives, among whom the numbers of the group in favor of union were constantly increasing, and the proposal by Scholarius of a new formula that was immediately accepted by Bessarion and Isidore but that the Latins considered to be still ambiguous.

On May 27 the pope spoke in person to the Greek synod; he reviewed the very painful history of the council and, when discussing union, spoke in accents that moved his audience. Isidore of Kiev justified the slow pace of the discussions and negotiations by pointing to the exceptional importance of the goal proposed; but shortly after, Bessarion, Dorotheus, and Methodius, metropolitan of Lacedemon, told the patriarch that they were now resolved on union with the Latins. When the emperor convoked the Greek synod once again on the Thursday after Pentecost, his address was a dramatic one: after so many discussions the only choice left was between being united, which was against justice, or remaining divided, which was also against justice. The Byzantine representatives had, therefore, to make their decision without inflicting harm on either soul or body but also bearing in mind the fate of Constantinople and remembering that anyone who cunningly hindered the union was more accursed than Judas. They all declared themselves to be in favor of the union, but then they immediately began again their discussions on the meaning of "from" and "through" and on the still-open question of the *Filioque*.

On the days that followed, the Byzantines in favor of union worked ceaselessly trying to gain a general agreement on the authenticity of the texts used by the Latins and a compromise on the *Filioque*. Finally, on June 2 and 3 a final vote was taken; those who accepted the equivalence of "from" and "through" were in the majority, and a text was composed saying that the Holy Spirit proceeds from the Father and from the Son as from a single principle and a single substance; he proceeds through the Son who has the same nature and the same substance; he proceeds from the Father and from the Son by a single spiration and procession.

The "senatorial" dignitaries likewise declared themselves in favor of the union, but only for political reasons, as did also the emperor's brother, Demetrius. All the officials of the court came out in favor of the union except for the "Staurophors," who abstained. Eugenicus, however, simply refused to sign the written declaration and spoke clearly against the union, as did six other prelates.

Once the dogmatic question that had made the agreement so difficult was at last resolved, the resolution of the other problems was accomplished much more quickly; it was helped by the negotiations which Isidore was carrying on at the same time with the pope in order to gain the help promised to Constantinople. On June 28 the Greeks accepted the corrections which the Latins had proposed in their statement on the procession of the Holy Spirit; on June 29 agreement was reached on the question of the bread to be used in the Eucharist.

Next it was decided, with regard to purgatory, that both the souls of the just and the souls of the wicked entered upon their definitive destiny after, but that there also existed an intermediate state of penance and testing; it was left undecided, however, whether souls in this state suffered a punishment of fire. The very difficult problem of the pope's place in the one Church was also settled by the full recognition that he possessed all the privileges he had enjoyed before the schism.

The troubled course of the council was, however, not yet ended. The Latins asked the Greeks why they had added the epiclesis, as they called it, to the formula of eucharistic consecration. They also requested a public discussion of a very controverted and sensitive point of Eastern theology: the relationship between God's essence and his works.[18] Finally, the pope himself demanded that the Byzantines explicitly state their position on (1) the procession of the Holy Spirit; (2) the leavened or unleavened bread used in the sacrament of the Eucharist; (3) papal primacy; (4) purgatory; and (5) the legitimacy of the addition of the *Filioque*.

This demand provoked a decided reaction from the emperor, who immediately sent his emissaries to Venice to prepare for a rapid departure to Constantinople. There was now no possibility of a union except on conditions set by the Latins, the obvious winners in a dispute in which political necessities had played a much greater part than the great skill and learning of the theologians. Even though serious disagreements remained, especially regarding the Latin formula of the Eucharist and Roman primacy, the Greek delegates said they were ready to accept the teachings of the Latins on all five points. But the disagreements were not yet ended. On June 18 there was renewed discussion aimed at getting a better understanding of the Greeks on the question of papal primacy and, further, on the relations between "matter" and "form" in the eucharistic sacrament; on June 22 Pope Eugene asked that he be given all the privileges that were his in his own Church: to be the supreme appellate judge, to rule the entire Church, to convoke an ecumenical synod whenever he thought necessary, and in addition, that all the patriarchs regard themselves as subject to his decisions.

Faced with these requests, the emperor lost all hope of reaching the agreement that had seemed almost settled, and he ordered his entourage to prepare for departure. This decision of his softened the demands of the Latins, who on June 25 met with the Greeks once again in the form of a commission comprising six delegates from each side. The pope agreed not to include in the decree of union the still-open question of the "form" of the eucharistic sacrament, while the Greeks said they were ready to accept papal primacy, without however, detracting from the rights and privileges of the patriarchs of the Eastern churches (Constantinople, Alexandria, Antioch, and Jerusalem). Cesarini was then able to report to the Greek synod the good progress made in the negotiations, which were now almost completed. Among the Greeks Eugenicus alone refused to sign the agreement no matter what, after he had been assured by the emperor that he would not be forced to sign it.

On the following days the decree of union was drawn up in both languages, the Greek version being edited principally by Traversari. The Greeks, followed by the Latins, signed the decree on July 5; Bessarion read a document on the "form" of the Eucharist that formally eliminated the final differences. As a result, the solemn ceremony in Florence, which was our starting point in this chapter, was held the next day. It was the final seal on an agreement that had been reached with such labor and difficulty and that, moreover, the two sides were ready to accept only with many mental reservations and to interpret according to their own customs and particular interests. It was not an accident that a few days later the Latins raised other difficulties: they asked that steps be taken against Eugenicus; they demanded assurances regarding the appointment of the new patriarch of Constantinople (Joseph II had died in Florence on June 10); and they called for the Orientals to adopt a different attitude toward divorce. But this time the requests were dropped, as John VIII Paleologus and the Byzantine delegations were now hastening their departure from Florence.

2. Giannozzo Manetti and Matthew Palmieri

To sum up: The uncertain unity achieved at Florence was more the result of a necessary political compromise than a genuine fulfillment of ecumenical hopes and hopes of reform. Both of the latter had a place in humanist culture, especially among those who longed for a return to the pure and uncontaminated Christianity of the beginnings and who had been and were devoting themselves to the reading of the Greek Fathers or who were beginning to think of the gospel message once again as the sole authentic wellspring of faith, a wellspring which (they said) had been muddied by the "disputational" and "dialectical" theology of the "moderns." In speaking earlier of Traversari, I noted the profound influence which this devout humanist had on the generation that grew to adulthood in Florence during the first decades of the fifteenth century, and I spoke of the meetings and conversations that took place in the Camaldolese monastery of Santa Maria degli Angeli. It is now time to call to mind, from among those closest to Traversari, two young humanists, Giannozzo Manetti and Matthew Palmieri, who manifested a very lively interest in religious matters and a very marked interest in subjects of a theological character and nature.

Manetti was born in 1396 and died an exile in Naples in 1459.[19] He also had close connections with Bruni and with others of the more important representatives of the humanist generation that had been formed under the influence of Salutati. His fine training in philology (he had a good knowledge of Greek and Hebrew) and his reading of the works of Paul and Augustine, but also of the *Nicomachean Ethics,* had led him to a solid combination of a pure Christian faith and a strict ethical and civic outlook. As Vespasian of Bisticci tells us, "He used to say that our faith ought to be called not faith but certainty."[20]

In his *Dialogus consolatorius,* written in 1438 on the occasion of a death of a young son, Manetti's religious spirit was already to be seen in his steadfast adherence to Paul and Augustine, whom he had taken as models of Christian thought and life. His knowledge of Hebrew enabled him even to attempt a Latin translation of the Psalms, which he defended in his *Apologeticus adversus suae novae Psalterii traductionis obtrectatores,* in which he connected his work as translator with the task of responding to Jewish accusations that Christians had falsified the Scriptures. He wrote that, on the contrary, the Jewish inability at this point to grasp the true meaning of revelation was the direct consequence of their intellectual isolation and their obsessive reading of the Old Testament, all of which had prevented them from understanding that only a broad and complete knowledge of all "liberal" learning could permit a genuine access even to the divine word.

The same ideas inspired Manetti's large and uncompleted apologetic work, *Adversus Judaeos et Gentes,* which, as Fioravanti has pointed out,[21] distinguished itself clearly from the "usual" controversialist tradition and attempted a clearly different approach. In Book I, in fact, he carried out, in his own fashion, an investigation of pre-Christian philosophies and religions and followed this with a history of the Hebrew people from Abraham to the promulgation of the Law. In Book II he told the life of Christ down to the resurrection of Lazarus; in Book III he expounded the "doctrine" of Christ; and in Book IV he picked up again the story of the Savior, recounting his capture, passion, death, and resurrection. Then in Books V to X he assembled an immense bio-bibliographical list of sacred and secular (but Christian) writers and of holy confessors, martyrs, and virgins; the list was to have been followed by a similar list of popes and emperors.

Fioravanti has undertaken a keen and complete analysis of the method followed by the humanist in assembling this vast material as well as of the sources he used and his judgments on the Law and the Hebrew tradition. In this analysis Fioravanti stresses the fact that in the work "there appears no reference to the rabbinic tradition" and that there is no obvious indication of the author's reading in, and knowledge of, the Jewish exegetical literature. It is also significant that Manetti lays no emphasis on the traditional motif of the crime of "deicide" attributed to the Jews or on the consequences to which it supposedly led for the Chosen People. Rather, having adopted the perspective of the conversion of all unbelievers and of the Jews in particular, Manetti seems to have opted for contrasting the "poets, historians, orators, philosophers, and scientists" of Christianity with the endless exegesis of the Jewish "doctors," who have now become incapable of looking beyond their Book and understanding the spiritual renewal that has been brought about in Christ.

Manetti's best-known work, however, is his *De dignitate et excellentia hominis,*[22] which he composed in 1451–52 and dedicated to King Alphonsus of Aragon. The work originated as a reply to the mediocre disquisition, *De excellentia et praestantia hominis,* of Ligurian humanist Bartholomew Fazio (1400?–1457), which did not depart from the models common to a lengthy tradition geared to the Scholastic palate. In Bartholomew's work the authentic sign of human excellence was seen in the immortality of the soul, a substance not subject to the corruption proper to all the things of nature.

Giannozzo, on the contrary, extolled the value of human actions and works and, along with these, the arts that enable human beings to master nature and show forth their likeness to God. Calling upon Cicero and Lactantius as witnesses to the dignity of the human person, he took over the hermetic motif of the power God has given to human beings as the focal point of reality and the link between the lower regions of the world and supreme, immortal wisdom. Indeed, in Manetti's view, the divine nature of human beings is manifested in their ability to understand and act, using their miraculous freedom of will. All the arts, doctrines, and sciences, from painting to sculpture, architecture to history, poetry to philosophy, astronomy to law, are thus called upon to prove that the human person continues and completes the work of creation:

> Everything that has made its appearance in the world after the first, formless creation seems to have been discovered, produced, and completed by us through the unique and superior keenness of our minds. All the things that we see, then, are ours and are therefore human because made by human beings: all the houses, villages, cities, all the buildings on earth, which are so many and of such a character that because of their wonderful excellence they ought to be taken as the work of angels rather than of human beings. Ours are the paintings, the sculptures, the arts, the sciences, ours the wisdom . . . ours the almost infinite number of inventions, our work the languages.[23]

Every form, custom, or thought in which human action can find expression bears witness to a creative will in which the divine destiny of human beings is revealed: the world is the place appointed to them in which to demonstrate their ability to govern it and thereby to carry out the task God has assigned to them.

Another who took part in the "conversations" at Santa Maria degli Angeli, first as an adolescent and then as a young man, was Matthew Palmieri (1406–75), a Florentine dealer in spices who spent a great part of his life in filling magistracies and offices of the republic.[24]

In his *Della vita civile,*[25] which he composed perhaps in 1438–39, he had praised those who "devoted all diligence and care to things honorable and worth knowing, and from which some private or public gain results"; he had considered useless the practice of "the very obscure arts" that do not teach human beings how to exercise their proper powers. No human work, in fact, could be "more outstanding, greater, or more worthy" than those which are devoted to "the growth and safety of the fatherland and the best state of a well-ordered republic, for the preservation of which men of virtue are best suited." It is understandable that he should recall Cicero and Quintilian and should offer as examples and models of a perfect ethical life the "noble citizens" of antiquity who had always dedicated themselves to the safety of their city and in this supreme duty had found glory for themselves and a reputation that resisted the destructive power of time.

Palmieri was thus repeating themes that had deep roots in the Florentine humanistic tradition and that writings of Bruni had already voiced with a rare effectiveness. However, right at the end of the book, following in the steps of Macrobius, Palmieri was already able to combine the Platonic myth of Er with Cicero's *Somnium Scipionis* and to make Dante the recipient of a revelation from the next world that located the praise of "civic life" on a special "terrace" (*Purgatory*, canto 5) that was rich in eschatological meanings and symbols. When the poet had for a long time looked for the body of a fallen friend on the battlefield of Campaldino, the latter, "either risen or not dead," had revealed to him "not without reason . . . by a special grace," what he had seen in the world beyond. His message, willed by "a light of the universe," gave divine confirmation to what Palmieri had written about the virtue and glory of the great men of old.

For "in the everlasting places" he had seen "the souls of all the citizens who in this world had governed their republics with justice"; among them he had recognized "Fabricius, Curius, Fabius, Scipio, and Metellus, and many others," who, for the "safety of the fatherland" had renounced every personal advantage of their own.[26] In short, the assumption of the classical heroes into the Platonic and Christian paradise proved that the "best" of all human works is "to see to the safety of the fatherland, preserve cities, and maintain the union and harmony of well ordered cities." But when, around 1465, almost thirty years later, Palmieri was completing his *Città di vita,*[27] a visionary poem evidently inspired by Dante, he gave voice, instead, to ideas that were obviously Pythagorean and Platonic in origin but that were perhaps also developed by his reading of some passages of Origen, an author who had earlier caught the interest of Traversari.

In this poem, life in the present world is regarded as a test granted to God by human souls, which are identified with those cowardly angels who, in face of Lucifer's rebellion, sided neither with him nor with God. Enclosed now in the "fleshly" prison of the body, they have been allowed to decide their lot in the daily battle of this world and in the struggle with evil, in which if they overcome they will win their deliverance.

> Thus the spirits in this place
> Go flying through the pleasant air
> Until the body exists that they have chosen.

> The Father, whom they did not heed
> In the purity of their first call,
> When he asked a response from all,

> Willed that their freedom be tested
> a second time, but only with such a companion
> are they to show the good will they have within them.[28]

Palmieri's emphasis on these eschatological motifs (which brought many suspicions on the poem and its author's orthodoxy) already made clear his aim of bringing human salvation and eternal blessedness into agreement with just and fruitful activity as the only way to the ultimate contemplation of God. The deeply Platonic inspiration of the poem, one theme of which is the soul's "re-membering" of its heavenly life, also shines through in the conception of the universe as an infinite, living "city" in which everything is joined and connected by the one "golden chain" of being:

> This is the great city in which dwells
> Everything that lives, thinks, feels or breathes. . . .

> Infinite life surrounds it all,
> Contains all and binds it in close unity,
> So that every part draws every part. . . .

> This knot descends from the supreme heaven,
> Binding all so that it may reach the depths.
> It is the chain of which Plato speaks.[29]

It is clear here how the idea of the government of the world, within the cosmic and providential order that prevails in it, establishes the principle of a supreme justice that unfolds in the eternity of an endless life.

3. Byzantine Teachers in Italy and the Dispute over Plato and Aristotle

Palmieri's poem was never published, but it did circulate among the educated Florentines of the day accompanied by a detailed commentary which Leonard Dati, a close friend of the author, composed in Latin. Of course, even the unmistakable "Pythagorean" and "Platonic" character of the poem was a sign of a new intellectual climate that had been developing during the decade of the council and of ecumenical and reform expectations. As historians of fif-teenth-century culture have often noted, the great Church event had brought to

Florence some of the greatest representatives of the Byzantine philosophical and theological tradition, which was the object of growing interest on the part of humanists, who were finding in it the heritage of ancient Greek "wisdom."

It hardly needs saying that among the Byzantines active during the months when the council was in Florence were persons destined to have an important influence on the religious and intellectual history of the time. I am referring to Bessarion, who was already foreshadowing a theological doctrine that was open to Platonic metaphysical motifs and bent on reasserting continuity with the "Oriental" patristic experience; to George Scholarius, a resolute Aristotelean and an admirer of Thomas Aquinas, and at that time also a resolute follower of the unionist party; and to those who, like philosopher George Gemistus Plethon,[30] during their stay in Florence spread ideas and suggestions that were destined to have a profound influence on the spiritual restlessness of the time.

In saying this, I do not mean to accept the historical hypotheses that make so many events of late-fifteenth-century culture depend on the presence of Plethon in Florence; still less do I mean to accept the personal and self-interested reconstruction of Marsilius Ficino, who traced back to the "impassioned discourses" of the elderly Gemistus (+ ca. 1450) the origins of Cosimo de'Medici's particular philosophical interests and his intention of reviving the ancient Platonic wisdom. The fact remains, however, that many testimonies agree in emphasizing the fascination exerted by this philosopher, who, as though in response to the fatal decay of the Byzantine Empire, had seen in Platonic and Neoplatonic teachings and in the "revelations" of the mythical Zarathustra the source of a radical ethical, political, and religious renewal and a rebirth of the most ancient truth, all of which were to be the beginning of a new cycle in human events.

Convinced that only a clear knowledge of the one truth could draw human beings out of the confused and darkened uncertainty of constantly opposed and hostile "dogmatic" opinions, Gemistus harked back to the ancient legislator-sages (Zarathustra, Eumolpus, Minos, Lycurgus, Iphytus, and Numa), to the first "wise men," and to the philosophers who were their direct successors and worthy heirs. He spoke, too, of the Brahmans, the Magi, the Curetes, the priests of Didona, and then of Tiresias, Cheiron, the seven wise men, and further, of Pythagoras, Plato, Timaeus, Plutarch, Porphyry, and Iamblichus, all of these being regarded as the trustees of an "original" teaching that belonged to the entire human race and was free of any contamination. But the fruit of his meditation on the *Chaldean Oracles* and the teachings of the ancients revealed itself later on when, already advanced in years, he had gathered around him a "phratry" of scholars, united by the common aim of rebuilding on the ruins of the old empire an ideal society on a Platonic plan, bound together by a common cult of the sun that was enriched by ancient Plotinian motifs and the heliolatry of Julian.

Similar ideas were set down by Gemistus in his *Laws*,[31] a work which Scholarius condemned to destruction when he later became the antiunionist patriarch of Constantinople under the name of Gennadius. But what we have already seen is enough to attest Gemistus' constant stress on the idea of an immutable, eternal universe, generated by the absolute Monad from which everything comes forth in an eternal, immutable process. In accordance with the perennial principles of the oldest "Greek theology," the philosopher placed above every being "the supreme God, invisible in his substance," father of "various sons, in varied descending orders, inferior and superior to one another, each of them charged with presiding over a more or less important part of the single great whole."

These "sons" or "eons" were different from the Father, because they possessed an inferior essence and a divinity quite different from that of the superessential Monad; "Greek theology" had indeed called them "gods" but only because, conceiving them as begotten by God, it did not intend, "when speaking of other divine beings, to distinguish between generation and creation, or to separate the divine nature from its action." Thus, from Zeus, "the king, the greatest and the best possible . . . father and first maker of everything," was descended Poseidon, "lord and maker of the heavens"; while from Zeus' "marriage to Hera," "producer of matter," came "the gods that dwell in the heavens, the heavenly breed of the stars, and the demons of earthly breed, a breed already close to ours." In fact, the souls of human beings, which are already like the gods, remained immortal and eternal and capable of uniting themselves in contemplation to the perfections of the divine intelligences, provided they were able to understand the eternal laws of the universe, avoid all evil, pursue the common good, and so ascend back again to the one Origin.[32]

The return to this luminous awareness of the supreme divine and cosmic unity and the recognition of the "solar" symbol as the sign of a wise and rational religion that can at last unite the entire human race, rescued now from the domination of opposing cults, beliefs and sects—this return was, in Plethon's view, the necessary condition for the coming advent of a new era of brotherhood and harmonious concord. The very events of the times seemed to him to demonstrate the inevitable end of a long and deadly period of history; for this reason, he sought new proofs of this end in the course of the heavens and the stars and in their conjunctions, which announced radical and decisive changes. If we can trust the bitter attack of his harsh adversary, George of Trebizond, Gemistus even claimed, right in Florence, that a few years would bring the end of the reign of the "positive religions," of Christianity and Islam, and all human beings would at last embrace "one and the same religion, with one heart, one mind, one preaching."[33]

We do not know whether Plethon actually spread such "dangerous" ideas among his Florentine listeners. It is certain, in any case, that his attack on Aristotle and his appeal to the *Chaldean Oracles*, that is, the teachings attributed to Zarathustra and the Persian Magi, did not go unheard. No less influential was his work *On the Difference Between Plato and Aristotle*,[34] composed in Florence, in which he brilliantly argued the superiority of the Platonic tradition against the Peripatetic teachings so dear to Western theologians. In fact, Gemistus accused Aristotle of being an "inferior" philosopher, ignorant of the supreme divine truths and therefore incapable of understanding the nature of souls and heavenly intelligences and the very causes of the motions of the heavens and the stars. In contrast, Gemistus exalted Plato, whom he regarded as the most enlightened guardian of the theological mysteries, knower and theoretician of the absolute divine unity and of pure spiritual and separated natures.

The strongest reactions against Plethon and his ideas came from the Byzantine side, beginning with a violent reply from Scholarius, who in 1443 bitterly attacked the elderly philosopher.[35] As I have already said, Scholarius was a master who had drawn extensively on Western Aristotelean traditions, with special attention to the commentators on the texts of the *Organon,* from Peter the Spaniard to Pseudo-Gilbert of Poitiers and, above all, to Thomas Aquinas. He had also translated some of their writings into Greek, conceiving in the process a deep admiration for the methods of Latin Scholasticism and for the philosophical culture of its greatest representatives, which in his judgment made them superior in theoretical debate and more capable, precisely because of their "Peripatetic" training, of developing and explaining the ancient elements of dogma. It is not surprising that he so strongly opposed one who maintained the superiority of Platonism and reduced Aristotelean teaching to a kind of "inferior doctrine."

However, the intervention in the debate, in 1455, of another master, George of Trebizond (1395–1484), already author of a *Rhetorica* and a *Dialectica,* both of them especially successful, certainly had a much greater echo.[36] George of Trebizond had not always been an intransigent Aristotelean; he had even translated the *Laws* of Plato and had extolled his merits as supreme philosopher in his dedication to Nicholas of Cusa of a translation of the *Parmenides.* Now, however, whether due to the oppositions that were increasingly dividing Byzantine intellectuals or due to concerns of a probably religious kind, he did not restrict himself to leveling very serious accusations again Gemistus, accusing him of being the Antichrist, but he also hurled an anathema at Plato and all the Platonists for their "godlessness," of which the "solar" prophecies and the astrological leanings were the most eloquent confirmation.[37] In response to the danger that the harm *(laevitas)* present in Platonic philosophy, the source of all heresies, might contaminate Christian truth, he called for the defense of sound Aristotelean teaching as the best foundation of theological studies and even as the only philosophy that a Christian mind could adopt when looking for rational and natural criteria for the preambles of faith.

This is not the place to go into the details of a lengthy invective that involved, in particular, some of the most learned masters of the Byzantine immigration, such as Theodore of Gaza, Michael Apostolios, and Andronicus Callistus. It is more important to recall that in response to George of Trebizond Bessarion himself (1403–72) intervened in a work published in 1469.[38] I have already spoken of Bessarion in connection with his interventions in the conciliar debates at Ferrara and Florence, where he was one of the most influential Byzantine delegates, a frank supporter of the union but also a defender of the "Oriental" cultural and doctrinal traditions, which he recognized as having a permanent value even in the reunited Christian Church.

After the union Bessarion became a cardinal of the Roman Church and soon became closely connected with Italian humanist circles but also with very prestigious Scholastic masters, such as Francis della Rovere, the future Sixtus IV. The Greek prelate had already shown his learning not only in his interventions at the council and in conciliar documents but also in short treatises, such as the *De Spiritus sancti processione* and the *Oratio dogmatica*. Anyone reading these works will see how he always kept to the teaching of the Greek Fathers and had behind him a philosophical and theological formation that had been much influenced by Platonic ideas and traditions, which he regarded as operative at a deep level in patristic reflection and in the culture of Byzantine Christianity. It is not surprising, therefore, that he decided to defend his teacher Plato, and Platonic philosophy in general, against accusations which he regarded as false and opportunistic and which threatened to label one of the supreme expressions of "Greek wisdom" as heresy and to transform Aristoteleanism into the single "orthodox" philosophy of the Christian world by ratifying the absolute primacy of Western Scholastic methods.

Nevertheless, his *In calumniatorem Platonis* was not simply a polemical document dictated by contingent circumstances. Both in its Greek version in three books and in its four-book Latin version, revised by Theodore of Gaza, it was a work that offered the philosophers and theologians of the time a complete and profound interpretation of Platonic teaching, one that claimed to be close to Christianity and at the same time stressed its obvious agreement with Aristoteleanism. Bessarion's intention was not, of course, to present Plato in the garments of an orthodox Catholic philosopher; he even acknowledged that it was impossible to dress Plato's philosophy in Christian robes. But if this was true of the Athenian thinker, it was no less true of Aristotle, loftiest of philosophers but likewise without the light of Christian revelation.

On the other hand, the teaching of Plato was closer to the essential principles of the faith, as the Greek Fathers, and Augustine among the Latin Fathers, had already recognized. This did not lessen the indisputable value of Aristotle, whose *Metaphysics* in particular Bessarion praised; nor, on the other hand, could it be denied that various Platonic ideas were and remained far removed from Christianity, such as the theory of the preexistence of souls, the multiplicity of gods, and the attribution of souls to the heavens and the stars. But the doctrine of God, conceived as absolute and unreachable unity, super-essential principle, and source of all beings, seemed to Bessarion much more congenial to Christianity and well-grounded in the *Parmenides* and others among the most important works of Plato. It was that teaching that fed the mysticism of Dionysius, a spiritual source common to Christians of both West and East. And, while certainly bearing in mind the use which Latin theologians had made of Aristotelean concepts and categories during the discussions at the council, the cardinal nonetheless denied that it was possible to find a real trinitarian doctrine in either Plato or Aristotle, even though he maintained that it was possible to find at least an allusion to the Son in the sixth book of the *Republic*.

This "some likeness" between Platonism and Christianity was then confirmed by an extensive discussion of the concept of the production of matter and form out of nothingness, as well as of what Bessarion had to say about Plato having always accepted the idea of Providence and the divine government of the world. It was true that he had expressed these ideas in the language of myth and poetry, just as even Moses, in fact, had attributed "hands and feet" to God in the story of creation. But the cardinal was sure that Plato, and for that matter, Proclus, Porphyry, Amelius, Iamblichus, Syrianus, Plotinus himself, and Hermes, had understood that the divine eternity is the sole cause of the production of all the multiplicity of beings and of their continuance in being.

Not only that: the demonstration given of the immortality of the soul in the *Phaedrus* and then the *Phaedo* was much closer to Christian truth than the ideas of Aristotle, which, according to Alexander of Aphrodisias, led to the acceptance of the soul's mortality. Nor could anyone point to the doctrine of metempsychosis, although taught by Plato, as a reason for condemning him as a supporter of utterly wicked ideas, since, in this case once again, the purpose of his "popular" discourse was simply to convince "the common people" that only unblemished and virtuous souls could receive heavenly blessedness.

In any case, it had always to be acknowledged that any philosopher not divinely enlightened could succeed only in apprehending the existence of a first efficient cause of all things. That had been the accomplishment of Plato and Aristotle, Avicenna and Proclus, when they speculated on a single God and the ensuing procession of "intelligences." But, since George of Trebizond had harshly condemned Plato, accusing him of adoring lesser divinities and demons, Bessarion gave proof that Aristotle had expounded similar teachings without on that account being in the least an idolater or blasphemer.

The remainder of the book is in large part a continuous, penetrating parallel analysis of the ideas of Plato and Aristotle on the human person and the world and on freedom and fate. The discussion is marked by a wide knowledge of ancient thought and by constant, detailed references to the teachings of Christian theologians and, in particular, to Western masters such as Thomas Aquinas and Duns Scotus. The author shows that the differences between the two greatest philosophers of antiquity were quite limited, since they agreed far more than they disagreed. He also shows that their ideas can be easily reconciled, provided one thinks of them as complementing each other in the search for a common, single, and sure truth. This had not been understood by George of Trebizond, whose erroneous interpretations and deliberate distortions of Platonic and Aristotelean texts Bessarion challenges in detail.

In the *In calumniatorem Platonis* the contrast between the two greatest philosophers of antiquity was thus transformed into a search for a basic and reciprocal agreement, out of which there emerged a proposal that the doctrinal foundations of Western theology be renewed through the contribution of a tradition of thought that had remained too foreign to it in recent centuries. Renascent Platonism found here its legitimation, and this in a perspective that was already looking beyond Plato himself to Plotinus and the Neoplatonists. Already emerging, too, was the plan of a new theology that abandoned the "syllogisms" and "sophistries" of the Scholastics and turned, instead, to those of the faithful who were educated but not accustomed to the subtleties of the masters and whose spiritual restlessness was beginning to manifest itself in the desire for an evangelical piety that would be based on the teaching of the divine word and the practice of charity.

4. Marsilius Ficino

In the past, and still today, there has been a great deal of debate about the influence that the work of the Byzantine cardinal may have had on a young philosopher, Marsilius Ficino (1433–99),[39] who right at the time when the *In calumniatorem Platonis* was published was already engaged in his labor as a Latin translator of the most important documents of the Platonic, Neoplatonic, and Hermetic tradition. As a young student trained in Scholasticism and a disciple of a physician, Nicholas Tignosi, who professed Peripatetic doctrines, Marsilius had begun works of a still-traditional kind connected with the texts of Aristotle and the interpretations of them by Averroes and other commentators. Later, around 1457, he had turned to the discussions being carried on regarding *voluptas,* and he had composed his *Commentariola lucretiana.*

In any case, the paucity of documents surviving from this early activity makes it impossible to gain complete clarity about his early speculative outlook. However, from 1456 to 1458 he composed a *De voluptate,* a *De virtutibus moralibus,* and his *De quattuor sectis philosophorum,* in which the discussion of these themes was based on the Platonic distinction between *gaudium* and *laetitia.* His precocious calling to speculative thought was confirmed during those same years by the composition of his *Institutiones ad Platonicam disciplinam* (now lost), which he wrote, it seems, at the urging of

Landino and the elderly Cosimo. Subsequently, however, Ficino always insisted on connecting the Platonic, Hermetic, "Chaldean," and "Orphic" renaissance, of which he was a major promotor, with the period of the council, when the "great" Cosimo had listened to Gemistus speaking of the "Platonic mysteries."

Although it is clear, as Garin has emphasized, that "Ficino's imaginative and rather fantastic stage scenario" had been deliberately used in order to "link" the supposed Medicean initiative with "supernatural interventions and 'signs' of spirits and the stars," the fact remains that Marsilius was not only the translator largely responsible for making known the most important documents of the Platonic and Neoplatonic traditions but also the most illustrious interpreter of the "fables" to which had been entrusted the memory of a very ancient theological wisdom, one that was independent of biblical revelation and had been granted by God to every people. This seems clear from his own activity as a translator, which was not limited to making known the Platonic corpus and the *Enneads* of Plotinus but included also the writings of Proclus and Psellus, the *De mysteriis* and *De secta pythagorica* of Iamblichus, and above all, the *Hermetica,* the *Symbola pythagorica,* and the *Carmina orphica.*[40]

If, as seems to be the case, the translation of the *Oracula chaldaica* that has been attributed to him is not his,[41] at least he made extensive use of it in his own works. As a result, the idea of a very ancient "archaic philosophy" and its continuation in the "devout philosophy" of the Platonists had a definitive seal set upon it. Moreover, the repeatedly asserted convergence between this wisdom and Christian revelation was expressed in language more congenial to a new public that was no longer made up of professional theologians but rather of "civilian" patricians, politicians, craftsmen, and artists.

In the case of Marsilius it will be necessary, once again, to give only a brief analysis and not to launch onto the wide sea of his complete writings, a body of work which, in its various expressions, covered so large a part of the late fifteenth century. There is no doubt, however, that the Latin translation of the *Hermetica,*[42] which Ficino completed in 1463 at the beginning of his labor as a translator, shows the direct connection which he made between the revival of the ancient Platonic wisdom and the sources of the primordial revelation of the most hidden divine secrets. This fact remains, even if we accept as true the story that Cosimo himself asked his young protégé to devote himself urgently to the task to putting into Latin the mysterious message of the father of Egyptian "theology."

There are, in any case, many indications suggesting that Ficino's spiritual experience had its "focal" point precisely in the years of the first printing of his very successful translation of the *Hermetica* (1471) and the publication, first in the vernacular (1474–75) and then in Latin (1476), of his *De christiana religione* and the completion of the first version of his *Theologia platonica,* works to which may be added the complex development of the *De amore* (completed, by any reckoning, before 1474) and, in my opinion, of the *De raptu Pauli* (1476).[43] In fact, it is not difficult to see in this sequence of works a carefully thought out and masterly program aimed at spreading and popularizing ideas truly alien to ordinary apologetics, aimed, that is, at offering a new image of Christian piety that was based on the supreme value of love and charity, and at showing in these the essential values of every true "philosophical religion" that drew its light from the teaching of the most ancient wise men no less than from the "splendor" of biblico-Christian revelation.

It is true that the *De christiana religione*[44] takes over from authors who were among the best known, such as Nicholas of Lyra, Paul of Burgos, and Ricoldo of Montecroce, many arguments typical of controversy with the Jews and the Muslims similar to those given also in the *Epistula Rabbi Samuelis,* which was turned into Latin and also translated into the vernacular by its very own author, Sebastian Salvini.[45] At the same time, however, there is the explicit and revealing assertion that the Christian religion is not founded on any worldly power and that it draws its life solely from the eternal divine wisdom. No less eloquent is Ficino's insistence on adding to his extended presentation of the Old Testament prophecies of Christ's coming the prophecies attributed to the oracles of the Sibyls and Hermes. At the same time, he gives decided prominence to the idea that all religions have always had something good in them and that perhaps their "variety . . . by God's arrangement lends a certain marvelous beauty to the universe."[46]

The controlling idea in this work in a more "popular" key seems to be a proclamation of the complete identity of piety and wisdom, that is, the inseparable connection between religion and philosophy, a connection that in turns calls for a faith that is always open to rational reflection and to a search for the motives innate in the soul due to its "heavenly" origin and its immortality. This enables the Florentine canon to appeal again to those "divinely inspired" learned men who in very earliest times were both priests and sages, searchers into the "causes of things" and organizers of the worship paid to the "first cause." Thus he could write that the biblical prophets were not only men of profound piety but also philosophers; that in ancient Egypt the priesthood was always awarded to those who had an expert knowledge of nature and were also masters of "things divine"; that likewise among the Persians the Magi, trustees of the mysteries of the world, "presided at sacrifices"; that the seven wise men of Greece also possessed the rank of priests; that the Celtic druids were the guardians of an occult philosophy no less than were the Indian Brahmans; and that at the beginnings of Christianity, when the faith was purer, "bishops" and "presbyters" combined the orthodox truth of their theological teachings with a no less certain and very useful knowledge of philosophy.

These were, however, examples and traditions from which Ficino meant to derive a teaching for the present time, a time of ever-clearer crisis in longstanding ways of teaching and in ecclesial institutions. He sees as depending on those examples and traditions the restoration of "right religion" no less than its universalist claim in a world divided by all kinds of conflict and threatened (he writes) by the godlessness of the philosophers. During recent centuries a divorce between piety and wisdom had in fact taken place; for this reason philosophy had become a tool of unbelief, while the guardianship of things divine had fallen into the hands of uncouth, ignorant, and unworthy priests who had made these things ridiculous in the eyes of the faithful, transforming them into ambiguous, superstitious practices and external ceremonies lacking in any spiritual meaning. To do away with this disastrous state of affairs, which Ficino regarded as fatal to the highest forms of the spiritual life, the only course was to reform both wisdom and religion, that is, to recover those common principles on which, ever since the origins of the human race, the eternity of revelation and the certainty of doctrine had rested. That meant returning to that most ancient and profound nucleus of a truth in which all human beings would participate, provided they rediscovered the original treasure of a knowledge that would ensure the exercise of their own exceptional powers.[47]

Marsilius undoubtedly also maintained that the Christian religion alone could effect this reunification, bring "piety" and "philosophy" back into the channel of a single spiritual experience, and come to know once again the great amount of truth which all the faiths and the not "ungodly" philosophies possessed when they were not "polluted" or deflected from their goal by the force of desires, passions, and worldly "idols," or infected with ignorance. It is clear, however, that the religion Ficino had in mind was, first and foremost, the teaching and practice of charity, that is, a faith and participation in the universal divine love, beyond all dogmatic formulas and beyond every cause of separation and disagreement. In short, a complete identification of the human person with the absolute life of the eternal Monad, of which the incarnate Son is the cosmic intermediary; a final communion with being, contemplated in the splendor of its changeless light, to the point of a total identification or deification.

From the outset Ficino sets such ideas under the sign of the most ancient "authorities," which he lists in the dedication of his translation of the *Hermetica* to Cosimo de'Medici. After recalling the very remote antiquity of Trismegistus and the Egyptian practice of awarding priesthood to the philosophers, he writes as follows:

> He [Trismegistus] was the first of the philosophers to turn from physics and mathematics to the contemplation of divine things; he was the first to speak of the divine majesty, the order of demons, and, with very great wisdom, of the transmigration of souls. For this reason he was called the first founder of theology. Orpheus, following him, took first place in ancient theology. Aglaophemus was initiated into the mysteries of Orpheus; his successor in theological learning was Pythagoras, who was followed by Philolaus, teacher of our divine Plato.[48]

Here Ficino already traces the harmonious tradition of the original theology ("a line, in agreement at every point, of a single original theology") on its journey from Hermes to Plato. But in the *De christiana religione* the picture of wisdom is different, since it is seen entirely in the perspective of Christian revelation, the "light" that has shown up the most "hidden" truth:

> The original theology of the Gentiles, on which Zarathustra, Mercury, Orpheus, Aglaophemus, and Pythagoras were all in agreement, is brought together in its entirety in the works of our Plato. And in his letters Plato announced the mysteries that were at last to be revealed to humanity after many centuries. That is exactly what happened when in the time of Philolaus and Numenius people began for the first time to grasp, from the pages of the Platonists, the intention of the early theologians, and this after the discourses and writings of the apostles and the disciples of the apostles. The Platonists would, in fact, use the divine light of the Christians for understanding the divine Plato.[49]

Later on, in the famous letter to Martin Uranius, the continuity of the "devout philosophy" went well beyond the apostolic and patristic ages and was seen also in the greatest "witnesses" of medieval Platonism and in clearly identified Scholastic "authorities." Dionysius the Areopagite, Augustine, Boethius, Apuleius, Chalcidius, and Macrobius, but also "Jews" and "Muslims," namely Avicebron, Alfarabi, and Avicenna, and Masters Henry of Ghent and Duns Scotus were all the trustees of a truth that was kept alive down to the most recent times by Cusa and Bessarion; of this truth Ficino declared himself the heir. This was a "royal road" of knowledge human and divine, the superiority of which is obvious, especially when compared with the "worldly" science of the Peripatetics:

> The divine Iamblichus describes two ways to happiness as found in the thinking of the Egyptians, the one philosophical, the other priestly; the former, he says, is more bent on discovering happiness, the latter a shorter way to reach it; the former is the way chosen mainly by the Peripatetics and the philosophers, the latter is the way trodden by the religious people. Our Plato marvelously combined these two ways into one, and at every point he is the subtle philosopher and debater, the devout priest, and the eloquent orator.[50]

It is understandable that this philosopher could be understood as completely in tune with biblical revelation and even with the prophetic announcement of Christ as universal "mediator," a point confirmed by the teaching of the Christian followers of Platonism.

It is clear from many of the most important eloquent passages of so lengthy a "search" that all this is indeed the dominant motif of Ficino's philosophical thought—and of its expression in a teaching that clearly distances itself from the tradition of the schools and has at its center the Platonic doctrine of the "soul," its immortality and cosmic centrality (as we can tell from the title of his most important work, *Theologia platonica, sive de immortalitate animae.*)[51] But perhaps even more revealing is the introduction to the translation of the *Enneads*,[52] in which the condemnation of the godless sects of Averroes and Alexander, which have "pervaded the entire world," is connected with the goal of developing "a religious philosophy that can be accepted by and be convincing to the philosophers."

Not even the explicit plan to "reconcile Plato and Aristotle" falls outside this outlook; the reconciliation is to be accomplished by acknowledging both their differences and their "complementarity" in the common search for a truth that is both natural and divine and has to do with the order of the world and its ground in the one absolute Principle. The search of the wise looks beyond the "images" and "symbols" that satisfy the minds of the simple; it seeks always to pass beyond the "letter" to the "spirit" and to ascend to the light and splendor of the divine, which manifests itself in this world only "in enigmas." Thus the task of the "devout philosopher" will be precisely to gather up the one wisdom in all the forms in which it reveals itself, in the sacred books as in the hidden teaching of the poets, in the Pythagorean harmony of the heavens and in the perfect arrangement of nature that finds expression in its perennial beauty. In this way "devout philosophy" is transformed into a "learned religion" that can grasp the divine roots of the universe and the marvelous unfolding of the eternal Oneness in the exhaustible multiplicity of its creation.

In dealing with the doctrine of the divine Monad, the Father and origin of being, Ficino's "theology" calls upon its Pythagorean, Platonic, Hermetic, and Plotinian sources, which agree in celebrating the "superessential" nature. But the most typical aspect of Ficino's thought here is its depiction of a cosmic order that is arranged in a hierarchical series of perfections and intermediaries and is understood to be a "mirror" of God. In it every reality is a "way" and "ladder" to the divine, and everything has reference to the Principle and, through its own unavoidable "insufficiency" reveals the Principle's absolute "sufficiency" and "power." In fact, Ficino considers the beings and "degrees" of the world to form an ascending line, the ultimate summit of which is always the One and the Eternal from which they descend. Sometimes his philosophical imagination seems to conceive them as being the various notes in a vast musical system in which each contributes to the harmony of the whole and in which that same harmony is realized in the perfect "adjustment" and absolute accord of the individual notes.

From corporeal beings, with their specific conditions of "matter" and "quality," to souls and from souls to the angels and God, the ascensional process of the universe unfolds, identical with but the inverse of that by which the multiple descends from the One. The Florentine canon intends, of course, to avoid any possible reduction of his Platonic and Neoplatonic thinking to the dreaded outcome of a pantheism in the Gnostic mode. He asserts, too, that God is outside the order of things, as a principle that is not identified with its "consequences," a supreme cause that does not exhaust itself in its "effects."

Nevertheless, although he is the infinite over against the finite, the absolute over against the changeable, he is the only goal and sole reason for all of the reality that descends from him. It is possible, moreover, to "climb back" to God through knowledge and "love" along the "chain" of the various cosmic natures, but, above all, through the "soul," which is the intermediary par excellence, since, participating as it does in the finite and the infinite, the temporal and the eternal, it is the "bond of the world *(copula mundi),*" the connection between the eternal Monad and the changeable flux of the "multiple."

The "soul" is, in fact, present and active in every part of the universe; it is the source of the life and movement of every corporeal entity. It contemplates the ideas, the divine Logos that thinks them, and the Monad that generates them. On the other hand, it is the "craftsman" who works in the bosom of nature and draws forth from it, as by the "power of its art," all the forms. It is an artist whose work is very much superior to the rough "imitation" practiced by human beings; it is therefore the "mind of nature joined to matter," the power continually applied to embodying in matter the eternal and immutable "forms."

It is precisely its function as "bond of the world" that is for Ficino the principle for proving its immortality. The soul, even that of the individual human being, is incorporeal and indivisible and, as form of the body, the source of all its activities and its unity; its own existence is identical with its essence, and it is compact in itself. On the other hand, its "simplicity" is relative, and therefore its being can only come from God. This means that in its origin and nature the soul is independent of the body and is immortal and free of all corruption. It possesses the "eternal reasons" that are present in the divine mind; it is, as it were, the "mirror" of the divinity, which is reflected in it. When it contemplates its own interiority, it achieves a knowledge, relative indeed, of God, a knowledge reflective of the forms stored up in his eternal mind.

On the foundation of this teaching that renews and transforms the ancient Platonic theme of the "soul of the world," Ficino is able to introduce Pythagorean and Orphic themes as well as the astrological ideas and even the magical suggestions that came to him from the Hermetic writings and the *Chaldean Oracles.* The entire universe—the heavens as well as the "elements," the planetary spheres as well as plants, animals, and human beings—seems to him permeated by life and "measure"; everything accords with the geometrically rigorous laws which an eternal mind has set down. Just as all souls participate in the soul that governs the entire cosmos, so all of them live by the immortality which derives from their divine origin.

But if the soul can be united with the higher minds, it is also able to enter, through the body subject to it, into the order of material things and to impose on them its higher, immortal power. Thus the "circle" of universal life is closed, and the soul can return to its origin, into the splendor from which it arose. God is in fact the light of light, the "Father of lights" whence derives and descends the angelic light, "intellectual certainty . . . and an overflowing joy of the will," from which in turn proceeds the sparkling of the stars, the strength and shaping power of fire, and the "spark" of the human intellect. To contemplate God is to understand that he is the life-giving warmth that gives existence to everything, the universal "love" from which every creature is begotten and due to which everything "begotten" tends without respite to unite itself to the "light" that has produced it.

This is why the persistent metaphors of light are continually interwoven, in Ficino's speech, with the motif of the Platonic eros, which a shrewd "strategy" links to Pauline teaching on charity. In a passage of the *De amore* Ficino writes: "The mind is moved and drawn from the inquiry into its own light to the discovery of the divine light, and this drawing is true love. . . . When God infused his light into the soul, he made it suited above all for this, that human beings should be led by it to blessedness, which consists in the possession of God."[53] It is true that God flees those who attempt to find this blessedness in things and deceive themselves that in the illusory beauty of bodies they are enjoying the divinity and his love. And yet, even the love of beautiful things is always also a desire for the divine, a "thirst" for that invisible splendor that is hidden behind the appearances of sensible light. When the soul, having been recalled to itself, really understands the divine nature of worldly beauty, it is immediately seized by an "inextinguishable fire" and becomes itself light and "fervor."

However, the passion that is born of the contemplation of beauty, the love that "lifts the human being above itself and changes it into God," is the most sublime form of a universal desire that turns each being toward its final and necessary end. In this sense Eros (the "ancient" and "youngest" god, the god of "origin" and "return") is, in Ficino's view, the hidden force that animates all things, the myth that best expresses the eternal alternation of a process that has in the One its origin and its end. And nothing expresses the "paradox of love" better than the ancient image of the beloved who enthralls the lover, for this symbolizes the deification that is the ultimate goal of the soul, when it is at last released from its ties to the body and restored to its pure nature as a spiritual and immortal creature, the "offspring" of God.

In this extraordinary fusion of all the motifs of the "archaic theology" and of Platonic thought, it was not possible to omit the emphatic appeal to the power of magic, understood as the "beneficent" art that makes it possible to understand the secret language of the world, to control the hidden forces, and to help the soul on its journey toward its "heavenly" destiny. Magic and astrology, a belief in the hidden connections that link the various orders of reality with one another and in the secret power of the stars and even, finally, a trust in the active power of "images" and the astrological "symbols": these are in fact motifs that continually recur in Ficino's work, down to the more disquieting pages of *De vita coelitus comparanda* (1489). For while Ficino rejected the more extreme and deterministic forms of "judicial" astrology and asserted the freedom and superiority of the soul, which is free of "servitude" to the body, he did not reject the idea that the world is in its entirety "ensouled" and that "heavenly" souls are superior in dignity and power to those of human beings.

Thus, in some of the most ambiguous pages of the *Libri de vita*,[54] he accepted the therapeutical and magical power of amulets and of astrological images cut into stones and metals and also the power of those "demonic" influences coming from creatures operating on the border between earth and the heavenly spaces. Here, again, Ficino appealed to traditions and teachings that were already widespread in medieval culture and that were now acquiring new power in a time of growing spiritual restlessness.

As a matter of fact, even these more obscure and "murky" elements in Ficino's work would contribute to the exceptional success of an author whose ideas were to have such a profound effect on the culture of sixteenth-century Europe, influencing, as they did, circles and personalities of great importance in the history of philosophical and religious ideas.[55]

5. Christopher Landino

Often linked with Ficino's name is that of another Florentine intellectual, Christopher Landino (1424–98),[56] whose closeness to and even dependence on the ideas of his more illustrious fellow citizen have been overly stressed. More recent studies have tended to emphasize the originality of Landino's approach to the Platonic tradition, which was independent of Ficino's "journey" and even preceded it in time, as well as the advice and help that he gave to the younger philosopher in the latter's first steps toward Platonism; it is not without significance that Ficino dedicated his now lost *Institutiones* to Landino. Landino was certainly calling on ideas that were always present in Florentine humanistic culture when, in his commentary on Petrarch, he revived the myth of "poetic theology" and looked to the poet's work for the signs of a divine truth expressed in poetic figures and allegories. Nor will it be necessary to remind the reader of Landino's commentary on Dante in the famous edition published by Nicholas della Magna (1481) and illustrated by Botticelli; this commentary interpreted the great journey through the kingdoms of the next world as a "vision" that revealed hidden Platonic truths and announced an imminent palingenesis.

This was an exegesis of Dante that in the course of the sixteenth century was to provide food for other typical examples of doctrinal poetry and for readings of the two "greatest" poets that were inspired by a fervent revival of the theological fable of Orpheus and its "civic" and "spiritual" meaning. It was, however, characteristic that even when commenting on Dante, Landino should cite his own dialogues *De anima*,[57] which he had published in 1472 at the beginning of the Platonic "rebirth."

These dialogues, in which the chief characters are Landino himself, Charles Marsuppini, and Paul of Pozzo Toscanelli, recapitulate many of the motifs destined to become philosophical and literary commonplaces, including the special emphasis on the profound affinity between Platonism and Christianity. In fact, the first two books already reject the theory that the soul is a kind of "harmony" or "blending" of corporeal elements and assert instead that the soul, in virtue of its power of understanding, is an immaterial form. Then, in the third book, the problem of the soul's immortality is tackled by an appeal to the inner consciousness which the soul has of itself and which reveals its divinely appointed central place in the "union" of the highest and the lowest (and corporeal) orders of creation.

Precisely for this reason Landino challenged the solutions proposed by Averroes and Avicenna and maintained that the agent and active intellects of which Aristotle speaks are two faculties proper to each individual soul. As "light," the agent intellect does indeed act on the "phantasm," which provides the material to be understood. But the soul belongs to the world of the "spirits" and is made in the likeness of God; nor does the destruction of the body and of the vegetative and sensitive functions proper to it mean that destruction must come also to the soul, whose intellectual faculty exists even independently of the body. For this reason Hermes and Plato rightly maintained that the soul "moves itself" and therefore cannot suffer corruption, since it is immaterial, is destined for eternal happiness or suffering, and always tends beyond the world and time to things eternal and divine. Or, as Landino writes: "It is, then, the mind that asserts its right against destruction; it is therefore immortal."

Three years later, in 1475, the humanist probably finished his *Disputationes camaldulenses*,[58] in which he himself plays a role along with Donatus Acciaiuoli, Alamannus Rinuccini, Mark Parenti, Ficino, Anthony Canigiani, Leonbaptist Alberti, and Lorenzo and Giuliano de'Medici. Their main subject is the question of the superiority of the active or the contemplative life. In the first book Landino seeks to answer by maintaining a correct combination of the two, since the human person is not a pure spirit and cannot neglect the body and, with it, the necessary concerns of life in the world. On the other hand, the human being is born to "speculate," and if it be true that "Martha and Mary are sisters, live in the same house," and both please God, then there is no doubt that the ultimate end for which the human soul longs is perfect contemplation that does not exclude active participation in works of the world.

That the supreme good, then, consists precisely in ascending to "divine things," according to the teaching of Plato, is explicitly stated in Book II. But in Books III and IV, in which Virgil is called to mind as the supreme example of the "theologian poet," the conclusion is even clearer and more explicit. Human beings should, it is true, "join Martha" so as not to neglect their place in the world; but they ought to desire even more to be united to Mary in order that their souls "may be fed with ambrosia and nectar," attain to the highest knowledge of God, and find in this "ultimate good" their "harbor of utmost tranquillity." The primacy of the wise person, who seeks his true destiny in the contemplation of the "supreme things," is thus reasserted in the image of Plato, teacher of the "honorable" and "happy life" to all of humanity and founder of values that transcend the passing affairs of the earthly order.

6. John Pico della Mirandola

The "return of Plato" and the spread of the fascinating myth of the "archaic theologians" were certainly signs of a radical change in the intellectual climate of the late fifteenth century, a period increasingly marked by a serious religious uneasiness and soon to be attracted by the revival of ancient millenniarist expectations and of prophetic preaching that proclaimed the imminent "renewal" *(renovatio)* of Christian life. It was precisely this period that saw the development and premature end of the intellectual experience of the other major Italian philosopher of the century, John Pico della Mirandola (1463–94).[59]

While still an adolescent this Paduan aristocrat had begun the study of law at the Studium of Bologna, where he had also been introduced to the study of astronomy and astrology. But more than by the short time spent in Bologna and more than by his initial stays in such prestigious intellectual centers as Florence and Ferrara (1479), his formation was influenced by the years he spent at the Studium of Padua, in direct contact with the philosophical world of the university, with teachers such as the very well-known "Averroist" Nicoletto Vernia and the young Nifo, with learned orientalists such as Jerome Ramusio, and humanist translators and commentators such as Jerome Danà (1480–82).

It was his study of the Aristotelean texts, which were the basis of the teaching of philosophy at Padua, that led Pico back to the primary sources of the medieval Peripatetic tradition, namely, to the great Arabic and Jewish masters. Thus Elias del Medico, a learned Jew and a faithful interpreter of Averroes whose intense intellectual mysticism he had strongly emphasized, was Pico's guide to authors and texts with which Ficino had been less familiar and which, as in the case of Averroes, he had decisively condemned. Nor is there any doubt that Pico acquired at this time (and strengthened during his stay in Paris in 1485–86) the stern speculative outlook that caused him to give a privileged place to the knowledge of things *(res)* and to exclude from the realm of philosophy (but not from ethical and religious "persuasion") the indiscriminate use of rhetorical devices. It will be enough to recall here the celebrated letter to Ermolaus Barbarus, which Pico wrote in Florence in June of 1485 and in which his defense of the "language of Paris" *(sermon parisiensis)* and of Scholastic vocabulary implied a rejection of a rhetorical art that would replace the philosophical quest of truth.[60]

Pico himself undoubtedly recognized the value and effectiveness of expressive form and the connection between the latter and the clarity and lucidity of philosophical discourse. But perhaps with Ficino, among others, in mind, he wanted to maintain a firm distinction between the rigorous structure of speculative language and the "eloquence" required by an "orator." Neither his passage through a climate so intensely linked to the renewal of Platonism, nor his friendship with Ficino, nor his reading of Plotinus and other Neoplatonic authors could narrow his philosophical interests, which were always drawn to constant conversation with the Aristotelean masters and with learned representatives of the Jewish speculative tradition.

His return from Paris in the spring of 1486 coincided, in fact, with the renewal of discussion with Elias del Medico on the opinions of Avicenna and Averroes and, most importantly, his studies of the Hebrew and Chaldean tongues and his introduction to the reading of texts of the Cabala (among them the *Zohar* and the *Sefer Yesirah*). In this reading he was also guided by a Jewish convert, Raymond of Moncada (Flavius Mithridates), an unusual personage who was involved in various "esoteric" events. Indeed, the Cabala, as a very high and pure form of gnosis, made known to Pico the only true hidden "wisdom," which had been revealed by God and had the power to interpret every language and every mystery on the basis of the divine word itself. He had now moved beyond even the documents of the "archaic theology" and had identified the supreme point of contact between human wisdom and revelation, between the teachings of the philosophers and the absolute manifestation of eternal and changeless truth.

Traces of the enthusiasm with which Pico accepted and made his own the experiences of the Cabalists are already obvious in his *Commento all canzone d'amore* of Jerome Benivieni,[61] a work which Pico described as a preliminary to a new commentary on the *Symposium* of Plato (not without polemical intentions regarding the *De amore* of Ficino). But even more than the evident Cabalistic ideas found in this work and the strong mystical bent to which the work attests, the thing that is striking about the *Commento* is the references to the great meeting of scholars that was to have taken place in Rome at Epiphany of 1487 in order to discuss the theses which Pico was preparing and, with these as the focus, to celebrate the harmony of all doctrines.

The origin of this project was to be found in many typical aspects of the spirituality of the time that had already found expression in Ficino's "theology": the expectation of a new era of peace and the hope of a Christian *renovatio,* which would be accomplished in the light of the inspiration drawn from the "archaic theology" and would culminate in the recognition of the radical unity of all the great religious and sapiential traditions. At the same time, however, Pico profoundly altered the character and purpose of the "devout philosophy"; above all, he interpreted his mission as philosopher of *concordia* to be the justification of the "unique" character of the human creature and of its significance in the cosmic order.

In his *Oratio de hominis dignitate*,[62] composed as a manifesto for the Roman meeting and as an introduction to his nine hundred theses (or *Conclusiones*), Pico harked back to a theme already frequently discussed by the humanists and, in a way, "consecrated" by Manetti's little work. But whereas the Florentine humanist had sung the praises of the human works, arts, and sciences in which our superiority to all other things of this world and our task of continuing the creation are manifested, the count of Mirandola wanted to celebrate the absolute value of the freedom which only human beings enjoy.

Unlike all other creatures, which are all conditioned by a "necessity-driven" nature and constrained by rigid laws that determine their destiny, to human beings alone God has given the power to "make themselves," to be the authors and "fathers" of their own "condition." Free as they are of every other situation except that of choosing their own lot, and therefore capable of ascending to the glory of the "children of God" or of degenerating to the lowest and murkiest kind of brutish nature, all individuals are, in Pico's view, masters of themselves and their own fate. But precisely because they always live suspended, as it were, between the downward pull of their natural and carnal desires and their divine vocation, human beings show that they possess a "dignity" loftier than that of any other nature and superior even to that of the angels. For to them alone is it permitted to rise deliberately to the perfection of God's living images by showing forth their "origin" not only by the supreme "nobility" of knowledge but also by every action and deed that is done in the light of the reason they possess and under the influence of the fervent aspirations of their faith:

> When the brute animals are born they bring with them from their mother's womb everything they will ever have. The heavenly spirits were, either from the beginning or from shortly afterward, what they will be through endless ages. In human beings coming to birth the Father places seeds of every kind and germs of every form of life. And these will bear their own fruit depending on how each individual cultivates them. If they are vegetal, they will be plants; if sensible, they will be brute animals; if rational, they will become heavenly animals; if intellectual, they will be angels and children of God. But if they are not content with the lot of any creature, and if they will gather themselves together at the center of their unity and become a single spirit with God, in the solitary darkness of the Father, then they who have been placed over all things will be above all things.[63]

The tragic greatness of human beings consists in this continual choosing between the infinite happiness of love of God, in which all their limitations are dissolved in the absolute identity, and the extremes of degradation. But only when they are capable of being "one with the Father" in the mystic "death of the kiss," of which the Jewish sages speak, will they truly have fulfilled their destiny.

It is not surprising, then, that Pico was able to appeal to Hermes, oldest master of the "archaic theology," and to write at the beginning of the *Oratio* the words that were so dear to Ficino as well: "A great miracle, O Asclepius, is man!" and that on the same page he should also recall that the Persians had called the human being "the bond and indeed the marriage of the world."[64] But we should not let ourselves be deceived by this presence of the authors on which Ficino based his "devout philosophy" or by Pico's clear propensity to accept the teachings and devices of speculative magic, for his conception of "wisdom" is radically different when viewed theoretically and historically. In his *Conclusiones* the philosophers called upon to weave the difficult tapestry of *concordia* are, it is true, the "Chaldean" theologians and Trismegistus, along with Plotinus, Abdalam the Arab, Porphyry, Iamblichus, Proclus, and Pythagoras, but they also include the masters of the Scholastic philosophical and theological tradition and the supreme interpreters of other great experiences of "classical" and "Oriental" thought: Albert the Great and Thomas Aquinas, John Duns Scotus, Francis of Meyronnes, Giles of Rome, along with Averroes, Avicenna, Alfarabi, Isaac of Narbonne, Abumaron of Babylon, Maimonides, Muhammad of Toledo, and Avempace; and in addition, Theophrastus, Ammonius, Simplicius, Alexander of Aphrodisias, and Themistius.

But at the summit of this new picture of wisdom there now stands the Cabala as the supreme key for interpreting the Scriptures and the world. By means of its secret exegesis, the Cabala does away with every opposition and contradiction and restores all forms of knowledge to their original and essential unity. In addition, it gives human action a power that no other form of knowledge can achieve. In fact, not even the magic song of the *Orphic Hymns* can obtain the wonderful effects of the Cabala, "which has the property of giving every formal, continuous, or discrete quality a practical effect." The reason is that only the language which the Cabalist is able to use—the sacred and original language in which God spoke to the Chosen People—contains his Name and thus reflects the Word by which the world was created and its principles and most hidden secrets were established. This language makes it possible "to win the powers of higher realities" and place them at the service of the human free will in its ascent to the divine.

For this reason the wise man must prepare himself to rise above all the orders of nature, every form and measure, beyond even the hidden power of the stars, toward the spheres and "supracelestial" waters; here even the spell cast by magical words fails, and only the knowledge of the divine discourse and language enables the sage to act in freedom from every "bond." Any magical and Cabalistic activity must always be directed toward God, the ultimate goal of every human desire and, at the same time, first cause of every power. Moreover, the "wise magician" has the duty of keeping silence, since nothing is more sacrilegious than to reveal the supreme "mysteries" to the unworthy and to put at their disposal the words that contain the highest power and place human beings in direct union with the angelic intelligences.

And yet, when Pico advances along the dazzling road of Cabalistic "theurgy," he has left behind the wisdom of the "archaic ones" *(prisci)* that granted human beings only the knowledge of the celestial powers and assigned them the cosmic role of *vinculum nundi*. Instead, the most secret and hidden exegesis now opens the way to the supreme union, which includes both birth and rebirth. Thus on the image of the wise magician-priest, embodied in Hermes, Zarathustra, and Orpheus, is superimposed the "sacral" figure of the one who possesses access to the infinite "mysteries" of Scripture, the devout "decoder" of a language that expresses both what God has communicated to all and what he has reserved to those who are able to understand and control the absolute power hidden in the energy of the divine names.

We know the fate of Pico's attempt to crown his plan for *concordia* with this invocation of the "divine" magic of the Cabala. The condemnation by the theologians and the supreme Roman hierarchy was decisive, affecting those "unusual" and "suspect" theses of his, the publication of which on December 7, 1486, in Rome, seemed like an act of defiance, one that was aggravated by the subsequent publication of the *Apologia*. Then, on August 5, 1488, there followed the definitive judgment of Pope Innocent VIII, who declared the *Conclusiones* to be in part heretical, in part close to heretical, inclined to the errors of the pagan philosophers, favorable to the "obstinacy" of the Jews, showing a penchant for dangerous arts and practices, alien from and even hostile to the Christian faith.

But not even the reaction of the ecclesiastical authorities could keep the combination of Hermetism and other traditions connected with the myth of the "archaic theology," together with a constant Platonic and Neoplatonic inspiration, from forming a doctrinal "complex" that had a strong influence on many events of fifteenth-century religious life. Nor could it prevent metaphysical and theological ideas obviously originating with Nicholas of Cusa, as well as the revival of techniques of calculation derived from the "art" of Raymond Lull, from combining to constitute the dominant themes of a philosophical religious outlook rich in esoteric and spiritualist modulations and always faithful to the idea of a supreme human "ascent," to be achieved by means of particular contemplatives and active practices.

As for Pico himself, he fortunately escaped papal condemnation and lived out the final short years of his life in retreat at Florence, where he dedicated himself increasingly to meditation on the deepest "mysteries" of the divine being and to religious and theological studies. In 1488–89 he devoted himself to a commentary on the psalms and a defense of Jerome's translation and the Greek translation of the Psalter; but he also translated from Hebrew the philosophical romance by Ibn Tufail. Not unconnected with his meditations were a renewed reading of the Pseudo-Dionysian writings, his friendship with Elias, and an association with another Jewish philosopher, Jochanon Alemannus, who worked rather closely with Pico in 1488 and 1489, when the latter was completing his *Heptaplus, de septiformi sex dierum Genesos enarratione,*[65] a Cabalistic commentary on the creation dedicated to Lorenzo the Magnificent, his protector and friend. This same period saw the writing of the *De ente et uno,*[66] a work conceived as an implicit debate with Ficino and his conception of the One.

In this work Pico invoked the Dionysian mystical tradition to deny that it was possible to know God by the methods and procedures of the intellect, over against which he set the supreme wisdom of negative theology. But the powerlessness of the intellect was counterbalanced by the power of the act of total adherence that can unite human beings to their "origin." Much less did that powerlessness imply a renunciation of the divine infinity, which is, in fact, a continual spur to our desire of being united with the "truest light" of the Father. God, the originating unity from which everything comes forth and to which everything returns, is absolute transcendence and, at the same time, constant presence, an invisible and therefore limitless point, an absolute instant and totality that cannot be measured by time, creation and perfect life, utterly perfect knowledge and "changeless permanence":

> When you think of God as living and knowing, consider, above all else, that the life and knowledge being attributed to him are free of all these imperfections. . . . Conceive of a life that is utterly perfect, that is, a life that is completely life and nothing but life, that has no element of mortality, no admixture of death, and that requires nothing outside itself in order to be constant and perduring. Conceive of a knowledge by which everything is known simultaneously and with utter completeness; then add that this knowledge by its nature knows everything, need not seek the truth outside itself, but is itself the truth. Nevertheless there are some other things, which, although most perfect in their kind and such as cannot exist outside of God, are unworthy of God when understood in this way and separately. He is, in fact, complete and infinite perfection, but not in the sense that he contains within himself all the various infinite perfections as such, since in this case he would not be infinite nor would the things be infinite that are in him. He would be an infinite made up of attributes many in number but finite in their perfection—an impious thing to say or think of God. . . . Let us therefore remove from life not only anything that makes it imperfect but even that which makes it only life, and let us do the same with all the other names we give to God. What will be left of it all will necessarily be what we want God to be conceived as: one, completely perfect, infinite, utterly simple.[67]

In order to understand God in this way and to refer to his essence, even in human modes and with human powers, it is necessary, in short, to think of him in terms of the most absolute oneness, beyond all multiplicity, even above and beyond the concept of being. God, being a pure essence that excludes any determination and any limit, is indeed, in a certain sense, a nonbeing, because, being the "fullness of existence," he is infinitely beyond any defined or definable reality. The only name, therefore, that can be attributed to him, though without claiming to grasp in it his inconceivable essence, is not "being," but "superbeing," a name that negates being but nonetheless has in it "more" than being. This is why when the human mind tries to think God, it is always forced to halt in the face of an impenetrable "absence": the point at which all the light of being seems to be extinguished in darkness. But, as the loftiest Jewish and Christian mystical wisdom teaches, the deepest darkness is identical with the most intense light in a splendor which the human eye is not capable of enduring. If our way seems thus to be enclosed between two barriers of darkness, between the darkness of its origins and the divine darkness which it always seeks to reach, then its final and certain goal is to drown in the infinite and the eternal, to be dissolved in the divine unity.

Moreover, it is to this kind of knowledge that we are urged by biblical revelation itself, when this is illumined by the Cabalistic exegesis that is for Pico, as we have seen, the height of all true wisdom. The interpretation of Genesis, when carried out in the light of millennia of philosophical and theological experience, reveals to us, in fact, that every particular reality arises out of the deep darkness of matter, that is, of pure and undetermined "potentiality." It also shows, however, that the entire universe is infused with a universal principle of reason, a norm that controls its entire system from the highest heavens to the lowest forms and natures. Everything in the cosmos, then, is reason and soul; in everything a "submerged and confused reason" is at work, an eternal revelation of the divine in the created world.

In this nature that is so permeated by the divine reason it is, then, possible to develop the speculative and operative capacity of the human mind, when the latter knows how to read the book of creation by understanding the hidden letters in which it is written. In this sense, the "magic" which Pico distinguishes in the most unyielding way from deadly "necromancy" and from the practices of sorcery is nothing else than a "practical part of the natural sciences." It allows human beings to make themselves "understood" by nature, to penetrate to nature's "soul," that is, the spiritual power that is at work in all things, and thereby to direct the unknown forces hidden in its innermost recesses. As controller of these forces, the magician can alter the order of things and impose on matter his own will, which carries out the plans of the Father.

Faithful to his defense of freedom as an absolute value of the human creature, Pico had to be resolutely opposed to the astrological doctrines[68] that were so widespread even in the humanist culture of his time and were accepted in so many writings of Ficino, especially in his *Libri de vita*. In an implicit disagreement with the same Marsilius, Pico once again asserted the freedom of the human being from any form of necessity whatsoever, even that produced by the movements of the heavens and the "conjunctions" of the stars. To Ficino's concept of "man the microcosm," who reflects in himself the necessary order of the universe and of the influences that govern it, Pico opposed a new image, that of the sage who is able to subject to his own will even the mysterious power of the stars and to penetrate to the ultimate sources of cosmic law.

Above all, however, in denying the rigid necessity of astrological determinism that was implicit in the most typical doctrines of judicial astrology, Pico meant to challenge an alleged science that was in fact based on age-old vestiges of very ancient religions and astral myths and to replace it with the model of a cosmic system that was certainly governed by necessary causes and laws but that was also liberated from the false belief in the hidden power of the stars. The "differences in human customs and wits," "all the activities and characteristics of the mind in relation to demons, higher minds, God, the efficacy of prayer, the secrets of consciences, the circumstances of the future life," certainly could not be made subject to the "rules of divination" which the "swindling" astrologers were selling "with shameless temerity."

But Pico also criticized those (here the reference to Ficino was quite clear) who tried to "hide their thoughts by prattling on at length about free will" and who said they "did not believe that the stars exert force on our freedom, because we receive from them only a preparation and an invitation which it is in our power to accept or reject." To such people Pico answered that this kind of talk was only a palliative intended to hide the radical and unavoidable denial of free will implicit in every doctrine that subjects human nature to conditions.

Undoubtedly, not even the count of Mirandola denied that the stars exert influences on natural phenomena through their luminous rays and their heat; these, after all, were studied by the "mathematical astronomers" with the proper instruments for acquiring a knowledge of nature. But it was utterly absurd to believe in the powers of amulets, magical stones, and astral exorcisms, which were regarded as capable of altering the course of natural events or human actions and of effecting marvelous changes in the decisions and destinies of individuals. It is understandable, too, that Pico was especially against those "prognosticators" who had drawn from the unusual astrological phenomena of the *annus mirabilis,* 1484, the grimmest prophecies of the proximate "destruction of Europe," as they foretold new schisms and heresies, the coming of the Antichrist, and a lengthy period of calamities and wars.

This is certainly not the place for recalling the bitter controversies that welcomed Pico's *Disputationes in astrologiam divinatricem* after their posthumous publication.[69] It is more important to stress the fact that this work was in perfect accord with those ideals of reform and religious renewal that, during the last years of his life, took a new direction under the influence of his close friendship with Jerome Savonarola and led him to devote himself to meditations marked by a stern ethical character and religious edification.

Increasingly close to the preacher from Ferrara and in agreement with him even during the first controversies caused by his prediction of a proximate terrible time of "repentance," Pico took part in the meetings in the Dominican convent of San Marco, where other intellectuals, such as Jerome Benivieni, also gathered, men already with ties to Ficino and likewise longing for the imminent reformation of Christianity. Pico's call for *concordia* had a deep appeal for them, just as it was to attract other great figures of European humanism, from Erasmus to Thomas More.

In 1497, only a few years after Pico's death, John Nesi, an admirer of Ficino and then an ardent disciple of Savonarola, was already extolling Pico in his *Oraculum de novo saeculo,*[70] along with the Dominican and Marsilius, as one of the prophets of the now proximate Christian rebirth and the coming of an age of peace and spiritual perfection.

BIBLIOGRAPHY

Giannozzo Manetti (Florence, 1436–Naples, 1459)

MANUSCRIPTS AND EDITIONS

De dignitate et excellentia hominis. Ed. E. R. Leonard. Padua, 1975.
Dialogus consolatorius de morte filii, ms. Florence, Biblioteca Riccardiana, 1200.
    Manetti's own Italian version: ed. A. De Petris. Rome, 1983.
Vita Socratis et Senecae. Ed. A. De Petris. Florence, 1979.
Adversus Judaeos et Gentes, ms. Biblioteca Apostolica Vaticana, Urb. lat. 5.
Apologeticus. Ed. A. De Petris. Rome, 1982.

STUDIES

Pagnotti, F. "La vita di Niccolò V scritta da Giannozzo Manetti." *Archivio della Società Romana di Storia patria* 14 (1891) 429–36.
Cassuto, U. *I manoscritti palatini ebraici della Biblioteca Apostolica Vaticana.* Vatican City, 1935.
Garofalo, S. "Gli umanisti italiani del secolo XV e la Bibbia." *Biblica* 27 (1946) 338–75.
Cagni, G. M. "I Codici vaticani palatino-latini appartenenti alla biblioteca di Giannozzo Manetti." *La bibliofilia* 62 (1960) 1–43.
Badaloni, N. "Filosofia della mente e filosofia delle arti in Giannozzo Manetti." *Critica storica* 2 (1963) 395–450.
Westfall, C. W. "Biblical Typology in the *Vita Nicolai V* by Giannozzo Manetti." *Acta conventus neo-latini lovaniensis.* Leuven-Munich, 1973. Pp. 701–9.
De Petris, A. "Il *Dialogus consolatorius* di Giannozzo Manetti e le sue fonti." *GSLI* 154 (1977) 76–106.
———. "Giannozzo Manetti and his *Consolatoria*." *BibHumRen* 41 (1979) 493–525.
Onofri, L. "Sacralità, immaginazione e proposte politiche: La *Vita di Niccolò V* di

Giannozzo Manetti." *Humanistica lovaniensia* 28 (1979) 27–77.

Fioravanti, G. "L'apologetica antigiudaica di Giannozzo Manetti." *Rinascimento, ser.* 2, 23 (1983) 3–32.

Grego, A. "Giannozzo Manetti nella biografia di un contemporaneo." *Res Publica Litterarum* 6 (1983) 155–70.

Fubini, R. "L'ebraismo nei riflessi della cultura umanistica. Leonardo Bruni, Giannozzo Manetti, Annio da Viterbo." *MedRin* 11 (1988) 283–324. Also in *Italia. Studi e ricerche sulla storia, la cultura e la letteratura degli Ebrei d'Italia* 8 (1989) 7–52.

Dröge, Ch. "Zur Idee der Menschenwürde in Giannozzo Manettis *Protesti di Giustizia.*" *Wolfenbütteler Renaissance Mitteilungen* 14 (1990) 109–26.

Martelli, M. "Umanesimo e vita politica: il caso di Giannozzo Manetti." *Conciliarismo, Stati Nazionali, inizi del'umanesimo.* Atti del XXV Convegno storico internazionale (Todi, Accademia Tudertina, 9–12 ottobre 1988). Spoleto, 1990. Pp. 265–85.

Matthew Palmieri (Florence, 1406–75)

EDITIONS

Via civile. Ed. G. Belloni. Florence, 1982.

La Città di vita. Ed. M. Rooke. Northampton, Mass.-Paris, 1927–28.

STUDIES

Bottari, E. *Matteo Palmieri.* Lucca, 1885.

Messeri, A. "Matteo Palmieri citadino di Firenze nel secolo XV." *Archivio storico italiano, Ser.* 5, 13 (1894) 256–340.

Boffito, G. "L'eresia di Matteo Palmieri." *GSLI* 37 (1901) 1–69.

Sarri, F. "La religione di Matteo Palmieri." *La Città di vita* 1 (1946) 301–23.

Varese, C. *Storia e politica nella prosa del Quattrocento.* See the index.

Buck, A. "Matteo Palmieri (1406–1475) als Repräsentant des Florentiner Bürgerhumanismus." *ArchKult* 47 (1965) 77–95.

Belloni, G. "Il 'protesto di Matteo Palmieri." *Studi e problemi di critica testuale* 16 (1978) 27–48.

————. "Intorno alla datazione della *Città di vita* di Matteo Palmieri." Ibid., 49–62.

Palermino, R. J. "Palmieri's *Città di vita*: More Evidence on Renaissance Humanism." *BibHumRen* 44 (1982) 601–4.

Martelli, M. "Palmeriana." *Interpres* 5 (1983–84) 277–301.

Carpetto, M. G. *The Humanism of Matteo Palmieri.* Rome, 1984.

Finzi, C. *Matteo Palmieri. Dalla "Vita civile" alla "Città di vita."* Milan, 1984.

Tanturli, G. "Tradizione di un testo in presenza del'autore. Il caso della *Vita civile* di Matteo Palmieri." *Studi medievali, ser.* 3, 29 (1988) 217–43.

George Gemistus Plethon (Constantinople, 1355–Sparta, 1450)

EDITIONS

The philosophical and theological writings are collected, in part, in PG 160. But see also *Traité des lois ou recueil des fragments, en partie inédits de cet ouvrage*. Ed. C. Alexandre. Paris, 1858; reprinted: Paris, 1982.
Peri aretôn. Ed. B. Tambrun-Krasker. Leiden–New York–Copenhagen-Cologne, 1987.
De differentiis. Ed. B. Lagarde. *Byzantion* 43 (1973) 312–43.
Contre les objections de Scholarios en faveur d'Aristote (Réplique). Ed. and trans. B. Lagarde. *Byzantion* 59 (1989) 354–507.

STUDIES

Taylor, J. Wilson. *Pleton's Criticism of Plato and Aristotle*. Menasha, Wis., 1921.
Masai, R., and F. Masai. "L'oeuvre de Georges Gemiste Pléthon." *Bulletin de l'Academie Royale de Belgique,* Cl. de lettres, 101 (1954) 536–55.
Derret, J. D. M. "Georges Pletho, the Essenes, and More's *Utopia*." *BibHumRen* 27 (1965) 579–600.
Masai, F. "Pléthon, l'Averroïsme et le problème religieux." *Le Néoplatonisme*. Actes du Colloque international sur le Néoplatonisme (Royaumont, 9–13 juin 1969). Paris, 1971. Pp. 435–46.
Lagarde, B. "Le *De differentiis* de Pléthon d'après l'autographe de la Marcienne." *Byzantion* 43 (1973) 312–43.
Bargelliotis, L. "Pletho as Forerunner of Neohellenic and Modern European Consciousness." *Diótima* 1 (1973) 33–60.
———. "Fate or Heimarmene According to Pletho." Ibid., 3 (1975) 137–49.
———. "The Problem of Evil in Pletho." Ibid., 4 (1976) 116–25.
Dedes, D. "Die Handschriften and das Werk der Géorgios Gemistòs (Plethon)." *Ellenika* 33 (1981) 66–81.
Woodhouse, C. M. "How Plato Won the West." *Essays by Divers Hands.* = *Transactions of the Royal Society of Literature,* N.S. 42 (1982) 121–42.
Medvedev, J. P. "Solar Cult in Plethon's Philosophy?" *Bysantiná* 13 (1986) 739–49.
Couloubaritsis, L. "*Physis* et *technê* dans le *De differentiis* de Pléthon." *L'homme et son univers au Moyen Age*. Actes du VII Congrès international de philosophie médiévale (30 août–4 septembre 1982). Ed. Ch. Wénin. Philosophes médiévaux 26. Louvain-La-Neuve, 1986. I, 333–40.
Woodhouse, C. M. *Gemistos Plethon: The Last of the Hellenes*. Oxford, 1986.
Thümmel, H. G. "Pleton und Florenz." *Annuarium Historiae Conciliorum* 21 (1989) 413–17.
Webb, R. "The *Nomoi* of Gemistos Plethon in the Light of Plato's *Laws*." *JWarCourt* 52 (1989) 214–19.

George Scholarius (Gennadius II, Patriarch of Constantinople) (Constantinople, ca. 1405–Prodromos, after 1472)

EDITIONS

Oeuvres complètes de Gennade Scholarios. Ed. L. Petit and others. 8 vols. Paris, 1928–36. The controversy with Plethon is in vol. 4.

STUDIES

Salaville, S. "Un thomiste à Byzance au XVe siècle: Gennade Scholarios." *Echos d'Orient* (1924) 129–36.
Jugie, M. "La polémique de Georges Scholarios contre Pléthon." *Byzantion* 10 (1935) 517–30.
Podalsky, G. "Die Rezeption der thomistischen Theologie bei Gennadios II Scholarios (ca. 1403–1472)." *Theologie und Philosophie* 14 (1974) 305–23.
Balfour, D. "Gennadios Scholarios." *Sobornost* [incorporating *Eastern Churches Review*] 5 (1983) 81–84.

George of Trapezond (Crete, 1395–Rome, 1472/73)

EDITIONS

Comparationes philosophorum Aristotelis et Platonis. Venice, 1523; reprinted: New York–Frankfurt a M., 1965.
De re dialectica. Cologne, 1539; reprinted: New York–Frankfurt a. M., 1965.
Two works of theological controversy: PG 161:769–868.

STUDIES

Castellani, G. "Giorgio di Trebisonda, maestro di eloquenza a Vicenza e a Venezia." *Nuovo Archivio Veneto* 11 (1896) 123–42.
Garin, E. "Le traduzioni umanistiche di Aristotele nel secolo XV." *Atti dell'Accademia fiorentina di scienze morali La Colombaria* 8 (1950) 55–104.
Vasoli, C. "Su una *Dialettica* attribuita all'Argiropulo." *Rinascimento* (1959) 157–64.
———. "La *Dialettica* di Giorgio Trapezunzio." *Atti dell'Accademia fiorentina di scienze morali La Colombaria* 17 (1959–60) 299–327.
Kristeller, O. "Platonismo bizantino e fiorentino e la controversia su Platone." *Venezia e l'Oriente fra tardo Medioevo a Rinascimento.* Florence, 1966. Pp. 103–16. In English, with notes: Kristeller. *Renaissance Concept of Man.* New York, 1972. Pp. 85–109.
Vasoli, C. *La dialettica e la retorica dell'Umaniesimo. "Invenzione" e "metodo" nella cultura del XV e XVI secolo.* Milan, 1968. See the index.
Garin, E. *L'età nuova.* Naples, 1969. Pp. 128–29, 278–80; 287–92.
Gaeta, F. "Giorgio di Trebisonda, le *Leggi* di Pletone e la constituzione di Venezia." *BIstStorArchMur* 82 (1970) 479–501.

Garin, E. "Il platonismo come ideologia della sovversione europea. La polemica antiplatonica di Giorgio Trapezunzio." *Studia humanitatis. Ernesto Grassi zum 70. Geburtstag.* Munich, 1973. Pp. 113–20.

Monfasani, J. *George of Trebizond: A Biography and a Study of His Rhetoric and Logic.* Leiden, 1976.

Balivet, M. "Deux partisans de la fusion religieuse des Chrétiens et des Musulmans au XVe siècle: le Turc Bedreddin de Samavna et le Grec Georges de Trébisona." *Byzantina* 10 (1980) 363–400.

Monfasani, J. *Collectanea Trapezuntiana: Texts, Documents, and Bibliographies of Georges of Trebisond.* Binghamton, N.Y., 1984.

Onofri, L. "Note su Giorgio di Trebisonda e il *De evangelica praeparatione* di Eusebio da Caesarea." *Cultura* 24 (1986) 211–30.

John Basil Bessarion (Trebizond, 1403–Ravenna, 1472)

EDITIONS

Opera philosophica et theologica and *Epistolae.* PG 161:137–746.

In calumniatorem Platonis. Critical edition of Greek and Latin texts in vol. II of L. Mohler. *Die Wiederbelebung des Platons* (see Studies, below).

Oratio dogmatica de unione and *De Spiritus sancti processione.* In *Concilium Florentinum. Documenta et scriptores.* Sect. B, VII/1–2. Rome, 1958.

STUDIES

Vast, H. *Le cardinal Bessarion, 1403–1472. Étude sur la chrétienté et la Renaissance vers le milieu du 15ᵉ sicle.* Paris, 1878; reprinted: Geneva, 1977.

Rocholl, R. *Bessarion.* Leipzig, 1904.

Mohler, L. *Die Wiederbelebung des Platons. Studium in der Zeit der Renaissance durch Kardinal Bessarion.* 2 vols. Cologne, 1921.

_____. *Kardinal Bessarion als Theologe, Humanist und Staatsman.* I. *Darstellung.* Quellen und Forschungen aus dem Gebiete der Geschichte 20. Paderborn, 1923; reprinted: Paderborn, 1967.

_____. *Aus Bessarions Gelehrtenkreis.* Paderborn, 1942.

Loenertz, R. L. "Pour la biographie du cardinal Bessarion." *OCP* 10 (1944) 116–49.

Gill, J. *The Council of Florence.* Cambridge, 1959. See the index.

Corsanego, C. "Il Cardinale Bessarione e l'unione dei cristiani." *Studi Romani* 11 (1963) 280–87.

Labovsky, L. "Bessarione, Giovanni Basilio." *DBI* 9 (Rome, 1967) 696–98. Published separately: Rome, 1968.

Rivista di studi bizantini e neoellenici 5 (1968). Special number devoted to Bessarion.

Gill, J. "East and West in the Time of Bessarion: Theology and Religion." *Rivista di studi bizantini e neoellenici* 5 (1968) 3–27.

Garin, E. "Copernico e Bessarione." *RCSF* 28 (1973) 664–84.

Capizzi, S. E. "Un piccolo contributo alla biografia del Bessarione." *OCP,* N.S., 11 (1974) 84–113.

Hevia Ballina, A. "Bessarion de Nicea humanista cristiano." *Studium ovetense* 2 (1974) 7–108.

Il Cardinale Bessarione nel V centenario della morte (1472–1972). Rome, 1974. = *Miscellanea francescana* 72 (1973) 265–386.

Gill, J. "The Sincerity of Bessarion the Unionist." *Journal of Theological Studies*, N.S. 26 (1975) 377–92.

Miscellanea marciana di studi bessarionei. Padua, 1976.

Gill, J. "Was Bessarion a Conciliarist or a Unionist Before the Council of Florence?" *Collectanea Byzantina*. Rome, 1977. Pp. 201–14.

Labovsky, L. *Bessarion's Library and the Biblioteca Marciana*. Rome, 1979.

Neuhausen, K., and E. Trapp. "Lateinische Humanistenbriefe zu Bessarion's Schrift *In calumniatorem Platonis*." *Jahrbuch der Österreichischen Byzanttinistk* 28 (1979) 141–65.

Bianca, C. "La formazione delle biblioteca latina del Bessarione." *Scrittura, biblioteche e stampa a Roma nel Quattrocento. Aspetti e problemi*. Atti del (primo) Seminario della Scuola Vaticana de Paleografia, Diplomatica e Archivistica (1–2 giugno 1979). Ed. C. Bianca and others. Littera antiqua 1. Vatican City, 1980. Pp. 103–65.

Hevia Ballina, A. "Bessarion de Nicea latinista." *Acta conventus neo-latini Turonensis*. IIIᵉ Congrès international (Tours, 6–10 Sept. 1976). Ed. J.-C. Margolin. Paris, 1980. I, 449–61.

Monfasani, J. "Bessarion latinus." *Rinascimento*, Ser. 2, 21 (1981) 165–209.

Stormon, E. J. "Bessarion Before the Council of Florence: A Survey of His Early Writings." *Byzantine Papers*. Proceedings of the First Australian Byzantine Studies Conference (Canberra, May 17–19, 1978). Ed. E. Jeffreys and others. Canberra, 1981. Pp. 128–56.

Monfasani, J. "Still More on Bessarion Latinus." *Rinascimento*, Ser. 2, 23 (1983) 217–35.

_____. "The Bessarion Missal Revisited (Vatican. Barb. lat. 562)." *Scriptorium* 37 (1983) 119–22.

Dieten, J. L. van. "Die Erklärung Bessarions zur Forma Eucharistiae. Kritische Fragen zu einem Protokoll." *Annuarium Historiae Conciliorum* 16 (1985) 369–84.

Bianca, C. "Una nuova testimonianza sul nome di battesimo del Bessarione." *RSCI* 38 (1984) 428–36.

_____. "L'Accademia del Bessarione tra Roma e Urbino." *Federico di Montefeltro. La cultura*. Ed. G. Cerboni Baiardi and others. Rome, 1986. 61–79.

Garin, E. *Umanisti, artisti, scienziati. Studi sul Rinascimento italiano*. Rome, 1989. See the index.

Bianca, C. "Un messale 'ritrovato' del Cardinal Bessarione." *RSCI* 44 (1990) 488–93.

_____. "Roma e l'accademia bessarionea." *Bessarione e l'umanesimo*. Catalogo della mostra (Venezia, Biblioteca Nazionale Marciana, 27 aprile–31 maggio 1994). Ed. G. Fiaccadori. Naples, 1994. Pp. 119–27.

D'Ascia, L. "Bessarione al concilio di Firenze: umanesimo ed ecumenismo." Ibid., 67–77.

Lotti, B. "Cultura filosofica di Bessarione: la tradizione platonica." Ibid., 79–102.

Rigo, A. "Le opere d'argomento teologico del giovane Bessarione." Ibid., 33–46.

Marsilius Ficino (Figline Valdarno, 1433–Florence, 1499)

EDITIONS

A complete list of Ficino's works—editions, manuscripts, and translation into various languages—is given in P. O. Kristeller, *Supplementum Ficinianum* (2 vols.; Florence, 1937; reprinted: Florence, 1973) I, LXXVII–CLXVII, with an updating in idem, "Marsilio Ficino and His Work After Five Hundred Years," in *Marsilio Ficino e il ritorno di Platone. Studi e documenti*, ed. G. C. Garfagnini (Istituto Nazionale di Studi sul Rinascimento, Studi e Testi, 15; 2 vols.; Florence, 1986) I, 15–196 (also published separately as Quaderno di *Rinascimento* 7; Florence, 1987).

I shall restrict myself here to the main editions and the more recent critical editions.

Opera omnia. Basel, 1561 and 1576; reprinted: Turin, 1959–62, 1983².

Numerous unpublished or now lost texts are in Kristeller, *Supplementum Ficinianum.*

Other unpublished texts and some documents are in idem, *Studies in Renaissance Thought and Letters.* I (Rome, 1956; reprinted: Rome, 1984), especially 35–247.

Come Sancto Paolo fu rapito al tertio cielo (Ficino's Italian version of his *De raptu Pauli*). Ed. in E. Garin, *Prosatori latini del Quattrocento* (Naples-Milan, 1952) 939–69.

Commentarium in Platonis Convivium de amore. Crit. ed., French trans., and commentary by R. Marcel. Paris, 1956.

Theologia platonica. Partial text and Italian trans. by M. Schiavone. 2 vols. Filosofi moderni 7–8. Bologna, 1965.

Théologie platonicienne de l'immortalité des âmes. Text, French trans., and commentary by R. Marcel. 3 vols. Paris, 1964–70.

Consiglio contro la pestilenza. Ed. B. Ferrari and S. Balossi. *Consigni contro la peste.* Pisa, 1966.

Commentarii in Philebum. Crit. ed. M. J. B. Allen. Berkeley, 1975 and 1979.

Dello amore (Ficino's own Italian version of the *Comm. in Platonis Convivium*). Crit. ed. S. Niccoli. Florence, 1987.

Libri de vita. Crit. ed. C. V. Kaske and J. R. Clark. Binghamton, N.Y., 1989.

Epistolarum libri XII. Crit. ed. S. Gentile. I: Florence, 1990.

BIBLIOGRAPHY

A very extensive bibliography is given in Kristeller, "Marsilio Ficino and His Work After Five Hundred Years" (see Editions, above), and updated in idem, *Il pensiero filosofico di Marsilio Ficino* (Florence, 1988²) 441–76. The reader is referred to these lists for a general bibliography and especially for the very many contributions of Kristeller himself, all of them very important for the study of Ficino.

Here I shall limit myself to some works of special importance for the development of the literature of this author and to some more recent studies.

STUDIES

Baron, H. "Willensfreiheit und Astrologie bei Marsilio Ficino und Pico della Mirandola." *Kultur- und Universalgeschichte, Walter Goetz zu seinem 60. Geburtstag dargebracht.* Leipzig-Berlin, 1927. Pp. 145–70.

Dress, W. *Die Mystik des Marsilius Ficino.* Berlin-Leipzig, 1929.

Horbert, W. *Metaphysik des Marsilius Ficinus.* Bonn-Koblenz, 1930.

Jedin, H. "Die Mystik des Marsilius Ficinus." *RömQ* 39 (1931) 281–87.

Heitzman, M. "L'agostinismo avicennizzante e il punto di partenza della filosofia di Marsilio Ficino." *GCFI* 16 (1935) 295–322, 46–80; 17 (1936) 1–11.

_____. "La libertà e il fato nella filosofia di Marsilio Ficino." *RivFilNeo* 28 (1936) 350–71; 29 (1937) 59–82.

Festugière, A. *La philosophie de l'amour de Marsile Ficin et son influence sur la littérature française au XVIe siècle.* Paris, 1942².

Kristeller, P.O. *The Philosophy of Marsilio Ficino.* New York, 1943. Expanded Italian edition: *Il pensiero filosofico di Marsilio Ficino.* Florence, 1953, 1988².

Saitta, G. *Marsilio Ficino e la filosofia dell'umanesimo.* Florence, 1943; Bologna, 1954².

Kristeller, P.O. "Ficino and Pomponazzi on the Place of Man in the Universe." *Journal of the History of Ideas* 5 (1944) 220–26.

Chastel, A. *Marsile Ficin et l'art.* Geneva, 1954.

Walker, D. P. "Ficino's *Spiritus* and Music." *Annales Musicologiques* 1 (1953) 133–50.

_____. "Le chante orphique de Marsile Ficin." *Musique et Poésie au XVIe siècle.* Paris, 1954. Pp. 17–33.

Garin, E. "Ritratto di Marsilio Ficino." *Libera cattedra della civiltà fiorentina. Il Quiattrocento.* Florence, 1954. 29–48. Also in *Belfagor* 6 (1951) 289–301.

Keller, A. "Two Byzantine Scholars and Their Reception in Italy: I. Marsilio Ficino and Gemistos Plethon on Fate and Free Will." *JWarCourt* 20 (1957) 363–66.

Kristeller, P. O. "Renaissance Platonism." *Facets of the Renaissance.* Ed. W. H. Werkmeister. Los Angeles, 1959. Pp. 87–107.

Gilson, E. "Marsilio Ficino et le *Contra Gentiles*." *AHDLMA* 32 (1957) 101–13.

Walker, D. P. *Spiritual and Demonic Magic from Ficino to Campanella.* London, 1958.

Marcel, R. *Marsile Ficin.* Paris, 1958.

Garin, E. *Studi sul platonismo medievale.* Florence, 1958.

Chastel, A. *Art et humanisme à Florence au temps de Laurent le Magnifique.* Paris, 1959.

De Gandillac, M. "Astres, anges et génies chez Marsile Ficin." *Umanesimo e Esoterismo.* Ed. E. Castelli. Padua, 1960. Pp. 85–109. = *ArchFil* 30 (1960).

Klein, R. "L'enfer de Ficin." Ibid., 111–21. Also in idem. *La forme et l'intelligible.* Paris, 1970. Pp. 89–124.

Garin, E. *La cultura filosofica del Rinascimento italiano.* Florence, 1961. See the index.

Jayne, S. R. *John Colet and Marsilio Ficino.* Oxford, 1963.

Klibansky, R., and others. *Saturn and Melancholy: Studies in the History of Natural Philosophy, Religion, and Art.* New York–London, 1964.

Kristeller, P. O. *Eight Philosophers of the Italian Renaissance.* Stanford, 1964.

_____. "Marsilio Ficino as Beginning Student of Plato." *Scriptorium* 20 (1966) 41–54.

_____. "The European Significance of Florentine Platonism." *Medieval and Renaissance Studies.* Proceedings of the Southeastern Institute of Medieval and Renaissance Studies (Summer 1967). Ed. J. H. Headley. Chapel Hill, 1968. Pp. 206–29.

Garin, E. *L'età nuova*. Naples, 1969. See the index.

Kristeller, P.O. "La diffusione europea del platonismo fiorentino." *Il pemsiero italiano del Rinascimento e il tempo nostro*. Atti del V Convegno Internazionale del Centro di Studi Umanistici (Montepulciano, 1968). Florence, 1970. Pp. 1–21.

Collins, A. B. "Love and Natural Desire in Ficino's Platonic Theology." *Journal of the History of Ideas* 9 (1971) 435–42.

Tarabocchia Canavero, A. "Agostino e Tommaso nel commento di Marsilio Ficino all'*Epistola ai Romani*." *RivFilNeo* 65 (1973) 815–24.

Zambelli, P. "Platone, Ficino e la magia." *Studia humanitatis. Ernesto Grassi zum 70. Geburtstag*. Munich, 1973. Pp. 121–43.

Allen, M. J. B. "The Absent Angel in Ficino's Philosophy." *Journal of the History of Ideas* 35 (1975) 219–40.

Garin, E. *Lo zodiaco della vita*. Rome-Bari, 1976. See the index.

Kristeller, P.O. "L'état présent des études sur Marsile Ficin." *Platon et Aristote à la Renaissance*. Paris, 1976. Pp. 59–77.

Allen, M. J. B. "Ficino's Lecture on the Good?" *Renaissance Quarterly* 30 (1977) 160–71.

Corradi, M. "Alle origine della letteratura neoplatonica del *Convivio*. Marsilio Ficino e il *De amore*." *RivFilNeo* 69 (177) 406–22.

Lupieri, E. "Marsilio Ficino e il *De resurrectione* di Atenagora." *Studi storico-religiosi* 1 (1977) 147–634. = New series of *Studi e materiali di storia della religione*.

Purnell, F. "Hermes and the Sibyll: A Note on Ficino's *Pimander*." *Renaissance Quarterly* 30 (1977) 305–10.

Tarabocchia Canavero, A. "Il *De Triplici vita* di Marsilio Ficino: una strana vicenda ermeneutica." *RevFilNeo* 69 (1977) 697–717.

Zanier, G. *La medicina astrologica e la sua teoria: Marsilio Ficino e i suoi critici contemporanei*. Rome, 1977.

Tarabocchia Canavero, A. "S. Agostino nella *theologia platonica* di Marsilio Ficino." *RivFilNeo* 70 (1978) 626–46.

Allen, M. J. B. "The Sibyl in Ficino's Oaktree." *Modern Language Notes* 95 (1980) 205–10.

Beierwaltes, W. *Marsilio Ficinos Theorie des Schönen im Kontext des Platonismus*. Sitzungsberichte der Heidelberger Akademie der Wissenschaften, Philos.-hist. Klasse 11. Heidelberg, 1980.

Sheppard, A. "The Influence of Hermias on Marsilio Ficino's Doctrine of Inspiration." *JWarCourt* 43 (1980) 97–109.

Gentile, S. "Per la storia del testo del *Commentarium in Convivium* di Marsilio Ficino." *Rinascimento,* Ser. 2, 21 (1981) 3–27.

Allen, M. J. B. "Cosmology and Love: The Role of the *Phaedrus* in Ficino's *Symposium Commentary*." *Journal of Medieval and Renaissance Studies* 10 (1980) 131–53.

_____. *Marsilio Ficino and the Phaedran Charioteer*. Berkeley, 1981.

_____. "Marsilio Ficino on Plato's Pythagorean Eye." *Modern Language Notes* 107 (1982) 171–82.

Kaske, C. V. "Marsilio and the Twelve Gods of the Zodiac." *JWarCourt* 45 (1982) 195–202.

Chastel, A. "Mercure et Saturne, lettres de Marsile Ficin." *Le Promeneur* 2, no. 8 (1983) 10–12.

Kristeller, P. O. "Marsilio Ficino e Venezia." *Miscellanea di studi in onore di Vittore Branca* III/2. Florence, 1983. Pp. 475–92.

Garin, E. *Il ritorno dei filosofi antichi.* Istituto Italiano per gli Studi Filosofici, Lezioni della Scuola di Studi Superiori in Napoli 1. Naples, 1984.

Allen, M. J. B. "Marsilio Ficino on Plato, the Neoplatonist, and the Christian Doctrine of the Trinity." *Renaissance Quarterly* 37 (1984) 555–84.

————. *The Platonism of Marsilio Ficino: A Study of His "Phaedrus" Commentary, Its Sources and Genesis.* Berkeley–New York, 1984.

Copenhaver, B. P. "Scholastic Philosophy and Renaissance Magic in the *De vita* of Marsilio Ficino." *Renaissance Quarterly* 37 (1984) 524–54.

Fubini, R. "Ficino e i Medici all'avvento di Lorenzo il Magnifico." *Rinascimento,* Ser. 2, 24 (1984) 3–52.

Kristeller, P. O. "Marsilio Ficino and the Roman Curia." *Roma humanistica. Studia in Honorem Rev.i adm. Dni. Iosaephi Ruysschaert.* Louvain, 1985. Pp. 83–98. = *Humanistica lovaniensia* 34 (1985).

Marsilio Ficino e il ritorno di Platone. Ed. G. C. Garfagnini. Florence, 1986.

Kristeller, P.O. "Marsilio Ficino e il ritorno di Platone." *La storia del Valdarno* 56 (1986) 162–74.

Garin, E. "Marsilio Ficino, medico dello spirito." Ibid., 34–45.

Vasoli, C. "Marsilio Ficino: una straordinaria fortuna europea." Ibid., 46–63.

Allen, M. J. B. "Marsilio Ficino's Interpretation of Plato's *Timaeus* and Its Myth of the Demiurge." *Supplementum festivum: Studies in Honor of Paul Oskar Kristeller.* Ed. J. Hankins and others. Medieval and Renaissance Texts and Studies 49. Binghamton, 1987. Pp. 399–439.

Copenhaver, B. P. "Jamblichus, Synesius, and the *Chaldean Oracles* in Marsilio Ficino's *De vita libri tres:* Hermetic Magic or Neoplatonic Magic." Ibid., 441–55.

Gentile, S. "Note sullo *Scrittoio* di Marsilio Ficino." Ibid., 339–97.

Watts, P. M. "Pseudo-Dionysius the Areopagite and Three Renaissance Platonists: Cusanus, Ficino, and Pico on Mind and Cosmos." Ibid., 279–98.

Branca, V. "Tra Ficino 'Orpheo ispirato' e Poliziano 'Ercole ironico.'" *Filologia e forme letterarie. Studi offerti a Francesco della Corte* V. Urbino, 1987. Pp. 445–59.

Fubini, R. "Ancora su Ficino e i Medici." *Rinascimento,* Ser. 2, 27 (1987) 275–91.

Klutstein, I. *Marsilio Ficino e la théologie ancienne. Oracles Chaldaïques, Hymnes Orphiques, Hymnes de Proclus.* Quaderni di "Rinascimento" 5. Florence, 1987.

Bourke, V. J. "A Millennium of Christian Platonism: Augustine, Anselm, and Ficino." *Anselm Studies* 2 (1988) 527–57.

Mojsisch, B. "Platon, Plotin, Ficino. 'Wichtigste Gattungen'—eine Theorie aus Platons *Sophistes.*" *Die Philosophie im 14. and 15. Jahrhundert. In memoriam Konstanty Michalski (1879–1947).* Bochumer Studien zur Philosophie 10. Ed. O. Pluta. Amsterdam, 1988. Pp. 19–38.

Vasoli, C. "Ficino e il *De christiana religione.*" Ibid., 151–90.

————. "Per le fonti del *De christiana religione* di Marsilio Ficino." *Rinascimento,* Ser. 2, 28 (1988) 135–233.

————. *Filosofia e religione nella cultura del Rinascimento.* Naples, 1988. Pp. 19–135.

Garin, E. *Umanisti, artisti, scienziati. Studi sul Rinascimento italiano.* Rome, 1989. See the index.

Allen, M. J. B. "Marsilio Ficino, Hermes Trismegistus, and the *Corpus Hermeticum.*" *New Perspectives on Renaissance Thought: Essays in the History of Science, Education, and Philosophy in Memory of Charles B. Schmitt.* Ed. J. Henry and S. Hutton. London, 1990. Pp. 38–47.

Bullard, M. M. "Marsilio Ficino and the Medici. The Inner Dimensions of Patronage." *Christianity and the Renaissance: Image and Religious Imagination in the Quattrocento.* Ed. T. Verdon and J. Henderson. Syracuse, N.Y., 1990. Pp. 467–92.

_____. "The Inward Zodiac: A Development in Ficino's Thought on Astrology." *Renaissance Quarterly* 43 (1990) 687–708.

Gentile, S. "Sulle prime traduzioni dal greco di Marsilio Ficino." *Rinascimento,* Ser. 2, 30 (1990) 57–104.

Zintzen, C. "Die Inspiration des Dichters. Ein Brief Ficinos aus dem Jahre 1457." *Pratum saravense. Festgabe für Peter Steinmetz.* Palingenesia 30. Ed. W. Gorler and S. Koster. Stuttgart, 1990. Pp. 189–203.

De Gandillac, M. "La renaissance du platonisme selon Marsile Ficin." *Diótima* 19 (1991) 83–89.

_____ "L'idée de Renaissance chez Marsile Ficin." *Historia Philosophiae Medii Aevi. Studien zur Geschichte der Philosophie des Mittelalters.* Ed. B. Mojsisch and O. Plaauta. 2 vols. Amsterdam, 1991. I, 321–28.

Vasoli, C. "Un 'medico' per i 'sapienti': Ficino e i *Libri de vita.*" Ibid., II, 1013–28.

Hankins, J. "The Myth of the Platonic Academy of Florence." *Renaissance Quarterly* 44 (1991) 429–75.

Beierwaltes, W. "Plotino e Ficino. L'autorelazione del pensiero." *RivFilNeo* 84 (1992) 293–324.

Allen, M. J. B. "Ficino and the Tutelary Spirit." *Il neoplatonismo nel Rinascimento.* Atti del Convegno internazionale (Roma-Firenze, 12–15 dicembre 1990). Ed. P. Prini. Rome, 1993. Pp. 173–84. Longer version in *Reconsidering the Renaissance.* Ed. M. A. Di Cesare. Binghamton, N.Y., 1992. Pp. 63–88.

Cristiani, M. "Dionigi dioniśiaco, Marsilio Ficino e il *Corpus Dionysianum.*" *Il neoplatonismo nel Rinascimento* (see Allen, above). Pp. 185–203.

Klutstein, I. "L'interprétation ficinienne des Oracles chaldaïques." Ibid., 53–64.

Vasoli, C. "La *prisca theologia* e il neoplatonismo religioso." Ibid., 83–101.

Christopher Landino (Pratovecchio, 1424–Florence, 1492)

EDITIONS

Disputationes camaldulenses. Ed. P. Lohe. Florence, 1980.

De anima. Ed. A. Paoli and G. Gentili. *Annali delle Universiotà toscane,* N.S. 35 (1915) 1–50; 36/2 (1916) 1–135; 37/3 (1917) 1–95.

De vera nobilitate. Ed. M. Lentzen. Geneva, 1970.

Testi inediti e rari di Cristoforo Landino e Francesco Filelfo. Ed. E. Garin, Florence, 1949.

Scritti critici e storici. Ed. R. Cardini. 2 vols. Rome, 1974.

Reden Cristoforo Landino. Ed. M. Lentzen. Munich, 1974.

STUDIES

Wolff, E. "Die allegorische Virgilierklärung des Cristoforo Landino." *Neue Jahrbücher für das klassische Altertum* 22 (1919) 453–79.

Gentile, G. "La cronologia del *De anima* di Cristoforo Landino." *Studi sul Rinascimento*. Florence, 1936², 1968³. Pp. 108–17.

Ricci, P. G. "Alla ricerca di Cristoforo Landino." *La Rinascita* 4 (1941) 733–44.

Buck, A. "Dichter und Dichtung bei Cristoforo Landino." *Romanische Forschungen* 58–59 (1947) 233–46.

Wadsworth, J. B. "Landino's *Disputationes camaldulenses,* Ficino's *De felicitate,* and *L'altercazione* of Lorenzo de'Medici." *Modern Philology* 50 (1952–53) 8–10 and 23.

Müller-Bochart, E. *Leon Battista Alberti und die Vergil-Deutung der "Disputationes camaldulenses." Zur allegorischen Dichtererklärung Cristofoto Landinos.* Cologne, 1968.

Cardini, R. "A propositio del *De vera nobilitate* landiniano." *La rassegna della letteratura italiana* 75 (1971) 451–59.

Lentzen, M. *Studien zur Dante-Exegese Cristoforo Landinos.* Cologne-Vienna-Böhlau, 1971.

Tigerstedt, E. "The Poet as Creator: Origin of a Metaphor." *Comparative Literature Studies* 20 (1970) 455–88.

Cardini, R. "Alle origini della filosofia landiniana." *Rinascimento,* Ser. 2, 9 (1970, but 1972) 119–49.

———. *La critica del Landino.* Florence, 1973.

Lentzen, M. "Cristoforo Landinos Dante-Kommentar." *Der Kommentar in der Renaissance.* Boppard, 1975. Pp. 167–89.

Weiss, R. *Cristoforo Landino: das Metaphorische in den "Disputationes camaldulenses."* Munich, 1981.

Field, A. "An Inaugural Oration by Cristoforo Landino in Praise of Virgil." *Rinascimento,* Ser. 2, 21 (1981, but 1982) 235–45.

Kallendorf, C. "Cristoforo Landino's *Aeneid* and the Humanist Critical Tradition." *Renaissance Quarterly* 36 (1983) 519–46.

Chance, J. "The Medieval Sources of Cristoforo Landino's Allegorization of the Judgement of Paris." *Studies in Philology* 81 (1984) 145–60.

Di Cesare, M. A. "Cristoforo Landino's *Disputationes camaldulenses." The Early Renaissance: Virgil and the Classical Tradition.* Ed. A. Pellegrini. Binghamton, 1984. Pp. 19–31.

La Brasca, F. "Tradition exégétique et vulgarisation néo-platonicienne dans la partie doctrinale du commentaire dantesque di Cristoforo Landino." *Culture et société en Italie du Moyen Age à la Renaissance. Homage à Henri Rochon.* Centre interuniversitaire de Recherche sur la Renaissance italienne 13. Paris, 1985. Pp. 117–29.

Lentzen, M. "Le lodi di Firenze di Cristoforo Landino." *Romanische Forschungen* 97 (1985) 36–46.

Cardini, R. "Cristoforo Landino." *Dizionario critico della letteratura italiana* 2 (Turin, 1986²) 528–31.

Di Cesare, M. A. "Cristoforo Landino on the Name and Nature of Poetry: The Critic as Hero." *Chaucer Review* 21 (1986) 155–81.

Field, A. "Cristoforo Landino's First Lectures on Dante." *Renaissance Quarterly* 39 (1986) 16–48.

La Brasca, F. "L'humanisme vulgaire et la genèse de la critique littéraire italienne: étude descriptive du commentaire dantesque di Cristoforo Landino." *Chroniques italiennes* 6 (1986) 7–96.

Zintzen, C. "Zur *Aeneis*-Interpretation des Cristoforo Landino." *Mittellateinisches Jahrbuch* 20 (1985, but 1986) 193–215.

Fabrizio Costa, S., and F. La Brasca. "De l'âge des auteurs à celui des polygraphes: les commentaires de la *Divine Comédie* de C. Landino (1481) et A. Vellutelo (1544). *Les commenaires et la naissance de la critique littéraire, France/Italie (XIVe-XVIe siècles*. Actes du Colloque international sur le Commentaire (Paris, mai 1988). Ed. G. Mathieu-Castellani and M. Plaisance. Paris, 1990. Pp. 175–93.

Garin, E. *Umanisti, artisti, scienzati. Studi sul Rinascimento italiano*. Rome, 1989. See the index.

La Brasca, F. "*Scriptor in cathedra:* les cours inauguraux de Cristoforo Landino au 'Studio' de Florence (1458–1474)." *L'Écrivain face à son public en France et en Italie à la Renaissance*. Actes du Colloque de Tours (4–6 déc. 1986). Ed. A. Fiorato and J.-C. Margolin. De Pétrarque à Descartes 53. Paris, 1989. Pp. 107–25.

Cardini, R. "Landino e Dante." *Rinascimento,* Ser. 2, 30 (1990) 175–90.

_____. "Satira e gerarchia delle arti: dall'Alberti al Landino." *Sapere e/è potere. Discipline, Dispute e Professioni nell'Università medievale e moderna: il caso bolognese a confronto*. Atti del 4º Convegno (Istituto per la Storia di Bologna, 13–15 aprile 1989). Ed. L. Avellini and others. Bologna, 1991. I, 171–96.

Lentzen, M. "Zur Problematik von *vita activa* und *vita contemplativa* in den *Disputationes camaldulenses* von Cristoforo Landino." *Wolfenbüttler Renaissance Mitteilungen* 14/2 (1990) 57–64.

_____. "Die Konzeption der *anima rationalis* im dritten Buch von Landinos Dialog *De anima.*" Ibid., 15/3 (1991) 104–14.

Rombach, U. *"Vita activa" und "vita contemplativa" bei Cristoforo Landino*. Beiträge zur Altertumskunde 17. Stuttgart, 1991.

McNair, B. G. "Cristoforo Landino's *De anima* and His Platonic Sources." *Rinascimento,* Ser. 2, 32 (1992) 227–45.

John Pico della Mirandola (Mirandola, 1463–Florence, 1494)

EDITIONS

The first edition of Pico's works was published in Bologna in 1496 in 2 vols. by his nephew John Francis, who prefaced them with a *Vita* (edited with translation and commentary by T. Sorbelli, Modena, 1963). Then:

Opera omnia. Ed. J. Wimpfeling. Strasbourg, 1519; Basel, 1557–73; reprinted: Hildesheim, 1969, and Turin, 1971, with the addition of other texts reproduced from the original editions with a preface by E. Garin, informing the reader of many other editions in the press. In the National Edition of the Classics of Italian Thought, edited with Italian translation, by E. Garin:

I. *De hominis dignitate, Heptaplus, De ente et uno,* and *Commento sopra una canzone d'amore*. Florence, 1942.

II–III. *Disputationes adversus astrologiam divinatricem.* Florence, 1946–52.

Oratio de hominis dignitate. Garin's translation, reprinted with a facing Latin text, introduction, and notes by G. Tognon. *Discorso sulla dignità dell'uomo.* Brescia, 1987.

Conclusiones (sive Theses DCCC Romae anno 1486 publicae disputandae, sed non admissae). Ed. B. Kieskowski. Geneva, 1973.

Unpublished writings and letters. E. Garin. *La cultura filosofica del Rinascimento italiano.* Florence, 1969. Pp. 229–89. And P. O. Kristeller. "Giovanni Pico della Mirandola and His Sources." *L'opera e il pensiero di Giovanni Pico della Mirandola nella storia dell'Umanesimo.* Convegno internazionale (Mirandola, 1963). 2 vols. Florence, 1965. I, 84–107.

Carmina latina. Ed. W. Speyer. Leiden, 1964.

STUDIES

Kibre, P. *The Library of Pico della Mirandola.* New York, 1936, 1966[2].

Semprini, G. *La filosofia di Giovanni Pico della Mirandola.* Milan, 1936.

Anagnine, E, *Giovanni Pico della Mirandola.* Bari, 1937.

Garin, E. *Giovanni Pico della Mirandola. Vita e dottrina.* Florence, 1937.

Gauthier-Vignal, L. *Pic de la Mirandole.* Paris, 1938.

Dulles, A. *Princeps Concordiae: Pico della Mirandola and the Scholastic Tradition.* Cambridge, 1941.

Cassirer, E. "Giovanni Pico della Mirandola." *Journal of the History of Ideas* 3 (1942) 123–44, 319–46.

Barone, G. *L'umanesimo filosofico e Giovanni Pico della Mirandola.* Milan, 1949.

Breen, Q. "Giovanni Pico della Mirandola on the Conflict of Philosophy and Rhetoric." *Journal of the History of Ideas* 13 (1952) 384–412.

Secret, F. "Pico della Mirandola e gli inizi della cabala cristiana." *Convivium* (1957) 31–37.

Cordier, P. M. *Jean Pic de la Mirandole ou la plus pure figure de l'humanisme chrétien.* Paris, 1957.

Monnerjahn, E. *Giovanni Pico della Mirandola.* Wiesbaden, 1960.

Garin, E. *La cultura filosofica del Rinascimento italiano.* Florence, 1961. See the index.

_____. *Giovanni Pico della Mirandola.* Mirandola-Parma, 1963.

Kieskowski, B. "Les rapports entre Elie del Medigo et Pic de la Mirandole." *Rinascimento,* Ser. 2, 4 (1964) 41–91.

L'opera e il pensiero di Giovanni Pico della Mirandola nella storia dell'Umanesimo. Convegno internazionale (Mirandola, 1963). 2 vols. Florence, 1965.

Crouzel, H. "Pic del a Mirandole et Origène." *BLE* 66 (1965) 81–106, 174–94, 272–88.

Di Napoli, G. *Giovanni Pico della Mirandola e la problematica dottrinale del suo tempo.* Rome, 1965.

Mayer, R. W. "Pico della Mirandola und der Orient." *Asiatische Studien* 18–19 (1965) 308–36.

Gabrieli, V. "Giovanni Pico and Thomas More." *La Cultura* 6 (1968) 313–32.

Berger, H. "Pico and Neoplatonist Idealism: Philosophy as Escape." *Centennial Review* 13 (1969) 38–83.

Wirszubski, Ch. "Giovanni Pico's Book of Job." *JWarCourt* 32 (1969) 171–99.

Waddington, R. B. "The Sun in the Center: Structure as Meaning in Pico della Mirandola's *Heptaplus*." *The Journal of Medieval and Renaissance Studies* 3 (1973) 69–86.

De Lubac, H. *Pic de la Mirandole, études et discssions*. Paris, 1974.

Maskell, D. "Robert Gaguin and Thomas More: Translators of Pico della Mirandola." *BibHumRen* 37 (1975) 63–68.

Colomer, E. *De la Edad Media al Renacimiento, Ramón Lull, Nicolas de Cusa, Juan Pico della Mirandola*. Barcelona, 1975.

Greive, H. "La kabbale chrétienne de Jean Pic de la Mirandole." *Kabbalistes chrétiens*. Paris, 1979. Pp. 159–79.

Scholem, G. "Considerations sur l'histoire des débuts de la Kabbale chrétien." Ibid., 17–46.

Wirszubski, C. "L'Ancien et le Nouveau dans la confirmation kabbalistique du Christianisme par Pic de le Mirandole." Ibid., 181–93.

Crouzel, H. *Une controverse sur Origène à la Renaissance: Jean Pic de la Mirandole et Pierre Garcia*. Textes présentés, traduits et annotés. Paris, 1977.

Battlori, M. "Giovanni Pico della Mirandola i el Lul.lisme italiá al segle XV." *A través de la história i la cultura*. Montserrat, 1980. Pp. 269–77.

Flasch, K. "Nikolaus von Kues und Pico della Mirandola." *MFCG* 14 (1980) 21–42.

Zanier, G. "Struttura e significato della *Disputationes* pichiane." *GCFI,* Ser. 5, 1 (1981) 54–86.

Craven, W. C. *Giovanni Pico della Mirandola, Symbol of His Age: Modern Interpretations of a Renaissance Philosopher*. Geneva, 1981. On this volume, see L. Valke, *Renaissance and Reformation,* N.S. 7 (1983) 79–88; E. Garin, *Belfagor* 40 (1985) 343–52.

Costa, D. "Stuck Sow or Broken Heart: Pico's *Oratio* as Ritual Sacrifice." *Journal of Medieval and Renaissance Studies* 12 (1982) 221–35.

Novak, B. C. "Giovanni Pico della Mirandola and Hochanan Alemanno." *JWarCourt* 45 (1982) 125–47.

Baker, D. *Giovanni Pico della Mirandola: 1463–1494. Sein Leben and seine Werke*. Dornach, 1983.

Weil, E. "Deux textes, I: Contre l'occultisme; II: Pic de la Mirandole et la critique de l'astrologie." *Archives de philosophie* 48 (1985) 563–75. Reprinted: idem. *La philosophie de Pietro Pomponazzi*. Paris, 1986.

Valcke, L. "Des *Conclusiones* aux *Disputationes*. Numérologie et mathématiques chez Jean Pic de la Mirandole." *Laval théologique et philosophique* 41 (1985) 43–56.

Heesakkers, C. L. "Pico della Mirandola en sijn *Oratio de dignitate hominis*." *Lampas* 18 (1985) 124–42.

Allen, M. J. B. "The Second Ficino-Pico Controversy: Parmedidean Poetry, Eristic, and the One." *Marsilio Ficino e il ritorn di Platone. Studi e documenti*. Ed. G. C. Garfagnin. 2 vols. Florence, 1986.

Desantis, G. "Pico, Pontano e la polemica astrologica." *Annali della Facoltà di lettere e filosofia dell'Università di Bari* 29 (1986) 155–91.

Lujan, N. "Pico della Mirandola." *Historia y vida* 221 (1986) 44–48.

Queron, J. *Pic de la Mirandole. Contribution à la connaissance de l'Humanisme philosophique renaissant.* Aix-en-Provence, 1986.

Bader, G. "*Theologgia poetica.* Begriff und Aufgabe." *Zeitschrift für Theologie und Kirche* 83 (1986) 188–237.

Jacobelli, J. *Pico della Mirandola.* Milan, 1986.

Valcke, L. "Entre raison et foi: le néoplatonisme de Pic de la Mirandole." *RTAM* 54 (1987) 186–237.

————. "Influence d'Augustin sur la pensée de Jean Pic de la Mirandole." *Atti del Congresso Internazionale su S. Agostino nel XVI centenario della Conversione (Roma, 15–20 sett. 1986).* Studia Ephemeridis "Augustinianum" 26. Rome, 1987. III, 203–23.

Watts, P. M. "Pseudo-Dionysius the Areopagite and Three Renaissance Neoplatonists: Cusanus, Ficino, and Pico on Mind and Cosmos." *Supplementum festivum: Studies in Honor of Paul Oskar Kristeller.* Ed. J. Hankins and others. Medieval and Renaissance Texts and Studies 40. Binghamton, 1987. Pp. 279–98.

Garin, E. *Umanisti, artisti, scienziati. Studi sul Rinascimento italiano.* Rome, 1989. See the index.

Roulier, F. *Jean Pic de la Mirandole (1462–1494), humaniste, philosophe et théologien.* Geneva, 1989.

Reinhardt, H. *Freiheit zu Gott. Der Grundgedanke des Systematikers Giovanni Pico della Mirandola.* Weinheim, 1989.

Valcke, L. "Humanisme et scolastique: le 'conflit des deux cultures' chez Jean Pic de la Mirandole." *RTAM* 56 (1989) 164–99.

————. "*Homo contemplator:* il doppio distacco dell'umanesimo pichiano." *Homo Sapiens, Homo Humanus* I. Atti del XXVII e del XXVIII Convegno internaz. del Centro di studi umanistici di Montepulciano (Palazzo Tarugi, 1985 e 1986). Ed. G. Tarugi. Florence, 1990. Pp. 233–45.

————. "L'itinerario filosofico di Giovanni Pico della Mirandola: fra libertà poetica e rigore scientifico." *Homo Sapiens, Homo Humanus* II. Atti del XXIX e del XXX Convegno internaz. . . . (Palazzo Tarugi, 1987 e 1988). Ed. G. Tarugi. Florence, 1990. Pp. 203–20.

Gosselin, E. A. "The 'Lord God's' Sun in Pico and Newton." *Renaissance Society and Culture: Essays in Honor of Eugene F. Rice, Jr..* Ed. J. Monfasani and R. G. Musto. New York, 1991. Pp. 51–58.

Raspanti, A. *Filosofia, teologia, religione. L'unità della visione in Giovanni Pico della Mirandola.* Palermo, 1991.

Valcke, L. "Le dionysisme appollinien de Jean Pic de la Mirandole." *Canadian Journal of Italian Studies* 15, no. 44 (1992) 1–10.

Vasoli, C. "La *prisca theologia* e il neoplatonismo religioso." *Il neoplatonismo nel Rinascimento.* Atti del Convegno internazionale (Roma-Firenze, 12–15 dicembre 1990). Ed. P. Prini. Rome, 1993. Pp. 83–101.

On Pico's connections with Cabalism see also, however, J. L. Blau. *The Christian Interpretation of the Cabala in the Renaissance.* London, 1944; and F. Secret. *Les kabbalistes chrétiens de la Renaissance.* Paris, 1964; new ed.: Milan, 1985 (see the index).

CHAPTER 5

Theology in Fifteenth-Century Spain

Isaac Vázquez Janeiro

I. Historiographical Introduction

At the end of the fifteenth and the beginning of the sixteenth centuries Spain regained its national unity: first, through the union of the two kingdoms of Aragón-Catalonia and Castile-León (1474), then through the reconquest of Granada (1492), and finally, the annexation of the kingdom of Navarre (1512–15).

The image—not only theological, but also political, ecclesial, social, cultural, and moral—of fifteenth-century Spain that has come down to modern times is one seen in the pale light of the "waning of the Middle Ages," to use Huizinga's phrase, or even wrapped in the darkness of deep night. In addition to the religious prejudices of both the Protestant Reformation and the Catholic Reform and Counterreformation, this distorted image can perhaps be also explained as a result of the enormous historiographical labors carried out at the end of the nineteenth and beginning of the twentieth centuries by Marcellino Menéndez Pelayo (+ 1912). This immensely learned and wide-ranging writer, as well as very fervent Catholic, wanted to exalt the sixteenth century in Spain, which was the country's "golden age" religiously, politically, and culturally. But in doing so he either forgot about the fifteenth century or hardly mentioned it except to give an entirely negative view of it from both the religious and the political aspects, especially in regard to Castile:

> All the bonds of the medieval organization of society seemed feeble and ready to come undone. Even religious fervor seemed to have weakened due to moral laxity, the loosening of discipline, the abuse of merely nominal prelatures and com-

mendam benefices, the intrusion of greedy foreigners who at their courts devoured the fruits of our churches without knowing these or ever having seen them. . . . The result of this disturbed state . . . was a decline of the religious spirit, which already manifested itself in the dearth of great theologians (with two or three well-known exceptions, although these were more famous and influential in the general history of the Church in the fifteenth century than in the history of the Church in Spain). . . . Even more diminished in prestige than the Church was the throne. With a single exception, that of the short reign of Henry III [of Castile; 1390–1406] . . . the dynasty of the Trastamara produced only weak princes, whose idleness, inability, and neglect kept increasing, from the dreams of greatness of John I [1379–90] to the vile and shameful actions of Henry IV [1454–74].[1]

Today, a hundred years after Menéndez Pelayo wrote, fifteenth-century Spain displays a different face. Despite its shadows, it also shows not a few bright spots. Rather than as the decline of the Middle Ages, it should be looked on as the dawn of a new age, the Spanish Golden Age. This changed outlook has been due to the historical research of our century, which has enriched us with plentiful editions of documentary and literary sources, monographs, research tools, and so on.

It is obviously not possible to give a complete list here. I shall list only a few titles: Sources: V. Beltrán de Heredia, *Bulario de la Universidad de Salamanca (1219–1549)* (3 vols.; Salamanca, 1966–67); idem, *Cartulario de la Universidad de Salamanca (1218–1600)* (6 vols.; Salamanca, 1970–73). Monographs: idem, *Miscelánea Beltrán de Heredia. Colección de artículos sobre historia de la teología española* (4 vols.; Salamanca, 1972–73); L. Suárez Fernández, *Castilla, el Cisma y la crisis conciliar* (Madrid, 1960). Research tools: *Repertorio de Historia de las Ciencias eclesiásticas en España* (7 vols.; Salamanca, 1967–79).

II. The Teaching of Theology: The Institutions

Even though, as we shall see, the writers of the fifteenth century did not, generally speaking, produce "academic" treatises on theology, they, or the majority of them, were nonetheless theologians and had therefore studied at some theological center. A word must be said, then, about the theological institutions of this period.

A. THE UNIVERSITY FACULTIES OF THEOLOGY

The teaching of theology at the university level was a relatively late phenomenon in Spain. After an unsuccessful attempt at Palencia (1208), theological faculties began to operate in Perpignan (1350), Huesca (1354), and Salamanca (1381), but they could not confer the "license to teach everywhere" *(licentia ubique docendi)*. This was a recognition that only the popes could grant and that the theological faculty of the Sorbonne, the *alma parens* ("nurturing parent"), as Gregory IV described it, continued jealously to claim as its exclusive privilege. As a result, anyone desiring this recognition had to "cross the Pyrenees," that is, travel to Paris.

This situation ended, however, right at the beginning of the fifteenth century, when Benedict XIII, the Avignon pope, who was annoyed at the hostility shown him by the Faculty of Theology in Paris, granted Salamanca the right to confer academic degrees and, in addition, decreed that no Spaniard should go to Paris to study theology. Later, in 1416, in the bull *Sincerae devotionis,* the same pope restructured the faculty of Salamanca by creating four chairs there: those of "morning" and "evening," which had their place in the halls of the university, and two others located in the Dominican convent of San Esteban and the convent of San Francisco. Students could attend the courses of any of these chairs. On February 20, 1422, in the bull *Sedis Apostolicae,* Pope Martin V approved the new constitutions of the Faculty of Theology of Salamanca, and these remained in force down to the modern period.

Another Faculty of Theology was established at Valladolid and obtained pontifical recognition in 1418, but it did not prosper during the fifteenth century. Finally, toward the end of the century, in 1489, the third and final Faculty of Theology founded in the kingdom of Castile in this century was established at Sigüenza.

In Aragon and Catalonia university chairs of theology were more numerous and probably more flourishing than those of Castile: that of Lérida, which was already in operation in 1300, was recognized in 1430; that of Perpignan, which began in 1350, had already won recognition in 1447; that of Huesca, established in 1354, was recognized in 1464; that of Barcelona, in 1450. Finally, toward the end of the century, in 1483, a Faculty of Theology was established in Palma de Mallorca, native land of Lullism.

B. THE CONVENTUAL STUDIA

It is a well-known fact that during the last centuries of the Middle Ages the secular clergy preferred the study of law to that of theology. On the other hand, theology found a generous welcome, in Spain as elsewhere in Christian Europe, in the convents of the mendicant orders, especially of the two most widespread, the Dominican and the Franciscan. As early as about 1226 the Dominicans and Franciscans, who had shortly before established themselves at the European "end of the earth" *(finis terrae),* namely, at St. James of Compostella, were borrowing books from the archdiocesan curia: the Dominicans borrowed, among others, the book of the *Sentences* of Peter Lombard; the Franciscans, on the other hand, made use of only a single book, the *Glossatura magna* of the same Peter Lombard, which he had used as a textbook before composing the *Sentences.*[2] During the thirteenth and fourteenth centuries the numbers of Spanish mendicants going to the great convents or *studia* (houses of study) opened by the two orders in Paris grew continually. In 1303, in the great Franciscan convent known as the convent of the "cordeliers," there were almost eighty-seven foreigners in residence, among them a large number of Spaniards.[3]

In the Middle Ages the most renowned general *studia* of theology of the Spanish Dominicans were undoubtedly those of Salamanca, established in 1290 and incorporated into the local university in 1416, and then of Barcelona, established in 1303; other flourishing centers of theology were in Tarragona, Lérida, Tortosa, Perpignan, Valencia, Murcia, Palma de Mallorca, Játiva, and Valladolid.

During the same period there were very many provincial or conventual *studia* of theology among the Spanish Franciscans; these were usually open also to members of the secular clergy. Among their general *studia* the oldest was that of Barcelona, which was already open in 1322; next, perhaps, was that of Salamanca, which, together with the Dominican center, formed one of the pillars of the local Faculty of Theology; then came those of Lérida, Valencia, Palma de Mallorca, Toledo, Valladolid, Palencia, and finally, Seville.

Although the theological institutions maintained by the other mendicant orders were less important because of their small number, mention must be made here of at least some of them. The Augustinians, for example, had very prosperous *studia* in Salamanca and Valencia. Beginning in the middle of the fourteenth century the Carmelites, too, cultivated theological studies at both the conventual and the provincial levels; moreover, in Barcelona from 1333 on and in Perpignan from 1345 on, they also had general *studia*.

III. The Creators of Spanish Theology in the Fifteenth Century

H. Hurter in his *Nomenclator litterarius Theologiae Catholicae* (Innsbruck, 1903–13) listed barely eighty Spanish theologians as having lived in the last three centuries of the Middle Ages. Yet even just the theologians we know of today as belonging to the fifteenth century number more than that. In fact, looking only at the biblical field, K. Reinhardt and H. Santiago Otero in their *Biblioteca bíblica ibérica medieval* (Madrid, 1986) manage to list at least fifty-three biblical scholars who lived or died in that century. It is not my intention in this section to fill up the lacunas in the aforementioned lists, even though I may add a few new names; I shall restrict myself to brief sketches of some personages who in one or other way were especially prominent in the history of fifteenth-century Spanish theology.

1. John of Monzón

John was born in Valencia in about 1340. He became a Dominican and, after his formation, devoted himself to teaching in the various convents of the kingdom of Aragon-Catalonia; in 1372 he lectured on the *Sentences* at Barcelona. Later on, he was called to take degrees in Paris; in 1379 he became a bachelor. Only in the first months of 1387 did he obtain the licentiate in theology; it was on this occasion that he showed for the first time the unquenchable controversial spirit that was to be the characteristic mark of his work throughout his life. He was tall of stature and arrogant of mind, according to Gerson's description of him. Thus in his *vesperiae* for obtaining the title of master and then in his first lecture as master—the so-called *resumpta*—he defended some decidedly rash propositions on the Trinity, on divine omnipotence, and, above all, on the conception of the Virgin Mary. He not only denied the Marian privilege, something which at that time did not cause any wonder, but he even declared that supporters of this privilege were heretics and opposed to the teaching of Thomas. He thus gave his hearers to understand that he was speaking not simply on his own account but in the name of the principal teachers of his order.

The response was vigorous. His teaching, summed up in fourteen propositions, was condemned by the University of Paris and even by the bishop. On the other hand, the entire Dominican convent of Saint-Jacques closed ranks around Fray John and put forward two theses that could not fail to provoke the academic authorities and the churchmen of Paris: the first, that the condemnation of teaching was exclusively the competence of the Holy See; the second, that the teaching of St. Thomas had been solemnly approved by the Church. The immediate result was that the university excluded Dominican professors and students from all academic activities. Twelve Dominican masters, with John of Monzón at their head, transferred to Avignon and sent a petition to the pope. A commission of four masters of the university, led by Peter d'Ailly, also went to the pope. Proceedings were begun, but before they could end, Monzón, who was increasingly backed into a corner by the rapid and coherent interventions of d'Ailly, fled in secret from Avignon and returned to Aragon. The papal tribunal condemned him by default, and in Paris the triumphant university intensified its boycott of the Dominican convent, which remained almost empty in the years that followed.

The only one who did not surrender was the intrepid and highly competent man from Valencia. Disappointed in the Avignon pope, he went over to the employ of the pope of Rome. In 1393 he traveled through Sicily and in 1395 was in Rome. In 1412 he carried out an assignment in Aragon; this is the last information about him that has reached us.

Some works: (a) *Brevis conspectus utrum beata et intemerata Virgo Maria in peccato originali sit concepta;* (b) *Dialogus super schismate Ecclesiae orto tempore Urbani VI;* (c) *Tractatus brevis de electione papae.*[4]

2. Jerome of the Holy Faith

This personage, a Jew named Yehoshua ha-Lorqui, was born around the middle of the fifteenth century. There is disagreement about whether the surname ha-Lorqui (Lorca, in Murcia) signifies his place of birth or simply his place of origin. In the latter case, it may be thought that he was born in Alcañiz (Teruel), where he lived and practiced his profession as a physician.

In 1390 he suffered a crisis of faith when his teacher, Rabbi Schlomo ha-Levi, became a Christian at Burgos and took the name Paul of Saint Mary. Only in 1412, however, as a result of serious conversations with Vincent Ferrer, did he ask to be baptized, and he received the name Jerome of the Holy Faith. With the zeal of a new convert he wrote a book to convince his former brethren about the faith; above all, he convinced Pope Benedict XIII to convoke some memorable Jewish-Christian disputations at Tortosa (1413–14).

Principal work: *Libri duo, quorum prior fidem et religionem (Judaeorum) impugnat, alter vero Talmud* (1412); first publication: Zurich, 1552.[5]

3. Fray James Moxena of Valencia

In this name I combine two surnames, "Moxena" and "of Valencia," that in the past were used for two different persons, both named James. The first was Fray James Moxena (Muxena, Mogena, Mugena, Mojena, Mujena), who was occasionally seen with the Avignon pope, Benedict XIII, and with Ferdinand I, king of Aragon, and also at the Council of Constance. The second was Fray James of Valencia, well known for his poetry, which was collected in the *Cancionero de Baena,* the most important anthology of Castilian poetry of the first decades of the fifteenth century. After years of research I have become firmly convinced that the two Jameses were in fact a single Castilian, who when abroad (in Aragon and at Constance) signed himself with the patronymic "Moxena," but at home with the toponymic "of Valencia" ("the man from Valencia").

Even when these two persons have been identified as one and the same, we know rather little about him. He was born in the early years of the second half of the fourteenth century, not at Valencia de Don Juan (province of León), as was thought in the past, but probably in the small town of Valencia de Alcántara (province of Cáceres), which was part of the old kingdom of León, but under the jurisdiction at that time of the Military Order of Alcántara. He entered the Franciscan Order, and from 1375 on, while simply a bachelor, he lectured on the *Sentences* in the convent of León. In 1348 Gregory XI authorized him to teach at Salamanca or in some other general *studium* so that he could gain the title of doctor or master. We do not know where or when he did so, but he certainly became a doctor and master; in fact, in 1410 he was one of the candidates for the "morning" chair of theology in the University of Salamanca.

Being, however, restless by nature, he preferred to throw himself into the game of diplomacy on the confused chessboard of the Great Western Schism. In fact, as early as 1405 he was appointed *familiaris domesticus commensalis* (a sharer in the table of the domestic household) of the Avignon pope,

Benedict XIII, for whom he seems to have been working for some time. During that same year we find him occasionally at the papal court in Nice and in Savona. In 1414, while in northern Italy, he abandoned Benedict XIII's party and secretly went to the Council of Constance, his participation in which is documented from November 28, 1414, on, in connection with the case of John Huss. In the late summer of 1415, with the council's authority, and in advance of Emperor Sigismond, who was likewise on the road to Catalonia, James appeared before his friend and protector, Ferdinand I of Aragon, in order to persuade him to abandon Pope Luna [Benedict VIII = Peter of Luna] and accept the council; Ferdinand himself would later say on at least two occasions that James had persuaded him *(nos suasit)*.

James later returned to Constance, but he was dissatisfied by the election of Martin V and returned to Benedict XIII; on May 19, 1418, the latter delegated a canon of Barcelona to absolve James of "apostasy" and reinstate him. There are some hints that his death occurred during the third decade of the fifteenth century.

This alienation from the official Church may perhaps explain sufficiently the eclipse, after his death, of the fame James seems to have enjoyed during his life. In circles at Constance, from the very first month after the opening of the council, it was commonly said, even among the papal gendarmes, that Fray James was "a very penetrating theologian." The head of the Aragonese delegation, which reached Constance at the beginning of 1415, used similar language when writing to King Ferdinand I regarding him; he wrote: "He is in high repute, has an excellent reputation, and is greatly respected at this meeting [the council]; and, my Lord, many of the matters here are in his hands." In his turn, the author or compiler of the above-mentioned *Cancionero* describes James as an outstanding person in the field of science and letters: "A very famous master of sacred theology" (*Cancionero,* no. 519, heading), "a great man of letters and a great master of all the liberal arts," "very competent in physics, astrology, and the science of mechanics, so much so that in his time there was no one so well grounded in all the sciences as he was" (*Cancionero,* no. 473, heading).

Despite his reputation among his contemporaries, until ten years ago our knowledge of James' works (even when the man was divided into two distinct personages) was limited to a Latin letter written from Constance to King Ferdinand and about forty Castilian poems in the *Cancionero de Baena.* My own researches have enabled me to assign James as the author of a series of anonymous texts that do full justice to the fame that surrounded him during his life. I therefore give below a provisory list of works written by him or attributable to him; those under letters *a* to *e* bear his name, the others are anonymous. The list is provisory in regard both to the number of works and to the validity of the attribution to James.

This list is thus not intended as a definitive inventory but rather as a working hypothesis.[6]

(a) 43 Castilian poems collected in the *Cancionero de Baena;*[7]

(b) Collection of records and other documents from the first sessions of the Council of Constance, sent to Ferdinand I of Aragon on May 14, 1415, "by his diligent ambassador, Master James de Moxena"; this autograph dedication is found in only one of the three known manuscripts, that of Barcelona, Archivio de la Corona de Aragón, sign. (modern): Biblioteca, Códices Varia, n. 7; 59ff., with 33 documents;[8]

(c) *Capitula agendorum in concilio generali Constanciensi,* ff. 41r–58r, in the above-mentioned Barcelona collection; it is an abridgment of the treatise of Dietrich of Niem, *De modis uniendi ac reformandi Ecclesiam in concilio universali;*[9]

(d) *Epistula* to Ferdinand I, from Constance, July 9, 1415 (original), Barcelona collection, Fernando I, Cartas Reales, Caja 18, doc. 3356;

(e) *Recepta ad memoriam secundum mag. Didacum Hispanum ordinis Minorum,* Parma, Bibl. Palatina, ms. Misti B 26, f. 129rv (fifteenth century);

(f) *Disputa entre Gonzalo Morante de la Ventura y un "mal cristiano" sobre la predestinación y el libre albedrío,* preserved in three manuscripts;[10]

(g) *Disputa entre un moro filósofo y Gonzalo Morante sobre la Trinidad y la Encarnación,* Rome, Bibl. Casanatense, ms. 1022, ff. 97rb–102vd;[11]

(h) *Disputatio saecularis et iacobitae,* also titled *Liber de conceptu virginali* (attributed in the past to Raymond Lull and to Raymond Astruc of Cortyelles); there are five manuscripts, several printings, and some Spanish translations;[12]

(i) *Cantilenae in Dei servitium et gloriosae Virginis eius matris et aliorum sanctorum compositae,* Rome, Bibl. Casanatense, ms. 1022, ff. 56c–60d;[13]

(j) *De sanctissima et purissima conceptione Virginis,* Copenhagen, Det Kongelige Bibliothek, Thot 105, 4°, ff. 78r–86v;[14]

(k) *Gracián* (an adaptation of Lull's *Felix de les maravelles del món*), Salamanca, Biblioteca Universitaria, ms. 1866, ff. 13r–174v.[15]

4. St. Vincent Ferrer

This eminent preacher was born in Valencia around the year 1350. He became a Dominican in 1367 in his native city; there he also began the study of philosophy and theology, which he continued at Lérida, Barcelona, and Toulouse, France. From 1385 to 1391 he taught theology at the cathedral of Valencia and in 1392 moved to Avignon. From the beginning of the Western Schism (1378) he was a follower of the Avignon popes and a friend especially of Benedict XIII; but from 1412 on he began to think that for the sake of Church unity Benedict ought to abdicate, and in fact it was Vincent who on January 6, 1416, at the behest of Ferdinand I, solemnly proclaimed at Perpignan the kingdom of Aragon's decision no longer to obey Benedict. As a preacher, he traveled throughout Aragon, Castile, Italy, Switzerland, and

France, attracting multitudes and fostering conversions; in his sermons he communicated, in addition to his personal charism, a solid biblical and theological teaching. He died at Vannes (Brittany) on April 5, 1419.

Some works: (a) *Scholia in Bibliam;* (b) *Sermones;* (c) *Tractatus contra Judaeos* (but today there is a tendency to attribute this to Jerome of the Holy Faith.[16]

5. Anthony Canals

Anthony was born in Valencia and entered the Dominican province of Aragon, where he studied theology; he continued this study at Toulouse in France. In 1387–88 he was a lector at Lérida, then probably at the cathedral of Valencia, and from 1398 on, at Barcelona in the royal *studium*. In 1402 he was appointed inquisitor of Valencia. Canals was a theologian, a spiritual writer, and a good representative of Catalan humanism. He died around 1419.

Some works: (a) *Escala de contemplació;* (b) *Tractat de confessió;* (c) translations from Latin to Catalan of *Liber Senecae de providentia; Epistola pseudo-Bernardi ad suam germanam;* the *Arrha animae* of Hugo of St. Victor; the *Africa* of Francis Petrarch.[17]

6. Peter of Luna (Benedict XIII)

Peter was born at Illueca (Saragossa); he studied and then taught canon law at Montpellier. On being appointed a cardinal by Gregory XI (1375) he went to Rome with him. He took part in the lively conclave of 1378 that elected Urban VI; being convinced that this election was irregular, he took part in the election of Clement VII at Avignon and returned there with Clement. It was due to his diplomatic missions that Castile, Aragon, and Navarre, as well as the great preacher Vincent Ferrer, accepted the new pope. In 1394, he himself succeeded Clement VII and took the name Benedict XIII. An austere but also headstrong man, he never doubted the legitimacy of his election. Even after the loss of the obedience of all the Spanish kingdoms in 1416 and then his excommunication by the Council of Constance, he continued to invoke constantly the "path of justice." He died at Peñiscola (Castile) on May 23, 1423.

His main contribution to the history of Spanish theology was to have restructured the Faculty of Theology at Salamanca and to have left behind him, in addition to his personal writing, a very rich library.

Some writings: (a) *Tractatus de concilio generali;* (b) *Tractatus de principali schismate;* (c) *Tractatus de novo subschismate;* (d) *Allegationes pro papa et contra revelantes.*[18]

7. Philip of Malla

A native of Barcelona, from 1392 to 1407/8 he studied at the University of Paris, where one of his teachers was John Gerson and where he obtained the degree of master in theology. He was one of the representatives of the king of Aragon at the Council of Constance and took part in the election of Martin V. He died at Barcelona in 1431.

He wrote, among other things, a theological summa entitled *Memorial del pecador remut* (Gerona, 1483; Barcelona, c. 1495; ibid., 1982).[19]

8. Paul of Saint Mary

Schlomo ha-Levi was born about 1350 into a distinguished Jewish family. At the age of thirty he was already Grand Rabbi of Burgos, but in 1390 he abandoned Judaism, received baptism in the cathedral of Burgos, and took the name of Paul of Saint Mary, although he is known also as Paul of Burgos ("Burgense"). His conversion had strong repercussions in Jewish circles. As I noted earlier, it led to the religious crisis that brought Jerome of the Holy Faith to embrace the Christian faith. After his conversion Paul studied theology at Paris (1391–95); he subsequently lived for a while in Avignon in the service of Benedict XIII. In 1403 he was appointed bishop of Cartagena and in 1415 of Burgos. He was also chief chaplain of Henry III and Grand Chancellor of John II of Castile. He died on August 30, 1435.

Paul was a man of great culture and, despite his many occupations, wrote some important works: (a) *Additiones 1–1100 ad postillam Nicolai de Lyra;* (b) *Quaestiones XII de nomine divino tetragrammato;* (c) *Scrutinium scripturarum contra perfidiam Judaeorum.*[20]

9. John of Casanova

John was born in Barcelona in 1387, became a Dominican in 1403, and a priest in 1414. He studied theology at Salamanca, where in 1419 he obtained the title of master. In 1420 Martin V appointed him Master of the Sacred Palace, then bishop of Borsano and of Elna. In 1431 he was created a cardinal by Eugene IV, whose rights he had defended against the Council of Basel. He died in Florence on February 24, 1436.

(a) *Tractatus de potestate papae et concilii,* ms. Bibl. Vaticana, Vat. lat. 4129, ff. 39ra–74rb; (b) *Tractatus de papa haeretico,* ibid., ff. 74va–86va.[21]

10. Raymond Sibiuda

Raymond Sibiuda (also Sabiende, Sabieude, Sabiuda, Sabunde, Sabundo, Sebeide, Sebeyde, Sebon, Sebond, Sebonde, Sebude, Sibiude) was probably born around 1385 in Gerona, Catalonia; he died on April 29, 1436, at Toulouse, France.

He was master of philosophy, medicine, and theology, and a licentiate in canon law. He taught philosophy in Toulouse before 1429, since in that year he was rector of the *studium,* a post that required a certain length of service in teaching; in 1434 and 1435 he was a teacher of theology and rector once again.

In 1434 he began drafting the work that was to make him famous: *Scientia libri creaturarum sive libri naturae et scientia de homine,* or more briefly, *Liber creaturarum,* the name the work has in a good part of the manuscript tradition. In the printed edition (Deventer, 1484), on the other hand, the work bore the title *Theologia naturalis sive Liber creaturarum,* which it kept in all subsequent Latin editions, with or without some indication of the second part. But the changes were not to stop there: in 1499 Carthusian Peter Dorland published the work in a shortened form under the title *Viola animae;* almost two centuries later, in 1661, Protestant humanist Johann Amos Komensky (Comenius), a Czech, reconstructed the book in its unabridged form and published it once more at Amsterdam with the title *Oculus fidei.*

The *Theologia naturalis* went through a good fifteen Latin printings, of which at least two were in the fifteenth century; it was published in French for the first time at Lyons in 1519, but the version that evoked the greatest interest was that of Michel de Montaigne, *La théologie naturelle de Raymond Sebond* (Paris, 1569; reprinted there in 1581 and 1611, at Rouen in 1603 and 1641, and at Tournon in 1605).

Even the *Viola animae* had a wide readership. As far as Spain is concerned, it is enough to mention the edition of 1500 and the Castilian translation *(Violeta del ánima)* of 1549, both at Toledo, and the more or less extensive adaptations under quite different titles: *Luz del alma* (Seville, 1542) by the Franciscan John of Cazalla; *Tesoro de ángeles* (Astorga, 1547), issued anonymously but to be attributed to Francis of Evia, another Franciscan; and finally the anonymous *Despertador del alma* (Seville, 1544, and Saragossa, 1552). Sibiuda's work was not only published, translated, and adapted but evidently also read and imitated. J. M. de Bujanda has been able to show its presence in sixteenth-century Spain in two important writers of spiritual literature: Fray James of Stella and Fray John of the Angels.

Raymond Sibiuda is thus of interest to theology because his thought became so widespread but even more because of his method, of which I shall speak further on.[22]

11. Alphonsus Fernández of Madrigal, "El Tostado"

"El Tostado" ("the sunburnt") or "el Abulense" ("the man from Avila") was born in Madrigal de las Altas Torres (Avila) around 1410. He studied Latin with the Franciscans of Arévalo. At a very young age he began to attend the University of Salamanca, first as a student, becoming in succession a master of arts (1432), a master of theology (1441), and at least a bachelor of canon law; subsequently he taught moral philosophy, exegesis, and theology in various chairs; he was also rector. In 1443 he traveled to Italy in fulfillment of a mission given him by the king of Castile; while in Siena at the papal court he publicly defended some theses in theology, among them three that were not well received by the Curia and were attacked in writing by Cardinal John of Torquemada, to whom Alphonsus replied in a *Defensorium*. Contrary to what has been supposed, he seems never to have been at the Council of Basel. He was elected bishop of Avila, but certainly in 1454 and not in 1445, as has repeatedly been asserted. He died in 1455 at Bonilla de la Sierra (Avila).

Though his life was short, he left a vast literary production that was perhaps not exceeded by any of his fellow countrymen in that same era. The inscription on his tomb calls attention to his universal learning: "Here lies the wonder of the world, who dealt with everything knowable."

Some writings: (a) Commentary on the historical books of the Old Testament and on the Gospel of St. Matthew; (b) *De la reformación de la Iglesia;* (c) *De indulgentiis;* (d) *De conciliis generalibus.*[23]

12. Alphonsus of Cartagena

This son of Paul of Saint Mary was born around 1385, probably at Burgos, and was baptized along with his father in 1390. His name was Alphonsus García of Saint Mary, but he kept the surname "of Cartagena," seemingly because he was his father's companion during the period when the latter was bishop of Cartagena. He studied canon and civil law at Salamanca for ten years. From 1434 to 1439 he took part in the Council of Basel as a delegate of John II of Castile and on the side of Eugene IV; in 1435, while at Basel, he received news of his father's death and of his own election to succeed him as bishop of Burgos. He died on June 23, 1456.

In addition to being a lawyer, he was a theologian, moralist, historian, and poet.

Some works: (a) *Oracional;* (b) *Apologia super psalmum Iudica me Deus;* (c) *Defensorium unitatis christianae.*[24]

13. John of Segovia

John was born in Segovia around 1395. His full name was John Alphonsus of Segovia. During the first and longer stage of his life he seems to have been closely associated with the University of Salamanca; although he was of poor and humble origin, he went to the university while still very young, and in 1413 he was already a bachelor of theology; he later taught exegesis and then theology. The second stage of his life began in 1433 when he went to the Council of Basel as a delegate of the university; there he played a prominent part in the more lively debates, especially in the debate on conciliarism; he also took part in the rejection of Eugene IV and the election of antipope Felix V, to whom he gave his allegiance. But when this minischism dissolved he was reconciled with Nicholas V, who appointed him a titular archbishop in exchange for his renunciation of the title of cardinal, which the antipope had granted him. He withdrew to the monastery of Ayton (Savoy) and devoted the last years of his life to the writing of new theological treatises and a history of the Council of Basel. He also collected a very extensive library, which he left in his will to his "nourishing mother," Salamanca. He died at Ayton on May 24, 1458.

He was one of the most important figures of fifteenth-century Spain.

B. Hernández Montes lists eighty-one writings of John's own and sixteen more composed in collaboration. Some titles: (a) *Tractatus decem avisamentorum ex Sacra Scriptura de sanctitate Ecclesiae et generalis concilii auctoritate;* (b) *Liber de Sancta Conceptione;* (c) *Tractatus de processione Spiritus Sancti a Patre et Filio;* (d) *Historia gestorum generalis synodi Basiliensis;* (e) *De gladio divi Spiritus in corda mittendo Saracenorum.*[25]

14. John of Torquemada

John was born in Valladolid around 1388; in 1404 he entered the Dominican convent of San Pablo in his native city. He accompanied his provincial, Louis of Valladolid, to the Council of Constance; he subsequently studied in the Faculty of Theology in Paris and obtained the title of master of theology in 1425. He attended the Council of Basel (1431–37) and there vigorously defended the superiority of the pope over a council. Eugene IV appointed him Master of the Sacred Palace in 1434 and then a member of the papal delegation to the diets of Nuremberg (1438) and Mainz (1439). In the latter year he was created a cardinal and spent the rest of his life in Rome. His death occurred on September 26, 1468.

The influence of his personality and his writings was strongly felt in almost all areas of Catholic theology in that period.

Some works: (a) *Tractatus de sacramento eucharistiae;* (b) *Tractatus de veritate Conceptionis beatissimae Virginis;* (c) *Impugnationes quorumdam propositionum* [of Alphonus Fernández of Madrigal]; (d) *Tractatus contra Madianitas et Ismaelitas;* (e) *Summa de Ecclesia.*[26]

15. John of Carvajal

John was born in Trujillo (Cáceres) around 1399 and studied civil and canon law at Salamanca. In 1438 he became an auditor of the Tribunal of the Roman Rota. He is of interest to the history of theology not only for his skill as a writer but above all as a diplomat in the service of the Holy See for almost thirty years and an active participant in the main politico-religious affairs of the Church of that period. During the pontificate of Eugene IV (1431–47) he led a papal mission to seven German diets (1441–46) in connection with the schism of Basel. On December 17, 1446, Eugene IV bestowed the cardinal's hat on him.

Under Nicholas V (1447–55) he was papal legate from 1447 to 1449 in Germany (where he promoted and signed the Concordat of Vienna in 1448), in Bohemia, and in Hungary; in the years that followed, he was sent to Florence, Venice, and Milan to promote the crusade against the Turks. Under Callistus III (1455–58) he returned to Germany, then Hungary (his mission reached its climax in the victory at Belgrade in 1456); he visited Bosnia and then went anew to Hungary. Under Pius II (1458–64) he was an adviser, along with Cardinal Bessarion, of the humanist pope and watched over the interests of Bohemia. Finally, under Paul II (1464–71), he helped form a league of Italian states at Venice in order to finance the cost of the crusade. After returning he spent the last two years of his life in Rome and died there on December 6, 1469.

His writings: (a) defenses of the Holy See; (b) summary reports of his missions; (c) letters; (d) discourses sacred and secular.[27]

16. Roderick Sánchez de Arévalo

He was born in Santa María de Nieva (Segovia) in 1404. From 1418 to 1429 he studied law at Salamanca; he seems also to have been a bachelor of arts and of theology. He was a member of the Castilian diplomatic mission to the Council of Basel from 1433 to 1439, and, in the name of the king of Castile and of the council, he was part of the delegation that met Emperor Albert II at Breslau in 1438. In the years that followed he fulfilled various other charges, but the most important stage of his life, as far as the history of theology is concerned, was the decade of the sixties which he spent in Rome, first as Referendary of Petitions and then as governor of Castel Sant'Angelo. This last office provided him with the occasion for developing contacts with the Roman humanists who were imprisoned after the unsuccessful plot against Paul II. Arévalo was bishop successively of Oviedo, Zamora, Calahorra, and Palencia, although he never set foot in any of these dioceses. He died at Rome in 1470.

Both in his diplomatic activity and in his writings Arévalo was a firm supporter of the power of the Roman pontiff against the conciliarism of Basel. He also fought against other errors of his age, such as that of the Fraticelli.

Some works: (a) *Dialogus de remediis schismatis;* (b) *Libellus de libera et irrefragabili auctoritate Romani Pontificis;* (c) *Libellus de paupertate Christ et Apostolorum.*[28]

17. Martin of Córdoba

He was born in Córdoba at the end of the fourteenth century, entered the Augustinian convent of his native city, and probably did his studies in

Salamanca. He was lector at Saragossa and obtained the degree of master of theology in Toulouse, France. In 1451 he turned up as a master at Salamanca and ten years later at Toulouse again. He died at Valladolid on July 5, 1476.

Among his works (some of which are still unpublished) these may be noted: (a) *Tratado de la predestinación;* (b) *Compendio de la fortuna;* (c) *Ara praedicandi.*[29]

18. John López of Salamanca

He was born around 1385 in Salamanca or its environs and took the Dominican habit in the convent of San Esteban, where he was a master and, from 1462 on, regent of studies. He attacked Peter Martínez of Osma for his teaching on penance. He died at Plasencia on April 13, 1479.

Some works: (a) *Concepción y nascencia de la Virgen;* (b) *Defensorium fidei contra garrulos praeceptores. Tratado de la penitencia según la Yglesia Romana;* (c) *Responsio ad Quodlibetum magistri de Osma.*[30]

19. Peter Martínez of Osma

He was born in Osma (Soria) around 1427–30 and in 1444 entered the college of San Bartolomeo in Salamanca, where he studied the arts and theology. He taught moral philosophy and in 1463 advanced to the chair of "morning" theology, which he filled until 1478. His treatise *De confessione* was condemned by the Inquisition of Saragossa and then by a commission of theologians in Alcalá, and finally by Sixtus IV. The author retracted his teaching and died at Alba de Tormes in 1480.

Some works: (a) *Commentarium in Symbolum Quicumque;* (b) *Quodlibetum;* (c) *Repetitio de comparatione Deitatis, proprietatis et personae;* (d) *Responsio ad quaedam deliramenta duorum huius temporis verbosistarum;* (e) *Dialogus in quo ostenditur fundamenta humanae philosophiae, quibus fulciunut verbosistae, plerumque in theologia deficere;* (f) *Repetitio de efficacia legis Christi eiusque a Lege Veteri differentia.*[31]

20. James Pérez of Valencia

Born around 1408 at Ayora (Valencia), he entered the Discalced Augustinians at Valencia in 1435; there he studied and taught canon law and theology. In 1468 he was appointed titular bishop of Christopolis and an auxiliary of Cardinal Roderick Borgia, the future Alexander VI. He died at Valencia on August 30, 1490.

His works are exegetical: (a) *Commentum in psalmos;* (b) *Quattuor opuscula exegetica* (the first of which is a *Tractatus contra Judaeos*); *Expositio in cantica canticorum.*[32]

21. Alphonsus of Espina

He was a Franciscan, but we do not know the place or year of his birth or anything about the early part of his life. He appears in 1452 as regent of the theological *studium* of San Francisco in Salamanca. He had the reputation of being a great preacher; in 1462 he finished his main work, *Fortalitium*.

He was in favor of the establishment of the Inquisition in Castile. In 1479 he played a part in the condemnation of Peter Martínez of Osma, at Alcalá. In 1491 he was appointed a titular bishop and an auxiliary of the diocese of Oviedo. He was still alive in 1495.

A work which had a great influence on the status of the *conversi* (converted Jews) was entitled *Fortalitiuum fidei contra Judaeos, Sarracenos et alios fidei christianae inimicos* (no place or date, but at Strasbourg before 1471; other editions).[33]

IV. Fifteenth-Century Theology in the Spanish Context

Since it is impossible here to analyze the teaching of the individual authors named and of others no less deserving of mention, I shall limit myself to sketching some historical, methodological, and thematic trends in the Spanish theology of the fifteenth century. In this section I shall concentrate on the Spanish context and in the next section on the European context.

A. Theology and Theological Methods

All the authors mentioned received an academic formation at either a university or a convent; many of them also occupied chairs of theology; all of them, therefore, were familiar with the Scholastic method that had been imposed on them in Paris and was then uniformly imitated in the other universities and conventual *studia*. But if we look at the scientific production of the authors considered and of others of their contemporaries, we easily recognize that it is not completely conformed to the programs and methods of academic teaching followed in the schools. Except in rare instances, it is a production that does not result from teaching and is not intended for teaching but results from the need to give an answer to problems that were arising in the society of the time. It was precisely this need of coping with concrete realities that drove the Spanish authors to look for a new way of doing theology which was in open contrast to the conceptualist formalism, empty of any real content, of late Scholasticism.

A first innovation to be mentioned was the use of the vernacular. Latin evidently continued to predominate, but it is of interest to note that precisely at this time the vernacular came to be used in theological discourse. If I am not mistaken, temporal priority belongs to James Moxena, who at the beginning of the century used Spanish in writing about predestination, the Trinity, and the incarnation. As the century drew on, the use of the vernacular became more frequent; we may think of Philip of Malla, El Tostado, and Martin of Córdoba. Spanish also served as a vehicle for the poets of the *Cancionero da Baena* who dealt with profound theological problems, among which, here again, were the three just mentioned: predestination, the Trinity, and the incarnation.

A second innovation of the Spanish theology of this period was the literary genres. There are indeed plenty of the genres of a clearly Scholastic kind: in theology, such genres as *quaestiones* and *tractatus* (we have these from various authors) and the *summa* (used by John of Torquemada; and in law, such as *allegationes* and *repetitiones;* but the commentaries on the *Sentences,* so numerous in the preceding century, are missing. On the other hand, the literary genres that characterize Spanish theology in the fifteenth century and can be regarded as predominant are the apologetic and the polemical. We also find an odd literary genre, which I would not call new, since it had been used a century before by Raymond Lull, and which was not very widespread elsewhere, but which is not less fascinating on that account: the genre of the theological novel, in which a profoundly theological subject is expounded in a lively dialogue between two or three participants and in a particular place, while obviously using names that are purely symbolical. Four of the writings I have assigned to James Moxena belong to this genre.

Let me call attention to still a third innovation having to do this time with method, that is, with the starting point of the theological argumentation. Unlike the formalists or *verbosistae* ("word-mongers"), who started with logical concepts and remained firmly anchored in them without relation to reality, the theologians and even the canonists I have been studying are all in agreement in starting from history, that is, from the fact of God's revelation to humankind. In this respect, it is true, our theologians did not in fact differ from their more classic medieval predecessors, who had made theology into a systematic reflection on the word of God, an *intelligentia fidei.* But what ways can be followed in coming to understand the word of God and in making it intelligible and persuasive to the people of one's own time? Risking a provisional response, a simple hypothesis for research, I would say that the Spanish theologians of the fifteenth century proposed three ways, each of which does not exclude but rather includes the others: the way of the Bible, the way of the Church, and the way of creation. It will be enough here to mention some names representative of each of these ways.

The Bible, the written word of God, evidently could not but be the privileged theological source *(locus theologicus)* for the converts from Judaism: Paul of Saint Mary, Jerome of the Holy Faith, and Alphonsus of Cartagena; El Tostado seems to take the same approach.

The way of the Church seems to have been the one most traveled: the witness of the early Church and of its tradition was in fact the warranty to which theologians and lawyers appealed in responding to the problems of the contemporary Church. Among others who followed this path was Peter Martínez of Osma, a man who would later be condemned by the Church of his day. It is worth noting that by finding themselves reflected in the "ancients," these theologians contributed to the reform of the fifteenth-century Church to a greater extent than did the formalists of the time, who wanted to be called *moderniores* ("more up-to-date").

The third way, that of creation, was expounded above all in the work *Theologia naturalis,* that is, Raymond Sibiuda's *Liber creaturarum seu de homine*. It is a truly ecumenical way, since it "teaches that every human being actually knows, without difficulty and toil, all the truths needed by human beings, about both the human person and God." It is a cosmic way, inasmuch as its starting point is the book of creation. God has revealed himself in two books: the Scriptures and nature, the latter being open to all and "cannot be falsified or wiped out or falsely interpreted." The human microcosm is a synthesis and completion of the whole creation. In addition to the three degrees of "being," "life," and "sensation," in which it shares with other creatures, the human being possesses a fourth degree, that of "understanding and volition," which it does not share with any other being.

It is this unique qualification that enables it to read the book of creation and even to read its own nature, which is a compendium of creation. Sibiuda's entire demonstration is aimed at showing how "the human person advances through creation to the understanding of God the creator." He emphasizes the point that this is a safe way, since it uses "infallible arguments" based on the very sure experience the human being has of itself and therefore of other creatures: "It argues from what is most certain to every human being as a result of experience, namely, from all creatures and from the nature of the human person itself. . . . And consequently this science does not look for other witnesses but only the person himself." The demand that the human being be the medium for knowing God leads Sibiuda to develop a christology (Christ is the true microcosm) and a theology of sin as that which breaks the communion with creation and with God: "The more you distance yourself from creatures, the more you distance yourself from yourself and from your creator."

Although original in many respects, Sibiuda does not seem to have been the only one to traverse the "infallible" way of creation. To limit ourselves to the fifteenth century: James Moxena, too, in the *Liber de conceptu virginali* (which I maintain is to be attributed to him) undertook to confirm the truth of the Immaculate Conception "by means of some cogent arguments"; and after expounding some of these, arguments to the effect that since from a rejection of the truth that the Virgin Mary was conceived without sin, it would necessarily follow that "not even God can do something," "the Trinity would cease to be," "the movements of nature would be nonexistent," "genera, species, and individuals would fail," and "it would be the destruction of the entire universe."

Two further examples: according to Moxena, too, God made the created world in order to make himself known and loved by human beings and, through them, by the entire world: "God created human beings that he might be known and loved; and that, through human beings, [the created world] might be united to him in greater love and knowledge." Then, too, Moxena understands sin as a "flight" of human beings from the Creator and from the created world, from being to nonbeing: "The creature, by inflicting deformity on itself and fleeing from the end for which God created it out of nonbeing, endeavors by this flight from its end to return to what it had been, which is nonbeing."

To sum up: it is evident that if we were to trace the use of this way back into the past, we would come upon Raymond Lull, St. Bonaventure, and the Victorines. On the other hand, originality in theology often consists not so much in discovering something new as in bringing back to the present things that seemed to have been made useless by the passage of time.

B. "ONE KINGDOM, ONE FAITH":
THEOLOGY AND THE POLITICO-SOCIAL UNITY OF SPAIN

1. Theology and Political Unity

In 589, with the abjuration of Arianism during the Third Council of Toledo, the kingdom of the Visigoths, which now embraced all the old Roman populations and all the other barbarian peoples who took root in Spain, became a Catholic kingdom. At that time the idea of Hispania as a geographical, political, religious, cultural, and social unit was born. At the next council, the Fourth of Toledo (633), liturgical unity was also achieved in the "Spanish liturgy," because, as Isidore of Seville, president of the assembly, said: "We are united in the same faith and form one and the same kingdom": *unum regnum, unum fides*.

But the golden age of close collaboration between *regnum* and *sacerdotium* (priesthood; the ecclesiastical hierarchy) came to a violent end in 711, when the Moors, or Arabs of Mauretania, invaded Spain. The majority of Christians were subject to the invaders, and only a very small minority managed to retain their independence in the mountains of the northern part of the peninsula. In fact, then, in that fateful year, Hispania, that is, united, Catholic Spain, did not "die" but was only "scattered"; it was possible, therefore, to "recover" it. The Neogothic consciousness, which came into being after the beginning of the invasion and was constantly stirred to life by preachers, theologians, canonists, poets, and chroniclers, would for centuries drive the small groups in the north, now set up as various kingdoms, to undertake the "reconquest" of "lost" Hispania. We must bear in mind that the creation of new and independent Christian kingdoms (Asturia, León, Castile, Navarre, Aragon) never weakened in the minds of their inhabitants the awareness of a common "fatherland," even if at times particularist interests made it less visible and effective in action.

We come thus to fifteenth-century Spain, which was filled with politico-religious expectations, the beneficiaries of which would be, according to the interpretation of certain biblical and late medieval prophecies, one or other of the two Spanish kingdoms, Castile and Aragon. A single monarch would, like the unconquered sun, shine resplendent over all of Spain, defeat the Arabs, conquer the Lord's tomb, purify the Church, bring back to it the Jews whom Alexander the Great had shut up behind the Gates of the Caucasus, organize his many children into as many Christian kingdoms, and, finally, like a second Lion of Judah, defend the unity of the faith against all enemies.

The "one kingdom, one faith" idea was thus being reborn in a future-oriented perspective. According to Fray James Moxena, the advent of this messianic age already had a date and a hero: it began on March 6, 1405, with the birth of the son and heir of Henry III of Castile: the future king John II. The theologian and poet wishes for the newborn child, among other things, that he may possess "the entire monarchy in great power," that he "recover the tomb of the glorious king," that he "shed his blood and be wounded for the Christian faith," that he "be the head *(caudillo)* of the Christian people," that he reopen "the gates that were closed"; in short, that he be an "unconquered lion" and shine more brightly than the sun.

In 1410, the Infante Ferdinand, who became regent of Castile after the premature death of his brother, Henry III, wrested the important city of Antequera from the Moors of Granada. The poets of the *Cancionero de Baena* praised him not so much for having overcome the invaders as for having defeated the "Arians." This was a clear allusion to the triumph of Hispania, the idea that had been born at the Third Council of Toledo.

Hardly two years later, in 1412, the same Infante and regent of Castile, Ferdinand, was called to become king of Aragon. Thus the two most powerful kingdoms of the Iberian peninsula were from this point on governed by sovereigns of the same dynasty, that of the Trastamara; this was a very important step toward the future political unification of Spain.

But we ought to speak of a religious unity more than of a political. Once again, our witness is James Moxena, spokesman for the new King Ferdinand at the Council of Constance. In a letter of July 9, 1415, Moxena advises Ferdinand to side with the council and abandon the schism; he offers him Visigothic Hispania as a model: "I have no doubt that whatever Hispania was able to accomplish in the past, that much it can still accomplish under your leadership." At this point in his letter Fray James repeats the words with which Francis Petrarch urged Cola di Rienzo to demonstrate that what ancient Rome had been, the Rome and Italy of their time could be again, if all Italians would agree. But the purpose of this consensus, for Petrarch, was nothing else than to get rid of those who "mock the name of Italy." Moxena, on the other hand, is calling upon his royal addressee for reasons of faith and the Church: "How much longer shall they mock the unity of the faith?"; ". . . and especially to meet the needs of your mother, the Church."

This resolutely ecclesial consciousness was shown at the Council of Basel in connection with the regrettable quarrel caused by the claim of the English delegation to have precedence over the Castilian ambassadors at the sessions of the council and in its balloting. Alphonsus of Cartagena, among others, came to the defense of the Castilians; he appealed not to arguments having to do more or less with political prestige but to historical reasons centered on membership in the church of Visigothic Hispania, of which the Castilians regarded themselves as heirs.

The Christian consciousness of Hispania was to find its historian in Roderick Sánchez de Arévalo, who devoted three works to it: (a) *Libellus de situ et descriptione Hispaniae* (1463); (b) *Liber de monarchia orbis et de differentia cuiusvis humani principatus tam imperialis quam regalis* (1467); (c) *Historia hispanica* (1469–70).

In 1474, Ferdinand of Aragon and Isabella of Castile married and thus united the crowns of the two kingdoms. In 1482, with the conquest of Granada and the expulsion of the Jews, the same Catholic monarchs restored and brought to completion the "one kingdom, one faith," the messianic kingdom. Only one further step remained: the complete destruction of the Muslims, and the messianic kingdom would become an eschatological kingdom. The hour now seemed near. The great Italian preacher at the century's end, Fra Bernardine de'Bustis, claims in fact that even the Saracens were persuaded by some prophecies that their sect was shortly to be wiped out; and Bernardine himself says he is convinced of this, pointing out as proof the fact that the sect had now been wiped out in Granada, where it had ruled for eight hundred years.

It would, then, be difficult to understand fifteenth-century Spain without taking into account its historical consciousness.[34]

2. Theology and the Socio-Religious Situation

Throughout the Middle Ages, Spain had been divided into two communities: Christian Spain and Muslim Spain. In social terms, each of these two communities in turn included three groups that were distinguished more by religion than by ethnicity: the Christian group (known in Muslim Spain as the Mozarab group), the Jewish, and the Muslim (in Christian Spain, the Mudéjars). Here I shall be concerned only with the social situation of the Christians, Jews, and Mudéjars (or Muslims) in Christian Spain.

The vast majority in Christian Spain were Christians; the Jews and Mudéjars were minorities, without legal rights from birth. In Castile, in fact, by common law the only legitimate citizens were those born of a Christian marriage that had been celebrated "as Holy Church prescribes."

Such citizens had considerable rights: from their parents and ancestors they inherited not only "wealth" but also "honors" and "good reputations"; in short, they were able "to live with the esteem of their fellow men and women." All the others, being born outside of Christian marriage, were simply "natural and not legitimate" and did not enjoy the same rights. This arrangement inevitably affected all converts *(conversos),* whether from the Jewish religion (the "Marranos") or from the Muslim religion (the "Moriscos"). Since they were born of non-Christian marriages, they remained legally "illegitimate" for life, even though they had received baptism. Only their children, when born of a Christian marriage, acquired legitimacy.

This legal situation, already distressing, was further aggravated by the presence, in the midst of genuine converts, of "Judaizers," or Jews who pretended a conversion to Christianity. This phenomenon became overt and worrying precisely at the beginning of the fifteenth century. During the tragic persecution of Jews that began in Seville in 1391, spread quickly to other cities, and produced thousands of victims, very many Jews who wanted to protect themselves against this and other foreseeable massacres asked for and received baptism en masse. They were, of course, not convinced Christians but secretly Jews or, as they came to be called in their own language, *anuzim,* "the forced."

It is necessary now to look at this complicated socio-religious map from the viewpoint of the Church and in the light of fifteenth-century Spanish theology. Let us begin with the Muslims. Insofar as they were a political community, that is, as the kingdom of Granada, the Church regarded them as enemies to be overthrown "even with the material sword." There was, however, a different attitude to the Mudéjars, or Muslims who remained in the reconquered territories; scattered as these were, here and there in distant localities along the frontier and usually occupied in lowly rural trades, they did not create any problems, either political or social. It may be said that in the Christian society they were not opposed *(adversi)* but simply different *(diversi)* by reason of their religious origin.

The Church and the theology of the time endeavored to remove even this "difference" through preaching and doctrinal debates, that is, by using the "sword of the spirit." There was an abundant literature in the service of this goal. As we have seen, burning issues in anti-Muslim polemics, such as the Trinity, the incarnation, and predestination, were discussed by James Moxena and Martin of Córdoba, among others. In order to facilitate knowledge of Muslim teaching and a peaceful dialogue in these discussions, John of Segovia wrote two works, today unfortunately lost: *Corano trilingue* (in Arabic, Latin, and Castilian) and *De mittendo gladio spiritus in corda Sarracenorum.* Also to be noted is the odd and little-known anonymous

Castilian adaptation, dating back to the beginning of the fifteenth century, of the *Dialogus de elementis catholicae fidei,* which Arnold of Villanueva had written a century before for the king of Aragon "for the education of his children." In the Latin text the disciple is called *dominus* ("Master"), but in the Castilian translation he becomes a "Moor," a clear sign that in the new version the work was intended for the instruction of the Mudéjars or the Moriscos.[35]

The presence of Jews was a more complicated and worrying matter. Unlike the Mudéjars, the Jews would change from mere *diversi* to *adversi.* Being employed by the dominant minority (king and nobles) as political and administrative advisers and usually as collectors of public taxes and lenders of capital at very high rates of interest, they could not avoid being regarded as responsible for serious, unremitting social injustices. The popular masses, who were the immediate victims of these injustices, responded with hatred and not infrequently with dreadful and uncontrollable massacres. The massacre of 1391 showed that the breakup of a state of peaceful coexistence was henceforth unavoidable. In addition to the social problem, which had been dragging on for a long time, there now arose, as I mentioned earlier, the religious problem created by the "Judaizers," who seriously undermined the credibility of authentic conversions and the identity of the Church, to the point where modern scholars have spoken of a "Marrano religion."

Coming now to the reaction of the Spanish church, let me say right off that it seems to have been more theological than practical, unlike what happened in Italy, for example, where the "Monti di Pietà" (credit banks) were established. But even if the reaction was perhaps less effective, it was nonetheless intense and fruitful in the areas both of preaching and of theological controversy. I shall limit myself here to some examples.

First place among the preachers undoubtedly goes to St. Vincent Ferrer. His fiery, apocalyptic words helped to stop the wave of terror that had spread almost everywhere after the events of 1391 and brought many Jews into the Church. A contemporary of the Dominican apostle was Blessed Matthew of Agrigento, an Italian Franciscan who deserves mention here for his effective preaching to the Jews in Valencia and Barcelona.[36] In the second half of the century, and still in the East, James Pérez of Valencia distinguished himself not only as a university professor but also as preacher and inquisitor; in Castile there was a quite similar personage in Alphonsus of Espina. These examples should not cause us to forget that during the fifteenth century preaching to the people was carried on by countless members of reformed religious communities, which were flourishing increasingly. From among the secular clergy I shall cite only one person who will serve to show the lively concern to preach to the Jews: Paul of Heredia (+ ca. 1490), a cleric, a convert from Judaism, "enfeebled" and "quite learned in the Hebrew language," who in 1489 asked Pope Innocent VIII for authorization "to preach the word of God in all places."[37]

It is worth at least referring to the doctrinal content of this preaching "to the Jews." Generally speaking, in the sermons of St. Vincent and those of Pérez of Valencia biblical themes predominate, especially the fulfillment of the messianic promises in Christ. Also biblical in subject matter but focused on the exaltation of the Name of Jesus (written as the monogram IHS) were the sermons which Matthew of Agrigento preached in Barcelona and Valencia, following the example of St. Bernardine of Siena; Alphonsus of Espina introduced the same theme into Castile. But the burning socioeconomic questions were also discussed in the pulpit; a good proof of this is the fact that in Segovia, where there was a sizable Jewish community, the Dominicans possessed two collections of sermons of St. Bernardine of Siena, *De restitutione* and *De contractis et usuris;* the Franciscans of the same city had another, *De restitutionibus,* a copy of which was made in 1474 by a young friar who took it with him to other convents of Old Castile.[38]

Anti-Jewish controversy was no less intense at the theological level. It developed in two directions. During the first half of the century the focus was above all on the question of the equality between old Christians and new Christians. It is to be remarked that the active participants on the Catholic side of the debates with the Jews were all, or almost all, converts of Jewish origin.

The debate on messianism reached its high point right at the beginning of the century in the Disputation of Tortosa (February 7, 1413, to November 13, 1414); this was probably the most important and longest doctrinal meeting held between Jews and Christians. Benedict XIII called for it and several times presided over it himself; it had as participants, on the Catholic side, the recently converted Jerome of the Holy Faith, and on the Jewish side, sixteen of the most qualified rabbis of the Jewish communities in the kingdom of Aragon. Both sides could count on a number of well-prepared supporters. The sessions were public and solemn and were usually attended by many spectators (between two and three thousand).

The subject of the debate was unvarying: Has the Messiah come, or has he not? In these discussions, the standard-bearer of the Christians, Jerome of the Holy Faith, played the lion's part. As in a duel, he chose the weapons which his interlocutors could not reject: the Old Testament, the Talmud, the books of the synagogue, the Midrashim, and even the Cabala; in the light of the prophetic literature and hewing to a literal exegesis, he expounded twenty-four conditions which were to determine the coming of the Messiah, and then demonstrated that all of them had been fulfilled in Jesus. He concluded: The Messiah has already come. The rabbis denied this, and he repeated, The Messiah has already come. And so it went for twenty months.

No official agreement was reached, but in practice the discussions did very serious damage to the Jews, both in their faith and in their public credibility. Even before the end of the sessions some rabbis and other influential Jews surrendered and asked for baptism; subsequently, many others followed their example.

Jerome of the Holy Faith handed on his own arguments to posterity in his book *Hebraeomastix*.

Although it might have seemed that the subject of the Messiah's coming had been exhaustively discussed, other apologetic writings on the same theme continued to appear. The most important was undoubtedly the *Scrutinium Scripturarum* of Paul of Saint Mary; it went through six printings in the fifteenth century. Also deserving of mention is the *Zelus Christi,* authored by Peter de la Caballería, a descendant of one of the most influential families that had converted during the Disputation of Tortosa; there were also the *Ensis Pauli* of Paul of Heredia as well as other writings of El Tostado.

In 1449 a riot broke out among the people in Toledo in which the Marranos were involved. As a result, the authorities of that city issued a condemnatory statute, according to which the *conversos* were declared "infamous, ineligible, incompetent, and disqualified" from holding any office or benefit, public or private, in the city. This would mark the start of the well-known inquiries into "purity of blood."

The hateful distinction between old Christians and new Christians became henceforth the key question in theological controversy. The most eminent personages in the Church and among the theologians at once attacked the "Toledo Condemnation." Among them were Cardinal John of Torquemada, who in that same year, 1149, obtained from Nicholas V the bull *Humani generis inimicus* and himself wrote a *Tractatus contra madianitas et ismaelitas;* Alphonsus of Cartagena, who wrote his *Defensorium unitatis christianae;* Bishop Lope of Barrientos prepared a treatise *Contra algunos zizañadores de la nación de los convertidos del pueblo de Israel;* Alphonsus of Oropesa wrote his *Lumen ad revelationem gentium;* and at the end of the century Fernand of Talavera published a *Católica impugnación.*

Both the papal bull and the authors mentioned were in agreement that the undiscriminating distinction made by the Condemnation of Toledo was anti-Christian and unjust. Their arguments were well founded and persuasive; in contrast, the arguments made by the defenders of the distinction, though doctrinally very weak, were supported by the heated social climate and ended up being de facto accepted in the statutes concerning "purity of blood." Alphonsus of Espina's book *Fortalitium fidei* was to contribute not a little to maintaining the atmosphere of suspicion of the *conversos.*

C. Theology and Heterodoxy

In fifteenth-century Spain there were no heresies of major significance, like that of John Wyclif in England or John Huss in Bohemia. There were not lacking here and there, however, isolated cases of deviations in faith and in orthopraxis. I shall mention only a few of these.

1. Anselm Turmeda

Born in Palma de Mallorca around 1352, Anselm appears as already a Franciscan in 1375; he studied first at the University of Lérida and, beginning in 1378, spent ten years at the University of Bologna and visited other cities of Italy. In 1387/88 he embraced the Muslim religion in Tunis and ostentatiously abjured his former faith in the presence of several Christians whom the king had summoned for the occasion. The motive for his apostasy does not seem to have been of a moral kind (as has hitherto been maintained) but was intellectual; scholars speak of possible Averroist influences brought to bear on him during his long stay in Italy. In any case, because of his decisive and sensational act as well as because of his reputation as a scholar, Anselm won not only the esteem of the king but responsible offices in the palace itself.

Some writings of his are known: (a) *Disputa dell'Asino;* (b) a collection of prophecies; (c) *Llibre dels bons amonestaments;* (d) *La Tuhfa,* or autobiography; and others.

Not satisfied with apostatizing, Anselm fought bitterly against Christianity, especially in his *Disputa dell'Asino;* in an attractive style he popularized the usual arguments of Muslim attacks on Christians.

In his lifetime he also succeeded in creating a somewhat legendary image of himself in the Western world; there were reports that he returned to the Church and even died a martyr. What is certain is that on September 22, 1412, after receiving a petition from him, Benedict XIII in the bull *Pium misericordis* absolved him from the guilt of apostasy and from the punishments for it and granted him permission to move freely in Christian territories. Today, however, we know that he died a Muslim around 1494.[39]

2. The Heretics of Durango

This was a sect that arose at mid-century in the little town of Durango (Biscay) in northern Spain. Its leader was Fray Alphonsus de Mella, born in Zamora and brother of Cardinal John de Mella. He belonged to the Franciscan Observantine movement and was probably in Italy when in 1434 some of his heterodox sermons caused a Roman commission of cardinals to sentence him to ten years of imprisonment in the Franciscan convent of Santa Maria del Monte in Perugia. Perhaps through the offices of his brother he obtained from Eugene IV a remission of the punishment. But in the years that followed, until 1438, he earned various other condemnations, again because of his sermons. Around 1442 we find him at the head of a large group of persons in Durango (most of them women) who fervently attended his sermons. As a result of some denunciations the public authorities intervened, but Fray Alphonsus, accompanied by his brother, Fray Guillén, and (it is said) by a large number of women, took refuge in the territory of the Moors. From there he wrote a lengthy letter to John II of Castile justifying his action and referring vaguely to his ideas. It seems that steps were taken against his followers who had stayed behind in Durango; there are reports even of death sentences.

Neither the ancient chroniclers nor modern historians seem to have managed to determine precisely the scope and nature of this sect. The chroniclers speak in general terms of a "great heresy." Opinions of its nature are divided: some think of the Fraticelli, others of Joachimism, or the sect of the Free Spirit, or precursors of Luther, and so on. In my opinion, both the facts and teachings regarding the so-called heretics of Durango need to be reexamined more carefully.[40]

3. Alphonsus González of Córdoba

Alphonsus was imprisoned on grounds of having written a book that contained errors in matters of faith; he defended himself, claiming he had bought the book through another without knowing its contents. Nicholas V intervened in the case on November 23, 1451.[41] We are unable to say anything further about the nature of the heresy or about its supposed author.

4. Peter Martínez of Osma

I have already spoken of this outstanding professor of Salamanca. His errors had to do with sacramental confession, penance, and indulgences, subjects with which he dealt for the first time in his *Tractatus de confessione,* published probably in 1476. The treatise seems to have anticipated the ninety-five theses of Martin Luther, not only in its teaching but also in the circumstances that led to its writing: it was offered as a critical response to the hasty announcement by the pope of a plenary indulgence for the Holy Year, 1475.

In summary, the author maintained the following theses: (1) the forgiveness of sins and the remission of the temporal punishments for it derive solely from contrition, which amounts to saying from a process that involves directly and exclusively God and the human person, without any mediation by the Church; (2) sacramental confession and absolution were not instituted by Christ but were introduced by the Church and can therefore be changed, not however, by the pope alone but by the universal Church; (3) the power of the keys that is granted to the Church does not extend to the direct relationships between God and human beings but only to the external order of the Church; (4) therefore, the Church cannot act as mediator in the forgiveness of sins nor can it remit, through indulgences, the temporal punishments of the living and the dead.

The theses of the elderly professor immediately gave rise to debates for and against throughout Spain. Among those who attacked him, in addition to the already mentioned Dominican John López, I may mention Salamanca theologian Peter Ximénez of Présamo, author of a *Confutatorium errorum contra claves Ecclesiae nuper editorum.* Martínez of Osma answered the accusations of his adversaries with *Quotlibet de confessione.*

The seriousness of the issue required, however, the intervention of the ecclesiastical authorities. The theses of the Salamanca theologian were condemned by the Inquisition of Saragossa in 1478; in May 1479 by a synod convoked at Alcalá by the archbishop of Toledo in which over sixty theologians took part; and finally, by Pope Sixtus IV in a bull on the subject dated August 9, 1479. From then on, the name of Peter Martínez of Osma appears in all the collections of decisions by the ecclesiastical magisterium. Peter died the following year, after having withdrawn his teaching.

V. Spanish Theology in the Context of Fifteenth-Century Europe

The preceding pages may have given the impression that the directions taken by fifteenth-century Spanish theology were decided solely by the need to give answers to the internal problems of the country: reconquest and controversies with the Saracens and with the Jews and their *conversos.* It is therefore fitting that I also describe the Spanish theology of this period in a European perspective, taking as points of reference two very important ecclesial events: the Council of Constance and the Council of Basel-Ferrara-Florence.

A. Spanish Doctrinal Presence at the Council of Constance

For reasons of ecclesiastical policy, the representatives of the several Spanish kingdoms were the last to arrive at the Council of Constance (1414–18). Aragon and Navarre gave their support to it on December 24, 1416; Castile only on June 18, 1417. From that point on, the Spaniards evidently had the possibility of influencing the decisions of the council by means of their votes.[42] For the most part, however, the questions were juridical and purely matters of protocol.

Much more important, however, for the history of theology are two subjects—hitherto studied only little or not at all—which, oddly enough, connected Spain with the council even before the official arrival of the Spaniards in Constance: recourse to the Visigothic conciliar tradition as a model, and the Spanish contribution to the condemnation of Huss.

1. The Visigothic Conciliar Tradition at Constance

At the very beginning of the first session, November 16, 1414, the fathers of Constance decided that as far as procedure was concerned, "we should have recourse to the practices of the ancient Fathers, which are best gathered from the canon of the Council of Toledo, the contents of which we have decided should be inserted here." And they cited Canon 1 of the Eleventh Council of Toledo (675).

We know also that the session of March 26, 1415, began with the prayer *Adsumus, Domine sancte Spiritus* and with the exhortation *Ecce sanctissimi sacerdotes,* with which the records of the national councils of Toledo began and which were then taken into the collection of Pseudo-Isidorean Decretals known as the *Collectio Hispanica.*

In this connection, we must bear in mind that from the Third Council (589) to the Eighteenth and last (702) the famous Councils of Toledo were convened by the king, who presided at the opening and presented the *tomus* or *desiderata* that in fact provided the agenda, and at the end by his own authority confirmed the conciliar decrees, which thus became laws of the Visigothic kingdom. The circumstances that led to and accompanied the Council of Constance were not dissimilar. Although convoked by John XXIII, the pope elected at Pisa, the council was desired and imposed by Emperor Sigismund, whose role in the conduct of the council became even more necessary from March 21, 1415, on, when John XXIII left Constance in headlong flight. It was Sigismund who kept the council unified: it was by his will and in his presence that the earlier-mentioned session presided over by Cardinal Peter d'Ailly was celebrated five days later.

I think it can be said that Sigismund was quite familiar with the Visigothic conciliar tradition. I offer two examples in confirmation. The first is a lengthy letter that a group of council fathers, who remained anonymous, wrote to Sigismund around mid-January 1415 to encourage him, who had barely arrived in Constance, to keep the council going without any indecision. As though to justify their action, at one point the signers introduced this statement: "And he who gives good counsel has support in the present life and will obtain the reward of an everlasting repayment"; although the source is not cited, it is from chapter 5 of the Ninth Council of Toledo (655). The second example is another anonymous document, probably drawn up by the same group of individuals, which lists the duties of the emperor in regard to the reform and peace of the Church. Oddly enough, the duties are identical, even in their verbal formulation, with those which Recared, king of the Visigoths, reserved to himself in his opening address at the Third Council of Toledo (589).

If these ancient texts were used as models in this fashion without even naming the source, it is obvious that they must have been well known to all, including Emperor Sigismund. The further conclusion can be drawn that in following a teaching and practice of incontrovertible antiquity, the council fathers of Constance showed themselves, at least in this area, less "innovators" than modern historians still continue to believe.[43]

2. The Intervention of Spain in the Condemnation of John Huss

The bitter experiences of John Huss of Bohemia at Constance are well known. The master from Prague came to the council at its beginning after being guaranteed personal immunity by a safe-conduct pass issued by Sigismund; but before the latter came himself to Constance, Huss was imprisoned on November 28, 1414, by order of the cardinals then present in the city of the council; then, when Sigismund's resistance had at last been overcome, Huss was condemned by the entire council on July 6, 1415, and sent to the stake.

As far as Spain's participation in the trial of Huss was concerned, two interventions are to be noted: (1) on the very day of Huss' imprisonment, November 28, James Moxena, perhaps the only Spaniard present at Constance as a rebel against Benedict XIII, was sent by the cardinals to interview Huss in jail "to . . . investigate Master [Huss]"; (2) on March 27, 1415, Ferdinand I, king of Aragon, wrote "in his own hand" a very harsh letter to Sigismund entreating him not to prevent but even to consent to this "false Christian" (Huss) being immediately condemned as he deserved.

Both interventions are well known to historians of the Council of Constance, although they have hitherto been studied only in relation to their political influence and to their more or less effective role in bringing about Huss' tragic end. Leaving aside these aspects, which are secondary, I would like to call attention to an aspect that was much more important for the history of theology: the doctrinal basis of the denunciation of Huss by both Fray James and King Ferdinand.

The stages in the dialogue between Moxena and Huss on that November 28 were reported by John of Chlum, a knight of Prague who was also present in the cell, to a young theologian and disciple of Huss, Peter Mladenovice, and included by the latter in the *Relatio de magistro Ioanne Hus* that was published for the first time at Wittenberg in 1537 with a preface by Martin Luther.

Fray James, pretending to be a simpleminded friar, began the interrogation with a question which everyone was asking about Huss, both in Prague and at Constance: "Do you maintain and assert, as people claim, that after the words of consecration the material bread remains in the sacrament of the altar?" James asked the question three times. But when he saw that Huss was being evasive in his answers, he changed the subject and straightway advanced to the question of the hypostatic union: "Of what nature is the union of the divinity with the humanity in Christ?" Huss lost control and began speaking in Czech to his companion: the friar (he said) seems simple and ignorant, but "he is not extremely simple, since he asks a very profound question."

The reason for Huss' discomfort was, however, not so much that he had to speak about "a very profound question" as that he saw all of his teaching being brought into very dangerous proximity to the doctrine of the hypostatic union, a central theme of Catholic dogma. Finally Huss calmed down and seemed to have answered the question, but we do not know how he formulated it, since Mladenovice preferred not to report it. We know, however, that Fray James abruptly ended the questioning and left convinced that Huss was in serious and stubborn error on the incarnation.

In fact, in the letter of March 28, 1415, which Ferdinand signed but which was undoubtedly dictated down to its least details by his "ambassador" in Constance, the error on the incarnation is precisely the only charge brought against Huss. In the words of St. Peter (2 Pet 2:1), both Huss and his teachers and followers are called "lying teachers" because "they deny the Lord who paid the price for them." The nature and seriousness of the heresy are further attested by five other New Testament texts (Matt 28:7; Rom 11:20; Titus 3:10-11; 1 John 2:28; 2 John 1:10-11). The error regarding the incarnation of the Word obviously could not but affect the doctrine of the Trinity, and the letter refers to this by citing a lengthy passage from the Old Testament (Deut 13:6-9) that calls for the death penalty for anyone promoting idolatry, that is, anyone who draws the people away from worship of the true God, the God of the fathers, which amounts to saying, the one and triune God.

It is of interest to us here to note that among the errors charged to Huss on July 6, 1415, before the death sentence was passed, were these two: (1) "The two natures, the divinity and the humanity, are one Christ"[44]; (2) "[It has] likewise [been attested] by a doctor of theology who says he heard from Huss' own mouth that he maintained the following: that the substance of the bread remains in the sacrament of the altar after the consecration. And he added that he also heard, during a disputation presided over by a certain Master Richard, that John Huss had agreed he was a person in the Godhead and there were more persons in God than three." The appearance of these two articles in the final list is puzzling for two reasons: they were not discussed during the trial, and they express trinitarian and christological propositions that were not really a part of Huss' theology. But Huss himself was the first to be surprised, especially by the second of these articles. After hearing the article read, he lost his control again and cried out in anger: "Name the doctor who testified against me on this point!" I myself am convinced that he was thinking at that moment of the "not extremely simple" friar who had questioned him in jail on November 28, 1414.

Earlier in this chapter I attributed to Fray James Moxena some *Cantilenae in Dei servitium*. The first four of them are a clear refutation of the three errors mentioned in the two articles: errors on transubstantiation, on the incarnation, and on the Trinity. Moreover, the very structure of the four *Cantilenae* shows that the christological error is central and the source of the other two; this idea, we know, was from the very beginning a fixed point of reference for Fray James. In the present context, however, I think it appropriate to ask on what basis he judged the teaching of Huss in function of the hypostatic union if it be true, as De Vooght remarks, that christology was not an organic part of Huss' teaching.

In my opinion, an answer to this question might be seen in the fact that Fray James, *subtilissimus theologus* (a most precise theologian), judged Huss not so much on the basis of his own writings as on the basis of those of his two teachers, whose spiritual heir and assiduous defender all considered him to be, namely, John Wyclif and Stanislas Znojmo. Now the first of the 260 errors for which Wyclif was condemned and which were well known at Constance starts from a denial of the hypostatic union in order then to deny the transubstantiation of the bread into the Body of Christ: "Just as Christ is God and man at the same time, so the consecrated bread is at the same time the body of Christ and true bread. . . . It is Christ's body at least *in figure* and true bread *in nature,* or . . . it is true bread naturally and Christ's body *figuratively*" (article 1, emphases added).

In like manner, the bringing together of the Trinity and transubstantiation in the second of Huss' condemned articles (the one that stirred his anger) is echoed in the teaching of Znojmo, who establishes an analogy between the transformation of every just person into a kind of god in virtue of grace, even while the person remains human, and the transformation ("transubstantiation") of the consecrated bread into the Body of Christ, even while it remains bread: "*Just as* in the fatherland the human being, while keeping its human nature, is through its beatification *completely transformed into God* and through it *is more incomparably God through participation . . . so . . .* it is possible that bread, while remaining bread in its proper nature . . . is transubstantiated into the body of Christ and becomes and afterwards is incomparably more the body of Christ through its sanctification . . . than it remains bread by its nature."

Thus Fray Diego did not lack for excuses, real or dialectical, for connecting the teaching of Huss with a denial of the fontal principle of Catholic dogma. In so doing, he showed himself to be not only an able dialectician but a formidable strategist; he knew that by shifting his adversary onto trinitarian and christological ground he could base his own criticism on the authority of the Eastern and Visigothic councils of the fifth to the seventh centuries, which had defined what the profession of faith in the Trinity and the incarnation was to be. And in fact we have the impression that Fray Diego made extensive use of these early documents both in the *Cantilenae* and in the letter which he inspired and Ferdinand signed. The need for brevity prevents me from going into details here, but it will nonetheless be appropriate to give two or three examples that will confirm the impression.

Let me begin with Ferdinand's letter to Sigismund. Some verbal and conceptual figures seem to hark back to the text and context of the *Tomus Leonis* (449), that is, the letter, later accepted by the Council of Chalcedon (451), in which Leo I rebuked the patriarch of Constantinople for his passivity in condemning the christological errors of Eutyches:

Tomus Leonis	Letter of Ferdinand
I am amazed that such an absurd and corrupt declaration of faith was not very severely censured by the *judges*	*I am amazed* at Your great Majesty . . . that one whom God has *judged* is not punished.
Therefore . . . we remind you, dearest brother, of your charity's *responsibility* . . .	*Therefore,* most serene prince, I ask you to punish *immediately* . . .
But when he had refused to be party to the anathematising of his wicked doctrine, your fraternity would have realised that he was *persisting in his false belief and that he deserved* a verdict of condemnation.	[Huss] who continually offends by his ongoing heresy, from which he has not turned away. . . . But *he persists in his wickedness*. . . . He certainly *deserves* punishment.

On the other hand, other verbal and conceptual elements of the letter suggest the Second Council of Constantinople or the "Three Chapters" (553), which Emperor Justinian convoked in order to condemn the christological errors and the very persons of Theodore of Mopsuestia, Theodoret of Cyr, and Ibas of Edessa.

Three Chapters	Letter of Ferdinand
Teachings . . . *full of darkness* *The Church of God* . . . further disturbed	words *full of darkness.*
Teach false doctrines *We were astonished* Since the Lord declares that the person is already *judged*	*False teachers* *I am astonished* Whom God *judged*
Were *straightway* burned up by divine fire	Let him be punished *straightway*
To the Apostle when he writes: "As for someone who is factious, after admonishing him once or twice, have nothing more to do with him (evita), knowing that such a person is perverted and sinful (perversus est et peccat); he is self-condemned"	*Through the Apostle when he writes:* "As for someone who is factious, after admonishing him once or twice, have nothing more to do with him (devita), knowing that he has been overthrown (subversus) and has done wrong (deliquit), being condemned by his own sentence.

Let me turn now to the *Cantilenae*. It is not an exaggeration to say that we will not find a single verse in them that does not direct us, through verbal or conceptual images, to the conciliar sources of which I have spoken. Simply by way of an example, let us look quickly at the third strophe of the fourth *Cantilena:*

> Each of the aforesaid
> is properly called "God,"
> but a plurality of gods
> is utterly denied;
> in this way *(hoc modo),* the true faith
> of Christians is maintained *(verificatur);*
> the wickedness of heretics
> is forever put to flight.

Verses 1–4 are a reply to the trinitarian error attributed to Huss; very similar words and concepts are to be found in the creed of the Eleventh Council of Toledo (675): "*Each* person is fully God; *each* individually is called God . . . while all three persons are called one God"; "one name is appropriate to the Trinity by its nature, so that there can be no *plural* in the three persons"; "but, the fact that we have said there are two natures in the Son does not allow us to speak of two persons in him, *nor does there seem to be—God forbid!—any quaternity in the Trinity*" (recall the accusation that had Huss maintaining a "*fourth* person"). A passage of Isidore's *Etymologiae* (PL 82:271C), which that council used as one of its main sources, reads: "The divinity is not tripled . . . because if it is, we introduced a *plurality of gods.*"

Verse 5 is taken from the fourteenth anathema of the Second Council of Constantinople: "Holy Cyril preached *the true faith of Christians.*" By way of completing this citation, verse 6 takes us back to the Second Letter of Cyril to Nestorius, which the Council of Ephesus accepted: "This is the account *(protestatur)* of *the true faith.* So *(in hoc sensu)* we shall find *(comperimus)* that the holy fathers believed." Note the correspondence between *in hoc modo* and *in hoc sensu,* and between *verificatur,* in the one case, and *protestatur* and *comperimus,* in the other.

Verses 7–8 sum up the christological meaning of the entire strophe in a happy image: "the wickedness of heretics" *(pravitas haereticorum)* was a technical formula referring not to just any heresy, but to the heresy, or set of heresies, against the divinity or humanity of Christ. It was coined by Leo the Great in connection with the faith professed by Peter: "You are the Christ, the Son of the living God" (Matt 16:16), on which Leo comments: "This is the faith that overcomes the devil. . . . So strongly is it fortified by God that the wickedness of heretics *(haeretica pravitas)* has been unable to corrupt it, or the faithlessness of the pagans overcome it." Pope Leo uses the same formula in his *Tomus.*

Equipped as he was with these theological tools, Fray James could not but expect a victory, which took concrete form in the condemnation of Huss immediately after that of Wyclif, on July 6, 1415. Three days later, on July 9, James hastened to send the news to Ferdinand: "The professors of heretical teachings have been committed to the fire."[45]

B. The Doctrinal Presence of Spain
at the Council of Basel-Ferrara-Florence-Rome (1431–45)

Few councils have had a more troubled history than the seventeenth ecumenical council, which began in Basel in 1431 and was transferred to Ferrara in 1437, to Florence in 1439, and finally to Rome in 1443. We may recall, in addition, that some fathers who were part of the council during its Basel period held a council of their own (1438–49), which, among other things, deposed Eugene IV (1431–47) and proclaimed Amadeus VIII of Savoy as pope with the name of Felix V (+ 1451), the last antipope in the history of the Church.

The Spanish kingdoms, like the other European states, took an active part in the council, especially during its first phase in Basel, by sending ambassadors, attorneys, and other experts in large numbers; the participants from Castile alone were about 130 in all. Spanish theology was thus well represented in the principal controversies of the council, such as those having to do with conciliarism, papal primacy, union with the Oriental Church, and, finally, the Immaculate Conception of Mary. I shall limit myself here to naming a few theologians who took part in each of these controversies.

Conciliarism, which had been ratified at the Council of Constance, had its strongest defenders present in Basel right from the beginning and especially, as is obvious, after a section of the participants turned schismatic. Conciliarism was embraced in its most radical form by John of Segovia and by two Franciscans, Bartholomew of Pelegrin, titular bishop of Hebron, and Andrew of Maluenda, master of theology. Segovia, who was one of the most dogged promotors of the schism, wrote, in addition to the works mentioned earlier, a treatise *De auctoritate Ecclesiae,* which was known also under the title *De insuperabili sanctitate et summa auctoritate generalium conciliorum.*

In reaction to the extreme defense of conciliarism, there was a strong movement in favor of the authority of the supreme pontiff, which had a skilled champion in the Spanish Dominican John of Torquemada, one of the most outstanding theologians of his age. From 1433 until his death (1468) he fought unwearyingly against conciliarism in his activities and by his writings. His ideas on the subjects had already been fully expressed in the addresses he prepared for the second Diet of Nuremberg (1438) and the Congress of Mainz (1439).

In his first address he developed three fundamental themes: the monarchical nature of the Church, the full power of the pope, and finally, the authority of the pope as the source of the other forms of ecclesiastical authority. In this final section, in order to establish with clarity the guidelines for the struggle against conciliarism, he set down ten theses, in which he drew on the practice of the early Church and on the teaching of the Fathers, councils, and theologians. In them he demonstrated that on his own authority the pope can, first of all, define those truths that are "matters of faith" and that it is solely in virtue of his authority that the fathers assembled in a general council have the right and power "to establish canons and define propositions." It is also within the competence of the pope alone to convoke, transfer, and break off general councils and to approve or quash their decisions.

In his address to the Congress of Mainz, Torquemada gave a detailed proof of the infallibility of the pope (he used the word *infallibilitas*) and returned again to the subject of the pope's authority, in relation this time not only to councils but to the entire Church. On this subject he developed the following three theses: (1) the pope is pastor of the Lord's entire flock; (2) he is head of the Mystical Body of Christ; (3) he is the leading member *(princeps)* of the universal Church and of the entire Christian people.

On his return from Germany the fearless Dominican took part in the Council of Florence and, among other things, delivered a great address that prepared the way for the conciliar bull *Moyses vir Dei* of September 4, 1439, against the schismatics in Basel. The ecclesiological ideas which Torquemada had maintained during the lively period of the council were incorporated into his *Summa de Ecclesia,* which he completed around 1450 and which was to become during the modern period a theological classic on the primacy and infallibility of the pope.

Torquemada was also the Spanish theologian most involved in the discussions with the Greeks at the Council of Florence: he wrote a treatise on the doctrine of the Eucharist, took part in the preparation (from June 28 to July 4, 1439) of the final text of the bull of union, and finally, used his ecclesiological ideas to challenge the claims of the Orientals regarding Roman primacy.[46] Mention is also to be made, along with Torquemada, of another Spaniard who played a less important role: Fray Gonzalo of Valbuena, titular bishop of Granada; we do not have any theological writings of his.

Finally, both before and after the schism, the Council of Basel dealt with the "troubled question" of the Immaculate Conception of the Virgin Mary. On September 17, 1438, the council issued a decree "defining" the doctrine and establishing the feast of this Marian privilege for the entire Church. Among the foremost champions of the decree was the already mentioned John of Segovia, with an extensive treatise entitled *Septem allegationes et totidem avisamenta . . . circa sacratissimae Virginis Mariae immaculatam conceptionem.*[47] In the interests of historical accuracy it should be noted, however, that the decree of Basel was not something entirely new, as has sometimes been claimed. On the doctrinal side, the treatise *Liber de conceptu virginali,* which I have attributed to James of Moxena, had already maintained the Immaculate Conception of Mary as a truth of faith and not as a mere "pious opinion."[48] On the liturgical side it is to be recalled that the Marian confraternity, which had its center in the royal palace of Barcelona, had begun a campaign on November 7, 1415, to have the Council of Constance decree the celebration of the feast of the Immaculate Conception for the entire Church.[49] These petitions, to which the Council of Constance gave no ear, would have their effect at the Council of Basel, even if the decree was issued during the schismatic phase.

VI. Some Conclusions

It seems possible to draw some conclusions from the necessarily schematic exposition that I have tried to sketch in this chapter:

1. From the cultural viewpoint, we have today a much more positive view of fifteenth-century Spain than the one current in the time of Menéndez Pelayo, a century ago.

2. The theological works produced in this century were perhaps superior, in numbers, to those of the preceding centuries.

3. The work of the theologians was marked by some of the signs of modernity: a discreet use of the vernaculars (Castilian and Catalan), a return to early Church sources, expositions in the form of dialogues and even novels, participation of laypersons, and so on.

4. As far as its content went, fifteenth-century Spanish theology devoted itself to answering the most urgent and current problems of the Church and of society at both the national and European levels.

5. It can be said, in summary, that the work of theologians in this period was herald and precursor of the mature theology of Spain's golden age.

BIBLIOGRAPHY

I

Bulario de la Universidad de Salamanca (1219–1549). Ed. V. Beltrán de Heredia. 2 vols. Salamanca, 1966–67.

Cancionero de Juan Alfonso de Baena. Critical ed. J. M. Azáceta. 2 vols. Madrid, 1966.

Cartulario de la Universidad de Salamanca. Ed. V. Beltrán de Heredia. 6 vols. Salamanca, 1970–73.

Miscelánea Beltrán de Heredia. Colección de artículos sobre Historia de la Teología española. 4 vols. Salamanca, 1972–73.

Repertorio de Historia de la Ciencias eclesiásticas en España. 7 vols. Instituto de Historia de la teología española 1–7. Salamanca, 1967–79.

Farinelli, A. *Italia e Spagna.* 2 vols. Turin, 1929.

García Oro, J. *La reforma de los religiosos españoles en tiempo de los Reyes Católicos.* Valladolid, 1969.

_____. *Cisneros y la reforma del clero español en tiempo de los Reyes Católicos.* Madrid, 1971.

Haebler, K. *Bibliografía ibérica del siglo XV.* 2 vols. Uppsala, 1908.

Izbicki, T. M. "A Collection of Ecclesiological Manuscripts in the Vatican Library: Vat. lat. 4106–4193." *Miscellanea Bibliothecae Apostolicae Vaticanae* 4 (Vatican City, 1990) 89–129.

Jorge Aragones, M. *Los movimientos y luchas sociales en la baja edad media.* Madrid, 1949.

Madurell i Marimón, J. M. "Antiguas ediciones de libros de autores eclesiásticos. Notas documentales." *Analecta sacra tarraconensia* 43 (1970) 97–182.

_____. "Regesta documental de biblias manuscritas e impresas (1336–1600)." Ibid., 47 (1974) 27–63.

Mendoza Negrillo, J. de D. *Fortuna y providencia en la literatura castellana del siglo XV.* Anejos del Boletín de la Real Academia Española 27. Madrid, 1973.

Reinhardt, K., and H. Santiago-Otero. *Biblioteca bíblica ibérica medieval.* Medievalia et humanistica 1. Madrid, 1986.

Schiff, M. *La bibliothèque du Marquis de Santillane.* Paris, 1905.

Suárez Fernández, L. *Nobleza y monarquía. Puntos de vista sobre la historia castellana del siglo XV.* Valladolid, 1959.

_____, A. Canellas Lopez, and J. Vicens Vives. "Los Trastámaras del siglo XV." *Historia de España* 15. Ed. R. Menénde Pidal. Madrid, 1982[3].

Tarsicio de Azcona. *La elección y reforma del episcopado español en tiempo de los Reyes Católicos.* Madrid, 1960.

_____. *Isabel la Católica. Estudio crítico de su vida y su reinado.* BAC 237. Madrid, 1964.

Vicens Vives, J. *Aproximación a la historia de España.* Barcelona, 1952.

II

Alcocer Martínez, M. *Historia de la Universidad de Valladolid.* 2 vols. Valladolid, 1918–25.

Andrés, M. *Historia de la Teología en España.* I. *Las instituciones (1470–1570).* Rome, 1962.

Aviles, M. "La teología española en el siglo XV." *Historia de la teología española* I. Madrid, 1983. Pp. 495–577.

Beltrán de Heredia, V. "Los dominicos y la enseñanza de la Teología en las catedrales del reino de Aragón." *Estudis franciscans* 34 (1934) 38–58.

_____. "La Universidad de Palencia." *Semana pro Ecclesia et Patria de Palencia.* Palencia, 1935. Pp. 215–43.

_____. *Historia de la reforma de la provincia dominicana de España (1450–1550).* Rome, 1939.

_____. "La formación intelectual del clero según nuestra antica legislación canónica (s. XIV–XV)." *Escorial* 3 (1941) 289–98.

_____. "La facultad de Teología en la Universidad de Sigüenza." *RevEspTeol* 2 (1942) 409–69.

_____. "La facultad de Teología en la Universidad de Toledo." Ibid., 3 (1943) 201–47.

_____. "Los orígenes de la Universidad de Salamanca." *Ciencia tomista* 81 (1954) 69–116.

_____. "El convento de san Esteban en sus relaciones con la Iglesia y la Universidad de Salamanca en los siglos XIII–XV." Ibid., 84 (1957) 95–116.

_____. "Primeros estatutos del colegio español de San Clemente de Bolonia." *Hispania sacra* 11 (1958) 187–224, 409–26.

Goñ Gaztambide, J. "Boletín bibliográfico sobre Universidades, Colegios y Seminarios." Ibid., 9 (1956) 429–47.

Las reformas en los siglos XV y XVI. Introducción a los orígenes de la Observancia en España. Archivo Ibero-Americano 18. Madrid, 1958.

Ruis i Serra, J. "L'Estudi general de Lleida." *Estudis universitaris catalans* 18 (1933) 160–74; 20 (1935) 98–141.

Sanahuja, P. "La enseñanza de la Teología en Lérida." *Archivo Ibero-Americano* 38 (1935) 418–48; new series, 1 (1941) 270–98.

_____. "La Universidad de Lérida y los franciscanos." Ibid., 6 (1947) 167–242.

San Martín Payo, J. *La antigua Universidad de Palencia.* Madrid, 1942.

Vázquez Janeiro, I. "La enseñanza del escotismo in España." *De doctrina Ioannis Duns Scoti* 4. *Scotismus decursu saeculorum.* Studia scolastico-scotista 4. Rome, 1968. Pp. 191–220.

_____. "Repertorio de franciscanos españoles graduados en Teología durante la edad media." *Repertorio de Historia de la Ciencias eclésiasticas en España* III. Salamanca, 1971. Pp. 235–320; VII. Salamanca, 1979. Pp. 411–49.

III

Alborg, Domínguez, A. "Jaime Pérez de Valencia, figura clave de los dos planteamientos hermenéuticos de la Bíblia en el siglo XV." *Actas del I Congreso de historia del País valenciano* (del 14 al 18 abril de 1971). Valencia, 1980. II, 793–802.

Alonso Getino, L. G. *Vida y obra de fray Lope de Barrientos.* Salamanca, 1927.

Arnau-García, R. *San Vicente Ferrer y las eclesiologías del Cisma.* Valencia, 1987.

Balasch i Recort, M. "El pensament biblic de Filip de Malla." *Revista catalana de Teología* 3 (1978) 99–126.

Beltrán de Heredia, V. "Noticias y documentos para la biografía del cardinal Juan de Torquemada." *AFP* 30 (1960) 53–148.

Belloso Martín, N. *Política y humanismo en el s. XV. El maestro Alfonso de Madrigal, el Tostado.* Valladolid, 1988.

Blásquez Fernández, J. "Teólogos españoles del siglo XV. El Tostado." *RevEspTeol* 1 (1940) 211–42.

_____. "El Tostado alumno graduato y profesor en la Universidad de Salamanca." *XV Semana bíblica española.* Madrid, 1956. Pp. 411–47.

_____. "El *tractatus absolutionis indulgentiarum* del Tostado." *Victoriensia* 35 (1975) 183–202.

Bonilla y San Martín, A. *Fernando de Córdoba (1425?–1486?) y los orígenes del renacimiento filosófico en España.* Madrid, 1911.

Bosi, S. *Alfonso Tostato. Vita ed opere.* Rome, 1952.

Cabanelas, D. "Juan de Segovia y el primier Alcorán trilingüe." *Al Andalus* 14 (1949) 149–73.

Calvo Moralejo, G. *Fray Ambrosio Montesino OFM (+ 1514) y el culto a la "Gloriosa Virgen María."* Humanismo, reforma y teología 10. Santiago de Compostela, 1980.

Carreras y Artau, J. "Las *repetitiones* salmantinas de Alfonso de Madrigal." *Revista de filosofía* 2 (1943) 211–36.

Castrillo, E. "Contribución a la historia de la exégesis en España. 1. La diócesis de Coria y los estudios bíblicos (siglos XV y XVI)." *Miscelánea Comillas* 2 (1944) 55–74.

Coll, J. M. "El maestro fray Antonio de Canals, discípulo y sucesor de san Vicente Ferrer." *Analecta sacra tarraconensia* 27 (1954) 9–21.

Díaz y Díaz, L. A. "Alonso de Oropesa y su obra." *Studia hieronymiana.* Madrid, 1973. I, 253–313.

Ehrle, F. "Die kirchenrechtlichen Schriften Peters von Luna (Benedikt XIII)." *ArchLitKirchMA* 7 (1900) 515–75.

Forcada, V. "El *Tratado del cisma moderno* de san Vicente Ferrer." *Anales de Centro de cultura valenciana* 35 (1975) 72–93.

_____. "Vicente Ferrer, predicador de la reforma de la 'Cristiandad.'" *Escritos del Vedat* 10 (1980) 151–81.

Foulche-Delbosc, R. "Étude biographique sur Fernán Pérez de Guzmán." *Revue hispanique* 16 (1907) 26–55.

Frias Balsa, J. V. "Pedro Martínez de Osma. Vida y obras." *Burgense* 20 (1979) 552–64.

_____. "Obras de Pedro Martínez de Osma." *Celtiberia* 30 (1980) 37–58.

_____. "El *Compendium metaphysicae* de Pedro de Osma. Estudio bibliográfico." *Revista de investigación* 9 (1980) 108–9.

García y García, A. "Un opúsculo inédito de Rodrigo Sánchez de Arévalo: *De libera et irrefragabili auctoritate Romani Pontificis.*" *Salmanticensis* 4 (1957) 474–502.

_____. "Nuevas obras de Clemente Sánchez, acerdiano de Valderas." *RevEspTeol* 34 (1974) 69–89.

_____, and V. Muñoz Delgado. *La "Suma" de Pedro de Osma sobre "La Politica" de Aristóteles.* Humanismo, reforma y teologia 37. Madrid, 1982.

Darganta, J. M. De, and V. Forcada. *Biografía y escritos de san Vicente Ferrer.* BAC 153. Madrid, 1956.

Gómez Canedo, L. *Un español al servicio de la Santa Sede. Don Juan de Carvajal, cardenal de Santángelo, legado en Alemania y Hungría (1399?–1469).* Madrid, 1947.

Gonzalo Maseo, D. "Alonso de Madrigal y su labor escrituraria." *Miscélanea de estudios árabes y hebraicos* 4 (1955) 143–86.

Goño Gatzambide. "Fray Juan de Monzón OP: su vida y sus obras (c. 1340–1412)." *Boletín de la Sociedad Castellonense de Cultura* 56 (1980) 506–23.

_____. "Estado actual de los estudios sobre Pedro Martínez de Osma." *Celtiberia* 30 (1980) 5–35.

_____. "Conclusiones y nuevas obras de Pedro Martínez de Osma." Ibid., 59–66.

_____. "Un tratado inédito de Pedro de Osma: *De officiis militis.*" *RevEspTeol* 43 (1983) 11–191.

Hernández Montes, B. "Obras de Juan de Segovia." *Repertorio de Historia de la Ciencias eclésiasticas en España* 6 (1977) 236–347.

_____. *Biblioteca de Juan de Segovia, Edición y comentario de su escritura de donación.* Madrid, 1984.

Huerga, A. "El *Tratado del cisma moderno* de san Vicente Ferrer." *RevEspTeol* 39–40 (1979–80) 145–61.

Iglesias, A. L. "María en la sagrada Escritura." *Estudios marianos* 23 (1962) 309–26.

Käppeli, Th. "Ioannes de Turrecremata." Idem. *Scriptores Ordinis Praedicatorum Medii Aevi* III. Rome, 1980. Pp. 24–42.

Laboa, J. M. *Rodrigo Sánchez de Arévalo, alcaide de Sant'Angelo.* Madrid, 1973.

Lange, W.-D. *El fraile trovador: Zeit, Leben und Werk des Diego de Valencia de León (1350?–1412?).* Analecta romanica 28. Frankfurt a. M., 1971.

Labajos Alonso, J. *Pedro de Osma y su Comentario a la "Metafísica" de Aristoteles.* With edition of text. Biblioteca Salmanticensis, Estudios 149. Salamanca, 1992.

Madurell i Marimón, J. M. "Mestre Felip de Malla." *Boletín de la Real Academia de Buenas Letras de Barcelona* 30 (1963–64) 499–626.

Marcos Rodríguez, F. "Algunos datos biográficos y testamento del maestro Pedro de Osma." *Salmanticensis* 2 (1955) 692–706.

_____. "Los manuscritos de Alfonso de Madrigal conservados en la Biblioteca Universitaria de Salamanca." Ibid., 4 (1957) 3–50.

Marquez, F. *Estudio preliminar a "Fray Hernando de Talavera O.S.H., Católica impugnación."* Espirituales españoles, A. 6. Barcelona, 1961. Pp. 1–53.

Martín Nieto, E. "Los libros deuterocanónicos del Viejo Testamento según el Tostado Alonso de Madrigal." *Estudios abulenses* 1 (1954) 56–74.

Meyuhas Ginio, A. "The Conversos and the Magic Arts in Alonso de Espina's *Fortalitium fidei.*" *Mediterranean Historical Review* 5 (1990) 169–82.

Millares, A. "Fray Gonzalo de Ocaña, escritor del siglo XV." *Boletín de la Universidad de Madrid* 3 (1931) 157–73.

Morreale, M. "Los Evangelios y Epístolas de Gonzalo García de Santa María y las biblias romanceadas de la edad media." *Archivio de filología aragonesa* 10–11 (1958–59) 277–89.

Müller, A. V. "Giacomo Pérez de Valencia O.S.A., vescovo di Chrysopoli e la teología di Lutero." *Bilychnis* 9 (1920) 391–403.

Peinado Muñoz, M. "Jaime Pérez de Valencia, un importante teólogo agustino valenciano del siglo XV: investigaciones sobre su vida y obra." *Confrontación de la teología y la cultura.* Actas del III Simposio de Teología histórica (7–9 mayo 1984). Publicaciones de la Facultad de Teología San Vicente Ferrer, Series Valentina 15. Valencia, 1984. Pp. 195–200.

_____. "Jaime Pérez de Valencia (1401–1490). En el quinto centenario de su muerte." *Archivo teológico granadino* 53 (1990) 131–60.

Perarnau Espelt, J. "Dos tratados 'espirituales' de Arnau de Vilanova en traducción castellana antigua." *AnthAn* 22–23 (1975–76) 477–630.

_____. "Els inventaris de la biblioteca papal de Peñíscola a la mort de Benet XIII." *Arxiu de textos catalans antics* 6 (1987) 7–295.

Puig i Oliver, J. de. "Saint Anselm i Ramon Sibiuda." *Arxiu de textos catalans antics* 7–8 (1989) 255–63.

_____. "Valoració crítica del pensament de Sibiuda al llarg del temps." Ibid., 9 (1990) 275–368.

_____. "Sobre el lul.lisme de Ramón Sibiuda." Ibid., 10 (1991) 225–60.

_____. "Cinc documents tolosans sobre Ramón Sibiuda." Ibid., 298–302.

_____. "Els manuscrits del *Liber creaturarum* de Ramón Sibiuda." Ibid., 303–19.

_____. "Complements a la valoració crítica del pensament de Sibiuda al llarg del temps." Ibid., 358–90.

Puig i Puig, S. *Pedro de Luna, último papa de Aviñón (1387–1430)*. Barcelona, 1920.

Reinhardt, K. "Pedro de Osma y su Comentario al Símbolo 'Quicumque.'" Madrid, 1977.

_____. "Das Werk des Nikolaus von Lyra im mittelalterlichen Spanien." *Traditio* 47 (1987) 321–58. References to Paul of Burgos, El Tostado, and James Pérez of Valencia.

Santiago Otero, H. "Savoir et méthode dans l'oeuvre théologique de Pedro Martínez de Osma (+ 1480)." *Knowledge and the Sciences in Medieval Philosophy*. Proceedings of the Eighth International Congress of Medieval Philosophy III. Ed. R. Työrinoja and others. Helsinki, 1990. Pp. 509–21.

Satorre, J. J. *La novela moral de Gracián (Un testo inédito del siglo XV)*. Palma de Mallorca, 1986.

Sconza, M. J. "Pablo de Santa María and his *Siete Edades del Mundo:* The Extant Manuscripts." *Manuscripta* 43 (1988) 185–96.

Stegmüller, F. "Pedro de Osma, Ein Beitrag zur spanischen Universitäts-, Konzils-, und Ketzergeschichte." *RömQ* 43 (1935) 205–66.

_____. "Das *Summarium Bibliae* des Fernandus Didaci de Carrione." *Spanische Forschungen der Görres-Gesellschaft,* Erste Reihe, 17 (1961) 234–36.

Suárez, P. L. "El matrimonio y la paternidad de san José en Ilmo. Jaime Pérez de Valencia." *Estudios josefinos* 13 (1959) 145–55.

_____. *Noemática bíblico-mesiánica de Alfonso Tostado de Madrigal*. Madrid, 1956.

_____. "Iacobi Pérez de Valencia in Magnificat Commentarium." *Ephemerides mariologicae* 8 (1958) 473–87.

Vázquez Janeiro, I. "Tres incunables más de los *Sermones* de san Vicente Ferrer, existentes in Santiago de Compostela." *RevEspTeol* 39–40 (1979–80) 325–30.

_____. *Tratados castellanos sobre la predestinación y sobre la Trinidad y la Encarnación del maestro fray Diego de Valencia OFM (siglo XV). Identificación de su Autoría y edición crítica*. Madrid, 1984.

_____. "En torno a la biblioteca de Juan de Segovia." *Antonianum* 60 (1985) 670–88.

_____. "'Gracián.' Un 'Felix' castigliano del secolo XV. Una ricerca sull'innominato autore." *Annali del'Istituto Universitario Orientale, Sezione Romanza,* 34 (1992) 293–37.

Werbeck, W. *Jacobus Pérez de Valencia. Untersuchungen zu seinem Psalmenkommentar*. Tübingen, 1959.

Zamora, H. "Un opúsculo biblico del Tostado desconocido." *Verdad y Vida* 31 (1973) 269–315.

On John of Torquemada and Roderick Sánchez de Arévalo see also the bibliography for the second chapter of this volume.

IV

Amore, A. "La predicazione del B. Matteo d'Agrigento a Barcellona e Valencia." *AFH* 49 (1956) 355–445.

Avalle-Arce, J. B. "Los herejes de Durango." *Homenaje a Rodríguez-Moñino.* Madrid, 1966. I, 39–55.

B. Matthaei Agrigentini OFM Sermones varii. Ed. A. Amore. Rome, 1960.

Beltrán de Heredia, V. "San Vicente Ferrer, predicador de las sinagogas." *Salmanticensis* 2 (1955) 669–76.

Benito Ruano, E. "La sentencia-estatuto de Pero Sarmiento contra los conversos toledanos." *Revista de la Universidad de Madrid* 6 (1957) 277–306.

Browe, P. *Die Judenmission im Mittelalter und die Päpste.* Rome, 1942.

Cabanelos, D. *Juan de Segovia y el problema islamico.* Madrid, 1952.

————. "Un franciscano heterodoxo en la Granada nasri, fray Alonso de Mella." *Al-Andalus* 15 (1950) 233–50.

Cantera Burgos, F. *Alvar García de Santa María. Historia de la judería de Burgos y de sus conversos más ilustres.* Madrid, 1952.

Cardo Guinaldo, M. T., and others. *Críticas y aportación de Pedro Martínez de Osma (+ 1480) al método teológico.* Humanismo, reforma y teología 57. Madrid, 1984.

Caro Borja, J. *Los judíos en la España moderna y contemporánea.* 3 vols. Madrid, 1961.

Carriazo, J. de M. "Precursores españoles de la Reforma. Los herejes de Durango (1442–1445)." *Actas y memorias de la Sociedad española de antropología, etnografía y prehistoria* 4 (1925) 35–69.

Castro, A. *La realidad histórica de España.* Mexico City, 1954.

Dahan, G. *La polémique chrétienne contra le judaïsme au Moyen Age.* Paris, 1991.

Epalza, M. de. *La Tuhfa, autobiografía y polémica islámica contra el Cristianismo de Abdallah al Taryuman (Fray Anselmo de Turmeda).* Rome, 1971.

Esposito, M. "Une secte d'hérétiques à Medina del Campo en 1459, d'après le *Fortalitium fidei* d'Alphonse de Spina." *RHE* 32 (1936) 350–60.

Fernández Conde, F. J. "Teología misionera, apologética y polemizante: judíos, mohametanos y cristianos." *Iglesia y cultura en las edades media y moderna: Santoral hispano-mozárabe en España.* Actas de congreso celebrado en Burgos (27 al 29 de julio de 1990). Ed. A. Hevia Ballina. Memoria Ecclesiae 3. Oviedo, 1992. Pp. 61–72.

Goñi Gaztambide, J. "Los herejes de Durango. Nuevas aportaciones (1442)." *Hispania sacra* 28 (1975) 225–35.

Groult, P. "Les courants spirituels dans la Peninsule Ibérique aux XVe, XVIe et XVIIe siècles." *Les lettres romanes* 9 (1955) 208–25.

López Martínez, N. *Los judaizantes castellanos y la inquisición en tiempos de Isabel la Católica.* Burgos, 1954.

López Rojo, M. "Los herejes de Durango (s. XV)." *Estudios de Deusto,* 2a epoca, 24 (1976) 303–18.

Maravall, J. A. *El concepto de España en la Edad Media.* Madrid, 1954.

Meseguer Fernandez, J. "Doctrina de Alfonos de Mella? Extraña attribución. Trágico final de fray Guillén OFM." *Archivo Ibero-Americano* 44 (1984) 361–72.

Orlandis, J. "Sobre el origen de España y de la cultura cristiana española." *Iglesia española y evangelización.* Toledo, 1993. Pp. 95–107.

Pacios López, A. *La disputa de Tortosa.* 2 vols. Madrid, 1957.

Rasmussen, T. "Jacob Pérez of Valencia's *Tractatus contra Judeos* (1484) in the Light of Medieval Anti-Judaic Traditions." *Augustine, the Harvest, and Theology (1300–1650). Essays Dedicated to Heiko Augustinus Oberman in Honor of His Sixtieth Birthday.* Leiden, 1990. Pp. 41–59.

Reinhardt, K. "Hebräische und spanische Bibeln auf dem Scheiterhaufen der Inquisition. Texte und Geschichte der Bibelzensur in Valencia um 1450." *HistJb* 101 (1981) 1–37.

Regla Campistol, J. "Los moriscos. Estado de la cuestión y nuevas interpretaciones documentales." *Sataibi* 10 (1960) 101–30.

Sánchez Albornoz, G. *España, un enigma histórico.* Barcelona, 1956.

Santiago-Otero, H., and K. Reinhardt. *Pedro Martínez de Osma y el método teológico. Edición de algunos escritos inéditos.* Madrid-Soria, 1987.

Secret, F. "*L'Ensis Pauli* de Paulus de Heredia." *Sefarad* 26 (1966) 79–102.

Serrano, L. *Los conversos don Pablo de Santa María y don Alfonso de Cartagena.* Madrid, 1942.

Sicroff, A. A. *Les controverses des statuts de 'pureté de sang' en Espagne du XVe au XVIIe siècle.* Paris, 1960.

Singerman, R. *The Jews in Spain and Portugal: A Bibliography.* New York, 1975.

Suárez Fernández, L. *Judíos españoles en la edad media.* Madrid, 1976.

Vázquez Janeiro, I. *San Bernardino de Sena y España. Notas para una historia de la predicación en la Castilla del siglo XV.* Humanismo, reforma y teología 22. Madrid, 1980.

Vendrell, F. "La actividad proselitista de san Vicente Ferrer durante el reinado de Fernando I de Aragón." *Sefarad* 13 (1953) 87–104.

V

Ameri, H. *Doctrina theologorum de Immaculata B. V. Mariae Conceptione tempore concilii Basiliensis.* Rome, 1954.

Baer, F. *Die Juden in christlichen Spanien.* 2 vols. Berlin, 1929–36.

Finke, H. *Acta concilii Constanciensis, II–IV.* Münster i. W., 1923–28.

Gómez Canedo, L. "Juan de Carvaly el Cisma de Basilea." *Archivo Ibero-Americano* 1 (1941) 29–55, 209–28, 369–420.

Goñi Gaztambide, J. "Los obispos de Pamplona del siglo XV y los navarros en los concilios de Constanza y Basilea." *Estudios de Edad Media de la Corona de Aragón,* VII. Saragossa, 1962. Pp. 31–423.

———. *Los españoles en el concilio de Constanza. Notas biográficas.* Madrid, 1966.

Hofmann, G. *Papato, conciliarismo, patriarcato (1438–1439).* Rome, 1940.

Izbicki, T. M. *Protector of the Faith: Cardinal Johannes de Turrecremata and the Defense of the Institutional Church.* Washington, D.C., 1981.

Jedin, H. "Sánchez de Arévalo und die Konzilsfrage unter Paul II." *HistJb* 3 (1954) 95–119.

López Martínez, N. "El cardenal Torquemada y la unidad de la Iglesia." *Burgense* 1 (1960) 45–71.

Martín Palma, J. "María y la Iglesia según Juan de Segovia y Juan de Torquemada." *Estudios marianos* 18 (1957) 207–30.

Perarnau Espelt, J. "Política, lul.lisme i Cisma d'Occident." *Arxiu de textos catalans antics* 3 (1984) 59–191.

Pozo, C. "Culto mariano y 'definición' de la Inmaculada en el concilio de Basiliea." *Scripta de Maria* 3 (1980) 609–31.

Suárez Fernández, L. *Castilla, el Cisma y la crisis conciliar*. Madrid, 1960.

Vázquez Janeiro, I. "Una collección de documentos del concilio de Constanza." *RevEspDerCan* (1986) 115–26.

_____. "San Ildefonso y los concilios visigóticos vistos desde el siglo XV." *Estudios marianos* 55 (1990) 309–34.

_____. "*Nominetur ille doctor*. El último deseo incumplido de Juan Hus en Constanza." *Antonianum* 66 (1991) 265–300.

_____. "El encomío mariano *Cunctas haereses sola interemisti*. Origen de su sentido inmaculista." Ibid., 497–531.

Vera-Fujardo, G. *La eclesiología de Juan de Segovia en la crisis conciliar*. Vitoria, 1968.

CHAPTER 6

Scholastic and Humanist Culture in France in the Fifteenth and Sixteenth Centuries

Anna Morisi

1. Between the Middle Ages and the Modern Age: Scholasticism

The Council of Constance had put an end to the Great Schism, but France had not yet found peace. The armies that met in battle during the endless Hundred Years' War devastated cities and countryside, sowing ruin and desolation; the domestic conflicts between Burgundians and Armagnacians created anxiety in the minds of the people; the entire country was subjected to profound suffering, and even the Church passed through a difficult period of impoverishment and anarchy that could not but have an effect on discipline.

Nicholas of Clamanges, who during the schism had composed his *De ruina et reparatione Ecclesiae,* twenty years later joined his voice to the many that were raised to complain of the decadence of religious life, the degeneration of morals, and the breakup of society:

> There is no emperor; there is no sure pope while the remnants of the schism still exist; we have no king, there is no law, there is no prophet, there is no faith in the land, there is no justice, there is no truth, there is no concern for salvation, no zeal for souls, no fear of God, no fear of hell, no practice of obedience, no pursuit of virtue nor fervent charity; the law is violated, impaired, and laid low.[1]

The preacher and theologian accompanied this sorrowful denunciation of a state of deep uneasiness with a specific accusation that was unsparing of the university. In his judgment the major responsibility had to be assigned to the Studium of Paris, which had distinguished itself "in disturbing, not to say pumping its arrows into, the affairs of the Church." The temple of knowledge had closed its doors to the reality of the life of religion; its teachers were not up to their task; like peacocks they showed off their degrees and their doctor's caps, they were proud of their teaching and their large number of hearers, but they had grown sluggish in their leisurely studies and did not preach, did not teach the people.[2]

Nevertheless, in the desolating picture which the voices of this period give us, it is possible to see at work the leaven of a spiritual rebirth that was to manifest itself in many forms and with varying degrees of success. Despite the lack of pastors, the devotion of the laity gave life to many confraternity movements, and the faithful gathered around preachers. The religious orders began the work of internal renewal: the Observance spread abroad in the Franciscan family; the Dominicans adopted the reform that had been tested by the Congregation of the Netherlands; many Benedictine monasteries took as a model the monastery of Santa Giustina in Padua. Toward the end of the century Jan Standonck, rector of the college of Montaigu and a man of great austerity who had been formed in the school of the *Devotio moderna,* imposed a very strict discipline on the students in an attempt to make the seminary a training ground for exemplary priests.

The extent to which devotional fervor influenced theological thought is perhaps the most intriguing question for those desirous of working through the history of religious thought in fifteenth-century France. The University of Paris, which had always been regarded as the major center of theological studies, the acknowledged arbiter in controversies, and a source of doctrine even for popes, was certainly not untouched by the general crisis. The English siege of that city ended only in 1437; the impoverishment of the clergy, both regular and secular, did not facilitate an influx of students, some of whom turned to other universities that had been founded at the end of the Middle Ages; political conflicts had kept many teachers away, and among these was Gerson, who died at Lyons in 1429 after a long exile. Nicholas of Clamanges had accused learned academicians of not meeting the spiritual needs of the time, and yet it was precisely from the Faculty of Theology that men would come who distinguished themselves in pastoral activity and did not disdain to use the vernacular in order to speak to the faithful.

It is not easy for the modern observer to uncover the signs of new perspectives in the work of the masters of that time; a long winter seemed to have descended on the halls of the famous Faculty of Theology, which was closely bound up with and conditioned by the schools of philosophy. The nominalists, who were regarded as bringers of dangerous innovations, were repeatedly condemned and subjected to recurrent "persecutions," but they were always there; they still clashed with the realists, but the disagreements did not depart from the lines already drawn in the past. At the beginning of the century, after a period in which the "moderns" predominated, the "old way" *(via antiqua)* seemed to have regained the upper hand. In 1407 the Dominican John Capreolus, "prince of Thomists," was lecturing on the *Sentences* in Paris; he then left to teach at Toulouse and ended his days in 1444 in the convent of the Friars Preachers in his native Rodez.

His name is tied to a monumental work in four volumes, the *Defensiones theologiae divi Thomae de Aquino,* which explained and defended Thomist teaching in the form of a commentary on the *Sentences.* Beginning with Peter Lombard's Prologue, Capreolus asked the "first question: Whether theology is a science," and then went on to study the ensuing problems while refuting the views of those who had distanced themselves from or were opposed to the theses of Thomas. This meant, first and foremost, Durandus of Saint-Pourçain, Scotus, Gregory of Rimini, Peter d'Ailly, and, in general, the nominalists. The result was a vast and rich encyclopedia of Scholastic thought that would be used and appreciated even a century later by the anti-Lutheran controversialists, such as Isidore Isolanus and Silvester Mazzolini of Priero, who thought of making a compendium of the work.

During those same years, among the ranks of the followers of the *via antiqua* in Paris, a school of Albertists flourished alongside the defenders of the Thomist tradition. The school originated with John of Neuhausen, perhaps a Fleming, who in 1410/11 was among the masters of the *natio Picardiae.* The aim of these masters was not simply to recover the thought of Albert the Great and to revive his memory and the veneration paid him, although this in fact had never been completely forgotten, especially within the Dominican Order and, in particular, among the German theologians. The new school intended rather to turn to advantage some motifs in the teaching of the Swabian master that would provide new weapons against the *moderni.* It went back, therefore, to those of his works in which the Neoplatonic heritage was more evident and the distance from the thought of Thomas greater.

This is what we see in the *De esse et essentia,* with its ten *quaestiones,* in which John of Neuhausen tackled the subject of the real difference between being and essence and, following Albert, concluded that there is no real distinction. In the great German mystics of the past the Albertist heritage had acted as a vital sap, feeding even the boldest aspects of their experience. In the fifteenth-century school, however, it would be difficult to detect the outlines of a new theological method. The school's representatives seemed to prefer to keep to the strictly philosophical realm, and there they remained even when they might have opened the door to other considerations and given expression to a different religious sensibility, as, for example, in John's seventh question, on the angels. Engaged on two fronts, against the followers of Ockham and the followers of Thomas, the Albertist school was harshly anti-Thomist in its fundamental motivations and showed itself to be such when it was transplanted to Germany, first in Cologne and then at other universities.[3]

Perhaps the broad, balanced, and reassuring intellectual structure erected by Aquinas no longer satisfied the restlessness of theologians who, within the limits of the *via antiqua,* tended rather toward Scotist voluntarism, without, however, moving beyond the models it provided. There was in fact a rich flowering of commentaries on the *Sentences* that were inspired by those of the "subtle Doctor," and even commentaries on the commentaries. Although written by men who were not unaware of the needs of their time, these commentaries concealed their deepest driving force in the very close-knit web of traditional methods and language. The greatest representative of this trend was a Breton Franciscan, William of Vaurillon (+ 1464), who taught in Paris in 1429 as a bachelor and returned there in 1448 with his *licentia docendi.* As an influential theologian, he took a part, in the time of Pius II, along with other representatives of his order, in the debate over the blood of Christ. He was the author of a commentary *Super quattuor libros sententiarum, iuxta doctrinam Joannis Scoti,* a *De principiis,* and a textbook (perhaps partly written by his students) entitled a *Vademecum* or *Collectarium* or *Repertorium* of Duns Scotus' *Opus Oxoniense.*

The teachings of the Scotist school found their most important popularizer and exponent in Nicholas of Orbellis (+ 1472/75), an Observant Franciscan, the author of commentaries on the *Sentences* that were basically didactic in character, as we can see from the title of the Venice edition of 1507, *Petri Lombardi quatuor sententiarum volumina cum doctissimis Nicolai de Orbellis theologi acutissimi interpretationibus, in quibus Scoti dicta quae obscura vulgo videbantur faciliter enarrantur. Ex quorum cognitione brevi omnes in Scoti dogmatibus sunt peritissimi evasuri.*

An author of like kind was Stephen Pillet, known also as Brûlefer, likewise a Franciscan, born in Saint-Malo (+ ca. 1501). He earned his doctoral degree in Paris and later taught in Metz and Mainz. He was called back from Germany to his native land by the famous preacher Oliver Maillard, who sent him to Brittany to oversee the reform of the order. He wrote *Formalitates in doctrinam Scoti* and some short works of a strictly theological kind, which he published in his *Opuscula.* His duties as Observant reformer, however, also roused his interest in his Franciscan origins and in the first great thinker of the order, whose writings he investigated, organized, and studied; the result was his *In quatuor Sancti Bonaventurae doctoris seraphici sententiarum libros, Scoti subtilis secundi.* Philosopher and theologian Peter Tataret (Tartaretus), who was rector in Paris in 1490 and commented on Aristotle, Porphyry, and Peter of Spain, has left us *Commentaria sive, ut vocant, reportata in quatuor libros sententiarum et Quodlibeta J. Duns Scoti.*

When the English army lifted its siege of Paris, the nominalists returned to the university and remained even though restrictive measures were taken against them on various occasions, as happened in the time of Louis XI. The representatives of this school likewise left no deep and original traces in the sphere of religious thought, even though they did not lack the opportunity to carry out experiments that might have become the leaven for a new kind of theological reflection. They were regarded as very prestigious teachers.

In addition, many of them devoted themselves to preaching and wrote on ethical subjects, as did, for example, Martin Lemaistre (De Magistris) of Tours (1432–82), who had been a student in the College of Navarre and had earned the degree of doctor in 1473. He authored various works on strictly philosophical subjects and left behind him *Quaestiones morales,* a kind of case-book in which he studied the virtues and then raised the question of their relationship with grace. His *Contemplatio* on the *Salve Regina,* which seems to be a collection of points for sermons, is a specimen of oratorical skill and at the same time of the author's capacity for psychological insight: the subject of hope is treated in a way that would touch all of the reader's or hearer's emotional chords, but it does not become the occasion for deeper reflection. Primarily philosophical, on the other hand, were the interests of Thomas Bricot, commentator on Aristotle and Buridan, who obtained his licentiate in theology in 1489/90 and taught logic at the university; he stuck to the path of nominalism but with something of a tendency to eclecticism.

Among the many debates in which the "ancients" and the "moderns" faced each other, the one on the eternal problem of future contingents in which the universities of Louvain and Paris were opposed had special repercussions, because it involved both philosophers and theologians and almost caused a diplomatic incident.[4] In 1465 Peter Rousseau (or van den Beken), a bachelor of Louvain, had discussed a question in which he explained the difficulties met in reading the prophecies in the Scriptures without having to accept a strict necessity. Henry of Zoemeren (Sommeren) and James Schelwaertus, two nominalist masters teaching at that time in the University of Paris, reacted strongly, and in 1470, against the advice of the theological faculty, submitted to Rome a detailed accusation of heresy. When consulted on the accusation, the masters of Cologne replied that they could find no heterodox elements in the bachelor's statements. The latter also asked for the opinion of twenty-four Paris theologians, all of them realists and probably Thomists, who gave him their approval. But Pope Sixtus IV, who was Francis della Rovere, a fervent Scotist and himself author of a work *De futuris contingentibus,* was not favorable toward him.

The case was discussed at length in the Curia, and in 1473 Peter Rousseau was forced to recant. The sentence was regarded in Paris as a challenge and an offense; the controversy saw personages of the political and university worlds being drawn into it and went far beyond the philosophical and theological importance of the initial question. In March of 1473/74 the king promulgated the Edict of Soissons, which banned the nominalists from teaching at the University of Paris. The action was not overly successful, but many left the city, and the faculty felt the effects of the crisis. Here again, modern readers would be disappointed if they looked for traces of a new sensibility in this debate, for the truth of the propositions was measured by the usual authorities, with syllogisms as weapons. The problem was a touchy one, for it had to do with God's foreknowledge and will; it raised, in other terms, the problem of freedom and necessity, but the debate also revealed the inability of the adversaries to frame it in a new way.

The lack of any orthodox development of doctrine was matched by the rarity of heretical views. The ghost of Wyclif and his heresy was indeed raised in the discussion of future contingents, but, unlike what happened in Germany where the survival of Wyclif's thought among the Bohemians and in some suspect conventicles was seen as a concrete and imminent danger, the threat seems to have remained somewhat remote in the debate between the Louvainians and the Parisians.

The name of the English theologian did reappear, however, in matters involving two personages, otherwise little known, who were suspected of heresy. On June 30, 1484, John Laillier, a scholarship student at the College of the Sorbonne, maintained in the theses for his doctorate that there is no evidence in Scripture to justify the primacy of Peter over the other apostles and, consequently, the preeminence of Rome over all the other Churches. Therefore, the doctoral candidate added, the decretals have no universal force. The arguments were, it seems, of an ecclesiological kind and an expression of an anti-Roman mood, but it was soon observed that some of the propositions reasserted the teaching of Wyclif. Proceedings for heresy were begun, but only in June of 1486 did the faculty issue a condemnation; Laillier had very powerful supporters who managed to postpone the sentence and who guaranteed him impunity, thanks to a belated retractation that was so unconvincing and lacking in credibility that Pope Innocent VIII intervened personally and asked that the guilty man be punished and that he be denied his degree as master.[5]

John Langlois was less fortunate and ended at the stake for having attacked a priest during the celebration of Mass in 1491, for profaning the chalice, and for saying that the body of Christ was not on the altar. The heretic, who had the title of master, had been out of France for a long time and on his travels had met heretics of various kinds: Bohemians, followers of the Free Spirit, Jews, and Averroists. His sacrilegious action was probably the expression of a eucharistic heresy, but the documents that have come down to us do not let us know anything further.[6]

2. Early Humanism

While the nominalists and realists were fighting their battles, a humanist culture was also making its way into France, although slowly. The fortunes of war had made exchanges with other countries difficult, but the papal court at

Avignon had been a meeting place for persons open to new experiences; it was there that a network of close relationships began to develop and soon spread to other centers. The memory of Petrarch had always remained alive in this city of the popes; his works, preserved in the library of the university, were read and copied. Not all French men of letters, however, shared his overly severe judgment: "There is no learned person in France. . . . Orators and poets are not to be looked for outside of Italy,"[7] and they cultivated a humanism more in accord with their own traditions. The new culture acted on many of them especially as a stimulus, urging them to look to distant but not overly remote times for the survival of that love of letters that had formerly flowered on the tree of Christian spirituality. Chancellor John of Montreuil claimed that he owed his interest in the classics to Lactantius, who had introduced him to the reading of Cicero and of "our Virgil." When Nicholas of Clamanges died, the chancellor delivered the eulogy of the friend who had been preacher, theologian, man of culture, and an example of how literary men of a high standard could be found even in France.[8]

Early humanism, which was more literary than philosophical, does not seem to have created serious problems by challenging medieval thought and traditional methods of study. Even John Gerson (1363–1429) was a diligent reader of the ancient writers, whose wisdom he appreciated, "since every truth, no matter who voices it, is from the Holy Spirit."[9] His zeal for preaching did not make him forget the importance of rhetoric and eloquence, and in this area (he said) the Fathers of the early centuries were an example for us. In addition, as a theologian and exegete he recognized the need of literary studies, "for the sacred scriptures, like the sciences of morality and history, have their own logic, which we call rhetoric."[10]

"The Church embraces all the sciences, all the arts," John of Montreuil used to say, but humanism brought a new mentality, a new way of assessing human beings and their works; as such, it inevitably came in conflict with the culture that preceded it. While John Dominici, in Italy, was writing his *Lucula noctis* to show that pagan literature was alien and harmful to the Christian universe, in France a comparable debate arose that involved Gerson and John of Montreuil, Christine of Pisan and the two Cols, Peter and Gontier. This time, however, the dispute concerned not ancient poetry but a work of medieval literature, the *Roman de la Rose*.

The most complete document of the debate is a short work, not lacking in literary ambition, which Gerson wrote in 1402.[11] In it he imagined that one morning—a morning in May—his heart took wing and reached the "holy court of Christendom," where, on the throne of equity, canonical Justice sat, with the scepter of reward in its right hand and the scepter of punishment in its left. In the presence of a noble chivalry consisting of all the virtues, a trial was being held, and Conscience had the task of presenting the complaints of Chastity against the Delirious Lover. The accused, Conscience said, leads people to moral disorder, devotes all his efforts to expelling Chastity from the face of the earth, is an offense to marriage, condemns young people who enter monasteries and convents on the grounds that they are doing violence to themselves, uses lustful words such as Venus, Cupid, and Genius, defames Lady Reason by saying things that cannot be repeated, talks of holy, divine, and spiritual subjects while mixing in with them what is dissolute and indecent, and promises paradise and glory to those who abandon themselves to the pleasures of the senses.

Since there were in that noble assembly not a few who declared themselves ready to take on the defense of the accused, Theological Eloquence came forward, ready to refute every justification and to show that human nature is of itself inclined to disorder and that there are only too many fools ready to be won over by imprudent talk. As the only authority in a position to judge the fruits of an eloquence that does not lead to virtue, Theological Eloquence concluded that the author of the work (the *Roman de la Rose*) had practiced an art like that of the harpies, showing, that is, the face of a woman and a body that was misshapen, bestial, and filthy. He had not obeyed the rules of the school, the laws of rhetoric that require consideration above all of the one who speaks, to whom he speaks, and on what occasion; therefore he deserved condemnation. At the end of a long harangue, while recognizing that judgment on human beings belongs to God alone, Theological Eloquence advised the banning "of all pictures or writings or words that incite to lewdness, since our weakness is of itself too inclined to this without inflaming it all the more, and too tottering or steeped in vices, far from the virtues and from God who is our glory, our love, our salvation, joy, and happiness."

On the other hand, John of Montreuil, who was a friend of Coluccio Salutati and probably up on what was being discussed in Florence at that time, sided firmly with the author of the *Roman,* "a satirist and very strict teacher." John disliked being regarded as a heretic for his favorable judgment of a work that revealed infinite riches, and he maintained that before uttering condemnation, persons had to have a thorough knowledge of what they were talking about.[12] A century later, Gerson's little work against the *Roman de la Rose* had not lost its relevance; it was translated into Latin, perhaps by James Wimpfeling, a fervent admirer and biographer of Gerson, who like the latter had found himself fighting against the freedom of poetry, in this case the poetry of the ancients, when it proved incompatible with Christian ethics.[13]

Gerson was influenced by the new climate but remained a man of the Middle Ages; he deprecated the decline of theological studies, but he did not cast doubt on the great learning of the Scholastics. His friends, on the other hand, and his younger disciples went a step further. Among them was Nicholas Poillevin of Clamanges (or Clémanges, Marne; ca. 1360–1437), a theologian, humanist, and preacher who loved Seneca and Petrarch and said that he had learned from Cicero the "Tullian eloquence" which his contemporaries recognized in him. He was a bachelor of theology and secretary to Benedict XIII, to whom he remained loyal even when France refused him obedience. After a period of withdrawal in the charterhouse of Valprofonde and then with the Augustinians of Fontaine-au-Bois,[14] he returned to Paris in 1423 and resumed his theological studies. He had learned from Gerson that theology is a wisdom of the heart rather than an exercise of the mind, an experience of God rather than intellectual speculation; he took this teaching to heart when he collected his reflections in a *Liber de studio theologico ad Johannem de Pedemontio Baccalarium*.[15]

In a letter to Peter d'Ailly, Gerson had spoken of the need of a reform of theological studies; he complained that future teachers would be devoting themselves to useless, captious debates, "while scorning the Bible and other doctors"; that they would change the language inherited from the Fathers; that they would thereby expose themselves to the criticism of those who would judge them to be uncouth or "fanciful"; and above all, that they would not pay attention to the instruction of the people.[16]

Nicholas of Clamanges took up these themes in his work, which abounds in polemical digs at doctors who shut themselves up in the idleness of the schools and refuse their pastoral duty; but he also called into question the very role of the faculty, assigning it a limited and subordinate role in the work of theology.

Nicholas' *Liber,* which is a lengthy letter-manifesto, seems to be continuing a dialogue already begun; the author reassures his young addressee and says that he has no intention of taking him from the study of the books of the *Sentences,* for he is well aware that in this apprenticeship the soldiers of Christ receive their training, the good farmers learn to cultivate the field of the Lord and to gather the seeds which they will later sow in abundance. Nicholas does, however, want to warn him to distrust those who are more interested in prestige than in learning, more in the blossoms than in the harvest; the important thing is not titles but attitudes. Paul said that there are in the Church apostles, prophets, evangelists, teachers, and pastors; Nicholas will prove that these last two roles are aspects of a single duty: "Let him who is a pastor realize that he must be a teacher, since to guide the flock is naught else but to teach it, by his own life, his word, and his example, how to reach wisdom. There are therefore no pastors who are not also teachers, nor can anyone be regarded as a teacher who is not also a pastor." The role of the theologian, then, coincides with that of the preacher; it consists, above all, in living according to God's will in imitation of Christ; therefore it is right "to begin not with doctrine but with action."

Certainly (Nicholas insists) theologians must devote themselves to meditation on the word of God but must at the same time keep in mind that meditation is an activity of the heart. *Lectio divina,* he says, is not an intellectual exercise but an ability to understand the deep mysteries hidden in the text, as can be seen from the commentaries of the Fathers, who were enlightened by the Spirit; these commentaries are streams of pure water gushing from the wellspring, for "the word of God is a fountain of wisdom" (Sir 1:5). Today, however (the author continues), theologians read the word of God distractedly and wear themselves out in empty subtleties; they have abandoned the fruit-rich tree and are wandering around among barren bushes and dying of hunger there; they have lost all enthusiasm because they are devoting themselves to useless knowledge; they provide the tools of their intellects but are unable to transmit any affection, because they have forgotten that "love is the fulfillment of the law" (Rom 13:10).

The law of Christ teaches that it is not the knowledge of theology that renders human beings blessed but action based on that knowledge. Study is therefore not useless, it helps to discern and combat errors; but it is the task of theologians to anticipate these errors by their commitment and example: "Is there anyone who cannot understand that it is more useful to expel errors from hearts than from books?" It is to be noted that the errors Nicholas lists are never doctrinal but only moral; they are manifestations of disorder, superstition, and ignorance. And they are, says the author, errors which the preacher can correct by falling back, always and exclusively, on the Scriptures, which are the sole source of authority and a ring joining heaven and earth: "Therefore, a house of theological studies is, so to speak, a workshop for pastors and preachers; from it those are to be called and chosen who have learned the art of pastoring, in order that they may be put in charge of flocks left empty by learning."

The work of Nicholas of Clamanges reflected the spiritual climate of France at the beginning of the fifteenth century. While his heritage from Gerson is evident, it is more difficult to determine the humanistic element. There are countless citations from the Bible, whereas the medieval theologians are completely absent; there is an explicit and repeated invitation to go back to the sources, the Scriptures and the Fathers, but the invitation is borne on the wave of a mystical impulse. There is a persistent attack on the schools, the training grounds on which future theologians were to be formed, and on the teachers there, who have forgotten that "it is the athlete, not the coach, who wins the prize." But the criticism does not touch the procedures and method of study; it looks more to the results than to the approach, although when we have finished reading, we have the impression that the ideal theologian-preacher, the teacher-pastor, should have little interest in discussing the proofs for the existence of God or metaphysical questions. The author strongly asserts that at the basis of the work of theology there is simply the act of faith and a trust in the assistance of the Spirit, who raises up prophets and through them speaks to human beings in order to help, exhort, and console them.

Nicholas' entire discourse is, as it were, left hanging: his religious experience seems to have the upper hand over any conceptual development of it, and the text is pervaded by an intense feeling that finds expression in a stream of vivid images, all from the Bible, which speak of springs and running water, trees and fruit. The limitation of this kind of reflection may perhaps be found in a failure to study deeply the relation of the theologian to his sources, in a lack of hermeneutical awareness. But humanism at that time was in its beginnings, and it would be unjust to look here for the presence of a more mature consciousness of problems.

The teaching of St. Bernard, of Hugo and Richard of St. Victor, and of the school of Citeaux, which had fed Gerson's mysticism, is present in the work of other personages of the first half of the century.

Among these was Robert Ciboule (Breteuil, Eure; ca. 1403–58), a theologian and politician, a collaborator (in 1452) of the king and Cardinal William of Estoutville in working out a plan for the reform of the university, and author of *Livre de la sainte méditation et connaissance de soi* and of *Livre de perfection.* He was one of the representatives of the "Christian Socratism"[17] that characterized the French spirituality of the fifteenth century. In his view, too, introspection and the recognition of one's own weakness were the premises for the encounter with the divine that takes place through love *(dilectio),* the ascent of the mind *(elevatio),* and detachment *(alienatio).* Like the others, he wanted to communicate his own religious experience. Ciboule was a popularizer and wrote in the language of the people so that all might understand him. In the writers of this period the influence of the *Devotio moderna* is undeniable but not predominant; the reception of the motifs peculiar to the religious spirit of northern Europe seems to have run up against a barrier in a tradition that would have been unable to assimilate them completely. But then Gerson, too, had shown himself suspicious of the overly audacious routes traveled by the mystics.[18]

Not unimportant in the present context is the fate of the *Imitation of Christ* in France. The work was widely read, and toward the end of the century it was even attributed to Gerson, but in its vernacular form it had undergone a revision that completely changed the approach taken in the original. The original, in four books, depicts an upward progress: it leads believers in their preparation for a spiritual life by teaching them detachment from earthly things, the renunciation of what is transitory, and the exercise of the virtues; then, as the first stage in the ascent to God, it leads them into themselves, into the most hidden part of the heart, from which they will derive the impulse to live according to the model of Christ. The soul thus enters into a relationship with the Creator, who consoles it and readies it for an indescribable union with him.

In the *Livre de l'internelle consolation,* the rewriter of the *Imitation* has chosen a more popular and pedagogical approach, while sacrificing the work's most authentic mystical motif; he begins with the third book, the title of which he takes for his own work, omits the fourth, and sets out to guide human beings on their journey of perfection by leading them into themselves in order that they may be able to hear the word of God, and then leading them out again to the practice of the virtues and to life as an imitation of Christ.[19]

3. Humanism in Paris from Fichet to Gaguin

During the first half of the century French humanism did not as yet have any plan, and it was only in January of 1457/58 that a chair of Greek was established in Paris and entrusted to an Italian, Gregory Tifernate. William Fichet may be regarded as the first real French humanist. Born in Upper Savoie in 1433, he went to the University of Avignon, where he discovered his literary calling and trained himself by reading the works of Petrarch. He then transferred to Paris to complete his studies, but in this famous city (he claims) he found a disheartening cultural situation: no one read Cicero, no one composed verse, and "the school of Paris had become unaccustomed to Latin and had descended to the language of rustics."[20] The young student became a bachelor at the Sorbonne in 1452, a doctor of theology in 1468, and had the opportunity to make his first journey to Italy in the winter of 1469–70, when Louis XI charged him with a diplomatic mission to Galeazzo Maria Sforza.

Fichet, who like many humanists had been trained in the school of the realists (he was probably Thomist in his tendencies), taught logic and theology in the morning, while in the evening he read the classics with a group of friends and disciples, among whom Robert Gaguin stood out. Fichet was open-minded and receptive of novelties; he was an enthusiastic defender of the usefulness of printing, a priceless invention which (he said) could shake the learned from their mental indolence by forcing them into a continual and direct comparison with one another. In 1470, while librarian of the Sorbonne, he introduced the first printery with the help of another theologian, John Heynlin von Stein, who brought three expert printers from Basel: Ulrich Gering, Michael Crantz, and Martin Friburger. Thus the first French publishing house came into existence; it began with the publication of the letters of Gaspar Barzizza and went on to the classics and the works of the Italian humanists, for which Fichet wrote a number of prefaces.

During these years the echo reached France of the disputes between the admirers of Plato, who had George Gemistus Plethon as their champion, and those who preferred Aristotle and were led by Theodore of Gaza and George of Trebizond. Also being read were the four books *Adversus calumniatorem Platonis,* which Bessarion had published in 1469 in an effort to settle the conflict and to show that Plato is more compatible than Aristotle with Christian thought. In Paris, the Aristoteleans were defended by Andrew of Trebizond, son of George, while Fichet sided with the supporters of the cardinal of Nicea, a volume of whose *Epistolae et orationes* he published (Paris, 1471). In 1472 Bessarion was in France as legate of Sixtus IV; when he returned to Italy, Fichet followed him and lived there the remainder of his life.

No important examples have survived of the work of this humanist theologian, who certainly had a great influence on the religious formation of his disciples in Paris. In the preface to a treatise of his on rhetoric (1471) he said that he was convinced that literary studies are an irreplaceable vehicle for the spread of Christ's message. A combining of ancient and modern, of traditional methods and humanist eloquence, can be seen in his final work, an address delivered to the court in Rome on December 26, 1476, in honor of St. Stephen; its main theme is the mercy of God.[21]

When Fichet left France, the humanists of Paris gathered around Robert Gaguin (Colline-Beaumont, Pas de Calais, ca. 1423–Paris, May 22, 1501), a well-known man of letters, a reader of Petrarch, a lover of philosophy, and a professor of rhetoric. At that time he was superior of the convent of Saint-Mathurin, and was soon to become general of the Trinitarians. Two members of the group were Martin of Delft, author of a treatise on the art of oratory, and his brother Giles (d. 1515), who had received a nominalist training and was a student of Aristotle,[22] a successful commentator on Ovid, and author of a *De causis ortus mortisque Christi,* of a metrical version of the penitential psalms,[23] and of a paraphrase of the letter to the Romans in Latin verse.[24]

Another member of the group was Charles Fernand of Bruges, director of music for Charles VIII. In 1492 he withdrew to the Benedictines of Chezal-Benoît in Berry, where he published a collection of *Epistolae familiares* (Paris, 1488), followed by other works: *De animi tranquillitate* (Paris, 1512), *Epistola paraenetica observationis disciplinae monasticae* (Paris, 1512), *Speculum disciplinae monasticae* (Paris, 1515), and *Confabulationes monasticae* (Paris, 1515). A short time later his brother John the Blind, author of *Horae divae crucis,* followed him into the convent. Another who frequented this coterie of Christian humanists was Guy Jouennau (+ 1505–7), at that time a Benedictine monk of Saint-Germain-des-Près, who in 1503 wrote a *Reformationis monasticae vindiciae seu defensio* in order to help his friends in their effort to reform the famous abbey. Then, too, there was Lawrence Bureau, a Carmelite, who spread knowledge of the poetry, written in a Christian Virgilian style, of his fellow religious, Baptist Spagnoli Mantovano.

These learned men read not only the classics but also the works of the monastic tradition: of St. Bernard and of Hugo and Richard of St. Victor. It was these that, on the one hand, guided them to the cloistered life and, on the other, led them to give voice to a religious spirit marked by a human sweetness and attentive to feelings and devotion. It was these cultural and psychological presuppositions that motivated them in favor of the Immaculate Conception during the period when the debates on the subject were at their hottest. Gaguin met the arguments of Vincent Bandelli with a poem *De mundissima virginis Mariae conceptione adversus Vincentium de Castronovo decertatio;*[25] this was followed by a second edition to which a commentary by Charles Fernand was attached.[26] In 1492 the general of the Trinitarians returned to the subject in a prose work. Giles of Delft also wrote some *Opuscula in laudem Virginis Mariae,* and the subject was later taken up by other theologians, such as Lefèvre d'Étaples and Josse Clichtove.

It is no simple matter to put a doctrinal disagreement into verse, but Gaguin succeeded, taking as his starting point the statement that everything is possible to God, "who creates the heavens and the earth, unbound by any law."[27] But his defense of the privilege of the Mother of Jesus in the name of Christian humanism had nothing in common with the typical Scholastic debates in which the theologians in their opposing armies faced off against each other. It took the form, rather, of a search through the pages of Scripture for passages and motifs capable of forming a Marian anthology; it was an appreciative recognition, offered as a probative argument, of the fact that belief in the absolute purity of the Blessed Virgin had always fed the piety of believers and that, as such, it could be a source of doctrine:

> What law do you follow? Piety.
> There are many books published without sacred texts,
> whose reliability and devout religious spirit stand firm.
> Not everything the Church observes proceeds
> from law. It is clear there is a place for morals.
> Very often human commands lead the Church:
> to resist them is forbidden, to obey them is salvation.[28]

But the learned piety *(docta pietas)* of the humanists, which seems so far removed from the thinking and language of the Scholastics, never led to an open contradiction of the latter; it did not call into doubt the didactic and scientific methods used in the faculties of theology; it did not keep any of them from taking an interest in the subjects and authors that filled the university curricula.[29] The theological faculty of Paris continued to have an unquestioned importance and prestige; many great preachers emerged from its halls.

Pico della Mirandola was in regular attendance there from July of 1485 to March of 1486: he was disappointed with the results produced by a type of humanistic culture that gave no answers to the most distressing questions of human beings and amused itself instead with the stories of the gods and the children of the gods. He preferred therefore to immerse himself in studies "that deal with and discuss the reasons for things human and divine."[30] His plan to merge in a higher unity the wisdom of antiquity, medieval wisdom, and the wisdom of the Cabala found attentive listeners in Paris, and when the young count was accused of heresy by Roman theologians, a professor on the faculty, John Cordier, defended him and saw to it that no condemnation of him was issued.

Ten years later, Erasmus came to Paris; he was to devote himself to theological studies, but he attended the lectures with little conviction and instead developed to the full the aversion to the old school that he had conceived during his years in the Netherlands. He was more at ease in the cosmopolitan atmosphere of the humanists, who gave him the opportunity for experiences that he had always desired. And yet he never came to agree completely with those who saw the monastery as the crown on their lives as Christian scholars.

He submitted the text of his *Antibarbari* to Robert Gaguin, who had given him a kind welcome and had introduced him to his own circle; in return Erasmus received a letter of praise: "You have undertaken a war against a contemptible gang of people who do not cease condemning the *studia humanitatis,* but it is a war more unpleasant than difficult; you will not defeat them with any weapon, and if you do succeed in defeating them, their ignorance will only make them more stubborn."[31] The elderly humanist joined in the condemnation of those who were opposed to the new culture, the new educational ideals; he had probably never heard such strong words and perhaps did not realize the consequences to which this criticism would lead. Erasmus owed a great deal to France, but he did not make it his homeland and even refused the invitation given to him later by Francis I, who would have liked him to join the circle of illustrious personages he had gathered around himself.

4. On the Eve of the Reformation: Briçonnet, Lefèvre, Budé

Other groups were formed in the years spanning the two centuries. Especially important was the group that formed around William Briçonnet, an unusual individual who agreed to and promoted one of the most troubling experiments of that age of reforms. He was the son of the cardinal and statesman of the same name and was born in Tours around 1470. In 1486 he went to Paris to the College of Navarre, where he attended the lectures on rhetoric; he then transferred to theological studies, in which he had as teachers two well-known conceptualists.

The first of the two, John Raulin (Toul, ca. 1443–Cluny, 1515) cultivated, in addition to speculative theology, an affective theology that was mindful of the needs of popular piety and found expression in his sermons, all of which were dictated by the desire for reform. In 1497 he entered Cluny and there dedicated to his fellow religious a *Collatio de perfecta religionis plantatione,* in which he exhorted them to follow the Rule of St. Benedict. After Raulin's departure, the position of leading master of the college was taken by Louis Pinelle (Montluçon, ca. 1465–Meaux, 1516), author of a work of intensely christocentric spirituality, *Les quinze fontaines vitales.*

With the support of his father the young Briçonnet began a rapid *cursus honorum* when he took the see of Lodève in 1489. In 1507 he was in Rome, heading an embassy to Julius II. While in Italy, he came in contact with humanists who combined a love for the study of antiquity with a sincere concern for the radical renewal of the Church and Christian society. On his return to his native land, he was appointed abbot of Saint-Germain-des-Prés and set about reforming the monastery, where he intensified studies and expanded the library, to which James Lefèvre d'Étaples, Josse Clichtove, and Hebraist Francis Guastablé, known as Vatable, all came to study. Here he received as a gift from a Florentine friend, Zanobi Acciaiuoli, a follower of Savonarola, the translation of the commentary of Ecclesiastes by Olympiodorus the Deacon; it was intended as a homage to one who, as the preface said, had decided to "abandon the stormy sea of the world and the swirling currents of the court" in order to prepare by recollection and meditation for a work of profound and, above all, personal renewal.

In 1511–12, still in his father's retinue, William took part in the schismatic Council of Pisa; the council's plan of reform was destined to fail, especially because of the primarily political meaning it had taken on, and yet this was once again the occasion of new experiences for Briçonnet. In Milan, to which council had been transferred, he took part in a meeting of a group of Francophile spiritualists, reformers, and troubled individuals, which met at the Cenacle of Eternal Wisdom, read prophetic and apocalyptic texts, and practiced a fervent devotion to Mary. He did not surrender his office as abbot of Saint-Germain even when in March of 1516 he entered Meaux as bishop, succeeding his former teacher, Pinelle. Here Briçonnet began an intense reforming activity, visiting the diocese, imposing discipline on the clergy, and promoting preaching. The news of his commitment to reform and his piety spread; the king's sister, Marguerite of Angoulême, chose him as her spiritual director,[32] and others turned to him who shared his ideas and would become "the leading group in Meaux."

The "case" of Luther had now burst on to the scene. On April 15, 1521, the Sorbonne had condemned 104 propositions taken from the heretic's works, while in Paris a climate of suspicion began to weigh upon many intellectuals. Lefèvre d'Étaples, who until then had lived and worked at Saint-Germain, moved to be near his former protector, and he was followed by Gerard Roussel, Michael d'Arande, Martial Masurier, William Farel, John Lecomte de la Croix, and Francis Vatable. The bishop used them as collaborators in vitalizing his pastoral plan and sent them as preachers to the various parishes of the diocese for the purpose of evangelizing both people and clergy. But the group also carried on intense theological and exegetical labors under the guidance of Lefèvre, who had proposed as a program: "Know the gospel, follow the gospel, make the gospel known." The plan of Gerson and Nicholas of Clamanges was now being realized: the "evangelicals" of Meaux were studying the Scriptures with satisfactory tools and making them known by offering them to the faithful in a language that all understood.

This great zeal could not fail to feed the suspicions of the theological faculty and Parliament of Paris, which would have intervened if the protection of the king had not prevented them. The bishop found himself in difficulties: in October of 1523 he convoked a synod in which he took measures against those who possessed Lutheran books or denied the doctrine of purgatory or the invocation of the saints[33]; in December he saw himself forced to withdraw the appointments of some preachers.[34] It was at this point that Farel departed, to turn up then at Basel. But others joined the initial group: Peter Charles (Caroli), John Lange (Angelus), Hellenist John Canaye (Canoeus), James Pauvan, and Matthew Saunier, and the work went on. In 1523 the French translation of the New Testament was published, in 1525 a volume of *Épistres et évangiles pour les cinquante et deux sepmaines de l'an*. Meanwhile, translations of other books were prepared, which were then brought together in the *Saincte Bible en Françoys,* published at Antwerp in 1530. In 1524 Lefèvre wrote to Farel:

> You cannot imagine the great fervor with which God has inflamed the souls of simple people in some places, after the publication of the New Testament in French. You regret, and rightly, that the book is not known widely enough. Some have tried to prevent its spread by having Parliament intervene, but our noble-minded king has been ready to take up the defense of Christ, because his desire is that in his kingdom the word of God may be heard without hindrance in the language people know. And now, on every feastday, and especially on Sundays, throughout our diocese the epistle and gospel are read to the people in the vernacular, and if the parish priest is to deliver some exhortation, he does so after the epistle or the gospel or both.[35]

The spread of Lutheran ideas was making it difficult to carry out the program to which Briçonnet and Lefèvre had devoted themselves. The theologians of Paris were keeping a suspicious watch and were not ignorant of the fact that the people in Meaux were in communication with Strasbourg and the Swiss cities; Caroli, Pauvan, and Saunier were censured by the Sorbonne.

When, after the battle of Pavia, the king's support failed, the group broke up. Briçonnet, who on more than one occasion had proved his orthodoxy and taken anti-Lutheran measures, escaped condemnation, but his collaborators scattered: some would go over to the Reformers, others would be put on trial. After a short period spent in Blois as tutor to the young princes, Lefèvre found refuge in Nérac with Marguérite, who had become queen of Navarre; there, in 1536 or 1537, he ended his days in silence.

James Lefèvre had been the central figure of the group. He was born in about 1460 at Étaples in Picardy and completed his studies in Paris; there, too, he had obtained the academic degrees that allowed him to teach philosophy at the college of Cardinal Lemoine, where he lectured on Aristotle. He was never a literary man, although, like the others, he loved the poetry of Baptist Mantovano. He was, however, a humanist, by reason of his demanding concern for philology, his intellectual curiosity, and the multiplicity of his interests in philosophy, mathematics, music, and astronomy, all of which came together in his religious thought. Like all the humanists of that time, Lefèvre too made a journey to Italy: in 1492 he visited Venice, then Florence, where

Pico della Mirandola made him a gift of the manuscript of Aristotle's *Metaphysics* in Bessarion's translation. His encounter with Ficino and with Neoplatonic and Hermetic culture was for him, an Aristotelean, a new experience. In Rome he was able to talk with Ermolaus Barbarus about Aristotle, whom both loved: an Aristotle read in the original and liberated from the interpretations and the dross laid down in the course of the centuries.

When he returned to France, he went back to teaching and began an intense editorial activity by publishing, with prefaces and notes, the authors who had been signposts on his own intellectual and spiritual journey: Aristotle above all, but also Ficino, the Hermetic writings, Boethius, Raymond Lull, John of Sacrobosco, Ricoldo of Montecroce, Richard of St. Victor, John Damascene, George of Trebizond, the writers of the apostolic and patristic periods, Ruysbroeck, and, most valued of all for their theological thought, Pseudo-Dionysius and Nicholas of Cusa. He was aided by a group of disciples, among them Josse Clichtove, Charles of Bouelles, John Molinier, Matthew Fortunatus from Pannonia, and later, Farel, the two Amerbachs of Basel, and Beatus Rhenanus.

Among the humanists of Paris, those who had formed Gaguin's circle, many had chosen the monastic life; Lefèvre did not enter a monastery, but when Briçonnet became abbot of Saint-Germain, Lefèvre moved there and in the quiet of the abbey continued his work with his closest collaborators around him. From that time on he devoted himself entirely to biblical studies and in 1509 published the *Quincuplex Psalterium,* an edition in parallel columns of the four Latin versions (the *Vetus* and the three of Jerome) along with a text containing the best readings. It has been said that "this book, written on the eve of the overwhelming events that were to turn Christian Europe upside down, is the most serene and beautiful book that can be imagined."[36] The Psalter was followed in 1512 by an edition of the letters of Paul in which the Vulgate text was given and, alongside it, a corrected version with a wealth of commentary[37]; later on, when he was already living at Meaux, he published the Gospels[38] and the Catholic Letters,[39] always accompanied by *Commentarii initiatorii.*

Lefèvre enjoyed a special status on the French and European religious scene during the first decades of the century; his disciples venerated him, Luther had a great regard for him, and Erasmus esteemed him for his doctrine and his piety, while the Sorbonne and Parliament of Paris kept an eye on him from a distance and suspected him of being a heretic. And yet this theologian, who had not obtained the title of doctor of theology, never wrote a doctrinal treatise, nor a guide, nor a comprehensive reflection on the many points which the reading of the sacred text suggested to him. Instead, he entrusted his thought to a broad-ranging work of exegesis that consisted of dedications, notes, and comments. In this work, then, can be traced the lines of a thinking that was unable and unwilling to offer itself as a closed and well-defined system; he used to say, "What else is the reading of the divine writings but a happy journey of our soul to God?"[40] And, like every journey, this one also had its North Star and was guided by some principles of interpretation.

When Lefèvre began his exegetical work, Erasmus had a short time before published the *Annotazioni al Nuovo Testamento* of Lawrence Valla (1505) and was working on the enterprise that would culminate in the publication of the *Novum Instrumentum* in 1516. Many problems had already been raised, and for anyone setting out to found a new biblical theology, philology was pointing out some specific preliminary questions about the text. Lefèvre was fully aware of these, but unlike Erasmus, he was not primarily a scholar of the word; he was working rather, but with great prudence, on pages that contained "the utterance of God, or the expression of his utterance." The *Quincuplex Psalterium* was a book in which the work of a philologist was most evident, but in this case he had at his disposal four versions, and this fact enabled him to advance with some freedom. In the later works interest in erudition seems to take second place. Like many humanists and biblicists, he was convinced that the Vulgate could not be attributed to St. Jerome; he therefore introduced some corrections that showed a knowledge of textual problems and, at times, a reading also of Valla's notes, but all this was not the guiding thread of his labors.

Lefèvre approached the Bible in a different spirit; his "journey" followed paths that were not those of the philologist, and in support of his choice he gave a privileged place to certain presuppositions. In the Scriptures (he said) God has given us the gift of his word: "Those who realize that this is a divine gift will be able to make progress, not by their own merits but by grace," because any profit derived is something surpassing human powers.[41] This is the first requirement for an understanding of the text. The second is the certitude that the Spirit, who is the author of the text, guides believers in their reading of it: the sacred pages are a place where God and creatures meet; God wrote these pages directly, guiding the hand of prophets and evangelists, and "Paul is only an instrument."[42]

If the writers were thus ready to be passive intermediaries, then readers, too, must adopt an attitude of complete readiness, "not to act but to be acted on." Lefèvre does not deny that there is a hermeneutical science, a practical discipline that teaches how to interpret a text. He warns that readers must keep in mind the language in which the text was written, and they must examine the context; but when dealing with a sacred text, the primary requirement is to read with the eyes of a believer. If this act of faith is not present, the truth remains silent and the reading barren or even an instrument of destruction.

> If soil that is not tilled, that does not feel the rain from heaven, produces anything at all, it is not anything that human beings can use: it produces only thorns, brambles, weeds. That is what happens to human minds that do not experience the divine ray: if they succeed in producing anything at all, it is usually more harmful than useful, and does not provide a lifegiving nourishment. The fruits

of minds lacking divine grace are weeds, thorns, burs, and things of that kind fill the works of those who write on human subjects and even on matters divine. . . . Left to themselves, human minds are barren, and if they think they can produce something, they sin by presumption, and if they do produce something, it is arid, wearying, opaque, and contrary to the mind rather than a lifegiving nourishment that is suited to the soul and to life.[43]

Not even the traditional four senses of Scripture seem to Lefèvre to be suitable instruments for reaching a full understanding; it is indeed true that there are stages calling for a moral reading and that the parables are allegories and must be read as such, but the key that opens up all the mysteries is different. There is a sense that is usually called literal but stops at the surface without grasping the true intention of the Spirit; this is the letter that kills. The authentic literal sense is different, being identical with the spiritual sense, with the intention of the Spirit who uttered it.[44] This is the only understanding that believers should seek: "We ought not ever or in any place seek anything but Christ";[45] "Those who have once understood that Christ is everything for us, as indeed he is, have understood everything."[46] And again: "The writings without Christ are only writings and a letter that kills."[47] The suggestion that there be an exclusively christological reading may not seem entirely new;[48] the problem is to decide what role the exegetical phase plays in the entire work of theology.

In 1514, in the dedication of his edition of Cusa's writings to Denis Briçonnet, Lefèvre wrote as follows:

I see that there are three theologies: the first and highest belongs to the intellect; in second place, there is a middle kind, a rational theology; the lowest involves the senses and imagination. The first seeks the truth in peace; the second fights error by rational arguments based on the truth; the third seeks to assail the truth by ambushes, making use even of falsehoods. In the first, the greater light absorbs the lesser; in the second, clarity is opposed to darkness; in the third, darkness to clarity. The first teaches in silence, the second in prudent speech, the third squawks in a torrent of words.[49]

The "first and supreme" theology, which dwells in the highest regions, is also the only one able to lead the faithful to the mystery, in the silence of contemplation, without the aid of the human sciences, by immersing them solely in the word of God.

A christological understanding profoundly changes the readers, leading them to imitation of Christ and advancing their *Christformitas,* the conformation or assimilation of believers to Christ.[50] This is the goal of Lefèvre's thought, and it is in the light of it that we may understand some themes by reason of which he has been compared to Luther: the assertion of the principle of "Scripture alone" *(sola scriptura),* the conviction that human beings cannot by their own powers do anything for their salvation, the commitment to making God's word known and spreading it with the help, among other things, of vernacular translations.[51]

But his biblicism did not involve a rejection of the tradition, and he was not alone in desiring that all might have access to a knowledge of the Scriptures. As for the more narrowly doctrinal subject of justification, which was then at the center of theological debate, his view was born of presuppositions not comparable to those of Luther:

> If you were to lead a life even more austere than that of Hilarion and all the hermits of the Thebaid, but were to look to yourself and think that your works could save you, you would indeed carry the cross but you would be following not Christ but yourself, because you would be thinking that your salvation lay in those works. Unlucky fellow, salvation comes not from your works but from those of Christ; it is not your cross but the cross of Christ that will save you. . . . As you bear the cross, then, look to him who saves you, and put your hope in his cross, that is, in his suffering, and not in your own, which does not save you.[52]

Lefèvre did not, however, deny the freedom of the human will, but he did approach the problem from another point of view. He maintained that the inherited sin was potential evil that becomes actual in the course of life, a blanket of darkness which Adam cast over his descendants and to which is added the cold in which each person encloses himself or herself by their own sins. But those who have truly died with Christ and have come to life with him and now follow him can no longer sin:

> He removes sin because his grace always erases it, just as when a ray of the sun strikes a place where there is cold and darkness, by its very nature it dispels the cold and darkness and brings light and warmth. The darkness is the seed of the evils which Adam has scattered over all; the cold is the individual sin that is added. The light is the universal justification that comes from on high, from the true sun of Justice, which is Christ. The warmth is the purification from one's own sins, those which each person has committed. The first justification comes through faith and is the work of the light; the second comes through charity and is the work of the warmth, but of a warmth combined with the light. In fact, if love, if charity is not immediately joined to and inseparable from faith and from him who is the cause of faith, it justifies no one and cannot be truly called love or charity. Realize, then, that the author of our salvation takes away all sins, the universal and the particular, and justifies us with a double justification.[53]

Commenting on the letter to the Romans, he explained further: "Neither faith nor works justify, but they prepare for justification, since God alone justifies. . . . The function of works, then, is to prepare and clear the way; faith is the goal, and is a kind of way by which God enters."[54]

Like Erasmus, Lefèvre thought that the work of theology had both its starting point and its highest point in the reading of the Scriptures, but the perspectives of the two scholars were profoundly different, with the result that there were opportunities for opposition and for misunderstanding. The most important instance arose in connection with the translation of a passage from the letter to the Hebrews (2:7) that refers to Jesus and cites verse 6 of Psalm 8. In his edition of the letters of Paul in 1512 Lefèvre had followed St. Jerome and translated the original as *minuisti eum paulominus a Deo* ("you have made him a little less than God"). Erasmus, on the other hand, in his *Novum Instrumentum* (1516), had accepted the more usual *minuisti eum paulominus ab angelis* and then stated that the adverb *paulominus* should be taken in a temporal sense: "you have made him for a short while less than the angels."

Here two theologies, two christologies, came face to face, and the exchange of accusations that followed was sometimes rather lively. Lefèvre's choice was dictated by a scrupulous piety. Respect for the dignity of the Son of God (he maintained) prevented him being made lower than other created things but not lower than the Father, since he himself said: "The Father is greater than I" (John 14:28). Erasmus, focusing as always on the human side of Christ, on that which had brought him closer to human beings and made him more intelligible to them, replied with the claim that by his translation Lefèvre was weakening the paradox of faith, playing down the reality of the incarnation and thereby slipping into a Docetist conception of it.[55]

Lefèvre, for his part, insisted on the argument of "convenience" or suitability as a principle that should always guide the interpretation of the sacred text. He had recourse to it on other occasions as well, for example, when he sought to show that the three women in the gospel stories whom a tradition originating with the Fathers identified with Mary Magdalene were in fact three different women. He compared the texts, appealed to the authority of the earliest commentators, and concluded that it would not be "suitable" to confuse Mary of Bethany, the devout sister of Lazarus and symbol of the contemplative life, with the women delivered from seven demons or with the sinful woman.[56] He followed the same principle when he took pen in hand to denounce the impious legend that had the mother of the Virgin being married three times.[57]

Lefèvre had left several disciples behind him in Paris. Among them was Charles of Bouelles, who was also called by the Latinized name Bovillus (Saucourt, Picardy, ca. 1470–ca. 1553). He was a man of many interests; he had inherited his teacher's passion for mathematical studies and had learned to love Nicholas of Cusa, Raymond Lull, and Pseudo-Dionysius. After a lengthy tour that took him to Germany, Switzerland, Italy, and Spain, he returned to France, devoted himself to the teaching of theology, and wrote many works of a spiritual, theological, and moral character. During his stay in Rome, in 1507, he had the opportunity to debate with a rabbi; from this came his *Dialogi de Trinitate,* which he dedicated to Lefèvre and later published in *Quaestionum Theologicarum Libri septem.*

Josse Clichtove, a Fleming (Nieuwport, 1472/73–Chartres, 1543), was also one of Lefèvre's most diligent collaborators in the publication of the works of Aristotle and of commentaries on him and also defended Lefèvre in the debates that arose on the subject of Mary Magdalene.[58] Clichtove, like his teacher, was interested in the revival of studies and the renewal of philosophy and theology and was in turn influenced by these, as the titles of other works show: an edition of the *Epistolae beati Pauli apostoli . . . necnon beati Jacobi, Petri, Joannis et Judae* (Paris, 1512); a *De mystica numerorum significatione opusculum, eorum praesertim qui in sacris litteris usitati habentur, spiritualem eorum designationem succincte elucidans* (Paris, 1513); and the numerous short works of a devotional kind, often dealing with marginal subjects as compared with the major problems of theology but indicative of the "practical theology" that was concerned with everything that could stimulate pity.[59]

When Lefèvre moved to Meaux, Clichtove did not follow him; from that point on, all his efforts seemed to be concentrated on the defense of orthodoxy and the tradition. Appealing to what he had learned from the works of Pseudo-Dionysius, he justified the dignity of the priesthood,[60] devoted himself to strenuously defending the validity of the veneration of the saints,[61] and won a reputation in Paris as the most important of controversialists, thanks to some polemical works: *Antilutherus* (1524), *Propugnaculum Ecclesiae adversus Lutheranos* (1526), *De sacramento eucharistiae, contra Oecolampadium* (1526), and *Compendium veritatum ad fidem pertinentium contra erroneas Lutheranorum assertiones* (1929).

William Budé (Paris, 1468–1540), one of the greatest of French humanists and known especially as a jurist and inaugurator of the science of economics, did not neglect theological studies. In his office as royal secretary, first of Charles VIII, then of Francis I, he endeavored to carry out a vast cultural program along humanistic lines. In 1522 he was director of the Royal Library; in 1530 he suggested to the sovereign the foundation of the Collège de France. As an attentive witness of the religious crisis of his age, Budé bitterly criticized the papacy of Julius II and was then hopeful that under Leo X a new era might begin. He was disappointed once again and, although he declared himself always opposed to the Reformation, he did share many of its motivations. But the rebirth of the spiritual life that he desired showed strongly cultural and aristocratic overtones that would have made it difficult to translate into a concrete program.

In his most important theological work, *De transitu Hellenismi ad Christianismum,* he studied the possibility of putting Greek philosophy at the service of theology, because (he maintained) wisdom is one and, like a golden chain, descends from heaven and draws to itself even those who resist it; it is Homer's golden chain, "extended through all the ages of the world by one and the same divinity." However, the ancients, who had first glimpsed the image of the truth, betrayed their duty, because "they thought they possessed everything," and like the Philistines, they stopped up and covered over the wells which Christianity would later have to clean out again. It is not without significance that Budé's works found an attentive reader in the Italian heretic Celius Secondus Curione, who published them at Basel in 1557.

BIBLIOGRAPHY

SOURCES

John Capreolus (+ Rodez, 1444)

Defensiones theologiae Thomae Aquinatis. . . . Venice, 1480–84, 1515, 1519, 1589; then, ed. C. Paban and Th. Pégues. 7 vols. Tours, 1900–8. Reprinted: New York, 1967.

John of Neehausen

De esse et essentia. In G. Meerssemann. *Geschichte des Albertismus.* I, 91–191. See below, under Studies.

William of Vaurillon (ca. 1400–1464)

Opus super quattuor libris Sententiarum iuxta doctrinam Johannis Scoti. Lyons, 1489; Venice, 1496; Basel, 1510.
Declaratio seu Retractatio. In I. Brady. "The *Declaratio seu Retractatio* of William of Vaurouillon." *AFH* 58 (1965) 399–416.
Liber de anima. In I. Brady. "The *Liber de anima* of William of Vaurouillon O.F.M." *Medieval Studies* 10 (1948) 224–97; 11 (1949) 247–307.
Repertorium magistri Guillelmi Varillonis, quod alio nomine dicitur vademecum, vel collectorium non opinionis Scoti, sed opinionum in Scoto nullatenus signatarum. Padua, [1485].

Nicholas of Orbellis (+ 1472/75)

Commentarii in quattuor libros Sententiarum. Paris, 1488.
Super sententias compendium perutile. Hagenau, 1503.
Petri Lombardi quatuor sententiarum volumina cum doctissimis Nicolai de Orbellis theologi acutissimi interpretationibus, in quibus Scoti dicta quae obscura vulgo videbantur faciliter enarrantur. Ex quorum cognitione brevi omnes in Scoti dogmatibus sunt peritissimi evasuri. Venice, 1507.

Stephen Pillet (Brûlefer) (+ 1500/2)

Formalitates in doctrinam Scoti. Paris, 1490.
In quatuor S. Bonaventurae doctoris seraphici Sententiarum libros, Scoti subtilis secundi. Basel, 1501.

Peter Tartaret (Tataret)

Commentaria sive, ut vocant, reportata in quatuor libros sententiarum et quodlibeta J. Duns Scoti. Venice, 1583.
Quaestiones morales. Paris, 1504, 1509, 1513.

Martin Lemaistre (De Magistris) (Tours, 1432–1482)

Quaestiones morales . . . de fortitudine. [Paris], 1489, 1510.
Quaestiones morales de temperantia. Paris, 1490, 1511.

Nicholas of Clamanges (Clémanges; Nicholas Poillevillain) (Clémanges, Marne, 1360–Paris, 1437)

Liber de studio theologico. In L. d'Achery. *Spicilegium sive Collectio veterum aliquot scriptorum.* I. Paris, 1723. Pp. 473–80.

Robert Ciboule (Breteuil, Eure, ca. 1403–Paris, 1458)

Livre de la perfection de la vie crestienne. [Paris, n.d.].
Le livre de la méditation sur soy mesme. [Paris], 1510.

Robert Gaguin (Colline Beaumont, Pas de Calais, 1420/25–Paris, 1501)

Epistolae et orationes. Ed. L. Thuasne. 2 vols. Paris, 1903.

John Raulin (Toul, ca. 1443–Cluny, 1515)

Opera quae inveniri potuerunt. 7 vols. Antwerp, 1611–12.

Louis Pinelle (Montluçon, ca. 1465–Meaux, 1516)

Les quinze fontaines vitales, utiles et salutaires. Ed. in Veissière. "Un précurseur." See Studies, below.

William Briçonnet (Tours, 1470–Meaux, 1534)

William Briçonnet and Marguerite of Angoulême. *Correspondance.* Ed. C. Martineau and others. 2 vols. Travaux d'humanisme et renaissance 141 and 173. Geneva, 1975–79.

James Lefèvre d'Étaples (Étaples, ca. 1460–Nérac, 1636)

Quincuplex Psalterium. Gallicum, Romanum, Hebraicum. Vetus. conciliatum. [Paris] 1509. Second printing, 1513. Reprinted Geneva, 1979. Travaux d'humanisme et renaissance 170.
[Pauli epistolae]. Commentarii in Pauli epistolas. [Paris] 1512.
Sanctum Evangelium secundum Matthaeum . . . , Marcum . . . , Commentarii. Meaux, 1522.
[Epistolae catholicae.] Commentarii in epistolas catholicas. Basel, 1527.
Psalterium David, argumentis adjectis hebraica et chaldaica multis in locis translatione illustratum. [Meaux] 1522.

Charles of Bouelles (Bovillus) (Sancourt, ca. 1470–Paris, ca. 1553)

Commentarius in primordiale Evangelium divi Johannis. [Paris] 1511.
Quaestionum theologicarum libri septem. [Paris] 1513.

Josse Clichtove (Nieuwport, 1472/73–Chartres, 1543)

De laude monasticae religionis. Paris, 1513.
Antilutherus. Paris, 1524.
Compendium veritatum ad fidem pertinentium contra erroneas Lutherorum asser-tiones. Paris, 1529.

William Budé (Paris, 1468–1540)

Opera omnia. Basel, 1557.
De transitu Hellenismi ad Christianismum. Recently translated with introduction and notes by M. M. de La Garanderie and D. Franklin Penham. *Le passage de l'hel-lénisme au christianisme.* Les classiques d'humanisme. Paris, 1993.

STUDIES (IN ALPHABETICAL ORDER BY AUTHOR)

Amann, E. "Lefèvre d'Étaples, Jacques." *DTC* 9 (Paris, 1926). Cols. 132–59.
Bedouelle, G. *Lefèvre d'Étaples et l'intelligence des Écritures.* Travaux d'humanisme et renaissance 152. Geneva, 1976.
_____. *Le "Quincuplex Psalterium" de Lefèvre d'Étaples. Une guide de lecture.* Travaux d'humanisme et renaissance 171. Geneva, 1979.
_____. "Raulin, Jean." *DSp* 13 (Paris, 1988). Cols. 154–56.
Berier, F. "Exégèse et ironie: à propos de l'*Expositio super septem capitula Ysaye* de Nicolas de Clamanges (ca. 1425)." *Recherches et travaux. Université de Grenoble. Bulletin* 41 (1991) 17–35.
Burrows, M. S. "Jean Gerson After Constance: *Via Media et Regia* as a Revision of the Ockhamist Covenant." *Church History* 59 (1990) 467–81.
Chantraine, G. "Josse Clichtove: témoin théologien de l'humanisme parisien. Scholastique et célibat au XVI siècle." *RHE* 66 (1971) 507–28.
Combes, A. "Ciboule, Robert." *DSp* 2 (Paris, 1953). Col. 887–90.
_____. *Essai sur la critique de Ruysbroeck par Gerson.* 3 vols. Paris, 1945–59.
_____. *Jean de Montreuil et le chancellier Gerson. Contribution à l'histoire de la théologie en France au début du XV* siècle. Études de philosophie médiévale 32. Paris, 1942.
Coville, A. *Gontier et Pierre Col et l'humanisme en France au temps de Charles VI.* Paris, 1934.
_____. *Le traité de la ruine de l'église de Nicolas de Clamanges et la traduction française de 1564.* Paris, 1935.
Delaruelle, L. *Guillaume Budé. Les origines, les débuts, les idées maîtresses.* Paris, 1907; reprinted: Geneva, 1970.
Dulieu, L. "Les 'Théologastres' de l'Université de Paris au temps d'Erasme et de Rabelais (1496–1536)." *Bibliothèque d'humanisme et renaissance* 27 (1965) 248–64.
Histoire des Universités en France. Ed. J. Verger. Toulouse, 1986.
Kerner, H. "Budé, Guillaume." *TRE* 7 (Berlin–New York, 1981) 335–38.
Kristeller, P. O. "An Unknown Humanist Sermon on St. Stephen by Guillaume Fichet." *Mélanges Eugène Tisserant* IV. Studi e Testi 236. Vatican City, 1964. Pp. 459–97.

La Garanderie, M. M. de. *Christianisme et lettres profanes (1515–1535). Essai sur les mentalités des milieux intellectuelles Parisiens et sur la pensée de Guillaume Budé.* Lille-Paris, 1976.

Langlois, E. "Le traité de Gerson contre le *Roman de la Rose." Romania* 45 (1918–19) 23–48.

Massaut, J. P. "France: Le 16ᵉ siècle." *DSp* 5 (Paris, 1964). Cols. 892–96.

————. *Josse Clichtove, l'humanisme et la réforme du clergé.* 2 vols. Bibliothèque de la Faculté de Philosophie et Lettres de l'Université de Liège 183. Paris, 1968.

McNeil, D. O. *Guillaume Budé and Humanism in the Reign of Francis I.* Travaux d'humanisme et renaissance 142. Geneva, 1975.

Meersseman, G. *Geschichte des Albertismus.* Heft I. *Die Pariser Anfänge des Kölner Albertismus.* Institutum Historicum FF. Praedicatorum, Rome. Dissertationes Historicae 3. Paris, 1933.

Ornato. E. *Jean Muret et ses amis Nicolas de Clamanges et Jean de Gerson. Contribution à l'étude des rapports entre les humanistes de Paris et ceux d'Avignon.* Geneva, 1969.

Rapp, F. "France: Le 15ᵉ siècle." *DSp* 5 (Paris, 1964). Cols. 880–91.

Renaudet, A. *Préréforme et humanisme à Paris pendant les premières guerres d'Italie (1494–1517).* Paris, 1953².

Simone, F. "Robert Gaguin e il suo cenacolo umanistico. I: 1473–1485." *Aevum* 13 (1939) 410–76.

Stegmann, A. "Erasme et la France (1495–1520)." *Colloquium Erasmianum . . .* (Mons, 26–29 octobre 1967). Mons, 1968. Pp. 275–95.

Tokarski, F. "Guillaume de Vaurillon et son commentaire sur les *Sentences* de Pierre Lombard." *Mediaevalia philosophica Polonorum* 29 (1988) 49–119.

Veissière, M. "Un précurseur de Guillaume Briçonnet, Louis Pinelle évêque de Meaux de 1511 à 1516. Avec l'édition de son traité spirituel: *Les quinze fontaines vitales." Bulletin de la Société d'Histoire et d'Art du diocèse de Meaux* 18 (1967) 7–62.

————. *L'évêque Guillaume Briçonnet (1470–1534). Contribution à la connaissance de la réforme catholique à la veille du Concile de Trente.* Provins, 1986.

CHAPTER 7

Traditionalism, Humanism, and Mystical Experience in Northern Europe and in the Germanic Areas in the Fifteenth and Sixteenth Centuries

Anna Morisi

*1. England at the Beginning of the Modern Age: Thomas Netter
and Reginald Pecock*

At the end of the fourteenth and the beginning of the fifteenth centuries, the period of the Great Schism, England was troubled by a serious crisis: to foreign wars, dynastic conflicts, and social tensions there was added a profound religious restlessness that found its most important expression in the Lollard movement. The world of the official culture was not unaffected by the general anxiety; the major centers of theological study in particular seemed to have suffered a decadence that would last for almost a century. During the long conflict with France relations with Paris had been interrupted, and this had led to the isolation of the English universities from those of the Continent; Oxford and Cambridge, which could not rely on personalities comparable to Gerson or Peter d'Ailly, seemed to have lost their former intellectual fervor. And yet, as in every transitional period, beneath a seeming lack of luster great changes were in preparation.

The century in which the foundations were laid for a new reading of the Bible and therefore for a new theology began in England under the sign of direct persecution of the followers of John Wyclif, the "Evangelical Doctor." In

March of 1401 Henry IV issued the edict *De haeretico comburendo,* which offered the support of the secular arm to the ecclesiastical hierarchy and provided Thomas Arundel, archbishop of Canterbury, with a suitable tool for suppressing the movement. Henry thus initiated a religious policy which the successive kings of the Lancaster family were to follow in a subtle and ambiguous power game aimed at maintaining a relationship with the papal court that was not openly hostile and, at the same time, to safeguard the freedom of the English church. But at this time the liveliest and most problematic part of the Wyclif heritage had been taken over by the Bohemians, while no outstanding religious personality emerged from the ranks of the English Lollards. As for the philosophical and theological motives that had been the basis for the teachings of Wyclif, the emphasis was being placed on the ethical and disciplinary aspect, with a strong anticlerical stamp: heresy acquired almost the connotations of social protest and political rebellion and thus was seen as high treason.

During the first thirty years of the fifteenth century the movement seemed to have exhausted its driving force; in fact, it disappeared as a political force, being suppressed by the enterprise of the ruling classes, and it survived only secretly in isolated conventicles, an underground stream that would emerge again a century later and flow into the great riverbed of the Reformation. And yet the English people kept the vernacular translation of the Bible that Wyclif had promoted, this despite some restrictive measures aimed at limiting its spread. In the plans of the Oxford doctor and his fellow workers, that undertaking certainly was not an anticipation, in either approach or method, of the biblicism that would be born on the soil of humanism. But, precisely because Wyclif's aim was to reach even those who had always been excluded from the world of theological speculation, he fostered a widespread knowledge of the sacred texts at all levels of society.

It is possible to make out in the antiheretical controversies of those years some new elements that portended a movement beyond Scholastic procedures, and this precisely in the works of the most convinced adversaries of the "evangelical men" *(viri evangelici),* that is, in the pages of such theologians as Thomas Netter and Reginald Pecock. These men lined up in defense of the tradition, but they were also able to discern and give a place to some fundamental demands of the culture of the time. It is perhaps not an accident that both men carried on their work outside the university environment, in more or less direct relationship with the world of politics and the court.

The first of the two, also known as Thomas Waldensis from the name of his native place (Saffron Walden, Essex), where he was born around 1377/80, entered the Carmelite convent in London as a very young man. After a period of theological studies at Oxford he became a court preacher and then a court confessor and was employed in various religious and diplomatic missions by his sovereigns. Thus in 1409 he went to the Council of Pisa by commission of

Henry IV; in the time of Henry V, in 1414, he became provincial of the English Carmelites and in that capacity took part in the Council of Constance. He was later sent to make peace between the grand master of the Teutonic Order and Ladislaus of Poland, with the specific aim of freeing the king from other commitments and inducing him to turn his weapons against the Hussites. On the occasion of these journeys Netter visited and reformed the convents of the order in Germany and founded other new convents in Prussia, Poland, and even distant Lithuania. He died at Rouen in 1430 while accompanying young Henry VI, who was to assume the crown of France. The fame of his teaching and integrity was such that he was regarded as a saint, and his tomb became a place of worship.

In his youth, during his years at Oxford, Netter had carefully studied the works of Wyclif and had felt the fascination of the heresy against which he then lavished all his talents. We do not know with certainty whether he was ever officially given the office of inquisitor, but he certainly contributed to the work of suppressing Lollardism. In particular, he was present at some famous trials, such as those of Peter Payne, John Oldcastle, William Whyte, and Thomas Scrope, and to him can be attributed in large measure the imposing collection of documents and records of the interrogations of heretics that is known by the name of *Fasciculi Zizaniorum.* His reputation, however, rests on his theological writings. The Council of Florence had condemned the teachings of the English heretic, and the flames of John Huss' pyre had already died out, when Master Thomas put his hand to his major work, the *Doctrinale antiquitatum fidei catholicae Ecclesiae,* against Wyclif and his followers, "who after having filled the churches of England now occupy all of Bohemia."[1]

This work, the only one of his many treatises of an exegetical and controversialist kind to have survived the snares of time in its entirety, was very favorably received: the subjects were exceptionally relevant and topical; the approach, the method, and the wealth of documentation would guarantee it a singular success even in later centuries. The argumentation, which was strictly theological and developed with great doctrinal consistency, took as its starting point Wyclif's fundamental assumption, namely, the sufficiency of Scripture as sole source of the faith and exclusive foundation of Christian life. Netter did not reject this premise, but he did propose to show the limitations and weakness of the approach taken by an adversary against whom he turned back the accusation of having betrayed the divine word.

The sacred text (he maintained) did need to be interpreted, but individual believers cannot arrogate such great authority to themselves, ignoring what has been said by the apostles, the Fathers, and then, by common consent, the entire community of the Church. If such a course were to be followed the door would be opened to heresy, and not only would Christian society lose all its cohesion, but the very continuity between the community of believers and its founder would be broken. Only a part of the truth was committed to the pages of the Gospels; there are other truths which the apostles and first Christians were able to learn from the living voice of Christ; they communicated these to the earliest exegetes, and these in turn passed them on to later generations. The magisterium of the Church has preserved this heritage; if today we seek to go back solely to the words of the Savior that are attested in the New Testament, we are renouncing part of his teaching, drastically reducing the patrimony of the faith, and separating the Mystical Body from its Head.

It is not possible, indeed, to say that no Father made mistakes, but it is also true that all the teachers have followed the same doctrines in their main lines. This unity and consistency have been the Church's guide especially in deciding which books are to be considered canonical, and the number of these cannot be increased since the law of Christ has already reached its completion. For this reason, where there is a lacuna, custom steps in, for "custom is the living faith of the Church."[2]

This line of argument was not new, but the manner of proceeding was unusual, for in carefully refuting Wyclif's statements Netter avoided getting involved in a "Scholastic game" *(ludus scholasticus)*. In matters of faith he did not think it permissible to have recourse to philosophy; he wanted to base his demonstration not on the empty speculation of human wisdom but solely on the word of God; he did not intend to erect a new conceptual edifice, as the heretic had done, but rather to gather up the records which come to the Church from its earliest tradition.[3] In replying to the claims of his adversary, whose disciples regarded him as a new Augustine, "John son of Augustine" *(Joannes Augustini)*, Netter chose the Fathers as his guide: first and foremost the real Augustine, but also Ambrose, Hilary, Basil, Jerome, and Cassian, whom the followers of Wyclif scorned as having little wisdom. Only rarely did Netter appeal to more recent theologians; in the practical and ecclesiological perspective which he adopted he preferred to leave aside all demonstrations of a Scholastic kind and make more room for a biblical and patristic line of reasoning.

During these same years the first humanists were readying themselves for a "rediscovery" of the early Christian writers, who were being newly esteemed in response to abuses of the Scholastic method. But Netter was not a humanist; he did not turn back to the pages of the Fathers in order to recover a purity that had been lost during long centuries of decadence; his aim rather was to seek in them the traces of a never-interrupted original tradition represented by the unity of the faithful in the Mystical Body of Christ. For these reasons, his work, which was located entirely in the setting of a renewed Augustinianism, was destined to become a precious repertory of patristic sources and would be extensively used by the controversialists of the Counterreformation and, first and foremost, by Bellarmine.

A very different approach is to be seen in the pages of Reginald Pecock. A generation younger than Netter (being born in Wales around 1395), Pecock likewise received his formation in the theological faculty of Oxford. He then left the world of the university for the world of the court, where he had a brilliant career with the support of Duke Humphrey of Gloucester, brother of Henry V. As bishop of St. Asaph (1444) and then of Chichester (1450) and a member of the king's privy council (1454), he linked his fortunes to the Lancaster family and shared their lot when, York having prevailed, he was accused of promoting heretical doctrines and fomenting rebellion (1457–58). He ended his days in obscurity around 1460 as a prisoner in the abbey of Thorney.

The many works of his that have survived make it possible to reconstruct a coherent system of thought that is clearly set forth in the language most familiar to his readers: from *The Donet* to *The Folewer to the Donet* (written respectively in 1440 and 1454), from *The Reule of Crysten Religion* (1443), which follows the outline of the *Summa contra Gentiles,* to the *Repressor of Over Much Blaming of the Clergy* (1449) and to his best-known work, the *Book of Faith* (written in 1455–56), Pecock, too, sets out to refute the Lollards, those "men of the Bible," and their key doctrine, namely, the conviction that Christians cannot be bound by any other law than the one attested in the Scriptures, which every individual can correctly interpret without fear of error.

Accustomed as he was to the Scholastic method, Pecock first of all distinguished between philosophy and theology: reason and faith (he maintained) are two different faculties, each with its own competence, its own limitations, its own conclusions, and neither of which can be used to prove the propositions of the other. There is an area that is closed to reason: the area of religious truths, in which the Scriptures alone provide the object of faith. As Thomas Aquinas himself had said, faith is a kind of knowledge *(cognitio quaedam)* that is different from the knowledge proper to science; it is a knowledge that can be *scientialis* or *opinionalis,* and it alone can human beings manage to reach, not however in virtue of their intellectual capacities but by the direct or indirect action of God. Only in the Scriptures, then, is the supernatural truth revealed that lies outside the realm of reason but is not contrary to it. Everything having to do with the moral law and with the behavior of the individual can be confirmed in the sacred text, but need not be sought there exclusively, to the extent that it falls within the scope of a natural law which reason can grasp; on the truths proved by reason, all human beings, whatever their culture, can reach agreement.

Pecock drew the ultimate conclusions from his reasoning and maintained that when reason speaks with a perfectly clear voice, it must be obeyed against every other law; but the certainties of reason are not limitless, and where it hesitates it must follow the lead of the Church, which, though fallible in principle, has in fact never erred. It is perhaps precisely in defining this uncertain borderline that we can see the limits of Pecock's rationalism, which was deeply rooted in the logic of medieval philosophy. It was on the basis of these premises that he adopted attitudes which contributed to making him an inconvenient person. His recognition of the universality of rational thought led him to become a champion of tolerance once it became possible to ask logic and the syllogism to provide the means of persuading heretics instead of suppressing them. Furthermore, in the same years in which Lawrence Valla was proving the *Constitutum Constantini* to be a forgery by a grammatical and rhetorical analysis of the document, Pecock was reaching the same conclusion from a line of argument that took into account chiefly the document's historical context.[4]

The real originality of what the English theologian had to offer, his response to the problems of his time, consisted above all in his having seen the necessity of enabling a public far more inclusive than the specialists to share in the work of the theologians. His experience at court had put him in contact with men involved in practical problems, with merchants and highly intelligent lawyers, who could not be denied direct access to the sacred texts nor deprived of the right to study them. For this reason he wrote his works in the language of everyday, suggested that the liturgy be revised to make it intelligible to the laity, and was in favor of the vernacular translation of the Bible. He himself did a translation of the Creed into English but left in it a trace of his personal theological views: he omitted the article on the descent into the lower world, and this was held against him at the trial that condemned him as a heretic, a new Abelard who had extended beyond due measure the rights of reason.

2. Humanism in England: Thomas More, John Colet, and John Fisher

In the second decade of the century the ecumenical council that brought representatives of all Christian Europe together at Constance was also an extraordinary opportunity for persons of diverse cultures and experience to meet and exchange views. Various humanists were there as secretaries in the entourage of the cardinals; then, when the papal court was transferred to Rome, some of these men entered it as writers for the Apostolic See and were often used for diplomatic missions. It was then that Italian humanism spread to England and found favor with prelates and churchmen who did not see in it, at least at the beginning, elements that were controversial and hostile to their traditions.

Although enthusiastic readers of Petrarch had not been lacking since the end of the preceding century, the direct contact with Italian culture can be dated to the moment when Henry Beaufort, bishop of Winchester, made the acquaintance of Poggio Bracciolini at Constance and invited him to visit England. Poggio accepted the offer, mistakenly thinking that on that island he could continue the profitable search for ancient manuscripts that he had already begun in Germany. His hopes were dashed; he wrote to a friend, "The libraries of the oldest monasteries have lost many precious books in the course of lengthy wars."[5]

But during his stay (1518–23) he was able to strike up new friendships; in addition, it was precisely in England that he developed his interest in the Fathers of the Church, the reading of whom seems to have replaced, at least temporarily, the reading of his beloved classics. He immersed himself there in the study of John Chrysostom's homilies on the Fourth Gospel, which he read in a Latin translation: "There is nothing more learned, serious, wonderful," he wrote. "It is a pity that the translator did not have the gift of eloquence!"[6]

Some years later, from 1435 to 1440, a disciple of Guarino, protonotary apostolic Pietro del Monte, who was also at Constance, sojourned in England as nuncio at a particularly difficult point in relations between the crown and the pope. He struck up a fruitful literary association with Henry Beaufort, who had become a cardinal; he made the acquaintance of abbots, professors, and noblemen, among them Duke Humphrey of Gloucester, who liked to surround himself with Italian secretaries and who promoted humanistic studies at Oxford, his own university. The exchange of persons and books between Italy and England became ever more extensive; it was not only the Greek and Latin classics that were being read but also the works of the Church Fathers. The latter were being translated, studied, and made the subject of commentaries, as being a key to the interpretation of the Scriptures, because in them, as Erasmus was to say, the word of heaven still lives and breathes.

While Oxford soon became the most important center for humanistic studies, Cambridge did not remain alien to the demands of the new culture; though more conservative and tied to tradition and a place where Scholasticism had deep roots and the *via antiqua* prevailed, it nonetheless became a location of lively discussions. Toward the end of the century a renewal of the curriculum of studies was gladly accepted and the teaching of Greek was introduced; subsequently, the influence of humanism on theology was seen chiefly in biblical and patristic studies, and it was in this school that a generation of men committed to the reform of the Church was trained.

Around the middle of the fifteenth century the number of Englishmen visiting Italy began to increase. Thus William Grey (+ 1478), who had studied at Balliol College, Oxford, came to know Guarino and struck up a friendship with Bessarion; on his return he was appointed bishop of Ely, devoted himself to theological studies, and collected an extensive library. William Shelling, a monk of Canterbury, obtained a doctorate in theology at Bologna, learned Greek, and brought home from Italy some valuable manuscripts: a Homer, a Euripides, a Synesius, but also a Basil and a John Chrysostom. It was he who directed the studies of Thomas Linacre (1470–1524), sending him first to Oxford; later, when William was appointed preacher for Innocent VIII, he took Thomas with him to Italy, had him visit Rome and Florence, and introduced him to Politian and Demetrius Calcondilla.

At Oxford, where Cornelius Vitelli, a Greek scholar from Cortona (ca. 1440–1500) was teaching both privately and at the university, the first official course in Greek language and literature was organized and taught by one of Shelling's disciples, William Grocyn (+ 1519), who had already been a professor of theology at Magdalen College since 1481. There he had among his listeners William Latimer (+ 1545), Thomas More, Cuthbert Tunstall (1474–1559), John Fisher, and William Lily (+ 1522), in short, the whole of that "Italy in England"[7] that at the end of the century welcomed Erasmus and had him as guest during his successive stays on the island. Aldo Manutius had a special esteem of the English humanists, who collaborated with him in his editions of the physicians and philosophers of antiquity. He saw in this a sign of destiny: in the distant past (he remarked), barbarous and unlearned letters came to us from Britain and settled throughout all of Italy, where even today they maintain their strongholds; now, from that same land, we are receiving help in overcoming the forms of barbarism and regaining our positions, so that "the very spear that inflicted the wound is now healing it."[8]

But in the lively circle of the English humanists who were resolved to renew theology by returning to the sources with the tools of the new philological science, there were not lacking debates and oppositions that were no less lively. Most of them had experienced the attraction of Florentine Neoplatonism; those, on the other hand, who, like Grocyn, had gained a knowledge of Aristotle at Padua, gave the palm to the Stagyrite: "In my opinion, there is as much difference between the supreme philosophers, Plato and Aristotle, as there is (I say this with due respect for all) between much learning and much wordiness *(polymathê kai polymythê).*"[9] Therefore, although all professed confidence in the same method and held that knowledge of the ancient languages was the first and necessary step in the study of theology, different approaches and perspectives inevitably led to different results. Grocyn, for example, followed the historical and philological method in explaining the works of Pseudo-Dionysius and, to the great consternation of the Neoplatonists, concluded that he could not have lived in the time of Paul the Apostle.

All this fervent study and discussion finally lapped against even the stern halls of the theological faculties. In 1517 Bishop Richard Fox, protector of the University of Oxford, drew up the statutes of Corpus Christi College, introduced an obligatory course in the Greek language for all students of theology, and required the instructors to lecture on the texts of the Fathers rather than on those of the medieval theologians. Reaction was swift; the more conservative elements, who felt surrounded and besieged by the new Greeks, prepared to defend themselves, like the ancient Trojans, under the leadership of a new Priam and with the help of a new Hector and of others who had adopted the names of the Homeric heroes. The game degenerated into open attacks and harsh insults from the pulpits, so much so that the king himself asked someone to intervene, and Thomas More was entrusted with the task of pacifying spirits. More wrote a lengthy letter to the authorities of the university, assuring them of the intentions of the practicioners of the new science, who did not have in mind to sacrifice truth to the art of speaking well nor intend to imprison the queen of all the sciences in literary straitjackets. They wanted only to make one point clear:

> Does she [theology] not dwell and abide in the Holy Scripture? Does she not pursue her pilgrim way through the cells of the holy Fathers: Augustine and Jerome; Ambrose and Cyprian; Chrysostom, Basil, and their like? The study of theology had been solidly based on these now despised expositors of fundamental truth during all the Christian centuries until the invention of these petty and meretricious "questions" which are today glibly tossed back and forth.[10]

The English humanists had put the traditionalist theologians in a difficult spot and had produced a climate that was open to new cultural needs and to the demands for a reform of Christian life. None of them, however, had the boldness or the time to draw from these premises a concrete plan for the work of theology. In his *Utopia* More did sketch a plan of an ideal society that was so arranged as to foster a religious experience in keeping with the natural aspirations of the human person: an experience that was adogmatic and based on a few simple suppositions, such as belief in the existence of God, the immortality of the soul, and a reward in a life beyond this world. He imagined that the laws of this happy state would not permit debates and disputes of a doctrinal kind, such as are useful only for embittering minds, nor would they even allow proselytism. But he was also convinced that once this community was trained to live in hardworking fellowship, it would show itself ready to receive the Christian message, which is the one closest to meeting the needs of the human soul and the only one able to enlighten it with the certainty of revelation.

Using all the freedom granted one who tells a good story, More had shown the prerequirements for religious tolerance, but he left it to others to draw the conclusions. His later works are the meditations of a profoundly devout, cultivated, and refined spirit that tended to seek peace with itself and the surrounding world rather than to be the agent of a new way of life. Consequently, when the Reformation threw the Christian West into confusion, More was unable to meet it with arguments much different from those of so many other anti-Lutheran controversialists.

John Colet, the most theological minded of the group, did not live to see the days of the great wounding. He too had begun his studies at Oxford and then finished them at Cambridge; during a lengthy journey that took him to France and Italy from 1493 to 1496 he developed his interest in the Bible and the Fathers. In Florence he may have met Pico, whose works he read with care; with Ficino he struck up a lasting friendship that left its traces in some letters. When he returned to his native land, he was ordained a deacon and later a priest and began a cycle of lectures on the letters of Paul at Oxford.

As Pico had already done, Colet also commented on the opening chapters of Genesis and meditated on the works of Pseudo-Dionysius, from which he drew the inspiration for two writings of his own, *De sacramento ecclesiae* and *De compositione corporis Christ mystici*. In 1504 he was appointed dean of St. Paul's in London, and in 1510 he founded there a school dedicated to "Jesus talking with the teachers"; in this school a good number of boys who had already begun their studies learned Latin and Greek so as to prepare themselves for a more consciously Christian life. He also compiled a Latin grammar and a catechism for his pupils. He died on September 16, 1519, when the movement of reform had already started, many aspects of which he seemed to have anticipated.

Erasmus, who came to know Colet during his first journey to England (1499–1500), said: "When I listen to Colet, I seem to be hearing Plato."[11] Two years after Colet's death, in an emotional letter, Erasmus drew a picture of Colet as a preacher and a teacher who had given of himself with great generosity. He was proudly opposed to Scholastic theology (Erasmus related); the Scotists, whom all regarded as gifted with unusual insight, seemed to him to be obtuse and dull-minded rather than clever; Thomas pleased him even less, and he said of him that "if he had not had a good bit of arrogance in him, he would not have so rashly and presumptuously tried to offer a definitive judgment in every matter; and if he had not had a certain worldly spirit, he would not have contaminated all of Christian doctrine with his secular philosophy." And yet there was no work, however heretical, that Colet did not read carefully and find some good in, much more, certainly, than can be learned from those who very arrogantly seek to settle every question for the sole purpose of winning applause for themselves. But above all (Erasmus concluded) Colet was a promotor of peace and convinced that for Christians no war is just.[12] This portrait has perhaps some traits that are autobiographical, or at least it emphasizes points on which the two friends were in agreement; at the same time, however, it does provide the basis for an understanding of the man.

Colet was certainly not a systematic theologian; nothing was more foreign to him than grand conceptual structures that were clearly defined and rounded off. His exegetical work on the texts of the Bible was a continual study along soteriological lines. His christocentric humanism fed on a variety of influences: Platonism and Neoplatonism, Augustinianism and the patristic tradition, with a tendency to harmonize all these that brought him close to his friends in Florence, although he did not fully share their intellectual boldness or their large philosophical plans. Colet had approached the culture of the humanists with a deeply religious intention, and from it he had learned to read the sacred texts as pages of high poetry, in which the individual authors, guided by the Spirit, communicate to their readers a love of God, each of them in his own style and according to the needs of his times and his readers. But Colet was not disposed to indulge in the enthusiasm of many for secular literature, perhaps because he saw the danger of esthetic study, even to itself.[13] Scripture by itself, he said, contains all the food the soul needs;[14]

he realized, however, that his goal was not to make known the mysteries of God but to make God loved: "Revelation, which is our wisdom, gives light to faith."[15]

In his zeal as preacher, teacher, and theologian Colet wanted a reform of the community of believers; he understood this reform as a return to the "form," the perfection of the beginnings, the faith that loves and believes. The themes of the relationship between faith and works, religious experience and moral experience, which were at the center of theological debate at the time, could be linked to Ficino's conception of love as a perennial force that elevates human beings to God and gives meaning to their activity. The justice that is born of faith is revealed in the Gospel, and no salvation is possible except through faith in Christ and in his mercy: "Everlasting life comes only from the justice which faith gives."[16] A recompense is due those who work, but justification is a freely given gift granted to those who believe; grace alone in fact justifies, whereas apart from the justice which faith gives, the works of the flesh and the body have no value.[17] But, Colet warned, "the faith that justifies has, as part of its meaning, the imitation of Christ and cooperation with him; Paul speaks of it elsewhere as the faith that works through love."[18]

Neoplatonic, too, are the basic lines of his anthropology: the sin of Adam was devastating for the human race, which acquired from it an inclination to evil, but evil in turn has no reality of its own; it is an alienation from God, the supreme good and supreme love; it is a resistance by matter, which is prey to chaos, to the action of grace, which works as a form capable of restoring a lost order.

In the circle of love that joins Creator and creature, faith and charity are not distinguishable. The absence of this lifegiving element leads to the corruption of the Christian community and delegitimizes its highest authorities, beginning with the pope, because (Colet said in his commentary on Pseudo-Dionysius) if God does not work in him, all of Christianity becomes infected—something that has been happening for many years now. The dignity of priests is superior to that of king and emperor, provided the priesthood be understood as service, commitment, the doing of good, and responsibility. Today, however, it is clear that the root of every evil is greed, as the apostle said (1 Tim 6:10). Not even the power to forgive sins can be acknowledged as present in one who is unworthy of it: the power of "binding and loosing" belongs only to God in heaven. The supreme authorities, the popes, know how much is bound and loosed for them

> by revelation, and they declare that they have received it, and in their words they carry out God's intention, not their own. But if they do not act on revelation and are not moved by the Spirit of God in all that they do and say, then inevitably they rave and speak foolishly from out of themselves and abuse the power given to them to blaspheme God and ruin the Church. . . . They are not executors of God's will, but doers of their own.[19]

While Colet was writing and preaching against abuses, externalism, and formalism, and longing for the recovery of a simpler and more intimate religious experience, the Lollard movement seemed to be regaining strength. In February of 1512 the province of Canterbury held a meeting, and Colet, who was commissioned to give the opening address, instead of uttering condemnations of the heretics urged those present to proceed first and foremost to a radical reform of the Church. His enemies collected from his works a series of suspect statements so that they could accuse him of heresy: they reproached him for his indifference to the veneration of saints and their relics and to pilgrimages, for his silence on the doctrine of purgatory, his attack on Church property, and his proposal to translate part of the Scriptures and the prayers of the liturgy into the vernacular. But Archbishop Wahram brought all his authority to bear and absolved him.

Another of Erasmus' friends was John Fisher, one of the central figures in the religious world of contemporary England. He was not, in fact, an original theologian; he always remained attached to the ancient traditions of the theological faculties and never hid his admiration for Thomas and Duns Scotus. He did, however, try to introduce new life into the ancient tree of Scholasticism by grafting onto it the new contributions of humanism, with a view to integrating two different traditions of thought which he did not consider irreconcilable.

Fisher was a northerner (born in Beverly, Yorkshire, in 1469); he entered Michaelhouse, Cambridge, where he obtained the academic degrees and became chancellor of the university in 1504, the same year in which he was also appointed bishop of Rochester, the second episcopal see in England after Canterbury. While Fisher was a student at Cambridge, he felt the influence of Italian humanism. Gaius Auberino stayed there from 1483 to 1504, but an important influence was also exercised by Lawrence William Traversagni, whose preaching fostered an interest in the Fathers; the works of Baptist Spagnoli of Mantua also enjoyed special favor. The chancellor devoted a great deal of care to his university; he was helped in this by the generosity of Lady Margaret Beaufort, whose confessor he was. He promoted the study of the biblical languages and welcomed Erasmus, who lectured there from 1511 to 1514.

Scholars have sought to find in his works, both Latin and English, an echo of Erasmus' "philosophy of Christ," but the dominant theme in Fisher's writings is the "increase of faith." Faith, Fisher maintained, exists in the agreement of the entire Church, the Mystical Body of Christ, in which truth dwells permanently because it has been handed on by the apostles to the Fathers and Doctors and is guaranteed by the leadership of the pope. When the Lutheran storm shook Christianity to its foundations, Fisher experienced no doubts; many think that to him, or to his suggestions, is owing the *Assertio septem sacramentorum* (1521),[20] in which Henry VIII answered Luther's *De captivitate Babylonica*. Certainly his are other controversial writings on particular problems in opposition to the teachings of the Reformers as well as sermons, prayers, commentaries on the seven penitential psalms, and an *Epistola de caritate,* in which he rebukes Luther's contempt for tradition and develops the theme of charity on the basis of passages from Augustine.

His works enjoyed a wide readership in Germany, where the Catholic controversialists made use of them. When Henry VIII opposed the pope, Fisher fell into disfavor; he had openly opposed the king's decision, but he was accused of having suggested the invasion of England to Charles V and was tried for high treason. In 1535 Paul III appointed him a cardinal, but this did not save him from execution.

3. Germany from the Middle Ages to the Modern Age: Universities, Theological Currents, the Devotio Moderna

Developments in late Scholasticism in Germany were closely connected with the history of its universities. The German universities had been founded late by comparison with those in other parts of Europe, and the most famous faculties of theology had begun their activity in the second half of the fourteenth century. These faculties had often taken over, as in the case of Cologne and Erfurt, the older *studia,* houses of study, of the monastic orders, which furnished the greater number of teachers and saw to the formation of their novices within the new structures.

In the fifteenth century other universities were established in Würzburg (1402), Leipzig (1409), Rostock (1419), Triers (1454), Greifswald (1456), Freiburg in Breisgau (1457), Mainz (1476), Ingolstadt (1472), and Tübingen (1477), the initiative being taken by particular municipalities or by princes or bishops or the emperor. In 1459 at the wish of Pius II, Basel transformed its general house of studies into a university; in 1502 the elector of Saxony, Frederick the Wise, wanted a university in Wittenberg to rival the one in nearby Leipzig; and a few years later the university of Frankfurt on the Oder was founded. Frequent exchanges with Paris, which always remained the great model; the consecutive emigrations of teachers from Prague; the presence of theologians sent by their respective faculties to the councils of Constance and Basel—all this meant that German theology remained closely linked to that of the other great European centers without, however, losing any of its specific characteristics.

In the fifteenth century, the conflicts continued between the supporters of the "old way" *(via antiqua)* and the nominalists, champions of the "modern way" *(via moderna)* and followers of William of Ockham, who had, in fact, spent his last years in Germany. But the repetitiousness of these disputes was perhaps more apparent than real, one reason being that within each of these parties quite distinct positions emerged: Scotists, Thomists, Albertists, often bitterly disagreeing among themselves. The name "nominalists" was given not only to the more orthodox Ockhamists but also to the disciples of

Marsilius of Inghen, who had taught at Heidelberg, and to the representatives of the Augustinian revival that harked back to the thought of Gregory of Rimini and Ugolino of Orvieto. In the two groups that faced off against each other in the faculties of the arts, the differences in principle had to do with the doctrine of universals; this was a specifically philosophical problem, but in Scholastic debates it ended up taking on theological implications that conditioned religious thought. In almost all universities instruction was given according to both "ways," but the predominance of the one or the other gave each faculty a more "conservative" or a more "modern" character.

Thus, on the one hand, Cologne was always and exclusively a field of action reserved to the realists, so much so that in 1425 it opposed the claim of the prince electors to favor the modern way. Heidelberg and Vienna, on the other hand, were ready to welcome the groups of nominalists that at the end of the fourteenth century had left Prague, where the university was controlled by supporters of Wyclif's thought, which had by then been introduced into Bohemia. The commitment of these philosophers and theologians was immediately manifested in their attack on those who had forced them to emigrate; they claimed that "real universals are the seedbed of heresy." But they soon found themselves side by side with the representatives of a second Prague diaspora who took an entirely opposite view.

Ever since the time of its foundation (1348) the Charles University of Prague had been controlled by its German element, because in the division of students and teachers into "nations," the Bohemians had but a single vote as compared with the Bavarians, Saxons, and Poles. During the last two decades of the fourteenth century tensions had increased: in 1384 the Czech students attacked the German rector with weapons; other disorders occurred in 1390. Finally, in 1409 the Bohemians gained the upper hand; Prague became increasingly nationalistic, and the Germans abandoned the field. In December of that same year the first nucleus of the University of Leipzig was established; its founder and first rector was theologian John Münsterberger (ca. 1377–1451), while John Hoffmann (1365–1460), author of a treatise on the Eucharist against the Hussites, also came from Prague. The new Faculty of Theology adopted a moderate Thomism that tended to distance itself from the extreme realism of a Scotist kind that marked the teachings of Wyclif.

But the real "stronghold of Thomism"[21] was Cologne, which was always conspicuous for its conservative choices and yet numbered among its students some profoundly innovative minds such as Nicholas of Cusa, or restless eccentrics such as Conrad Celtis and Agrippa of Nettesheim. It was also the first German university to introduce Hellenistic and Oriental studies. The city, which was one of the oldest centers of culture and gloried in its famous charterhouse, still kept alive the memory of John Duns Scotus, who had taught in the Franciscan house of studies there, and of Albert the Great and Thomas Aquinas, the greatest glories of the Dominican general house of studies. But the old way, which predominated, was not united: alongside of and in competition with the prevailing Thomist tendency Albertism had developed and was spreading from there to other university centers. The movement had started in Paris during the years of the bitterest conflicts between realists and nominalists and was the work of some masters who, in order to combat Ockhamist terminism, had taken advantage of some motifs in the teaching of Albert the Great.

The greatest exponent of this line of thought was John of Neuhausen, who had as one of his students a Fleming, Eimeric of Kampen. In 1423 the latter came to Cologne, where, according to him, the university world was being torn apart by the same "tripartite controversy" that was going on in Paris. While the bitterest attack against the Thomist school was certainly stirred up by Eimeric, it is also a fact that this attack must have found ready sympathy in many admirers of the Swabian master, Albert. Veneration of Albert had always remained strong in Germany: there were those who read his writings in the natural sciences; others were attracted by the Neoplatonic motifs present in his thought, as made known for the most part through the *Summa theologica* of one of his greatest disciples, Ulrich Engelbert of Strassburg. This tradition had fed German and especially Dominican mysticism, then that of the Netherlands; it also influenced Nicholas of Cusa, who had been a student of Eimeric; and even in the sixteenth century there were those who looked with pride to Albert, "the public glory of all Germany in letters," "the philosopher of the Germans."[22] Even Reuchlin, who was completely removed from Scholastic controversies, numbered Albert among the greatest glories of his native land.[23]

Around 1438 Eimeric circulated a treatise of his own on *Problemata inter Albertum Magnum et sanctum Thomam* consisting of two parts: in the first he set forth his critique of the nominalist interpretation of the universals; in the second and much longer part he explained the themes which divided the realists, breaking these down into eighteen points that covered all the problems of philosophy, from logic to ethics, from metaphysics to cosmology. The theological implications of these questions could lead to serious doctrinal differences: a different conception of the soul suggested different interpretations of the consequences of original sin; the problem of knowledge could lead to disagreements regarding ecstasy, prophecy, and divination. But in Eimeric's work all this was simply alluded to, and the debate remained on the philosophical level.

In 1456 the response of a secular master, Gerard de Monte, was made known: in his *Tractatus ostendens concordiam sancti Thomae et venerabilis domini Alberti in quibus dicuntur esse contrarii* he tried to minimize the difference between the two thinkers. The controversy continued in sometimes bitter tones, and the divisions between the parties became so deep that different colleges were established for the Albertists and the Thomists: the *Bursa*

Laurentiana and the *Bursa Montana*. From Cologne, Albertism spread to other universities, such as Heidelberg, and was especially vigorous in Cracow, where special courses in this teaching were established.

The masters of Cologne, who were always careful guardians of orthodoxy, were involved in other problems during those years. The Bohemian heresy, which had taken on a strongly nationalist character and had produced a vast literature in the Czech language, had also found a by no means negligible echo in the German world. In Prague sermons were given to Hussites of German origin, and care was taken to provide them with a liturgy in their language. In the first half of the century some personages went there who would later spread the teaching of the Taborites in Germany, Austria, and Switzerland; among these was Friedrich Reiser (1402–58), author of short theological works and of a translation of the New Testament into German that became widespread thanks to the help of the Waldensian communities.

During the war of King Sigismund against the heretics the city of Cologne, though not directly taking part in it, declared itself in favor of the sovereign's enterprise, and the theological faculty issued a document against the teaching being spread by Procopius the Great, a Taborite: *Replicationes almi Coloniensis studii contra litteras et rationes Procopii heretici et articulos Hussitarum ac errores Bohemorum et heresim Wicleff.* Eimeric represented the university at the Council of Basel and wrote an *Epistola contra Johannem de Rokozano de communione sub utraque specie.*

Another who attacked the Bohemian heresy in his numerous works was a Dutchman, Henry of Gorcum, who after his studies in Paris went to Cologne and remained there until his death in 1431. His treatise *Contra articulos Hussitarum* explained the position taken by the university, but the author took up the subject again in other theological and exegetical writings in order to show the dangerous consequences to which a radical metaphysical realism, on the one hand, and Ockhamist nominalism, on the other, could lead. Both of these schools were guilty (he said) of having abandoned the teachings of Thomas on the soul and on the order of the universe, understood as a manifestation in multiplicity of the divine simplicity and beauty. In this conception, which saw in the natural order a parallel to the order of grace and rejected Ockhamist arbitrariness, there was also room for an ecclesiology that opposed the extreme spiritualism of the heretics.

In the disagreements that divided the world of the theologians, Henry of Gorcum tried to keep to the middle way which the Angelic Doctor had traced out for him; he thus contributed to the rebirth of Thomism that would be seen especially in the sixteenth century. But there was another note characteristic of his approach that showed him attentive to the new needs of the age: the lesser importance given to abstract disputes and the greater interest in a practical theology that looks primarily to pastoral practice and edification.

Another who studied the works of Aquinas in Cologne during the years 1421–25 was Denis of Louvain, better known as Denis the Carthusian, the "Ecstatic Doctor." He was born in Rijkel, Belgium, in 1402/3 and received a rather varied education: after having attended the Benedictine school in St. Truiden and then that of the Brothers of the Common Life in Zwolle, he obtained the title of "master of arts" at Cologne; later he entered the charterhouse of Roermond, where he died in 1471. His extraordinary capacity for work and his intellectual curiosity, which makes him seem in many respects a modern man, were prodigious.

He read, in translation, the Greek, Hebrew, and Arab philosophers and got to know thinkers and theologians of various schools; from these he collected ideas and thoughts but was not always able to work these up into a new synthesis. On more than one occasion he had ecstatic experiences. But his life was not devoted exclusively to meditation and contemplation: beginning in 1433 he became regent of his monastery; in 1451–52 he accompanied Nicholas of Cusa, then a cardinal legate, on his visit to the provinces of the Meuse and the Rhine and with him founded the charterhouse of 'sHertogenbosch. His works, which number over two hundred, are theological and philosophical (commentaries on the Books of the *Sentence* and on Boethius, a *Summa fidei orthodoxae,* which he describes as "the quintessence of the works of St. Thomas") and scriptural.

His greatest fame, however, is due to his dogmatico-ascetic writings: the commentaries on the works of Pseudo-Dionysius; the *De donis spiritus sancti;* the *De contemplatione,* which contains the most complete systematic exposition of his teaching on mysticism; and the *De fonte lucis ac semitis vitae.* Even in these it is possible to trace the presence of various sources: Bernard, Bonaventure, Tauler, Suso, and at bottom, Pseudo-Dionysius, whose negative theology is here transfused into the Scholastic heritage.

The writings of this Carthusian do not provide simply a teaching on mysticism, nor are they simply a diary of the soul. As one who shared a new religious sensibility, Denis set out rather to provide monks and the simple faithful with guidelines for embarking on the way of mystical union through the exercise of pure prayer, which helps the soul free itself of all earthly shadows, so much so that it need not fall back even on the support of the imagination. By following this way and concentrating on one thing, human beings may succeed in detaching themselves from the multiplicity of things and, thanks to the gift of wisdom, may transform their prayer into an act of perfect love of God, the center of the universe, to whom all things tend by a natural desire and who is not perceived by the eyes of the mind but only by the interior gaze.

In other universities, such as Vienna, Heidelberg, Erfurt, and later on, Tübingen, the modern school of philosophy was in control. Theologians who paid allegiance to it focused their attention chiefly on soteriological themes, but the presence of two different traditions of thought led them to radically different results. The followers of Ockham developed especially the themes of a theology of covenant that was leading to a veiled Pelagianism. Parallel to this, others were vigorously pursuing a more rigidly Augustinian course that aimed at emphasizing the exclusive power of grace in the process of salvation.

Outstanding among the representatives of the first of these two currents of thought was Gabriel Biel, "the last of the Scholastics," who was a nominalist but showed himself open to numerous influences. He studied at Heidelberg, Erfurt, and Cologne, and was for many years a preacher in the cathedral of Mainz. During this period he entered the Brothers of the Common Life and took part in the founding of various houses of the community. He was rector of the community in Urach when, in 1484, Count Eberhard of Württemberg, who wanted to keep the realists from taking over in his young university, called him to the chair of theology in Tübingen. Here, however, it happened that the encounter of the two ways, instead of giving rise to new conflicts, led to a degree of convergence.

The problems that had passionately engaged and tormented the theologians of earlier generations no longer occupied a central place; those disputes had by now lost their intensity and given way to other urgent needs. The result was the formation of a "middle way" in which a variety of experiences came together and which was characterized by an interest in ethical problems, including those of a social and economic kind. From this point of view the work of Conrad Summenhart played a fundamental role; he was a realist but closer to Duns Scotus than to Thomas, a canonist, and along with Biel, was one of the inaugurators of the "early Tübingen school."

In his first year of teaching Biel gave his students a course of lectures which he then put together in his *Canonis missae expositio* (Ruetlingen, 1488). This work had, in all likelihood, been thought out and developed during his years in Mainz; in character it is a manual of practical pastoral theology, born of the experience of a preacher who had achieved a wide-ranging culture and who showed this in numerous citations from the Scriptures, the Fathers, and the medieval theologians. The introductory letter was the work of a realist theologian, John Heynlin von Stein (Johannes a Lapide), who had preceded Biel as a teacher in Tübingen and was himself the author of a *Resolutorium dubiorum circa celebrationem missarum occurrentium* (Basel, 1492). The many printings of the *Canonis missae expositio* attest to the success of the work among Biel's contemporaries; it influenced Luther, who in Erfurt had attended the lectures of Bartolomew Arnoldi, a student of Biel's.

In the following year, Biel published another course of lectures, which were collected in a volume that was more academic and more explicitly Ockhamist in character: the *Epitome pariter et collectorium circa IV Sententiarim libros* (Tübingen, 1989), one of the countless commentaries on Peter Lombard. The guiding thread of this treatise was provided by Ockham's commentary, but Biel did not neglect other authorities, especially in places where the "Venerable Beginner" seemed to have left blanks. The result was a clear and orderly exposition based on many sources and controlled by an exceptionally balanced mind and a great prudence in definitions.

The writings that best reveal Biel's moral and pastoral concern are, however, the sermons, which amount to a good half of what he produced. He elaborated especially on the problems of grace and salvation; as a faithful Ockhamist, he taught that out of the abyssal darkness of the absolute and inaccessible will of God one segment, which represents his ordered will, has been made known by the Creator himself, who has revealed himself to humanity and entered into a covenant with it. In this setting, none who do what is in their power will see grace denied them *(facienti quod est in se Deus non denegat gratiam)*. By their own powers and works, said Biel, human beings could never win salvation *de condigno* (by meriting it); but God's acceptance, precisely in virtue of the covenant, will obtain justification for them *de congruo* (it is appropriate for God to grant it). Such was the teaching which many theologian preachers gave from the pulpit and which, in response to the need to reassure and console consciences, left a great deal of room for an optimistic interpretation of human activity.

During the fifteenth century the best representatives of the Augustinian revival also taught at Erfurt: Angelus Dobelinus (+ after 1420), John Zachariae (+ 1428), and John of Dorsten (+ 1481). All of them were in the tradition that began with Gregory of Rimini, the "Gregorian way" *(via Gregorii),* although they had been deeply influenced by Scotism in regard to the formal principle of justification. They maintained that there is no causal relation between possession of the "habit of grace" *(habitus gratiae)* by human beings and their justification but only a harmony established by the plan of God, who, in virtue of his absolute will, could still deny his acceptance and refuse the reward of eternal life. So radical and dramatic a doctrine was the subject of debate in the higher circles of university theologians; in the pulpit preachers emphasized the motif of the divine mercy. John Staupitz, an Augustinian who had been trained in Cologne and Leipzig and had also undergone the influence of the mystical tradition, maintained the principle of absolute predestination, but he exhorted the faithful to throw themselves trustingly on Christ by an act of love, which itself is also a gift of God.

John of Paltz, a disciple of John of Dorsten, was even accused of a certain laxism; he was a teacher of theology at Erfurt from 1485 to 1495, a preacher of crusades against the Turks and the Bohemians, and involved in the reform of convents of his order. He was a typical representative of a new generation of theologians who set themselves the task of making the principles of speculative theology bear fruit in a concrete care of souls that was suitable for promoting the formation of Christian life. He preached the Augustinian doctrine of sin, but still following the lead of Augustine, he urged the faithful to take refuge from the thought of God's anger and to trust in his mercy; to draw strength and consolation from the certainty that every shortcoming will be forgiven thanks to the infinite goodness of God, the love of Christ, the maternal protection of Mary, the friendship of the saints, and the efficacy of the sacraments.

Not a few of the leading figures in the German theological culture of the fifteenth century had been trained in the atmosphere of the *Devotio moderna;* many, in their youth, had studied in the schools of the Windesheim congregation or, like Biel, had in their maturity entered the Brothers of the Common Life and then contributed to the spread of the movement. This movement, which in its beginnings had encountered not a few difficulties, also overcame the resistance that showed itself during a council: at Constance, in 1418, the Beghard communities were charged with being suspect groups. The concern here was disciplinary rather than moral; in any case, the denunciation was allowed to lapse, which amounted to an implicit absolution. The *Devotio moderna* received a definitive recognition at Basel and from then on spread far and wide, as can be seen from the many manuscripts and editions of its major representatives that are to be found in monastic and university libraries.

The influence of the movement was very soon felt in a widespread effort to reform convents and ecclesiastical institutions. At the beginning of the fifteenth century John Eustatius pushed reform in the foundations of the Cistercians. John Rode (+ 1439), abbot of St. Matthias in Trier, introduced the spirit of the *Devotio* there with the help of monks from St. James in Liège; his example was quickly followed by the Premonstratensians of Magdeburg. A man outstanding in this work was John Busch, chronicler of the Windesheim congregation, who by order of Nicholas of Cusa promoted the reform of convents of various orders and, in particular, played a part in the reform of the famous Benedictine abbey of Bursfeld, which then served as an example for other monasteries of the same congregation. In this setting, and in the spirit of Windesheim, a vast literature of meditations for the use of monks flourished.

It is not easy to measure the influence that the *Devotio moderna* had on the directions taken by theological thought in the fifteenth century; its self-distancing from intellectualism and its leaning toward interior religious experience certainly contributed, directly or indirectly, to the lessening of interest in doctrinal disputes and to the turn toward a "romantic" theology, that is, one more attentive to the feelings, experience, and piety of the ordinary human being. However, there were not lacking theologians who explicitly linked themselves to the mystical experiences that had prepared the way for the *Devotio* and then flowed into it.

When Gerson pointed to the dangers of a pantheistic conception that were present in the works of Ruysbroeck, John of Schoonhaven went to the latter's defense and, appealing to the teaching of St. Thomas, maintained that a passing foretaste of the beatific vision is possible in the present life. This very learned Dutchman, who had studied in Paris and then entered the Canons of Windesheim, was the author of letters that had an exceptionally wide readership and of four sermons delivered at chapters of the congregation. He dealt with themes dear to the new form of devotion and proposed christocentric meditation as a way to asceticism and mystical union. By concentrating his thoughts on the humanity and the sufferings of Christ (he said), one may reach contemplation of the divinity through the four stages of ecstatic love, starting with the moment in which God visits and inflames the soul and leading on to the highest degree, when he wins the soul over to himself.

Henry Herp, too, had been formed by the works of Ruysbroeck; he had been rector of the brothers of the house in Delft, but later, during a journey to Italy in 1450, he entered the convent of the Franciscan Observantines on Aracoeli. In his sermons but especially in his ascetical works, *Spieghel der Volcomenheit* and *Theologia mystica,* the themes of Franciscan spirituality and those of Flemish and Cistercian mysticism come together. He, too, proposed a way for undertaking the life of contemplation; it had a series of stages, from the exercise of the virtues in the world, to purification, then to abnegation of the will, and finally to the vision of God.

The spirit of the *Devotio moderna* is also to be seen in Wessel Gansfort of Groningen, who did not belong either to the Brothers of the Common Life or to the Canons Regular, although he did think at one time of becoming a monk. A restless spirit, he attended several universities: Cologne, Heidelberg, Paris, and was influenced first by realism and then by nominalism. He learned Greek, Hebrew, and Arabic, read the classics and the Fathers, and because of his learning was called "Light of the world" and the "Master of contradictions." After many travels and a lengthy stay in Italy he returned to his native land and busied himself in the convent of Mount St. Agnes, where he associated with Thomas à Kempis. He expounded a systematic method of meditation in his *Tractatus de modo constituendarum meditationum,* in which he proposed a "ladder of meditation" with twenty-three rungs based on the ascending order of the three faculties of memory, intellect, and will.

His most original works, however, are those dealing with theological and ecclesiological themes: *De benignissima Dei providentia, De causis incarnationis, De magnitudine passionis, De dignitate et potestate ecclesiastica, De oratione,* and *De sacramento eucharistiae,* in all of which readers found heterodox motifs that seemed to anticipate positions of the Reformers. The need of interiorizing religious experience led himself to reduce to second place everything external, in a spiritualist perspective that bordered on heresy. In writing of the Eucharist he did not deny the doctrine of transubstantiation, but he did emphasize the psychological element of the commemoration and insisted on the necessity of meditating on the passion, because this was the moment in which the union of the suffering Christ with the faithful took place; in taking this tack, however, he seemed to deny the efficacy of the sacrament. And in discussing confession he maintained that simple attrition is not enough to obtain forgiveness of sin; in fact, absolution is not the work of the priest but of the Holy Spirit, who takes possession of the heart of the penitent and transforms it through perfect contrition.

4. Humanism in Germany

When humanism spread north of the Alps, it brought to maturity many preexisting elements and found expressions that were completely new and peculiar to that world. It is not an easy matter to pinpoint the time and manner of this spread: relations between Italy and Germany had always been very close for both political and commercial reasons, and with the passage of time they became even more frequent. At the beginning of the modern age there was an increasingly large number of German students who enrolled in the ancient universities of Bologna and Padua, Ferrara and Pavia, in order to study law and medicine. At the time of the councils of Constance and Basel such well-known figures as Poggio Bracciolini and Aeneas Silvius Piccolomini spent long periods north of the Alps. The result was a multiplication of opportunities for establishing new relationships and forming new friendships.

The men of the north, who had already learned to know and love Petrarch and to acquire from his works a desire for a different kind of religious life, brought to the encounter with humanist culture an intellectual and moral patrimony of their own. This they had acquired in the faculties of arts or theology, and it had often been influenced by the spirituality of the *Devotio moderna*. Among them were those who realized that there was an irremediable break between the perspectives that were opening up and the tradition of Scholastic thought; but there were also not lacking others who had been formed in the traditions of the *via antiqua* or the *via moderna* but were disposed also to accept and make their own the motifs of the "new knowledge."

The *Devotio moderna* was not without its role in preparing a soil favorable to the spread of humanism, even though it could not be considered an anticipation of this new culture. The two movements had had radically different origins and motivations: the presence of the Brothers of the Common Life in the schools was ensured especially by the hostels in which young people found hospitality; the canons of Windesheim, for their part, did not offer curricula of a humanistic type, and if they preferred to read the Fathers rather than the more recent theologians, their choice was motivated by considerations purely of edification. Nevertheless, it was the very presence of humanists such as Hegius and Agricola in the schools of the congregation that opened the doors to the new knowledge and made a renewal of studies necessary. On the other hand, the scant interest and sometimes even open aversion of the "devout" when it came to Scholastic disputations helped guide the upcoming generations toward a new theology.

In a cultural environment so rich in new ideas as the German world was, each humanist developed his experience along paths of his own as he came to grips with the novelties offered to him; but all this required a lengthy period, and it is therefore difficult to find original personalities in the first half of the fifteenth century. As in other countries of Europe, so in Germany: there was no educated person who did not cultivate a desire to travel to Italy in order to complete his formation through contact with the primary sources of humanism; but once they returned to their homeland, German scholars set themselves to rival the Italians and developed, along with patriotic motifs, others which they considered to be lacking southern humanism: a religious dimension capable of combining piety and learning.

Rudolf Agricola (Rudolf Huusman or Huisman) is regarded as the father of northern humanism: "For the cisalpine world, so lacking in all literary gifts, has never produced anything such as this."[24] He was born in Baflo on February 17, 1447, and received his early education first in nearby Groningen, in the school of St. Martin and in an environment influenced by the Brothers of the Common Life, and later in Deventer. Then, as a young man, he attended the universities of Erfurt, Cologne, and Louvain, thus coming in contact with several different cultures. His decisive experience, however, was his lengthy stay in Italy, in Padua, Pavia, Rome, Florence, and above all, Ferrara. After returning to his homeland he continued his study of rhetoric and was called to teach at Heidelberg, where he died on October 27, 1485.

Agricola was a great man of letters, an admirer of Petrarch (whose biography he wrote), a tireless reader of the Greek and Latin poets, historians, and philosophers, and publisher and editor of many of their works, "very Greek among the Greeks, very Latin among the Latins," in the judgment of Erasmus, who had met him in Deventer. In the final years of his short life he devoted himself to biblical studies and for this purpose also learned Hebrew, but fate did not allow him to leave any mark of himself in this field.

Nowadays Agricola does not occupy an important place in the history of religious thought, and yet a short page written a year before his death is enough to warrant numbering him among those who posed, with great clarity, the problem of integrating ancient culture into Christian spirituality. I am referring to the letter to James Barbirano, known by the title *De formando studio;* its thirty-eight printings in the sixteenth century show the influence which this humanist exerted on his very many disciples and admirers, who included not only men of letters but theologians as well. The short document, which initiated a series of programmatic manifestos for a reform of teaching, was intended chiefly as a defense of classical studies, a set of guidelines and counsels, and a discourse on method, but it was also this Christian humanist's profession of faith. The letter clearly rejects the old system of studies, which led students into a labyrinth of tortuous disputes and riddles that in the course of so many centuries never found their Oedipus.

In the presence of so many useless conflicts that torment and ruin young minds (says Agricola), the sense is lost of the central place of moral philosophy, which recapitulates "the whole plan of a life lived uprightly and religiously." Therefore, take as guide, instead, the works of the philosophers, of Aristotle, Cicero, and Seneca, but also of the historians, poets, and orators, who provide very effective examples of what is to be done and avoided. Then, "passing through these studies, ascend to the sacred writings, and order our life as prescribed in them, and believe that we shall be saved by these most salutary guides."[25] It is true that the ancients did not have the means of knowing the true end of human life; they had only a hazy notion of it, but they spoke of it always and constantly despite not having faith, for it is the Scriptures alone that made the goal known without error. Education, dialectic, and rhetoric are not the servants of theology, but they do constitute an indispensable route to true knowledge and are presupposed by it. For this reason, the author hopes that the "corrupt speech practices" prevailing in the schools will be quickly changed, because they hinder an accurate preservation and transmission of learning, which needs to be made accessible to all, and this through the use of the national languages.

Agricola's message was not accepted by all of his disciples; only Erasmus would succeed in expressing with equal clarity the role of "good letters" in the process of forming the human being, reforming the Church and Christianity, and proposing a new theology. And yet, even though they did not come up with especially innovative ideas, many humanists did take part in the theological debates of their time. They were often laymen who had been trained in German universities where they learned the several "ways" but who later found ways of expressing themselves more easily in the *sodalitates* or fellowships, the circles which were being formed in various cities and which included professors, students, poets, churchmen, and educated men who were involved in practical everyday life.

Some of these sodalities, like the one in Erfurt, cultivated primarily literary interests and only secondarily found themselves caught up in religious disputes. Its members, among them Conrad Muth (Conradus Mutianus, Rufus), Eoban Hessus, Crotus Rubianus, and Euricius Cordus, admired Erasmus but were enthusiastic above all for the nationalistic humanism of Ulrich von Hutten. But these men were not disinterested in the religious problems of their day; this was true especially of Muth, who had been influenced by the thinking of Ficino and had reached the point of a radical spiritualization of the Judeo-Christian heritage. In any case, all of them contributed to the formation of a generation of philologists, many of whom took up biblical studies.

Other circles, such as the one in Strasbourg, were more open to problems of a religious and moral nature and entertained projects for reform; among its members were James Wimpfeling, Sebastian Brant, James Sturm, and Matthis Schürer. *Pia eruditio,* "devout learning," was for them a way of life; their humanistic interest in education made them certain that better educated and more learned human beings would have produced a better society, but their reflection on the importance which classical antiquity might have for Christian culture did not go beyond a recognition of the propaideutic and subsidiary value of literary studies. Consequently they rejected Scholastic disputations and their philosophico-juridical language, but they were unwilling to contribute to the rebirth of the ancient world. For this reason they were suspect to contemporary Italian writers, who regarded them as tainted with paganism.

They read Petrarch, with a preference for his *Secretum* and *De remediis utriusque fortunae;*[26] among the more recent authors they had taken as their model Baptist of Mantua, the Christian Virgil.[27] Among the philosophers they preferred Pico, who had shifted from secular to sacred studies; they saw to the publication of his works and maintained close ties with his nephew, John Francis, a disciple of Savonarola.[28] They also read the Fathers of the Church, in whom they found the room for new freedom in which their spirits could expand, but they did not reject continuity with a tradition that had found expression in medieval culture, in which they discovered the reasons for and roots of the devotion of the entire people.

In the early years of their formation these humanists had almost all been influenced by the spirituality of the Brothers of the Common Life, from whom they had learned to prefer withdrawal into the interior life over the manifestations of an external religiosity; now they found in the theology of Gerson a guide for their spiritual needs.[29] At the time when disagreements in Mariology were most fierce they took a position against the doctrines maintained by the Dominicans. Wimpfeling voiced his own burning devotion to the Blessed Virgin in two poems: *De nuntio angelico* (1490) and *De triplici candore Mariae* (1492). Brant composed a doctrinal poem, *Contra Judaeos et haereticos conceptionem virginalem fuisse possibilem argumentatio,* as well as other poems on the same subject. Such were the spiritual themes of the group of intellectuals, most of them Alsatians, who had founded the *Sodalitas literaria Argentinensis* and who had adopted as their moral guide the preacher John Geiler of Kaisersberg, perhaps the personage most representative of a tendency that was strongly critical of the decadence of the Church and yet at the same time faithful to tradition.

Geiler, too, had university experience: he had studied at Freiburg and had even become dean of the Faculty of Arts (1469); then at Basel he had devoted himself to theological studies, following the new nominalist school of William Textor. From the writings of Gerson he had learned that pastoral practice is not a secondary activity for a theologian, and he found Gabriel Biel agreeing with and supporting him in this concern for the care of souls. He therefore abandoned teaching and became a preacher at the cathedral of Strasbourg, a role in which he showed an extraordinary ability to translate the most difficult and abstract concepts into language intelligible to all.

The central theme of his preaching was justification; he explained this to his hearers basically along the lines of Ockhamist theology, that is, emphasizing the infinite power of God but also his boundless mercy and urging the faithful to act as if their actions could lead them to salvation. At the same time, he did not neglect other themes; in particular, he recommended prayer as the most useful way of disposing oneself for grace. He was unwilling to investigate how this activity could begin; it was not necessary to know "whether it comes about by a natural disposition or by a general influence of God, as Scotus would have it, or by a special movement from God, according to the teaching of St. Thomas; if a human being asks for mercy, God will certainly not refuse it."

Thus spoke Geiler in 1498, at the beginning of one of his famous Lenten series that took as its guiding thread the list of human vices and follies given in Sebastian Brant's *Ship of Fools*.[30] Observance of the commandments, patience, humility, and generosity were the foundations of a theology of discipleship that was very like Erasmus' program.[31] Geiler maintained that the teaching in the decretals had nothing to do with theology, but he was also very careful about rejecting the medieval Scholastic tradition. Thus he advised those about to devote themselves to theological studies against turning directly to the ancient Fathers, even though these are the lights and pillars of our religion. He suggested instead that they begin with the Scholastics and more recent Doctors, since these could serve as guides in the use of the mind and in the analysis of the sacred text. This was true especially of William of Auxerre, Thomas, Bonaventure, Scotus, and Marsilius, who had performed the service of gathering together and organizing the vast patrimony of the Christian tradition and explaining it clearly as well as of providing explanations for new doubts and new cases of conscience than had not yet emerged or been clarified. Above all, he advised them to read Gabriel Biel as a sure guide.[32]

Geiler's biographer, James Wimpfeling (Schlettstadt, 1450–Strasbourg, 1528), was a humanist, a man of letters, a poet, and a preacher for fourteen years in the cathedral of Speyer. He had made the restoration of Christianity his life's project. As a young man he had studied at the faculties of Arts in Freiburg, Erfurt, and Heidelberg; he then devoted himself to theology but had soon felt a distaste for the "empty and disgusting" sophisms of Scholasticism, which had arisen from the wrongful mingling of logic, metaphysics, and grammar, and were far removed from the elegance and simplicity of the Fathers. During his years of study he had treasured his reading of Lawrence Valla, and when he was called in 1498 to teach in Heidelberg, he began his lectures by commenting on the letters of St. Jerome and the poetry of Prudentius. In his writings on pedagogy, *Isidoneus Germanicus* and *Adolescentia* (1496), he maintained that the evils of society and Church were due to the poor education given in the schools and universities. In his *Apologia pro republica Christiana* (1505) he bemoaned the fact that theological and biblical studies were so neglected, even by the clergy, but he also warned of the danger of an education based on the reading of obscene poets.

In his own life he sought to show the way to a Christian humanism or a Christianity capable of using humanistic culture, and he put his own literary powers at the service of the liturgy: in 1499 he published *De hymnorum et sequentiarum auctoribus generibusque carminum* and, in the following year, *Castigationes locorum in canticis ecclesiasticis et divinis officiis depravatorum.*

Later on, he had an opportunity to make his own ideas explicit and adopted a position that was even overly radical. In 1503 James Locher, a professor at Freiburg, "the friend of the Muses," wrote to assert the value of poetry and its independence from theology. Wimpfeling replied with *Contra turpem libellum Philomusi defensio theologiae scholasticae et neotericorum* (Oppenheim, 1510),[33] in which he showed all his prudence and his suspicion of the classics. The goal of education and culture (he maintained) is ethics, not eloquence; theology is the queen of all the arts and sciences.

To many the tone of the little book seemed too harsh, and the author felt some embarrassment. He was, after all, a sincere admirer of Erasmus, had worked hard for the Strasbourg edition of the *Praise of Folly,* and had advised the reading of the *Adagia* in the schools. On this occasion, he felt the need of writing to Erasmus in order to clarify his thought and to confirm their common ideas of moral reform.[34] He was also bound to Erasmus by his desire for harmony and his suspicion of theological disputes. He avoided getting involved in the harrowing controversy that had flared up around Reuchlin. During the Reformation he wrote a letter to Zwingli and Luther, the *Canonis missae defensio,* in which he tried to win them back by persuading them that the Canon of the Mass contained nothing contrary to the teaching and customs of the early Church. But even though he looked on Erasmus as a model, he was not capable of following him along unexplored ways.

The poet Sebastian Brant (Strasbourg, 1457–1521), who adopted the Latin name Titius, was involved in the political life of his city, whose chancellor he first became in 1503. He had completed his university studies and was led by Heynlin in Basel to adopt a moderate realism; later, however, his thinking was shaped by the works of Augustine, and he edited the sermons of the Doctor of Hippo, accompanying them with additions and notes and preceding them with a poem.[35] Augustine also inspired his didactico-moral poems, from the successful *Ship of Fools*[36] to the *Invectiva contra mundi delicias* and the *De periculoso scacorum ludo inter mortem et humanam conditions.* In other poems of a spiritual character, which he collected in *Varia carmina* (1498), he developed the theme of human beings shattering the harmony of creation by their sins. He translated into the vernacular various hymns and liturgical sequences, such as the *Pange lingua,* but also passages of St. Bernard under the title *Rosenkranz.*

The humanists of Strasbourg were also skilled in using the tools made available to them by the art of printing in order to spread knowledge of the Scriptures. At Basel, in 1498, Brant published an edition of the Latin Bible along with the *Glossa ordinaria* and Nicholas of Lyra's commentary, to which he added comments of the more important doctors. In 1504, likewise at Basel, Wimpfeling published a *Biblia latina cum postillis Hugonis a sancto Caro*. Geiler translated into German the harmony of the Gospels that had been compiled by Matthias Ringmann,[37] and Brant saw to the publication of the biblical concordances of Conrad of Halberstadt.[38] The contribution of these men to the vast number of editions of the Bible, which placed Germany in the forefront of this kind of publishing,[39] was evidently a response to a particular cultural need.

Among the German theologians of the fifteenth century there were not lacking individuals who were inclined to look to the Scriptures as the sole origin of doctrine; this was the view not only of Wessel Gansfort but also of John Pupper of Goch and John Rucherat of Wesel, the latter of whom was accused of having elements in common with the Wycliffites and Hussites. The biblicism of these men, however, was not directed to the elaboration of a new biblical theology but retained a predominantly ecclesiological outlook. The humanists' concern was to make clear the need of a return to the sources, and they were applying new methods for the recovery and publication of texts, even sacred texts, but their enthusiasm did not yet find expression in new religious thinking.

A study of the first Bibles edited by promotors of the new knowledge does not show any substantial novelties apart from a painstaking care: the text they published was always that of the Paris edition of the Vulgate, which went back to the end of the twelfth century; this they revised and accompanied with notes giving cross-references to other passages. In short, there was nothing more than had already been done in preceding centuries. Meanwhile, however, the need of reading the Bible in its original languages was becoming increasingly clear. Students of Greek began to read the New Testament text as philologists; in the wake of their studies came a renewed critical interest in the Hebrew text.

In Germany the most important representative in this field of studies was John Reuchlin, who Grecized his name as "Kapnion." While not the only one, he was certainly the most original, and in addition, fate found him at the center of a quarrel that echoed throughout the entire Christian world and involved humanists and theologians of every stripe. He had studied philosophy, grammar, and rhetoric, first at Paris and then at Basel, where he had obtained his academic degrees and the license to teach; later he had opted for law, had returned to the Sorbonne, and then had completed, at Orleans and Poitiers, the studies that would open the way to a career in law and politics.

His meeting with Rudolf Agricola brought a decisive turn in his life: without neglecting codices and pandects, he began to study Greek and Hebrew and in a short time became one of the greatest experts in the three sacred languages. In 1478 he wrote a Greek grammar and in 1506 his *De rudimentis hebraicis,* which was the first attempt at an introduction to the language of the Old Testament that was intended for Latins and printed. However, though a diligent student of the sacred text, Reuchlin was not one of those who proposed a philological revision or a new translation of it. He used his knowledge of the biblical languages for an exegesis that would bring out the hidden wisdom contained in the deepest meaning of every word and letter. He shared the conviction of those who regarded Hebrew as the oldest and most enduring of languages: born at the dawn of the world and destined to be the language of the entire race at the end of time, it was created directly by God ("voice of God," "holy language") along with all other things, because it reflected God's inner nature. Such premises led logically to an investigation of the ontological significance of words; once engaged in this search, scholars were inevitably drawn to the Hebrew Cabalistic tradition.

Reuchlin had an opportunity to advance his studies and fill out his intellectual experience during three journeys to Italy in 1482, 1490, and 1498, during which he perfected his knowledge of Hebrew. His encounter with Florentine culture and with Lorenzo de'Medici, Marsilius Ficino, and especially John Pico della Mirandola suggested to him the development of a system that not only could Christianize Jewish mysticism but also use the latter in a new and vast synthesis of the cultures of all times.

In his first work on this subject, *De verbo mirifico* (1494), three sages discuss it among themselves; they are Sidonius, an Epicurean, who embodies an insatiable desire for knowledge; Baruchias, a Jewish sage; and Kapnion himself, a Christian. In the end, all agree that truth resides in the unsearchable abyss of the divine mind and is therefore inaccessible to the human intellect; God and human beings, however, come in contact through the mysterious word of power, the tetragrammaton that may not be uttered, which contains not only the *mysterium tremendum* of the Most High but also the mystery of his manifestation in the universe, of his work in creation. Only thanks to the miracle of redemption has the ineffable name of the Mosaic God become utterable in the letters that make up the name Jesus, who has united divinity to humanity. In his attempt to construct a biblical theology Reuchlin used the interpretational techniques of the Cabala and dissolved Hebrew theosophy into a christosophy.

In the year in which the *De verbo mirifico* was published Pico died; Reuchlin was resolved to gather up the heritage of the prince of Mirandola and continue the work which he had left unfinished. In 1517 the *De arte cabalistica* appeared, in the form of a dialogue between a Jew, a Muslim, and a Pythagorean philosopher. In dedicating the work to Leo X the author predicted the return of a new spring that would bring back the age of Lorenzo the Magnificent. To this new flowering of studies he, the author, had made his own contribution; Marsilius Ficino had given Italy its Plato; Lefèvre d'Étaples had honored France with its Aristotle; to Germany would be given the oldest

Italian philosophy, the Pythagorean teaching that had for centuries been buried in oblivion. All this would come to pass thanks to the use of the art of the Cabala in the reading of the sacred texts; Pythagoras had, in fact, gotten the principles of his own teaching from the earliest sages, the Cabalists, who were the custodians of Mosaic wisdom; his philosophy had been transmitted orally from father to son and from Magna Graecia had passed once again into the works of the Cabalists.

Many influences, philosophical, theological, and theosophical, can be seen at work in the great synthesis that Reuchlin attempted; etymologies and demonstrations came in part from the tradition of Christian Cabalism and had already been used to show how the Hebrew doctors had, more or less consciously, foreshadowed in their works the main truths of Christianity. Pico's heir brought these elements into a unity and showed in the science of words the way leading to a deeper wisdom.

While writing, Reuchlin was also involved in a controversy that embittered the last years of his life; the dedication of his work to Leo X may also have been an attempt to gain the pontiff's good will. It happened that in 1507 a Jewish convert, John Pfefferkorn, had published a *Judenspiegel* in which he maintained that Jews were second-class *(minoris iuris)* citizens who had no right to engage in controversy with Christians and that it would therefore be a good thing to deprive them of all the tools they needed for controversy, namely, their books, except for the Torah. The petition was not something new, and this would not have been the first burning of Jewish books; therefore the Jewish communities of Germany appealed to Emperor Maximilian, who asked for Reuchlin's legal advice.

The latter replied that in Roman law the Jews were full citizens; as for their books, he held it appropriate to destroy their manuals of magic and other works offensive to Christians, especially their histories of Jesus, which were blasphemous imitations of the Gospels. Everything else should be preserved, either because they were books containing ancient traditions, such as treatises on medicine or agriculture, or because some texts could prove useful to all; special care should be taken to preserve their biblical commentaries, which were extremely valuable to Christians. The matter did not stop there. Pfefferkorn won the support of James Hoogstraten and other Dominican theologians of Cologne, who sought and obtained the approval of the universities of Paris and Louvain. Reuchlin, for his part, published under the title of *Epistolae clarorum virorum* testimonials in his favor from the most important intellectuals of his time.

The controversy expanded when the group of humanists in Erfurt issued a collection of *Epistolae obscurorum virorum* addressed to Ortwin Gratius, a master in Cologne, and supposedly written by professors in that university. In light of the success of the first edition of this work, its authors decided to follow it up with other enlarged and augmented editions. In these pages they did not explicitly raise questions of a religious nature, nor did they line up in defense of the studies which Reuchlin was pursuing. They intended simply to use the occasion to show their adversaries as apostles of ignorance, caricaturing them as sunk in their vices, enemies of all liberal studies, ignorant of grammar, and unrefined. There followed a series of violent pamphlets that made no contribution either to clarity or to the resolution of the dispute.[40] The case was finally submitted to Rome, but by this time the question was mixed up with the Lutheran question, and after many postponements and uncertainties, the court issued a sentence unfavorable to Reuchlin.

Whatever may have been the religious commitment of the humanists who intervened in the controversy, they had succeeded in radicalizing the clash between the "old" and the "new" and had launched themselves headlong into the attack on the representatives of a backward culture that was closed to every innovation, refugees in the fortress of their privileges secure in the authority of the faculties of theology and the support of powerful religious orders. But the discontent crept into even the ranks of the Dominicans, and young Martin Butzer, who at that time wore the habit of St. Dominic, was not alone in his distress when he confessed that he felt ill at ease wearing his cowl.[41]

The memory of this incident was decisive for many when it came to making a choice of field. That is what happened to Willibald Pirckheimer, perhaps the most Erasmian of the German humanists because of his conviction that Christians should regard no field of knowledge as closed to them, since God can make his presence known everywhere; in particular, Christians ought to cultivate the humanities.[42] He had hopes of the Reformation and was among the first to launch the movement of renewal at Nuremberg, but he was soon disillusioned with it. He had been formed by the reading of the Greek Fathers and soon discovered in the quarrels among the Reformers the danger of a relapse into the sophistries of Scholasticism[43] and in their behavior a betrayal of the Christian freedom which they proclaimed.[44]

His was the tragedy of many humanists who ended feeling ill at ease in either camp, as he was forced to admit a few years later in a sorrowful letter to Pope Hadrian. He explained to the pontiff that the root of all the evils was to be sought in the unacceptable behavior of some religious who were arrogantly opposed to every kind of culture and were bitter enemies of the better persons who hindered their plots. First they attacked Reuchlin and, using religion as a pretext, attempted to destroy him; then they behaved in an unseemly way during the preaching of indulgences, when they went about saying they had the authority to absolve even those who had used violence against the Blessed Virgin, since in this matter they were not inferior even to Christ. "The godlessness of these criminals has forever tainted Pope Leo, has rendered the *dominicastri* [so-called men of the Lord, i.e., the Dominicans] hateful in the eyes of all, and, more seriously, has forced the best individuals, the most learned, to transfer quickly to the Lutheran camp."[45]

5. Erasmus of Rotterdam

Erasmus (Rotterdam, 1466?–Basel, 1536), who more than anyone else had mocked the ignorance and self-conceit of monks and theologians, preferred to remain aloof. He found the first *Epistolae obscurorum virorum* to be amusing, but he was annoyed by some examples of intemperance in later editions; he was disturbed by the bitterness of the attacks, tried to intervene and soothe spirits, and even wrote to Hoogstraten to express his puzzlement and fears: one does not defend the faith, he warned, by acting cruelly toward the Jews, and yet "if it is a Christian act to hate the Jews, then in this respect we are all Christians in a very high degree."[46]

He felt bound to Reuchlin by a high esteem for him and a sincere friendship, but he did not hide his distrust of Cabalistic studies and declared that he would prefer to see the world infected by the Scotist plague rather than by these barren fancies.[47] It is likely that, in addition to the problem he had with their methodology, he was unconvinced by the central position given to this kind of Old Testament studies; his own formation led him to give priority to the gospel message, so much so that he allowed this bitter admission to escape his lips: "I would even prefer that, provided the New Testament be safeguarded, the whole Old Testament might be suppressed rather than that the peace of Christians be torn away because of the books of the Jews."[48]

When Reuchlin died, however, Erasmus paid him the tribute of a very moving eulogy, the *Apotheosis Capnionis*.[49] He recounted the dream that had been sent to a holy monk on the very day of the death of that learned and devout man, who was expert in the three biblical languages that are the basic tools of the true theologian. The monk seemed to see Reuchlin crossing a little bridge between the two banks of a river that is the border between the world of mortals and the world of the blessed; on the far side, in a field jewelled with flowers, St. Jerome, the saint of the humanists, was waiting for him wearing a white robe embroidered with the blue, red, and green letters of the Hebrew, Greek, and Latin alphabets. The newcomer was given a similar robe and then, accompanied by a crowd of the blessed spirits, was welcomed into heaven. The monk, who remained on earth, was then able to offer to God a prayer of thanksgiving for having given human beings a new saint, a model to follow. The hubbub of controversy was now dying away; the time had come to recognize how much lasting value there was in the toilsome labors of Reuchlin.

When Erasmus wrote these pages, he was at the peak of his fame; he had already published his major works, the ones that marked the fundamental stages in the development of his theological thought, which had been reached only after a long journey. His education had not been much different from that of so many of his contemporaries: while still a child he had entered the school of Deventer, then transferred to that of s'Hertogenbosch, and had eventually been accepted among the Canons Regular of St. Augustine in their house at Steyn near Gouda, where he pronounced his vows and in 1492 was ordained a priest. During these years he had been influenced by the spirituality of the *Devotio moderna,* but at Deventer he had also heard Alexander Hegius and had come to know Rudolf Agricola, who had opened wider horizons to him. Thus he had read the Fathers of the Church, especially Augustine and Jerome, but had also developed literary interests and had carefully studied Valla's *Elegantiae.*

In 1493 he left the cloister never to return: he had accepted the office of secretary to the bishop of Cambrai and had subsequently obtained permission to go to Paris and follow the course in the theological faculty. The Scholastic method in which he was trained at the famous university did not satisfy him, but the city offered other resources, and through contacts with the humanist circles of Paris he was able to pursue the study of the classics that was his preferred occupation. It seems that up to this point he had not managed to bring his seemingly contradictory interests into harmony, but in the summer of 1499 he was given the opportunity of traveling to England for several months, and this was the occasion for him of decisive new and stimulating experiences. He met Thomas More, John Colet, William Grocyn, and Thomas Linacre; through them he became acquainted with Italian culture at the century's end and with Florentine Neoplatonism, about which his English friends were so enthusiastic. He certainly did not adopt the great plans of Ficino and Pico, who were proposing comprehensive philosophico-religious syntheses that could absorb all knowledge and all cultures into a higher unity, but they did make a strong impression on him.

As he listened to Colet's lectures on St. Paul, he was fascinated by them, and the two men soon developed a deep understanding of each other. Both gave first place to a religious spirit that was fed by feeling and spiritual inwardness and was indifferent to formalism and external practices. Both were suspect in the eyes of the "up-to-date theologians and their ilk" who showed off in barren and quarrelsome controversies. Erasmus recognized that amid countless difficulties and conflicts Colet had devoted himself to ridding sacred science of the tangle of thorns in which it had become wrapped and restoring to favor the ancient theology of the Fathers: adding nothing, keeping only to some few principles, and leaving to divine omnipotence the reasons and ways according to which he wills to reveal his mysteries.[50]

Erasmus had found an ideal partner for conversation, one with whom he could even disagree, provided the disagreement became an occasion for learning; in fact, the two friends did have different views on the interpretation of some passages of Scripture. In October of 1499 we find them commenting on the gospel story of the "sadness" of Jesus in Gethsemane (Matt 26:38-39).[51] Colet adopted Jerome's interpretation, according to which Jesus was weeping at the fate of his people, who were preparing to put him to death. Erasmus answered that in this passage there was no mention of the Jewish people and that a correct historical and philological reading of the text did not allow the introduction of extraneous elements. On the other hand (Erasmus wrote), the meaning was perfectly clear if one bears in mind that Jesus had a genuine human nature and for this reason was distressed by the thought of death, just as he suffered from the lack of food or sleep; in that time of anguish his determination to sacrifice himself was not lessened, but it did contradict his natural inclination; his love for the human race was not diminished but became even more intense.

The disagreement arose from differing approaches to exegesis. Colet maintained that since the Spirit is one, the sacred text conceals a single true meaning that cannot be wholly grasped by human beings. If different interpretations are given of the same passage (the manna does not have the same taste for everyone), this depends on the fragmentation of that single meaning in the multiplicity of earthly experiences. The different readings of Scripture really impoverish its meaning, being born not of Scripture's "fruitfulness" but of the "barrenness" of the human mind, and yet they ought not become an occasion of conflict but of mutual understanding and charity.

Erasmus was less inclined to accept a presupposition that could introduce confusion, and he asserted instead the polysemy of the Scriptures, the inexhaustible wealth of its many meanings, which, furthermore, do not allow themselves to be contained in the traditional scheme of the four senses. But he also drew from the passage in question a further teaching to which he would always remain faithful: on this occasion (in Gethsemane) Jesus once again intended to give an example not of heroism or courage but of gentleness and patience; he showed that human beings are not asked to go against nature but rather to entrust themselves to the Father's will and face up to the suffering which is the fruit of sin in our nature. We are called, therefore, to the "imitation of Christ," which does not mean simply the straight imitation of a model but springs from the ability to grasp the deeper motives for every action and every attitude. The Gospels do not present a repertory of paradigmatic behaviors to which we are to conform; they offer an ethic not of norms but of intentions. Colet had started from his conception of God; Erasmus took the viewpoint of human beings who must interpret God's word. It was the first time that Erasmus had met such views; he tested his abilities, realized the gaps in his preparation, and in the coming years took steps to fill them.

After leaving England at the beginning of the new century, Erasmus plunged into feverish activity: he resumed his study of Greek and got wrapped up in his reading of Fathers and of St. Jerome in particular; in 1501 he set to work on his *Enchiridion militis Christiani,* which he published in 1503. This handbook, or dagger, of the Christian soldier was meant not as a treatise but as a guide to devotion; life, he said, is a battle against the forces of evil, and human beings have two weapons at their disposal for fighting it: prayer, which springs from trust in God, and education, which enables them to draw from the sources the precepts of Christian life. In twenty-two canons the author gives some basic pieces of advice to those who desire to follow in the footsteps of Christ. The work subsequently became one of the most read books and was translated into all the languages.

In 1504 Erasmus made a discovery that decisively contributed to the maturation of his plans: while he was "hunting" for ancient codices in the library of the Premonstratensian convent of Parc, he found the *Annotationes in Novum Testamentum* of Lawrence Valla. The philological and grammatical notes which the Italian humanist had compiled as he was collating some Greek manuscripts and correcting the text of the Vulgate showed Erasmus how even the sacred books can be subjected to scientific study and how a philological reading can yield a new exegesis. He found the very structure of the work congenial, because the observations, which could be read as notes at the foot of each page, were not presented as linked together to form a system of thought but did allow the appearance of various guiding threads that were interwoven, separated, and brought back together again along ever new paths. Erasmus published Valla's work in Paris in the following year, with a dedication to John Fisher in which he claimed for philologists the right to use the tools of their science in tackling the pages that contained the word of God so as to be able to understand it fully.

Valla's work served Erasmus as a valuable guide during the ten years in which he was preparing his Greek-Latin edition of the New Testament. During that period, however, he was also studying and traveling: in 1506 he went to Italy and earned a doctorate in theology at Turin; in 1509 he went to England once again and, as a guest of Thomas More, completed the writing of the *Praise of Folly,* which has remained his best-known work. In 1514 he moved to Basel in order to correct and finish his work on the New Testament, which he published in February 1516.

Under the title *Novum Instrumentum* he offered an edition of the Greek text, which was the result of the collation of a number of manuscripts and was set side by side with a new Latin translation and accompanied by an extensive store of annotations. The dedication to Leo X was meant to ensure protection for the work at the highest level, but the author thought it wise to preface the work with some pages explaining his intentions and at the same time forestalling criticisms: a *paraclesis* to the reader, a *methodus,* and an *apologia.* As could be anticipated, these precautions were not sufficient, and in the years that followed Erasmus had to defend himself against rebukes and objections from all sides: from Luther and Lefèvre d'Étaples, Stunica and Latomus, Edward Lee and Nicholas Baechem of Egmond. Some accused him of sacrilegious boldness in daring to interpret the Scriptures with the tools which the grammarian used for analyzing secular texts and, a more serious matter, in casting doubt on the accuracy of the Vulgate, in which the Christian West had for over a thousand years seen its own face and which the Church had authoritatively adopted as its official text.

In fact, the work Erasmus was presenting was not an isolated phenomenon, but the many *Correctoria Bibliae* that had been compiled in the last centuries of the Middle Ages were no longer sufficient; the "new science" of philology and the multiplication of editions had shown the need of a radical revision of the sacred text. Pope Leo himself could not have been unaware of the problem, since during these years he had been presented with several specimens of new translations,[52] while Cardinal Francisco Ximenes de Cisneros was supervising the work of the *Biblia Poliglotta Complutensis.*

Erasmus' work, on the other hand, showed itself immediately to be dangerously innovative. The preference given to some readings of the Greek text, the boldness shown in the translation, the numerous notes justifying the editor's choices or offering other possible options, were received as vehicles for interpretations differing from the traditional ones or even as heretical. In the new Greek text, for example, the "Johannine comma" (1 John 5:7) no longer appeared because it was not attested by the earliest manuscripts. There was an outcry of scandal, and suspicion grew that Erasmus was leaning dangerously toward the Arian heresy. The humanist answered that to surrender a text confirming the doctrine of the Trinity did not mean denying a doctrine accepted by all.

In other passages his proposal of new words betrayed (it was said) an intolerance of expressions which he regarded as inadequate; for example, he had translated the *logos* of the Fourth Gospel as *sermo* instead of *verbum,* and although no one at that time could imagine what use might be made of this translation, criticism was not long in coming. Erasmus defended himself by showing that the word was found in Cyprian, Tertullian, Hilary, and even in Augustine and Thomas; *verbum* corresponds to the Greek *rhêma,* while *logos* can also signify *oratio, ratio,* and *sapientia;* these are all words, and "no human expression can completely convey the divine reality."[53] But in replacing a more static term "that would even be unpalatable if habit did not make it acceptable," *sermo* manifests a different sensibility, one that grasps the divine in the exercise of its creative and redemptive power, as the reason that is immanent in the universe and speaks continually to human beings.

In 1519 a Louvain professor, James Masson (Latomus), acted as spokesman for the dissatisfaction of his colleagues and attacked the very foundation of Erasmus' enterprise. Erasmus the humanist maintained that only those who knew the biblical languages could rightly call themselves theologians; he had signed himself "the least of theologians" in his dedication to Leo X, and in 1517 he had played an active part in the foundation of the Collegium Trilingue Lovaniense. The presence of what he regarded as an authentic school of theology alongside the famous university faculty had given rise to a great deal of debate; some objected that the knowledge of Hebrew, Greek, and Latin is indeed very useful, but it does not exhaust the work of the theologian because concepts have a value of their own that is completely independent of the language in which they are expressed, and it is precisely with these concepts that those doing theology must concern themselves. Latomus' argument revealed the irreconcilability of the two positions at the level of logic and method.

Others raised more or less penetrating objections, but all agreed on one point: Erasmus, who was not a theologian, had had the effrontery to enter clumsily on a terrain with which he had little familiarity. Attacked on several fronts, Erasmus found himself forced to answer censure with defense,[54] and this led him better to define his own thinking and to clarify both his method and his purposes.

The New Testament text which he had printed in 1516 did not satisfy him; it had been "rushed out rather than edited"[55] because Froben, the publisher, had kept tugging his hand, perhaps in his haste to have the work appear before the text of the *Complutense*. The new edition of 1519 was thoroughly revised as compared with the preceding; the helps given to readers as they explored the text were more abundant; furthermore, instead of the previous short *methodus* there was a *Ratio seu compendium verae theologiae,* which was much fuller and had been published as a short independent volume during the previous year.

It was to this work, which was brought up to date and expanded in successive editions, that Erasmus entrusted his reflections on the methodological foundations of his research, ideas that had been developed through those years of intense work and hot debate.[56] Instead of a systematic treatment he preferred the clear and discursive manner of one who makes his experience available and offers his advice as a guide to the reading of the Scriptures. In fact, in providing this little *Summa* he was proposing a radical reversal of the Scholastic method and demonstrating that exegetical work and theological work were in harmony. Unlike the other sciences (Erasmus claimed), theology not only required the engagement of the intellect but involved the most hidden recesses of the human soul, the feelings, and the passions.[57] It is a science of the mind and heart, and for this reason the theologian ought to be initially moved by enthusiasm and ought to dispose himself to be changed, entranced, inspired, and transformed into what he is learning.[58]

Above all, he should be clear on the object and purpose of his diligence: theology is not a human discourse on divine matters but a listening to God's word to humanity; the candidate will thus be *theodidaktos,* taught by God, and will have to submit himself to a true and proper initiation if he is to be introduced to the "philosophy of Christ," which is the only one capable of taking possession of him and transforming his entire being.[59] That was what Hippocrates required of his disciples, and that is what was claimed also by those who were initiated into the pagan mysteries. Only in this way will the theologian receive the wisdom needed to "speak the divine writings," since the "speaking," as Paul says (1 Cor 14:6), is not philosophy but prophecy, which is a gift of the Holy Spirit.[60]

Since love and knowledge nourish each other, it will be the duty of neophytes to enter ever more deeply into the understanding of the Scriptures by devoting to them all the care and attention that they give to any literary work. They must make sure, above all, to have a correct text. Then they must interpret it by drawing on the various fields of knowledge: on history and geography first of all, but it will be useful to them to know also the names of the plants, animals, and stars in order that when each story is set in its context and all its details are explained, it may be filled with light and life. Before anything else, however, neophytes must make their own the language in which the work is written. A translation causes us to see things through the eyes of others inasmuch as each language has its own peculiarities, its syntactic constructions, its ways of saying things, and it is difficult to translate all these without impoverishing them. It is not to be forgotten, moreover, that from this point of view the Bible presents special difficulties, since Hebrew and Greek differ structurally from each other, and in addition, some passages of the New Testament, though written in Greek, were thought out in Hebrew. The subsequent translation into Latin created misunderstandings on which absurd interpretations were subsequently built.

The introductory work exemplified here was that specifically of a philologist, but this did not mean that philology and the other sciences had a purely propaideutic and instrumental value as "handmaids" of theology. In fact, according to Erasmus, to put the matter in these terms is to put it badly. Whether dependence or interdependence be the proper descriptive term, one thing is certain: there is no doing of theology without an extensive store of information.[61] For their part, the representatives of official science, "our Masters," who regard it as useless or even harmful for theologians to worry about this aspect of their preparation, are not concerned by the fact that theology as professed today in the schools had lost its identity; it has been transformed into philosophy and has borrowed from Aristotle its language, method, and ways of proceeding. From being queen it has turned into a slave and had dissolved into pettifogging disputes and paralyzing definitions that have fed the quarrelsomeness of people but have not made them better.

Theology is, Erasmus maintained, a special kind of thought, knowledge, and experience, and as such, it has a language of its own which it learns from the sacred texts. Augustine had noted long ago that both the Old and the New Testaments teem with images, allegories, comparisons; Jesus preferred to teach in parables, as Socrates too had done, taking his examples from very simple things that are part of everyone's experience. There are those who think that by using figurative language God wanted to make himself more readily understood, or that he was testing our capacity for understanding, or, again, that in this way he was hiding the truth from those who were not worthy of it. In any case, one thing emerges clearly: the use of comparisons, stories, and images catches the attention of people and moves them; it penetrates directly to the depths of the soul, where reason and affectivity rub elbows.

The parable of the prodigal son conveys a teaching that would not have been so effective if it had used the terminology of moral doctrine; the image of the vine and the branches conveys to our intuitive grasp the idea of our incorporation into Christ; the image of the seed that dies in the womb of the earth in order to be reborn to new life rouses in us a hope which no philosophical demonstration could give. Examples could be multiplied (Erasmus said), but it is enough to observe that there are things that "offer a more pleasing sight when seen through crystal or amber than if seen directly. And, I know not why, sacred things are more majestic when set before the eyes under a veil than if they are seen completely uncovered."[62]

Truth cannot reveal itself in its unbearable splendor, and perhaps the language of images is the means by which the eternal wisdom makes itself understandable to us as in a kind of stammering.[63] This language, which is closer to that of the poets than to that of the philosophers, presents not a few difficulties, and Erasmus was aware that the exploration of the sacred text could prove tricky, for he advises beginners to hold firm to some precise points of reference: those contained in the creed commonly known as the "Apostles' Creed" because it reflects the simplicity of apostolic times. Later on, he noted, as faith grew weaker, creeds multiplied and to them were added theological definitions that kill the religious sense by imposing entirely human ideas or, more often, opinions.

Just what these definitions were that Erasmus loathed can be seen in all his works: he rejected formulations extracted from the simple truths of faith by means of dialectical artifices; it was enough for him to believe in the humanity of Christ without asking whether the Son of God could have assumed the nature of a vegetable or an animal instead of a human being; he maintained that the trinitarian mysteries, the modes and causes of the procession of the Holy Spirit, will be perfectly clear on the day of judgment; here on earth the prudent thing is not to enter into the obscure labyrinths of a truth that is beyond the capacities of our mind.

But he also rejected customs that had been laid down like deposits of soil over the centuries and that now burdened the consciences of the faithful: rituals, fasts, more or less superstitious practices. In this area, however, his doubts led him much further: as he read the Fathers, he seemed to see a quite different manner of life, one marked by the simplicity of the Christian community in the earliest times, when not only were no vows taken but baptism was administered to adults and marriage was not considered a sacrament. The reading of the writers of the early centuries absorbed him for many years and produced concrete results in numerous editions and translations: Jerome (1516), Cyprian (1520), Arnobius (1522), Hilary (1523), Chrysostom (1525–33), Irenaeus (1526), Origen (1527), Ambrose (1527), Augustine (1528–29).

6. Erasmus and Luther

Even when it was now clear that an unmendable rent had been made in the Christian world, Erasmus continued to display a freedom of mind that only increased suspicions of him. He did not go over to Luther's camp, even though he acknowledged the reformer's sincerity, genuine religious spirit, and many good points, regretting only that these were expressed in unsuitable ways. He himself, moreover, had with great anticipation given free play to his irony with regard to the corruption and madness of the Christian world; as a result, there was some foundation for the common saying that Erasmus had laid the egg which Luther then hatched. And yet right from the outset it was clear that the two men could never become fellow travelers.

In December 1516, when the *Novum Instrumentum* was in the hands of everyone, George Spalatin, chaplain of Frederick the Wise, wrote a letter to Erasmus in which he submitted the doubts of a young monk. In Erasmus' notes on the letter to the Romans (Spalatin said), the humanist had interpreted the justice that comes from the law or works as meaning the external observance of ceremonies; this was too literal and reductive an interpretation. In addition, he had denied that the apostle made any reference to original sin. The causes of the disagreement that would later oppose the two exegetes were already present in these brief remarks.

Luther, who shortly before had completed a course of lectures on the same epistle, was afraid that Erasmus was reducing religious experience to its ethical dimensions; this would pave the way for a positive appraisal of works which, apart from faith, and even if done by persons whom all judge to be most upright, have nothing to do with justice.[64] Perhaps Erasmus did not even answer, but in the years that followed he could no longer ignore the voice of his correspondent. Once Luther had given up hope of numbering the prince of humanists among his own supporters, he asked Erasmus to remain a simple spectator at the conflict, but meanwhile, in the opposing camp the latter was under increasing pressure to take up his pen against the heresiarch.

No one any longer deluded himself into thinking that a debate could help shed light on the controversies and restore peace to souls, and Erasmus was asked to make a clear choice. He found himself compelled, though reluctant and unwilling, to descend to the field of battle, and he did so in his own way: he went straight to the heart of the problem by choosing the subject of free will. Instead of discussing it in polemical fashion, however, he preferred to compare the different opinions. In September 1524 his book *De libero arbitrio diatribé sive collatio* was published in Basel. The work left both parties disappointed and dissatisfied, and it once again won for its author the reproach of having ventured incautiously, as a mere grammarian, onto the difficult terrain of theology.[65]

Readers who had been following Erasmus' publications for some years could believe that his outlook was not diametrically opposed to that of Luther.

More than once he had acknowledged that grace alone justifies; in the *Ratio* he had said, with Paul, that "we are not saved otherwise than through the justice which is from faith";[66] in the months preceding the publication of the *Diatribé* he had published his *Inquisitio de fide*,[67] a courageous and sincere work in which the recognition of the littleness of human beings, who can do nothing without divine help, seemed to provide a meeting ground. Now, in the *Diatribé*, the subject he had chosen led him to give a thorough explanation of the reasons that divided him from Luther, and the issue, once again, was a problem of method.

He divided the work into four parts: a preface, a study of the biblical passages that confirm the doctrine of free will, an analysis of texts that seemed to favor an opposite interpretation, and, finally, concluding thoughts. Setting aside all Scholastic ways of proceeding, he said that he was sure to reach agreement with his adversary if the discussion were conducted on the plane of exegesis, since only by inquiring of the Scriptures was it possible to bring the truth to light; but for this very reason he maintained the necessity of establishing in advance a norm of interpretation. The distance between the two disputants showed itself clearly from the very first lines: whereas Luther proclaimed the absolute simplicity and perfect clarity of the sacred text, Erasmus answered that on the contrary the reader comes at times on obscure passages which, if tackled rashly, lead into labyrinths from which there is no way out. That was what had happened in debates on the subject of freedom and necessity, which the philosophers had taken up first, followed by the theologians, who struck blows with dogmatically asserted definitions but without appreciable results:

> There are, in fact, in the divine pages secret passages into which God has not willed that we should enter in excessive depth, because, if we do, we will find ourselves wrapped in increasingly thick darkness and will be forced to acknowledge the unsearchable majesty of the divine wisdom and our own weakness. Pomponius Mela reports something similar about the cave of Corico, which at first sight was pleasant and agreeable, but those who ventured too far into it felt driven to flee, struck by a sacred terror at the majesty of the divinity that dwelt in it.[68]

After being felicitously introduced by this "myth of the cave," the discussion gradually brings out the uneasiness of those who feel compelled to confront the sacred texts with statements that in principle either deny or affirm the free choice of human beings in regard to their salvation. Luther had denied the freedom of the will in his *Assertiones*,[69] and Erasmus admitted: "Dogmatically assertive statements please me so little that I more readily turn to skeptical views." We can (he said) reach absolute certainties only if, sometimes for noble purposes, we approach the text of Scripture with an interpretative key that preordains the answer. That is how Pelagius acted, who, though condemned and abhorred, was in fact sustained by a strong ethical drive and wanted to bring everyone back to a sense of their own responsibility; that is also how Augustine acted, who, fearing the loss of the Christian dimension of human experience, emphasized the theme of grace. But careful readers will note that only after the debate with Pelagius did Augustine declare himself clearly opposed to the doctrine of free will.

When we turn to the study of the Scriptures, difficulties arise from the fact that in both the Old and New Testaments we come upon passages that seem to contradict each other, even though they all come from the same Spirit. We must therefore ask ourselves how they are to be read, without seeking, however, to plumb the depths of the divine will. According to Erasmus' way of reading the Scriptures, the factor that gives unity, even here, is the echo which the words of Scripture awaken in the minds of the faithful. The choice seems to incline in favor of the ability human beings have of grasping the way of the good and of therefore accepting the intervention of grace, but the emphasis is always on what can be "attributed to free will." There is never a dogmatic assertion of a presumed freedom of choice but only the suggestion of a hope that sustains each individual in daily living. The scriptural passages that exhort to good are to be interpreted literally, because it would be absurd to think that God gives a command or counsel in order to deceive human beings; the passages that seem to deny freedom are to be read in their context and put back into perspective or else read as if their purpose were to check the insolence of those who attribute their successes not to the Lord but to their own strength or their own wisdom. The very wrath of God and his repentance, which lead him to change a decision, are to be interpreted as metaphors of his freedom.

In the final section, Erasmus pulls together the threads of the entire analysis, touching on various themes and emphasizing that which he regards, from an exegetical viewpoint, as the basic motif, namely, that when we proceed by means of axioms in our search for truth, we are moving between Scylla and Charybdis, which means, in this case, between pride and despair. Human beings should live as if their salvation depended on themselves but also with the awareness that everything comes from God's grace, beginning with the first grace, the natural freedom which is given to all, even to pagans, and which persuades them to live responsibly and to make the choices that become them.

At the end of 1525 Luther published his *De servo arbitrio,*[70] a bitter and at times contemptuous reply, in which he again studied the biblical passages cited by his adversary in order to reverse the latter's interpretation of them and to show that only a reading guided by the Spirit can lead to the understanding of the Scriptures. The Wittenberg theologian delved deeply to show that human nature, wounded by sin and turned in on itself, is now incapable of even a passive collaboration in its salvation, because human beings, however they behave, lack any ability at all to will the good and, by an irreversible inversion of the will, are turned to love of themselves and not of God.

On this occasion, the two contestants manifested their different sensibilities; they could not understand each other, and Erasmus' answer was not a help to clarity.[71] Luther accused him of remaining the prisoner of a legalistic ethic that quantified the value of each action and presumed it could get rid of the debt by ransoming the sinner. The humanist, in his turn, rebuked the reformer for forcing the meaning of the Scriptures by using a dogmatic presupposition; but Erasmus perhaps did not perceive the tragic aspect of Luther's thought, did not have the same desperate sense of sin, did not share the outlook of those who "vastly exaggerate original sin."[72] Luther had made the cross his interpretive key: "I understand nothing anywhere in scripture except Christ crucified";[73] he saw at the basis of Christian experience the tension between the two poles of the Fall and the redemption; he was a theologian of the passion. Erasmus was a theologian of the nativity; for him Christianity is a rebirth, a gift of light, the beginning of a new life that gives meaning to the whole of human history, because, as he says in a famous *Colloquium:* "I believe that the Spirit is poured out more extensively than we can possibly imagine."[74]

BIBLIOGRAPHY

SOURCES

Thomas Netter (Saffron Walden, ca. 1380–Rouen, November 2, 1430)

Fasciculi Zizaniorum Magistri Johannis Wyclif cum tritico, ascribed to Thomas Netter of Walden. Ed. W. W. Shirley. Rerum Brittanicarum Medii Aevi Scriptores 5. London, 1858.

Doctrinale antiquitatum fidei catholicae Ecclesiae. Ed. B. Blanciotti. 3 vols. Venice, 1757–58.

Some letters: ed. B. Zimmerman, in *Monumenta Historica Carmelitana* I, 4. Lerins, 1907. Pp. 441–82.

Reginald Pecock (ca. 1395–Thorney, 1460)

The Donet. Ed. E. V. Hitchcock. London, 1921.

The Reule of Crysten Religioun. Ed. W. Cabell Greet. London, 1924.

Repressor of Over Much Blaming of the Clergy. Ed. C. Babington. 2 vols. London, 1860.

The Folewer to the Donet. Ed. E. V. Hitchcock. London, 1924.

Book of Faith. Ed. J. B. Morison. Glasgow, 1909.

Johannis de Whethamstede Narratio, ante hac inedita, de Reginaldi Pecockii adjuratione. In W. Hemingford. *Historia de rebus gestis Edvardi I, Edvardi II et Edvardi III.* Oxford, 1731. II, 480–89.

Thomas More (London, 1477–78—July 6, 1535)

The Complete Works of St. Thomas More. New Haven–London, 1963ff.

The Correspondence of St. Thomas More. Ed. E. F. Rogers. Princeton, 1947.

John Colet (London, 1467–September 16, 1519)

Opus de sacramentis Ecclesiae. Ed. J. H. Lupton. London, 1867.

Super opera Dionysii (Opus de Caelesti Dionysii Hierarchia and *In Ecclesiasticam Divi Dionysii Hierarchiam).* Ed. J. H. Lupton. London, 1869.

Enarratio in Epistolam S. Pauli ad Romanos. Ed. J. H. Lupton. London, 1873.

Opuscula quaedam theologica (In principium Geneseos; De corpore Christi mystico; Epistola B. Pauli ad Romanos Expositio litteralis). Ed. J. H. Lupton. London, 1876.

Enarratio in Primam Epistolam S. Pauli ad Corinthios. Ed. J. H. Lupton. London, 1874. This and all the preceding works were reprinted in four vols.: Farnborough, 1965–66, 1968[2].

Commentary on First Corinthians: A New Edition. Ed. B. O'Kelly and C. A. L. Jarrot. Medieval and Renaissance Texts and Studies 21. Binghamton, N.Y., 1985.

Oratio ad Clerum in Convocatione. In S. Knight. *The Life of Dr. John Colet.* London, 1724. Pp. 273–85.

Statuta Ecclesiae Cathedralis S. Pauli. Exhibita to Cardinal Wolsey. Statuta Fraternitatis Jesu. In *Registrum Statutorum et Consuetudinum Ecclesae Cathedralis Sancti Pauli Londinensis.* Ed. W. Sparrow Simpson. London, 1873. Pp. 217–36, 237–49, 446–52.

John Fisher (Beverley, ca. 1469–London, June 22, 1535)

Opera quae hactenus inveniri potuerunt. Würzburg, 1597; reprinted: Farnsborough, 1967.

Sacri Sacerdotii defensio. Cologne, 1525. Ed. H. Klein Schmeink. Corpus Catholicorum 9. Münster, 1925.

Rouschausse, J. *Erasmus and Fischer, Their Correspondence.* Paris, 1968.

The English Works I. Ed. J. E. B. Mayor. London, 1876; reprinted, 1935.

Eimeric of Kampen (Heimerik van den Velde) (Zon, ca. 1395–Louvain, 1460)

Problemata inter Albertum Magnum et sanctum Thomam ad utriusque intelligentiam multum conferentia (1468). Cologne, 1496.

Epistola Heymerici De Campo contra Johannem de Rokozano de communione sub utraque soecie. In Ladner, *Heimericus de Campo* (see Studies, below). Pp. 304–8. With a list of unpublished works.

Gerard de Monte (Gerhard Ter Stegen) (ca. 1400–Cologne, December 31, 1480)

Decisionum S. Thomae quae ad invicem oppositae quibusdam dicuntur concordantiae. Ed. G. G. Meersseman. Rome, 1934.

Henry of Gorcum (+ 1431)

Quaestiones in Summam Sancti Thomae. Esslingen, 1473.

Conclusiones super IV libros Sententiarum. Brussels, ca. 1480.

Tractatus de praedestinatione et reprobatione divina. No place, 1474.
List of the works, including the unpublished, in Weiler, *Heinrich von Gorcum* (see Studies, below). Pp. 88–92.

Denis the Carthusian (Denis van Leeuven) (Ryckel, 1402/3–Roermond, March 12, 1471)

Opera omnia. 44 vols. Vols. 1–14 and 17–18: Montrueil, 1896–1901. Vols. 14bis, 15–16, 19–42: Tournai, 1902–13. Vol. 25bis: Parkminster, 1935.

Gabriel Biel (Speyer, before 1410–Schönbuch, December 7, 1495)

Canonis missae expositio. Ed. H. A. Oberman and W. J. Courtenay. 2 vols. Veröffentlichungen des Instituts für Europäische Geschichte 31–32. Wiesbaden, 1963–65.
Collectorium circa quattuor libros Sententiarum. Ed. W. Werbeck and U. Hofmann. Tübingen, 1973ff.
Defensorium oboedientiae apostolicae (1500). Ed. H. A. Oberman and others. Cambridge, Mass., 1968.
Sermones de festivitatibus Christi. Hagenau, 1510.
Sermones dominicales de tempore. Hagenau, 1510.

Conrad Summenhart (Calw ?–Schuttern, 1502)

Septimpertitum opus de contractibus pro foro conscientiae atque theologico per centum quaestiones digestum. Hagenau, 1500.
Tractatus bipartitus de decimis. Hagenau, 1500.

John Staupitz (Motterwitz, ca. 1468–Salzburg, December 28, 1524)

Lateinische Schriften. 2 vols. I. Ed. R. Wetzel. Berlin–New York, 1987. II. Ed. L. Graf zu Dohna and R. Wetzel. Berlin–New York, 1979. Spätmittelalter und Reformation 13–14.
Deutsche Werken. I. Ed. W., Schneider-Lastin. Berlin–New York, 1990. Seven volumes in all are planned.

John of Paltz (Johannes Jeuser) (Pfalzel, 1445–Mühlheim, March 13, 1511)

De septem foribus sive portis beatae Virginis. Leipzig, 1491.
Die hymelische Fundgrube. Leipzig, 1490. Latin revision: *Coelifodina.* Erfurt, 1502. Ed. Ch. Burger and F. Stasch. Berlin–New York, 1983.
Supplementum Coelifodine. Erfurt, 1504. Ed. B. Hamm. Berlin–New York, 1983.
Opuscula. Ed. Ch. Burger. Spätmittlelater und Reformation 2–4. Berlin–New York, 1989.
A. Zumkeller. *Manuskripte von Werken der Autoren Augustiner-Eremitenordens.* Würzburg, 1966. Pp. 255–60 and 604.
M. Ferdigg. *AnalAug* 30 (1967) 256–86.

John of Schoonhaven (or Schoonhoven) (Schoonhoven, 1356/7–January 22, 1432)

Exortatorium Spirituale. Ed. W. Becker. *De Katholiek* 86 (1884) 204–10, 352–61; 87 (1885) 126–41.

Bonum certamen. In *Divinitas* 11 (1967) 792–95.

Epistola responsalis super epistolam cancellarii and *Commendatio sive defensio libri fratris Johannis Ruusbroec De ornatu spiritualium nuptiarum.* Ed. A. Combes. *Essai sur la critique de Ruysbroeck par Gerson* I. Paris, 1945. Pp. 716–71 and 683–716.

List of works in A. Gruis. *DSp* 8 (Paris, 1974). Cols. 724–35.

Henry Herp (Hendrik Herp) (Erp, beginning of fifteenth century–Malines, 1477)

Speculum aureum de praeceptis divinae legis. Mainz, 1474.

Sermones de tempore, de sanctis, de tribus partibus poenitentiae. Speyer, 1484.

Spieghel der Voncomenkeit. Mainz, 1475. Ed. L. Vershueren. 2 vols. Antwerp, 1931.

Theologia mystica. Cologne, 1538. Contains *Soliloquium divini amoris; Directorium contemplativorum; Eden seu Paradisus contemplativorum.*

Description of manuscripts, editions, and translations: B. de Troeyer, in *Die deutsche Literatur des Mittelalters. Verfasserlexikon* III. Berlin–New York. Cols. 1127–35.

Wessel Gansfort (Groningen, ca. 1419–October 4, 1489)

Opera. Groningen, 1614. Reprinted: Monumenta Humanistica Belgica 1. 1966.

John Busch (Zwolle, 1399–Sülte, 1479)

Des Augustinerpropstes Johannes Busch Chronicon Winderheimense und Liber de reformatione monasteriorum. Ed. K. Grube. Halle, 1886.

John Geiler of Kaiserberg (Schaffhausen, March 16, 1445–Strasbourg, March 10, 1510)

Navicula sive speculum fatuorum. Strasbourg, 1511.

Editions of sermons: see H. Kraume in *Die deutsache Literatur des Mittelalters. Verfasserlexikon* II. Berlin–New York, 1980. Cols. 1141–52.

Jakob Wimpfeling and Beatus Rhenanus. *Das Leben des Johannes Geiler von Kaysersberg.* Ed. D. Mertens and O. Herding. Munich, 1970.

John Pupper (Goch, ca. 1420–1475)

De libertate Christiana. Ed. F. Pijper. Bibliotheca Reformatorica Neerlandica 6. Den Haag, 1910. Pp. 41–255.

De quattuor erroribus circa legem evangelicam exortis de votis et religionibus facticiis Dialogus. Ed. C. W. F. Walch. *Monimenta Medii Aevi* I, 4. Göttingen, 1760; reprinted: 1966. Pp. 74–239.

De scholasticorum scriptis et religiosorum votis epistola. Ed. Walch, ibid., II. 1. Göttingen, 1761. Pp. 3–24.

John Rucherat (or Ruchrat) of Oberwesel (+ after 1479)

Disputatio adversus indulgentias. Ed. C. W. F. Walch. *Monimenta Medii Aevi* I. Göttingen, 1757. Pp. 111–56.

John Reuchlin (Pforzheim, February 22, 1455– Bad Liebenzell, June 30, 1552)

De verbo mirifico. Basel, 1994.
De arte cabalistica. Hagenau, 1517. Both works reprinted: Stuttgart–Bad Cannstadt, 1964.
De arte praedicandi. Pforzheim, 1504.
Defensio contra calumniatores suos Colonienses. Tübingen, 1514.
Briefwechsel. Ed. L. Geiger. Stuttgart, 1875; reprinted: Hildesheim, 1962.

Willibald Pirckheimer (Eichstätt, December 3, 1470– Nuremberg, December 22, 1530)

Opera politica, historica, philosophica et epistolica. Frankfurt, 1610.
Briefwechsel. Munich, 1940.
De vera Christi carne et de vero eius sanguine ad Ioan. Oecolampadium responsio. Nuremberg, 1526.
Responsio secunda. Nuremberg, 1527.

Erasmus of Rotterdam (Rotterdam, October 28, 1466 or 1469– Basel, July 12, 1536)

Opera. Ed. L. Le Clerc. 10 vols. in 11 books. Leiden (Lugduni Batavorum), 1703–5; reprinted: Hildeheim, 1961.
Opera omnia. Amsterdam-Oxford, 1969ff.
Opuscula. Ed. W. K. Ferguson. Den Haag, 1933.
Opus epistolarum Des. Erasmi Roterodami. Ed. P. S. Allen. 12 vols. Oxford, 1906–58.

STUDIES

Contemporaries of Erasmus: A Biographical Register of the Renaissance and Reformation. Ed. P. G. Bietenholz and Th. B. Deutscher. 3 vols. Toronto-Buffalo-London, 1985–87.
German Humanism and Reformation. Ed. R. P. Becker. New York, 1982.
L'humanisme allemande (1480–1540). Colloque international de Tours (1975). Munich-Paris, 1979.
Pre-Reformation Germany. Ed. G. Strauss. London, 1972.
Die Reformationszeit. Ed. M. Greschat. 2 vols. Stuttgart-Berlin-Cologne-Mainz, 1981.
Wegbereiter der Reformation. Ed. G. Benrath. Bremen, 1967.
Beer, M. *Dionysius' des Kartausers Lehre vom Desiderium Naturale des Menschen nach der Gotteschau.* Münchener Theologische Studien 28. Munich, 1963.
Béné, C. "Érasme et saint Augustin: Influence de saint Augustin sur l'humanisme d'Érasme. État de la question." *Atti del Congresso internazionale su S. Agostino nel XVI centenario della Conversione (Roma, 15–20 settembre 1986).* Studia

Ephemeridis "Augustinianum" 26. Rome, 1987. III, 225–39.

Bradshaw, B., and E. Duffy. *Humanism, Reform, and Reformation: The Career of Bishop John Fisher.* Cambridge, 1989.

Brouette, E. "Dionysius Cartusianus." *TRE* 9 (Berlin, 1982) 4–6.

_____. "Devotio Moderna, I." Ibid., 8 (Berlin, 1981) 152–75.

Buck, A. "Der Rückgriff des Renaissance-Humanismus auf die Patristik." *Festschrift Walter von Wartburg.* Tübingen, 1968. Pp. 153–75.

Chambers, R. W. *Thomas More.* London, 1935.

Chantraine, G. "L'*Apologia ad Latomum.* Deux conceptions de la théologie." *Scrinium Erasmianum* II. Leiden, 1969. Pp. 51–75.

_____. *Érasme et Luther, libre et serf arbitre. Étude historique et théologique.* Paris-Namur, 1981. With bibliography.

Coogan, R. *Erasmus, Lee, and the Correction of the Vulgate: The Shaking of the Foundation.* Travaux h'humanisme et renaissance 261. Geneva, 1992.

Courtenay, W. J. "Nominalism and Late Medieval Religion." *The Pursuit of Holiness in Late Medieval and Renaissance Religion.* Ed. Ch. Trinkaus and H. A. Oberman. Studies in Medieval and Reformation Thought 10. Leiden, 1974. Pp. 26–59.

Crompton, J. "Fasciculi Zizaniorum." *Journal of Ecclesiastical History* 12 (1961) 35–45, 155–66.

Crusius, I. "Gabriel Biel und die Oberdeutschen Stifte der Devotio Moderna." *Publications du Centre européen d'études bourguignonnes (XIVe–XVI^2 s.)* 29 (1989) 77–87.

Debongnie, "Dévotion Moderne." *DSp* 3 (Paris, 1967). Cols. 727–47.

_____. "Busch, Johannes." Ibid., 1 (Paris, 1937). Cols. 1983–84.

Dettloff, W. "Biel, Gabriel." *TRE* 6 (Berlin, 1980) 488–91.

Dolfen, C. *Die Stellung des Erasmus von Rotterdam zum scholastischen Methode.* Osnabrück, 1936.

Eckert, W. P. "Heimericus de Campo." *Neue Deutsche Biographie* 9 (Berlin, 1972) 92.

_____. "Nicolaus von Kues und Johannes Reuchlin." *Niccolò Cusano agli inizi del mondo moderno.* Atti del V congresso internazionale (Bressanone, 6–10 settembre 1964). Florence, 1970. Pp. 195–209.

Geiger, L. *Johannes Reuchlin. Sein Leben und seine Werke.* Leipzig, 1871; reprinted: Nieuwkoop, 1964.

Gleason, J. B. *John Colet.* Berkeley, 1989.

Godfrey, W. R. "John Colet of Cambridge." *ArchRef* 65 (1975) 6–17.

Gorce, D. "La patristique dans la réforme d'Érasme." *Festgabe J. Lortz* I. Baden-Baden, 1958. Pp. 233–76.

Grabmann, M. *Mittelalterliches Geistesleben.* 3 vols. Munich, 1926–56. See the index.

Greenslade, S. L. "The Faculty of Theology." *The History of Universities* VII. Oxford, 1986. Pp. 295–334.

Guellouy, R. "L'évolution des méthodes théologiques à Louvain d'Érasme à Jansenius." *RHE* 37 (1941) 31–144.

Gullick, E., and O. de Vegel. "Henri de Herp." *DSp* 7 (Paris, 1968). Cols. 346–66.

Haber, P. *Traditionsfestigkeit und Traditionskritik bei Thomas More.* Basel, 1953.

Haines, R. M. "Reginald Pecock: A Tolerant Man in an Age of Intolerance." *Persecution and Toleration.* Ed. W. J. Shiels. Pp. 124–37. = *Studies in Church History* 21 (1984).

Hamm, B. "Frömmigkeit als Gegenstand theologiegeschichtlicher Forschung. Methodische-historische Überlegung am Beispiel vom Mittelalter und Reformation." *Zeitschrift für Theologie und Kirche* 74 (1977) 464–97.

_____. *Frömmigkeitstheologie am Anfang des XVI Jahrhunderts. Studien zum Johannes von Paltz und seinem Umkreis.* Tübingen, 1982.

Harvey, M. "The Diffusion of the *Doctrinale* of Thomas Netter in the Fifteenth and Sixteenth Centuries." *Intellectual Life in the Middle Ages: Essays Presented to Margaret Gibson.* Ed. L. Smith and B. Ward. London, 1991. Pp. 281–94.

Haubst, R. *Zum Fortleben Alberts des Grossen bei Heymerich von Kamp und Nikolaus von Kues.* BGPTM, Suppl. 4. Münster i. W., 1952.

Holeczek, H. *Humanistische Bibelphilologie als Reformproblem bei Erasmus von Rotterdam, Thomas More und William Tyndale.* Studies in the History of Christian Thought 9. Leiden, 1975.

Hudson, A. "The Debate on Bible Translation, Oxford 1401." *English Historical Review* 354 (1975) 1–18.

Humbert, A. *Les origines de la théologie moderne. I. La renaissance de l'antiquité chrétienne (1420–1521).* Paris, 1911.

Hunt, E. W. *Dean Colet and His Theology.* London, 1956.

Hurley, M. "*Scriptura sola*: Wyclif and His Critics." *Traditio* 16 (1960) 275–352.

Jayne, S. R. *John Colet and Marsilio Ficino.* Oxford, 1963.

Jacob, B. F. "Reginald Pecock, Bishop of Chichester." *Proceedings of the British Academy* 37 (1951) 121–53.

Joachimsen, P. A. "Humanism and the Development of the German Mind." *Pre-Reformation Germany* (see above). Pp. 161–224.

Kohls, E. W. *Die Theologie des Erasmus.* 2 vols. Basel, 1966.

Ladner, P. "Der Ablass-Traktat des Heimericus de Campo." *Zeitschrift für Schweizere Kirchengeschichte* 71 (1977) 93–140.

_____. "Heymericus de Campo an Johannes Rokycana. Zur Laienkelchdiskussion am Basler Konzil." *Variorum Munera Florum. Festschrift für Hans H. Haefele.* Sigmaringen, 1985. Pp. 301–8.

Levine, J. J. "Reginald Pecock and Lorenzo Valla on the 'Donation of Constantine.'" *Studies in the Renaissance* 20 (1973) 118–43.

Leube, H. *Reformation und Humanismus in England.* Leipzig, 1930.

Lytle, G. F., "The Church Fathers and Oxford Professors in the Late Middle Ages, Renaissance, and Reformation." *Actas conventus neo-latini Bononiensis. Proceedings of the Fourth International Congress of Neo-Latin Studies (Bologna, 26 August to 1 September 1979).* Ed. R. J. Schoeck. Medieval and Renaissance Texts and Studies 37. Binghamton, N.Y., 1985. Pp. 101–15.

Lohse, B. "Zum Wittenberger Augustinismus. Augustinus Schrift *De spiritu et littera* in der Auslegung bei Staupitz, Luther und Karlstadt." *Essays Dedicated to Heiko Augustinus Oberman.* Leiden-New York-Copenhagen, 1990. Pp. 89–109.

Lourdaux, W. "Dévotion moderne et humanisme chrétien." *The Late Middle Ages and the Dawn of Humanism Outside Italy.* Leuven-Den Haag, 1972. Pp. 17–77.

Lupton, J. H. *A Life of John Colet: With an Appendix of Some of His English Writings.* London, 1887; reprinted: Hamden, Conn., 1961.

Macek, J. "Die bömische und die deutsche radikale Reformation bis zum Jahre 1515." *Zeitschrift für Kirchengeschichte* 85, no. 2 (1974) 5–29.

Mara, M. G. "Esegesi biblica e riforma della vita cristiana nel pensiero erasmiano." *Annali di Storia dell'Esegesi* 4 (1987) 175–95.

Marcel, R. "Les 'découvertes' d'Erasme en Angleterre." *BibHumRen* 14 (1952) 117–23.

Margolin, J.-C. "Erasme et le néoplatomisme." *Il neoplatonismo nel Rinascimento.* Atti del Convegno internazionale (Roma-Firenze, 12–15 dicembre 1990). Ed. P. Prini. Rome, 1993. Pp. 147–71.

Marius, R. C. "Thomas More and the Early Church Fathers." *Traditio* 24 (1969) 379–407.

McLaughlin, R. E. "Universities, Scholasticism, and the Origins of the German Reformation." *The History of Universities* IX (Oxford, 1990) 1–43.

Meersseman, G. *Geschichte des Albertismus.* I. *Die Pariser Anfänge des Kölner Albertismus.* Paris, 1933. II. *Die ersten Kölner Kontroversen.* Rome, 1935.

Mercier, J. "Netter, Thomas." *DTC* 15 (1950). Cols. 3505–6.

Miles, L. *John Colet and the Platonic Tradition.* London, 1962.

Moeller, B. "Religious Life in Germany on the Eve of the Reformation." *Pre-Reformation Germany* (see above). Pp. 13–42.

Mokrosch, R. "Devotio moderna, II." *TRE* 8 (Berlin, 1981) 609–16.

Oberman, H. A. *Forerunners of the Reformation.* New York, 1966.

_____. *The Harvest of Late Medieval Theology: Gabriel Biel and Late Medieval Nominalism.* Cambridge, Mass., 1963.

_____. *Master of the Reformation.* Cambridge, Mass., 1981.

_____. "Some Notes on the Theology of Nominalism with Attention to Its Relation to the Renaissance." *Harvard Theological Review* 54 (1960) 47–76.

_____. "*Duplex misericordia:* Der Teufel und die Kirche in der Theologie des jungen Johann von Staupitz." *Theologische Zeitschrift* 45 (1989) 231–43.

O'Malley, J. W. "Erasmus and Luther: Continuity and Discontinuity as Key of Their Conflict." *Sixteenth Century Journal* 5 (1974) 47–65.

Post, R. *The Modern Devotion: Confrontation with Reformation and Humanism.* Studies in Medieval and Renaissance Thought 3. Leiden, 1968.

Prévost, A. *Thomas More (1477–1535) et la crise de la pensée européenne.* Paris, 1968.

Punzo, L. "Influssi del neoplatonismo sulla cultura rinascimentale inglese." *Il neoplatonismo nel Rinascimento* (see Margolin, above). Pp. 245–62.

Raeder, S. "Johannes Reuchlin." *Die Reformationzeit* (see above). I, 33–51.

Reeves, S. D. "Gansfort, Wessel." *TRE* 12 (Berlin, 1984) 25–28.

Rex, R. *The Theology of John Fischer.* Cambridge, 1991.

Rhein, S. "Religiosità individuale e riforma della società: un contributo alla teologia di Johannes Reuchlin." *Homo Sapiens, Homo Humanus.* Atti del XXIX e XXX Convegno del Centro di studi umanistici (Montepulciano, Palazzo Tarugi, 1987 e 1988). Ed. G. Tarugi. Florence, 1990. II, 421–33.

Ritter, G. "Studien zur Spätscholastik." *Sitzungsberichte der Heidelberger Akademie der Wissenschaften, Phil.-Lit. Klasse,* 1921, no. 4; 1922, no. 7; 1926–27, no. 5.

Rolof, H.-G. "Brant, Sebastian." *TRE* 7 (Berlin, 1981) 136–40.

Rummel, E. *Erasmus' Annotations on the New Testament: From Philologist to Theologian.* Toronto, 1986.

Schulze, M. "Der Hiob-Prediger Johannes von Staupitz aud der Kanzel der Tübingen Augustinerkirche." *Augustine, the Harvest, and Theology (1300–1650).* Essays

Dedicated to Heiko Augustinus Oberman in Honor of His Sixtieth Birthday. Leiden, 1990. Pp. 60–88.

———. *"Contra rectam rationem:* Gabriel Biel's Reading of Gregory of Rimini, Versus Gregory." *Via Augustini: Augustine in the Later Middle Ages, Renaissance, and Reformation.* Essays in Honor of Damasus Trapp, O.S.A. Ed. H. A. Oberman and F. A. James. Studies in Medieval and Reformation Thought 48. Leiden, 1991. III, 55–71.

Seeberg, N. "Netter, Thomas." *Realencyklopädie für protestantische Theologie und Kirche* 12 (Leipzig, 1903) 749–53.

Seebohm, F. *The Oxford Reformers.* London, 1887³.

Spitz, L. *The Religious Renaissance of German Humanists.* Cambridge, Mass., 1963.

———. "Reuchlin's Philosophy: Pythagoras and Cabala for Christ." *ArchRef* 47 (1956) 1–20.

Steinmetz, D. C. *Misericordia Dei: The Theology of Johannes von Staupitz in Its Late Medieval Setting.* Studies in Medieval and Renaissance Thought 4. Leiden, 1968.

Stoelen, A. "Denis le Chartreux." *DSp* 3 (Paris, 1976). Cols. 430–49.

Stupperich, A. "Devotio moderna und reformatorische Frömmigkeit." *Jahrbuch der Vereins für Schlesische Kirchengeschichte* 60 (1967) 11–26.

Trapp, J. B. "John Colet and the 'Hierarchies' of the Ps.-Dionysius." *Studies in Church History* 17 (1981) 127ff.

Vinay, V. "Friedrich Reiser e la diaspora valdese di lingua tedesca nel XV secolo." *Bollettino della Società di Studi Valdesi* 109 (1961) 35–56.

Weiler, A. G. *Heinrich von Gorkum (1431). Seine Stellung in der Philosophie und der Theologie des Spätmittelalters.* Hilversum-Einsiedeln-Zurich-Cologne, 1962.

Weiss, R. *Humanism in England During the Fifteenth Century.* Oxford, 1967³.

Winckler, G. *Erasmus von Rotterdam und die Einleitungsschriften zum Neuen Testament.* Munich, 1974.

Zika, C. "Reuchlin and Erasmus: Humanism and Occult Philosophy." *Journal of Religious History* 9 (1976–77) 233–46.

Zumkeller, A. *Erbsünde, Gnade, Rechtfertigung und Verdienst nach der Lehre der Erfurter Augustinertheologen des Spätmittelalters.* Cassiciacum 35. Würzburg, 1984.

———. "Paltz, Jean." *DSp* 12 (Paris, 1984). Cols. 145–48.

———. "Staupitz, Jean." *DSp* 14 (Paris, 1990). Cols. 1184–89.

CHAPTER 8

The Crisis of Late Humanism and Expectations of Reform in Italy at the End of the Fifteenth and Beginning of the Sixteenth Centuries

Cesare Vasoli

1. The Religious and Speculative Problems of Late Italian Humanism

It is commonly held in an extensive historiographical literature that the twenty years spanning the last decade of the fifteenth century and the first of the sixteenth were a time of growing apprehensions and spiritual crises. These, it is said, foreboded deep rents in the ancient unified fabric of Western Christianity and radical changes in the ways of understanding and living the gospel tradition. These changes would come about during the new century and would cause a growing proliferation of new ecclesial institutions and of movements that rebelled against every dogmatic and magisterial structure, but they were also premonitory symptoms of what post-Tridentine Catholic discipline would be.[1]

Increasingly extensive and detailed research in the area of textual and documentary analysis has, in fact, shown how widespread the expectation of a radical renewal of Christian life was at the most diverse levels of intellectual experience and social life. This renewal would mean a return to the purity of Christian origins; it would rid religious life of every unworthy superstition and all power, greed, and worldly pomp; it would put an end to the corruption of the hierarchy and clergy; above all, it would restore to all believers their rights

371

and duties as "children of God" and their peaceful coexistence with all other human beings in the one flock that is safeguarded by the eternal "spouse of Christ."

These themes found expression especially in the many prophecies, erudite and popular,[2] that during these decades proclaimed either the proximate coming of the long-awaited reform under the leadership of an "angelic pope" or "reforming" sovereign, or an imminent age of punishment and penance, the proximate appearance of the Antichrist, and the approach of the final judgment "at the end of days." These predictions received their most powerful and profound expression in the words of Savonarola and in the predictions which he addressed chiefly to the lower classes of a city overwhelmed by incurable crises and political and social conflicts. But quite similar ideas were becoming widespread also in upper class and aristocratic humanist circles among men who had enthusiastically welcomed Ficino's conception of a "devout philosophy" *(pia philosophia)* with its esoteric and Hermeticist attractions.

Moreover, the criticism by not a few humanists of the more external forms of devotional practice, their rejection of traditional forms of asceticism and poverty, which they regarded as plebeian and hypocritical, their distrust of any flight from the world to monastery or hermitage, their rejection of the theology of the *magistri* and its "barbarous" language—all these were so many aspects of a radical call for renewal that would lead, by way of Valla's stringent "philology," to Erasmus' proposed "philosophy of Christ" *(philosophia Christi)*. Not only that: the insistent recall to the teaching of the Fathers against that of the Scholastic *magistri* was often interwoven with the rediscovery of the extraordinary diversity and riches of the philosophical experience of antiquity (which was not reducible to that of Aristotle alone or even of Plato alone); with the reappraisal of Epicureanism, which was discovered to be not irreconcilable with the Christian faith; and finally, with the growing interest in classical skepticism, which attracted even persons and circles marked by an intense religious spirit, such as the Florentine convent of San Marco itself.[3]

All these were ideas, aspirations, and ways of thinking that often made their way even into the schools and the conventual and monastic *studia*. Nor, at times, were even the professional theologians unaffected, men often torn between fidelity to the impressive legacy of their tradition, the demand for a new language, the fascination of the literary and philosophical experiences of the humanists, the awareness of the need of a profound change in the life of the Church, and the persistent summons to obey the hierarchic discipline of the Church. Even in the universities and among the philosophers who continued to regard Aristotle as the supreme if no longer the only philosopher, an increasingly penetrating and refined exegesis was being practiced that was conformed to the critical canons of the humanists and based on an extensive knowledge of the interpreters and ancient commentators. This exegesis kept alive or reopened the discussion of those very difficult topics (the unity of the intellect, the mortality of the soul, the eternity of the world, the impossibility of a "creation out of nothing," and so on) that had already been constant subjects of controversy between the "natural philosophers" and the theologians.[4]

Another factor not to be forgotten was the presence, sometimes open but more often hidden and concealed, of ancient and new currents of unbelief. These were frequently connected with the idea that all the religions were simply human laws and skillful deceptions thought up by shrewd legislators in order to make the obedience of their subjects more certain and secure.

I wrote earlier of the "dandies" in the Roman Academy of Pomponius Laetus and of one of their most typical representatives, Callimachus Esperiens; I mentioned also the writings that were sent from Poland to Ficino and Pico toward the end of the century.[5] But other testimonies and clues lead us to believe that attitudes similar to theirs were present, even if masked or else put forward by means of skillful "stratagems," in intellectual circles connected with the ancient Scholastic institutions no less than among humanist masters especially responsive to the attacks on monastic institutions and the worldly power of the ecclesiastical hierarchies.

Moreover, it is not difficult to see already present at the beginning of the century some very obviously symptomatic incidents that had quite varying outcomes and conclusions. There is, for example, the case of a learned and eloquent humanist, Paul Cortesi, a Roman (1456–1510).[6] He was a stylish man of letters, first a "writer" and then an apostolic secretary in the Curia with close ties to some of the more important exponents of humanistic culture. He was also fairly well known for an attack on Politian on the subject of "imitation" and as the author of *De cardinalatu,* a book that aimed at instructing others in the excellent behavior, more civil, political, and worldly than religious, of the princes of the Church.[7]

Now, in 1504, shortly after leaving the Curia, Cortesi wrote an unusual book, *In quattuor libros Sententiarum disputationes,* which was an attempt to reconcile the traditional "wisdom" of the theologians with the "eloquence" of the humanists by expounding the Scholastic teachings in a limpid and resonant Ciceronian Latin.[8] He undoubtedly had in mind John Pico's defense of the "Parisian style" in which he opposed Ermolaus Barbarus' renewed condemnation of Scholastic language.[9] Cortesi also seemed committed to the project of showing how the same truths can be expressed perfectly in a new language that was no longer "barbarous" and was even conformed to the best standard of stylistic elegance and purity.

This was, admittedly, an attempt that remained on the surface of the real problem, which was the humanist rejection of Scholastic theology and of a kind of discourse regarded now as locked into a "jargon" and incapable of teaching the faithful the word of Christ and the religious message of the Gospel. Yet it was symptomatic that a humanist, a man disposed to consider in a primarily political perspective even the problems raised by heresy and schism, should see the need of shaping a new theological language even as he opposed to the new "devout philosophies" a substantial fidelity to Scholastic methods. In this he set a pattern that would be followed by many sixteenth-century *magistri,* who were likewise concerned about their own ways of expressing themselves.

A few years later, in 1507, another powerful and unbiased man of the Curia, one accustomed to all the chances and tricks of diplomacy, a schemer often involved in obscure incidents of corruption and conspiracy, Cardinal Adrian Castellesi (ca. 1461–1521),[10] likewise wrote a book. To his protector, Henry VII, king of England, he dedicated a volume with the no less significant title *De vera philosophia ex quattuor doctoribus ecclesiae.*[11] His philosophy was based on an abundant collection of passages drawn from sacred Scripture but even more from Jerome, Ambrose, Augustine, and Gregory the Great. The purpose of the book was explicit and clearly opposed both to Scholastic theology and to the new attempts to establish "Platonic theologies" or to look to the ancient philosophers for doctrinal and apologetic tools in place of those of the *magistri.*

Castellesi had, in fact, no confidence in the ability of human reason to understand and interpret the truths of Christianity; evidence of this was the author's obvious indifference, in the content of his work, to subtle and complex doctrinal questions as well as the irritation he felt at the language and theoretical developments of the theologians. He asserted that, for his part, he wanted to appeal always and exclusively to the Scriptures and to those "ancient" interpreters who seemed closer to the letter and the spirit of the Scriptures and who had not uselessly tainted the divine word with empty human philosophies nor had tried to transform the divine word into a system of abstruse doctrines that were entirely lacking in certainty. On this point, the cardinal was peremptory: only the faith that had inspired those "Fathers" of Christian learning could make possible a knowledge that is both true and necessary for our salvation, because it is based on the only word that does not lie, the divine word of biblical and evangelical revelation.

This attitude of Castellesi has sometimes been likened to Erasmus' insistent call for an evangelical theology that would take the form of a humble, simple exegesis of the sacred text in unyielding respect for its letter and its spirit. Scholars have also reminded us that around 1516 Erasmus supposedly tried to translate some books of the Bible from Hebrew; this suggestion is confirmed by his friendship with such an outstanding Hebraist as Giles of Viterbo and by his relationship with Reuchlin, who dedicated to him his *De accentibus et orthographia linguae hebraicae.* In my opinion, a reading of the *De vera philosophia* does not bring to mind such exalted parallels, even though it is true that Castellesi was friendly with the same English humanist circles that greatly influenced the thinking of the young Erasmus and his religious and evangelical experience.

A rather more interesting man of culture and thought was John Francis Pico della Mirandola (1470–1533), who lived his entire life cultivating the memory of his great uncle, John Pico, and Savonarola the "martyr."[12] In his early youth he was quite close to the final thinking of John Pico, to his attacks on astrology, his stern religious spirituality, and his admiration for the friar of San Marco, and he wanted to continue his uncle's work while also profoundly altering its goals and meaning. He was a very well educated man and had a good knowledge of the ancient philosophers; he shared with other Savonarolians a strong interest in the teaching of the skeptics and in Sextus Empiricus in particular. He also nourished his intense fideism and his criticism of pagan philosophies by reading Jewish thinkers, especially Hasday Crescas. But whereas his uncle had intended to celebrate the concord among all the teachings due to their shared truth, John Francis aimed rather at denouncing their emptiness and errors, which he could escape only by seeking in revelation and faith a solid ground of certainty.

In collaboration with John Mainardi, John Francis published his uncle's *Disputationes in astrologiam divinatricem* and then, in his own *De rerum praenotione* (1502–5),[13] repeated the condemnation of the astrologers, fortunetellers, and all who deceived themselves into thinking that they could obtain a knowledge of the future by human learning or devices. Either such people were blinded by the darkest superstition or they were victims of or accomplices in obscure diabolical snares. On the other hand, John Francis was utterly certain that true prophecy, such as that of Fra Jerome, was inspired by the supernatural light of the divine intellect. The human mind, which is the lowest of the intelligences, is forced to use the weak instrument that is reason, which rarely grasps even a shadow of the truth. But on this road of darkness and error a person may at times be unexpectedly enlightened by a revelation that God grants by his own completely unconditioned decree. Thus Pico did not hesitate to appeal to the Avicennian doctrine of the "prophetic intellect" and to the speculations of Alghazali and Maimonides in his defense of the divine "gift" of prophecy, which is a knowledge of the future that is won through the very close union of the human mind with eternal divine truth.

In the certainty, then, that the only truth we can reach is always, in one or other manner, a revelation, John Francis did not hesitate to claim in his *Examen vanitatis doctrinae gentium et veritatis disciplinae christianae* (1520)[14] that not only were the "wonderful" philosophies of the ancients, so admired by the humanists, irreducibly opposed and contrary among themselves but also that this opposition proved their "emptiness" and condemned them to an incurable powerlessness. Even the disagreements among theologians were still, and always would be, useless philosophical oppositions that in no way helped to the attainment of the truth of the Christian faith, which resides wholly in the divine word of the Scriptures.

It is not surprising that this protector of the last Savonarolian prophets[15] should radically criticize not only all the pagan philosophies but even all logical methods and procedures, thus including in the one condemnation literature, the arts, grammar, rhetoric, and finally and above all, mathematics and geometry, which were, and not by chance, the tools of the "mad" astrologers. However, there was one philosophy that John Francis rebutted with special tenacity: Aristoteleanism, or the very doctrine which the Scholastic theologians had often claimed was the one most in harmony with the Christian faith.

Nor did he limit himself to condemning the disastrous godlessness of Averroes' interpretation or the "barbarousness" of the medieval translations. On the contrary, he judged the very philosophy of Aristotle to be utterly uncertain in its principles and in its conclusions, for it was based (he claimed) on deceitful appearances and on the misleading evidence of the senses.[16] This was shown by the insuperable contradiction in his teaching on time and space when it came to the question of the eternity or the creation of the world, a point that Crescas had already attacked. It was confirmed by the many irreducible oppositions between the teachings of Aristotle and scriptural revelation, oppositions which no clever pretenses of the philosophers or theologians could do away with. These "errors" of Aristotle threw the harshest light on the weakness of the human intellect, which was capable only of getting lost in endless disputes and getting mixed up in fights between consistently opposed and irreconcilable doctrines where there was no point and no possibility of expecting an eventual harmony.

In short, John Francis, with his deeply religious spirit and his certainty that faith alone offered a way of salvation amid the dark "drift" of useless human attempts, ended up in the most radical skepticism. As a result his work was to contribute in coming decades to the gradual breakup of the vast Aristotelean "encyclopedia" and the questioning of his cosmology and physics. Many aspects of the "Pyrrhonism" typical of various late-fifteenth-century writers were to find sustenance in the writings of this devout Savonarolian, even though he always remained faithful to the humanist theme of a return to the gospel message.

2. Paduan Aristoteleanism and the Controversy over the Immortality of the Soul

John Francis Pico had seen in Aristotle (but also in the equivocal Ficinian notion of a "devout philosophy") the basis of a dangerous theological intermingling of "empty" philosophy, which was alien and contrary to Christian revelation, with the absolute truth of the faith. But during the very years when he was working out his critique, Aristoteleanism, often in its most radical forms and conclusions, continued to be the solid institutional "bulwark" of Scholastic learning and to control intellectual experience at the great university centers, such as Padua and Bologna.

In the Studium of Padua at the end of the fifteenth century the reputation of one master, Nicholas Vernia (1420–99),[17] was still rather high, even though, if we may believe his most important disciple, he did not hide his own "unbelief" and had for a long time been interpreting Aristotle according to strictly Averroist norms. Nicholas had been a student of Paul of Pergola and Gaetano of Thiene and had succeeded them as teacher in 1468. The majority of his writings that have come down to us (but that certainly represent only a small part of his activity, most of which took the form of lecturing) show that his education, gained from the study of the *suiseticae calculationes* and the teaching of two students of Paul of Venice, had quickly made him open to Averroist influences. In fact, Vernia not only followed the opinions of the Commentator in his commentary on the "physical books"; he also accepted the doctrine of the unicity of the intellect and often got into controversy with the Thomists and the Scotists.[18]

Later on, however, the professor from the Abruzzi definitely changed his opinion, due perhaps in part to the edict of Peter Barozzi, bishop of Padua, to which reference was made earlier. In fact, after a failed attempt to transfer to Pisa, he hastened to write his *Quaestiones de pluralitate intellectus contra falsam et ab omni veritate remotam opinionem Averroes de animae felicitate,*[19] which he began in 1491 and finished at last in 1499. It was a true and proper recantation of the positions he had previously held; in it he clearly rejected and committed himself to refute the Averroist conception of the unicity of the intellect, declaring that he had previously maintained it solely "for the sake of arguing the question and sharpening his mind."

In any case, it cannot be said that Barozzi's edict or the earlier mentioned attacks of Scotist Anthony Trombetta[20] prevented Averroism from continuing to have open followers in Padua. These included such men as Mark Anthony Zimara from Apulia (ca. 1470–before 1537); Tiberius Bacilieri, a follower of Siger of Brabant and professor in the Padua *Studium* between 1503 and 1511; and the more moderate Peter Trapolin (1451–1506), in whose writings doctrinal fluctuations even in the direction of Thomism have been pointed out. During these decades that bridged the two centuries Alexander Achillini in Bologna was maintaining views that were, if not strictly Averroistic, at least those of Siger; thus in 1494, perhaps in the presence of Pico and Augustine Nifo, he discussed his *Quodlibeta de intelligentiis,* in which similar points of doctrine were clearly identifiable.

A good deal more complex and nuanced, however, was the outlook of a master who, in the course of a long teaching career that took him on many journeys to various Italian universities, had to write on very diverse subjects and produced an exceptionally rich body of writings, but without ever making his real theoretical views entirely clear. The man was Augustine Nifo (ca. 1473–ca. 1546).[21] He himself recalls that, at least when he was young and under the direct influence of Vernia, he had professed the teachings of Averroes, and he mentions, among other things, some *collectanea* on the *De anima* that had been circulated without his knowledge; he also mentions a commentary on the *De substantia orbis* of Averroes, which he later emended and reworked. But when in 1492 he finished writing the first version of his *De intellectu,*[22] the work that interests us especially here, he acknowledged the many corrections the work had undergone and he sang the praises of Barozzi, but his concern was rather to combat "Alexandrian" teaching, which he regarded as the more dangerous and deadly.

The radically negative conclusions of the Alexandrians on the immortality of the soul (this last being given, naturally, its Aristotelean meaning) seemed to Augustine to make human life wholly like that of the brute animals, to deny its special and higher end, and even to undermine every moral principle or law. It is not surprising, then, that in the following years and decades (both in the period of his controversy with Pomponazzi, to which I shall return,[23] and in other writings and on other occasions) he appealed increasingly to Plato and the Platonists as defenders of the human soul's freedom and superiority and always remained substantially faithful to the idea that perfection and speculative happiness consist in the union of the individual intellect with the higher intelligences. Moreover, as has been often pointed out and as was in keeping with the rather eclectic nature of his thinking, there were not lacking in his writings hints of Hermeticism and ideas originating far back in Pythagoras.

A great deal more coherence and speculative power marked the thinking of Peter Pomponazzi of Mantua (1462–1525), who, while still very young, began to teach philosophy at Padua in 1488 and continued to do so at Bologna, where he succeeded Achillini in 1512.[24] He was trained in the world of Padua, far removed from the more intense kind of Peripatetic exegesis and from the increasingly tense and polemical opposition between very different and contrary interpretative positions. As a result, he too knew the Averroist tradition and its "Sigerian" variant, which had been so familiar to his teachers and colleagues since the time of Paul of Venice.

He also had a sure knowledge of Thomist teachings as expounded by Dominican master Francis Securus of Nardò; for a while, these attracted him for their direct refutation of the Commentator [Averroes], who was excessively exalted in Padua and regarded as the sole depositary of the "truth of the Philosopher [Aristotle]." Soon, however, he distanced himself from Thomism as well, being attracted by the theses of Alexander of Aphrodisias, whose commentary, already known, became much more widespread in the Latin translation of it by Jerome Donà. Far from attributing immortality, as Averroes was to do later on, to the one "possible intellect" common to the human species, Alexander regarded only the divine and immortal agent intellect as eternal, while considering as transitory the individual human intellect that is so closely bound up with the lot of the body of which it is the form.

This is not to say that Pomponazzi's teaching conformed, then or later, to the "Alexandrian" Scholastic line which had its supporters and followers even in Padua. In fact, in all his mature activity this philosopher did not hesitate to deal in a very critical way with the most widespread teachings of the schools. Thus in his *Quaestio de intensione et remissione formarum* (1514) he reacted against the useless subtleties of the logicians and against what Gaetano of Thiene had maintained on the subject.[25] It is really not possible to understand his personality unless we set aside the overworked distinctions of the masters and reflect on the originality of his ideas, which could not be reduced to the usual Scholastic "classifications."

This emerges clearly from Pomponazzi's most famous work, *De immortalitate animae,* which was dedicated to Mark Flavius Contarini and published in Bologna in 1516.[26] The work took the form of a reply to Dominican Jerome Natale of Ragusa, who had asked him to explain Aristotle's teaching on the soul using only philosophical arguments and not having recourse to any principle foreign to them. From the outset, however, the philosopher took the occasion to emphasize rather a theme that was extensively developed in fifteenth-century humanist thinking: the "middle position" of human beings, who live "between things eternal and things temporal, being neither unqualifiedly eternal nor unqualifiedly temporal" but participating simultaneously in the rationality that makes them like the gods, in at least the possibility of living according to the moral virtues that free them from enslavement to the body and, finally, in the pure sensuality that in one way makes them no different from the animals.

Human beings are, therefore, not "simple" but "multiple," being endowed with a "double" nature that situates them, as Pico had said, halfway between mortal things and those immortal things that are the objects of their desire. But Pomponazzi refused to regard this halfway position as a juxtaposition of two natures, one spiritual and the other merely corporeal, which after death would be completely separate and belong to two different realms of reality. Instead he noted that in the natural order there is a continuity from the plants, which are endowed with a soul that presides only over nutritive and generative functions, to animals that have only the senses of taste and touch, and on to those animals that are endowed with imagination and special instincts and seem even to approximate to intelligence (for example, the bees, which seem superior to many human beings).

Not only that: there are also halfway animals that come between the plants and the beasts, or between the animal realm and human beings, such as the monkeys, of whom it is difficult to say whether they are closer to the brute animals or to human beings. In like manner, the "intellectual" soul of the human person is regarded as intermediate between temporal reality and eternal. It is, therefore, mortal, when considered as such, but immortal in a certain respect, as is shown by its undeniable desire of immortality.

Given this position, Pomponazzi's attack is turned, first of all, on the Averroists, who considered the intelligence of the human species to be eternal, akin to the intelligences of the celestial spheres, which were entirely separated from matter. But while he shows his appreciation of the Thomistic critique of Averroist teaching, which it correctly destroys and "annihilates," he stresses with equal decisiveness the fact that human intellection is impossible apart from the "phantasm" and that it can therefore never be completely independent of the body. Consequently, even though it be not united to any corporeal organ, it remains connected with it for the indispensable content of its act of knowing. In short, it is not possible to claim that the intellectual soul is ever separated from the body, no matter what its condition or activity. Those, therefore, who claim that they can, following a rational process and on the basis of Aristotelean teaching, prove the immortality and separability of the soul have clearly fallen into an error no less serious than that of the Platonists (such as Ficino), who were convinced that the soul is self-moving and utterly independent of the body. In fact, the sensitive power and the intellectual power are always closely linked in the human being; the soul will always be both sense and intellect.

These theses are still close to the Thomist solution. But Pomponazzi clarifies his position when he denies that it is possible, given these foundations, to deduce, as Thomas does, that the soul is "unqualifiedly immortal, and mortal only in an improper sense." The Christian faith does, of course, teach us, in accordance with the Scriptures, that the human soul is immortal; and it is our duty to accept this teaching that lies beyond all human reasoning or experience. The teaching is one that goes well beyond the limits of the human mind and requires a revelation from on high that is utterly at odds with the teachings of Aristotle. In fact, an analysis of the human cognoscitive functions, which are so linked to the senses and the body, show us that from the standpoint of reason the soul is, if anything, unqualifiedly mortal and only improperly and in a certain respect immortal. Moreover, human beings are very rarely rational, and the majority of them seem rather close to the animals in their behavior and thinking; even those regarded as "rational" are such only in comparison with those considered to be entirely bestial. Since the human soul is very uncertain in its sense knowledge and is able only rarely to achieve intellectual knowledge, it seems, in a word, to have a corporeal and corruptible essence that is unworthy of immortality.

Such a state is not enough. In order to be truly separated from the body, the soul would have to be completely independent not only of material organs but also of an imaging power. It is, however, beyond dispute that the intellect depends on the imaging power and that this in turn depends on the senses, that is, on corporeal matter. This relationship and dependence can, of course, be denied. But then it will be necessary to explain how it is possible, apart from such links, to understand the reciprocal action of body and soul. If, according to Aristotle, it is not possible to understand apart from the "phantasm," it is no less difficult to explain how the soul, separated by nature and origin from the body, could undergo the pains of hell in the other life or enjoy the delights of heaven, for both of these conditions presuppose a degree of sensibility. The only state possible for the separated soul would be one of complete ease *(otium)* or else of repeated transmigration, as the Pythagoreans thought. But both of these views are contrary both to reason and to faith. Consequently, the only conclusion possible for reason is that in the human being the rational soul is identical with the sensitive soul and that it is essentially and truly mortal and immortal only in a certain respect.

As Pomponazzi goes on to explain, the soul, which is unqualifiedly material, does carry within itself a "shadow," as it were, a "perfume," a "longing" for immortality, that makes it always aspire to transcend the limits of matter and time in which it is enclosed. It is thus on the border, as it were, between two realms; the fact that it is the noblest of material realities allows it to "push beyond" and to demand for itself a destiny that is not closed within the limits of ephemeral matter and time. Though not immortal or even spiritual in an unqualified sense, human beings, who are conscious of their death and the end of their bodies, constantly hope for an eternity that cannot, however, be demonstrated with certainty by reason.

Pomponazzi does not, of course, fail to grasp the ethical and social usefulness of the belief in immortality on which is based the threat of the condemnation and everlasting punishment that will come upon even those who escape human laws and punishments. He knows, too, that this very argument has always been made against those who cast doubt on human survival outside the bounds of time. But (he says) the answer to those who appeal to such arguments is that the "true" morality of human beings as well as the "happiness" which the just enjoy consists in the harmony of the soul with itself and in its interior peace and perfect dispositions. The reward of the virtuous is, as the Stoics taught, the very virtue that renders them happy within this complete order and frees them from the only real punishment, namely, disorder, interior dissension, or even a fall into a savage bestiality. Everlasting retributions and chastisements are only possible rewards and punishments that would be added to this "destiny," of which each human being is master through his or her own choices.

In summary: there are no philosophical arguments of any kind that can demonstrate the immortality of the soul. Faith, however, does assert it, and believers are "firmly and solidly" sure in their beliefs, which are based on a revelation that is accepted as absolutely true. Philosophers do not discuss these certainties, which have nothing to do with reason and philosophy and belong, therefore, to a different order of experience, of which it is not the task of philosophy to take a position. It is therefore obvious that as far as reason is concerned, the human soul (as understood by philosophers in accordance with the doctrine of Aristotle, their teacher) is only the highest "form" in the natural order and is destined to perish, in obedience to the lot of all things that are generated and corruptible.

The publication of the *De immortalitate animae* immediately gave rise to bitter and irresolvable controversies. The work was refuted by theologians of different backgrounds, such as the Dominican Bartholomew of Spina and the Augustinian Ambrose Fiandino. It was also the subject of criticism and objection even by philosophers who had been trained in the school of Padua. The first to enter into a resolute but friendly debate with Pomponazzi was Gaspar Contarini, a patrician of Venice (1458–1542),[27] a former student of his, and a scholar destined to be, later on, the most important personality of the Catholic Reform movement. Shortly after the publication of *De immortalitate animae* Contarini sent its author a first refutation, which the philosopher made public by printing it along with his own *Apologia*.[28] Contarini (who had a good philosophical training, as is clear from his various writings and especially from his *Compendium della Metafisica*) had initially taken a sympathetic view of Alexander's exegesis and had himself had strong doubts about the possibility of a philosophical demonstration of the soul's immortality. He had subsequently become convinced of the Thomist positions, as was shown by the definitive version of his refutation, a version that included his answers to Pomponazzi's reply.

His critique starts from the principle that the soul, insofar as it is an "act in act," is also a "separable substance"; furthermore, although its act of intellectual understanding is undoubtedly connected with the sensible "phantasm," it cannot be concluded from this that the soul is not capable of other forms of life and knowledge that are not dependent on union with the material body. In this regard Contarini made an important appeal to Avicenna and cited the existence of the heavenly intelligences, which move the spheres but do not inform them and are therefore wholly separated. And since Pomponazzi had laid such stress on the intrinsic dependence of the intellect on the phantasm and the senses, his former student replied that according to Aristotle the soul was also capable of understanding first principles, universals, and forms abstracted from their matter. If the possible intellect is able to understand the forms, then it certainly cannot be determined by any material form or have any kind of corporeal conditioning.

Contarini did not limit himself, however, solely to these objections of an essentially Thomist kind. He reminded his readers that the intellect is also able to know itself and its own operations, and this without the need of any corporeal instrument or intermediary. Here Contarini could again appeal to Avicenna and his argument about the "flying human being" in order to assert that this kind of activity proves the purely spiritual and separable nature of the soul. This was an argument that Ficino, too, had cited in confirming and concluding his lengthy defense of the immortality of the soul. It was symptomatic that it come up again from the pen of an Aristotelean and Thomist philosopher in claiming the legitimacy, before the bar of reason, of a proof of the immortality of the soul that was at the same time in keeping with Aristotle's teaching. Not by chance did he assert at the end of Book II that anyone who, like himself and Pomponazzi, accepted an intellect that was indivisible, not determined in time and space, and the sole subject of intellection must also conclude that the intellect is a form that cannot be simply the act of the body but is also "act by its nature, existing in act." Such a form, however, was necessarily incorruptible and therefore not mortal.

Pomponazzi, as was mentioned above, answered with an *Apologia* that also contained answers to other opponents: Ambrose Fiandino[29] and Dominican Vincent Colzade. He asserted once again the indissoluble connection of the intellect with the body, while emphasizing the purely aspirational character of the human "fragrance" of immortality. Otherwise he would have had to admit openly the complete separation of soul from body according to the theory of the Platonists and Averroists, with all the consequences that this implied. Pomponazzi's answer was evidently a way of turning back the Platonizing arguments of Contarini and stressing their departure from a correct exegesis of Aristotle.

The debate did not end but became even more tense and relentless with the intervention of Nifo in his *Libellus de immortalitate*.[30] This former colleague of Pomponazzi at Padua did indeed very prudently limit himself to setting forth some theses of a more Platonic than Averroist kind and insisting on the complete separability of the soul, which cannot be at all conditioned by and linked to corporeal matter. He stressed the intellect's knowledge of abstract universals, something possible only to a separated substance that is independent of the senses. He reminded his readers, as Contarini had done before him, that all Aristoteleans, including Pomponazzi himself, considered the intelligences that moved the heavenly spheres to be separate and that, consequently, it was entirely possible to have an "act in act" that was not always united to matter. He, too, ended by appealing to the teaching of Plato in the *Phaedo* and the *Phaedrus* and by making his own the concept of the soul as absolute principle of motion and life (and therefore entirely autonomous and immortal), a concept that was also an element in the extraordinary success of Ficino's *Theologia platonica*.

On the other hand, there was a good deal of ambiguity in Nifo's shifting back and forth between conclusions of an Averroist kind (in his limited acceptance of the unicity of the possible intellect) and an integral acceptance of Platonic doctrines and, in particular, of Ficino's apologetics. Nevertheless, the *Libellus* was meant to be, and was, very clearly opposed to Pomponazzi's theses; it was based on a rather eclectic convergence of traditions that were especially widespread during those years, even in circles unconnected with the culture of the universities.

The new reply which Pomponazzi set forth in his *Defensorium* of 1519[31] did not and could not change the terms of a debate that had its origin in such very different and opposed interpretations of the texts of Aristotle. His strictly naturalistic position was unaffected by Nifo's appeal to the testimony of the "heroic" virtues of human beings and the mind's lofty speculative powers as proof of a heavenly destiny that was not reducible to the inescapable laws of matter. In fact, both in his university courses and in his *De nutritione et augmentatione* (1521) Peretto (a nickname of Pomponazzi) repeated and even stressed more strongly his teaching on the soul and made even clearer his distinction between the sphere of argumentation and philosophical exegesis and the sphere of the truths of faith, which (he asserted again) could not be rationally demonstrated or argued.

There were other episodes in the controversy connected with the *De immortalitate animae,* but I need not mention these here. In the years that followed Pomponazzi did, however, write two other works that are especially important for students of the philosophical and theological ideas of the sixteenth century: *De naturalium effectuum admirandorum causis, sive de incantationibus*[32] and *De fato, libero arbitrio et praedestinatione.*[33] These writings, composed around 1520, were published in print a good deal later on, between 1556 and 1567, by William Gratarol, a physician of Bergamo who lived in exile "for religion's sake" *(religionis causa)*. They then enjoyed a wide circulation, especially among authors and controversialists who have often been regarded as the begetters of "libertinism." The main concern of these men was undoubtedly to postulate and defend the sphere in which philosophical study and its rational procedures ought to operate.

This sphere seems extremely large, since Pomponazzi does not hesitate to discuss the causes of religions and their variations; following an ancient astrological tradition, he traces these back to the influence of the heavens and the stars. The analysis naturally takes as its subject the religions of the "ancient," whose "prodigies" *(portenta)* are considered to be the effects of rationally determinable physical events and causes. But the reader is immediately struck by the similarity between these miracles and those of the Christian religion, and it is clear that Pomponazzi intended to go as far as reason can go in understanding, explaining, and demonstrating without appealing to supernatural or occult powers and influences. He thus banishes all the superstitious and imaginative hypotheses that end up populating the world with illusory fictions and distorting the purest values of religion itself. While asserting that no spirit can ever act on matter, since it can have no connection with it, he also maintains that forces and "powers" still unknown to us are active in the universe but that clear and certain knowledge of them will come as human learning becomes more complete.

On the other hand, Pomponazzi also wanted to show how it is possible for the human person, who is the center of cosmic reality, halfway between the eternal and the corruptible, between heaven and earth, to take possession of these forces and "powers" through knowledge and suitable instruments. Therefore (he says) the accusation of practicing a perverse and satanic magic, which has so often been leveled at wise persons who act according to their knowledge of nature and the heavens, is utterly baseless, just as many wonders which the common people think have been worked by holy thaumaturges or even through the mediation of angelic powers have in fact been the fruit of knowledge and rational intelligence.

It is understandable that some of these wise men promoted such popular beliefs and used them to increase their own prestige, just as the founders of alleged religions, which were in fact only "laws," made use of any and every kind of imposture. The credulity of "common" and almost bestial men and women has even led them to imagine that the divinity itself is controlled by human sentiments and passions that determine its behavior and that are postulated as the causes of many of the most far-reaching and fearful events. But reason teaches us that these events, too, are only the effect of immutable heavenly laws that regulate the entire order of the world and bring about all phenomena.

For this very reason Pomponazzi strongly criticized Pico, who had denied any scientific value to astrology and had rejected the doctrine of astral influences. Testifying against him were the undeniable fact of many previsions and the usefulness of astrology as an indispensable tool in the practice of medicine. In addition, Peretto had no doubt that the very power of religious beliefs and the prodigies, or unexpected events, that this power could produce were linked to the dominance of various stars, which also played a part in the historical destiny of religions. Even the miracles that have usually accompanied the birth of all the religions were simply the effect of the wonderful and powerful heavenly causes that act to bring about major changes in the "laws" and radical renewals of the human "orders."

A conception that so unyieldingly reduces every event, phenomenon, and human activity to a perfect system of laws and cosmic "powers" seems to entail the disappearance of all freedom and the denial of any choice that is not already unalterably determined. It was therefore natural that during those same years Pomponazzi should be led to take up the great philosophical and theological themes of fate, free will, and predestination, which had begun again to be so topical, especially now that a lengthy controversy had started that was destined to continue well beyond the end of the sixteenth century.

Pomponazzi took up these themes from the philosophical angle, starting, that is, with Alexander of Aphrodisias' criticisms of the Stoic conception of fate, which Pomponazzi for his part defended in its substance and regarded as not unreasonable. This conception had the merit of regarding God as "knowledge" and, at the same time, as "first cause" of everything that has been or will be and therefore of a reality that is ruled by an already completely determined system of laws, in which the human will has a part as a specific and necessary cause of single determinate events. The problem of free will, which such a doctrine excludes in the most complete way, certainly remains open, but Pomponazzi stresses the point that Christian teaching itself makes it difficult to explain free will. This is especially true since faith in the immortality of the soul and in the penalties and rewards that await human beings in the other life seem to make God and his utterly free will the first cause of sin and human failings. It would seem difficult, therefore, to prevent him from being accused of cruelty, since he knows from eternity that very few people will be saved.[34]

The philosopher was not unaware that at a period still recent, masters and theologians had taken up the bitter debate on future contingents in an attempt to work out a solution that would safeguard the divine omnipotence and fore-knowledge and, at the same time, the real freedom of human volition. But he regarded it as an absurdity to speak of contingency in the presence of the divine knowledge, which is outside of time and embraces everything in its own eternity. He did not think that any of the solutions offered really succeeded in reconciling the absolute power of God and human free will, these being the opposed terms of a dilemma which the human mind was incapable of resolving. The Stoic conception, which identified God with the order of the world and its laws, certainly avoided the most terrible consequences of doctrines that, when pushed to their extremes, seemed to render inevitable every kind of sin and fault, these having been already decreed from eternity by a will, such as that of God, that is by supposition utterly free and sovereign. But even Stoicism, however reasonable and "more probable" in its teaching on fate, could not be accepted without denying to human beings any freedom that is not merely apparent and illusory.

In the presence of these tragic alternatives from which there is no escape, Pomponazzi stressed the contrast between the opposed demands, the irresolvable conflict in which there is no meeting ground. On the one hand, it is impossible to think that in reality everything is contingent and the result of chance; but, on the other, the acceptance of a strict system of causes can end only with the acknowledgment of fate, over against which can be set only an exaltation of an absolute will whose reasons no one can know and whose eternal choices remain always independent of any human merit or demerit. In the end, then, the philosopher's conclusion, which is set down in the "epilogue or peroration" of Book V, remains ambiguous and undecided.[35]

The order of the world (he writes) has always been what it is through endless ages, and it always will be, for it is based on necessary causes and is clearly divided between the immutable perfection of the heavens and the corruptible nature of earthly things," which are, as it were, the "excrement" of the everlasting "animal" that is the universe. God, who produces this universe, knows generatable and corruptible things only according to their "species," for in their individuality they are foreign to him. At the same time, human wisdom is almost always in error, nor will a purely natural knowledge ever allow it to rise up to the supreme truth and the divine secrets *(arcana),* regarding which we must hold to the decisions of the Church, "which is guided by the Holy Spirit."

Consequently (and this is already clear from the conclusion of chapter 9), we must accept that God knows from eternity the number of the elect, who are already destined for salvation, while other human beings are free to follow or not follow the laws of nature and will be judged according to their choice. Nevertheless the divinity will always be able, by his free choice, to forgive the sins of any whom he chooses and to hear or not hear their prayers without thereby doing anyone an injustice. In his infinite power God certainly could have created a "greater and more beautiful" universe, just as it was in his power to produce created things that were more numerous and more perfect. It is not possible, however, for the human mind to try to know the impenetrable reasons for his sovereign decisions.

Pomponazzi did not hesitate to write that in the ears of a philosopher such statements sound like the ravings of a deranged mind, but he concluded, nonetheless, that we ought to rely on the authority of the "divinely given" Scriptures. He also makes statements in which it is difficult to discern the subtle and ambiguous distinction between, on the one hand, obvious reasons of convenience and obedience to ecclesiastical authority, and on the other hand, the sense of an insuperable antinomy, in the presence of which even reason is forced to surrender in order not to deny either the necessary order of causes or the human aspiration to its own freedom and to the responsibility that follows from it.

3. Thomism at the End of the Fifteenth and the Beginning of the Sixteenth Century: Thomas de Vio

Peter Pomponazzi was the most important philosopher of the early sixteenth century and, at the same time, the representative of a culture that, boldly and with great speculative care, tackled even some of the most difficult problems of speculative theology. We have seen, however, that one factor in his complex doctrinal formation was the teaching and influence of a Thomist master, both of which could be seen in the courses which Peretto taught at Padua. Admittedly we do not have a great deal of information about the teaching of that master, Francis Securus of Nardò (+ 1489), although he was the best-known representative of Paduan Thomism toward the end of the century.[36] The reason for our ignorance is that no written evidence remains of this teacher whom Pomponazzi described as "very wordy"; we have only the information given in the writings of his friends and adversaries, that is, Trombetta, Vernia, and Nifo, in addition, of course, to his most famous student.

The information that has come down to us, however, is enough to tell of his activity as a resolute and lucid defender of Thomist teachings in constant discussions not only with his "Averroist" or "Alexandrian" colleagues but also with his Scotist rivals. He occupied himself with all the most sensitive and topical subjects of Scholastic controversy: from the techniques used in the *suiseticae calculationes* to the theory of how the "separated" intelligences "informed" the heavens; from the refutation of the logical and epistemological doctrine of the *regressus* to the distinction between the infinite-in-act in the line of continuous quantity and the infinite-in-act in the line of discrete quantity. His critical thinking was, however, devoted first and foremost to proving the conceptual superiority of the Thomist doctrine of the soul. We know that while he refuted the conclusions reached by the Scotists, he maintained that the soul's immortality, as well as its "individuation" and its connection with the body in the ordinary process of "natural" knowledge, were rationally demonstrable.

Clear traces of his teaching and of the tradition he so resolutely defended at Padua can be seen both in the objections which Gaspar Contarini raised against Pomponazzi and in the views of other Paduan masters involved in the debate on the immortality of the soul, a debate destined to go on a good deal longer, through most of the sixteenth century. But the combative revival of Thomism at the most important university center in Italy takes on special importance when we recall that Thomas de Vio (1468–1534), the future Cardinal Cajetan, one of the greatest of the commentators on Aquinas and one of the most outstanding personalities in the history of sixteenth-century theology, spent the most decisive years of his training at this *studium*.[37]

After completing his early studies in the Dominican schools of Naples and Bologna, de Vio arrived in Padua around 1491 and began his career as teacher in the local *studium* of his order before becoming a professor of metaphysics at the University of Padua in 1494. Here he immediately had to deal with Trombetta, his rival in the chair of Scotism, and with the still-influential Averroist professors. He was also a colleague of Pomponazzi and Nifo as well as of the elderly Vernia, who had by now forgotten his former enthusiasm for the teachings of the Commentator. Later on, after having gone on to teach in Pavia and Milan, Cajetan ("Il Gaetano," the man from Gaeta, his birthplace, of which he was bishop from 1519 on) was to become a high-ranking official of his order (procurator general, 1500–7; vicar general, 1507–8); and finally (still in 1508) its general, an office he filled for ten years.

The part he played in bringing about the failure of the so-called Council of Pisa (1511–12) is well known. He accomplished this by writing, among other things, his *Auctoritas papae et concilii sive Ecclesiae comparata* (1511),[38] in which with great determination he defended the thesis of the superiority of the pope over councils, which he alone had authority to convoke, and challenged the conciliarist doctrines. A response to this work (which

Louis XII submitted to the Sorbonne for condemnation) came from French theologian and jurist James Almain in his *Libellus de auctoritate Ecclesiae* (1512), which in turn elicited a reply from the Dominican *(Apologia tractatus de comparata auctoritate Papae)*[39] in which he also rejected the censures issued by the theologians of Paris.

Later on, Cajetan was one of those who persuaded Julius II to convoke the Fifth Lateran Council; during the work of this great Church assembly he had an opportunity to express his own ideas on reform with great clarity.[40] At the opening of its second session (as we shall see) he delivered a very important address in which he stated the need for a reform of the Church, a restoration of good morals among the clergy and the Christian people, the elimination of schisms, the conversion of unbelievers, and the return of heretics to orthodoxy. These were goals to be achieved through preaching, persuasion, and above all, the establishment of holy and just laws.

In 1517 Cajetan was raised to the cardinalate. Then in May of 1518 he began his work as legate in Germany, where his purpose was to persuade Emperor Maximilian to make war on the Turks; in fact, however, he ended up devoting himself to a last effort to persuade Luther to retract. Even though he used all the resources of "paternal" persuasion, he failed in his purpose. At the end of October after Luther had left Augsburg, Cajetan was forced to acknowledge that the now-spreading religious crisis in Germany could no longer be controlled and that Luther would never abandon his views and his increasingly open and radical attack on the Curia and Roman institutions. Cajetan did, however, help to secure the imperial succession for Charles V.

His behavior toward Luther was considered to be overly weak and uncertain, nor were there lacking those who took advantage of his failure in order to block his influence in the Curia, an influence marked by an austere and stern view of Christian life. He did, however, take part in the Roman discussion of Luther, his teachings, and his rebellion; the discussion ended with a definitive condemnation that was set down in the bull *Exsurge Domine* of June 14, 1520.

After the death of Leo X, Cajetan was among the chief electors of Pope Hadrian VI, who charged him with a new mission to Hungary, Bohemia, and Poland, still with the view to meeting the Turkish threat. During the pontificate of Clement VII, de Vio (who had already been appointed bishop of Gaeta in 1519) spent years in retirement and study, devoting himself primarily to important works of biblical exegesis. He was also caught up in the terrible events accompanying the sack of Rome; he was imprisoned by the mercenaries (the *landknechts* or *lansquenets*) and forced to pay a very high ransom. He then withdrew to Gaeta, where he remained until 1529, when among other things he was charged by the pope with examining the thorny question of the divorce requested by Henry VIII; he dealt with it in a very balanced way, pointing out that polygamy could not be considered against the laws of nature and was not explicitly prohibited by the Scriptures.

Linked as he was with some of the more important representatives of the group of "reform prelates" (Seripando, Sadoleto, Giles of Viterbo), he was spoken of in 1534 as one of the most influential candidates for the pontifical throne. But he died on October 10 of that year at the height of the religious and spiritual crisis that had now opened up the most serious fissure in the history of Christianity.

Despite the fact that a great part of his life was thus committed to his duties as a churchman, diplomat, and member of the Curia, de Vio was above all else a scholar, who, even during periods of the most intense ecclesiastical activity, produced works of great importance in the history of sixteenth-century theology and in the complete systematic development of Thomist teaching. This is clear from the imposing list of his philosophical, theological, and exegetical writings, and it is confirmed by their far-reaching success and by the discussions and controversies to which they gave rise even within the Dominican Order itself, where his freedom of judgment and the acuteness and complexity of his conclusions were not always judged positively. Indeed, his continuous presence at the center of some of the most important philosophical and theological debates in the Scholastic culture of the time points to the exceptional qualities and intellectual keenness of a scholar who was able to meet some of the essential requirements of the radical intellectual renewal that was already going on. He was also a man who knew how to adapt his very firm doctrinal fidelity to the many problems of a theoretical, didactic, methodological, and spiritual kind emerging from a culture that was extraordinarily rich but also troubled by crises and conflicts of every kind.

Even during his teaching as a young man in Padua, de Vio found himself defending Thomist ideas against the contrasting criticisms of Averroist and Alexandrian masters and of his most important competitor, the Scotist Trombetta. His commentary on the *De ente et essentia*[41] of Thomas Aquinas (in which he clearly explained Thomist ontology along lines that would lead him to develop the basic conception of "the analogy of proportion")[42] attests to the skill and subtle intelligence with which this Dominican was able to confront the criticisms of the Scotists even while accepting some of their essential ideas, which he found useful for a better interpretation of Aquinas' ideas.

Even more interesting, however, is his commentary on the *De anima*,[43] written around 1512, in which, of course, he defended Thomist teachings on psychology but also explicitly claimed that Aristotle had conceived of the soul in the manner later explained by Averroes, whose theses on the unity and oneness of the human intellectual soul corresponded (he said) to the words of the "Philosopher."[44] We can understand then, why, when (as we shall see) the Lateran Council in 1513 condemned all teachings that presupposed the mortality of the soul and obliged professors of philosophy to justify the conclusions of faith in their lectures, de Vio uttered his *non placet*. He was in fact convinced that such a task belonged only to theologians and not to philosophers, who must work with exclusively rational arguments and methods. His doubts went even further in 1519 when, commenting on Paul's letter to the Romans, he made clear his own conviction that human reason is incapable by its own powers of proving the immortality of the soul and perhaps even providence.[45]

Bartholomew of Spina, a Dominican whose harsh criticisms of Pomponazzi we have already seen, did not hesitate to take up the cudgels even against the most illustrious master of his own order. In 1518 he published a set of three writings *(Propugnaculum Aristotelis de immortalitate animae contra Thomam Cajetanum*; *Tutela veritatis de immortalitate animae contra Petrum Pomponatium*; and *Flagellum in tres libros apologiae eiusdem)*[46] that had for their purpose to defend "correct" Aristotelean teaching, which he regarded as completely consonant with that of Thomas, and to accuse Pomponazzi and Cajetan of having weakened belief in the immortality of the soul by their arguments, since these reduced the belief to a matter solely of faith, unconnected with philosophical proofs.

As a theologian, de Vio was a faithful and systematic interpreter of Thomas and composed a monumental commentary on the *Summa theologica* that took probably twenty years and was completed in 1522.[47] The work was reprinted a number of times and also emended to eliminate passages that seemed too daring; ideas that could seem ambiguous, especially in the intellectual climate of the Counterreformation; and expressions regarded as insufficiently clear. It was, nonetheless, a fine tool for work and study for generation upon generation of theologians (and not only Thomists) and made a decisive contribution to the anti-Lutheran controversy, especially in its critique of the doctrine of "justification by faith alone," its emphasis on the cooperation of human beings with divine grace, its defense of works, and a conception of "free will" that elicited not a few reservations from theologians of the Augustinian tradition and often came up for discussion in the next century. On the other hand, even Cajetan's theological teachings were examined by the theologians of the Sorbonne, who censured sixteen of them.

But an even more bitter attack was made on the cardinal by one of his religious brothers, Ambrose Catarino Politi (ca. 1484–1553), a former Savonarolian who later became one of the leading men of the Counterreformation and an unrelenting prosecutor of any doctrinal deviation. In 1535—and in Paris!—he published his *Annotationes in excerpta quaedam de commentariis reverendissimi cardinalis Cajetani S. Xisti,*[48] which had a second expanded edition in Lyons in 1544. It was a skillful but factious examination of Cajetan's theological ideas with a denunciation of certain dangerous "deviations." In any case, in 1544 the Sorbonne again censured Cajetan's commentaries as well as his responses to the earlier criticisms of the Parisian theologians.

The final period of de Vio's literary activity was devoted chiefly to studies and writings on biblical exegesis. As early as 1523 he began the composition of his *Ientacula,* which contained explanations of passages of the

Gospels. In subsequent years and until the end of his life he devoted himself mainly to translating and commenting on the Scriptures, under the clear influence of humanist methods and ideas and while using the help of learned experts in Hebrew and Aramaic. He used the "scholia" of Erasmus and the commentaries of Lefèvre d'Étaples on the text of the New Testament; he also exchanged letters with the Dutch humanist, for whom he showed a keen and sincere appreciation.

In his work as exegete,[49] which he did not only as a theologian but also as an informed critic, he did not avoid touching on particularly thorny subjects or proposing opinions that in the eyes of some contemporaries and of Politi seemed dangerous and rash, as when he advanced reasons for doubting the authenticity of the last chapter of Mark's Gospel or discussed the attribution of various of the canonical letters.

The other major Thomistic commentator of that period, Dominican Francis Silvestri of Ferrara (1474–1528), was a good deal more cautious and traditional.[50] He composed a successful commentary on the *Summa contra Gentes*[51] that in some respects was no less important than Cajetan's monumental exegesis of the *Summa theologica*. A subtle metaphysician and a polished logician, he did not hesitate to criticize the teachings of Cajetan, without naming him but often citing his commentary verbatim. Above all, working as he was on a text that contained evident traces of Avicenna and suggestions of a Platonist type, it was not difficult for him to reject certain interpretations which he regarded as too compliant toward non-Christian philosophies and to deny in a decisive way that rational argument could not supply a clear demonstration of the immortality of the soul. In this context he maintained that for Aristotle the agent intellect is only a faculty of the soul and not an external power acting on it; that the agent intellect and the possible intellect are equally incorruptible; and that the fact that the soul is extrinsically joined to the body can by no means imply that it is separate and distinct from the agent intellect.

Especially important was his challenge to Cajetan's interpretation of and commentary on the most difficult and obscure passage in the third book of the *De anima,* which that great theologian had regarded as very close to the doctrine expounded by Averroes.[52] Silvestri was no less combative in dealing with the Scotists, whom he attacked with subtle dialectical skill on many sensitive points of trinitarian theology and even on the very concept of revelation. During the last years of his life Silvestri, too, entered the lists against Luther in a work published in 1525, the controversialist purposes of which are clear from the title: *Apologia de convenientia institutorum Romanae Ecclesiae cum evangelica liberatate tractatus adversus Lutherum de hoc pessime sentientem.*[53]

Another Dominican master rather heavily involved in the discussion of the doctrine of the soul was Chrysostom Javelli of Casale (1470–ca. 1538). He wrote *Solutiones rationum quae continentur in tractatu De immortalitate animae* and *Solutiones rationum quae formantur in Defensorio,*[54] which would accompany the 1519 edition of Pomponazzi's work.

This theologian, as we know, acknowledged the legitimacy of Pomponazzi's conclusions in the realm of philosophical exegesis, but he also maintained that these must be opposed by conclusions based on faith. But he had well understood the importance of the Mantuan professor's outlook, for he returned to it later on in his *Tractatus de animae humanae indeficientia in quadruplici via scilicet Peripatetica, Academica, Naturali et Christiana* (1536)[55] and in his *Quaestiones subtilissimae, in quibus clarissime resolvuntur dubia Aristotelis et Commentatoris, eaque ut plurimum decisa habentur iuxta Thomisticum dogma* (1532),[56] in which he also openly criticized Cajetan, attributing to him the teaching of Pomponazzi.[57]

Although a Thomist and fairly knowledgeable about Aristotle, Javelli had strong Platonic sympathies and inclinations and sought to show the agreement *(concordia)* between these two greatest philosophers of antiquity, whom he claimed were in substantial agreement on all the most difficult and decisive points of metaphysics. Thus he did not hesitate to say that Aristotelean philosophy, while completely valid in the realm of knowledge of nature, needed to be completed by the ethics and "theology" of Plato, a "divine seer and priest," who by his "prophetic style" spurs human beings to free themselves from the wretched flesh and rise to the level of a very devout and religious meditation. Such ideas as these found expression especially in his *De Christiana religione,* a work of his old age published in 1534, in which he revived many ideas already dear to late-fifteenth-century philosophy and which clearly showed the combined influence of Thomas and Ficino. But he followed the same inspirations in his attack on Lutheranism, set forth in his *Quaestio perpulchra et resolutissima de Dei praedestinatione et reprobatione,* which, not without reason, was accused of leaning toward "Pelagian" solutions.[58]

4. The Fifth Lateran Council and Hopes of Reform

As I mentioned earlier, Cajetan had played quite an important part in the preparation and debates of the Fifth Lateran Council, at which he was an eloquent defender of the prerogatives and work of "religious" and in particular of the mendicant orders. It is time now to speak of this important event in the history of the Church in the early sixteenth century. It was important because not only did it confirm the definitive waning, in practice, of the renewed attempts to set the great assembly of the "Christian people" over against the pope; in many of its addresses it also confirmed the state of deep crisis in ecclesial institutions; the growing spiritual restlessness that had by now reached its height in so many circles, personalities, and experiences of the religious life of the times; and the demand for a decisive reform as the only way of escaping from a state of decadence, the increasing dangers of which were being realized.

As is well known, the council was the answer of Julius II to the "furtive gathering" in Pisa, that is, to the conciliarist attempt made by cardinals

Bernardine Carvajal, Francis Borgia, William Briçonnet, de Prie, and Sanseverino, who had ties to the French party and Emperor Maximilian and who were joined by Hippolytus d'Este.[59] In addition to the council's political importance and to the skill with which Pope Della Rovere was able to confront an extremely dangerous political maneuver, the council also made possible the public and very eloquent expression of calls for a reform of the Church that could renew Christian life in head and members and provide a defense against now-imminent dangers and threats.

Giles of Viterbo, general of the Augustinians,[60] served as interpreter of these demands from the beginning of the council (May 3, 1512) a short time after the battle of Ravenna, which had seriously threatened the power of the papacy. He asserted that that defeat had been a warning from providence telling the Church, which had been defeated when it had sought its strength in weapons alien to it, that it should turn back to the weapons Christ intended for it: piety, prayer, faith, and "the sword of the light." The pope's duty, therefore, was to reform the Church, to bring peace to it and the Christian people, and to remove the new wounds inflicted on the "Mystical Body." But Giles also linked this reform to a renewal of the war against Islam and Muhammad, the implacable enemy of Christ, for this war was the condition of a renewal that would bring Christianity back to its origins.

Similar ideas were repeated in the address of Cardinal Alexander Farnese, although he emphasized mainly the need of overcoming "schism," which was the work of Satan. Bernardine Zeno, who spoke at the opening of the first session (May 10), repeated the same ideas, while likewise shifting the focus of his discussion to the twofold danger represented by the schismatics and the Turks, both of whom were tools of the devil.

It was left, however, to Cajetan at the beginning of the second session (May 17) to face up to the essential problem: Catholic teaching on the Church and councils. He described the Church as the Holy Jerusalem, with its means of salvation (the sacraments), the apostles, pastors, teachers, and gifts of grace, and with its citizens who are, as it were, the members of a single body. Precisely because the Church is a "holy city," it is also the "city of peace" that has come down from heaven and has been divinely shaped according to the "form" of the heavenly city. Governed by the vicar of Christ, to whom all owe obedience, the Church is a complete and universal community which cannot be divided in any of its members.

Such a division was what the followers of the "furtive assembly in Pisa" *(conciliabulum pisanum)* had tried to bring about, these members of an assembly that was neither universal nor legitimate and was, instead, infected with error, since it wanted to subordinate "Peter" to the Church, the pope to a council, the "shepherd" to the "flock." Their sole purpose (Cajetan said) was to overturn and not reform the magnificent order of the Church. At the same time, however, while exhorting Julius II to make use of his two "swords," the temporal and the spiritual, against errors and schisms, Cajetan reminded him that power was weak without "perfection" and that he ought to seek his inspiration in the "wisdom" of a Church restored to its original form.

The third session was held on December 3, when the political and military situation had already been radically altered, as was shown by the acceptance of the council by Emperor Maximilian, who dissociated himself entirely from the *conciliabulum,* which he condemned, along with the Gallican "tiny assembly" *(conventicula)* in Tours. Julius II went resolutely on the offensive, summoning the French clergy and laity to appear because of their acceptance of the "pragmatic sanction," reiterating previous papal decrees on that document, and declaring completely void the acts of the Pisan *conciliabulum* (fourth session, December 10). His first reward was the celebration of himself as "second God on earth" by protonotary apostolic Christopher Marcello, who gave the opening address.

The pope, who was by now quite ill, died on February 20, 1513; he was succeeded, after a short conclave, by Cardinal John de'Medici, Leo X. As soon as he was elected, he convoked the sixth session for April 27. Once again, the speaker who opened it, Simon Begni, bishop of Modrussa, chose as his theme the struggle against the Turkish peril and the moral decadence of the Church, whose reform he called for in order to do away with all doubts and make religion sure and solid. At this session it was decided to set up three "deputations," partly elected by the fathers and partly appointed by the pope; quite specific tasks were delegated to them: (1) the restoration of peace in Christendom and the final elimination of the schism; (2) the reform of the Curia; and (3) the discussion of the "pragmatic sanction" and the safeguarding of the principles of the faith. Thus the council was finally able to face up to some subjects that had been constantly raised in the addresses but never discussed in an explicit and substantive way.

The seventh session (June 17, 1513) was devoted once again to the Turkish peril; there, too, the commission on the reform of the Curia was divided into five subcommissions, each charged with studying particular problems. The eighth session (December 19) was a good deal more important, since it not only confirmed the official end of the very minor "Pisan schism" that came with the acceptance of the Lateran Council by the kingdom of France, but it also decreed the condemnation of all doctrines that in any way denied the immortality of the soul. It will be useful to note that the council regarded as heterodox the assertion that the rational soul of human beings is mortal, the Averroist thesis on the oneness of the possible intellect of the human species, and finally, the doctrine that maintained this last assertion to be true at least at the philosophical level. The principle that the soul is the form of the body and that each human being has its own personal and individual soul was proclaimed as an incontrovertible truth. Utter falsity was predicated of any statement contrary to these truths of faith, which even teachers of philosophy were obliged to maintain and demonstrate in their teaching.

Nor was that all. During the same eighth session it was decided to proclaim a crusade that would bring the Bohemians back to Catholic orthodoxy. A decree was also issued on the reform of the Curia; it considerably lowered taxes and struck hard at various abuses practiced by "curial officials," but it did not go further to a more radical renewal of the institution, for it was prevented from doing so by the conflict of particular interests that in fact blocked the decrees of the council.

The council's work began anew on May 5, 1514, with the ninth session, which opened with a homily by Anthony Pucci, chamberlain. He again called for the improvement of the Church and for an immediate stop to the moral decadence of the religious orders, the clergy, and the laity. His address was a kind of introduction to the bull on Church reform that was issued at this session. But after all the emotional pleas, eloquent denunciations, and heartfelt appeals, the reform had rather modest results. It was decreed that bishoprics and abbacies be entrusted to worthy persons and in accordance with canonical norms; regulations were set for granting "provisions" and carrying out consistorial trials so as to make "dispositions" and "translations" more difficult; there was an effort to rein in the aberrant practice of "commendams," while possession of four or more benefices was prohibited.

The same bull established stricter rules for the behavior of cardinals and their households; it was concerned to promote the better religious formation of clergy and laity, whose growing moral decadence and serious ignorance of the principles and essential teachings of the faith it deplored. Finally, it confirmed the serious punishments intended for the sacrilegious and for loose-living and simoniacal priests; it called for the riddance of every kind of superstition (the reference was probably to the increasing spread of magical practices and "witchcraft" at the most varied levels of society); and false, pretended Christians were to be unmasked and harshly persecuted. In summary: the bull contained a series of purely disciplinary norms and interventions that did not come to grips with the deeper causes of the unrest and spiritual malaise of the time and of a situation already close to exploding at the call of Luther.

In the following months the work of the council was in practice hindered or made quite difficult by the very sharp opposition between the bishops, who were aiming to strengthen and extend their jurisdictional powers, and the religious orders, which banded together in an obstinate defense of their "prerogatives" and "exemptions." Only on May 4, 1515, after a new call for reform by the bishop of Patrasso during the tenth session, was a bull promulgated that set new limits to "exemptions" and strengthened the authority of the bishops while also repeating the traditional principles of ecclesiastical "freedom." The Monti di pietà (credit banks) were definitively approved.

In the next session another bull was issued on the press; this was especially important because it showed that Church authorities had indeed understood both the opportunities and the dangers which this new means of communication could bring into the life of the Church, its institutions, and the discipline of the "faithful." The bull opened with a real and true celebration of the importance of this "wonderful" invention; but it immediately went on to establish a strict control by prohibiting, under pain of excommunication, the printing of any writing whatsoever that had not received episcopal and inquisitorial approval.

The tenth session also tackled the now age-old problem of the reform of the Church calendar by appointing a commission to study the various proposals already advanced. Then the work of the council went on wearily for months until December 19, 1516, and the opening of the eleventh session, in which for the first time a bishop of an "American" diocese, Santo Domingo, took part. The malaise and crisis in the society of the Church were daily more open and evident, as was shown by the growing success of a ceaseless apocalyptic preaching that connected the needed reform with the coming of disastrous and terrifying times or with an appeal for the "angelic pope" who would inaugurate a new age of Christianity under the sign of the "reign of the Spirit."

The council fathers, however, responded with an absolute prohibition barring any priest, secular or regular or even one belonging to a mendicant order, from preaching without first receiving permission from his superior; they threatened with excommunication anyone announcing future disasters, the coming of the Antichrist, or the imminence of the final judgment; and they required that authors or promulgators of supposed revelations submit them to the irrevocable judgment of the ecclesiastical authorities. Nor do they seem to have been overly concerned to understand the reasons for a phenomenon that was an obvious "sign of the times" and that expressed not only the anxieties and fears of a society now caught up in the tragedy of "dreadful wars" but also the desire for religious renewal and a return to a pure evangelical piety. At the same time, however, as the events of the following years were to show, even on the upper levels of the hierarchy and in those orders in which the spiritual restlessness and the call for reform were most deeply felt, faith in prophecy had not, in fact, died out at so crucial a moment in religious and civil history and on the eve of the greatest wounding of the Christian world.

Leo X did not intend to protract further the celebration of Fifth Lateran, and he proposed and discussed its closing at a consistory on February 1, 1517. John Francis Pico had addressed a new and sorrowful appeal for reform to the pope and the cardinals.[61] He had said that the pope could save the Church only by reforming it in its every part and delivering it from the many evils that afflicted it. In accents reminiscent of Savonarola's prophecy and preaching, he had attacked the wealth and pomp of the Church's magnates, the ambitiousness of prelates and the lustfulness of men whose duty it was to administer spiritual gifts, and the suspect way of life of too many priests and friars, for whom he asked punishments and very harsh penalties. He also asked that some forms of worship and liturgy be purified and that all ceremonies be stripped of a pomp that was utterly at odds with evangelical humility and charity.

These were proposals that certainly could not expect a ready acceptance from the pope and a large part of the college of cardinals, who were still constantly engaged in their struggles for power. As a result the council, which had now become inconvenient and perhaps dangerous, closed on March 16, 1517, with a final summons to evangelical truth as the source of all knowledge and all virtue. But the council had not effected the so long-awaited reform that in a few days' time would become Luther's battle cry. And yet, even in Italy a reform movement was already afoot that in the coming years and decades would aim at the renewal of theological teaching and Church life, at the beginning of a long process of development soon destined to have very different outcomes: from the acceptance of Lutheran or Calvinist doctrines to a stern program of Catholic restoration, from the practice of "Nicodemism" to the development of the most radical religious ideas.

5. The Platonic-Esoteric-Theological Synthesis of Francis Zorzi

Franciscan philosopher and theologian Francis Zorzi, better known as Francis George Veneto (1466–1540), had close connections with reform-minded circles in Venice.[62] He was the most typical representative of a tradition that was both speculative and religious, one grounded in the great themes of Ficino and Pico but, above all, radically dominated by constant recourse to "Gnostic" sources and doctrines, from the Hermetic and Cabalistic writings to the *Chaldean Oracles* and ideas clearly inspired by Origen. He was a person who played an important part in Venetian religious life during the first decades of the sixteenth century; we know of his connections with the young Contarini, with the first spiritual coteries that gathered around Ignatius Cipelli and Trypho Gabriele, and also with Giles of Viterbo.

In 1525 Zorzi published his *De harmonia mundi cantica tria*[63] and in 1536 his *In Sacram Scripturam problemata*, two works destined for noteworthy success in the sixteenth-century philosophical and religious world, especially in France and England and in some strata of German esotericism. In addition to other writings of Zorzi that have remained unpublished, mention must be made especially of a lengthy doctrinal poem in the vernacular *(L'elegante poema)*, which was accompanied by a commentary that drew on the same ideas as were put forward in the *Problemata*.[64]

The Franciscan begins with the Ficinian myth of an "archaic theology" *(prisca theologia)*, enriched now by a continuous appeal to "more recondite" Jewish "theologians" *(secretiores theologi)*, that is, the Cabalists. On this basis he asserts that every true "divine philosophy" that seeks to understand the ancient, changeless wisdom and shed on it the "splendid light" of biblico-Christian revelation must above all else meditate on the eternal "Monad," the One, the source that contains everything in itself and brings everything into being in its lasting perfection. From its creative power, which is prior to every other principle and all "multiplicity," the entire universe proceeds, the totality of all forms and all beings, the images of which coexist eternally in the divine mind.

This teaching (which was meant to bring into agreement the truths taught by the Platonists, the Hermetics, the very earliest wise men, and the Christian Doctor-saints) is only the starting point for a complex and sometimes obscure meditation that is at once philosophical and theological, ethical and mystical, and has obvious traces of Gnosticism. It is intended to bring out the spiritual value of the human person as "center" and "bond" of creation and of the hierarchical world order. But it is also intended as a celebration of the cosmic role of Christ, who is thought of both as "mediator" between the eternal "Monad" and the "many-sided" universe and as the supreme way of a "return to the One" *(reductio ad unum),* a way to be traveled according to the Franciscan "imitation of Christ" and culminating in the ineffable experience of "deification."

More than that: recourse to the Pythagorean mysticism of numbers, to the sacral mathematics of the Neoplatonists, and, of course, to the *Hermetica,* together with the Cabalistic exegesis of the Scriptures, provides the method for unlocking the deepest mysteries both of the "Book of God" and of that "other book," no less divine, that is opened to us in the perfection of nature. Citing Hermes [Trimegistus], Zorzi maintains that God governs everything with wisdom and establishes the measure and harmony of the world by introducing into formless matter the three principles of *heimarmenê* (fate), order, and necessity, which together establish the cohesive arrangement of the universe. He adds that these three principles, like the number, weight, and measure with which God organizes nature (see Wis 11:21), are the visible image of the Trinity, which is symbolized perfectly by the Hermetic image of the sphere.

I shall not dwell further on Zorzi's teaching about the soul, which, following Ficino, is conceived of as an individual vital, active principle that is at work in all the things that are, as it were, its "body" and individual "members." Nor on his revival of the famous Hermetic idea which, in order to explain the inexhaustible creative fruitfulness of the Monad, thinks of God as "having the fecundity of both sexes" and "as the source of all the sexes." Instead, I draw the reader's attention to the fact that the Franciscan calls God the "supramundane sun" and attributes to him, in relation to the universe as a whole, the same life-giving function which the sun exercises on the things of our earth, and to the way in which he describes in great detail God's "government" of the world, which he accomplishes by means of the influences and powers that descend from the seven heavenly intelligences and from the stars to which they give life.

The doctrine of the Trinity is also interpreted, in the light of Hermetic and Zoroastrian teachings, as the principle at work in the generative process that leads from the changeless and "solitary" oneness of the Monad to the limitless multiplicity of things and then back to the eternal Source. In pages made up of interwoven texts from Ficino and Pico and of echoes of Plato, Proclus, Porphyry, and Iamblichus, Pseudo-Dionysius and Boethius, Zorzi shows from "the most fruitful primal spirit" there originates a first "utterly like progeny," the authentic image of the Father, the "loftiest intellect" and true "Word of God," which Hermes had already revealed and which Plato called "Son." He is the "second source," which generates understanding and love of the divine goodness and thus links every being and every mind through the unitive bond of the Spirit.

Citations from Richard of St. Victor, Origen, and the "common opinion" of the Platonists are then used to prove that the "Word" is the "universal mediator" from whom the hierarchy of beings, the order of divine "governors," and the life-giving soul of the world all descend. For this reason we are obliged to fight against the "godlessness" of those "proud ones" (among whom that "dog," Averroes, takes first place) who stubbornly deny that God can generate and who are incapable of grasping the mystery of a limitless fecundity. They deny that the incarnation of the "Word" was the decisive cosmic event to which are owed not only the redemption of a human nature corrupted by its first sin but also the regeneration of the entire universe as it is brought back to the final salvation in the One that generated it.

It is not surprising that such teachings later elicited worried reactions even from his "spiritual" friends, such as Contarini and the Benedictine Gregory Cortese,[65] who were also made suspicious by the unclear allusions to magic and alchemy that were to be found in the *De harmonia mundi.* These friends were even more alarmed by the publication of the *Problemata,* which not only confirmed Zorzi's intellectual preferences but emphasized even further the esotericism of his religious outlook as he undertook a detailed examination and discussion of the many problems that emerged from a study of various biblical passages and from the fact of their at least seeming divergence and of the different meanings that would be given depending on the application of various exegetical methods.

It was also quite clear that in taking the approach he did, the Franciscan could suggest rather dangerous opinions (for example, on the symbolic rather than real meaning of paradise, on the Cabalistic interpretation of the Trinity, and on the purely "sign" value of baptism); these were views that became very suspect in light of the great disputes and controversies of the age. When Contarini learned of the censures leveled at the *Problemata* by Dominican Thomas Badia, Master of the Sacred Palace, and then at an *Apologia* written by Zorzi, he fully agreed with Badia's judgment and himself condemned the opinions of the elderly friar whose holy life and sincere and deep spirituality he admired. Later on, both the *De harmonia* and the *Problemata* were put on the Index "until corrected," but the corrections required included a quite extensive part of the works and would destroy their complex doctrinal fabric.[66]

6. Giles of Viterbo

Another major personage in the Italian religious life of the early sixteenth century, Augustinian Hermit Giles Canisio (Antonini) of Viterbo (1469–1532), shared Zorzi's interest in the secret exegesis of the Cabalists while interpreting it on Christian lines.[67] He was a religious who in 1506 became the highest authority in his order before becoming a cardinal in 1517. His career as scholar and teacher in the major Augustinian studia of the time is well known, as is his great interest in the philosophy of Ficino and, later on, in some aspects of John Pico's thinking. So too is his lengthy study of Hebrew and the other Oriental languages (a study he had taken up because, like the humanists, he wanted to go back to the original sources of biblical wisdom) and his association with some of the major representatives of the Jewish culture of that age (for example, Elias Levita) as well as his friendship with other learned Hebraists, first among them Reuchlin himself.[68]

Eloquent proofs of his impassioned participation in the debate on the present evils of the Church and on the needed reform were his address to the Fifth Lateran Council, which I have mentioned,[69] his *Promemoria ad Hadrianum papam IV de depravato statu romanae Ecclesiae et quomodo reformari possit et debeat,* and in addition, many passages from his letters and a number of as yet unpublished writings. Only recently have we had the extensive study by J. W. O'Malley, who has very meticulously brought together the ideas of the Augustinian cardinal on the Church and its needed reform.

It is now clear that the prelate did not confine himself to asking that the government of the Church be entrusted to men of faith and purity of life or condemning the ambitiousness and greed of the clergy and disapproving the abuses of indulgences, the amassing of benefices, and other "scandals." Rather, like many of the "reformers" of his time, he maintained that the salvation of Christian society depended on a return to the earliest and "original" biblico-evangelical traditions and to the earliest shared "wisdom" that had already been extolled by Marsilius Ficino. It was no accident that the young Giles had cultivated a relationship of admiring friendship with the Platonic philosopher, agreeing with the latter's views on the coming of a new "age of Saturn," a golden age of authentic knowledge brought about by a return to the truths taught by Plato.[70]

But in the course of his wide-ranging and even turbulent reflection, and following the path already traveled by Pico, he looked to the Cabala for the key to an understanding of the most hidden mysteries of revelation. Moreover, like other religious who were fairly close to him—Theseus Ambrogio and

Franciscan Peter Galatino—he was especially open to the revival of prophecy at the beginning of the century and, above all, to the renewed circulation of the Joachimite and Pseudo-Joachimite "predictions" which another Augustinian Hermit, Sylvester Meucci, published in Venice between 1516 and 1522.[71]

Giles' mental outlook is clearly attested in his *Sententiae ad mentem Platonis*,[72] composed in all likelihood between 1510 and 1512. It is a work in which the author is obviously attempting to use, even for a clearly "Scholastic" purpose (a commentary on the *Sentences* of Lombard), the metaphysical principles of Platonism, this philosophy's peculiar logical procedures, and methodological criteria utterly different from those of traditional theology, which he, like many humanists, saw to be inadequate and caught up in a profound crisis when it came to dealing with the spiritual problems of the age. In short, this reader of various Platonic and Neoplatonic works (his marginal notes in writings of Iamblichus, Porphyry, and Proclus have come down to us) made his own the Ficinian program of founding a new theology that would abandon the debatable Aristotelean foundations of Scholasticism and return to the philosopher who was more in agreement with the thinking of the Fathers: the Plato who of all the pagans had been closest to the truth of Christianity and had even had insight into essential elements of that truth.

Later on, without ever repudiating his Platonic sympathies, Giles turned to the Cabala, which he regarded as a more "hidden" but also "deeper" way of access to the divine wisdom of the Scriptures. Beginning especially in 1513–14 he collected numerous writings from the Talmud, the books of the Cabala, and the Midrashim, and had them translated; some of them he translated himself (at least in part, the rest done by others) even in the course of his intense activity as a churchman involved in the reform of his order and of the ecclesial community as well as in difficult missions. These books included the *Zohar,* the *Book of Creation,* the *Gate of Light,* the *Sefer ha temunah,* the *Ginnot Egoz,* the *Bahir,* and the *Ma'arekhet ha-elohut.*

The fruit of this intense meditation on the Cabalistic literature and the teachings of the "more recondite theologians" as well of his familiarity with the writings of Giustiniani, Augustine, Paul Ricci, and Felix of Prato, a former rabbi, now an Augustinian Hermit, is to be seen mainly in two works that stand out in the thick forest of Giles' manuscripts: the *Libellus de litteris hebraicis aut sanctis* and the *Scechina.*[73] The first, which is clearly based on the *Sefer ha temunah,* takes the form of an introduction to a study of Scripture that follows Plato's advice in the *Cratylus,* where he says that names were not invented by human beings but are the work of God. Giles therefore falls back on the *De divinis nominibus* of Pseudo-Dionysius and on the wise men of more recent times: John Pico, Paul Ricci, and Reuchlin, who were the first to turn to a study of the Cabala. He writes, however, that we need only read the Scriptures in order to see how necessary this study of "names" is for breaking through to the ultimate meaning of the scriptural word. Christian exegetes (he says) too often ignore the "holy language" and readily open themselves to the destructive criticisms of Hebrew sages. The cardinal hopes, therefore, that, heeding the words of Augustine, the pope will urge the study of the language of the prophets and invite all to slake their thirst at this primal fountain of truth.

God (Giles writes) revealed himself to Moses through the mouth of Jehurah, that is, "fire," giving himself the name "Tetragrammaton" and others that can be understood only with the aid of the ten numbers which the Hebrews and Arameans call "numerations" or "measures" and which Plato calls "ideas." In God, three of these constitute the higher world and seven the lower world; it is therefore necessary to apply the Cabalistic method and understand the meaning and value of each of their letters and of the hidden message these contain.[74]

I shall not pursue this complicated explanation or the list of names in the *sefirot* and the thirty-two "paths of wisdom" open to those who follow this exegesis. Instead I shall speak briefly of the *Scechina,* a work whose reference to the events surrounding the sack of Rome and the flooding of the Tiber in 1530 provides interesting chronological data that allows us to date its writing to the last years of its author's life. Though dedicated to Clement VII, the book is really addressed to Charles V, to whom it aims to reveal the secrets of authentic Cabalistic wisdom under the name of *Scechina,* which means "God's dwelling in the midst of humanity." It was necessary for the emperor, no less than for the pope, to know these mysteries at a time that was certainly one of tribulations and tragic events but was also bringing knowledge of new lands open to the gospel, a rebirth of the "holy language," and the advent of a new "Cyrus," Charles V. This new Cyrus, together with Clement VII, was to deliver the Christian world not only from the external peril of the Turks but also from the internal danger of cupidity.[75]

Giles does not doubt that the moment has come for the opening of the door to the most hidden revelation, the key to which is provided by the Cabala, the only method that is "not extraneous" but "interior" to the very Scriptures that enable us to understand all the "secrets" of the divine word. The exegetes of the sacred literature, in their ignorance of the mysteries it contains, have indeed chosen to use dialectic or eloquence and to give "ornaments" priority over the hidden truths and the most puerile *quaestiunculae* priority over the language of God. But access to revelation is not to be found in Pliny or Dioscurides, Theophrastus or Aristotle, or in philosophy and human science, which mislead their practicioners and render them as blind as those who would look for fish on the mountain tops or bears in the depths of the sea.[76] On the contrary, we must follow the Arameans, the learned writers of the *Zohar,* to an intimate knowledge of the words of Scripture, which, unlike the words used by human beings, are not mere conventional signs but a gift from the divinity.

And because the Gospel did not abrogate the older revelation, the Cabalistic method must be applied to the entire scriptural tradition, New Testament as well as Old, in search of meanings which the human writers were unable to grasp but in which the most resplendent "light" shines forth. Revelation is therefore continuous and uninterrupted down the centuries; the guide to its understanding is the *Scechina,* that is, the Holy Spirit granted to the prophets, the last of the *sefirot,* the tenth, which in the tenth "age" brings to completion the manifestation of the eternal Wisdom.[77]

Giles combined the wealth of doctrine he possessed as a "Hebraizer" with the use of a literary and philosophical symbology drawn from the pagan poets, the ancient "oracles," and Platonic and Neoplatonic writings. As a result, he was able to produce a highly extraordinary work in which his doctrinal intentions were overwhelmed by the striking nature and fascination of images, words, and symbols, as he continually explored the secrets of a discourse that was not only that of the Scriptures but also found its voice in the order and hidden connections between everything in the universe and in the dazzling power of prophecy both biblical and modern. His work is divided into three parts that are devoted respectively to numbers, letters, and the divine names. But central to the *Scechina* is the controlling doctrine of the *sefirot,* which are divided into three tripartite orders to which in turn correspond the various worlds and the divine names that reveal them. To these are added the *Scechina* that is in charge of the world of human beings, at the end of a journey which Giles was unable to complete.

Light is cast on its goal and end, however, by another work no less revealing of his spirituality and culture. That work is the *Historia viginti saeculorum,* in which the entire history, first of revelation and then of the Church, is presented in the same Cabalistic, mystical, and prophetic key and based on the same symbolism of names and numbers, the intention being to confirm the coming of the ultimate renewal by means of "the most hidden theology."[78]

7. The Concordism of Augustine Steuco

In his youth Augustine Steuco of Gubbio (ca. 1497–1548), a Canon Regular, had been at least initially distrustful of the "mysteries" of Cabalism and of "Platonic theology."[79] During his years of study in Bologna he had perhaps accepted the teaching of Pomponazzi. It was no accident, then, that he had written a *Liber contra theologiam platonicam* and a *Liber contra cabbalisticas superstitiones.* Later on, however, after his lengthy stay in Venice (beginning in 1525), this strong defender of Catholic unity and its supreme spiritual authority was attracted by the apologetic potential of a "devout philosophy" that was no longer constrained by the arid dialectic of traditional Scholastic discourse but could instead speak an especially bewitching language while developing the theme of a single, eternal "sapiential" truth.

In short, Steuco undertook a struggle on two fronts: against the old theology and the godless philosophy that had polluted it and against every doctrine or intellectual outlook that could detract from the dignity of the Catholic magisterium. His purpose in all this was to restore (as Ficino had wanted to do) the original identification of wisdom and religion. His aim was already made clear in such works as his *Recognitio Veteris Testamenti* and his *Adversus Luteranos*[80] and was confirmed by his brief controversy with Erasmus, whom he admired as a man of culture and learning but whom, nevertheless, he accused of having opened the way for Luther by his very radical criticisms of ecclesiastical institutions and authorities.[81] The result of his lengthy laborious study of the works of the Platonists and Neoplatonists, the *Hermetica,* the *Chaldean Oracles,* and other documents of the "archaic philosophy," was his *De perenni philosophia.*[82] He published this work in Lyons in 1540, on the eve of that turning point in sixteenth-century Italian religious history that was marked by the failure of the irenic efforts of Contarini, the definitive hardening of opposed confessional theologies, and the disappearance of every peaceful solution of a religious crisis that was henceforth inevitable.

Steuco's book reflected this period when there was still hope of a peaceful settlement, for it expressed a conviction that it was still possible, through philosophical persuasion, to resolve even the most serious conflicts and ruptures, and that the appeal to truths shared not only by all Christians but even by all "true" philosophers was the best antidote for theological conflicts too often caused also by "polemicist" and "proud" theologians. This is why the *De perenni philosophia* took as its starting point the theme of the original knowledge granted by God to Adam in the act of creation, when God allowed him to grasp the divine origin of all things and to know God in the immediate freedom of the creative act. This truth had, however, been immediately lost by Adam's sin, which was the beginning of a long sequence of sins and errors and, consequently, of the darkening of human knowledge, the confusion of tongues, and the loss of the sense of the supernatural destiny of the human person. Only a distant "gleam" of it survived, especially among those who, being born in the very land of Adam, had remained closest to the original state of things.[83]

The Chaldeans, Armenians, Babylonians, Assyrians, Egyptians, and Phoenicians had, then, been the trustees of those last traces of the Adamic revelation, which reappeared from time to time in a clearer and more certain way. It is not surprising that Steuco should have appealed to the authors whom Ficino had earlier regarded as "devout philosophers," and especially to Zarathustra, master of "the wisdom of the Chaldeans," to Hermes (of whose historical reality and antiquity he seems to have had no doubt), and to the other witnesses of the "most ancient" theology. To him these were solid proof of a single body of thought that was present in every age and among all peoples.[84]

This means that Steuco's undoubted knowledge of languages and his humanist formation did not keep him from accepting myths that were, in any case, accepted by so many learned men of his time and were to dominate, to the point of "madness," the great Orientalist William Postel. More than that, Steuco transformed Ficino's notion of an "archaic theology" into the idea of a single "eternal" and immutable tradition, the traces of which seemed obvious and in harmony and the providential nature of which was undeniable. As Ficino had said, this tradition had been deeply religious and had not distinguished at all between theology and natural philosophy or between the understanding of "revelation" and reflection on the creative work of God that is seen in the world.

In any event, it was the path set out in Hermetic "wisdom" and the "philosophy of the Mages" that all the great Greek wise men had followed (Orpheus, Homer, Hesiod, Thales, Pythagoras, Anaxagoras, and Empedocles, and then Plato and his most authentic disciples: Plotinus, Iamblichus, Porphyry, and Philo).[85] But some parts of Aristotle's doctrine (the "metaphysics") were also accepted into the canon of the "perennial philosophy," along with the philosophy of Cicero, Ovid, Virgil, and Seneca and the "dogmas" of Epictetus and Plutarch. Nor was there missing from this renewed call for "harmony," so reminiscent of Pico's attempt, an appeal to the "new Platonists," that is, George Gemistus Plethon and Bessarion, whom Steuco regarded as the first leaders in the return to "true wisdom."[86]

The perennial philosophy thus outlined by Steuco was necessarily in agreement with biblical and Christian revelation. This was demonstrated by the fact that all human beings and all the wise men had always agreed in recognizing that "piety" and "wisdom" are the supreme goods. Admittedly, in the long age that had passed before the coming of Christ the Savior, the truth, although expressed in myths and fables, had been threatened by the darkness of ignorance and superstition and by the godless arrogance of "false philosophers." But in the end that truth had been confirmed and taken over into faith in the redemption proclaimed by Christ and then acknowledged in the "holy teaching" of the Christian Fathers.

Its principles were simple and essential, since they included (1) certainty about the existence of a God who is One and Triune; (2) the obviousness of the creation by God of the world and the angelic intelligences; (3) acknowledgment of the divine creation of human beings and of the immortality of their individual souls; and (4) a belief in the eschatological destiny of human beings, who are destined for punishments or rewards in a life beyond nature, depending on their behavior. In addition (and departing in this respect even from Ficino), Steuco attributed to Hermes, Plato, the *Chaldean Oracles,* and the *Sibylline Books* the first announcement of the mystery of the Trinity; he was trying to remove every suspicion of heterodoxy from those authors.[87]

Clearly, this idea of a "perennial philosophy" had an obvious orthodox, if not outright apologetic, purpose, since it was marked by the search for a meeting point common to all the Christian philosophies, which were bound to agree on immutable "principles." In making Zarathustra, Hermes, and Plato serve this purpose rather than Thomas Aquinas or Duns Scotus, Steuco not only displayed a radical distrust of the principles at work in the so-called second Scholasticism, but he also made a rather difficult choice that was dangerous from the viewpoint of the theology of the "masters." This was because his incorporation of Hermeticism, "Magism," and Platonism into a new "Christian philosophy" could reduce Christianity to being just one form, even if the highest, of a sapiential experience that was common to the entire human race, with "wise and true philosophers" as its only authentic interpreters.

8. The Beginnings of the Reform Movement in Italy and the Theological Tendencies of the Catholic Reformers: Seripando and Sadoleto

A history of theological thought in Italy cannot but speak, at least briefly, about the beginnings of the reform movements or, to put it more accurately, of the various tendencies and outlooks that showed themselves and then acquired increasingly distinct and even contrasting traits in the years preceding and the decades immediately following upon the irreversible break opened up by the German Reformation. I shall, of course, be speaking here only of events proper to the religious history of Italy during those years. I shall not expatiate even on the rapid inroads made by Lutheran and, later, Zwinglian and Calvinist teachings. Nor shall I dwell on the undoubted attraction which these teachings had for various intellectual circles among laity, clergy, and "religious," especially in those orders (such as the Augustinian Hermits, the Franciscans, and the Canons Regular but also the Benedictines with their various congregations) in which spiritual restlessness was more intense and in which the Augustinian theological tradition was more fully at work with its emphasis on the great themes of justification, grace, and predestination.

Nor will it be possible to examine in depth the hold which these new teachings acquired on humanist culture and on intellectuals who for some time now had been granting a hearing to Ficino's theological views, to Pico's call for *concordia*, and above all, to Erasmus' ideal of the "philosophy of Christ."

Quite recent studies, among which it will be enough to mention those of Seidel Menchi,[88] have shown clearly how extensive and operative the influence of Erasmus was, even in Italy, and how this influence not seldom became the most direct vehicle for the acceptance of Reformation doctrines or, in any case, for the development of reformist attitudes and feelings. It is difficult to trace these new attitudes back to strict confessional positions; in fact, they were even marked by a growing impatience with theological controversies, a call for a return to the essential purity of "faith in Christ," and a more or less explicit rejection of the traditional "magisterium."

It must also be said, however, that for at least about twenty years, until the turning point at the beginning of the forties, it is not easy to locate the increasingly fine line between official orthodoxy, open adherence to the Reformation, and the various movements in which calls for reform, already so strong even in Italy during the first two decades of the sixteenth century, acquired forms and self-awareness over a vast doctrinal area. What we see is, in fact, a continuous process of deepening and differentiation that, starting from the original attitude of the "spirituals" or "evangelicals," either led to a crossing over to various Reformed denominations (or even to the more radical "heresies," such as the Anabaptists or the Antitrinitarians) or else exhausted itself in the call for a strict and rigorous renewal of Catholic morals and institutions, ending finally in an imperative call for a "Counterreformation."

The fact is that for not a few years men increasingly won over to the ideas of the reform movement, such as Peter Martyr Vermigli and Bernardine Ochino, would continue to work in Catholic institutions (sometimes in high positions), just as among the reforming prelates there would be individuals who differed profoundly among themselves, such as Contarini, Reginald Pole, and John Peter Carafa, the future Paul IV and real initiator of the Counterreformation. And it is certain that, given Erasmianism, indifference to dogma, "pretense," and "Nicodemism," the way was opened in the Italian Catholic Church for a movement of dissent which we know today to have been very broad, especially in intellectual groups. All this makes it clear that great caution is always needed in analyzing the religious history of the first half of the century. This is all the truer because the very manifestations of dissent could often not be defined in doctrinal terms but were expressed in deliberately cryptic language, while real intentions might be masked by a simple and substantial piety.

In any case, during the twenties and thirties it was already possible to identify some tendencies that were to characterize the history of the Reformation in Italy. The first was the acceptance of Reformed doctrines (often generically described even by the inquisitors in the summary term "Lutheran"), with a greater leaning toward the theological theses of Calvin and Zwingli. Perhaps the best-known representative of this tendency was Vermigli (1500–62), who was to become an eminent "Reformed" theologian of the Calvinist stripe. The second tendency was the criticism of all magisterial teaching and even the acceptance of the doctrine of justification "by faith alone" *(sola fide)* (not infrequently accompanied by a rejection of Calvin's teaching on predestination). The third was the longing for an "evangelical" Christianity based solely on the Word while also substantially accepting some essential Reformation themes, even if these were set forth in a cautious and nuanced fashion.

This last was the line taken by many of the "Waldensians," the followers or friends of John Valdés (whose concrete relations with the theological doctrines of the Reformation are better known to us today); some of these followers and friends, however, also had close relations with the "spiritual" circles that gathered around Cardinal Pole and other important churchmen.

Finally, reference must be made to the presence of Anabaptist and Antitrinitarian tendencies and, more generally, to "radical" views inspired by the principles of tolerance and religious freedom. These radical views were strongly opposed to any form of religious authoritarianism and inclined to an interpretation of Christianity that was filled with fermenting criticism under the influence of, among other things, the humanist philological tradition. Thus there took shape the rather new and original trend in the Italian Reformation that would manifest itself in such men as Celius Secundus Curione, Matthew Gribaldi Mofa, Camillus Renato, and Laelius and Faustus Socini, who were at the source of a tradition of thought that would have a very large influence on the modern "liberal" spirit and on the assertion of religious freedom. Nor may I pass over in silence another leader in our sixteenth-century religious history: Bernardine Ochino, general of the Capuchins, who, from a Franciscan experience that was fed by the spirituality of Bonaventure and his own Christocentrism, went on to accept the doctrines of the Reformation according to his own personal interpretation of them before ending his life in distant Moravia, among the most radical of communities.

It is clear that the reconstruction of the theological ideas of these "Reformed" Italians can be complete only when placed in the framework of the heated doctrinal debate that took place among the main tendencies and "confessions" of the Reformation. It was necessary, nonetheless, to refer to them in order better to understand the complexity and even the ambiguity of that other "reform" movement that remained within the Catholic Church and, with its ups and downs, played so important a role in the ecclesial events of the twenties and thirties as it fought for a radical renewal of Catholic morals, life, and institutions. But its most thoughtful representatives sought also to change theological methods and doctrines so as to promote the hoped-for religious peace and to bring an acceptance of those demands of the Reformers which they regarded as in keeping with the shared Christian spirit and its original traditions.

As we shall see, even in this case it is not easy to establish overly detailed interpretive norms or, above all, to sum up in short doctrinal definitions attitudes that were often transitory and in the course of time took on different meanings and goals. Thus while all the individuals of whom I shall speak were agreed on the necessity and inevitability of a reform of the Church "in head and members," they were not equally in agreement in defining the nature of this reform, the goals to be set for it, and its institutional, disciplinary, and doctrinal limits. So too, there was not yet full clarity on the role of anyone who continued for a long time to act within the not very tight meshes of a not yet clearly defined orthodoxy, moving between "simulation" and a firm belief in the wholly "Catholic" character of doctrines on justification and grace for which Augustine could be claimed as father in the distant past.

In any case, one trait seems to have been shared by many of the more important representatives of the Italian "Catholic Reform": their familiarity with the work and thought of Erasmus, with his idea of the "philosophy of Christ," and with his critical method and his call to irenicism to which he held so tenaciously even amid crises and ruptures now beyond healing. This was a characteristic found in such churchmen as the Augustinian Hermit Jerome Seripando, who was formed in the school of Giles of Viterbo; future bishop James Sadoleto, who corresponded so faithfully with Erasmus; and Cardinal Reginald Pole, who was so deeply influenced by the Dutch humanist and by Thomas More, to say nothing of the numerous men of letters, the secretaries, and the chaplains attached to the households of reform-minded cardinals and bishops, of such religious as the two Benedictine blood-brothers, Theophilus and John Baptist Folengo, and of persons to whom it is pointless to apply post-Tridentine standards and try to rank among the "orthodox" or the "heretics."

Admittedly, even the concept of "Erasmianism" must be used with care in order to prevent readings of him and sympathies common to so many educated men of sixteenth-century Italy (or on the contrary, aversions and disagreements quite widespread in many literary circles) from taking on too narrow a doctrinal significance, which they really never had. The fact remains, nonetheless, that across the entire range of reform movements, groups, and tendencies the Dutch humanist had a vast and deep influence, even if its results proved very diverse and in any case difficult to compare among themselves.

Take the case of Seripando (1493–1563),[89] who, as the favorite student of Giles of Viterbo, was directed by the latter to the study of Greek, Hebrew, and "Chaldean" as well as to a solid philosophical and theological formation that was inspired by the favorite doctrines of the Augustinian cardinal. After becoming a well-known preacher and a highly educated teacher, Seripando was vicar general of the Augustinians as early as 1538 and prior general in 1539; in that role he found himself faced with a serious crisis in his order. That order was for practical purposes dissolved in Germany and was elsewhere reduced by the passage of many religious to the Reformation; it was also the object of attacks and accusations because of the preaching of some of the friars, this being regarded as especially close to Lutheran views. In this difficult situation Seripando did not hesitate to condemn the teachings of the Reformers, but he was equally firm in defending Augustine's views on grace, justification, and predestination while also accepting the humanists' exegetical methods and their call for a return to the biblical and evangelical sources and to the teaching of the Fathers.

All this can be clearly seen in some of his more important theological writings that were composed during the period when the discussion of these subjects was especially searching and when it was becoming increasingly difficult to find a possible agreement with the Reformers through dialogue and peaceful theological debate. Such works were his *De duplici iustitia* and *Pro confirmanda sententia de duplici iustitia catholicorum quorundam doctrina* (1546), *De iustificatione* (1543), and *De peccato originali* (1546). In these writings the debate with the Reformed theologians was always closely connected with the intention of basing "Catholic" doctrine on original testimonies and "documents" and explaining, by recourse to Augustine and the Fathers and ancient Doctors, the meaning of these essential concepts that were now caught up in a controversialist clash in which there was danger of restoring, in masked form, Pelagian or Semipelagian teachings.

It is not surprising that Seripando should urge Paul III to convoke a council as the last hope of healing the "schism" and that he drew increasingly close to Reginald Pole and to his friends in the "Viterbian Church"—Victoria Colonna, Alvise Priuli, Victor Soranzo, and Mark Anthony Flaminio—although it is not clear how far he shared their more extreme theological views. Later on, when he had become archbishop of Salerno in 1554, he would continue to pursue reform goals; nor would he hide his disagreements with the very harsh and repressive pontificate of Paul IV, who would always be suspicious of him because of his relations with Pole and with Cardinal Morone, who had been put on trial for heresy. After the election of Pius IV, he would have a lengthy meeting with this pope in 1560 to ask him to resume the council and the reform of the Church. As secretary of the council after its resumption and as a cardinal, he would play a quite important and combative part in the debates on justification, in the drafting of the documents, and in plans for the drafting of the corresponding "decrees," although the sharp conflict with Cardinal Simonetta would cause him to fall into disfavor with the Roman See.

In keeping with the character of his education, Seripando was also an exegete who devoted his efforts as an expert and an educated reader of the sacred texts to his commentaries on the Pauline letters to the Corinthians, Thessalonians, Romans, and Galatians.[90] These works were published at a time of intense discussion of and great interest in the texts of Paul and Augustine, which were so often reprinted and read and publicly commented on in the thirties and early forties. This explains why this Augustinian's commentaries quickly became the object of criticism and suspicion regarding their orthodoxy.

This was also the period in which another reform-minded individual, James Sadoleto (1477–1547),[91] a graceful scholar and a secretary in the Curia, also gave himself to exegetical study (for example, a commentary on Psalm 90 dedicated to Frederick Fregoso and an interpretation, which today may seem ambiguous, of the letter to the Romans).[92] More than that: in 1530, in the serene shelter of his diocese of Carpentras, where he had taken refuge on the eve of the sack of Rome, Sadoleto wrote his *De liberis recte instituendis*,[93] followed by his *Hortensius, seu de laudibus philosophiae*,[94] a defense of humane letters and philosophical learning, inspired, like the *De liberis,* by the pedagogical writings of Erasmus. Sadoleto, too, considered a humanistic education to be the best way of turning students into wise and moral adults, while helping them at the same time to realize that they were "naturally" Christian. For this reason, after having been entrusted in their infancy to the family, children should learn grammar and rhetoric, poetry and music, arithmetic and geometry, from teachers. But the crown on their education was reached in the teaching of philosophy, which meant, of course, not the abstract science of the "Scholastics" but the ethical wisdom and "divine" metaphysics of Plato and Aristotle.

Sadoleto had no doubt that it is easy to lead children to goodness, because at their age they are naturally "good." For this reason he made his own the humanist norms of pedagogy and held that along with the development of a sincere and aware faith children should develop a sense of a personal, free, joyous participation in learning.

As a critic of the profoundly decadent state of the priesthood and ecclesiastical institutions and of the errors of popes and their advisers, Sadoleto found himself increasingly close to Erasmus, while also cultivating close but always rather reserved relations with the group of "reformers," for whom he had the natural sympathy of a religious man who was attracted by Erasmus' "philosophy of Christ." He was certainly a sincere opponent of Lutheran ideas, but he was this after the manner of Erasmus, even if more timidly and even ambiguously. His correspondence with the Dutch humanist sheds light on his deep spirituality and his thinking about the state of the Church and the possibility of surmounting a crisis that he felt as extremely "desolating."

In his view, in fact, the Reformation was not a rebellion to be put down with the usual means of suppression but a sign of the dissolution of Christian unity, a state hastened by the corruption of the Church and by the end of its primacy due to the power of princes no less than to the abuses of the hierarchy. He despaired of seeing the end of the "schism," being convinced that any possibility of reconciliation had now vanished. This did not keep him from disagreeing with Erasmus' excessively violent attacks on his Catholic critics and from cautioning him to proceed along the "peaceful" way of a constructive teaching of the true faith. But Erasmus was quick to reply that the doubts of the hierarchy about his orthodoxy were completely unjust and to contrast his "sincere" interventions against Luther with the "abuses" he himself had suffered from Jerome Aleandro and John Eck.[95]

Even after his return to Italy Sadoleto maintained a truly "Erasmian" outlook, based on the certainty that only by staying away from the factions that were tearing Christianity apart was it possible to work for the restoration of Christian unity. He was convinced that only men of letters, the members of Erasmus' "republic of letters," could work to this end, which was unattainable by those who involved themselves solely in "worldly" affairs. To the clashes of theological ideas, which he felt to be alien to his humanistic outlook, he opposed the search for a common Christian solidarity that would make it possible to find right in the gospel message, when this was interpreted with fraternal love, the resolution of the tragic ruptures of the Church's life.

9. The Theological Tendencies of the Catholic Reformers: Gaspar Contarini

The most outstanding individual in the reform movement within the Catholic Church was, however, Gaspar Contarini (1483–1542),[96] a member of one of the most important families of the Venetian patriciate; his participation in the controversies caused by Pomponazzi's *De immortalitate animae* was mentioned earlier.

After his initial studies at the School of San Marco and the School of the Rialto, he went on, in 1501, to the University of Padua as a student in the Faculty of Arts. Here he not only improved his knowledge of the classical language but also studied mathematics, astronomy, and philosophy under famous teachers, among them Pomponazzi himself, Alexander Achillini, Mark Musuro from Crete, and Benedict del Tiriaca. His real teacher was Pomponazzi, whom he followed in his esteem for Alexander of Aphrodisias' exegesis before settling for the Thomist conclusions, although these had not entirely done away with his serious doubts about a rational proof of the immortality of the soul.

The very serious political crisis of the Venetian state during and after the war with the League of Cambrai (which had led, among other things, to the closing of the studium in Padua) was the reason for his return to Venice in 1508. He continued, however, to develop his philosophical, mathematical, and theological interests, opening a kind of academy of friends that was soon frequented by some patricians of his own age (Thomas Giustiniani, Vincent Quirini, Nicholas Tiepolo, and Sebastian Zorzi) as well as by other intellectuals, such as John Baptist Egnazio and Trypho Gabriele, all of them linked by the same religious experiences.

Like Contarini, these men greatly desired a reform of their own Christian life, to be accomplished through a return to a pure gospel ethics, the study of Christian doctrine, personal meditation, and prayer. Like him again, and under the influence of criticism now widespread in many intellectual circles, they intended to abandon the secular sciences and the "empty sophisms" of Scholastic theology and turn to the reading of the Scriptures and the Fathers. For these, as Contarini wrote, "are wont to enlighten the minds of human beings and feed them with the very sweet food of truth, showing them how deep the darkness is of all worldly, I shall not say sciences, but follies."[97] The attitude of these men was, in short, not far removed from that which lay behind the skeptical attacks of John Francis Pico. In 1510, this continuous meditation on the transiency of all earthly goods and the "false" truths of the world led Giustiniani and then Quirini and Zorzi to abandon lay life, become Camaldolese monks, and submit themselves to a stern eremitical rule.[98]

For more than a decade, from 1511 to 1523, Contarini, who had not made the same choice and had prepared himself for the difficult course of a political and diplomatic career proper to a patrician, kept up a continuous correspondence with his Camaldolese friends. The letters are a mirror of his restless interior life, torn as it was between the attraction to the purity of ascetical meditation and the humanistic commitment to the "civic life" of dedication to the neighbor and of "service" to family and "city."[99] It is noteworthy, in particular, that in response to Giustiniani, who extolled the monastic and eremitical life as the highest level of Christian experience, the patrician insisted on regarding all forms of Christian life as fully equivalent when lived conscientiously and with an evangelical spiritual outlook; he denied that any one of them could be regarded as really "superior" and privileged. Nor was he disposed to accept the Camaldolese monk's radical rejection of secular studies (and of the classics, in particular), for he was convinced that the natural light of reason, too, is a gift from God and that even the ancient philosophers succeeded in grasping the correct ethical norms for human behavior.

Jedin has laid special emphasis on the intellectual and spiritual conflict which the still-young Contarini endured during those years, when he was still torn between participation in public life, philosophical studies, and a close association with the Benedictine circle of San Giorgio Maggiore; when, too, he was so filled with restlessness and religious tensions and so attentive, ever since the first news of them, to the religious innovations in Germany. The German historian had even seen emerging from Contarini's writings and memoirs a spiritual experience that in certain respects was very like that of Luther[100] but that, on the other hand, had a basis in frequently recurring themes in the preaching and books of devotion of that period.

Some of these themes were the inability of human beings to attain to salvation by their own powers; the insufficiency of any penance whatsoever or of any other human action really to satisfy the justice of God; and consequently, the need to trust solely in God's infinite goodness and in the "merits" and "favor" of Christ. This experience (according to Jedin) reached its dramatic climax on Holy Saturday, 1511, when Contarini became convinced that he could never cancel out his past sins and pay the debt he owed to God, so that his only hope was faith in Christ and in his suffering and death. Later on, his meditation on the second letter of Paul to the Corinthians would make him even surer that human beings are incapable of either thinking or doing any "good thing" by themselves.

During those years, Contarini did not give developed expression to this experience in a doctrinal form, although Jedin regarded it as decisive even for understanding his attitude to Luther and the Reformation. In fact, the point has frequently been made that Contarini's reading of the German reformer's writings went back only to the years around 1523, when the doctrine of justification became the focus of his theological reflection, which was always based on the idea of the "justice of Christ" as the sole cause of our salvation. He continued, however, his intense conversations with his Camaldolese friends; and in 1515 and 1516, in addition to cultivating friendly relations with the Florentine circle at the "Lichen Gardens" (in particular, with Ficinian philosopher, Francis Cattani of Diacceto),[101] he also became interested in Savonarola. He defended the latter's refusal to submit to ecclesiastical censures, and he seemed to approve the Dominican's prophetic interpretation of the Scriptures, concluding that the reform of the Church was demanded by "natural and divine reason."[102]

In this context, I shall say nothing more about the part Contarini played in the controversy over Pomponazzi's *De immortalitate animae,* which I discussed earlier.[103] I call attention rather to the fact that in 1517 he composed a work that already shows how he understood the needed reform: his *De officio viri boni ac probi episcopi.*[104] After explaining in Book I of this work the human and religious virtues he regarded as necessary for a bishop, he undertook to explain, above all, a bishop's duties, namely, a diligent participation in every activity of ecclesiastical service and ritual, and this in a pure evangelical spirit; a very great care of the faithful entrusted to him; a wise and just administration of the Church's possessions, which are to be regarded primarily as for the benefit of "the poor of Christ"; and a generous and constant beneficence.

The book extolled, and proposed as a model, Peter Barozzi, bishop of Padua, the one who had sternly forbidden discussions of the immortality of the soul.[105] In fact, however, even the picture of this prelate served to render even more explicit the writer's condemnation of many aspects of the spiritual and disciplinary decadence of the Church: the worldly power and pomp of the hierarchy; the failure of bishops to reside in their diocese and their lack of pastoral care; the profound ignorance of too many churchmen; the superstition fostered in the interests of some orders; the moral corruption of many monastic institutes, especially those of women. These were conclusions in harmony with what his Camaldolese friends had written as early as 1513, in their *Libellus ad Leonem X,* a free and eloquent denunciation of the many evils and corruptions of the Church's life.[106]

In 1520, when elected by the republic as its "orator," or spokesman at the imperial court of Charles V, Contarini had his first direct encounter with the German Reformation, and though he did not meet Luther and criticized his attitude to the Diet of Worms, he did not hide his good opinion of some of the reformers' demands. Then, after going to Spain in the emperor's retinue, he began to reflect again, in his *Primae philosophiae compendium,* on the limits of the human mind and its inability to grasp the very mysterious divine truth but also on the virtues of reason, which can free human beings from the passions and make them more able to turn to God. Thus he used reason to describe in this book the wise order of the universe, which he conceived as a system of hierarchically ordered perfections with God at its summit as source and foundation of everything, followed by the angelic intelligences, the heavenly bodies, human beings, animals, plants, metals and the elements, all of these bound together in a single cosmic harmony.

This was evidently a philosophical treatise that drew its inspiration from both Aristotle and Plato but that was also close, in more than one respect, to the Ficinian thinking of Francesco Cattani of Diacceto. The theme of "order," meaning the source and foundation of every right natural and human arrangement, also played a central role in *De magistratibus et Republica Venetorum,* the work in which Contarini extolled the Venetian constitution and which contributed so much to the spread throughout Europe of the "myth of Venice" as a model of the greatest political and institutional stability.

This is not the place for speaking of the years between 1525, when Contarini returned to Venice, and 1535, which were devoted first and foremost to an intense political, administrative, and diplomatic activity in the service of the republic. These labors, however, did not prevent him either from engaging in theologico-political controversy with his *De potestate pontificis quod divinitus sit tradita,* which was a staunch defense of the spiritual authority of the Roman pontiff, or from cultivating increasingly close relations with Reginald Pole, Alvise Priuli, Mark Anthony Flaminio, John Matthew Giberti, Ludovico Beccadelli, some members of the *Compagnia del Divino Amore,* and also with John Peter Carafa (the future Paul IV), with whose severe ideas on reform he agreed but not with his plan for a harsh repression of heresy. These were the circles in which, after the general agreement on reform that marked the early days, contrasting views and increasingly visible ruptures were emerging as ideas of an obviously "reformation" kind were circulating.

But even in these years, as is shown by the writings addressed to Trypho Gabriele from 1530 to 1532, Contarini remained faithful to his philosophical formation. Thus when discussing the relation between will and intellect, between the speculative virtues and the ethical virtues, he voiced his preference for a "middle way" of acting, between pure speculation and action, even though he appealed to Pseudo-Dionysius to show that supreme happiness consists in the final union and complete "absorption" of the human person in God. Nor had he forgotten his scientific and philosophical interests when, in 1531, he wrote a commentary on the *Homocentrica* of Jerome Fracastoro, and when, in his *De elementis et eorum mixtione,* in which he argued against divinational astronomy, he turned to his beloved ancient philosophers and made full use of the teachings of Aristotle and Galen.

On the other hand, in 1530 he directed a fully argued criticism against the *Confessio augustana* in his *Confutatio articulorum seu quaestionum lutheranorum.* But in its tone his discourse was completely lacking in polemical violence and was marked rather by a sustained, sincere call for *concordia* and by a concern for ethical reform that was influenced hardly at all by the inescapable implications of certain doctrinal and institutional changes.

When, despite curial resistance, Paul III appointed Contarini a cardinal on May 21, 1535, the action seemed to signify the definitive acceptance of the reform party. He immediately devoted himself with great zeal to sacred studies, along with Beccadelli, John of Kempen, and Peter Danès, who was rather close to the Reformation. In 1535 he intervened in a controversy that arose between Sadoleto and Thomas Badia, Master of the Sacred Palace, with regard to the banning of Sadoleto's *In Pauli Epistolam ad Romanos libri tres*. Contarini acknowledged that the author had departed too much from Augustinian teaching on justification, but he looked for some way to achieve reconciliation; in 1537, on the other hand, he associated himself with the condemnation of the ambiguous Cabalism and "problematic" exegesis of Francis Zorzi, which had likewise so worried Frederick Fregoso and Paul Cortese.[107]

The moment of Contarini's loftiest and final commitment was drawing near. On April 8, 1536, the consistory had already appointed him to the commission charged with establishing the dogmatic directions for the coming council; his colleagues on the commission were Carafa, Sadoleto, Pole, Fregoso, Giberti, Aleandro, Badia, and Cortese. A few months later, having been appointed bishop of Cividale and Belluno, he made known his own pastoral intentions in his *Modus concinandi,*[108] an instruction for the preachers of that diocese. In it he exhorted them to express themselves in clear and simple languages and to make the faithful aware that human weakness will not allow them to arise from sin without divine help, which is granted through the merits of Christ. But he forbade them to preach justification "without works" and obliged them not to insist too much on the "weakness" of our will, lest the "uninstructed" surrender to a "lethargy of will."

The commission began its work in November 1536 and ended it in March 1537 when it presented Paul III with its *Consilium de emendanda Ecclesia,* of which I shall speak further on.[109] It is impossible, of course, to determine precisely the part that Contarini played in the composition of a document that was so important in the ecclesiastical history of the sixteenth century. But it has been correctly observed that the *Consilium* bore the strong imprint of the spirituality of Venetian reform circles, some of whose demands and fundamental proposals it accepted.[110]

The document immediately elicited strong reactions from curial circles, and these became even harsher when Contarini and Carafa, subsequently joined by Badia and Aleandro, were delegated to reform the datary. Contarini thought, in fact, that many decisions made by this office were at odds with the very foundations of Church law and were even suspect of simony; at least initially, Carafa, too, seemed to accept his thinking, which was expressed, although with some inevitable softening, in the *Consilium quattuor delectorum cardinalium* and confirmed by the Venetian cardinal in his *De potestate papae in compositionibus* (an *epistola* written in the summer of 1538) and in his *De potestate clavium,*[111] in which, without challenging the authority of the pope, he maintained that papal authority was indeed subject to the "power of reason."

In 1539, when his first disagreements with Carafa were already emerging, Contarini was also assigned to the reform of the Penitentiary, for which he had a plan that was already complete in the summer of 1540. But he devoted his greatest efforts to the commission "for matters having to do with the council," since he was convinced that only the supreme assembly in Christendom could heal the rupture that had shattered it. He did not fail, however, to tackle once again the great theological subject of "justification," sending Lactantius Tolomei a letter, *Della predestinazione,*[112] as early as 1537. As soon as this letter became known, it gave rise to very lively discussions and disputes, in which Flaminio, Seripando, and Dominic de Cupis, among others, took part.

The cardinal once again took a position against those of a Pelagian mentality who attributed too much value to the human will and "played down" divine grace, forgetting our radical weakness from which Christ alone can deliver us. But he distinguished his position from that of the strictest followers of Augustinian teaching, because, he said, God grants "prevenient grace" even to the reprobate, who, by use of free will, can either accept it or refuse it. Historians have given very different and even opposed assessments of this attempt of Contarini to "mediate" between the theological views that doubtless prevailed in the theological debate of the time but were now irreconcilable. They have frequently underscored, in addition to the subtlety and cleverness of Contarini's views, the impossibility of coping with a doctrinal conflict that went far beyond formulas and efforts to achieve a balance in teaching. Some historians have also seen Contarini displaying increasingly the cautious attitude of a diplomat who was aware of the extreme complexity of the political and religious crisis but who was, for this very reason, far removed now from the spiritual tension he had experienced in his youth.

In any case, even Contarini's enlightened attitude as "mediator" and the irenicist cast of his ecclesiastical policy were checkmated for good by the failure of the last attempt which he made to achieve religious peace during his unsuccessful mission in Germany in 1541. It is not possible to reconstruct with certainty the complex events of an episode that was in many respects decisive for the religious history of the sixteenth century: from the compilation by Bucer and Gropper of the so-called Book of Ratisbon (examined by Morone, Badia, and Contarini himself) to the difficult and endless discussions of the doctrine of the Eucharist, penance, and the ecclesiastical hierarchy and to the working out of the theory of "double justification," which was put forward as the basis for a last attempt at agreement. Contarini explained this theory in the *Epistola de justificatione* that was sent to Cardinal Ercole Gonzaga on May 25, 1541.[113] In it he argued that salvation is based solely on the "justice of Christ" and not on a justice inherent in the human being, which is utterly insufficient unless it is completed by that which is imputed by Christ.

As is well known, this letter, the author of which was initially unknown, immediately gave rise to new controversies. Even Sadoleto wrote a decisive criticism of it in his *De iustitia nobis inhaerente, et de iustitia Christi imputata,* where his judgment was that the doctrine maintained was closer to Lutheran than to orthodox teaching. Like Sadoleto, other theologians were of the opinion that the letter undervalued works to a dangerous degree, whereas in fact works were an assertion of the human capacity for cooperating with divine grace.

In addition, the laboriously achieved agreement on predestination, which was immediately disavowed by both sides, and the growing controversies over his teachings had now weakened Contarini's position as a churchman; there were accusations of heresy and of having violated the pope's instructions. The final failure of the talks put an end to his mission and allowed him to return, as early as the autumn, to his never-interrupted work of preparation for the conciliar assembly, which he wanted to see convoked for the spring of 1542 in Mantua. But even during these very difficult and bitter years he continued to compose new works for the theological formation of clergy and preachers (*De sacramentis christianae legis et catholicae Ecclesiae,* 1540; *Instructio pro praedicatoribus,* 1541); to work for the reform of the episcopate; and to prepare in advance, together with other "spiritual" men, the defense of the reformist principles which he now felt were threatened by the return in force of the conservatives and by Carafa's doctrinal and disciplinary inflexibility.

His appointment as legate in Bologna in January of 1542 marked the end of his influence. Still close to Pole and Sadoleto but bitterly attacked by Dominican Ambrose Catarino Politi, Contarini found time to compose the *Formulario di fede* that was signed in September by a group in Modena who were suspected of heterodoxy and to defend them in his *De poenitentia* against the objections of some friends. But by August 17 he had been stricken with the illness that was to bring him to the grave in a few days. Shortly before his death he had a conversation with Bernardine Ochino, who had been summoned to Rome by the Inquisition; but we do not know whether the cardinal really advised the celebrated Capuchin preacher to flee. What is certain is that Contarini's death, together with the banishment of two such very well known "spirituals" as Ochino and Vermigli, marked a turning point in the religious history of the sixteenth century: the passage from a plan for the radical renewal of institutions and doctrines to the disciplinary severity and doctrinal intransigence of the age of the Counterreformation.

10. The Theological Tendencies of the Catholic Reformers: Reginald Pole

Among the "reform-minded" churchmen who worked closely with Contarini was an English prelate, a member of the House of York, Cardinal Reginald Pole (1500–58).[114] We know the events of his life as a young man:

he studied in Cambridge, in Padua, where he lived from 1521 to 1527, and in Paris, where he was in 1530. While in Paris, despite his personal opposition he was compelled to ask the Sorbonne for a declaration of nullity of the marriage of Catherine of Aragon with Henry VIII, the king who had given him patronage and protection and for whom, at that time, he felt loyalty and admiration. This attitude of his changed radically, however, in the years that followed, when, despite his being offered the archepiscopal See of York, he refused to agree with the ecclesiastical policy of the English king and defended his own position in a work that has not come down to us.

In 1532 Pole was once again in Italy, where, admirer that he was of Erasmus and Thomas More, he quickly became friendly with the reform-minded humanists and the "spirituals," such as Sadoleto, Bembo, and above all, Contarini and Cortese. As was customary in those years, he also devoted himself to a close reading and study of the sacred texts. Two years later he rejected a new attempt of Henry VIII to recall him to England; the break became final in 1535 when Thomas More and John Fisher were executed. After that, in 1536, he wrote his *Pro ecclesiasticae unitatis defensione libri quattuor,*[115] a sharp indictment of the king and a strong defense of Catholic unity, though it did not exclude and even fully accepted the necessity of a reform.

In November of 1536 Pole was named a cardinal and, shortly afterwards, became a member of the commission on reform. But he was also papal legate to England and, in this capacity, did his best to convince Charles V to declare war on the schismatic king. It was around 1538, the year in which his brother Henry was executed, that he wrote the work that is the most important for understanding his spirituality, a work of great charm and evidence of a prophetic calling: his *Apologia.*[116] The work remained unpublished for a long time, but it was undoubtedly known in some intellectual circles. It was not only an indictment and irrevocable condemnation of Henry VIII but a persistent, radical attack on Machiavelli, whose "satanic" teachings had, via the advice of Thomas Cromwell, inspired the entire conduct of the king. Pole had no doubt that Machiavelli's teaching was entirely hostile to and subversive of Christianity and that it was even an expression of a diabolical plan meant to set up a world of pretense against revelation. This teaching was the work of the Antichrist who, according to Pole's apocalyptic vision of history, will show himself in the age of the new coming of Christ and before his final victory.

Evidently, even Machiavellianism with its godless reduction of religion to a mere tool of power was, in the cardinal's view, a sign of a proximate *renovatio.* For to oppose this renewal, a diabolical plot had been hatched that relied on the circulation of *The Prince,* this being a kind of satanic "apocryphon" or "secret book" to be drawn on by wicked advisers, "the messengers" of the Antichrist and the corruptors of rulers. Clearly, too, Pole considered that the duty of unmasking this most terrible of deceptions was connected with his own prophetic destiny as one called upon to work with others for the return of the Christian world to unity and harmony in the true evangelical and apostolic faith.

This explains why, in the years that followed, Pole was always at Contarini's side in the search for a possible meeting ground with the Protestants and especially with the Protestant theologians who were humanists, such as Melanchthon, and with the followers of Erasmus, who certainly were not lacking among them. Two theological themes in particular attracted him and undoubtedly brought him close to the spirituality of the Reformers: justification based on faith and salvation through the "imputed" justice of Christ. We can understand why his household was made up of persons of a stern and sincere religious spirit, some of whom subsequently went over to the Reformation, and why he cultivated friendships with intellectuals such as Flaminio and Carnesecchi, whom the teaching of Valdés had persuaded to adhere in conscience to doctrines difficult to distinguish from those of the Reformers.

The failure of the talks in Ratisbon, the death of Contarini, and the crisis among the "spirituals" after the first flights: all these affected Pole in some measure. In 1541 he was sent to Viterbo as legate to the Patrimony of St. Peter. Around him there gradually formed what was later called "the Church of Viterbo" *(ecclesia viterbiensis),* which was composed of persons who, in the following years, were to be the focus of serious suspicions, growing accusations, and even trials and condemnations: Carnesecchi, Flaminio, Bartholomew and Francis Stella, Apollonius Merenda, who fled to Geneva, Fregoso, and Vittoria Colonna. Recent historiography has been especially attentive to the doctrinal and spiritual tendencies of this group and of its protector and has emphasized their great similarity to the theological ideas of the Reformers.[117] It has also debated the part which Pole may have had in promoting the writing and circulation of *Beneficio di Cristo,* the work of Benedictine Benedict Fontanini but revised and reworked by Flaminio and Carnesecchi.[118]

This is certainly not the place to enter into the still-recent discussion of the complex circumstances of this little book and of its special fortunes. It is more to the point here to recall that after being appointed papal legate to the Council of Trent in 1545, Pole not only disapproved of the draft decree on justification, but on June 28, 1546, he even left Trent and withdrew to Treville to the country house of his very close friend, Alvise Priuli, giving illness as an excuse. Jedin has recognized that the "decisive motive" for his absence and then of his resignation was his disagreement with a dogmatic decree which he judged inopportune and opposed to the doctrine of "double justification," which he interpreted in a way "nearer to Luther."[119]

Then came the conclave of 1549, at which Pole seemed the most likely to be elected pope, thanks to a complex interplay of political interests that coalesced around his name, to the support of a large number of the Catholic reformers, but also to the plans of powerful and ambitious churchmen. Carafa openly accused him of heresy, and, while he then withdrew his charge, the arrival of the French cardinals, led by Charles of Guise, and the renewal of suspicion and accusations barred the way to the cardinal from England. He was again a candidate for the papacy in the two conclaves of 1555, even though he had already retired to private life at the abbey of Maguzzano; and the Inquisition, led by Carafa, was already carefully examining his views.

But Pole, who had already begun his *De summo pontifice in terris vicario, eiusque officio et potestate liber,* a full reassertion of his loyalty to the Roman Church and its supreme hierarchy,[120] was henceforth involved in the final and most dramatic events of his life: the new mission to England after the ascent of Mary the Catholic to the throne.

Although he left Maguzzano in September of 1553, complicated questions of high-level European politics along with his own diplomatic mistakes prevented his returning to his native land until the late autumn of 1554. As papal legate and then, beginning in 1556, as archbishop of Canterbury and primate of England, he became involved in the attempted Catholic restoration and in the rebellions and bloody repressions and persecutions that followed from it. He was thus, once again, the object of very strong attacks by Peter Paul Vergerio (the Younger), who reproached him for his acceptance of the doctrine of "justification by faith alone" and his lengthy "pretence."[121] Next, his zeal against the English heretics did not keep Carafa, now pope, from beginning a formal inquisitorial process against him in 1555, removing him as legate, and demanding his return to Rome in order to clear himself of the charge of heresy.

Death, which came on November 18, 1558, saved him from this final trial. But in the *Apologia* which he wrote in his defense, while once again stating his loyalty to the Roman See, he did not avoid reconstructing the history of his long disagreement with Carafa, condemning papal policy which he regarded as mistaken and dangerous and fervently reminding the pope of his "paternal" obligations.[122]

11. John Peter Carafa and the Consilium de Emendanda Ecclesia

Fenlon has written that the incident of the *Apologia* (which, it is said, the author threw into the fire, but a copy was saved) was in keeping with the history of the Italian "spirituals" (and, I may add, of their unavoidable "ambiguity" in their lengthy attempt to find agreements, convergences, and "harmonies" that were by now impossible). On the other hand, John Peter Carafa (1476–1559), bishop of Chieti, then cardinal, and finally Pope Paul IV, was a man who never had any doubts and always had as his fundamental goal the full restoration of the power, authority, and supreme "rank" *(dignitas)* of the Church.[123] And yet, for a by no means short time, his activity as a churchman who looked solely to a stern ethical and disciplinary reform of institutions brought him rather close to the "spirituals," with whom he collaborated on the cardinalatial commission for reform and with whom he cultivated relations and friendships that were due, above all, to agreement on certain goals.

He was an inflexible guardian of orthodoxy and always very distrustful of any possible disciplinary or theoretical softening. He remained always faithful to the program of restoration of the traditional traits of the Church, whose decadence he did not hide and whose most serious ills he identified and attacked but without acknowledging, and while even rejecting, the new religious sensibility that was being manifested in the theological views of Contarini and Pole. It must be said that this outlook always guided his behavior, whether as bishop, or as a "brother" of the "Oratory of Divine Love," which numbered various "spirituals" among its members, or as founder, along with St. Gaetano of Thiene (+ 1547), of one of the most rigid and combative orders of the Counterreformation, or as a member of the commission on reform, or as the soul of the Roman Inquisition, or finally, as pope.

In any case, a reading of the *Memoriale per la Controriforma* (actually a letter-instruction sent to Clement VII on October 4, 1552, from Venice, where Carafa had taken refuge with some Theatines after the sack of Rome and where he engaged in caritative activity at the Ospedale degli Incurabili) leaves no doubts about how the bishop of Chieti conceived the reform. It leaves no doubts about his intention to transform an ethical renewal and a renewal of ecclesiastical discipline into a strong tool in the fight against heresy, which had to be stamped out everywhere and in any way, and in the restoration of Catholic unity under the banner of intransigence and the unwearying defense of orthodoxy and the Church's interests.

Carafa was undoubtedly the first (and remained this until he became pope, when he yielded for a while to the ancient temptation of "nepotism") to respect, and make others respect, his austere sense of morality, order, and Catholic discipline. For that reason he did not hesitate to oppose papal demands that seemed to him at odds with the norms of justice and the standards of right government of the Church's institutions. He was also a model of sincere piety and fervent charity, in keeping with some tendencies already typical of the first Italian movements for renewal of the Church. But when faced with the trauma of the Reformation and the spiritual and political crises to which it led, his reaction was essentially repressive. We know, too, the decisive part he played in preparing the tools of inquisition and control that subsequently were characteristic of the Counterreformation, especially after the failure of the final attempt to secure religious peace.

We can understand, then, his growing mistrust and aversion for the "spirituals," his special hostility toward Pole (whom he soon suspected of secret sympathy for the Reformation), the support he gave to the most resolute enemies of every "suspect" innovation, the energy he put into unmasking "Nicodemite" attitudes and coming down hard on any "deviation" whatsoever, and finally, his great fear, which was almost an obsession, that heresy might take hold of the Roman Church by creeping into the highest levels of the hierarchy. Inspired as he was during the first phase of the council by the most rigid theological tendencies but distrustful of an institution so difficult to control and so subject to the influence of powers outside the Church, he did not convoke it again after its suspension in 1552. As a result, his pontificate was characterized above all by steps to improve the morality of the clergy and hierarchy (with the imposition of a stern discipline even on the cardinals of the Curia) and by reforms that required a shrewd choice of bishops, combatted priestly concubinage, and obliged all "regulars" to return to common life.

The Roman Curia, too, was reorganized through the formation of commissions and congregations that were the embryonic forms of the future Roman congregations; at the same time, in measures that had long been desired by reformers, the revenues of the datary were stopped and those that came to cardinals from the bestowal of benefices were lessened. But the pope's favorite tool and one whose jurisdiction and powers were increased to an extraordinary degree was the Roman Inquisition, which was commissioned to proceed even against blasphemy, failures to fast, rapists, pimps, and sodomites. In 1555, when he had barely taken office, he issued the bull *Cum quorundam hominum* in which he set down very strict norms for dealing with Antitrinitarians and with deniers of Christ's divinity or his conception by the Holy Spirit and the virginity of Our Lady.

Moreover, as everyone knows, he was the first pope to publish an *Index* of books that were contrary to the faith and were to be burned. He did not fail to take steps no less harsh against the Jews, who were compelled to wear distinctive signs and were enclosed in ghettoes in Rome and Bologna; he revived the persecution of the "marranos" and the order to destroy Jewish books. Finally, his hunt for heresy reached even the highest places in the Church with the famous trial of Cardinal Morone, the inquisition prepared against Pole, and the arrest and sentencing of other bishops and dignitaries of the Church and the orders.

In any accounting, Carafa's pontificate meant the definitive downfall of the theological and, in a broad sense, political line taken by Contarini, Pole, and their fellows. And yet, not many years before, this same future pope had collaborated with them in composing a document that represented, as I pointed out earlier, the joint proposal of the reformers: the *Consilium delectorum cardinalium et aliorum praelatorum de emendanda Ecclesia*.[124]

The *Consilium*, which had been drawn up in 1537, was a plan that brought together very different concerns and proposals while forcefully attacking the causes of the decadence of the Roman Church. It locates these causes, in the first place, in the boundless extension of papal "power" resulting from the adulation of the canonists, who had come to think of the pope not as the "administrator" of benefices but as their "master." The document also condemned the poor observance of laws that, in the Church as in all societies, should form a strong and sure rule; in particular it regarded as harmful the excessive granting of "dispensations" of every kind, even though these should have been rare exceptions granted only for extraordinary reasons and without any thought of gain.

The cardinals then dealt at length with the difficult question of benefices, which were granted without checking to see whether the petitioners were worthy of them and which were the source then of many abuses connected with the waiver of residence, of the many tricks used to get around the canonical regulations, and of the disorders that always followed from them. Above all, the cardinals emphasized the crisis in discipline and ecclesiastical morals. The care of souls was being seriously neglected because priests and bishops did not reside among their "flocks"; too many convents and monasteries, especially of women, were places of corruption; schools and the circulation of books were not properly controlled; meanwhile, the Curia generously granted dispensations and other "favors," especially in the areas of sensitive marriage questions, the absolution of simoniacs, and release from vows. Finally, even in Rome itself, divine worship had degenerated, as though to signal the universal abandonment of pure and holy Christian morals.

The remedies for this tragic situation were proposed no less explicitly and firmly. It was necessary to exercise the greatest strictness in observing, and seeing to the observance of, all ecclesiastical laws. Priests and bishops had to be chosen from among persons worthy of their ministry and always to be supervised by the better prelates; residence had to be required of clergy and bishops, and those who lived at a distance were to be excluded from ecclesiastical benefices. Another urgently needed step was a prohibition against bestowing more than one benefice on the same person, thus putting an end to the scandalous disorders resulting from waivers of residence.

But it was no less essential that the cardinals no longer allow the conferral of bishoprics by princes, lest the bishops lose their independence. In addition, the disciplinary norms to be immediately put into practice were no less drastic. Convents "ruined" beyond repair were to be abandoned to their lot or allowed to disappear; all monasteries of women were to be placed under the discipline of the bishops, to whom was also given the task of choosing, with the greatest care, preachers and confessors for these monasteries; a strict watchfulness over schools and printeries would stem the spread of "insane" teachings, while it was also necessary to avoid any public discussion of difficult and complicated theological questions. Above all, the *Consilium* asked that all concessions by the Curia be limited to the greatest possible degree, especially those having to do with the abuse of indulgences. It also asked the pope to look out for divine worship everywhere so as to restore it, especially in Rome, to its ancient purity; to enforce respect for morality; and to raise up and promote caritative institutions.

As the reader sees, these demands were primarily of the disciplinary kind and did not touch on the basic reasons for the theological opposition between the Roman Church and the various Protestant confessions, as if the return to a "holy way" of Christian life could heal this most serious rupture within Western Christianity. They were, however, in addition, a response to the many accusations that had been directed, even before the Reformation, at the Curia and the Roman hierarchies and that Luther had repeated in his harshly eloquent way and in full agreement with Erasmus and so many other religious men, who remained, then and later, loyal to Catholic orthodoxy. It was also possible to hear in the *Consilium* echoes of the now-distant preaching of Savonarola that had not been silenced even by the pyre in 1498.

But, while the plan of these reformers, which was implemented in great part later on in the disciplinary measures of the post-Tridentine Church, implicitly confirmed the existence of the "scandals" attacked by the Protestants, it did not offer any way of untangling the knots of theological controversy that had already acquired inflexible dogmatic forms. Nor did it recognize the henceforth unbridgeable opposition between increasingly divergent ways of understanding and living the gospel message, divergent ways that were for that matter present even in the Church and in the Catholic hierarchy itself.

It was not by chance that the *Consilium,* which was meant to be secret, was instead soon made public in Rome and Milan, as early as the beginning of 1538, thus providing new food for Protestant attacks. Shortly afterwards, Reformed humanist John Sturm reprinted it at Strasbourg. In his introduction, Sturm credited Contarini in particular with having proposed drastic and courageous measures; but he regretted that the Catholic reformers had missed the deepest cause of the evils afflicting Christianity and the significance of doctrines that called for a return to the truth of its origins.

12. The Theological Literature of the Early Sixteenth Century in Southern Italy

This short survey of theological ideas in the first half of the sixteenth century needs to be completed by at least a reference to those literary and poetical works that spread knowledge of especially important theological doctrines and problems among educated circles, especially in the culture of the south. The first and most interesting of the authors in question was James Sannazzaro (1457–1530),[125] a refined humanist at the court of Aragon. After returning home in the retinue of Frederick of Aragon from his exile in France, he shifted the focus of his poetry from love to meditation on the mystery of the incarnation and of Christ's saving mediation—a subject which, as we have seen, was also central to the experience of the "spirituals." He was a friend and correspondent of Sadoleto.

He devoted the last part of his life to the composition of his *De partu Virginis,*[126] a poem marked by the purest humanism but based on the reading of ancient Christian writers such as Sedulius, Juvencus, Prudentius, and

Paulinus of Nola. It took a long time to complete: from a first draft in 1513, to an unauthorized and semiclandestine printing in 1520–23, to its definitive publication in 1526. In its three books Sannazzaro dealt respectively with the annunciation, the nativity, and the adoration of the shepherds and the Magi, putting a classical style at the service of the most profound Christian doctrine. It was obviously his intention to devote the epic-heroic structure of the poem to the exaltation of the God-man who had rescued the human race from its original guilt and made it able once again to receive divine grace.

Anthony de Ferraris, known as Il Galateo (1448–1517),[127] belonged to the same cultural environment as Sannazzaro. Anthony was a humanist who had gone from his native Apulia to Naples and then to Florence before becoming a physician at the court of King Ferdinand I in about 1490. In his relations with humanist circles in the south and especially with Ermolaus Barbarus (to whom in 1491 he addressed a rather polemical letter against the classical "barbarian" philosophers and in defense of *eloquentia,* but equally critical of the *grammatici* and even of Valla) Il Galateo was a firm defender of the Church's temporal power and descended into the arena against Valla's refutation of the authenticity of the Donation of Constantine.[128]

For us, however, his most interesting works are his *Epistola ad Antonium Lupiensem episcopum de distinctione humani generis et nobilitate* and his *Dialogus de heremita.*[129] The *Epistola* is a typical humanist composition on the wholly interior nature of human "nobility." In the *Heremita* the protagonist is Il Galateo himself, a faithful Christian who decides to withdraw from life in the world and to devote himself in solitude to contemplation. The humanist tells of how feeling close to death, he realized that his soul, which the angels had defended in vain, would fall into the devil's power if it did not succeed in an effort to free itself from its captivity and take refuge in the realm of the blessed. This is a clear poetic allusion to the power of faith, which can deliver human beings from their sins and destine them for salvation.

In the second part of the dialogue, however, the humanist undertakes a bold satire on the behavior of various saints and patriarchs who had acted weakly and inconstantly during their lives on earth; then he offers proof, though in a somewhat rationalistic way, that God is supreme wisdom.

The same motifs are again fairly clear in the *Esposizione del Pater Noster,*[130] which de Ferraris sent as a homage to Isabella of Aragon in 1507–8 and which is striking in its insistent references to the political and religious decadence of the age. But these were attitudes rather widespread in the contemporary culture, especially in the world of the humanists, who were so involved in religious dissent during the decades bridging the two centuries.

Scipio Capece (1480–1551), a jurist and an important personage in the government of the kingdom of Naples, belonged to a younger generation of humanists.[131] At an advanced age he was strongly attracted by the preaching of Bernardine Ochino and the teaching of Valdés. Julius Basalù's *Memoriale* to the Venetian Inquisition in 1555 denounced him as one who denied the divinity of Christ and championed a "justification by faith alone." It was undoubtedly due to suspicions, religious and political, that he was ousted as councilor of the sacred royal council and exiled to Salerno, where he was protected by Prince Ferrante Sanseverino. In 1533 he had written his *De vate maximo,* three books of hexameters on the life of John the Baptist, evidently written to rival and oppose Sannazzaro's *De partu Virginis.* Now, in Salerno, in 1546, he finished his best-known work, *De principiis rerum.* In it he criticized the teachings of Epicurus and Lucretius and rejected the hypothesis that matter is eternal. In addition, his Christianity, so rich in echoes of Erasmus and the Gospel, manifested a religious attitude that was rather opposed to the incipient Counterreformation climate and that even his cautious and closely monitored language did not succeed in concealing.

A philosopher, Simon Porzio (1496–1554), also belonged to this world of the south.[132] The events of his academic career are well known, from his studies in Pavia to his teaching at the universities of Pisa and Naples. He produced various works (I shall mention only his *De fato, De arbitrio, De animi motibus,* and *De partibus animi*) that were partly translated into the vernacular by John Baptist Gelli. He was above all, however, a learned commentator on the works of Aristotle, which he discussed with critical acumen, and a resolute supporter of a sharp separation between philosophical exegesis and theological doctrine.

In his *Disputatio de humana mente,*[133] published in Florence in 1555, he criticized all interpretations of Aristotle that regarded the agent intellect as completely "separated" or identified it even with God and thereby rendered the real process of human understanding incomprehensible. Thus he rejected both the Averroist and the Alexandrian solutions, behind which he saw a hidden Platonic propensity constantly reappearing and an inevitable commingling of theological concerns with pure philosophical analysis. As a man rather attentive to the development of the scientific ideas of his age, his intention was to see the human intellect *(mens)* as a work of nature completely integrated into the "composite" of matter and form, while he left it to the theologians to deal with the souls according to the norms of faith. He also admitted, indeed, that in its activity this intellect diffuses into things a power or, better still, a divine light that is impassible and immutable. This did not mean, however, that the soul's role as "instrument" implied its immortality, at least not according to the standards and demonstrative abilities of reason.

Porzio maintained this position in its essence even in his *Apologia* (published by James Anthony Marta only in 1578), in which the distinction between philosophical reflection and theological dogma was still kept, although the acknowledgment of the illuminative role and the impassibility of the intellectual faculty was more explicit and more eloquently put. But his innermost conviction was certainly best expressed in his *De rerum naturalium principiis*, published at Naples in 1553, in which his Aristoteleanism took on an openly naturalistic tonality and reached openly naturalistic conclusions. Nor was it a matter of chance that in approximately the same time period, when discussing freedom and fate as a philosopher (in his *An homo bonus vel malus volens fiat*, published in Florence in 1551), he acknowledged that it was impossible on a rational basis to attribute to the human person the freedom of will that belongs only to one who exists of himself *(gratia sui)*.

Porzio's thinking, which contained ideas and reflections rather close to those of Pomponazzi, thus once again, at mid-century, dealt with themes and doctrines that were to acquire a special polemical force not many years later in the naturalistic philosophies of the late sixteenth century. Above all, it was a sign of a new speculative trend that was emerging from the lengthy exegetical controversies on the works of Aristotle and his commentators and was leading to a new way of looking at nature. The processes and "forces" of nature were to be investigated without any theological purpose or regard, and this new outlook was already inclined to present itself as the only teaching capable of bringing to light the intrinsic divinity of a universe that could henceforth no longer be separated from its absolute Cause.

BIBLIOGRAPHY

Paul Cortesi (Cortesius, de Cortesiis) (Rome, 1465–San Gimignano, 1510)

EDITIONS

In quattuor libros Sententiarum disputationes. Rome, 1504.
De cardinalatu. San Gimignano, 1510 (?).

STUDIES

Pintor, F. *Da lettere inedite dei due fratelli umanisti, Alessandro e Paolo Cortesi*. Perugia, 1907.
Zabughin, V. *Giulio Pomponio Leto* I. Rome, 1909. Pp. 12–14, 160–62.
Dorez, L. "Les maîtres intellectuels du pape Paul III." *Études italiennes,* N.S. 1 (1931) 5–13.
Garin, E. "Il carteggio di Pico della Mirandola." *La Rinascita* 5 (1942) 590.
Paschini, P. "Tre illustri prelati del Rinascimento, Ermolao Barbaro, Adriano Castellesi, Giovanni Grimani." *Lateranum,* N.S. 23 (1957) 43–130 at 113 and 118.
_____. "Una familglia di curiali di Rome nel Quattrocento: i Cortesi." *RSCI* 11 (1957) 1–48.

Dionisotto, C. "Chierici e laici nella letteratura italiana." *Atti del Convegno di storia della Chiesa in Italia*. Bologna, 1958. Pp. 176–85.

————. "Umanisti dimenticati?" *Italia medioevale e umanistica* 4 (1961) 287–321 at 302–3.

————. "Questioncine sulle opere progettate da Paolo Cortesi." *Studi di bibliografia e di storia in onore di Tammaro de Marinis* I. Verone, 1963. Pp. 273–80.

Graziosi, M. T. "Note su Paolo Cortesi e il dialogo *De hominibus doctis*." *Annuali dell'Istituto Universitario Orientale* 10 (1968) 351–76.

Farris, G. *Eloquenza e teologia nel "Proemium in librum primum Sententiarum" di Paolo Cortesi*. Savona, 1972.

Graziosi, M. T. "Spigolature cortesiane." *Atti e memorie dell'Arcadia,* Ser. 3, 7 (1977) 67–84.

Ricciardi, R. "Cortesi (Cortesius, de Cortesiis), Paolo." *DBI* 29 (Rome, 1983) 766–70.

D'Amico, J. F. "Paolo Cortesi's Rehabilitation of Giovanni Pico della Mirandola." *BibHumRen* 44 (1982) 37–51.

————. "*Contra divinationem:* Paolo Cortesi's Attack on Astrology." *Renaissance Studies in Honor of Craig Hugh Smyth*. Florence, 1985. Pp. 281–91.

Cardini, R. "'Antichi e moderni' in Paolo Cortesi." *Rassegna della letteratura italiana,* Ser. 8, 95/3 (1991) 20–28.

(In the press: the proceedings of a congress of studies on Alexander and Paul Cortesi, held at San Gimignano in June of 1991.)

Adrian Castellesi (Adrian of Corneto) (Tarquinia, ca. 1461–1521 [?])

EDITIONS

De vera philosophia ex quattuor doctoribus ecclesiae. Bologna, 1507; Rome, 1514; Cologna, 1540; Rome, 1775.

STUDIES

Schrek, A. S. *La biografia del cardinale Adriano da Corneto*. Trent, 1837.

Gebhardt, B. B. *Adrian von Corneto, ein Beitrag zur Geschichte der Curie und der Renaissance*. Breslau, 1886.

Pollard, A. F. *Henry VIII.* London, 1905. Pp. 112–55.

Imbart de la Tour, G. *Les origines de la Réforme* II. *L'Église catholique, la crise et la renaissance*. Paris, 1909. Pp. 567–71.

Ferrajoli, A. *La congiura dei cardinali contro Leone X*. Rome, 1919.

Cantimori, D. *Eretici italiani del Cinquecento*. Florence, 1939. See the index.

Paschini, P. *Roma nel Cinquecento*. Bologna, 1940. Pp. 368, 423, 437.

Doussinague, J. M. *Fernando el Católico y el cisma de Pisa*. Madrid, 1946. See the index.

Paschini, P. "Tre illustri prelati del Rinascimento, Ermolao Barbaro, Adriano Castellesi, Giovanni Grimani." *Lateranum,* N.S. 23 (1957) 43–130.

Fragnito, G. "Castellesi, Adriano." *DBI* 21 (Rome, 1978) 665–71.

John Francis Pico della Mirandola (Mirandola, 1469–1533)

WORKS AND EDITIONS

Opera omnia. In vol. II of the works of John Pico della Mirandola. Basel, 1557, 1573, 1601; reprinted: Hildesheim, 1969; Turin, 1972. Editions of individual works:

De morte Christi et propria cogitanda. With *De studio divinae et humanae philosophiae, libri duo.* Bologna, 1497, and in *Opere,* Venice, 1503, and Paris, 1538.

Liber de imaginatione. Venice, 1501; Basel, 1536; Wittenberg, 1588; and in recent times, New Haven, 1930.

De rerum praenotatione and *Theoremata numero XXV de fide et ordine credendi,* with other works and the three preceding works. Strasbourg, 1506–7.

Opusculum de sententia excommunicationis iniustae pro Hieronymi Savonarola viri prophetae innocentia. Florence, 1497. In *Opere.* Venice, 1528; Wittenberg, 1521; Leipzig, ca. 1605. In M. Goldast. *Monarchia S. Romani Imperii.* Frankfurt a. M., 1614. II, 1635–48. Paris, 1674, with a *Vita* of Savonarola by John Francis.

Vita Fratris Hieronymi Savonarolae. Paris, 1674, and in *Vitae selectorum aliquot virorum . . .* London, 1681.

Defensio Hieronymi Savonarolae Ferrariensis ordinis praedicatorum adversus Samuelem Cassinensem. Florence, 1497. In *Opere.* Venice, 1528. And "In metropoli qua Francia mixta Suevis," 1615.

Epistola del conte Zoanfrancesco de la Mirandula in favore de fra Hieronymo da Ferrara dappoi la sua captura. Modena, 1498.

Operecta in defensione della opera di Piero Bernardo da Firenze. Ed. P. Cherubelli, in *Per le nozze Bellini Manfredi.* Florence, 1943.

De providentia Dei contra philosophastros. Novi, 1508; Strasbourg, 1509; Leipzig or Heidelberg, ca. 1615.

De amore divino. Rome, 1516.

Physici libri duo. Basel, 1518; Bologna, 1523.

De veris calamitatum causis nostrorum temporum. Modena, 1860.

Ad Leonem pontificem . . . de reformandis moribus oratio. Hagenau, 1520; Bologna, 1523 (together with *Strix* and other works). Then in *Fasciculus rerum expetendarum et fugiendarum.* Cologne (?), 1535. Cols. 208v–210v. In *Speculum ecclesiae pontificiae.* London, 1616. Pp. 250–74. In *Discursus epistolares politico-theologici de statu reipublicae christianae degenerantis. . . .* Frankfurt a. M., 1610.

Examen vanitatis doctrinae gentium. Mirandola, 1520.

Strix sive de ludificatione daemonum. Bologna, 1523 (with other works); Bologna, 1524 (vernacular translation by L. Alberti); Venice, 1556 (Alberti's translation again); Strasbourg, 1612; Milan, 1864 (Alberti's translation); Genoa, 1988.

De immortalitate animae digressio. Bologna, 1523; Paris, 1541; Padua, 1553.

Pro asserendis a calumnia libris Dionysii Areopagitae epistola. Bologna, 1523 (with *Strix*); Ingolstadt (?), 1526.

De auro libri tres (doubtful). Venice, 1586; Ferrara, 1587; Wittenberg, 1588; Ursel, 1598. In *Theatrum chemicum.* Ursel, 1602. Strasbourg, 1613 and 1659. In I. J. Manget. *Bibliotheca chemica curiosa.* Geneva, 1702.

Compendium rerum admirabilium coelicae virginis Catherinae Raconisiae (but always published in the vernacular). Turin, 1622; Bologna, ca. 1681; Chieri and Turin, 1856.

Epistola to Cardinal John Peter Carafa, and *Agli amatori del vero*. Ed. E. Garin, in his edition of John Pico's *Disputationes adversus theologian divinitricem*.

Epistolae de imitatione (two) to Peter Bembo. Ed. H. Caplan, Ithaca, N.Y., 1930.

Quaestio de falsitate astrologiae. Ed. W. Cavini. "Un inedito di Giovan Francesco Pico. La *Quaestio de falsitate astrologiae*." *Rinascimento*, Ser. 2, 13 (1973) 133–71.

STUDIES

Strowski, F. "Une source italienne des *Essais* de Montaigne. L'*Examen vanitatis doctrinae gentium* de François Pic de la Mirandole." *Bulletin italien* 5 (1905) 309–13.

Corsano, A. *Per la storia del Rinascimento religioso in Italia: dal Traversari a Giovan Francesco Pico*. Naples, 1935.

Cantimori, D. *Eretici italiani del Cinquecento*. Florence, 1939. Pp. 5–9.

Trinkaus, Ch. *Adversity's Noblemen*. New York, 1940. Pp. 130–32.

Walker, D. P. *Spiritual and Demonic Magic from Ficino to Campanella*. London, 1958. See the index.

Popkin, R. H. *A History of Scepticism from Erasmus to Descartes*. Assen, 1960. Pp. 19–21.

Schmitt, Ch. B. "Henry Ghent, Duns Scotus, and Gianfrancesco Pico on Illumination." *Medieval Studies* 25 (1963) 231–58.

———. "Who Read Gian Francesco Pico della Mirandola?" *Studies in the Renaissance* 11 (1964).

———. "Gianfrancesco Pico's Attitude Toward His Uncle." *L'opera e pensiero di Giovanni Pico della Mirandola nella storia dell'Umanesimo*. Florence, 1965. II. 305–13.

Vasoli, C. "Pietro Bernardino e Gian Francesco Pico." Ibid., 281–99.

Schmitt, Ch. B. *Gianfrancesco Pico della Mirandola (1469–1533) and His Critique of Aristotle*. Den Haag, 1967.

Raith, W. *Die Macht des Bildes. Ein humanistisches Problem bei Gianfranscesco Pico della Mirandola*. Munich, 1967.

Schmitt, Ch. B. "Gianfrancesco Pico della Mirandola and the Fifth Lateran Council." *ArchRef* 61 (1970) 161–78.

———. *"Cicero Scepticus": A Study of the Influence of the "Academica" in the Renaissance*. Den Haag, 1972. See the index.

Garin, E. "Gian Francesco Pico della Mirandola, Savonarolan Apologetics, and the Critique of Ancient Thought." *Christianity and the Renaissance: Image and Religious Imagination in the Quattrocento*. Ed. T. Verdon and J. Henderson. Syracuse, N.Y., 1990. Pp. 523–32.

Nicholas Vernia (Chieti, 1420–Vicenza, 1499)

WORKS AND EDITIONS

Quaestio an ens mobile sit totius philosophiae naturalis subjectum. Padua, 1480.

Quaestio an Medicina nobilior ac praestantiopr sit Iure civili. Venice, 1482. Ed. E. Garin. *La disputa delle Arti nel Quattrocento.* Florence, 1974. Pp. 111–23.

Quaestio an coelum sit animatum. 1491. Ed. P. Ragnisco, "Documenti inediti e rari intorno alla vita e agli scritti di Nicoletto Vernia e di Elia del Medigo." *Atti e Memorie dell'Accademia di Scienze, Lettere ed Arti di Padova* 292 (1890–92) 285–91.

Quaestio an dentur universalia realia. Venice, 1504.

Quaestiones de pluralitate intellectus versus falsam et ab omni veritate remotam opinionem Averroys et de animae felicitate. Venice, 1504.

For later publications of all these works see B. Nardi, *Saggio sull'aristotelismo padovano dal secolo XIV al XVI.* Florence, 1958. Pp. 102–4 and 108.

STUDIES

Ragnisco, P. "Nicoletto Vernia, studi storici sulla filosofia padovana della seconda metà del secolo decimoquinto." *Atti del Regio Istituto Veneto di scienze, lettere ed arti,* Ser. 7, 25 (1890–91) 241–66 and 617–64.

Nardi, B. *Saggi sull'aristotelismo padovano dal secolo XIV al XVI.* Florence, 1958. Pp. 125–28, and see the index.

Garin, E. *La cultura filosofica del Rinascimento italiano.* Florence, 1961. Pp. 293–99.

Di Napoli, G. *L'immortalità dell'anima nel Rinascimento.* Turin, 1963. See the index.

Nardi, B. *Studi su Pietro Pomponazzi.* Florence, 1965. See the index.

Pagallo, G. F. "Sull'autore (Nicoletto vernia ?) di un'anonima e inedita *quaestio* sull'anima del secolo XV." *La filosofia della natura nel Medioevo.* Milan, 1966. Pp. 670–82.

Vasoli, C. *Studi sulla cultura del Rinascimento.* Manduria, 1968. Pp. 241–56.

Mahoney, E. P. "Nicoletto Vernia and Agostino Nifo on Alexander of Aphrodisias: An Unnoticed Dispute." *RCSF* 23 (1968) 268–96.

_____. "Nicoletto Vernia's Question on Seminal Reasons." *Franciscan Studies* 16 (1978) 303–9.

_____. "Nicoletto Vernia on the Soul and Immortality." *Philosophy and Humanism: Renaissance Essays in Honor of Paul Oskar Kristeller.* Leiden, 1976. Pp. 144–63.

Pagallo, G. F. "Di un'inedita *expositio* di Nicoletto Vernia *In posteriorum librum priorem.*" *Aristotelismo Veneto e scienza moderna.* Atti del 25° Anno Accademico del Centro per la storia della tradizione aristotelica nel Veneto. Ed. L. Olivieri. 2 vols. Padua, 1983. II, 813–52.

Mahoney, E. P. "Philosophy and Sciences in Nicoletto Vernia and Agostino Nifo." *Scienza e filosofia all'Univesità di Padova nel Quattrocento.* Centro per la storia dell'Università di Padova 1. Ed. P. Poppi. Pp. 135–202.

_____. "Marsilio Ficino's Influence on Nicoletto Vernia, Agostino Nifo, and Marcantonio Zimara." *Marsilio Ficino e il ritorno di Platone. Studi e documenti.* 2 vols. Istituto Nazionale di Studi sul Rinascimento. Studi e Testi 15. Ed. G. C. Garfagnini. Florence, 1986. II, 509–31.

Hissette, R. "En marge des éditions de la *Métaphysique* d'Averroès. Sur les traces de Nicoleto Vernia." *Medioevo* 13 (1987) 195–221.

Schneider, N. "Der Gegenstand der Naturphilosophie Nicoletto Vernias und seine

Auseinandersetzung mit den Auffassungen des Mittelalters." *Mensch und Natur im Mittelalter.* Miscellanea Medievalia 21. Ed. A. Zimmermann and A. Speer. Berlin, 1991. Pp. 406–27.

Augustine Nifo (Sessa, 1473?–Salerno, 1546?)

EDITIONS

De intellectu et daemonibus. Padua, 1492.

In librum Destructio destructionum commentarii. Venice, 1497; Lyons, 1529.

De infinitate primi motoris. Venice, 1504.

De immortalitate animae libellus adversus Petrum Pomponacium. Venice, 1518.

Lilucidarium Augustini Nifi metaphysicarum disputationum in Aristotelis libros meta-physices. Venice, 1518 and 1559.

De regnandi peritia. Naples, 1523 (a rewriting of Machiavelli's *Prince*).

De pulchro et amore. Rome, 1531.

Commentarium in tres libros Aristotelis de anima. Venice, 1559.

Opucula moralia et politica. 2 vols. Paris, 1645.

STUDIES

Fiorentino, F. "Del *Principe* di Nicolò Machiavelli e di un libro di Agostino Nifo." *Giornale napoletano di filosofia e letteratura,* 1879, 94–114.

Werner, K. "Der Averroismus in der christlich-peripatetischen Psychologie des späten Mittelalters." *Sitzungsbreichte der Wiener Akademie der Wissenschaften,* 1881, 117–47. Reprinted: Amsterdam, 1964.

Tuozzi, P. "Agostino Nifo e le sue opere." *Atti e Memorie della R. Accademia si scienze, lettere e arti di Padova,* 1903–4, 63–86.

Tommasino, P. G. *Tre umanisti e filosofi. Una nobile figura sessana di letterato e di uomo attraverso l'epoca del pieno Rinascimento: Philalethes.* Maddaloni, 1921. Part I, 123–47.

Thorndike, L. *A History of Magic and Experimental Science* V. New York, 1941. Pp. 69–93.

Nardi, B. *Sigieri di Brabante nel pensiero del Rinascimento italiano.* Rome, 1945. See the index.

Giorgiantonio, M. "Un nostro filosofo dimenticato del Quattrocento: Luca Prassico e Agostino Nifo." *Sophia* 16 (1948) 212–14 and 312–13.

Nardi, B. *Saggi sull'aristotelismo padovano dal secolo XIV al XVI.* Florence, 1958. See the index.

Cassese, L. "Agostino Nifo a Salerno." *Rassegna storica salernitana* 19 (1958) 2–17.

Randall, H. "Scientific Method in the School of Padua." *Roots of Scientific Thought.* New York, 1960.

Garin, E. *La cultura filosofica del Rinascimento italiano.* Florence, 1961. See the index and especially pp. 299–303.

Di Napoli, G. *L'immortalità dell'anima nel Rinascimento.* Turin, 1963. See the index and especially pp. 203–14.

Poppi, A. *Causalità e infinità nella scuola padovana dal 1480 al 1513*. Padua, 1964. See the index.

Nardi, B. *Studi su Pietro Pomponazzi*. Florence, 1965. See the index.

Mahoney, E. P. *The Early Psychology of Agostino Nifo*. New York, 1965–66. Unpublished dissertation; see the abstract in *Dissertation Abstracts* 27 (1967) 2559A.

_____. "Nicoletto Vernia and Agostino Nifo on Alexander of Aphrodisias: An Unnoticed Dispute." *RCSF* 23 (1968) 268–96.

_____. "Agostino Nifo's Early Views on Immortality." *Journal of the History of Philosophy* 7 (1970) 451–60.

_____. "Pier Nicola Castellani and Agostino Nifo on Averroes' Doctrine of the Agent Intellect." *RCSF* 25 (1970) 387–409.

_____. "A Note on Agostino Nifo." *Philological Quarterly* 1 (1971) 125–32.

_____. "Agostino Nifo's *De sensu agente*." *Archiv für die Geschichte der Philosophie* 53 (1971) 119–42.

Nardi, B. *Saggi sulla cultura veneta del Quattro e Cinquecento*. Padua, 1971. See the index.

Mahoney, E. P. "Agostino Nifo." *Dictionary of Scientific Biography* 10 (New York, 1974) 122–24.

Zambelli, P. "I problemi metodologici del necromanta Agostino Nifo." *Medioevo* 1 (1975) 129–71.

Mahoney, E. P. "Agostino Nifo and St. Thomas Aquinas." *MemDom,* N.S. 7 (1976) 195–225.

Borraro, P. "Agostino Nifo, umanista e filosofo." *Archivio storico di terra di lavoro* 5 (1976–77) 169–92.

Jardine, L. "Dialectic or Dialectical Rhetoric: Agostino Nifo's Criticism of Lorenzo Valla." *RCSF* 36 (1981) 253–70.

Mahoney, E. P. "Philosophy and Sciences in Nicoletto Vernia and Agostino Nifo." *Scienza a filosofia all'Università di Padova nel Quattrocento*. Ed. A. Poppi. Padua, 1983. Pp. 135–202.

Aristotelismo veneto e scienza moderna. Atti del 25° Anno Accademico del Centro per la storia della tradizione aristotelica nel Veneto. Ed. L. Olivieri. 2 vols. Padua, 1983. See the index.

Larivaille, P. "Nifo, Machiavelli, principato civile." *Interpres* 9 (1989, but 1990) 150–95.

Mahoney, E. P. "Plato and Aristotle in the Thought of Agostino Nifo (ca. 1470–1538)." *Platonismo e aristotelismo nel Mezzogiorno d'Italia (sec. XIV–XVI)*. Ed. G. Roccaro. Palermo, 1989. Pp. 81–102.

_____. "Agostino Nifo (ca. 1470–1538) on the *Scientia de anima* as a 'Mathematical' or 'Middle' Science." *Knowledge and the Sciences in Medieval Philosophy*. Proceedings of the Eighth International Congress of Medieval Philosophy. III. Ed. R. Työrinoja and others. Helsinki, 1990. Pp. 629–36.

Tateo, F. "Le armi e le lettere in una disputa fra Agostino Nifo e Luca Prassicio." *Sapere e/è potere. Discipline, Dispute e Professioni nell'Università medievale e moderna: il caso bolognese a confronto*. Atti del 4° Convegno (Istituto per la Storia di Bologna, 13–15 aprile 1989). Ed. L. Avellini and others. Bologna, 1991. I, 85–99.

Mahoney, E. P. "Pico, Plato, and Albert the Great: The Testimony and Evaluation of Agostino Nifo." *Medieval Philosophy and Theology* 2 (1992) 165–92.

_____. "Agostino Nifo and Neoplatonism." *Il neoplatonismo nel Rinascimento.* Atti del Convegno internazionale (Roma-Firenze, 12–15 dicembre 1990). Ed. P. Prini. Rome, 1993. Pp. 205–31.

Peter Pomponazzi (Mantua, 1462–Bologna, 1525)

EDITIONS

De immortalitate animae. Bologna, 1516. Then: in *Opera,* Venice, 1525; ed. G. Gentile. Messina, 1925; ed. F. Morra. Bologna, 1954 (with bibliography, 17–31).

De naturalitate effectuum admirandorum causis, sive de incantationibus. Basel, 1556 and 1567.

De fato, de libero arbitrio et de praedestinatione. Ed. R. Lemay. Lugano, 1957.

Corsi inediti dell'insegnamento padovano. Ed. A. Poppi. Padua, 1970.

STUDIES

Fiorentino, F. *Pietro Pomponazzi. Studi storici sulla scuola bolognese e padovana del secolo XVI con documenti inediti.* Florence, 1868.

Ferri, L. "La psicologia di Pietro Pomponazzi secondo un manuscritto inedito dell'Angelica di Roma." *Atti della R. Accademia dei Lincei,* Ser. 2, 3, parte II. Cl. di scienze morali, storiche e filosofiche (1875–76). Pp. 333–548.

Fiorentino, F. *Studi e ritratti della Rinascenza.* Bari, 1911. Essays dating 1877–87.

Davari, S. "Lettere inedite di Pietro Pomponazzi filosofo mantovano." *Per nozze Tedaldi-Panini.* Modena, 1877.

Costa, E. "Nuovi documenti intorno a Pietro Pomponazzi." *Atti e memorie della R. Deputazione di storia patria per le Provincie di Romagna,* Ser. 3, 21 (1903) 277–318.

Douglas, A. H. *The Philosophy and Psychology of Pietro Pomponazzi.* Cambridge, 1910.

Breit, E. *Die Engel- und Dämonenlehre des Pomponatius und Cäsalpinus.* Bonn, 1912.

Betzendorfer, W. *Die Lehre des zweifachen Wahrheit bei Pietro Pomponazzi.* Tübingen, 1919.

Sante Felici, G. "Pomponazzi e la dottrina della predestinazione." *GCFI* 7 (1926) 24–43.

Oliva, C. "Note sull'insegnamento di Pietro Pomponazzi." *Ibid.,* 83–103, 179–90, and 354–75.

Weil, E. "Die Philosophie des Pietro Pomponazzi." *Archiv für Geschichte der Philosophie* 41 (1932) 127–77.

Corsano, A. *Il pensiero religioso italiano dall'umanesimo al giurisdizionalismo.* Bari, 1937. Pp. 65–97.

Thorndike, L. *A History of Magic and Experimental Science* V. New York, 1941. Pp. 95–110.

Kristeller, P. O. "Ficino and Pomponazzi on the Place of Man in the Universe." *Journal of the History of Ideas* 5 (1944) 220–26. Reprinted in idem. *Studies in Renaissance Thought and Letters*. Rome, 1956, 1969². I, 279–86.

———. "A New Manuscript Source for Pomponazzi's Theory of the Soul from His Paduan Period." *Revue internationale de philosophie* 16 (1951) 144–57.

———. "Two Unpublished Questions on the Soul of Pomponazzi." *Mediaevalia et humanistica* 9 (1955) 76–101; 10 (1956) 151.

Nardi, B. *Saggi sull'aristotelismo padovano dal secolo XIV al XVI*. Florence, 1958. See the index.

Gilson, E. "L'affaire de l'immortalité de l'âme à Venise au début du XVIe siècle." *Umanesimo europea e umanesimo venetiano*. Florence, 1963. Pp. 31–61.

Di Napoli, G. *L'immortalità dell'anima nel Rinascimento*. Turin, 1963. See the index.

Jorio, D. A. "The Problem of the Soul and the Unity of Man in Pietro Pomponazzi." *The New Scholasticism* 37 (1963) 293–311.

Kristeller, P. O. *Eight Philosophers of the Italian Renaissance*. Stanford, 1964. Pp. 72–90.

Nardi, B. *Studi zu Pietro Pomponazzi*. Florence, 1965. Passim.

Poppi, A. *Causalità e infinità nella scuola padovana dal 1480 al 1513*. Padua, 1964. Passim.

Fiorentino, F. *Pietro Pomponazzi*. Florence, 1968.

Poppi, A. *Saggi sul pensiero inedito di Pietro Pomponazzi*. Padua, 1970.

Di Napoli, G. "Libertà e fato in Pietro Pomponazzi." *Studi in onore di Antonio Corsano*. Manduria, 1970. Pp. 175–220.

Dieter, H. "Enkele *quaestiones* van Pietro Pomponazzi over de Ziel (1500–1516)." *Tijdschrift van de Vrije Universiteit Brussel* 13 (1970–71) 127–60. Also in *Dialog* 12 (1970–71) 16–76.

Pine, M. "Pietro Pomponazzi and the Scholastic Doctrine of Free Will." *RCSF* 28 (1973) 3–27.

Doni, M. "Il *De incantationibus* di Pietro Pomponazzi e l'edizione di Guglielmo Grataroli." *Rinascimento,* Ser. 2, 15 (1975) 183–230.

Graiff, F. "Aspetti del pensiero di Pietro Pomponazzi nelle opere e nei corsi del periodo bolognese." *Annali dell'Istituto di Filosofia* (Università di Firenze, Facoltà di Lettere e Filosofia) 1 (1979) 69–130.

Zanier, G. C. *Ricerche sulla diffusione e fortuna del "De incantationibus" di Pomponazzi*. Florence, 1975.

Céard, J. "Matérialisme et théorie de l'âme dans la pensée padouane: le *Traité de l'immortalité de l'âme* de Pomponazzi." *Revue philosophique de France and de l'Etranger* 171 (1981) 25–48.

Galimberti, A. "Intelletto e libertà nell'ultimo Pomponazzi." *Aristotelismo veneto e scienza moderna*. 2 vols. Ed. L. Olivieri. Padua, 1983. II, 685–94.

Kristeller, P. O. "Aristotelismo e sincretismo nel pensiero di Pomponazzi." Ibid., II, 1077–100.

Olivieri, L. "La scientificità della teoria dell'anima nell'insegnamento padovano di Pietro Pomponazzi." *Scienza e filosofia all'Università di Padova nel Quattrocento*. Ed. A. Poppi. Padua, 1983. Pp. 203–22.

———. *Certezza e gerarchia del sapere. Crisi dell'idea di scientificità nell'aristotelismo del sec. XVI. Con un'appendice di testi inediti di Pomponazzi, Pendasio, Cremonini*. Padua, 1983.

Pine, M. L. *Pietro Pomponazzi, Radical Philosopher of the Renaissance.* Padua, 1986.
Dethier, H. "Pomponazzi's Criticism of Calculator." *Knowledge and the Sciences in Medieval Philosophy.* Ed. R. Työrinoja and others. Helsinki, 1990. Pp. 58–191.
Olivieri, L. "Filosofia e teologia in Pietro Pomponazzi tra Padova e Bologna." *Sapere e/è potere.* Ed. L. Avellini and others. Bologna, 1991. II, 65–84.

Thomas de Vio (Cardinal Gaetano or Cajetan) (Gaeta, 1468–Rome, 1533)

EDITIONS

Opera omnia quotquot in Sacrae Scripturae excpositiones reperiuntur. 5 vols. Lyons, 1639. Reprint in progress: Hildesheim.
Opuscula omnia. 3 vols. Lyons, 1587. Reprint in progress: Hildesheim.
Scripta philosophica. 6 vols. Rome, 1934–39.
Scripta theologica I. Ed. V. M. Pollet. Rome, 1936.
Commentaria in Summam theologicam. In the Leonine edition of the works of Aquinas, vols. 4–11. Rome, 1882ff.
Commentarium in De ente et essentia. Venice, 1496. Ed. M.-H. Laurent. Turin, 1934.
Commentaria in tres libros Aristotelis De anima. Rome, 1509. Ed. J. Coquelle, Rome, 1938–39. Book III, ed. G. Picard and G. Pelland. Bruges, 1965.

BIBLIOGRAPHIES

Bozza, T. "Saggio bibliografico." *Il Cardinale Tomaso De Vio nel 4° centenario della sua morte.* Milan, 1935. = *RivFilNeo* 27 (1935) 63–66.
Congar, M. J. *Bio-bibliographie de Cajétan.* Saint-Maxim, 1935. = *Revue thomiste* 39 (1934) 3–49.
Groner, J. F. *Kardinal Cajetanus. Eine Gestalt aus der Reformationszeit.* Fribourg-Louvain, 1951.
Marega, J. "Operum Caietani indices. Bibliographicum specimen." In *Scripta philosophica* (see Editions, above) I. Rome, 1936. Pp. LXVI–LXXXVII.

STUDIES

Cossio, A. *Il cardinale Gaetano e la Riforma.* Cividale, 1920.
Laurent, M.-H. "La pensée de Sylvestre de Ferrare et Cajétan sur la justice originelle." *Revue thomiste* 11 (1928) 428–41.
Garrigou-Lagrange, R. "De personalitate iuxta Cajetanum speciatim de personalitate Christi." *Angelicum* 11 (1934) 539–46.
Grabmann, M. "Die Stellung des Cardinal Cajetanus in der Geschichte des Thomismus in der Thomistenschule." Ibid., 547–60. Also in idem. *Mittelalterliches Geistesleben* I. Munich, 1926. Pp. 602–13.
Loher, G. "De Cajetano reformatore Ordinis Praedicatorum." Ibid., 593–602.
Cajétan. = Special number of *Revue thomiste* 17 (1934).

Meersseman, G. G. "Cajetanus en de Nederlanden." *Kulturleven* 5 (1934) 262–74.

Il Cardinale Tomaso De Vio nel 4° centenario della sua morte. Milan, 1935.

Garrigou-Lagrange, R. "Le sens du mystère chez Cajétan." *Angelicum* 12 (1935) 3–18.

Vosté, J. *Thomas de Vio Cardinalis Cajetanus Sacrae Paginae Magister.* Rome, 1935.

Zimara, C. "Die Lehre Cajetano's und des Franz von Vitoria über das christliche Glaubwürdigkeitsurteil." *Divus Thomas* (Fribourg) 14 (1936) 421–34.

Cairo, V. "Cayetano y la tradición teológica medieval en los problemas de la gracia." *Ciencia tomista* 54 (1936) 289–311; 55 (1937) 5–32.

Goergen, A. *Die Lehre von der Analogie nach Kardinal Cajetanus und ihre Verhältnis zu Thomas von Aquin.* Speyer, 1938.

Carosi, P. "La sussistenza, ossia il formale costitutivo del supposto. Esame delle sentenze tomiste: Capreolo, Caetano." *Divus Thomas* (Piacenza) 43 (1940) 364–89.

Giers, J. *Gerechtigkeit und Liebe. Die Grundpfeiler gesellschaftlicher Ordnung in der Sozialethik des Kardinal Cajetanus.* Düsseldorf, 1941.

Degli'Innocenti, U. "L'opinione giovanile des Gaetano sulla costituzione ontologica della persona." *Divus Thomas* (Piacenza) 44 (1941) 154–66.

Giacon, C. *La seconda Scolastica. I. I grandi commentatori di S. Tommaso: il Gaetano, il Ferrarese, Il Vitoria.* Milan, 1944. Passim.

Alfaro Jiménez, J. "Posición de Cayetano en el problema del sobre-natural. Su crítica a la teoría de Escoto." *Archivo teológico granadino* 12 (1949) 49–160.

Quarello, E. *Il problema scolastico della persona nel Gaetano e nel Capreolo.* Florence, 1952.

Alfaro Jiménez, J. *La natural y lo sobrenatural. Estudio histórico desde S. Tomas hasta Cayetano.* Madrid, 1952.

Baur, G. *Die thomistische Naturrechtslehre und ihre Interpretation bei Kardinal Cajetanus.* Freiburg i. B., 1952.

Gilson, E. "Cajétan et l'existence." *TijdFil* 15 (1953) 78–85.

_____. "Notes sur le 'révélable' selon Cajétan." *Mediaeval Studies* 15 (1953) 199–206.

Mori, E. G. *Il motivo della fede da Gaetano a Suárez.* Rome, 1953.

Schwartz, T. H. "Analogy in St. Thomas and Cajetan." *New Scholasticism* 28 (1954) 127–44.

Bauer, R. *Gotteserkenntnis und Gottesbeweis bei Kardinal Kajetanus.* Regensburg, 1955.

Collins, T. A. "Cardinal Cajetan's Fundamental Biblical Principles." *Catholic Biblical Quarterly* 17 (1955) 363–78.

Degli Innocenti, U. "Capreolo d'accordo col Gaetano a proposito della personalità?" *Euntes docete* (1955) 168–203.

Gilson, E. "Cayétan et l'humanisme théologique." *AHDLMA* 22 (1955) 113–36.

Soleri, G. "Naturale e sopranaturale da S. Tommaso a Gaetano" *Sophia* (1955) 53–81.

Caba Rubio, J. "La personalidad en su dimensión metafisica según Cayetano" *(Crisis)* 1956, 169–99.

Hegyi, J. *Die Bedeutung des Seins bei den klassischen Kommentatoren des hl. Thomas von Aquin.* Pullach-Munich, 1959. See the index.

Reichmann, J. B. "St. Thomas, Capreolus, Cajetan, and the Created Person." *New Scholasticism* 33 (1959) 450–60.

Seaver, W. "Cardinal Cajetan Renaissance" *(Dominicana)* 1959, 354–70.

Gilson, E. "Autour de Pomponazzi. Problématique de l'immortalité de l'âme au début du XVIᵉ siècle." *AHDLMA* 28 (1961) 163–279.

Harrison, F. H. "The Cajetan Tradition of Analogy." *Franciscan Studies* 23 (1963) 179–204.

Beumer, J. "Suffizenz und Insuffizenz der Heiligen Schrift nach Kardinal Thomas de Vio." *Gregorianum* 45 (1964) 810–24.

Kuc, L. "Die Seins-Idee bei Thomas de Vio." *Studia philosophiae christianae* 5 (1965) 101–50.

Di Napoli, *L'immortalità dell'anima nel Rinascimento.* Turin, 1963. See the index.

Poppi, A. *Causalità e infinità nella scuola padovana dal 1480 al 1513.* Padua, 1964. Pp. 170–85.

Henning, C. *Cajetanus und Luther. Ein historischer Beitrag zur Begegnung vom Thomismus und Reformation.* Stuttgart, 1966.

Daudenault, G. *De la superiorité de la justice légale sur la religion d'apres Cajétan et Jean de St. Thomas.* Rome, 1966.

Horst, U. "Der Streit um die heilige Schrift zwischen Kardinal Cajetanus und Ambrosius Cattarinus." *Wahrheit und Verkündigung. Festschrift M. Schmaus.* I. Paderborn, 1967. Pp. 551–77.

Anderson, M. V. "Thomas Cajetanus' *scientia Christi.*" *Theologische Zeitschrift* 26 (1970) 99–108.

Bodem, A. *Das Wesen der Kirche nach Cardinal Cajetanus. Ein Beitrag zur Ekklesiologie im Zeitalter der Reformation.* Mainz, 1971.

Reilly, J. P. *Cajetan's Notion of Existence.* Den Haag–Paris, 1971.

Wicks, J. "Thomism Between Renaissance and Reformation: The Case of Cajetan." *ArchRef* 68 (1977) 9–32.

_____. *Cajetan's Response: A Reader in Reformation Controversy.* Washington, D.C., 1978.

Elders, L. "La théorie scotiste de l'acte indifférent et sa critique par Cajétan." *Tradizione scotista veneto-padovano.* Padua, 1979. Pp. 207–14. = *Regnum Hominis et Regnum Dei. Acta quarti Congressus scotistici internationalis.* Patavii, 24–29 septembris 1978. Rome, 1978.

Muzzarelli, M. G. "Il Gaetano e il Bariani: per una revisione della tematica dei Monti di pietà." *RSLR* 16 (1980) 3–19.

Dominguez Asensio, J. A. "Iglesia y transmisión de la fe. Comentarios de Cayetano a la *Second Secundae.*" *Scripta theologica* 12 (1980) 687–716.

_____. "Infallibilidad y *determinatio de fide* en la polémica antiluterana del Cardinal Cayetano." *Archivo teológico granadino* 44 (1981) 5–61.

Janz, D. "Cajetan: A Thomist Reformer?" *Renaissance and Reformation/Renaissance et Réforme* 6 (1982) 94–102.

Dominguez Asensio, J. "Amplitud objectiva de las nociones de fe y herejía en la teología del Cardinal Cayetano." *Archivo teológico granadino* 45 (1982) 5–50.

Belda-Plans, J. "Cayetano y la controversia sobre la inmortalidad de l'alma humana." *Scripta theologica* 16 (1984) 417–22.

Hallensleben, B. *Communication. Anthropologie und Gnadenlehre bei Thomas de Vio.* Münster, 1985.

Kuntz, D. G. "*De analogia graduum entis:* On Cardinal Cajetan's Neglect of Thomistic Hierarchy." *Acta Conventus Neo-latini Bononiensis.* Proceedings of the Fourth

International Congress of Neo-Latin Studies (Bologna, 26 Aug. to 1 Sept. 1979). Medieval and Renaissance Texts and Studies 37. Ed. R. J. Schoeck. Binghamton, N.Y., 1985. Pp. 72–79.

Pinchard, B. *Métaphysicque et sémantique autour de Cajétan*. Paris, 1987.

Ashworth, E. J. "Analogical Concepts: The Fourteenth-Century Background to Cajetan." *Dialogue (Canadian Philosophical Review)* 31 (1992) 299–413.

Guíu, I. "Puede la razón demonstrar la inmortalidad del alma?" *Los límites de la razón en el pensiamento medieval*. Actas del I Congreso Nacional de Filosofía Medieval (Zaragoza, 12–14 de Diciembre 1990). Saragossa, 1992. Pp. 357–71. On St. Thomas and Cajetan.

Francis Silvestri of Ferrara (Ferrara, 1474–Rome, 1528)

EDITIONS

In libros santi Thomas Aquinatis Contra Genetes Commentaria. Venice, 1524; Lyons, 1567; Antwerp, 1568. Then in the editions of the *Opera omnia* of St. Thomas from the Rome edition of 1570–71 to the Paris edition of 1660, and then in the Leonine edition, vols. 13–15, Rome, 1918–30. Ed. G. Sestili. 4 vols. Rome, 1898–1902.

Adnotationes in libros posteriorum Aristotelis et sancti Thomae. Venice, 1535.

Quaestionum libri De anima quam subtilissimae et praeclarissimae decisiones. Venice, 1535.

Apologia de convenientia institutorum Romanae Ecclesiae com evangelica libertate. Rome, 1525. Ed. G. Sestili. Rome, 1906.

STUDIES

Sestili, G. "Franscesco Silvestri." *Gli scienziati italiani* I. Rome, 1923. Pp. 128–37.

Gorce, M. M. "Silvestri, François." *DTC* 14 (Paris, 1941). Cols. 2085–87.

Gazzana, A. "La *materia signata* di S. Tommaso secondo la diversa interpretazione del Gaetano e del Ferrarese." *Gregorianum* 24 (1943) 128–37.

Giacon, G. *La seconda Scolastica*. I. *I grandi commentatori di S. Tommaso: il Gaetano, il Ferrarese, il Vitoria*. Milan, 1944. See the index.

Hegyi, J. *Die Bedeutung des Seins bei den klassischen Kommentatoren des hl. Thomas von Aquin*. Pullach-Munich, 1959. See the index.

Degli Innocenti, U. "Il Ferrarese e la nozione di persona." *Aquinas* 4 (1961) 369–74.

Di Napoli, G. *L'immortalità dell'anima nel Rinascimento*. Turin, 1963. See the index.

Kennedy, L. A. "Silvestri of Ferrara and Agent Sense." *New Scholasticism* 40 (1966) 464–77.

John Chrysostom Javelli (Chrysostom of Casale) (Canavese, ca. 1470–Bologna, ca. 1538)

EDITIONS

Opera omnia. Lyons, 1567; Venice, 1580.

Solutiones rationum animi mortalitatem probantium. An appendix in the *Defensorium*
of Peter Pomponazzi against Augustine Nifo. Bologna, 1519. Later, by
Pomponazzi's own wish, included with his *Opera.* Venice, 1525.

Quaestiones super XII libros metaphysicae ad mentem S. Thomae. Cremona, 1532.

Christiana philosophia seu ethica in octo partes divisa. Venice, 1540.

Philosophiae politicae seu civilis christianae dispositio. Venice, 1540.

*Tractatus de animae humanae indeficientia in quadruplici via, scilicet Peripatetica,
Academica, Naturali et Christiana.* Venice, 1536.

*Quaestiones subtilissimae, in quibus clarissime resolvunter dubia Aristotelis et
Commentatoris, eaque ut plurimum decisa habentur iuxta Thomisticum dogma.*
Venice, 1552.

For a list of Javelli's writings, published and unpublished, see J. Quétif and J. Echard.
Scriptores Ordinis Praedicatorum II. Paris, 1721. Pp. 104–5.

STUDIES

Fiorentino, F. *Pietro Pomponazzi.* Florence, 1968. Pp. 46–66 and 351–55.

Busson, H. *Les sources et le devéloppement du rationalisme dans la littérature
française de la Renaissance.* Paris, 1922, 1957[2]. Pp. 32–40.

Chenu, M.-D. "Javelli, en religion Christostome de Casale." *DTC* 8 (Paris, 1924). Cols.
535–37.

Giacon, G. *La seconda Scolastica* I. Milan, 1944. See the index.

Gilson, E. "Autour de Pomponazzi." *AHDLMA* 28 (1961) 163–279.

Di Napoli, G. *L'immortalità dell'anima nel Rinascimento.* Turin, 1963. Pp. 325–38.

Kristeller, P. O. *Le thomisme et la pensée italienne de la Renaissance.* Paris, 1967. See
the index.

Francis Zorzi (Francesco Giorgio Veneto)
(Venice, 1460/66–Asolo, 1540)

EDITIONS

De harmonia mundi. Venice, 1525; Paris, 1545 and 1546. In this last edition it bears
the name *Liber prontuarium rerum theologicarum et philosophicarum.*

In Sacram Scripturam problemata. Venice, 1536; Paris, 1574, 1575, and 1622.

L'elegante poema and *Commento sopra il poema.* Ed. J.-F. Maillard. Milan, 1991.

STUDIES

Wittkower, R. *Architectural Principles in the Age of Humanism.* London, 1949. See the
index.

Vicentini, U. "Il P. Zorzi e la Terrasanta." *Le Venezie francescane* 19 (1942) 174–76.

———. "Francesco Zorzi O.F.M. teologo cabalista." Ibid., 21 (1954) 121–59,
174–214; 24 (1957) 25–56.

Walker, D. P. *Spiritual and Demonic Magic from Ficino to Campanella.* London, 1958.
See the index.

Wind, E. *Pagan Mysteries of the Renaissance*. London, 1958. Harmondsworth, 1967. See the index.

Garin, E. *Il pensiero filosofico del Rinascimento*. Florence, 1961. Pp. 145–49.

Yates, F. A. *Giordano Bruno and the Hermetic Tradition*. London, 1964.

Secret, F. *Les kabbalistes chrétiens de la Renaissance*. Paris, 1964. New edition: Milan, 1985. See the index.

————. *Le Zôhar chez les kabbalistes chrétiens de la Renaissance*. Paris–Den Haag, 1964. See the index.

Yates, F. A. *Theatre of the World*. London, 1969. See the index.

Garin, E. *L'età nuova*. Naples, 1969. See the index.

Maillard, J.-F. "Le *De harmonia mundi* de Georges de Venise." *Revue de l'histoire des religions* 179 (1971) 181–202.

————. "Henri VIII et Georges de Venise. Documents sur l'affaire du divorce." Ibid., 181 (1972) 157–86.

Walker, D. P. *The Ancient Theology: Studies in Christian Platonism from the Fifteenth to the Eighteenth Century*. London, 1972. See the index.

French, P. J. *John Dee: The World of an Elizabethan Magus*. London, 1972. Pp. 139–42.

Rotondò, A. "La censura ecclesiastica e la cultura." *Storia d'Italia* V. *I documenti*. Turin, 1973. Pp. 1397–1492 at 1436–40.

Vasoli, C. *Profezia e ragione. Studi sulla cultura del Cinquecento e del Seicento*. Naples, 1974. Pp. 129–403, and see the index.

Secret, F. "Franciscus Georgius Venetus et ses réferences à Proclus." *BibHumRen* 26 (1974) 78–81.

————. "Franciscus Georgius Venetus et les *Oracula chaldaica*." Ibid., 81–82.

Maillard, J.-F. "Sous l'invocation de Dante et de Pic de la Mirandole. Les manuscrits inédits de Georges de Venise (Francesco Zorzi)." Ibid., 47–61.

Wirzubsky, C. "Francesco Giorgio's Commentary on Giovanni Pico's Kabbalistic Theses." *JWarCourt* 37 (1974) 145–56.

Zanier, G. "Un frammento di Giulio Camillo Delminio su un poema italiano di Francesco Giorgio Veneto." *GCFI*, 1976, 128–31.

Yates, F. A. *Elizabethan Neoplatonism Reconsidered: Spencer and Francesco Giorgio*. London, 1977.

Vasoli, C. *I miti e gli astri*. Naples, 1977. See the index.

Yates, F. A. *Occult Philosophy in the Elizabethan Age*. London, 1979. See the index.

Vasoli, C. "Vers la crise de l'hermétisme: le Père Mersenne et Fr. Zorzo." *L'Automne de la Renaissance*. XXIIᵉ Colloques internationale d'études humanistes (Tours, 2–13 juillet 1979). Paris, 1981. Pp. 281–95.

Franco, M. T. "San Francesco della Vigna e Francesco Giorgi." *Architettura e utopia nella Venezia del Cinquecento*. Milan, 1981. Pp. 410–11.

Magagnato, L. *Istruzione e promemoria di Francesco Giori per San Francesco della Vigna architettura di Jacopo Sanseverino*. Milan, 1982.

Foscari, A., and M. Tafuri. *L'armonia e i conflitti. La Chiesa di San Francesco della Vigna nella Venezia del Cinquecento*. Turin, 1983.

Perrone Compagni, V. "Una fonte di Cornelio Agrippa: il *De harmonia mundi* di Francesco Zorzi." *Annali dell'Istituto di Filosofia* (Università di Firenze, Facoltà di Lettere e Filosofia) 4 (1982) 45–74.

Vasoli, C. *Immagini umanistiche.* Naples, 1983. See the index.
Pierozzi, L. "Note su un inedito zorziano. Il *Commento sopra il poema del R. P. fra Francesco Giorgio." Rinascimento,* Ser. 2, 27 (1987) 349–86.
Scapparone, E. "'Sapienza riposta' e lingua volgare: note sull'*Elegante Poema* di Francesco Giorgio Veneto." *Studi veneziani* 13 (1987) 147–92.
Vasoli, C. "L'hermétique à Venise, de Giorgio à Patrizi." *Présence d'Hermès Trismégiste.* Paris, 1988.
_____. *Filosofia e religione nella cultura del Rinascimento.* Naples, 1988. See the index.
Scapparone, E. "Temi filosofi e teologici nell'*Elegante Poema* di Francesco Giorgio Veneto." *Rivista di storia della filosofia,* N.S. 45 (1990) 37–80.

Giles of Viterbo (Egidio Canisio, Egidio Antonini) (Viterbo, 1465/69–1532)

WORKS AND EDITIONS

For the most part Giles' works are unpublished. For the manuscripts containing them see J. W. O'Malley, *Giles of Viterbo on Church and Reform: A Study in Renaissance Thought* (Leiden, 1968) 192–97. Published works:
Lettere inedite del Cardinale Egidio Canisio Viterbese. Ed. F. G. Pazzaglia. Rome, 1915.
Lettere Familiari. Ed. A. M. Voci Roth. 2 vols. Fontes historiae Ordinis Sancti Augustini, Series altera, 1–2. Rome, 1990.
Letters as Augustinian General (1506–1517). Ed. C. O'Reilly. Fontes. . . , Series altera, 3. Rome, 1992.
Registrum generalatius (1514–1518). Ed. A. de Meijer. Fontes. . . , Prima series, 18. Rome, 1984.
Oratio habita post tertiam sacri lateranensis concilii sessionem. Ed. C. O'Reilly. *Augustiniana* 22 (1970) 80–117.
De aurea aetate. Ed. J. W. O'Malley. *Traditio* 25 (1969) 265–338.
Scechina and *Libellus de litteria hebraicis.* Ed. F. Secret. 2 vols. Rome, 1959.
Primus Sententiarum Liber ad mentem Platonis. Only a few excerpts have been published in E. Mazzi, *I fondamenti metafisici della "dignitas hominis" e testi inediti di Egidio da Viterbo* (Turin, 1954) 54–110.

STUDIES

Geiger, L. *Johann Reuchlin: Sein Leben und seine Werke.* Leipzig, 1871; reprinted: Nieuwkoop, 1964. Pp. 399, 404, 437, 450.
Kolde, T. *Die deutsche Augustiner-Kongregation und Johann von Staupitz: ein Beitrag zur Ordens- und Reformationsgeschichte.* Gotha, 1879. See the index.
Fiorentino, F. "Egidio da Viterbo e i Pontaniani di Napoli." *Archivio storico per le Provincie napoletane* 9 (1884) 43–52.
Pelissier, L.-G. *De opere historico Aegidii Cardinalis Viterbiensis.* Montpellier, 1896.
_____. "Manuscrits du Cardinal Gilles de Viterbe à la Bibliothèque Angélique." *Revue des Bibliothèques* 2 (1892) 228–40.

_____. "Pour la biographie du Cardinal Gilles de Viterbe." *Miscellanea di studi storici edita in onore di Arturo Graf.* Bergamo, 1903. Pp. 789–915.

Paquier, J. "Un essai de théologie platonicienne à la Renaissance: le commentaire de Gilles de Viterbe sur le premier livre des *Sentences.*" *Recherches de science religieuse* 13 (1923) 293–312 and 419–36.

Signorelli, G. *Il cardinale Egidio da Viterbo: Agostiniano, umanista e riformatore.* Florence, 1929.

Massa, E. "Egidio da Viterbo, Machiavelli, Lutero e il pessimismo cristiano." *Umanesimo e Machiavellismo.* Padua, 1949. Pp. 75–123. = *ArchFil* 5 (1949).

_____. "Egidio da Viterbo e la metodologia del sapere nel Cinquecento." *Pensée humaniste et tradition chretienne aux XV et XVI siècles.* Ed. H. Bédarida. Paris, 1950. Pp. 15–239.

_____. "L'anima e l'uomo in Egidio da Viterbo e nelle fonti classiche e medievale." *Testi umanistici inediti sul De anima.* Padua, 1951. Pp. 37–138. = *ArchFil* 9 (1951).

_____. *I fondamenti metafisici della "dignitas hominis" e testi inediti di Egidio da Viterbo.* Turin, 1954.

Martin, F. X. "The Problem of Giles of Viterbo: A Historiographical Survey." *Augustiniana* 9 (1959) 357–79; 10 (1960) 43–60.

Secret, F. "Le symbolisme de la Kabbale chrétienne dans la *Scechina* de Egidio da Viterbo." *Umanesimo e simbolismo.* Padua, 1958. Pp. 131–54. = *ArchFil* 26 (1958).

Astruc, C., and J. Monfrin. "Livres latins et hébreux du Cardinal Gilles de Viterbe." *BibHumRen* 23 (1961) 551–54.

_____. "Aegidiana hebraica." *Revue des études juives* 121 (1962) 409–16.

Martin, F. X. "The Registers of Giles of Viterbo." *Augustiniana* 12 (1962) 142–60.

_____. "Giles of Viterbo and the Monastery of Lecceto: The Making of a Reformer." *Analecta augustiniana* 25 (1962) 225–53.

Secret, F. "Notes sur les hébraisants chrétiens de la Renaissance." *Sefarad* 22 (1962) 107–27.

Cilento, V. "Glosse di Egidio da Viterbo alla tradizione ficiniana delle Enneadi in un incunabolo del 1492." *Studi di bibliografia e Storia in onore di R. de Marinis.* Verona, 1964. I, 281–96.

Massa, E. "Intorno ad Erasmo: una polemica che si credeva perduta." *Classical, Medieval, and Renaissance Studies in Honor of Berthold Louis Ullman* II. Rome, 1964. Pp. 435–54.

Secret, F. "Notes sur Egidio da Viterbo." *Augustiniana* 15 (1965) 68–72, 414–18; 18 (1968) 134–50; 27 (1977) 205–37.

_____. *Les kabbaistes chrétiens de la Renaissance.* Paris, 1964. See the index.

_____. "Egidio da Viterbo et quelques-uns de ses contemporains." *Augustiniana* 16 (1966) 371–85.

Martin, F. X. "The Augustinian Order on the Eve of the Reformation." *Miscellanea historiae ecclesiasticae* II. Louvain, 1967. Pp. 71–104.

O'Malley, J. W. *Giles of Viterbo on Church and Reform: A Study in Renaissance Thought.* Leiden, 1968.

_____. "Giles of Viterbo: A Sixteenth-Century Text on Doctrinal Development." *Traditio* 22 (1966) 445–50.

_____. "Giles of Viterbo: A Reformer's Thought on Renaissance Rome." *Renaissance Quarterly* 20 (1967) 1–11.

_____. "Historical Thought of Giles of Viterbo and the Reform Crisis of the Early XVIth Century." *Theological Studies* 18 (1967) 531–48.

_____. "Fulfillment of the Golden Age Under Pope Jules II: Text of a Discourse of Giles of Viterbo, 1507." *Traditio* 25 (1969) 445–50.

O'Reilly, Cl. *"Maximus Caesar et Pontifex maximus.* Giles of Viterbo Proclaims the Alliance Between Emperor Maximilian I and Pope Jules II." *Augustiniana* 22 (1972) 80–117.

O'Malley, J. W. "Man's Dignity, God's Love, and the Destiny of Rome: A Text of Giles of Viterbo." *Viator* 3 (1972) 389–416.

Giacone, F., and G. Bedoulle. "Une lettre de Gilles de Viterbe (1469–1532) à Jacques Lefèvre d'Étaples (c. 1460–1536) au sujet de l'affaire Reuchlin." *BibHumRen* 36 (1974) 335–45.

Pfeiffer, H. *Zur Ikonographie von Raffaels Disputa. Egidio da Viterbo und die christlich-platonische Konzeption der Stanza della Segnatura.* Rome, 1975.

O'Reilly, Cl. "'Without Councils We Cannot Be Saved.' Giles of Viterbo Addresses the Fifth Lateran Council." *Augustiniana* 27 (1977) 168–204.

Whittaker, J. "Greek Manuscripts from the Library of Giles of Viterbo in the Biblioteca Angelica in Rome." *Scriptorium* 31 (1977) 168–204.

Cristicini, S. *Egidio da Viterbo e i manoscritti della Biblioteca Angelica. Bibliografia.* Rome, 1978.

Martin, F. X. "The Writings of Giles of Viterbo." *Augustiniana* 29 (1979) 141–93.

Sed-Rajna, G. "Un diagramme kabbalistique de la bibliothèque de Gilles de Viterbe." *Homage à Georges Vajda. Études d'histoire et de pensée juives.* Ed. G. Nahon and Ch. Touati, Louvain, 1980. Pp. 365–76.

Javary, G., "De Malchut à Bina, ou De la lumière de loi à la lumière du Messie d'après le traité *Schechina* du cardinal Egide de Viterbe." *Lumière et cosmos. Courants occultes de la philosophie de la nature.* Paris, 1981. Pp. 111–18.

Egidio da Viterbo O.S.A. e il suo tempo. Atti del V Convegno dell'Istituto Storico Agostiniano (Roma-Viterbo, 20–23 ottobre 1982). Studia Augustiniana Historica 9. Rome, 1983.

Voci, A. M. "Marsilio Ficino ed Egidio da Viterbo." *Marsilio Ficino e il ritorno di Platone. Studi e documenti.* Ed. G. C. Garfagnini. 2 vols. Florence, 1986. II. 477–508.

Gionta, D. *"Augustinus deus meus:* La teologia poetica *ad mentem Platonis* di Egidio da Viterbo O.S.A." *Atti del Congresso Internazionale su S. Agostino nel XVI centenario della Coversione* (Rome, 15–20 sett. 1986). Studia Ephemeridis "Augustinianum" 26. Rome, 1987. III, 132–53.

_____. "Scholastik und Platonismus im Prolog zum Sentenzenkommentar des Aegidius von Viterbo." *Augustiniana* 39 (1989) 132–53.

_____. "Filosofi precristiani e Rivelazione: analogie e contrasti tra Ugolino da Orvieto e Egidio da Viterbo." *Schwerpunkte und Wirkungen des Sentenzenkommentars Hugolins von Orvieti O.E.S.A.* Ed. W. Eckermann. Würzburg, 1990. Pp. 123–33.

Secret, F. "Néoplatonisme et Kabbale dans la *Schechina* d'Egidio da Viterbo." *Il neoplatonismo nel Rinascimento.* Atti del Convegno internazionale (Roma-Firenze, 12–15 dicembre 1990). Ed. P. Prini. Rome, 1983. Pp. 29–44.

Augustine Steuco (Gubbio, 1497/98–Venice, 1548)

EDITIONS

Opera omnia. Paris, 1577–78; Venice, 1590 and 1601.
Recognitio Veteris Testamenti ad Hebraicam Veritatem. Venice, 1529.
Pro religione christiana adversus Luteranos. Bologna, 1530.
Cosmopoeia. Lyons, 1535.
Psalmorum XVIII and CXXXVIII Interpretatio and *De perenni philosophia.* Lyons, 1540; reprinted: New York–London, 1972.

STUDIES

Ebert, H. "Augustinus Steuchus und seine *Philosophia perennis:* Ein kritischer Beitrag zur Geschichte der Philosophie." *Philosophisches Jahrbuch* 42 (1929) 342–56, 510–26; 43 (1930) 92–100.

Freudenberger, T. *Augustinus Steuchus aus Gubbio, Augustinerchorherr und päpstlicher Bibliothekar (1479–1548) und sein literarisches Lebenswerk.* Münster, 1935. With information on earlier bibliography.

D'Angers, J.-E. "Epictète et Sénèque d'après le *De perenni philosophia* d'Augustin Steuco (1496–1549)." *Revue des sciences religieuses* 35 (1961) 1–31.

Schmitt, Ch. B. "Perennial Philosophy: Steuco to Leibniz." *Journal of the History of Ideas* 27 (1966) 503–32.

Di Napoli, G. "Il concetto di *philosophia perennis* di Agostino Steuco nel quadro della tematica rinascimentale." *Filosofia e cultura in Umbria tra Medioevo e Rinascimento.* Atti del IV convegno di studi umbri (Gubbio, 22–26 maggio 1966). Perugia, 1967. Pp. 459–89.

Wiedmann, F. "Das Problem der 'Christlichen Philosophie' nach Agostino Steuco." Ibid., 491–99.

Round Table on the Concept of *Philosophia perennis.* Ibid., 627–762.

De Vleschhauwer, H. J. "Perennis quaedam philosophia." *Studia leibiziana* Suppl. 1 (1968) 102–22.

Schmitt, Ch. B. *"Prisca theologia* e *philosophia perennis:* due temi del Rinascimento italiano." *Il pensiero italiano del Rinascimento e il tempo nostro.* Atti del V Convegno internazionale del Centro di studi umanistici (Montepulciano, 8–13 agosto 1968). Florence, 1970. Pp. 211–36.

———. Introduction to a reprint of *De perenni philosophia.* New York–London, 1972. Pp. V–XVII.

———. *Studies in Renaissance Philosophy and Science.* London, 1981. Chapters I and II.

Vasoli, C. "A proposito di Agostino Steuco e della *Perennis philosophia." Atti e memorie dell'Accademia Petrarca di lettere, arti e scienze,* N.S. 46 (1983–84, but 1986) 263–92.

Crociata, M. "Umanesimo e teologia in Agostino Steuco. Neoplatonismo e teologia nel *De perenni philosophia." Rinascimento,* Ser. 2, 28 (1988) 41–111.

Jerome Seripando (Naples, 1493–Trent, 1563)

WORKS AND EDITIONS

Juvenilia. Latin distichs in honor of Peter and Paul.

De summo bono. See Jedin, *Seripando,* II, 382 (see Studies).

Lettera on predestination to Mark Anthony Flaminio and *Lettera* on divine foreknowledge and free will to the prince of Salerno, in Jedin, ibid., II, 468–88.

Annotationes in epistolas ad Corinthios et Thessalonicenses. Ms. Naples, Bib. Naz., VII. A. 36.

Trattato della giustificazione. In *Concilium Tridentinum* 12 (Freiburg i. B., 1930) 824–49.

De potestate concilii.

Commentaria in epistolam Pauli ad Galatas. Eiusdem ad nonnullas quaestiones ex textis epistolae catholicae responsiones. Antwerp, 1567.

In Divi Pauli epistolas ad Romanos et Galatas commentaria. Naples, 1601.

De iustitia et libertate christiana. Ed. A. Forster. Münster, 1969.

Prediche or *Expositio* on the Apostles' Creed. Venice, 1567.

Prediche on the Our Father. Ed. in Abbondanza, *Seripando,* 85–299 (see Studies).

Doctrina orandi, sive expositio Orationis Dominicae. Latin version of the preceding. Louvain, 1689.

Quaestiones de natura divina. Ms. Naples, Bib. Naz., VIII. E. 40.

Farrago gestorum in concilio tridentino. Ms. Naples, Bib. Naz., IX. A. 48–50.

Diario (1513–52) *(Hieronimi Seripandi de vita sua).* Published in part, with some letters, in G. Calenzio, *Documenti inediti e nuovi lavori letterari sul Concilio di Trento* (Rome, 1874) 425–66.

Diario (1546–52). Ed. S. Merkle in *Concilium Tridentinum* 2 (Freiburg i. B., 1911) 432–68.

Diario (complete). Ed. D. Gutierrez in *Analecta Augustiniana* 26 (1963) 15–149; 27 (1964) 334–40.

Epistolae. Many are published in N. Paulus, *Der Augustinmönch Johannes Hoffmeister* (Freiburg i. B., 1891) 396–438, and in J. Susta, *Die römische Kurie und das Concil von Trent unter Pius IV* (4 vols.; Vienna, 1904–14).

Registrum generalatus. Fontes historiae Ordinis Sancti Augustini, Prima series, 25–26. Ed. D. Gutiérrez. Rome, 1982–83.

STUDIES

Jedin, H. *Girolamo Seripando. Sein Leben und Denken im Geisteskampf des 16. Jahrhunderts.* 2 vols. Würzburg, 1937, 1984².

Trapé, A. "La doctrina de Seripando acerca de la concupiscencia." *La Ciudad de Dios* 159 (1946) 501–33.

Jedin, H. "Seelenleitung und Vollkommenheitstreben bei Kardinal Seripando." *Sanctus Augustinus vitae spiritualis magister* II. Rome, 1959. Pp. 389–410.

Balducci, A. *Girolamo Seripando arcivescovo di Salerno.* Cava dei Tirreni, 1963.

Pontieri, E. "Figure e aspetti della riforma. Girolamo Seripando a Salerno." Idem. *Divagazioni storiche* II. Naples, 1971. Pp. 281–403.

De Frede, C. *La restaurazione cattolica in Inghilterra sotto Maria Tudor nel carteggio di Girolamo Seripando.* Naples, 1971.

Abbondanza, R. M. *Girolamo Seripando tra evangelismo e riforma cattolica.* Naples, 1980.

Marranzini, A. *Dibattito Lutero-Seripando su "giustizia e libertà del cristiano."* Brescia, 1981.

Gutiérrez, D. "De nuevo en defensa de Seripando." *La Ciudad de Dios* 197 (1984) 47–64.

James Sadoleto (Modena, 1477–Rome, 1547)

EDITIONS

Opera omnia. 4 vols. Venice, 1737; reprinted: London-Ridgewood, 1964.

Commentarius in Paulii epistolam ad Romanos. Lyons, 1535.

Hortensius, seu De laudibus philosophiae. Lyons, 1538. Ed. A. Altamura, Naples, 1950.

De liberis recte instituendis. Venice, 1533.

De republica christiana (fragment). Ed. Lazzeri, 1754.

De exstructione catholicae Ecclesiae. Ed. A. Mai. *Spicilegium romanum* II. Rome, 1839. Pp. 101ff.

De peccato originali. In S. Ritter. *Un umanista teologo: Iacopo Sadoleto.* Rome, 1912. Pp. 139–79.

Epistolae quotquot extant proprio nomine scriptae. Ed. V. A. Constanzi. 3 vols. Rome, 1760–64; reprinted: Stuttgart-Bad Cannstadt, 1965.

Epistolarum Appendix. Rome, 1767.

Lettere del Cardinal Jacopo Sadoleto e di suo nipote, tratte dagli originali. Ed. A. Ronchini. Modena, 1871.

Malagola, C. *Una lettera inedita del Bembo e due del Sadoleto.* Turin, 1875.

A Reformation Debate: Sadoleto's Letter to the Genevans and Calvin's Reply. Ed. J. C. Olin. New York, 1966.

STUDIES

Ritter, S. *Un umanista theologo: Iacopo Sadoleto.* Rome, 1912.

Cadier, J. "Sadolet et Calvin." *RHPR* 45 (1955) 79–92.

Douglas, R. M. *Jacopo Sadoleto, 1477–1547: Humanist and Reformer.* Cambridge, Mass., 1955.

Piscopo, U. "Cristianesimo e cultura del Cardinale Sadoleto." *Delta,* Ser. 3, 1 (1962) 45–64.

Reinhard, W. *Die Reform in der Diozese Carpentras unter den Bischöfen Jacopo Sadoleto, Paolo Sadoleto, Jacopo Sacrali und Francesco Sadoleto, 1517–1596.* Freiburg i. B., 1963.

Montano, R. "One of the Greatest Documents of Ecumenism of All Time: Letter to the Senate and People of Geneva by Cardinal Sadoleto." *Umanesimo* 1 (1966) 46–66.

Gesicora, G. "Probleme humanistischer Psalmenexegese dargestellt am Beispiel des Reformbischofs und Kardinal Jacopo Sadoleto." *Der Kommentar in der Renaissance.* Boppard, 1975. Pp. 35–46.

Venard, M. "Jacques Sadoleto, évêque de Carpentras, et les Vaudois." *Bollettino della Società di Studi Valdesi* 98 (1978) 37–49.
Waterbolk, E. H. "Erasmus en Sadoletus in de Weegs." Idem, *Verspeide Opstellen.* Amsterdam, 1981. See the index.
Feld, H. "Um die reinere Lehre des Evangeliums: Calvins Kontroverse mit Sadoleto." *Catholica* 36 (1982) 150–80.

Gaspar Contarini (Venice, 1483–Bologna, 1542)

EDITIONS

Opera. Paris, 1571; Venice, 1578 and 1589. The *Opera* include the following:
De elementis et eorum mixtionibus libri V. Paris, 1548.
Primae philosophiae compendium. Paris, 1556.
De immortalitate animae libri II. The first book was published anonymously with the *Apologia magistri Petri Pomponatii* (Bologna, 1518) and independently, under the author's name, at Venice, 1525.
Non dari quartam figuram syllogismorum secundum Galenum.
De homocentris. A commentary on the *Homocentrica sive de stellis* of Jerome Fracastoro.
De ratione animi. Two letters to J. G. de Sepúlveda, first printed in *Epistolae clarorum virorum* (Lyons, 1561) 36–39.
De magistratibus et republica Venetorum libri V. Paris, 1543.
De sacramentis christianae legis et catholicae ecclesiae libri IV. Florence, 1553.
Scholia in epistolas divi Pauli.
De officio episcopi libri II. The dedicatory letter to Peter Lippomano is in Fragnito, *Cultura.* See Studies.
Katechesiss sive chriatiana instructio, or *Formulario di fede,* written for the heterodox in Modena. Florence, 1553.
Instruttion Christiana volgare di monsignor Gasparo Contarini. The preceding in the vernacular. Crit. ed. in M. Firpo and D. Marcatto, *Il processo inquisitoriale del Cardinal Giovane Morone. Edizione critica* III. *I documenti difensivi.* Rome, 1985. Pp. 190–221.
Conciliorum magis illustrium summa. Florence, 1553.
Confutatio articulorum seu quaestionum Lutheranorum. Ed. Hünermann, in G. Contarini, *Gegenreformatorische Schriften* (see Studies) 1–22.
De potestate pontificis, quod divinitus sit tradita. Florence, 1553. Ed. Hünermann, ibid., 35–43.
De iustificatione. Ed. Hünermann, ibid., 23–34, and in *Concilium Tridentinum* 12 (Freiburg i. B., 1966) 314–22.
De libero arbitrio. Ed. of the original put in the vernacular by Vittoria Colonna in *Quattro lettere di mons. Gasparo Contarini Cardinale* (Florence, 1558) 57–67.
De praedestinatione. Ed. Hünermann, 44–67. Ed. of the original in the vernacular in A. Stella, "La lettera del cardinale Contarini sulla predestinazione." *RSCI* 15 (1961) 421–41.
Explanatio in psalmum "Ad te levavi oculos meos."

WRITINGS NOT IN THE *OPERA*

Consiglio facto sopra le cose del Rev.do padre fra Hieronimo Savonaraola. In F. Gilbert, "Contarini on Savonarola: An Unknown Document of 1516," *ArchRef* 59 (1968) 145–50.

Letter to Trypho Gabriele (December 24, 1530) on *Qual differenza fosse tra mente et intelletto,* in *Delle lettere volgari di diversi nobilissimi huomini et eccellenti ingegni* (Venice, 1544) 110–14.

Other letters to Trypho Gabriele on the relation between intellect and will and between speculative sciences and moral virtues, in *Quattro lettere di mons. Gasparo Contarini Cardinale* (Florence, 1558) 9–40.

Ad apologiam fratris Francisci Georgii. In F. Dittrich, *Regesten und Briefe des Cardinal Gasparo Contarini* (Braunsberg, 1881) 271–77.

Oratio ad deputatos de reformanda ecclesia habita. In *Concilium Tridentum* 12 (Freiburg i. B., 1966) 153–55.

De usu potestatis clavium. Ibid., 151–53.

De concilii celebratione sententia. Ibid., 4:108–16.

De potestate pontificis in compositionibus epistola. In J. Le Plat, *Monumentorum ad historiam Concilii Tridentini . . . illustrandam amplissima collectio* II. Louvain, 1784. Pp. 608–15.

Modus concionandi. In Dittrich, *Regesten,* 305–9.

De poenitentia. Ibid., 353–61.

STUDIES

Pasztor, L. von. "Die Korrespondenz des Kardinal Contarini während seiner deutschen Legation." *Historisches Jahrbuch der Görres-Gesellschaft* 1 (1880) 321–93 and 473–501.

Dittrich, F. "Die Nuntiaturberichte Morones vom Reichstag zu Regensburg." Ibid., 4 (1883) 395–402 and 618–97.

_____. *Gasparo Contarini, 1483–1542. Eine Monographie.* Braunsberg, 1885; reprinted: Nieuwkoop, 1972.

_____. "Nachträge zur Biographie Gasparo Contarinin." *Historisches Jahrbuch der Görres-Gesellschaft* 8 (1887) 71–83.

Friedensburg, W. "Der Briefwechsel Gasparo Contarinis mit Ercole Gonzaga." *Quellen und Forschungen aus italienischen Archiven und Bibliotheken* 2 (1899) 161–222.

Braun, W. *Kardinal Gasparo Contarini oder der Reformkatholizismus unserer Tagen im Lichte der Geschichte.* Leipzig, 1903.

Solmi, E. "Lettere inedite del Cardinale Gasparo Contarini nel carteggio del Cardinale Ercole Gonzagaa." *Nuovo Archivio Veneto,* N.S. 7 (1904) 245–74.

_____. "Gasparo Contarini alla Dieta di Ratisbona secondo i documenti inediti dell'Archivio Gonzaga di Mantova." Ibid., 13 (1907) 5–33 and 69–93.

Hünermann, F. "Die Rechtfertigungslehre des Kardinal Gasparo Contarini." *Theologische Quartalscrift* 102 (1926) 1–22.

Rückert, H. *Die theologische Entwicklung Gasparo Contarinis.* Bonn, 1926.

Jedin, H. "Ein Streit um den Augustinismus vor dem Tridentinum." *RömQ* 35 (1927) 351–68.

Hackert, H. *Die Staatschrift Contarinis und die politischen Verhältnisse Venedigs im 16. Jahrhundert.* Heidelberg, 1940.

Thorndike, L. *A History of Magic and Experimental Science* V. New York, 1941. Pp. 552–56.

Jedin, H. *Il tipo ideale di vescovo secondo la Riforma cattolica.* Brescia, 1950. Pp. 32–37.

_____. "Ein Turmerlebnis des jungen Contarini." *HistJb* 70 (1951) 115–20.

_____. "Contarini und Camaldoli." *Archivio italiano per la storia della pietà* 2 (1953) 59–118.

Cessi, R. "Paolinismo preluterano." *Rendiconti dell'Accademia dei Lincei, Cl. di scienze morali, storiche e filologische,* Ser. 8, 12 (1957) 3–30.

Mackenson, H. "The Diplomatic Role of Gasparo Contarini at the Colloquy of Ratisbon." *Church History* 27 (1958) 312–37.

Jedin, H. "Gasparo Contarini e il contributo veneziano alla Riforma cattolica." *La civiltà veneziana del Rinascimento.* Florence, 1958. Pp.103–24.

Casadei, A. "Lettere del cardinale Contarini durante la sua legazione di Bologna." *Archivio storico italiano* 118 (1960) 77–130 and 220–85.

Mackenson, H. "Contarini's Theological Role at Ratisbon in 1541." *ArchRef* 51 (1960) 36–57.

Gaeta, F. "Sul *De potestate pontificis* di Gasparo Contarini." *RSCI* 13 (1959) 391–96.

Giacon, C. "L'aristotelismo avicennistico di Gasparo Contari." *Atti del XII Congresso internazionale di filosofia* IX. Florence, 1961. Pp. 109–19.

Gaeta, F. "Alcune considerazioni sul mito di Venezia." *BibHumRen* 23 (1981) 58–75.

Di Napoli, G. *L'immortalità dell'anima nel Rinascimento.* Turin, 1963. Pp. 277–97 and see the index.

Gilson, E. "L'affaire de l'immortalité de l'âme à Venise au début du XVIe siècle." *Umanesimo europeo e umanesimo veneziano.* Florence, 1963. Pp. 43–59.

Jedin, H. *Kirche des Glaubens Kirche der Geschichte.* 2 vols. Freiburg i. B.–Basel–Vienna, 1966.

Tramontin, S. "Il *De officio episcopi* di Gasparo Contarini." *Studia patavina* 12 (1966) 292–303.

Cervelli, I. "Storiografia e problemi intorno alla vita religiosa e spirituale di Venezia nella prima metà del '500." *Studi veneziani* 8 (1966) 447–76.

Gilbert, F. "Cristianesimo, umanesimo e la bolla *Apostolici Regiminis* del 1513." *Rivista Storica Italiana* 79 (1967) 686–707.

Anderson, M. W. "Biblical Humanism and Roman Catholic Reform (1501–1542): Contarini, Pole and Giberti." *Concordia Theological Monthly* 39 (1968) 686–707.

Pallucchini, A, "Considerazioni sui grandi teleri del Tintoretto alla Madonna dell'Orto." *Arte veneta* 23 (1969) 54–68.

Fragnito, G. "Cultura umanistica e riforma religiosa. Il *De officio boni ac probi episcopi* di Gasparo Contarini." *Studi veneziani* 11 (1969) 75–189.

Gilbert, "Religion and Politics in the Thought of Gasparo Contarini." *Action and Conviction in Early Modern Europe: Essays in Memory of E. H. Harbison.* Princeton, 1969. Pp. 90–116.

Ross, J. B. "Gasparo Contarini and His Friends." *Studies in the Renaissance* 17 (1970) 192–232.

_____. "The Emergence of Gasparo Contarini: A Bibliographical Essay." *Church History* 41 (1972) 1–24.

Mathesen, P. *Cardinal Contarini at Regensburg.* Oxford, 1972.

Fragnito, G. "Ancora sul 'Beneficio di Cristo.'" *Studi urbinati* 40 (1971–72) 2–16.

_____. "Gli 'spirituali' e la fuga di Bernardino Ochino." *Rivista storica italiana* 84 (1972) 777–813.

Rosa, M. "In margine al *Trattato del beneficio di Cristo.*" *Quaderni storici* 12 (1973) 284–88.

Alberigo, G. "Vita attiva e vita contemplativa in un'esperienza cristiana del XVI secolo." *Studi veneziani* 16 (1974) 177–225.

Cantimori, D. *Umanesimo e religione nel Rinascimento.* Turin, 1975. Pp. 247–58.

Bozza, T. *Nuovi studi sulla Riforma in Italia.* Rome, 1976. See the index.

Logan, O. "The Ideal of the Bishop and the Venetian Patriciate: c. 1430–c. 1630." *Journal of Ecclesiastical History* 29 (1978) 415–50.

Settis, S. *La "Tempesta" interpretata. Giogione, i committenti, il soggetto.* Turin, 1978. Pp. 137–42.

Fragnito, G. *Memoria individuale e costruzione biografica. Beccadelli, Della Casa, Vettori alle origini di un mito.* Urbino, 1978.

Peyronel Rambaldi, S. *Speranze e crisi nel Cinquecento modenese. Tensioni religiose e vita cittadina ai tempi di Giovanni Morone.* Milan, 1979. Pp. 263–71.

Fragnito, G. "Contarini, Gasparo." *DBI* 28 (Rome, 1983) 172–92.

_____. "Il contributo du Hubert Jedin agli studi su Gasparo Contarini (1483–1542)." *Humanitas* 38 (1983) 629–43 and 668–71.

Firpo, M. "Gli 'spirituali,' l'Accademia Modena e il Formulario di Fede del 1542: controllo del dissenso religioso e nicodemismo." *RSLR* 20 (1984) 40–111.

Peruzzi, E. "Note e ricerche sugli *Homocentrica* di Girolamo Fracastoro." *Rinascimento,* Ser. 2, 25 (1985) 252–58.

Fragnito, G. "Aspetti della censura ecclesiastica nell'Europa delle Controriforma: l'edizione parigina delle opere di Gasparo Contarini." *RSLR* 21 (1985) 3–48.

Gasparo Contarino e il suo tempo. Atti del Convegno (Venezia, 1–3 marzo 1985). Ed. F. Cavazzana Romanelli. Venice, 1988. Includes a bibliography on Contarini by G. Fragnito.

Fragnito, G. *Gasparo Contarini. Un magistrato veneziano al servizio di cristianità.* Bibliotheca della *RSLR,* Studi e testi 9. Florence, 1988. Many of the articles of this author listed above are reprinted here.

Reginald Pole (or de la Pole) (Stourton Castle, Staffordshire, 1500–London, 1558)

EDITIONS

Pro ecclesiastica unitatis defensione. Rome, 1537; reprinted: Farnborough, 1965. Ed. and English trans. J. G. Dwyer. Westminster, Md., 1965.

Discorso di pace. No place, 1554–55.

De concilio liber, De baptismo Constanti Imperatoris, Reformatio Angliae ex decretis (Poli). Rome, 1562; Venice, 1562.

De summo pontifice in terris vicario. Louvain, 1569.

Apologia. In Tellechea Idigora, "Pole y Paolo V" (see Studies, below). Pp. 133–54.
Epistolae Reginaldi Pole S. R. E. Cardinalis et aliorum ad ipsum. 5 vols. Ed. A.
Quirini. Brescia, 1744–57.

STUDIES

Zimmermann, A. *Kardinal Pole, sein Leben und seine Schriften.* Regensburg, 1893.

Baxter, D. *Cardinal Pole: A Memoir.* London, 1901.

Haile, M. *Life of Reginald Pole.* London, 1910.

Paschini, P. *Un amico del Cardinal Pole: Alvise Priuli.* Rome, 1921.

Gasquet, F. A. *Cardinal Pole and His Early Friends.* London, 1927.

Jedin, H. "Il Cardinale Pole e Vittoria Colonna." *Italia francescana* 22 (1947) 13–30.

Crehan, J. "St. Ignatius and Cardinal Pole." *Archivum Historicum Societatis Jesu* 25
(1956) 72–98.

Dionisotti, C. "Monumenti Beccadelli." *Miscellanea Pio Paschini. Studi su storia ecclesiastica.* Rome, 1959. II, 251–68.

Parks, G. B. "The Parma Letters and the Dangers to Cardinal Pole." *Catholic
Historical Review* 16 (1960–61) 299–317.

Tellechea Idigoras, J. I. "Pole y Paolo IV. Una célebre Apologia inedita del cardinal in-
glès (1557)." *Archivum Historiae Pontificiae* 6 (1966) 105–54.

————. "Una denuncia de los Cardenales Pole y Morone por el Cardenal Francisco
Mendoza (1560)." *RevEspTeol* 27 (1967) 33–51.

Bruskevitz, F. *The Theology of Justification of Reginald Pole.* Rome, 1969.

Prosperi, A. *Tra Evangelismo e Controriforma, G. M. Giberti.* Rome, 1969. See the
index.

De Frede, C. *La Restaurazione cattolica in Inghilterra sotto Maria Tudor.* Naples,
1971. See the index.

Fenlon, D. *Heresy and Obedience in Tridentine Italy: Cardinal Pole and the Counter
Reformation.* Cambridge, 1972.

Eresia e Riforma nell'Italia del Cinquecento. Florence-Chicago, 1974. See the index.

Ginzburg, C., and A. Prosperi. *Giochi di pazienza. Un Seminario sul "Beneficio di
Cristo."* Turin, 1975.

Simoncelli, P. "Nuove ipotesi e studi sul 'Beneficio di Cristo.'" *Critica storica* 12
(1975) 320–88.

Marmion, J. "Cardinal Pole in Recent Studies." *Recusant History* 13 (1975) 56–61.

Pogson, R. H. "Reginald Pole and the Priorities of Government in Mary Tudor's
Church." *Historical Journal* 18 (1975) 3–20.

Bozza, T. *Nuovi studi sulla Riforma in Italia. I. Il "Beneficio di Cristo."* Rome, 1976.

Simoncelli, P. *Il caso Reginald Pole. Eresia e santità nelle polemiche religiose del
Cinquecento.* Rome, 1977.

Tellechea Idigoras, J. I. *Fray Barolomé de Carranza y el cardenal Pole. Un navarro en
la restauración católica de Inglaterra (1554–1558).* Pamplona, 1977.

Parks, B. "Italian Tributes to Cardinal Pole." *Studies in the Continental Background of
Renaissance English Literature.* Durham, 1977.

Jedin, H. "Kardinal Poles letzten Gewissenskonflikt." *Saeculum* 30 (1979) 256–63.

Pastore, A. "Due biblioteche umanistiche del Cinquecento (I libri del Cardinal Pole e
di Marcantonio Flaminio)." *Rinascimento,* Ser. 2, 19 (1979) 269–90.

Firpo, M. "Sulla legazione di pace del Cardinal Pole." *Rivista storica italiana.* 93 (1981) 821–37.

Pastore, A. *Marcantonio Flaminio. Fortune e sfortune di un chierico nell'Italia del Cinquecento.* Milan, 1981. Passim.

Gibaud, H. "Reginald Pole: le silence de Thomas More." *Moreana* 20 (1983) 85–89.

Mayer, Th. F. "Reginald Pole in Paolo Giovio's *Descriptio.* A Strategy for Reconversion." *Sixteenth-Century Journal* 16 (1985) 431–50.

Dainotti, T. *La via media: Reginald Pole.* Bologna, 1987.

Donaldson, P. S. *Machiavelli and the Mystery of State.* New York–New Rochelle, 1988. Passim.

James Sannazzaro (Naples, 1457–1530)

EDITIONS

De partu Viriginis. Ed. A. Altamura. Naples, 1948.

BIBLIOGRAPHY

Corti, M. "Sannazzaro, Jacopo." *Dizionario critico della letteratura italiana* 4 (Turin, 1986²) 82–88.

STUDIES (OF HIS RELIGIOUS THOUGHT)

Morpurgo, G. *La poesia religiosa di Jacopo Sannazzaro.* Ancona, 1909.

Calisti, G. *Il "De partu Virginis" di Jacopo Sannazzaro.* Città di Castello, 1926.

D'Alessio, C. *Sul "De partu Virginis."* Florence, 1955.

Sainati, A. *Studi di letteratura medievale e umanistica raccolti per il suo ottantac-inquesimo compleanno.* Padua, 1972. See the index.

Fiorini, P. L. "Lettere inedite di Jacopo Sannazzaro." *Italia medioevale e umanistica* 23 (1980) 315–39.

Vecce, C. "*Multiplex hic anguis*: gli epigrammi di Sannazzaro contro Politiano." *Rinascimento,* Ser. 2, 30 (1990) 235–55.

Anthony de Ferraris, called "Il Galateo" (Galatone, 1448–Lecce, 1517)

EDITIONS

Dialogus de heremita. Ed. in E. Garin. *Prosatori latini del Quattrocento.* Milan-Naples, 1952. Pp. 1065–125.

The most complete edition of the Latin and vernacular writings is by S. Grande in the Collana degli scrittori di Terra d'Otranto, vols. 2, 4, 18, 22. Lecce, 1867–71.

De educatione. Ed. C. Vecce, in *Studi e problemi di critica testuale* 36 (1988) 23–82.

BIBLIOGRAPHIES

Lisio, P. A. "L'umanesimo problematico di Antonio de Ferraris Galateo." In Idem, *Studi sull'umanesimo meridionale*. Naples, 1973. See the index.

Andreoli Nemola, P. *Catalogo delle opere di Antonio de Ferraris (Galateo)*. Lecce, 1982.

Griggio, C. "De Ferraris, Antoni, detto Galateo." *Dizionario critico della letteratura italiana* 2 (Turin, 1986²) 116–22.

STUDIES

De Fabrizi, A. *Antonio de Ferraris Galateo, pensatore e moralista del Rinascimento*. Trani, 1908.

Croce, B. *La Spagna nella vita italiana durante le Rinascenza*. Bari, 1917. See the index.

_____. "Antonio de Ferraris detto il Galateo." *BibHumRen* 4 (1937) 366–93. And in idem. *Poeti e scrittori del pieno e tardo Rinascimento* I. Bari, 1945. Pp. 17–35.

Studi su Antonio de Ferraris. Atti delle giornate (Galatone, 15–16 novembre 1969). Galatone, 1970.

Tateo, F. *L'umanesimo meridionale*. Bari, 1972. See the index.

Corsano, A. "Note sul pensiero religioso del Galateo." *Atti del Congresso internazionale di studi sull'età aragonese (Bari, 1968)*. Bari, 1972.

Griggio, C. "Tradizione e rinnovamento nella cultura del Galateo." *Lettere italiane* 26 (1974) 415–33.

Vallone, A. "Galateo, Venezia e il De educatione." *Vittorino e la sua scuola. Umanesimo, pedagogia, arti*. Florence, 1981. Pp. 299–311.

Jurilli, A. "Coordinate cronologiche dell'*Esposizione del Pater noster* di Antonio Galateo." *GSLI* 159 (1982) 536–50.

Vecce, C. "Antonio Galateo e la difesa della Donazione di Costantino." *Aevum* 59 (1985) 353–60.

_____. "Il *De educatione* di Antonio Galateo." *Lettere italiane* 40 (1988) 325–43.

Scipio Capece (Naples, 1480–1551)

EDITIONS

De vate maximo. Naples, 1533.
De principiis rerum libri II. Naples, 1546.

STUDIES

Miniero Ricci, C. *Biografie degli accademici alfonsini detti poi pontaniani dal 1442 al 1543*. Naples, 1880–82. P. 229.

Amabile, L. *Il S. Officio della Inquisizione in Napoli* I. Città di Castello, 1892. Pp. 134, 163, 193.

Schiavello, G. *Scipione Capese umanista del secolo XVI.* Naples, 1900.
Billanovich, G. *Tra don Teofilo Folengo e Merlin Cicaio.* Naples, 1948. Pp. 135–47.
Altamura, A. "Un 'rarissimo' del Cinquecento." In idem. *Studi di filologia italiana.* Naples, 1972. Pp. 183–97.
_____. "Per la biografia di scipione Capece." Ibid., 159–82.
Parenti, G. "Capece, Scipione." *DBI* 18 (Rome, 1975) 425–28.

Simon Porzio (Porta) (Naples, 1496–1554)

EDITIONS

De rerum naturalium principiis. Naples, 1553.
De humana mente disputatio. Florence, 1555.
An homo bonus vel malus volens fiat. Florence, 1551.
Opuscula. Naples, 1578.

STUDIES

Amenduni, G. *Di alcuni particolari della vita letteraria di Simone Porzio incerti o ignoti sinora.* Naples, 1910.
Fiorentino, F. "Simone Porzio." In idem. *Studi e ritratti della Rinascenza.* Bari, 1911. Pp. 81–153.
Saitta, G. "L'aristotelico Simone Porzio." *GCFI* 28 (1949) 279–306.
Di Napoli, G. *L'immortalità dell'anima nel Rinascimento.* Turin, 1963. See the index.
Gregory, T. "Aristotelismo." *Grande antologia Filosofica* 6 (Milan, 1964) 630–31.
De Gaetano, A. L. "Gelli's Eclecticism on the Question of Immortality and the Italian Version of Porzio's *De humana mente.*" *Philological Quarterly* 47 (1968) 532–46.
Montù, A. "La traduzione del *De mente humana* di Simone Porzio: storia ed esame di un manoscritto inedito." *Filosofia* 19 (1968) 187–94.

Chronological Tables

Giulio d'Onofrio

Date	Historical Context	Ecclesiastical Events	Doctrinal and Cultural Aspects
1365		On a visit to Avignon Emperor Charles IV asks Pope Urban V to return to Rome.	Niccolò Acciaiuoli dies at Naples. Foundation of the University of Vienna.
1366	Urban VI excommunicates mercenary troops and from Avignon organizes the League of Florence (which includes the Papal States, Naples, and Tuscany) against them.	Petrarch writes to the pope in the name of the Italians asking him to return to Rome. Same strong appeal from the clairvoyant Bridget of Sweden, who has lived in Rome since the Jubilee of 1350.	In Venice Petrarch completes his *De remediis utriusque fortunae* and writes *De sui ipsius et multorum ignorantia*. Death of Heinrich Seuse.
1367	Ferdinand, king of Portugal, dies, ending the Burgundy dynasty. Succeeded by John I the Great, of Aviz. War against the Hanseatic League and Denmark for control of the Baltic.	First return of Urban V to Rome.	Death of John Columbini, founder of the Congregation of the Gesuati.
1368		A provincial council at Lavaur compiles a book of laws for the moral and disciplinary reform of the church in Languedoc. At a provincial council in Périgueux, in which Edward, Prince of Wales, takes part as governor of Aquitaine, Bishop Austentius of Sarlat	

compares him hyperboli-
cally to the Son of God.
The French prelates
strongly criticize the incident and denounce it to
the pope.

1369   Henry II of Transtamara
has his half brother, Peter
the Cruel, king of Léon
and Castile, murdered.
Thus the struggle for the
succession in Castile ends
tragically with a change
of dynasty.
Gradual renewal in
French territories of the
Hundred Years' War.

Austentius of Sarlat goes
to Urban V in Rome to
apologize, but the matter
is not followed up. At this
time, the pope asks him
whether it is permissible
to rejoice at the murder
of Peter the Cruel, who
had been guilty of rela-
tions with the Muslims
and Jews.
At a provincial council in
London, with William
Wittlesey, archbishop of
Canterbury, presiding, the
clergy commit them-
selves to aid the state in
its economic difficulties
by increasing their offer-
ings.

John Wyclif becomes a
bachelor of theology at
Oxford and begins to
teach and compose his
theological writings.

1370   Relations between the
pope and Bernabò
Visconti, lord of the eastern possessions of the
Milanese, already tense
because of the latter's
meddling in central Italy,
worsen with the return of
Urban V to Avignon. The
election of Gregory XI,
displeasing to Florence,
which fears his territorial
ambitions in Tuscany,
leads to a reconciliation
of the Papal States with
the Visconti. Florentine
diplomacy effects a large
number of revolts in the
Papal States; the repres-
sion at Cesena is espe-
cially bloody.
With the Peace of
Stralsund, the Hanseatic
League is assured of po-
litical and economic

In April Urban VI returns
to Avignon, where he dies
in December. Election of
Gregory XI (Peter Robert
of Beaufort, 1370–78).

supremacy in northern
Europe.
In Poland, at the death of
Casimir II the Great, his
nephew, Louis I the Great
of Anjou, combines the
crowns of Poland and
Hungary.

1373	An epidemic of the Black Death in England, the third in twenty years, leads to serious economic and social disorders. During these years the monarchy promotes the spread of the social and religious teachings preached by John Wyclif, which assert the independence and superiority of the state in relation to the Church, deny the privileges of the papacy, and authorize sovereigns to confiscate ecclesiastical possessions.	A new provincial council in London, presided over by Wittlesey, at which Edward III asks that tithes be raised in his favor because of the country's internal difficulties and the expenses of war.	Giovanni Boccaccio delivers public lectures on the *Divine Comedy* in the church of Santo Stefano di Badia in Florence (1373–74). Death of Bridget of Sweden.
1374		Last provincial council in London celebrated by Wittlesey. The English clergy asks to be freed from many of the taxes they pay to the pope so that they may better meet the demands of the king. Gregory XI answers by promising to consider the request, but economic matters are henceforth the cause of high tension between the English crown and the papacy.	Francis Petrarch dies at Arquà. Preacher Milíc of Kromeritz dies at Prague; by his homilies, apocalyptic in tone and inspired by principles of poverty, he began the movement of reform in Bohemia.
1375	War between Florence and the pope, called the War of the Eight Saints from the popular nickname for the War Eight, the Florentine magistrates in charge of directing hostilities. Florence	Catherine of Siena goes in person to Avignon to convince the pope to return to Italy. A provincial council in Genoa, with Archbishop Andrea della Torre presiding,	Death of Boccaccio, who leaves his library to the Augustinians of Santo Spirito in Florence. Coluccio Salutati is chancellor of the Florentine Signoria. Wyclif publishes his *De dominio divino*.

obtains the support of
Bernabò Visconti (but not
of Galeazzo, master of
the western possessions)
and sets itself up as deliv-
erer of Italy from the papacy, which is called an
alien enemy. The re-
belling cities of the
Romagna display a red
banner with the word
"Freedom" on it.

reorganizes the canon law
for Liguria.
John Wyclif enters the
service of the English
crown as "special cleric
of the king" and takes the
lead in the movement for
Church reform: the
preachers whom he sends
throughout the country
are known as "poor
priesters," a name soon
changed by the people to
"Lollards" (from "lollen"
or "lullen," = to sing
hymns of praise).

1376   The pope interdicts
Florence and excommu-
nicates the Eight Saints,
causing serious harm to
the commercial economy
of the republic.

Wyclif publishes his *De
civil dominio.*

1377   The pope's return to Italy
weakens the theoretical
reasons for the War of the
Eight Saints.
At the death of Edward
III of England, his still-
young nephew, Richard
II, becomes king, under
the regency of John of
Gaunt, duke of Lancaster.
A period of dynastic and
social unrest begins: the
regent renews the conflict
in France in order to
make up for the recent
losses of Edward III, pro-
tects the Lollards, and begins a policy of tolerance
toward the peasants.

Definitive return of Pope
Gregory XI to Rome due
to the insistence of
Catherine of Siena.
At a provincial council in
London with Simon of
Sudbury, archbishop of
Canterbury, presiding, the
clergy ask Richard II for
a reduction of their financial burdens. John Wyclif
is summoned to appear
before Sudbury and
William Courtenay,
bishop of London; he
goes accompanied by
John of Gaunt, an enemy
of both bishops. Fifty of
Wyclif's propositions are
sent to Gregory XI in
Rome. In five bulls the
pope declares the teach-
ings to be erroneous and
dangerous, especially the
nineteen propositions
from the *De civili do-
minio,* and tells Wyclif to
appear before the papal

court. Judging this summons to be an attack on English freedoms, the University of Oxford refuses to condemn Wyclif, as the two bishops do; the theologian replies with his *Protestatio* and his *Conclusiones,* in which he identifies the pope with the Antichrist.

1378	In June the revolt of the Ciompi begins: they are lower rank workers of the Wool Guild, who demand the establishment of an autonomous workers' guild; Michele di Lando, one of the leaders of the revolt, takes the title of magistrate (Gonfaloniere) of justice and imposes a new democratic constitution on the guild. End of the War of the Eight Saints with the treaty of Tivoli (in July) which ratifies a pardon of the Florentines by Urban VI in exchange for the payment of an indemnity. Criticized by his own fellows, Michele leads a bourgeois reaction that suppresses the revolt (August) and begins an oligarchic regime under the domination of the major guilds. Death of Galeazzo Visconti, who is succeeded by his son Gian Galeazzo in the western territories of the signoria of Milan. The Venetian victory over the Genoese at Capo d'Anzio marks the beginning of the War of Chioggia (1378–81), the last great conflict	Death of Gregory XI (March). Twelve French and four Italian cardinals take part in the conclave in Rome. In April, under pressure from the people, Bartolomew Priganani of Naples is chosen as Urban VI (1378–89). A few months later the French cardinals, at odds with the new pope, gather at Fondi, in the territory of Joanna of Anjou, queen of Naples, and elect an antipope, Clement VII (Robert of Geneva; 1378–94), who makes Avignon his see. Beginning of the Great Western Schism (1378–1417). A united Spanish council meets at Alcalá to decide which pope the Iberian clergy should recognize. No agreement is reached and the decision is made to remain neutral.	Wyclif publishes his *De veritate scripturae, De ecclesia,* and *De officio regis.* In his preachings he proposes a conception of the Church as the "Gathering of all the Predestined," and a standard that makes Scripture alone the norm of all morality and behavior; he accepts only the sacraments authorized by the Bible and rejects the doctrine of transubstantiation as intellectualist.

between the two maritime republics.

Death of Emperor Charles V. He is succeeded by Wenceslaus of Luxembourg, known as The Lazy, already king of Bohemia (as Wenceslaus IV).

1379   Charles V, king of France, forestalls a Navarese-British plot. With the support of Henry II of Castile, he attacks Carlo II the Wicked, king of Navarre, in his own domains, curbing for good his expansionist ambitions. Following a worsening fiscal situation, a fierce social rebellion breaks out in England led by Wat Tyler and John Ball a Wyclifite preacher, who calls for ecclesiastical poverty and social equality.

An attempt of Clement VII to take Rome by force is thwarted; the antipope moves to Avignon and there sets up a new court, obtaining the obedience of France, Naples, Savoy, and Scotland. The two popes excommunicate each other and the other's followers. Everything is done to have the pope of Rome recognized, with the support of the emperor, St. Catherine of Siena, the jurist Baldo degli Ubaldi, Coluccio Salutati, and Henry of Langenstein. Vincent Ferrer comes out in favor of Clement VII, and under pressure from the king of France, so do the masters of the University of Paris. In response, the University of Heidelberg, loyal to the emperor's views, refuses to accept masters from Paris. Henry II of Castile convokes various provincial meetings and then a national council at Burgos to take a position on the schism, but he dies during the celebration of the council. His son, John I, seeks to influence the bishops in favor of Clement VII, but the

Foundation of the Fransciscan University of Erfurt with the help of Clement VII; only in 1389 is it recognized by Urban VI.

Wyclif publishes his *De potestate papae, De ordine christiano, De apostasia,* and *De eucharistia.*

council decides to main-
tain the neutral position
that is favored by Prince
Pedro of Aragon, whom
the people regard as a
saint and a prophet.

1380	Bernabò Visconti pro-poses for the Italian states a law against foreign rulers and mercenaries. After the death of Charles V of France, his son, Charles VI, becomes king, under the supervision of his uncles, Louis of Anjou, Philip the Bold of Burgundy, Louis Bourbon, and John of Barry. France is laid waste by English mercenaries. Excessive fiscal demands lead, in France too, to a popular uprising that casts a pall over the incoronation ceremony. At the river Don the first Russian victory over the Tatars of the Golden Horde: Demetrius IV Danskoj, prince of Moscow, begins Muscovite rule over the Russian states.		Death of St. Catherine of Siena. Wyclif has the Bible translated into the vernacular by his friends Hereford and Purney.
1381	The War of Chioggia ends with success for the Venetians, who are, however, obliged to come to terms with the king of Hungary and give up Dalmatia. Joanna of Anjou, queen of Naples, excommunicated by Urban VI, who favors Carlo of Durazzo against her, calls upon Louis of Anjou, uncle of the king of France for help and makes him her heir.	Following upon debates at the councils of Medina del Campo and Salamanca and yielding to pressure from the king of France and Cardinal Pedro de Luna, John I of Castile and León decides in favor of the pope in Avignon. During the troubles in England Archbishop Sudbury is assassinated. The new archbishop is William Courtenay, who considers Wyclif	Coluccio Salutati writes his *De saeculo et religione*. Peter d'Ailly is licensed in theology by the University of Paris. His conciliarist views are already known. Death of Jan Ruysbroeck.

responsible for the incident and, with the support of the king, undertakes a harsh repression of the Lollards. John Ball is captured and hanged.

1382   In Florence, with the exile of Michele di Lando, the turn to oligarchy is definitive. Joanna I is captured and put to death, but in Naples Louis of Anjou reigns. While social disorders are disturbing the territories of Genoa and Venice, the Habsburgs make their way into Istria and annex Trieste, thereby beginning their expansion into the Tyrol and the Alto Adige, at the expense of the Venetian Republic.
Popular revolts break out in Paris (rising of the Maillotins, named from the lead clubs used by the common people), in Rouen, Orleans, and Languedoc (rising of the Tuchins, named from the *touches,* the briars in which rebels took refuge). The Flemish cities under French control also rebel against heavy tributes, but they are defeated at Roosebeke by Philip II, duke of Burgundy, known as "The Bold" (an uncle of Charles VI), who receives Flanders as a reward (united territorially with the Duchy of Burgundy from 1405 on). In Poland-Hungary, at his death Louis I of Anjou is succeeded by his

Courtenay convokes two successive provincial councils in London (the first known as the Council of the Earthquake, from the tremor that closed it), at which ten propositions of Wyclif are condemned as heretical (among them the denial of transubstantiation, episcopal jurisdiction, and priestly ordination); another fourteen are declared contrary to ecclesiastical practice. The extremism of his eucharistic teachings costs Wyclif the support of his protector, John of Gaunt, and of Oxford University, which had already been deprived of its independence by ecclesiastical authority. Courtenay therefore requires Wyclif to appear before a new council convoked at Oxford; the preacher offers two professions of faith, one in Latin, the other in English, but in them he still has strong criticisms of the Church. The council decides to suspend him from teaching and to remove him from the University.

Wyclif, removed from Oxford, publishes his *Trialogus,* in which he holds the realist conception of creation as the best possible result of an intelligent and nonarbitrary divine will.

daughter Marie (known as "King Marie") with her mother, Elizabeth, as regent.

| 1383 | Death of the Green Count, Amadeus VI of Savoy; he is succeeded by Amadeus VII, the Red Count. | | Death of Nicolas Oresme. John Huss is a bachelor at the University of Prague. |

1384 — Death of Louis of Anjou; the throne of Naples goes to the papal candidate, Charles III, remaining Angevin of the Durazzo branch. Following the abdication of Marie of Anjou, challenged by her subjects, Charles becomes the last Angevin king of Hungary.

Philip the Bold convokes a provincial synod in Lille, to which he invites the delegates of the University of Paris in order to bring Flanders into obedience to Avignon. At the Sorbonne, however, the conciliarist party also becomes increasingly strong, finding supporters among the *moderni*.

Sudden death of John Wyclif, who had retired to Lutterworth. Death of Gert de Groote, inspirer of the Brothers of the Common Life.

1385 — Gian Galeazzo Visconti arrests his uncle Bernabò and his sons, and is sole master of the Milanese territory. The Infante Henry the Navigator, son of John I of Portugal, promotes exploration of the west coast of Africa in order to combat Islam (continuation of the *reconquista*) and increase Portuguese trade.

Vincent Ferrer teaches theology at Valencia. Foundation of the University of Heidelberg.

1386 — Charles III, king of Naples and Hungary, is assassinated. Struggle for the succession in Naples between his son Ladislaus and Louis II, son of Louis of Anjou. In Hungary, Sigismund of Luxembourg, brother of Wenceslaus, becomes king following on his marriage with Marie of

In Milan Gian Galeazzo Visconti begins work on the building of the cathedral. Geoffrey Chaucer begins his *Canterbury Tales*.

Anjou, who abdicates in his favor.

After an interregnum the throne of Poland is ascended by the Lithuanian grand duke Ladislaus II Jagellone, husband of Hedwig (sister of Marie); he converts to Christianity with all of Lithuania, which is henceforth a grand duchy under Polish sovereignty.

1387	The Scaliger dynasty dies out and Gian Galeazzo Visconti occupies Verona and Vicenza, expanding the power of the Visconti house. Louis, duke of Orleans, brother of the king of France, marries Gian Galeazzo's daughter, Valentina, who brings Asti as a dowry (thus giving rise of the Italian ambitions of the house of Orleans).	Foundation of the convent of Windesheim, directed by Geert de Groote, under a rule written by Thomas à Kempis and modeled on the Augustinian Rule.	Dominican John of Monzón is licensed in theology in Paris. His Thomist theses against the Immaculate Conception are condemned by the university authorities and the bishop of Paris, despite his defense by the Dominicans of Saint-Jacques. Put on trial at Avignon by a commission of university masters, with Peter d'Ailly presiding, he flees and takes refuge in Aragon.
1388	Charles VI of France attains his majority and freedom from his uncles' control. A group of British nobles, among which the names of those of Lancaster and York appear for the first time, crush Richard II and impose their own authority on the royal government.	Peter of Luna, as cardinal legate, presides over a council of Palencia for the moral and disciplinary reform of the Church; in the presence of the king of Castile the council decrees a prohibition against alienating ecclesiastical possessions, excommunication for public adultery, and the isolation of Muslims and Jews in ghetto cities or quarters.	Foundation of the University of Cologne.
1389	Richard II regains power and slaughters the barons. Henry of Lancaster, his	Urban VI dies in Rome. Election of Boniface IX (Peter Tomacelli,	John Gherardi da Prato writes his *Paradiso degli Alberti*.

cousin, flees to the continent.
Emperor Wenceslaus succeeds in breaking the autonomous Swedish and Rhenish leagues, but does not subdue the resistance of the Swiss.
The Serbs are badly defeated at Kosovo by the Turks, who henceforth control the Balkans, but Sultan Murad I loses his life in battle. His son Bayasid (Baiazet) I succeeds him.

1389–1404) as Roman pontiff.
Archbishop Courtenay of Canterbury takes part in a secret trial in the monastery of the Lancasters that condemns the Lollards for heresy.

Peter d'Ailly is chancellor of the University of Paris and confessor of the king.

1390   At the death of John I, the new king of Castile is his son, Henry III, called "The Feeble."

At the Council of Pamplona the adherence of Navarre to the party of Clement VII is officially announced in the presence of Peter of Luna, who promises in exchange the coronation of King Charles III (who recently succeeded his father, Charles II).

Coluccio Salutati writes his *De verecundia*.
Rabbi Selemó ha-Levi of Burgos receives Christian baptism under the name of Paul of St. Mary (Paul of Burgos) together with his son, who takes the name of Alphonsus García of St. Mary (Alphonsus of Cartagena).
Death of Albert of Saxony.

1391   Death of Amadeus VII, count of Savoy, who is succeeded by Amadeus VIII.

Fierce persecution of Jews in Spain, spreading rapidly from Seville, where it began.
In a provincial council at Paris John Gerson exhorts the French people to pray for and devote themselves to the ending of the schism.

1392   During a campaign against the duke of Britain, Charles VI of France goes mad. The regency is entrusted his uncle, Philip the Bold, and to his brother, Louis of Orleans, husband of Valentina Visconti.

John Dominici writes his *Libro d'amor di carità*.

1393		Assassination of John Nepomuk, vicar general of Prague, drowned in the Moldau by hired killers for having opposed the interference of Wenceslaus IV in Church affairs.	Nicholas of Clamanges is rector of the University of Paris.
1394	Louis of Orleans occupies Savoy. Emperor Wenceslaus is imprisoned in Prague and ousted from the throne of Bohemia.	Death of Clement VII, the antipope in Avignon. Election there of antipope Benedict XIII (the Spaniard Peter of Luna, 1394–1409). The choice disappoints the clergy and court of France, now less motivated to continue the schism against a Spanish pope. In a council at Paris the French cardinals decide that Benedict XIII should resign if they think it necessary for the good of the Church. In a provincial council in London, Courtenay presiding, the acts of condemnation of the Lancasters are made public in order to call upon the secular arm against the followers of Wyclif (on this occasion they are officially called "Lollards" for the first time).	Death of Louis Marsili, guiding spirit of the humanist group that gathered around Salutati in the Santo Spirito convent of the Augustinians. Augustine Favaroni writes his *Commentarium in Apochalypsim,* some extracts from which would be condemned at the Council of Constance.
1395	Wenceslaus manages to flee and returns to the throne, but he is opposed by the Bohemian nobility.	The French government, confirming its different interests from those of the new Avignon pope, calls a national council in Paris to discuss means of ending the schism. In a council in Oxford the kingdom of England ratifies its obedience to the Roman pope.	John Gerson succeeds to Peter d'Ailly as chancellor of the University of Paris.

1396	Louis of Orleans occupies Genoa. Richard II of England concludes the thirty-year truce of Ardes with France and marries Isabella, daughter of Charles VI. Invasion of Habsburg territory by the Turks: Serbia and Bulgaria become Ottoman provinces. Byzantine emperor Manuel II travels to Europe (Rome, Paris, London) seeking help. Sigismund of Luxembourg attempts a crusade but is defeated at Nikopolis. The Turkish janissaries set about besieging Constantinople, but pressure from the East by Tamerlane, creator of the second Mongol empire in Asia, forces Bayazid to let up pressure on the Byzantines.	At the request of the University of Oxford, eighteen articles from the *Trilogus* of Wyclif are condemned at a provincial council in London, with the archbishop of Canterbury and papal legate Thomas Arundel presiding.	Coluccio Salutati controverts John Dominici's criticisms of his ethical activism. Death of Vallombrosan hermit John dalle Celle and of Francis Landino, author of a poem in praise of Ockham. Death of Marsilius of Inghen.
1397	Wenceslaus is imprisoned again in Vienna, then released. Union of Kalmar: Sweden, Denmark, and Norway combine their respective crowns under Erik of Pomerania, but with a guarantee of political and administrative autonomy. A champion of the union is Marguerite, daughter of Waldemar IV of Denmark and wife of Haakon VI of Norway, aunt of Erik, and real governor in his place until 1412.		Humanist Anthony Loschi writes his *Invectiva in Florentinos* in support of the Visconti political propaganda. Coluccio Salutati, a former teacher of Loschi, replies on behalf of Florence in his *Invectiva in Antonium Luscum de florentina republica male sentientem* (reworked at length until 1403), as does Cino Rinuccini with a *Responsiva*. At Salutati's urging the learned Byzantine, Manuel Chrysoloras, translator of Plato's *Republic*, is called to the Studium of Florence to

take the first official chair
of Greek.
Death of Henry of
Langenstein.

1398		At a French national council called by Charles VI, after lengthy and lively debate France decrees its "withdrawal" from obedience to Benedict XIII. The formula says that while continuing to regard the Avignon pope as the legitimate pope, France will no longer obey him in order to force him to devote himself to ending the schism. In fact, the decision follows upon a considerable intensification of Gallican tendencies.	

1399   In the kingdom of Naples Ladislaus of Anjou prevails on Louis II and continues his father's plan of expanding into Latium. Henry of Lancaster (Henry Bolinbroke) returns to England, gathers his supporters, deposes Richard II, and has himself elected king as Henry IV. His reign is opposed by some of the nobility, who remain loyal to the Plantagenets.

The religious movement of the flagellants known as the Bianchi, brought about in Chieri by a popular revolt in response to the damage done by the mercenary troops of Facino Cane, spreads rapidly throughout Italy, their cry being "Peace and mercy!" After a series of demonstrations in various Italian cities, about ten thousand Bianchi gather at Orvieto in September, to present themselves to Boniface IX, who does not hide his sympathy for their religious enthusiasm. Rome becomes a gathering center for pilgrims, and the pope proclaims the following year as a jubilee of collective penance. The plague, which

Coluccio Salutati completes his *De fato et fortuna* (begun three years before) and writes his *De nobilitate legum et medicinae*. John Dominici, for thirteen years reader in theology at the Dominican *Studium* in Venice, is banished from the territories of the Most Serene Republic for having introduced the devotion of the Bianchi.

spreads rapidly through southern Italy, overwhelms the movement, which dies out in a short time without having crossed the borders of the peninsula.

The bishops of Castile, gathered at Alcalá de Henares, decide to join the French church in refusing obedience to Benedict XIII.

At a provincial council in London, held prior to the coronation of Henry IV, Archbishop Arundel, who had shortly before returned to his see after some years in exile, strongly condemns interference by the royal authority, which is spurred by the heresy of the Lollards.

| 1400 | Perugia surrenders to Visconti and opens the way for him to the Papal States, as far as Spoleto. The Visconti power is at its height and extends to the Veneto (Verona, Vicenza, Padua, Belluno) and to the south of the Appennines (Pisa, Lucca, Siena, Perugia), threatening Venice and Florence. Some German princes depose Wenceslaus, who flees to Bohemia, and replace him with the Palatine elector Rupert of Wittelsbach ("The Little"). | Provincial council of London, Arundel presiding, aiming at reform: the moral improvement of the clergy and the prevention of Lollardism. Pier Paolo Vergerio the Elder writes his *De ingenuis moribus et liberalibus adolescentiae studiis*. Active in the Faculty of Arts in Paris between 1400 and 1415: John of Neuhausen, author of a *De ente et essentia* in which he denies the Thomist distinction and opts for the Albertist view. John Gerson writes various treatises on catechetical subjects in the vernacular, among them *Traité des dix commandments* and *Bref traité des* |

tentations. His little work against the *Roman de la Rose* gives rise to a dispute about the permissibility of a secular culture; participants include John of Montreuil, the two brothers Peter and Gontier Col, and Christine of Pisan (who attributes misogynist views to the author of the *Roman*).

Death of Geoffrey Chaucer.

Writing at Sachsenhausen (near Frankfurt) of the anonymous *Theologia deutsch,* a little work that sets forth the principles of the faith in an elementary form; it was to be very popular among German Protestants.

John Huss, dean of the Faculty of Arts at the University of Prague, is ordained a priest and begins his activity as a preacher.

1401   Rupert of Wittelsbach is elected king of Germany, but not all the German princes acknowledge the deposition of Wenceslaus; a schism of about ten years thus begins. An attempt by Rupert to conquer Milanese territory fails with his defeat at Brescia.

To prepare for coping with the difficult situation created for ecclesiastical administration by the refusal of obedience to Benedict XIII, a meeting of prelates at Senlis promotes the calling of a council of those under Avignon obedience. Pope Luna, still committed to obtaining a reversal of the decisions made in 1398, energetically opposes this convocation.

With the Lollards in mind Henry IV of England issues the decree *De haeretico comburendo,* which establishes the

Cino Rinuccini composes his *Invectiva contro a cierti calunniatori di Dante, Petrarca e Boccaccio.*

Between 1401 and 1405 Leonardo Bruni works on his *Dialogi ad Petrum Paulum Istrum* (i.e., dedicated to Piero Paolo Vergerio).

Huss is chosen as preacher at Bethlehem Chapel, a center for the spread of reformist ideas and meant for preaching in the Czech language. The theological faculty of Prague condemns Wyclif's theological

penalty of the pyre (pre-
viously the punishment
was hanging).

works, brought from
England, spread by
Jerome of Prague, and
defended by Stanislas
Znojmo, Huss' teacher.
Znojmo openly joins
Wyclif in denying tran-
substantiation, while
Huss for the moment
does not take a stand on
this aspect and protests
only against incorrect citations of the incrimi-
nated articles.

1402   Visconti occupies
Bologna but dies of the
plague. While the re-
gency is assumed by
Caterina Visconti,
Bernabò's daughter and
second wife of Gian
Galeazzo, the state that
has been built up, divided
now between three heirs
who are minors
(Giovanni Maria, Filippo
Maria, and Gabriele
Maria) falls apart; some
cities are occupied by
such soldiers of fortune
as Facino Cane (who be-
comes lord of
Alessandria, Novara,
Tortona, and Piacenza);
others return to their former owners. Ladislaus of
Anjou wishes to profit by
Gian Galeazzo's death to
establish a large Italian
kingdom for himself, but
he meets with resistance
from Florence and the
pope.
Bayazid I is defeated by
Tamerlane in the battle of
Ankara and dies a pris-
oner. Temporary dynastic
and political crisis in the
Ottoman Empire.

1403		France temporarily renews its obedience to Avignon. A council meets at Valladolid to confirm the decisions of the Cortes of Tordesillas, but the alternating threats of denial and restoration of obedience and the perpetuation of disagreements between Henry III and Benedict XIII are a sign of the extent to which political interests prevail in these twists and turns.	Between 1403 and 1408 canonist Francesco Zabarella writes his *De schismate* in which he proposes conciliarism as the only way of ending the schism. Lorenzo Ghiberti begins the doors of the baptistery in Florence (1403–24). John Gerson writes his *Médicine de l'ame.*
1404	Death of Caterina Visconti; Archbishop Pietro di Candia is regent for Giovanni Maria. Philip the Bold dies. He is succeeded as duke of Burgundy and as regent of France by his son John the Fearless, who continues to use the crown of the Valois to promote Burgundy's autonomy and expansionist ambitions. On an impulse he changes his political direction, becomes hostile to the royal house, and allies himself with the English.	Death of Boniface IX. Election in Rome of Pope Innocent VIII (Cosma Migliorati of Sulmona, 1404–6). Benedict XIII gathers his bishops in Paris to decree some disciplinary regulations.	John Dominici writes his *Trattato delle dieci quistioni.* Death of Jean Froissart, author of *Chroniques* covering 1327 to 1400. Huss becomes a bachelor in theology and gives courses in theology at the University.
1405	Death of Tamerlane and decline of his empire. The Ottoman Empire is weakened by internal conflicts.	The University of Paris, like that of Bologna before it, lines up against the Avignon pope.	Foundation of the University of Turin. John Dominici writes his *Lucula noctis.* John Gerson writes *Dialogus cordis, conscientiae rationis et quinque sensuum* and *Dialogue "Dame raison, ma bonne mère."* Huss, perhaps in collaboration with Znojmo, writes a treatise *De sanguine Christi* in which he

strongly condemns the cult of an appearance "of the blood of Christ" at Wilsnack in Brandenburg, already a place of pilgrimage; this intervention increases his popularity. Despite the campaign of repression begun by Rome in order to prevent the spread of the Wyclifite heresy in Bohemia, Huss also publishes a *De corpore Christi* inspired by Wyclif's *De eucharistia,* although he still does not agree with the denial of transubstantiation.

1406	Florence subjugates Pisa, which has been sold to Gabriele Maria Visconti. Henry III of Castile dies; succeeded by John II.	Death of Innocent VIII. Election in Rome of Gregory XII (Angelo Correr of Venice, 1406–9).	Death of Coluccio Salutati, after having finished his *De laboribus Herculis,* which, following in the line of Boccaccio's *Genealogiae doerum gentilium,* seeks to rehabilitate ancient poetry and religion.
1407	Louis of Orleans, now a dangerous adversary of his ambitious cousin, John the Fearless, is assassinated on a Paris street. Bernard VII of Armagnac sides with the Orleanists in the name of Louis' son, Charles (Bernard's son-in-law, married to his daughter Bona). The civil war reaches its height in the battles between the supporters of the families of Burgundy, or "Burgundians," and of Orleans, the "Armagnacians."	The new Roman pontiff tries to open negotiations with Benedict XIII. In April the agreement of Marseilles, where the Avignon pope was residing for several months, provides for a meeting between the two popes at Savona at the end of December. But an unexpected hardening of Gregory's position, due chiefly to the influence of Ladislaus of Naples, prevents the meeting. Charles VI of France calls a national council in Paris, at which the theologians of the university declare themselves in	After the assassination of Louis of Orleans, Master John Petit maintains the liceity of tyrannicide to justify John the Fearless. John Gerson asks and obtains from the university a condemnation of these propositions, thus drawing upon himself the enmity of the Burgundians. John Capreolus teaches in Paris. Huss begins his own commentary *Super quatuor libros Sententiarum* and meanwhile publishes various short theological and exegetical works in the Czech language. In his

favor of a new refusal of obedience to Benedict XIII. It is decided to ask the Avignon pope to commit himself to ending the schism, but the divergent tendencies in the French episcopate are not yet reconciled.

De orthographia bohemica he proposes a successful reform of Czech spelling.

1408

At a new French national council in Paris the bishops favoring Benedict XIII absent themselves; once again, at the request of representatives of the university, the council approves the withdrawal of obedience and the neutrality of the kingdom of France in relation to the two popes. Later, thirteen cardinals obedient to Rome and the entire Avignon Curia meet in Livorno (June) and decide to call a general council at Pisa on March 24, 1409. The two popes do not accept this initiative and separately convoke two synods, at Cividale del Friuli and Perpignan respectively, which have no special success.

A provincial council called by Arundel in London in order to forestall the harm caused by the schism proposes to reform pastoral preaching, forbids translation of the Bible into the vernacular, and preaching by masters with no doctorate in theology. Another provincial council, at Oxford, publishes thirteen decrees against the Lollards with a view

Gasparino Barzizza opens a school in Padua.

In Padua Paul of Venice (Paolo Nicoletti da Udine) begins to teach and will do so until 1415, when he begins to travel about among the Italian universities. During this period he composes his *Summa naturalium* and compiles his commentary on the *De anima* and his *Expositio* of Aristotle's physics.

to definitively suppressing their errors; among other things, disputations, in the schools or elsewhere, on thorny theological subjects are forbidden, and it is decreed that every book be approved either by Oxford University or Cambridge University. Wenceslaus IV of Bohemia, who continues his struggle with Emperor Rupert, aligns himself with the king of France in deciding to remain neutral in the schism; the Czech masters of Prague University and John Huss agree with him, but he is opposed by the Germans and the representatives of the upper clergy, led by Archbishop Zaijc Sbinco. The latter convenes a provincial council in Prague that condemns the teachings of Wyclif and has his books burned; then, thanks to the majority of Germans among the masters of theology, he wins a condemnation of Huss by the university.

| 1409 | Urged by the Florentines, the newly elected Alexander V recognizes the rights of Louis II against Ladislaus of Anjou, reopening the war of succession in the territory of Naples. The kingdom of Sicily passes by inheritance to the firstborn branch of the Aragonese in Spain. | The Council of Pisa begins with the support of the theologians of Paris and Bologna. The cardinals of the two obediences declare the two popes, Gregory XII and Benedict XIII, to be deposed and elect a third pope, Alexander V (Pietro Filargo of Candia, 1409–10). But the two deposed popes do not renounce their claims until the Council of Constance. | Foundation of the University of Alcalá de Henares. Foundation of the University of Aix-en-Provence. Gerson writes his treatises on political theology: *De unitate Ecclesiae* and *De auferibilitate papae ab Ecclesia,* which confirm his authority in this area until the Council of Constance. John Münsterberg is first |

At the insistence of Jerome of Prague, Wenceslaus of Bohemia intervenes in the dispute at the University of Prague over Huss' teaching; he assigns, for the future, three votes to the masters of the Czech "nation" and only one to each of the other "nations" (decree of Kutná Hora). The entire German "nation" abandons Prague and goes off to found the University of Leipzig. Huss is elected rector at Prague but is excommunicated by the archbishop, who puts the city under interdict. Huss is examined by the Inquisition but emerges from the inquiry unharmed; Sbinco, however, has Alexander V forbid Huss to preach.

rector of the University of Leipzig. Among the masters from Prague who came to Leipzig is John Hoffmann, author of the treatise on the Eucharist against the Hussites. In reply to the decree of destruction of Wyclif's works, Huss writes his *De libris haereticis legendis,* in which, while acknowledging that Wyclif's works may contain errors, he maintains the timeliness of reading and reflecting on the works of heretics generally and of Wyclif in particular.

1410	Death of Rupert of Wittelsbach. The imperial schism is made more acute, while Wenceslaus is still alive, by the election of two more emperors: Sigismund of Luxembourg, king of Hungary and brother of Wenceslaus, and Jobst (or Josse) of Brandenburg, son of the margave of Moravia. German society is permeated by serious disturbances and social revolts, especially due to the prevalent system of large landed estates that harms the peasants. At Tannenberg-Grünewald Ladislaus II Jagellone of Poland defeats the Teutonic	Death of Alexander V and his replacement by John XXIII (Baldassarre Cossa of Naples, 1410–15). At the urging again of Sbinco John XXIII orders that the accusations against Huss be examined by the University of Bologna and by Cardinal Oddone Colonna: in both cases the resultant condemnation is for disobedience and not for heresy.	In his treatise *De modis uniendi ac reformandi ecclesiam in concilio universali,* Dietrich of Niem (or Nieheim, in Westphalia) maintains the need of a universal council to settle the schism.

Order, the grand master
of which, Heinrich of
Plauen, takes refuge in
Mareenburg.

1411	Henry IV of Lancaster procrastinates in the war against France and for this reason is opposed by his son Henry (the future Henry V), who calls for his abdication. Following the death of Jobst, Sigismund remains sole emperor. The first Peace of Thorn limits the territories of the Teutonic Order, to the advantage of Poland.	John the Fearless compels the parish priests of his territory to apply to Charles of Orleans and the followers of the Armagnac ruler (who are gathering troops to oppose John) the papal bull (1336) excommunicating the looters of the mercenary companies. John of Sens, bishop of Orleans and archbishop of Sens, calls a regional council at Orleans, which decrees that the bull in question cannot be applied to the young duke of Orleans and instead issues a solemn excommunication of the duke of Burgundy. Wenceslaus IV, who has been unsuccessful in protecting Huss against the Roman Curia, retaliates against Archbishop Sbinco, telling the people of Prague not to obey his renewed interdict. The archbishop flees Prague and dies in Bratislava.	John Gerson writes his *Doctrina pro pueris ecclesiae parisiensis.* Foundation of the University of St. Andrews in Scotland. In his *Positio contra Anglicum Stokes* and in his exegesis of the first seven chapters of 1 Corinthians, Huss does not hide his devotion to Wyclif. Then, in his *Quaestio de indulgentiis* and his *Contra bullam papae* he begins the battle against the promulgation of new indulgences by John XXIII.
1412	At the death of his brothers Philip Maria Visconti remains sole duke and works to rebuild and expand his dominions once again. He marries Beatrice of Tenda, widow of Facino Cane, thereby inheriting his possessions and army, and he recruits condottiere Francesco Bussone, "Il Carmagnola," to head the rebuilt Milanese army.	Huss' resistance to papal authority and to indulgences causes some of his supporters, among them Wenceslaus IV and Stanislaus Znojimo, to distance themselves from his teaching. From Rome comes a condemnation demanding his submission to ecclesiastical authority and the closing of Bethlehem Chapel. At the	Jehoshua-ha-Lorqui receives baptism as Jerome of the Holy Faith and writes his *Libri duo, quorum prior fidem et religionem iudaeorum impugnat, alter vero Talmud.* John Capreolus teaches at Toulouse. Huss publishes his *Defensio articulorum Wyclef;* then, in exile, *Explanation of the Creed,*

king's urging, Huss leaves Prague. A Roman synod convoked by John XXIII (the "Owl Synod") has no concrete results for reform.

the Decalogue, and the Lord's Prayer in Czech, the main purpose being to spread his teachings among the people and the lower clergy.

1413

The popular uprising is renewed in Paris, fed by the nobles of the Burgundian party against the monarchy: revolt of the "Cabochians" (from their leader, Caboche), who attack the Bastile and invade the Louvre. Ferdinand II of Transtamara ends the struggle for the succession in Aragon. Henry V of Lancaster ascends the throne of England. Muhammad I, son of Bayazid I, becomes sultan and begins to restore the unity of the Ottoman Empire.

In Tortosa Benedict XIII holds a solemn debate between Christian and Jewish Iberian scholars. Huss returns to Prague and begins to preach again in his chapel. During the following months, in obedience to Wenceslaus, he alternates his presence in Prague and periods of prudent exile. Meanwhile, in the countryside and provinces of Bohemia Hussitism spreads in bolder and more radical forms.

Jacopo della Quercia builds the tomb of Ilaria del Carretto in the cathedral of Lucca. Huss publishes his *De ecclesia,* which is heavily dependent on Wyclif; it soon reaches France and Italy.

1414

Ladislaus of Naples dies and is succeeded by his weak sister Joanna II, while Louis II, distracted by the development of the war against England, returns to France, where he dies a short time later. The weak reign of Joanna II is afflicted by quarrels between favorites, feudal lords, and soldiers of fortune. Sigismund, crowned king of Germany at Aachen, is at odds with Venice and tries unsuccessfully to send an expedition into Lombardy.

At the insistent requests of Emperor Sigismund, John XXIII calls a council at Constance (it will later be recognized at the sixteenth ecumenical council, 1414–18), endeavoring to have it accepted as a continuation of the Council of Pisa, which elected him. The right to vote is given not only to the cardinals, archbishops, bishops, and prelates but to representative of the king, the doctors, and the proxies of the universities and chapters; since this amounts to an impossible 128,000

Prague master Jacobello of Stribro teaches the right of the laity to Communion under both species. Huss immediately approves this teaching and while at Constance writes a short treatise, *Utrum expediat laicis fidelibus sumere sanguinem Christi sub specie vini,* which was to be very important in later years for the spread of the doctrine of the Utruquists. Immediately after his arrest in Constance, Huss is questioned by James Moxena.

voters, it is proposed that votes be by nation. John Huss agrees to go to Constance, accompanied by his disciple, Peter of Mladonovice, with a safe-conduct from Sigismund (brother of Wenceslaus IV) and a guarantee of safety from the pope to the representatives of the emperor. But Cardinal Peter d'Ailly, in agreement with other cardinals, has him arrested (on the basis of a decree signed by John XXIII), because, contrary to a formal prohibition, Huss celebrates Mass and does not stop spreading his own doctrines. When Sigismund reaches Constance, he is unable to win Huss' freedom because the cardinals threaten to break off the council. Huss is imprisoned in the fortress of Gottlieben. When allowed to speak to the council, he is unable to have it prove his errors from Scripture. When condemned, he protests strongly because no heresy has been shown in his Latin writings, while the Czech writings are not even read; he is put to death at the stake and his ashes are scattered in the Rhine.

| 1415 | Henry V of England flees a plot of the nobles who want to replace the Lancaster usurper with Plantagenet Edmund Mortimer, heir designated by Richard II; Henry de | Fearing deposition, John XXIII flees from Constance but is followed and arrested at Breisache on the Rhine. Aided by Gerson, the emperor manages to control the | Death of Manuel Chrysoloras. English theologian Thomas Netter (Thomas Waldensis) writes his *Doctrinale antiquitatum fidei catholicae Ecclesiae.* |

votes himself to renewing the war in France. The English disembark at the mouth of the Seine and besiege and conquer Harfleur; but despite the weak response of the Armagnacian government in Paris, at the onset of winter instead of moving into the interior of the country, the English seem to want to go back to Calais and Brittany. The Armagnacians bar their way, but at the battle of Agincourt the French are badly defeated. Paris and part of the Norman territory are occupied, Charles VI is taken prisoner, and the Burgundy of John the Fearless recognizes Henry V of England as king of France.

general unrest. The council (sessions 3–4) then issues decrees that present conciliarism (the superiority of ecumenical councils over the pope) as the official teaching of the Church and declares itself responsible for unity (i.e., the unity of the Church, with power to elect and depose popes), for reformation (the reform and moral improvement of the Church), and faith (the purity of doctrine against heretics). On March 2 John XXIII is deposed as a promotor of schism and a simoniac and is imprisoned. The Holy See is declared vacant as of May 5. Gregory XII offers his resignation through his legate, Charles Malatesta. Sigismund goes to Perpignan to persuade Benedict XIII to do the same, but in vain; after lengthy efforts, diplomatic measures get the kingdoms of Aragon, Navarre, and Castile to cease their obedience to Pope Luna (treaty of Narbonne, December 13). The prelates of all Spain are then able to join the council.

Jerome of Prague, who came to Constance and was imprisoned as he attempted to leave Switzerland after the death of Huss, is also condemned and burned at the stake. The council decides against the use of the chalice in the public Eucharist; in reaction, the

This persistent adversary of Wyclif and the Hussites is also considered to be the author, or perhaps partial compiler, of the *Fasciculi Zizaniorum,* a collection of anti-Wyclif documents.

Hussites of Bohemia
make use of the chalice
their standard in the
battle against Rome, the
result being the birth of a
local Urtraquist church (a
church based on the prin-
ciple of Communion
under both species for all
of the faithful).

| 1416 | Amadeus VIII obtains from Sigismund the title of duke of Savoy and Piedmont. The king of Aragon, Ferdinand I the Just, dies. His successor, Alphonsus I, who will be known as the Magnanimous, free now from internal concerns turns to the conquest of southern Italy. Emperor Sigismund, whom the duke of Armagnac has asked in vain to serve as mediator between France and England, allies himself with Henry V at Canterbury and plans a partition of France, a plan that has no follow-up. | The bishops of the province of Tarragona meet at a provincial council in Barcelona for the purpose of having Ferdinand of Aragon return to obedience to Benedict XIII, but the king replies that only an ecumenical council has authority to decide on this matter, Alphonsus takes the same position, and the effort at Barcelona is the last vain attempt by the partisans of Pope Luna. | Death of Biagio Palecani of Parma. |

| 1417 | In England Sir John Oldcastle (Lord Cobham) sides with the Lollards and rebels against the sovereign. The little war in Normandy continues. | Deposed pope Gregory XII dies at Recanati. The council condemns Benedict XIII as a perjurer, schismatic, and heretic. This sentence makes it possible to begin efforts to elect a legitimate pope, and after two years of an empty papal see, at a conclave combining cardinals and laymen, the council elects Pope Martin V (Oddo Colonna, 1417–31). It is determined that general | Francis Zabarella dies at Constance, where he had devoted himself energetically to the resolution of the schism. George of Trebizond, called to Venice by Francis Barbaro, studies Latin with Guarino Guarini of Verona and Vittorino de'Rambaldoni of Feltre. In Florence Donatus de'Bardi, or Donatello, executes his *St. George,* while Philip Brunelleschi begins his work on |

councils shall meet periodically.

the dome of Santa Maria del Fiore. Jacopo della Quercia begins the baptismal font in the baptistery of Siena (work finished in 1434).

1418   Amadeus VIII annexes the Piedmont territories of the Savoy-Acaia branch, now extinct, and acquires Vercelli, thus enlarging his duchy in Italy; Turin becomes its capital.

After dealing in a very general way with the problems of Church reform and postponing further work on them to a later ecumenical council (to meet in Pavia), the Council of Constance is officially closed by Martin V, who takes up permanent residence in Rome.
A provincial council in Perth decrees the shift of Scotland's obedience from Benedict XIII to Martin V.

At the invitation of Henry Beaufort, bishop of Winchester, Poggio Bracciolini stays in England (until 1423), where he further develops his interest in patristic literature. John Dominici is sent to Bohemia by Martin V to stem the Hussite crisis. Between 1418 and 1446 Philip Brunelleschi executes the dome of Santa Maria del Fiore in Florence.
At the end of the work of the Council of Constance, Augustinian theologian Theodoric Vrie gives Emperor Sigismund a detailed theological history of the assembly, entitled *De consolatione Ecclesiae*. After the close of the council John Gerson does not dare return to France from fear of John the Fearless and takes refuge in Austria at the Abbey of Mölk and then in Vienna; there, imitating the exiled Boethius, he writes his *De consolatione theologiae*.

1419   The Portuguese colonize Madeira and the Canaries.
Normandy and Rouen go over to the English, Paris falls into the hands of the Burgundians. The Armagnacians are

Former pope John XXIII is released from his imprisonment in Mannheim after paying a heavy ransom and dies shortly after as cardinal bishop of Frascati.

Augustine Favaroni is elected general of the Augustinians. John Dominici dies at Buda. Death of Anthony Canals, author of the *Escala de contemplación*. Death of decimated, the mad king and the queen are imprisoned; only Dauphin Charles is saved by flight. John the Fearless is assassinated at Montereau by killers on the Armagnacian side. In reaction to the condemnation of Huss and Jerome of Prague at Constance, a popular and aristocratic revolt against Wenceslaus breaks out led by John Zizka. Wenceslaus dies and Emperor Sigismund, his brother, is elected king of Bohemia; he takes charge of the repressive crusade.

As a condition for recognizing Sigismund as king, the Hussites present him with the *Four Articles of Prague,* in which they sum up their religious claims: freedom to preach the word of God on the basis of the supremacy of Scripture in theology and moral doctrine, use of the chalice in the Eucharist, expropriation of ecclesiastical possessions by the state, and punishment of public sins, especially those of the clergy.

Vincent Ferrer at Vannes in Brittany. After the death of John the Fearless Gerson returns to France and settles in Lyons with a brother who is prior of a convent of the Celestines. During this stay he writes his principal mystical works, among them *Considerationes de theologia mystica speculativa* and *Tractatus de elucidatione scholastica mysticae theologiae.* Foundation of the University of Rostock in Germany.

1420
Treaty of Troyes between Henry V and Charles VI, the latter a prisoner of the English, who disinherits the dauphin, recognizes the king of England as heir to the throne of France, and gives him his daughter Catherine as wife; the next year she bears a son, the future Henry VI. The guiding spirit behind the treaty is the new duke of Burgundy, Philip the Good, who shares with Henry the government of the conquered territories of France.
In order to restore peace to the territory of Naples, Pope Martin V, supported by Florence, opposes Joanna II and gives the kingdom to the son of Louis II of Anjou, Louis III, who prepares to invade Italy. Meanwhile, Alphonsus V of Aragon has occupied Sardinian and Corsica; Joanna II

A bull of Martin V proclaims a crusade against the Hussites, but the only effect is to intensify a fanatical religious nationalism. After agreeing to a truce with Sigismund, Zizka withdraws to the countryside and establishes Tabor, a fortified center of resistance for the radical Hussites: whence the name "Taborites" for the extreme wing, with its apocalypticism and its emphasis on strict poverty.

Death of Peter d'Ailly and of Augustinian theologian Angelo Dobelin, a master at Paris and Erfurt.

appears him her heir
against Louis, thereby
starting a new war of succession.

1421   While extending the domains of Philip Maria
Visconti, Carmagnola oc-
cupies Genoa.
At the death of
Muhammad I Murad II
becomes the new Turkish
sultan.

Conrad of Vechta, arch-
bishop of Prague, ap-
proves Utraquist teaching
at a council in Prague,
while Zizka's army wins
all of eastern Bohemia
for Hussitism. But the
spread in this country of
a doctrine opposed to
adoration of the eucharistic sacrament and known
as Piccardism (from the
Picards, who spread it
when they fled from the
Inquisition and took
refuge in Bohemia) is op-
posed by the Utraquists
of Prague but tolerated by
the Taborites, thus widen-
ing the gap between the
two churches. The
Taborites unite in a theocratic and revolutionary
brotherhood, whose
leader, after the death of
Zizka, is Procopius the
Great.

From 1421 to 1444 Philip
Brunelleschi works on
the Ospedale degli
Innocenti in Florence.
The Faculty of Theology
of Cologne issues an official statement against the
Taborites: *Replicationes
. . . contra literas et rationes Procopii heretici et
articulos Hussitarum.*

1422   Death of Henry V of
England and, shortly
after, of Charles VI of
Valois. The new king,
Henry VI, is under the
protection of John of
Lancaster (duke of
Bedford), who takes it on
himself to pursue the war
in France. Sharing the
government with him in
England are the duke of
Gloucester and Henry
Beaufort, bishop of
Winchester. The dauphin,
Charles of Valois, is
crowned King Charles
VII at Méhun by a few
loyal followers.

Foundation of the
University of Parma.
Gaetano of Thiene begins
to teach at the University
of Padua.

A first Ottoman attempt
to besiege Constantinople
fails.

1423   Francesco Foscari is
elected doge of Venice;
he represents the party of
expansion on the main-
land, which his predeces-
sor, Thomas Mocenigo,
had opposed.

Martin V convokes the
Council of Pavia for the
purpose chiefly of tack-
ling the problems of the
national churches. The
council is interrupted by
a plague and is trans-
ferred to Siena; at a
single general session and
in the absence of the
pope, the decrees of
Constance against Wyclif
and Huss and its condem-
nation of Benedict XIII
are confirmed, union with
the Oriental Church is favored, and tribunals of
the Inquisition are or-
dered and established
everywhere.
Benedict XIII dies at
Peñiscola, near Valencia.
A council meets in
Nuremberg, in the pres-
ence of Sigismund and
with Cardinal Julian
Cesarini as president, for
the purpose of organizing
the suppression of the
Hussites. In the name of
the pope Cesarini
promises a plenary indul-
gence to all who vote for
the undertaking.

Nicholas of Cusa receives
a licentiate in canon law
at Padua. Between 1423
and 1426 Leonard Bruni
writes his *De studiis et
litteris*. Vittorino of
Feltre, active at the
Gonzaga court, opens a
school in Mantua at a
villa known as La Zoiosa,
where some of the lead-
ers of mature Italian hu-
manism will be trained.

1424   Death of Muzio
Attendolo Sforza, a con-
dottiere who had amassed
large estates in the kingdom of Naples.

The Council of Pavia-
Siena (the ecumenical
character of which was
not recognized by later
popes) ends in February,
while appointing Basel as
the place of a future ecumenical meeting.
A year after the death of
deposed antipope
Benedict XIII, his loyal
cardinals in Spain elect

Leonard Bruni writes his
*Isagogicon moralis disci-
plinae ad Galeottum
Ricasolanum,* conceived
as an introduction to the
ethics of Aristotle; then,
in his *De recta interpretatione* (written between
1424 and 1426 but left
incomplete) he challenges
the accuracy and authen-
ticity of the medieval

his successor in the person of antipope Clement VIII (Giles Sancho Muñoz), who is favored by Alphonsus V of Aragon for political reasons.

translations from the Greek.

1425   Venice allies with Florence against Philip Maria Visconti. Carmagnola enters the service of La Serenissima. John II of Castile conquers Navarre by diplomacy.

Intense negotiations by Cardinal Peter of Foix bring about a reconciliation of Martin V with the king of Aragon and the end of the new schism.

Anthony Beccadelli, known as Panormitano, publishes a collection of erotic and satiric epigrams entitled *Hermaphroditus*. Jacopo della Quercia begins the sculptural decoration of the main door of San Petronio in Bologna (he will work on it until his death in 1438). John of Torquemada is master of theology at the University of Paris. Foundation of the University of Louvain, in the Brabant. Resistance of the University of Cologne to the prince electors, who seek the introduction of nominalism. Nicholas of Cusa follows the philosophical-theological courses of Eimeric of Kampen at Cologne.

1426   The war of Venice and Florence against Visconti begins; a coalition of the lords of Ferrara, Mantua, Monferrati, and Savoy also takes part. Florentine humanism is colored by patriotic and republican ideals against Visconti. The war in the Po Valley will last about thirty years and change Venice from a maritime to a mainland republic at the expense of the Visconti;

A Portuguese national council held in Braga succeeds in reining in the abuses of King John II against the religious and economic freedom of the clergy.

Tommasi di of Ser Giovanni Cassai, known as Masaccio, begins the frescoes in the Brancacci Chapel in Florence. Gerson writes his *De concordia metaphysicae cum logica*. Flemist painter Jan van Eyck paints the *Altar of the Mystical Lamb* (1426–32); the period of the Duchy of Burgundy's splendor under Philip the Good coincides but it will also play a role in ending the autonomy of Florence as a commune.

with the triumphal beginnings of Flemish realistic painting.

1427   Venice defeats the Milanese at Maclodio. The victor is Carmagnola, but he is accused of agreements with the Visconti and is executed.
In Bohemia the Taborites, led by Procopius the Great, triumph over the imperial armies and invade surrounding lands, spreading their doctrines widely in Central Europe.

Preacher Bernardine of Siena (Bernardino degli Albzzeschi) is accused of sacrilegious and superstitious practices because of his propagation of devotion to the Name of Christ. Tried for heresy, he is defended by Franciscan John of Capistrano and is found innocent. Death of Hubert Decembrio (father of Peter Candido), author of a *De republica* and translator of Plato's dialogue of that name. Leonard Bruni becomes chancellor of the Florentine signoria.

1428   The English prepare for a new attack south of the Loire, toward Orleans and Bourges (capital of Charles VII). The siege of Orleans begins. The Estates General, assembled at Chinon, decide to help Charles VII, and all the French cities send help to Orleans.

Poggio Bracciolini writes his *De avaritia* (1428–29).
Eimeric of Kampen writes his *Problemata inter Albertum Magnum et sanctum Thomam,* in which, while criticizing nominalism, he identifies the reasons for the disagreement among the exponents of realism. Death of Augustinian theologian John Zachariae, master at Erfurt and promotor, at Constance, of efforts to overcome the schism.

1429   As Orleans resists and Charles VII hesitates to intervene, Joan of Arc, a young peasant girl of Lorraine who claims to be inspired by God, gets the commander of the

In Peñiscola, Clement VIII officially renounces his alleged rank in the name of peace, handing his abdication to Peter of Foix, papal legate, and to two representatives of the

Paul of Venice dies at Padua, to which he had returned the previous year.
Between 1429 and 1444 Philip Brunelleschi builds the Capella dei Pazzi in

fortress of Vancouleurs to bring her to the king, whom she persuades to make a supreme effort to liberate Orleans. After three days of fighting, the English, who are attacked from within and without, are forced to abandon the city. Joan of Arc, sure of the favor of the French people, boldly leads Charles VII to Rheims and has him crowned king of France.

king of Aragon. Absolved and restored to "his original state," the former antipope is made bishop of Majorca. The papal legate holds a general Council of Aragon at Tortosa, at which the problems connected with the schism are finally resolved and religious unity is restored throughout the Spanish realms.

Florence. John Gerson dies at Lyons.

1430   Amadeus VIII reorganizes the duchy by introducing the Estates General.
Joan of Arc transfers the center of the struggle to Normandy but is not followed by Charles VII. She succeeds in delivering Compiègne from the English siege, but she is captured in a raid and handed over to the English.
Murad II again invades Serbia. Byzantine emperor John VIII looks to the West for help against the Turkish threat and, to this end, favors the reunion of the Oriental Church and the Roman Church.

Alphonsus of Cartagena writes his *Libellus contra Leonardum,* in which he criticizes Bruni's translation of the *Nicomachean Ethics;* the sharp controversy between the two contrasts two different views of the role of a translator and, in the final analysis, the Scholastic and the humanist ideals of philosophy.
Nicholas Niccoli leaves his library to the convent of Santa Maria degli Angeli (in 1444 it will become part of the library of San Marco). Thomas Netter dies at Rouen. German painter Stephan Lochner, one of the greatest representatives of late Rhenish Gothic, paints the *Final Judgment* altarpiece in Cologne.

1431   The Portuguese reach the Azores.
Joan of Arc is burned at the stake in Rouen, without any attempt to free her by Charles VII and his ministers. The duke of

Death of Martin V. Election of Eugene IV (Gabriele Condulmer of Venice, nephew of the deposed Gregory XII; 1431–47), who confirms the convocation, already decided on by Martin V

A new trial for heresy against Bernardine of Siena, but it is broken off by Eugene IV, who in the following years issues a bull praising Bernardine's life and teaching.
Augustine Favaroni is

Bedford has Henry VI crowned in Paris.

shortly before his death, of a new ecumenical council (the 17th) at Basel (1431–49), aimed above all at resolving the Bohemian question. But from the outset the new pope is ill disposed toward a council because he fears a new dominance of conciliarist tendencies. Therefore, ill informed about the poor attendance of bishops at the site of the council, he charges Cardinal Julian Cesarini, whom Martin V had appointed president, to close that council and convoke another for a year and a half later in Bologna, the place which suited the Greeks for the discussion of reunion.

appointed archbishop of Nazareth. Lawrence Valla teaches rhetoric in Pavia, where he attacks the jurists and the representatives of the university culture and writes the first version of his *De voluptate*. Ambrose Traversari, active at the convent of Santo Maria degli Angeli in Florence, translator of Diogenes Laertius and many patristic Greek works, is appointed general of the Camaldolensians; to report on the visits aimed at reform that he makes in this office, he writes, in the following years, his *Hodoeporicon,* a basic document on the religious life of the time. Luca della Robbia sculpts the *Cantoria* of Santa Maria del Fiore in Florence (1431–38).
Death in Barcelona of Philip of Malla, author of the *Memorial del pecador remut.*
Foundation of the University of Poitiers.
Death in Cologne of theologian Henry of Gorcum, who expressed the university's official position in a work *Contra articulos hussitarum.*
Eimeric of Kampen, representative of the university at the Council of Basel, also writes, against the Taborites, an *Epistola de communione sub utraque specie.*
Nichols of Pelhrimov, the chief Taborite theologian, writes the Taborite *Confessio* and an

			Apologia in defense of his beliefs.
1432		Cesarini, who has meanwhile held the first session of the council, asks the pope to reverse his decision, while the council continues its work and confirms the decrees of Constance of the superiority of a council over the pope, declaring itself the legitimate representative of the Church.	Carmelite painter Filippo Lippi paints the *Madonna dell'Umiltà*. John Capreolus completes his *Defensiones theologiae divi Thomae de Aquino,* a monumental exposition of Thomist wisdom in the form of a commentary on the *Sentences*.
1433	In the war of Florence against the Visconti the truce of Ferrara gives the exhausted city a respite. Death of John I of Portugal, who is succeeded by his son Edward. Sigismund of Luxembourg is crowned emperor in Rome by Eugene IV.	Seven sovereigns, among them Emperor Sigismund, support the council. Eugene IV is compelled to withdraw his decree closing the council and to recognize it as legitimate. After fruitless discussions in Basel between representatives of Hussitism and the council fathers, an agreement is signed in Prague (the *Compactata* of Prague) by the Utraquists and the council's legates: in order to help the return of Sigismund to the throne of Bohemia the legates tell the Bohemians of their intention to recognize the use of the chalice and to accept the expropriation of Church property.	Lawrence Valla begins to rework his *De voluptate* in the form of his *De vero falsoque bono,* which he will continue to revise until 1449; he begins the composition of his *Elegantiae linguae latinae* (finished in 1444). Nicholas of Cusa, present at the Council of Basel, writes his *De concordantia catholica,* in which he supports moderate conciliarist views.
1434	The Florentine Consorteria indicts and exiles Cosimo de'Medici, son of banker Giovanni di Bicci (called "father of the poor," and gonfaloniere from 1420 to 1429) and leader of the	Fransciscan Observant preacher Alphonsus of Mella is condemned by a commission of cardinals for heterodoxy. In the following years he will be leader of the "heretics of Durango."	George of Trebizond writes an especially successful *Rhetorica* and *Dialectica*. Raymond Sibiuda, master of theology and rector of the University of Toulouse, begins the

opposition to the oligarchy that governed the city since the wiping out of the Ciompi. But, shortly after, the new signoria, composed of supporters of the Medicean sympathizers with the people's party, calls Cosimo back; the oligarchs, led by Rinaldo degli Albizzi, object in vain and are exiled. Although without a formal title (for the time being Cosimo is gonfaloniere and Father of the Fatherland), the hereditary Medicean signoria now begins. Amadeus VIII of Savoy abdicates in favor of his son Ludovic and withdraws to a semiecclesiastical life in the monastery of Ripaglia (on Lake Geneva, to which his father, the Red Count, had already retired). In Normandy a general revolt against the English breaks out, rousing Charles VII and his friends from their torpor. In Poland, death of Ladislaus II Jagellone, who is succeeded by his son, Ladislaus III.

The Utraquists acknowledge Sigismund as nominal king and, in the name of peace and in defense of the *Compactata,* openly fight the Taborites and defeat them near Lipany. The military leader of the Taborites, Procopius the Great, dies on the battlefield.

writing of his *Liber creaturarum (Scientia libri creaturarum sive libri naturae et scientia de homine).* Nicholas of Cusa writes his *De auctoritate praesidendi in concilio generali).* German painter Konrad Witz, a follower of the Flemish painters, paints the altar piece of Basel. Jan van Eyck paints his *Portrait of the Arnolfinis.*

1435   Deaths, in quick succession, of Louis III of Anjou and Joanna II, both without heirs. Alphonsus V of Aragon enters Campania and besieges Gaeta, but Filippo Maria Visconti opposes him and appoints Renato of Anjou, brother of Louis III, as king of

Panormita enters the service of Alphonsus of Aragon. He follows the king to Naples and in subsequent years founds the Accademia Antoniana (later, Pontaniana). Death of Augustinian humanist Andrew Biglia, translator of works of Aristotle and author of a history of Milan.

Naples. The sending of
Genoese ships enables
Visconti to defeat the
Aragonese navy at Ponza
and take Alphonsus pris-
oner.
Paris is surrounded by
Charles VII's men. Death
of the Duke of Bedford.
Philip the Good of
Burgundy makes an al-
liance with Charles VII at
Arras.

Death of Paul of Burgos,
who is succeeded as
bishop by his son,
Alphonsus of Cartagena.
He leaves behind a
*Scrutinium scripturarum
contra perfidiam
Iudaeorum* and successful
Additiones to the *Postilla*
of Nicholas of Lyra.

1436   Alphonsus V, a prisoner,
manages to bring Filippo
Maria over to his side,
since Filippo is afraid of
being encircled by the
French. While he is re-
newing, with different alliances, the war of
succession in Naples,
Genoa rebels against
Visconti and enters a
league with Venice,
Florence, and the pope.
Charles VII makes a tri-
umphant entry into liber-
ated Paris. In England
there is a sharp dispute
between the peace party
(which had been
Bedford's party) and the
war party (led by
Gloucester); France is
struggling with a finan-
cial crisis, and the Estates
General are compelled to
restore the indirect taxes
abolished by Charles VII.

Nicholas of Cusa is sent
as papal legate to
Constantinople to invite
Emperor John VIII and
Patriarch Joseph II to
take part in the council
for the reunion of the
churches. The Concordat
of Prague is signed at
Jihlava: it recognizes the
national church of the
Utraquists, now led by
John Rokycana, a dis-
ciple of Huss, in ex-
change for tolerance of
the Catholic minority that
has survived the revolu-
tion.

Guarino of Verona opens
a school at the court of
Ferrara, whither he has
been called as tutor of
Lionello d'Este. Guido di
Pietro, known as Blessed
Angelicus, does frescoes
in the Florentine convent
of San Marco (1436–45).
Death of Raymond
Sibiuda at Toulouse.
Death of Salamanca theo-
logian John of Casanova,
author of a *Tractatus de
potestate papae et con-
cilii,* defending Eugene
IV against the council of
Basel.

1437

New rupture between the
council and the pope,
who has again made
known his plan of mov-
ing the assembly and for
this reason is summoned
to appear before the tri-
bunal of the council.
Offended by this insult,

Lawrence Valla settles at
the court of Alphonsus of
Aragon. Anthony
Pierozzi is vicar general
of the Dominican
Observance in Italy.
Death of Florentine hu-
manist Nicholas Niccoli.

Eugene decrees the disso-
lution of the Council of
Basel and its transfer to
Ferrara. Only a minority
loyal to the pope obeys,
with Cesarini and
Nicholas of Cusa at its
head.

Filippo Lippi paints the
Madonna of Tarquinia.
Death of Nicholas of
Clamanges. Foundation
of the University of Caen.
Flemish painter Rogier
van der Weyden paints
his *Deposition from the
Cross*.

1438   Death of Edward of
Portugal, who is suc-
ceeded by his brother
Alphonsus V, "the
African," with his mother,
Eleanor of Aragon, as re-
gent.
Death of Sigismund of
Luxembourg. A diet at
Basel elects, as emperor
and king of Hungary,
Albert II of Habsburg,
duke of Austria, who has
married Sigismund's
daughter Elizabeth.

Opening of the council at
Ferrara in October, after
preliminary sessions in
May and June, at which
the main reasons for the
disagreement between the
Oriental Church and the
Latin Church are dis-
cussed. The meetings in
Ferrara continue until
December 13, dealing
chiefly with the problems
of reunion. But after the
invasion of the Romagna
by Visconti, and yielding
to the urgent invitations
of Cosimo de'Medici
(who promises sizable
monetary aid), in
December Eugene de-
cides to move the council
to Florence.
The fathers of Basel, with
Louis the German, arch-
bishop of Arles, presid-
ing, issue a bull
suspending the pope, who
answers with an excom-
munication.
In a national council at
Bourges, Charles VII of
France has the *Pragmatic
Sanction* approved: this
takes over some of the
basic conciliarist decrees
of Basel and lays the
foundations for an au-
tonomous Gallican
Church.
The diet of Basel (which
consecrates Alphonsus II

Preceded by Mark
Eugenicus and Bessarion,
the official speakers at
the Council of Florence,
many Byzantine masters
come to Italy in the ret-
inue of the emperor;
among them are George
Gemistus Plethon,
George Scholarius, and
Theodore of Gaza.

as emperor) declares the neutrality of the prince electors in the conflict between pope and council.

1439　In France the direct tax on persons, known as the *taille royale,* becomes a fixed tax; the nobles, the clergy, and the burghers of certain cities are exempt from it.
Albert II dies fighting the Turks; he leaves no direct heirs.
Deposition of Erik of Pomerania: the Northern Union is maintained by his nephew, Christopher III of Bavaria, king of Denmark and Sweden from 1441, of Norway from 1442; and then by Christian I of Oldenburg, from 1448.

The Council of Florence is already at work in the early days of January. The pope's arrival is followed on February 1 by that of the Byzantine emperor John VIII Paleologus and the patriarch of Constantinople, Joseph II (who dies in Florence on June 10). The promise of a crusade against the Turks (which will not be fulfilled) is the foundational motive for carrying out the planned reunification of the two churches, which is proclaimed at a plenary session on July 6. In the month of November the council welcomes the Armenian church into the reunited world of the Church.
The Russian church rejects the union and breaks away from the Greek, becoming a national church.
The fathers of Basel declare Eugene IV deposed and in July elect as antipope Felix V (1439–49), who is Amadeus VIII, former duke of Savoy. This is the origin of the "Little Schism."
In a diet at Mainz the German electors abandon neutrality in practice by adopting in the *Instrumentum acceptationis,* a series of reform decrees issued by the Council of Basel.

In Florence George Gemistus Plethon writes his *Sulla differenza tra Platone ed Aristotele,* in which he urges a rebirth of Plato studies to counter the rampant Aristoteleanism of the Western Scholastics. Matthew Palmieri writes his dialogue *De vita civile.* Death of Ambrose Traversari. Anthony de Carlenis teaches, as a bachelor, at the Dominican Studium of Bologna; one result of this teaching, which will continue until 1442, is his *Quaestiones* on Aristotle and on the *Sentences.*
For his defense of papal authority at the council, John of Torquemada is given the title "Defender of the Faith" by Eugene IV and made a cardinal; he settles at the Roman Curia.

1440   Victory of Florence over Visconti's troops, led by Nicholas Piccinino, at the battle of Anghiari.
Social rebellion in France (known as the *Praguerie,* for its similarity to the Hussite rebellion), led by nobles of the recently liberated southern regions; the dauphin, the future Louis XI, takes part in it but is then forced by Charles VII to flee to Philip the Good of Burgundy.
The new king of Germany, and then emperor, is Frederick II of Habsburg, son of Duke Ernest of Styria. But Ladislaus III of Poland is elected king of Hungary.

Consecration of Felix V at Basel (July). Only Savoy, part of Switzerland, and some German princes formally side with the antipope.

Nicholas of Cusa writes his *De docta ignorantia,* which is followed, between 1440 and 1447, by a great many of his other philosophico-theological works, among them the *De coniecturis* (1441–44), the *De quaerendo Deum,* the *De filiatione Dei,* and the *De dato Patris luminum.*
Poggio Bracciolini writes his *De nobilitate,* in which he shows that true nobility is not a privilege of birth but a virtue of the soul. Lawrence Valla completes his *Dialectica* (or *Repastinatio dialecticae et rhetoricae*) and then writes his *De falso credita et ementita Constantini donatione.*
Tolentine humanist Francis Filelfo, at the Visconti court, composes his *Convivia Mediolanensia* (1440–42). Anthony Pierozzi begins the composition of his *Summa theologica* (or *Summa moralis*) and continues to work on it until the year of his death (1459).
Aeneas Silvius Piccolomini writes *Commentarii de gestis Basiliensis concilii* and *Libellus dialogorum de generalis concilii auctoritate et gestis Basiliensium,* in which he takes conciliarist positions.
Death in Rome of St. Frances of Rome, foundress (in 1433) of the women's Order of the Oblates of Tor

de'Specchi, which had
caritative and philan-
thropic goals.
Reginald Pecock writes
The Donet.
Death of Jan van Eyck.

| 1441 | The War in the Po valley becomes a direct struggle between the troops of Piccinino and those of Francis Sforza, who is fighting for Venice. To limit the growing power of Piccinino, who is carving out a personal domain in the Parma region, Filippo Maria Visconti halts hostilities with the Peace of Cremona (or of Carriana), in which he gives up Genoa and Ravenna and offers his illegitimate daughter, Bianca Maria, to Francesco Sforza as wife. | The Copts also subscribe to the bull reuniting the churches. | Byzantine master John Argiropulo teaches the Greek language and philosophy at Padua, then in Florence and Rome. Establishment of the University of Bordeaux. |

| 1442 | With the support of Filippo Maria Visconti, Alphonsus V of Aragnon succeeds in having himself crowned king of Naples, while Renato of Anjou returns to France. Henry VI of England comes of age and is freed from his protectors; he strikes a treaty with France and marries Margherita, daughter of Renato of Anjou. The marriage strengthens the peace party and, under Margherita's influence, Henry decides to abandon Maine. | | Lawrence Valla follows Alphonsus V to Naples and writes his *De professione religiosorum.* |

| 1443 | Continuation of the duel between Sforza and Piccinino, who is | In February Eugene IV decrees the transfer of the council from Ferrara to | Plethon's work on Plato elicits a violent reply, *Sui dubbi di Pletone intorno ad Aristotele,* from |

defeated at Montelauro. Eugene IV recognizes Alphonsus V as king of Naples.

Rome, where he intends to reside henceforth after a long absence. The Roman sessions achieve union with the Syrians of Mesopotamia, the Chaldeans and Maronites of Cyprus (as a result of Chrysoberges' effective action), and the Patarine heretics of Bosnia.

George Scholarius, who defends the compatibility of Aristoteleanism and Christianity and is an admirer of St. Thomas. Before returning to Greece, Plethon answers with his *Contra Scholarii defensionem Aristotelis.* Death of Augustine Favaroni. Poggio Bracciolini completes his *De varietate fortunae* (begun in 1431) and his *De infelicitate principum.* Leon Battista Alberti writes his *Momus* or *De principe* and begins *De re aedificatoria,* which he will complete in 1452. Gaetano of Thiene writes his commentary on the *De anima* of Aristotle and a *Quaestio de perpetuitate intellectus.* In Padua Donatello produces his equestrian statue of Gattamelata and the altar of the Santo in the Antonine Basilica. On a mission to Italy for the king of Castile, Alphonsus Fernández of Madrigal, known as El Tostado, defends some theological theses in the presence of the pope at Siena; three of them are challenged by John of Torquemada. El Tostado answers with a *Defensorium.* Reginald Pecock writes *The Reule of Crysten Religioun.* Rogier van der Weyden paints his *Polyptych of the Final Judgment.*

1444   Piccinino is called back to Milan by the duke,

George of Trebizond, appointed an apostolic

who is jealous of his success: his troops are again
routed by Sforza at
Montolmo, and the con-
dottiere dies of hydropsy
a few months later.
Ladislaus III Jagellone,
king of Poland and
Hungary, is urged on by
high ecclesiastical authorities, especially Zbigniev
Olesnicki, bishop of
Cracow, to a crusade
against the Turks; after
initial good results for the
Christians, Ladislaus is
defeated and dies in the
battle of Varna.
The Byzantine Empire is
now reduced to
Constantinople and its
suburbs.

secretary, teaches at the
Sapienza and translates
various works of Aristotle
from the Greek. Theodore
of Gaza stays with
Vittorino of Feltre.
Deaths of Bernardine of
Siena, Leonard Bruni,
and Peter Paul Vergerio.
Francis Della Rovere (the
future Sixtus IV) is re-
gent of the Santo
Studium in Padua.
Lawrence Valla meets Fra
Anthony of Bitonto, a
preacher in Naples, in a
debate on the origin of
the Apostles' Creed;
questioned on suspicion
of heresy, he defends
himself to Eugene IV in
his *Apologia contra ca-
lumniatores*. Cosimo
de'Medici establishes the
Biblioteca Laurenziana in
Florence. Foundation of
the University of Geneva.
Death of John Capreolus.
Konrad Witz paints the
altar piece in Geneva.

1445	Portuguese navigators reach the Cape Verde islands. Charles VII undertakes a reform of the military in France in order to reorganize the country and to renew hostilities. In Poland Casimir IV, brother of Ladislaus III, is crowned king and begins a policy of alliance with the lower nobility. Hungary is ruled by John Hunyadi, governor during the minority of Ladislaus V, the "Posthumous," son of Albert II of Habsburg.	The ending of the council allows Eugene IV to consecrate the successful universal reunification of the Church. With Aeneas Silvius Piccolomini (the future Pius II) as mediator, Frederick III of Habsburg officially recognizes the authority of Eugene IV in exchange for a promise of election as emperor in Rome.	Piero della Francesca paints the polyptych *Our Lady of Mercy* (1445–48) and, in the following years, the *Scourging of Christ*.

1446		Eugene IV declares the Council of Constance to be ecumenical. Death of deposed antipope Clement VIII. The German princes, disturbed by the interference of Eugene IV against the archbishop-electors, meet at the Diet of Frankfurt to decide whether to accept the urging of Frederick III and drop their neutrality. Through the mediation of Piccolomini and Legates Nicholas of Cusa and John of Carvajal, they acknowledge the authority of Eugene IV shortly before his death.	Anthony Pierozzi is archbishop of Florence. Biondo Flavio dedicates his *Roma instaurata* to Eugene IV.
1447	As the Peace of Carriana is broken and the Po valley war begins anew, Filippo Maria Visconti dies unexpectedly. Various claimants to the succession appear in Milan, among them Charles of Orleans (duke of Asti and son of Valentina Visconti), who has been freed from prison in England; Ludovic, duke of Savoy; Alphonsus V, king of Aragon, Sicily, and Naples; Francesco Sforza, husband of Bianca Maria Visconti. As the Venetians advance into the territory of the duchy occupying the Brianza district, Lodi, and Piacenza, the Milanese declare the signoria to be ended and establish the Ambrosian Republic, calling on Sforza to defend the freedoms of its citizens.	Death of Pope Eugene IV in Florence. Election of Nicholas V (Tommaso Parentucelli of Sarzana). In a diet-council at Aschaffenburg in the presence of Piccolomini, the entire "German nation" acknowledges Nicholas as legitimate pope against the claims of Felix V.	Theodore of Gaza teaches Greek at Ferrara. In 1447–48 Poggio Bracciolini writes his dialogue *Contra hypocritas,* in which he criticizes the Observantine Congregations of the mendicant orders, and his *Historia florentina* (from 1350 to the Peace of Lodi). Nicholas V begins to set up the future Vatican Library.

In England Gloucester is
accused of high treason
and imprisoned.

| 1448 | A new Ottoman victory at Kossovo over the Hungarians of John Hunyadi. | The Concordat of Venice between the pope and the emperor, fruit of Carvajal's mediation, confirms the agreements of Aschaffenburg. Frederick III revokes the safe-conducts for the council fathers in the imperial city of Basel, and the schismatic council must move to Lausanne and Felix V. Nicholas V appoints Nicholas of Cusa cardinal of St. Peter in Chains. | Lawrence Valla returns to Rome. By assignment from Nicholas V he devotes himself to translating Thucydides and then Herodotus. John of Torquemada gives a systematic presentation of his own preaching on papal power in his *Summa de Ecclesia.* William of Vaurillon teaches theology in Paris. |
| 1449 | The French free Rouen and Normandy, then Harfleur. | After lengthy mediation and negotiations with the Roman See, Charles VII, king of France, agrees to recognize the authority of Nicholas V and convokes a council in Lyons to put an end to the schism. On this same occasion the foundation is laid for a reform of the Gallican church, made necessary especially by the corrupt morals of the clergy. Felix V abdicates because the conflict is now so one-sided. In proclaiming the close of their council the fathers gathered in Lausanne obtain pardon and restoration to their offices. Nicholas V even makes Felix V cardinal of Santa Sabina and a papal legate, but Felix prefers to withdraw to a solitary life near Geneva. | Theodore of Gaza teaches philosophy and works as a translator in Rome. George Scholarius, on returning to Greece, withdraws to monastic life and takes the name of Gennadius. Lawrence Valla finishes his *Collatio Novi Testamenti* (later published as *Annotationes in Novum Testamentum*). In reply to the *De ignota litterature* of John Wenk of Herrenberg, rector of Heidelberg, Nicholas of Cusa writes his *Apologia doctae ignorantiae,* then two short works *De quadratura circuli.* Death of Anthony de Carlenis, recently made archbishop of Amalfi. Fra Angelico paints the frescoes of the Cappella Niccolina in the Vatican. Reginald Pecock writes his *Repressor of Over Much Blaming of the Clergy.* |

1450   In Milan Francesco Sforza clashes with the commune that had appointed him guardian of the Ambrosian Republic; he besieges the city and after capturing it declares himself legitimate lord, since he is direct heir of Visconti. By ceding some fortresses he frees himself from the duke of Savoy and then, with the support of Cosimo de'Medici, takes arms against Venice and Naples.
English defeat at Formigny. After the difficult recapture of Bordeaux, the French liberate the Guyenne, a possession of the English crown for three centuries. England is torn by internal conflicts. Insurrection of Jack Cade, who leads the common people of Kent, Sussex, and Surrey in a revival of Lollardism. The insurgents ask that Richard of York, direct descendant of the Plantagenets and presently governor in Ireland, take over the government. Henry VI (like his grandfather, Charles VI of France) loses his mind.

Nicholas V proclaims a holy year to celebrate the end of the schism. Nicholas of Cusa is appointed prince-bishop of Bressanone.

George Gemistus Plethon dies (between 1450 and 1452) at Mistra, near Sparta. Among the works written after his return to Greece are, in addition to the *Laws* (or *Code of Laws*) in three books, a treatise on fate, one on the virtues, and an exegesis of the *Chaldean Oracles*.
In Rieti, near Fabriano, Nicholas of Cusa writes his dialogues on the *Idiota*. Aeneas Silvius Piccolomini retracts his conciliarist views in his *De rebus Basileae gestis stante vel dissoluto concilio;* he then completes his *De viris aetate sua claris* and *De liberorum educatione*. Death of preacher Albert Bertini of Sarteano. A cycle of sermons in Ferrara by Franciscan John of Prato occasions a hostile exchange of letters with Guarino of Verona. Francis Della Rovere is regent of the Studium of Santa Croce in Florence. Leon Battista Alberti builds the *Tempio Malatestiano* in Rimini. French painter and miniaturist Jean Fouquet paints the *Diptych of Melun* and, between 1450 and 1460, the miniatures in the *Book of Hours* of Étienne Chevalier.

1451   Muhammad II, son and successor of Murad II, organizes his forces for a new attack on Constantinople.

Death of deposed antipope Felix V. Nicholas of Cusa undertakes a mission to Germany as papal legate. He is accompanied by

Matthew Palmieri begins the composition of his poem (in tercets) on *La città di vita* (completed ca. 1465). Young Marsilius Ficino studies

Denis of Louvain (known as Denis the Carthusian); together they found the charterhouse of s'Hertogenbosch. A provincial council over which Nicholas presides at Magdeburg discusses the legitimacy of indulgences and problems of monastic reform. John of Capistrano begins a mission in eastern Europe aimed at the conversion of the Hussites (with little success) and the preaching of the crusade against the Turks.

in Florence under Nicholas Tignosi. Foundation of the University of Glasgow.

| 1452 | Frederick III of Habsburg is crowned emperor in Rome and marries Eleanor, sister of the king of Portugal. | A provincial council in Cologne, Nicholas of Cusa presiding, issues various pastoral and disciplinary norms for the reform of the clergy; among other things, religious are urged to study the *De articulis fidei et sacramentis ecclesiae* of Thomas Aquinas; uninstructed priests are not to hear confessions; the superstitious veneration of images is to be avoided; Jews are to wear a mark by which they may be recognized. Nicholas settles in Bressanone, where he comes into conflict with the resistant cathedral chapter and the nuns of Sonnenburg, who are protected by Sigismund, Duke of the Tyrol. In Bohemia the Taborite community strikes a definitive peace with the Utraquists and submits to Rokycana's authority. Byzantine emperor | Dispute between Lawrence Valla and Poggio Bracciolini (who is supported by Panormita) over translations from Greek. Giannozzo Manetti writes his *De dignitate et excellentia hominis* as a reply to Bartholomew Fazio's *De excellentia et praestantia hominis*. Dominic Malatesta establishes the Biblioteca Malatestiana in Cesena. Filippo Lippi paints the *Pitti Madonna*. The University of Valence is founded. Cardinal legate William of Estouteville develops a plan for the reform of the University of Paris; among his collaborators is theologian Robert Ciboule. Rogier van der Weyden paints the *Bracque Triptych* and the *Bladelin Triptych* (1552–60). |

Constantine VI (brother and successor of John VIII) calls for Western help against the Turks and assures papal legate Isidore of Kiev of the union of the churches, while passing over the still-lively resistance of the Greek antiunionist party.

1453	After the battle of Chatillon in the Dordogne, the English possess only Calais in France. The Hundred Years War ends without a peace, due to the exhaustion and lack of interest of both sides. In England Richard of York is appointed regent for the insane Henry VI. Frederick III changes Austria into an archduchy. On April 5 the Turks advance from Adrianopolis to assault and besiege Constantinople. The Turkish fleet blocks the sea-lanes, and no Western power comes to the aid of the Byzantines except for four Genoese ships which try in vain to run the blockade. On May 29 the fortifications yield, despite the resistance of Genoese captain Giustiniani. Constantinople is in Turkish hands, and with it all the Genoese possessions in the Mediterranean except for Chios, which is saved by payment of a heavy tribute.	A provincial council in Limerick undertakes a reorganization of the Irish church, emphasizing its dependence on the Apostolic See.	Giannozzo Manetti opposes the Medici and is forced into exile, first in Rome with Nicholas V, then in Naples with Alphonsus. In Bressanone Nicholas of Cusa writes his *De visione Dei* and *Complementum theologicum*. Roderick Sánchez de Arévalo writes *De arte, disciplina et modo alendi et erudiendi filios*.

1454   An agreement, mediated by the Medici, between Sforza and Venice receives the approval of all the Italian lords; thus the Peace of Lodi is achieved, which recognizes Francesco Sforza as duke of Milan and Alphonsus of Aragon as king of Naples and paves the way for a policy of balance between the various powers in the peninsula.
Death of John II of Castile, who is succeeded by his son Henry IV (the Helpless). New war between the Teutonic Order and Poland, which is backed by the Prussian League (nobles and cities of northern Germany).

Gennadius Scholarius, imprisoned at the fall of Constantinople, wins the favor of Muhammad II and is made patriarch of Constantinople, an office he keeps until 1465. In this role he condemns Plethon's *Laws*.
Poggio Bracciolini writes his *De miseria humanae conditionis*. Piero della Francesca paints the fresco of the *Leggenda della croce* (1454–66) in the choir of the church of San Franscesco in Arezzo.
Reginald Pecock writes his *Folewer to the Donet*.

1455   After the Peace of Lodi an Italian (or Holy) League is formed by Milan, Florence, Venice, Rome, and Naples on the basis of a twenty-five-year pact founded on the principle of balance: respect for established borders and control of violations through a system of alliances that also enables each to face foreign enemies.
In England the civil War of the Roses (1455–85) breaks out between the houses of York (white rose) and Lancaster (red rose), which support respectively the parties of regent Richard of York and of Henry VI and his very young heir, Edward. The war upsets the legal and civic order of the

Death of Nicholas V. Election of Callistus III (Alfonso Borgia, 1455–58), becomes one of the first popes to practice nepotism, appointing his nephew, the future Alexander VI, a cardinal. In one of his first acts of government the new pope launches an unsuccessful crusade against the Turks in support of John Hunyadi.

George of Trebizond intervenes in the debate over Plato and Aristotle by attacking Plethon's Platonism in a *Comparatio philosophorum Aristotelis et Platonis*. Venetian theologian and reformer Dominic Dominici writes his *De potestate pontificio* (1455–58) in defense of papal authority.
Death in Bonilla de la Sierra of El Tostado, recently made bishop of Avila.
Reginald Pecock, bishop of the Lancaster party, writes his *Book of Faith*. His bold theological teachings, developed against the Lollards but obviously inspired by the humanists (he doubts the

state. The first encounter, at St. Albans, is won by York.
The prince electors present Frederick III with a plan for an administrative reform of the empire and for the pacification of the German territories: the heart of the plan is a centralized administration in a place different from that of the emperor's hereditary lords; financial reorganization based on regular taxes; legal reform.

authenticity of the Donation of Constantine and the Mosaic authorship of the Pentateuch, and anticipates deist views basing moral laws on natural reason) provide the York part with an opportunity for harsh criticism.
Foundation of the University of Freiburg in Breisgau. Invention of printing; Johann Gutenberg publishes his folio Bible in Mainz.

1456	John Hunyadi, leading a Christian crusade, hunts the Turks from Belgrade.	Controversy between the University of Paris and the four mendicant orders, which claim privileges granted by a papal bull of Nicholas V and renewed by Callistus III. Despite papal support of the orders, the authorities of the University refuse to grant the privileges and threaten the masters of the orders with expulsion and the loss of their academic degrees. Rehearing of the trial of Joan of Arc. At a diet in Frankfurt with Archbishop Theodoric of Mainz presiding, the *Gravamina nationis Germanicae* formulate for the first time the complaints of the German clergy and nobility about excessive monetary demands of the Holy See and its constant recourse to the weapons of excommunication and interdict.	Between 1456 and 1458 Marsilius Ficino writes his *Commentariola lucretiana,* his *De virtutibus moralium,* his *De quatuor sectis philosophorum,* and the lost *Institutiones ad Platonicam disciplinam.* John of Capistrano, who takes an active part in the battle of Belgrade by leading the left wing of the crusaders, dies a few months later at Villaco. Gerard de Monte, a secular master of Cologne, criticizes the *Problemata* of Eimeric of Kampen in his *Tractatus ostendens concordiam sancti Thomae et venerabilis domini Alberti.*
1457	Francesco Foscari, doge of Venice and promotor	A provincial council called in Avignon	Death of Lawrence Valla. Death of Paduan jurist

of a continental policy, is deposed for having neglected the defense of the eastern domains.
Sigismund Malatesta, lord of Rimini and a papal vassal, rebels against Rome's control and starts the first Italian conflict (1457–63) since the Peace of Lodi. The conflict is exacerbated by the intervention of Venice and Naples and then of Frederick of Montefeltro, lord of Urbino, and of condottiere Giacomo Piccolomini, son of Nicholas.
Emperor Frederick II is at war over the Habsburg heritage with his brother Albert, who raises Upper Austria against the emperor.
The Poles capture Marienburg, a stronghold of the Teutonic Order.

by Peter of Foix, archbishop of Arles, for the purpose of restoring Church discipline, confirms the decrees of the Council of Basel on the Immaculate Conception and bars further discussion of the subject.
A provincial council at Lambeth with Thomas Bourchier, archbishop of Canterbury, presiding, condemns the teachings of Reginald Pecock, who is forced to retract and is imprisoned until his death (ca. 1460) in the Abbey of Thorney, near Cambridge.

Peter del Monte, author of writings in defense of papal primacy, such as his *De summi pontificis origine et potestate* and *Liber contra impugnatores sedis apaostolicae ad Eugenium IV,* and of a practical and successful *Repertorium iuris.*
Roderick Sánchez de Arévalo writes his *Vergel de los principes.*
The University of Paris assigns Gregory Tifernate to its first chair of Greek.

1458   Death of Alphonsus V the Magnanimous, king of Aragon, Sicily, and Naples. He is succeeded in Aragon and Sicily by his brother, John II, while his natural son, Ferdinand I (the Bastard), becomes king of Naples and must face anew the claims of the Angevins in the person of John of Anjou, who is supported by Piccinino but opposed by Sforza and the pope. After being freed of this first danger, Ferdinand is concerned to reduce the power of the barons, who have opposed him, by cancelling their privileges in favor of the

Death of Callistus II and election of Pius II (Aeneas Silvius Picolomini of Corsignano, 1458–64). With the renunciation by the mendicant orders of their claimed privileges, the controversy between them and the University of Paris ends.

Nicholas of Cusa, after returning to Rome, writes his *De mathematica perfectione* and *De beryllo.*
Dominic Dominici dedicates his *Tractatus de reformatione Romanae Curiae* to Pius II.
Death of theologian John of Segovia, the author of, among other books, the *Liber de sancta conceptione,* the *Tractatus de processione Spiritus Sancti,* and a *Historia gestorum generalis synodi Basiliensis.*
Death of Robert Ciboule, author of *Livre de la sainte méditation et connaissance de soi* and *Livre de perfection.* Jean

bourgeoisie and opening
credit banks to avoid the
ruin of small farming
landowners.
Frederick III loses control
of Hungary and Bohemia:
at the death of Ladislaus
V the Posthumous,
Matthias Corvino, son of
John Hunyadi, is pro-
claimed king of Hungary
and endeavors to free
Hungary from the em-
pire; Bohemia, however,
is ruled by George
Podiebrad, a Hussite, first
as general administrator
of the realm, then as
king.

Foquet executes his
Boccaccio miniato.
Death of German
Taborite theologian
Frederick Reiser, who
translated the New
Testament into German
and thus helped the union
of the German-speaking
Waldensians with the
Hussites.

1459

Congress of Mantua: Pius
tries in vain to persuade
the European sovereigns
to a crusade against the
Turks.

Biondo Flavio dedicates
his *Roma triumphans* to
Pius II. Death of Poggio
Bracciolini, Anthony
Pierozzi, and Giannozzo
Manetti, who leaves in-
complete his *Adversus
Judaeos et Gentiles*.
Marsilius Ficino is intro-
duced to Cosimo
de'Medici, who encour-
ages his enthusiastic love
of Platonism.
Foundation of the first
Swiss university, in
Basel.

1460

Defeat of York at the
battle of Wakefield;
Henry VI of Lancaster is
restored to the throne.
The Yorkists favor
Edward, son of Richard.
The Swiss Federation
takes possession of
Turgovia at the expense
of the Habsburgs. In re-
sponse, Frederick III
pushes the expansionist
aims of the hereditary
prince of Burgundy,

Pius II declares concil-
iarism to be heretical.
In Calabria St. Francis of
Paola (who will die in
1507) founds the Minims,
a Mendicant order with a
Franciscan Rule on the
strict side.
The pope sends Cardinal
Bessarion to Germany
(1460–61) and then to
Venice (1463) to preach
the crusade against the

Francis Della Rovere
teaches at the Sapienza in
Rome. Nicholas of Cusa
writes his *De possest*.
Death of Eimeric of
Kampen.

Charles the Rash, son of
Philip the Good, offering
him as a pledge the
Habsburg possessions in
Alsace. The death of
Albert of Habsburg puts
an end to the rebellion of
Upper Austria against
Frederick III.

Turks, with disappointing
results.

1461

With his victory at
Towton, Edward of York
takes the crown as
Edward IV.
In France, death of
Charles VII, who is suc-
ceeded by his son, Louis
XI.

Shortly after ascending
the throne, Louis XI re-
vokes the *Pragmatic
Sanction* of Bourges as
contrary to the rights of
the Church and harmful
to universal order. Pius II
grants him the title of
"Most Christian King."

1462

Fall of Trebizond, the last
Christian-Byzantine out-
post against the Turks.

The triumph of Hussitism
in Bohemia, supported by
Podiebrad, worries Pius
II, who decides to nullify
the *Concordata* of
Prague. As a result, there
are new armed conflicts
between Utraquists and
Catholics.

After a temporary return
to Bressanone, Nicholas
of Cusa settles in
Orvieto, where he writes
his *De non-aliud*. A fierce
dispute arises between
Franciscan James of the
Marches and James of
Brescia, Dominican in-
quisitor for Lombardy,
over the liceity of veneration of the relics of the
blood of Christ in
Mantua: the bitterness of
the controversy, which
opposes numerous mem-
bers of the two orders,
worries the pope, who
forbids any public discussion of the subject but
urges the theologians of
the two sides to explain
their views in writing. On
this occasion Francis
Della Rovere writes his
De sanguine Christi.
Marsilius Ficino is guest
of Cosimo de'Medici at
the villa of Montevecchio
at Careggi, which

becomes the site of the revived Accademia Platonica; there Ficino begins his translation of the dialogues of Plato, which occupies him until 1477. Dominic of Flanders studies theology at Bologna from 1462 to 1470, the years in which he writes the first books of his *Summa divinae philosophiae* and his main philosophical works.

Franciscan preacher Alphonsus of Espina completes his *Fortalitium fidei contra Judaeos, Sarracenos et alios christianae fidei inimicos.*

1463		Death of Biondo Flavio and the mystic Catherine of Bologna. Marsilius Ficino translates the *Hermetica* into Latin, to be printed in 1471. Pius II writes his *Commentarii rerum memorabilium,* a history of his pontificate. Commissioned by the pope, architect Bernardo Rossellini (Bernardo Gambarelli) completes his rebuilding of the suburb and new piazza of Pienza.
		Foundation of the universities of Nantes and Bourges.
		Working-class satirical poet François Villon is condemned to death for criminal activities, but the sentence is changed to exile.
1464	Death of Cosimo the Elder. His son, Piero il Gottoso (the Gouty) begins a weak reign that	Death of Pius II at Ancona, whither he had gone in order to carry out in person his dream of	Nicholas of Cusa writes his *De ludo globi, De apice theoriae,* and *De venatione sapientiae.*

hardly opposes the aspirations of the oligarchs.

gathering troops for the crusade against the Turks. Election of Paul II (Pietro Barbo of Venice, 1464–71), who continues in vain to promote the crusade.

Ordered by Pius II to go ahead of him to Ancona on the business of the crusade, he dies on the way, at Todi.
Roderick Sánchez de Arévalo writes his *Tractatus ad quendam religiosum cartusianum.* Death of William of Vaurillon, author of a Scotist commentary on the *Sentences* and a *De principiis.*

1465   Paul II combats the power of the great feudal vassals of the papal states and expropriates the lands usurped by the Anguillara.
The nobles of southern France, concerned about the social troubles of the land, form the League for the Public Good against their former ally, Louis XI. The League is headed by the king's younger brother, Charles, duke of Berry, but is managed in practice by Charles the Rash of Burgundy. The ensuing peace of Conflans marks a weakening of the monarchy, which is forced to make large concessions to the rebellious nobles.

Death in Padua of Gaetano of Thiene and beginning of the teaching of Nicholas Vernia at Padua. Julius Pomponius Lactus, called by Paul II to teach at the Sapienza, is the guiding spirit in Rome of a circle of scholars who meet in his house on the Quirinal: the Accademia Romana (or Pomponiana). Members, among others: Bartholomew Sacchi, known as Platina, and Philip Bonaccorsi, known as Callimachus Esperiens. Between 1465 and 1475, architect Luciano Laurana, in the service of Federico da Montefeltro, completes the rebuilding of the ducal palace in Urbino. Louvain bachelor Peter of Rivo discusses a question in which he maintains a strict theological determinism and elicits an energetic response from two nominalist masters of Paris, Henry of Zoemeren and James Schelwaertus.

1466	Francesco Sforza dies and is succeeded by his son Galeazzo Maria, who in his first years is associated with his mother, Bianca Maria Visconti. His inflexible and foolish rule endangers the political work of his father. The Habsburgs occupy Fiume. The second Peace of Thorn ends the war against the Teutonic Order, whose domains, to the advantage of Poland, are now reduced to eastern Prussia. Special privileges granted to Danzig by the Polish crown give rise to the so-called Corridor.		Filippo Lippi paints the frescoes of the *History of the Virgin* in the Cathedral of Spoleto (1466–69). Death in Padua of canonist Anthony Roselli, author of *Monarchia seu tractatus de potestate imperatoris et papae,* in which he defends the supremacy of pope over council and also fully legitimizes the autonomy of the imperial power. Roderick Sánchez de Arévalo, on the other hand, attributes complete monarchical power over the entire world to the pope, in his *Defensorium ecclesiae.*
1467	Florence opposes Venetian plans for expansion into Lombardy; Rome and Naples intervene against Venice in order to avoid a crisis of balance. Death of Philip the Good; Charles the Rash, new duke of Burgundy, begins a policy of alliance with England and Castile in order to isolate France.	Pomponius Laetus, following disagreements with the pope over money, leaves Rome for Venice.	Francis Della Rovere, now a cardinal, writes his *De potentia Dei.* Benozzo Gozzoli begins to paint *Stories from the Old Testament* in the Camposanto of Pisa (finished in 1484). Roderick Sánchez de Arévalo again sets forth his theocratic and reformist ideas in *Speculum vitae humanae* and *Liber de monarchia orbis.* John of Torquemada writes *Meditationes de ipsius Mandato* and, in disagreement with Arévalo, *Opusculum ad honorem Romani imperii,* in which he repeats Dante's idea of the parallelism between the spiritual and temporal powers.
1468	In response to Charles the Rash, Louis XI calls delegates from sixty	Denunciation in Rome of an alleged conspiracy against Paul II, in which are involved, among	During his imprisonment Platina begins to compose his *De falso et vero bono,* while Roderick

cities to Tours and cancels the agreements reached at Conflans. Charles reacts with arms, captures Louis almost without a fight, and at Péronne, obliges him to confirm and increase the concessions made three years before.
Second descent of Frederick III of Habsburg into Italy.
With the defeat and death of national hero George Castriota, known as Scandenberg, Albania too falls into Turkish hands.

others, the principal men of the Accademia Romana; they are accused of immorality and spreading dangerous ideas and are imprisoned in Castel Sant'Angelo. Even Pomponius Laetus is extradited from Venice and imprisoned with his fellows for more than a year.

Sánchez de Arévalo, his warder in Castel Sant'Angelo, writes a dialogue engaging Platina's pacifist ideas: the *De pace et bello*. A gift from Bessarion forms the nucleus of the Biblioteca Marciana in Venice.
John of Torquemada dies in Rome.
Gabriel Biel enters the Brothers of the Common Life.

1469	Death of Piero de'Medici. The government of Florence passes to his two young sons, Lorenzo and Giuliano. Marriage of Ferdinand (who rules with his father, John II of Aragon) and Isabella, heir designate of her brother, Henry IV of Castile, is the basic premise for the reunification of Spain. Reorganization of Hungary, where Matthias Corvino with his wife, Beatrice of Aragon, daughter of Ferdinand, king of Naples, promotes the introduction of Italian renaissance culture. Matthias prepares for a military crusade against George Podiebrad and assumes the crown of Bohemia. The Hussite party leads Bohemian resistance and proclaims Ladislaus, son of Casimir IV of Poland, as king under the protection of		In reply to the anti-Platonist treatise of George of Trebizond, Bessarion writes his *In calumniatorem Platonis.* Others who subsequently enter the controversy over Plato and Aristotle are Theodore of Gaza with an *Adversus Plethonem pro Aristotele de substantia,* which elicits objections from Michael Apostolio and Andronicus Callistus with his *Risposte* to the anti-Aristoteleanism of Plethon. In the service of the king of France, Paris theologian William Fichet completes a mission to Milan, where he comes in contact with the Italian humanists.

Podiebrad. Casimir is in
conflict with the Roman
Curia, which does not ap-
prove of the Peace of
Thorn, and he is regarded
as a defender of Slavism
against the interferences
of Rome.

1470   Richard of Warwick,
principal supporter of the
Yorkists, goes over to
Henry VI Lancaster.
At the death of George
Podiebrad, Casimir IV is
reconciled with the
Roman Curia, and
Ladislaus is recognized
as king of Bohemia (as
Ladislaus VII).

The debate over deter-
minism and future contin-
gents, begun by Peter of
Rivo, shifts to Rome,
where the nominalists
have sent an accusation
of heresy against Peter,
who is defended by the
realist theologians of
Paris and Cologne. Della
Rovere enters the debate
with a *De futuris contin-
gentibus,* as does Salviati
with a *De libertate et im-
mutabilitate Dei.* Philip
Bonaccorsi, freed from
prison, takes refuge in
Poland, where he is pro-
tected by Archbishop
Gregory Sanok of
Leopoli. Bartholomew
Platina takes refuge, in-
stead, with the Gonzagas,
to whom he dedicates his
De principe. Agnolo
Ambrogini, known as
Politian, translates the
Iliad into Latin for
Lorenzo the Magnificent.
Roderick Sánchez de
Arévalo dies in Rome
after completing his
Historia Hispanica.
Foundation of the
University of Barcelona.
William Fichet and John
Heynlin von Stein open
the first printery in Paris.
Jean Foquet paints the
miniatures for the *Jewish
Antiquities* of Flavius
Josephus.

1471   Battles of Parnet and Tewkesbury; Edward IV defeats and orders the assassination of Henry VI, his principal heir, Edward of Lancaster, and Warwick. Under Edward's rule ten years of enforced peace follow, due to the terrorist methods of his brother Richard, duke of Lancaster. Louis XI succeeds in politically isolating Charles the Rash; at a new assembly of important men at Tours he nullifies the agreements of Péronne, raises the cities against the nobles, and forces Charles to sign a truce.

Death of Pope Paul II. Election of Sixtus IV (Francis Della Rovere of Savona, general of the Franciscans, 1471–84).

Anthony Trombetta is master of theology in Padua and sees to the printing of the first book of Duns Scotus' commentary on the *Sentences*. First edition in Rome of the *Postilla* of Nicholas of Lyra, along with the *Additiones* of Paul of Burgos and the *Defensorium Postillae* of Saxon Franciscan Matthias Döring. Andrea Mantegna paints the frescoes in the *Camera degli Sposi* of the ducal palace of Mantua (1471–74). While Andrew, son of George of Trebizond, maintains the superiority of Aristoteleanism at the University of Paris, William Fichet publishes a volume of *Epistolae et orationes* in which he comes out on the side of Bessarion in the humanists' dispute over Plato and Aristotle. Death of Thomas à Kempis, presumed author of the *Imitation of Christ*. Death of Denis the Carthusian, who leaves a vast production of over two hundred titles in speculative and mystical theology, including commentaries on the *Sentences*, Boethius, and Dionysius the Areopagite, a *Summa fidei orthodoxae*, which follows in detail the structure and divisions of Thomas' *Summa*, a *De donis Spiritus Sancti*, a *De contemplatione*, a *De fonte lucis ac semitis vitae*, an *Elementatio theologica*,

and a *De lumine chris-*
tianae theoriae on the
reasonableness of the
Christian faith.

1472			Death of George Scholarius, who had retired to the monastery of the Prodromos. John Gatto (or Gatti) is appointed bishop of Cefalù. Christopher Landino writes a treatise *De vera nobilitate* and publishes his dialogues *De anima*. Closing of the Studium of Florence. Andrea del Verrocchio sculpts the Medici tomb in San Lorenzo, Florence. Death (between 1472 and 1475) of Franciscan Nicholas de Orbellis, who leaves a commentary on the *Sentences* that is conceived as an exposition of Scotist thought. William Fichet follows Bessarion to Italy, where he remains until his death. Foundation of the University of Ingolstadt.
1473	The Venetians conquer Cyprus. The city manages to retain some important commercial strongholds in the Mediterranean.	Sixtus IV introduces the feast of the Immaculate Conception.	Pomponius Laetus again obtains a chair at the Sapienza, where he teaches until his death. Bernardino di Betto, known as Pinturicchio, paints the *Incidents in the Life of St. Bernardine of Siena* in the church of S. Maria in Aracoeli in Rome. At the intervention of Sixtus IV, Peter of Rivo is forced to retract, but the condemnation has repercussions in Paris,

where the realist masters
obtain from the king, in
the Edict of Soissons, the
expulsion of the nominal-
ists from the university.
German painter and en-
graver Martin
Schongauer paints the
Madonna del Roseto at
Colmar.

1474   At the death of Henry IV
of Castile, Isabella is
queen, with her consort
Ferdinand (II of Aragon,
V of Castile). The new
rulers must face the re-
bellion of the nobles of
Castile and the dynastic
claims of the Portuguese.
Alarmed by the expan-
sionist aims of the duke
of Burgundy, the
Habsburgs, through the
mediation of France,
make a "perpetual peace"
with Switzerland.

Platina, having been reha-
bilitated under Sixtus IV,
dedicates his *De vita
Christi ac omnium pontif-
icum* to the pope.
Marsilius Ficino com-
pletes his *De amore.*
Antonello da Messina
paints his *St. Jerome in
His Study* and his
Annunciation. Venetian
Giovanni Bellini paints
the altarpiece of Pesaro
with its *Crowning of the
Virgin* and his *Fugger*
portrait.
Foundation of the
University of Saragoosa.
Florentine geographer
Paolo dal Pozzo
Toscanelli presents to
Fernand Martines, geog-
rapher of the king of
Portugal, the idea that the
way to the Indies can be
reached by sailing west-
ward.
The nominalists of the
University of Paris write
a manifesto justifying the
via moderna, in which
they appeal to the author-
ity of Gerson.

1475   Following a landing of
the English in France,
done in agreement with
Charles the Rash, Louis
XI signs the Peace of
Pecquigny, in which he

Peter of Bergamo pub-
lishes his *Tabula aurea* in
Bologna. Vincent
Bandello speaks out on
the subject of the
Immaculate Conception,
defending the Thomist

obliges himself to pay a large annual compensation that strengthens the finances of the Yorkists.

position against Sixtus IV in his *Libellus recollectorius de veritate conceptionis Beatae Mariae Virginis,* and discusses the subject publicly with John Sansone, general of the Franciscans. Marsilius Ficino publishes in Italian and the next year in Latin his *De christiana religione.* Christopher Landino writes his *Disputationes camaldulenses.* Death of Matthew Palmieri in Florence. Between 1474 and 1478 Politian composes his *Stanze per la giostra,* which are incomplete at the death of the one for whom they are intended, Giuliano de'Medici, and will be published in 1494. Matteo Maria Boiardo finishes his collection of verses, *Amorum libri tres,* and begins his poem of chivalry, *Orlando innamorato.* Sixtus IV has the Sistine Chapel built from 1475 to 1481; then he has the premises of the Vatican Library redone. Platina, who is made director of the library, compiles a catalogue of 2527 volumes, prefixed with an alphabetical index entitled *Tabula ad inveniendos codices.* Antonello da Messina is in Venice, where, between 1475 and 1479 (the year of his death), he paints, among other things, his *Crucifixion,* his *Saint Sebastian,* and the altarpiece in San Cassiano. Death of Dutch reformer

John (Pupper) of Goch, who preached the acceptance only of those religious truths that could be proved from Scripture and who refuses to assign a special merit to monastic vows. Polish jurist Stanislaus Otrorog, teaching in Cracow, composes his *Monumentum pro reipublicae ordinatione,* a "handbook for the prince," which proposes an organization of the Polish state as an absolute monarchy, without privileges for the nobility and with fiscal parity.

| 1476 | A plot hatched by Cola Montano leads to the assassination of Galeazzo Maria Sforza. He is succeeded by his very young son, Gian Galeazzo, who governs with his mother, Bona of Savoy, as regent but under the de facto protection of his paternal uncle, Ludovic the Black, effective ruler of Milan from 1479 to 1510. Progressive strengthening of the French crown against local aristocracies: after occupying Barrois and Anjou, Louis XI persuades Louis, son of Charles of Orleans, to marry his daughter Jeanne, and Peter II Beaujeau Bourbon to marry his elder daughter, Anna. With French support, the Helvetic Confederation defeats Charles the Rash. Peasant revolt in Germany, known as the "Piping of Niklashausen." | Sixtus IV approves the Office of the Immaculate Conception composed by Leonard of Nogarola. | Death of James of the Marches. In Padua Anthony Trombetta regains the chair of Scotist metaphysics. Marsilius Ficino writes his *De raptu Pauli.* Andrea del Verrocchio sculpts the *David* in the Bargello. Death at Valladolid of theologian Martin of Cordoba, author of a *Tratado de la predestinación* and an *Ars praedicandi.* Peter Martínez of Osma publishes a *Tractatus de confessione* that criticizes the granting of a plenary indulgence for the 1475 Holy Year and anticipates some of Luther's anti-Roman theses; two years later he is condemned by the Inquisition. Death in Rome of William Fichet. Flemish painter Hugo van der Goes paints the *Portinari Polyptych.* |

1477	To win acceptance as king, Charles the Rash offers the hand of his daughter Maria to Maximilian of Habsburg, son of Frederick III, but he dies fighting against Swiss mercenaries hired by Renato II of Lorraine, whose little state he had invaded.		John Gatto is appointed archbishop of Catania. Death of humanist Peter Candidus Decembrio, author of biographies of Francesco Sforza and Filippo Maria Visconti. Foundation of the universities of Uppsala and Tübingen. Between 1477 and 1489 German sculptor and engraver Veit Stoss carves the wooden polyptych of the main altar in St. Mary of Cracow. Death of Flemish mystic Henry Herp, author of the *Speculum aureum praeceptorum Dei,* the *Spieghel der Volcomenheit,* and a *Theologia mystica.*
1478	Florentine oligarchs opposed to the Medici unite around the Guelph families of the Pazzi, led by Jacopo and Franceschino and the Albizzi. With the approval of Sixtus IV, who wants Florence for his nephew Gerolamo Riarlo (who with his help is already lord of Imola), and of Francesco Salviati, archbishop of Pisa, they hatch a plot to free themselves from Medici rule (the Pazzi Conspiracy). During an attack by the plotters in Santa Maria del Fiore Giuliano is killed, but Lorenzo is saved and the people rise up in his defense. The death of the archbishop, who is executed along with the plotters, and the arrest of a cardinal draw down the	Following upon the Florentine interdict, Louis XI of France convokes a national council in Orleans to pass judgment on the nepotism of Sixtus IV: on this occasion the king, now in control of the French clergy, reinstates the *Pragmatic Sanction* (reasserting, in particular, the authority of council over pope) and challenges the liceity of sending French money to the Holy See. Isabella of Castile and Ferdinand of Aragon convoke a national council in Seville to win from the pope the privilege of distributing as they choose ecclesiastical benefices that carry greater authority. The council also decrees a first expulsion of	Luigi Pulci publishes the first version of his comic-heroic poem, *Morgante* (the second, expanded version, dates to 1483). Death of Dominic Dominici. Christopher Landino publishes a commentary on the *Aeneid.* Sandro Filipepi, known as Botticelli, paints his *Primavera.*

wrath of Sixtus IV, who puts Florence under interdict; but the same actions kindle the ambition of Ferdinand I of Naples, who hopes to acquire land in Tuscany. With Milan as mediator and with the weapons of diplomacy, Lorenzo succeeds in avoiding a war with Naples and the Holy See and begins a period of splendor for the Florentine signoria that earns him the title "the Magnificent." Frederick III of Habsburg marries his son Maximilian to Maria of Burgundy; their son, Philip the Handsome, is born the next year.

Jews from the important commercial cities of Seville and Cadiz. A tribunal of the Inquisition is established in Castile, its main purpose being to investigate sham conversions of Jews.

| 1479 | Peace of Venice with the Turks, to Venice's disadvantage. War between France and the Habsburgs for the Burgundian inheritance: Maximilian defeats Louis XI in the battle of Guinegatte. | In Florence, Alamanno Rinucini writes his *Dialogus de libertate* against the absolutism of Lorenzo the Magnificent. Death in Florence of Dominic of Flanders, for three years regent of the Dominican Studium. Young John Pico della Mirandola goes to Ferrara and Florence to study. Venetian Gentile Bellini (brother of Giovanni) goes to Constantinople to paint the portrait of Muhammad II. Death in Plasencia of theologian John López of Salamanca, author of a *Responsio* to Peter Martínez of Osma. Rudolf Agricola writes a *De inventione dialectica* in which he reduces dialectic to an art of persuasion. |

Flemish painter Hans
Memling paints *The
Mystical Marriage of St.
Catherine*
and *The Adoration of the
Magi* for the Hospital of
St. John of Bruges.
Foundation of the
University of
Copenhagen.

1480   Maintaining that the prin-   New expulsion of Jews   In Mantua Politian com-
cipate is a hereditary   from Cadiz and Seville.   poses the pastoral play
right and does not need   *Orfeo*. Then, between
investiture by the people,   1480 and 1493, he com-
Ludovic the Moor cuts   poses his *Odae* and
his ties with Cicco   *Sylvae*. Pico della
Simonetta, adviser of   Mirandola studies in
Bona of Savoy, and pro-   Padua (1480–82), where
claims himself legitimate   he follows the lectures of
duke of Milan, while   Nicholas Vernia and, pri-
Gian Galeazzo Sforza is   vately, of Elias del
banished to Pavia.   Medico (or Medigo).
Lorenzo de'Medici sup-   Bosnian Franciscan Jurai
ports the first revival of   Dragisic, who in Italy has
the Italian League for the   taken the name George
express purpose of cur-   Benignus Salviati, pub-
tailing the ambitions of   lishes a *Logica nova se-*
Venice.   *cundum mentem Scoti et*
Ivan III of Russia defeats   *sancti Thomae Aquinatis,*
the Tatars of the Golden   which will be reedited
Horde.   twice in later years.
Peter Martínez of Osma
dies after retracting his
indicted teachings.

1481   Death in Portugal of   Vincent Bandello speaks
Alphonsus V; he is suc-   out again on the subject
ceeded by John II, who   of Mary Immaculate in
increases voyages of ex-   his *Tractatus de singulari*
ploration and coloniza-   *puritate et praerogativa*
tion to Atlantic Africa.   *conceptionis Salvatoris*
At the death of Renato of   *nostri Iesu Christi.*
Anjou, the king of France   Christopher Landino pub-
unites Anjou to the   lishes a commentary on
crown.   the *Divine Comedy* that is
Death of Christian I of   elegantly printed by
Denmark, Norway, and   Nicholas della Magna,
Sweden, who is suc-   with illustrations by
ceeded by his son John.   Botticelli. Cycles of fres-
Death of Muhammad II;   coes by Pinturicchio,

the new sultan is his son, Bayazid II.

Perugino (Petro Vanucci), Botticelli, Ghirlandaio (Domenico Bigordi) on the side walls of the Sistine Chapel (1481–83). In Florence, Leonardo da Vinci paints his *Annunciation* and *Adoration of the Magi*. Death of theologian and preacher John (Ruchrat) of Wesel, defender of the *sola scriptura* principle and persistent enemy of indulgences in his *Disputatio adversus indulgentias*. When investigated for suspicious connections with the Hussites, he had retracted his errors and lived as a prisoner in the Augustinian convent in Mainz. Death of Augustinian theologian John of Dorsten, a realist master in Erfurt.

1482   Temporarily free of worries about the Turks, Venice renews its expansionist goals on the mainland by invading the signoria of the Estes in the War of Ferrara. Lorenzo saves the balance of power by persuading Milan and Naples to join him against Venice. The Portuguese reach the mouth of the Congo. The partition of Burgundian territory becomes definitive in the Peace of Arras between France and the empire. In his kingdom Louis XI promotes a mercantilist economic policy with an increase in industry,

In the bull *Gravis nimis* Sixtus IV condemns adversaries of the Immaculate Conception.

Marsilius Ficino publishes *Theologia platonica de immortalitate animae*. Nicholas of Vernia publishes a dissertation *An dentur universalia realia?* Death of Peter of Bergamo. Piero della Francesca writes a treatise on the theory of painting, *De quinque corporibus regularibus*. Leonardo da Vinci moves to Milan and the service of Ludovico the Moor. Death of nominalist theologian Martin Lemaistre (De Magistris), author of *Quaestiones morales* and a *Contemplatio* on the Salve Regina.

planning for a commercial organization that would have a monopoly on trade with the East and restrictions both on luxury imports from Italy and on individual economic enterprises.

| 1483 | Death of Edward IV of York. Richard of Gloucester becomes regent for his twelve-year-old nephew, Edward V. After eliminating his potential enemies and having young Edward and his brother Richard, duke of York, strangled in the Tower of London, Richard has himself crowned as Richard III. Lord Buckingham, constable of England, revives the Lancaster party by supporting the candidacy of Henry Tudor, who is connected with the Lancasters through his mother; Buckingham also gets southern England to revolt. Failure of the revolt, beheading of Buckingham, and new repression. | The Inquisition is introduced into Aragon. | |
| 1484 | The Peace of Bagnolo ends the War of Ferrara by allowing Venice to annex Polesine and Rovigo. Second revival of the Italian League. Portuguese protectorate over the mouth of the Congo. Death of Louis XI of France; he is succeeded by his son Charles VIII, at whose court many Italian exiles who had opposed the local lords | Death of Pope Sixtus IV. Election of Innocent VIII (Giovanni Baptista Cybo of Genoa, 1484–92). A few months after his election he issues a bull against witches. A reunion of the Estates General of France at Tours invokes the need of a reform for the entire church of France. Thomas of Torquemada, nephew of Cardinal John, is made head of the | Death of John Gatto. At Rome, in the presence of the pope, Vincent Bandello undertakes a solemn disputation to obtain the title of master. Marsilius Ficino publishes his translation of Plato. Pico della Mirandola is in Florence, where he comes in contact with Lorenzo the Magnificent, Politian, and the Accademia Platonica. |

work to gain a victory over their enemies.

General Inquisition of Spain; he strengthens and reorganizes its mandate by publishing an *Instruction.* A strict and zealous theoretician of the authority of the Inquisition, he heads it until his death (1498) with implacable steadfastness in dealing with heretics and Jews.

Thomas Linacre journeys to Italy in the retinue of William Shelling, who has been appointed orator to Innocent VIII. First printed edition, in Deventer, of Raymond Sibiuda's *Liber creaturarum* (under the title *Theologia naturalis*). Gabriel Biel, rector of the house of the Brothers of the Common Life in Urach, is called by Count Eberhard of Wüttenberg to the University of Tübingen in order to offset the hegemony of the realists. Rudolf Agricola writes his *De firmando studio*, a treatise in the form of a letter to James Barbirano, which is intended as a programmatic manifesto for European humanism. Albrecht Dürer draws his *Self-Portrait* in pencil.

1485   A conspiracy of barons against the king of Naples is supported by the new pope, who occupies Aquila where he intends to create a new kingdom for the Cybo family to the detriment of Ferdinand I. Lorenzo the Magnificent intervenes again to preserve the balance of power. Three-year revolt (dubbed the "Mad War") of Louis of Orleans against Charles VIII.
In England the attempt to overthrow Richard III is renewed with the help of the new constable, Lord Stanley: Henry Tudor, a refugee on the continent,

Lorenzo the Magnificent wins the pope's trust by diplomacy and in exchange obtains the cardinalate for his son Giovanni (the future Leo X).
Peace of Kutná Hora between the Catholics of Bohemia and the Hussites: the *Compactata* of Prague is accepted as the law of the land. In this way, the coexistence of the two religions is ensured for about a century.

Vincent Bandello publishes his *Liber ducentorum et sexaginta sanctorum virginem Mariam in originali peccato conceptam dicentium dicta continens.* Pico della Mirandola writes a famous letter to Ermolaus Barbarus in which he explains his own ideas about moving beyond the more formal and schematic aspects of humanism; from June until the following March he stays in Paris, where he comes in contact with university circles.
Architect Giuliano da Sangallo (Giuliano Giamberti) builds the

lands in Wales and at Bosworth defeats Richard, who dies on the field. This ends the War of the Roses: Henry marries Elizabeth, daughter of Edward IV, and begins the Tudor dynasty as Henry VII. A plan for reforming the imperial administration and for monetary unification (along the lines of the 1455 plan) is put forward by the elector of Mainz at the Diet of Frankfurt.

Medici Villa at Poggio di Caiano and the church of Santa Maria delle Carceri in Prato. Augustinian preacher John of Paltz, a disciple of John of Dorsten, teaches theology at Erfurt and writes his major work, *Coelifodina* (translated into the vernacular as *Die hymmlicsche Fundgrube*).

| 1486 | Cruel repression in Naples of the barons defeated by the king; many of them are exiled and have their goods confiscated. Innocent VIII excommunicates Ferdinand. | The University of Paris condemns as a heretic John Laillier, who two years earlier, before the theological faculty, had defended theses in ecclesiology that smacked of Wyclifitism. | On his return to Italy John Pico begins his study of hermetic and Cabalistic works; writes his *Comento alla Canzione d'amore di Girolamo Benivieni* and his *Conclusiones sive theses DCCCC*, which he intends to defend in Rome at a public debate on philosophical and theological subjects; he composes his *Oratio de hominis dignitate* as an introduction to the theses. George Benignus Salviati, in Florence as tutor of the sons of Lorenzo the Magnificent, debates at court with Hungarian Dominican John de Mirabilibus on the causes and consequences of Adam's sin. In that same year he writes his *In Opus septem quaestionum,* a commentary on a theological sonnet of Lorenzo. Botticelli paints his *Birth of Venus.* German humanist Conrad Celtis (Conrad Pickel), |

on a journey to Rome,
admires the Accademia
Romana founded by
Pomponius Laetus and
proposes to establish
similar institutions in
Germany: his plan will
lead to the "Sodalitas lit-
teraria" of Cracow.

1487   Count Sigismund of the
Tyrol and the bishops of
Trent and Bressanone,
both of them vassals of
the Habsburgs, repeatedly
challenge and defeat
Venice, thus renewing the
German threat to north-
east Italy.

The Roman debate
sought by John Pico is
put off and censured by a
papal commission: thir-
teen of the *Conclusions*
are condemned as suspect
of heresy, and Pico is
forced to withdraw them.
He then drafts an
Apologia, but is con-
demned in a bull of
Innocent VIII and forced
to flee to France, where
he is captured and imprisoned in Vincennes.

1488   In France Louis of
Orleans and Charles VIII
are reconciled, and Louis,
who claims rights over
Visconti territory, urges
the king to go down into
Italy and reclaim them.
Frederick III of Habsburg
has Maximilian elected
King of the Romans and
associates him with the
empire.

Innocent VIII issues a decree against the Hussite
heresy.

George Benignus Salviati
writes his *In opus de
natura angelica.* John
Pico, freed through the
mediation of Lorenzo the
Magnificent, finds a letter
waiting for him in Turin
that invites him to
Florence, where he takes
up permanent residence.
Here he begins a com-
mentary on the Psalms
that remains incomplete.
Peter Pomponazzi begins
to teach in Padua. In
Venice Giovanni Bellini
paints the *Triptych* in
Santa Maria dei Frari,
and Andrea del
Verrocchio completes his
equestrian statue of
Colleoni.
Gabriel Biel collects the
lectures in theology
given in his first year of

teaching in Tübingen in his *Canonis missae expositio,* published in Basel with an introduction by realist theologian John Heylin von Stein. The lectures of his second year are part of *Epitomae et collectorium circa IV Sententiarum libros,* which follows Ockham's commentary in detail.

1489	Flanders acknowledges the territorial rights of Maximilian.	In an edict *Contra disputantes de unitate intellectus* Peter Barozzi, bishop of Padua, condemns masters who maintain the Averroist theses; the condemnation is directed mainly against the *De intellectu* of Nicholas of Vernia. Death of Paduan Thomist Francis Securus of Nardò. Politian publishes his *Miscellanea.* Marsilius Ficino writes his *Libri de vita,* the third of which is the *De vita coelitus comparanda.* John Pico dedicates to Lorenzo his *Heptaplus,* a Platonic-Hermetic commentary on the first verses of Genesis. William Briçonnet is appointed bishop of Lodève. Robert Gaguin speaks out on behalf of the Immaculate Conception in a poem *De mundissima virginis Mariae conceptione* and in other prose writings. In discussions on Mary against the Thomists, representatives of the humanist group in Strasbourg also take part, among them James

Wimpfeling, who writes
two hymns in praise of
the Virgin, and Sebastian
Brant, who composes a
poetic *Contra Judaeos et
haereticos conceptionem
virginalem fuisse possi-
bilem argumentatio.*
Death of Wessel
Gansfort, a disciple of the
Brothers of the Common
Life; dubbed by his ad-
versaries "Master of con-
tradictions," he leaves
some ecclesiological and
theological writings,
among them his *Farrago,*
his *Mare magnum,* and
his *Scala meditationum*
(or *Tractatus de modo
constituendarum medita-
tionum*), for which Luther
will have high esteem.

| 1490 | At the death of Matthias Corvino the crown of Hungary, due to the leanings of the upper Magyar nobility, passes to Ladislaus, king of Bohemia, despite the claims of Matthias' brother, John Albert. Ladislaus, who thus combines the Bohemian and Hungarian crowns (as Ladislaus VII of Bohemia, V of Hungary), marries Matthias' widow, Beatrice of Aragon. | | John Pico comes in contact with Savonarola and persuades Lorenzo to call him to Florence. Piero della Francesca writes his treatise *De prospectiva pingendi.* In Milan Leonardo da Vinci paints *The Virgin of the Rocks.* Giuliano sa Sangallo builds the Gondi Palace in Florence. Death of theologian and exegete James Pérez of Valencia. Scotist theologian Peter Tartaret (or Tataret) is rector of the University of Paris. Nominalist Thomas Bricot receives his licentiate in theology. |
| 1491 | Charles VIII of France marries Anne of Brittany, divorced wife of Maximilian I, thus assuring the crown of the | In Paris Master John Langlois, who has persisted in a eucharistic heresy, is executed at the stake. | John Pico dedicates his *De ente et uno* to Politian and begins his *Disputationes adversus astrologiam divinatricem,* |

duchy. Genoa, too, though a feudal territory of the duke of Milan, is under the direct control of the king of France. In the Peace of Pressburg (= Bratislava) Ladislaus of Bohemia-Hungary acknowledges the hereditary claims of the Habsburgs in Bohemia. Nzinga, king of the Congo, signs a trade agreement with the Portuguese and converts to Christianity under the name of Alphonsus I.

which will be completed by his nephew, John Francis. Anthony de Ferraris, known as Galateo, addresses to Ermolaus Barbarus a letter in defense of eloquence against the Scholastics but also criticizing the excessive liking of the humanists for form. Jerome Savonarola is prior of the Dominican convent of San Marco in Florence and writes his *Trattato dell'umiltà.*

1492   Death of Lorenzo the Magnificent, who is succeeded by his son Piero. After some years of war, the Most Catholic rulers of Spain gain the upper hand over the emirate of Granada, the last Islamic bastion in the Iberian peninsula, which was strenuously defended by Abu Abdallah. Treaty of Étaples between France and England: With a payment of gold Charles VIII ensures England's neutrality toward his ambitions in Italy. Death of Casimir IV of Poland, who is succeeded by his son John Albert I (already a claimant to Hungary against his brother Ladislaus). Sailing from Palos on August 3, Christopher Columbus, in the service of Spain, reaches the new world (San Salvador, now Watling, in the Bahamas) on October 12. He then discovers Cuba and Haiti (named Hispaniola or Española).

Death of Innocent VIII. Election of Alexander VI (Rodrigo Lanzol-Borgia of Jativa, 1492–1503). The Catholic kings, at the urging of Inquisitor Thomas of Torquemada, order the mass expulsion of all Jews and "Moriscos" from Aragon and Castile with confiscation of their property.

Marsilius Ficino publishes his translation of Plotinus' *Enneads.* Carmelite Baptist Spagnoli of Mantua writes *Opus aureum in thomistas* in defense of his confrere Peter Nebulario (Peter Gavassetti of Novellara), who maintained the legitimacy of the worship of Christ's blood against the Dominicans. Death of Franciscan John of Ferrara, who departed from Scotist teaching by maintaining in his *Liber de coelesti vita et de animarum immortalitate* the demonstrability of the soul's immortality. Jerome Savonarola publishes his *Compendium logicae,* his *Apologeticus de ratione poeticae artis,* and his *Trattato dello amore di Iesu Christo.* Augustine Nifo completes the first version of his *De intellectu et daemonibus.* Death of Piero della Francesca. Donato di Pascuccio d'Antonio, known as Bramante, raises the dome of S. Maria delle Grazie in Milan. Journey to Italy of James Lefèvre d'Étaples, who meets Pico and Ficino in Florence and Ermolaus Barbarus in Rome. Between 1492 and 1498 John Reuchlin makes three trips to Italy and comes in contact with the Florentine humanists, especially Pico. John Heynlin von Stein publishes a *Resolutorium dubiorum circa celebrationem missarum occurrentium.*

1493   Repeated petitions from Ludovic the Moor to the king of France for protection and defense against the king of Naples and his possible allies. In response to an agreement between Florence and Naples that promotes the territorial ambitions of Roman baron Virginio Orsini (thereby angering the pope and the Sforzas), the Moor enters into an alliance with Rome and Venice, the text of which contains a formal alliance with France. By the treaty of Barcelona in January, the king of France ensures the neutrality of Spain in regard to his aims in Italy; he cedes the Rossiglione and Cerdaña, the last Pyrenese provinces in French hands. In May in the

John II, King of Portugal, claims that the Spanish attempt to find a way to the Indies is opposed to the rights over those countries that the Church had always acknowledged as belonging to his country, and he says he is ready to hinder by force any new colonial efforts of Castile. Pope Alexander VI issues two bulls (on May 2 and 3) that recognize and confirm the rights of the Portuguese over west Africa, but grant equal privileges to Spain over lands colonized by Columbus and over future discoveries beyond the meridian (the "Alexandrian Line") running a hundred leagues from the Azores and the Cape Verde Islands. Another bull in September confirms

Thomas de Vio, known as Cajetan, begins his teaching of metaphysics at the University of Padua. Anthony Trombetta publishes his *Opus doctrinae scotisticae in thomistas.* John Colet finishes a stay of about four years in Italy, where he becomes a friend of Ficino, and in France. Young Erasmus of Rotterdam leaves the Augustinian monastery of Steyn, enters the service of the bishop of Cambrai, and then goes to Paris to study theology. German painter and engraver Hans Holbein paints the *Weingarten Altar* in Augsburg. Sculptor Tilmann Riemenschneider sculpts the statues of Adam and Eve for the cathedral of Würzburg.

Peace of Senlis and for the same purpose, Charles VIII renounces his rights to a Burgundian inheritance (Franche-Comté and Artois) in favor of the Habsburgs. Frederick III of Habsburg dies in Lenz. Maximilian I is elected king of Germany. In German territories a peasant revolt breaks out, known as the Bundschuh (from the rough shoes worn by the peasants). Return of Christopher Columbus to Spain and announcement of his adventure (March).

Spanish possession of lands already discovered.

1494   Death of Ferdinand I, king of Naples, who is succeeded by his son Alphonsus II. In September Charles VIII of France descends into Italy. Overcoming the opposition of the Neapolitans in Liguria, the French army enters Lombardy. In October Gian Galeazzo Sforza dies, and the Moor obtains the title of duke from Maximilian of Austria; from that point on, he changes his attitude to Charles VIII, whom he now fears as an invader. The advance of the French into Tuscany causes riots in Florence, which has been in upheaval due to the emergence of the Savonarola party. In November, when Piero de'Medici comes to an agreement with Charles that assures the

Death of Pico della Mirandola, Politian, and Boiardo. Jerome Savonarola preaches his sermons on Genesis; then, after the fall of the Medici, those on the Psalms and Haggai. Following the death of Lorenzo the Magnificent, the Platonic Academy of Careggi is for practical purposes closed, and Marsilius Ficino must defend his followers against the surge of reaction from the Piagnoni. Because of his connections with the Medici, George Benignus Salviati leaves Florence and takes refuge in Ragusa (Dubrovnik). In Bologna Alexander Achillini discusses his *Quodlibeta de intelligentiis,* inspired by Siger, in which he tries to soften the difference between Averroism and orthodoxy; he is answered by latter a free passage through Tuscan territory, the king of France is welcomed as a liberator by the Pisans; this final insult leads to the revolt of Florence against the Medici. Piero returns in haste to the city but is forced into flight and exile. The new republic, dominated by Savonarola, comes to an agreement with Charles, who now has a free way to the south.

Maximilian of Habsburg enters a second marriage with Bianca Maria (+ 1510), daughter of Galeazzo Maria Sforza and niece of the Moor. Ivan III, who has succeeded with the help of the faithful court nobility (the boyars) in transforming the Moscovite principality into a unified state with emblems and court ceremonial of Byzantine origin, appoints himself ruler of all the Russias; this marks the beginning of the eastern myth of Moscow as "the Third Rome," center of a universal Christian empire. In the treaty of Tordesillas the Spanish and Portuguese define their respective spheres of action in the new world, following the guidelines set by the pope but moving the dividing line from 100 to 370 leagues from Cape Verde. Second voyage of Columbus (1494–96), on which he discovers the Antilles and Jamaica.

Paduan Averroist Mark Anthony Zimara in *Quaestio de triplici causalitate intelligentiae.* Death of Paul Barbo of Soncino, whose *Quaestiones super Metaphysicam* are published posthumously a few months later. In Verona Aldo Manutius begins an activity as publisher that is marked by a special care for esthetic quality and distinguished by the first publication of catalogues with prices. Foundation of the University of Aberdeen in Scotland.

Sebastian Brant publishes his successful allegorical poem *The Ship of Fools (Das Narrenschyeff)* with woodcuts by Albrecht Dürer.

John Reuchlin writes his *De verbo mirifico.*

1495   Pope Alexander VI comes to an agreement with Charles VIII and has him accompanied on his expedition to the south by the pope's son, Rodrigo Borgia, cardinal of Valencia, as surety for the agreement. Alphonsus II of Naples abdicates in favor of his son, Ferdinand II, known as Ferrandino. In February Charles enters Naples and Ferrandino flees to Sicily. In Naples a popular middle-class government (a *Sedile*) is established that tolerates violent reactions against the Aragonese nobility. In March a Holy League is formed in which the Moor unites Milan, Venice, the pope, Emperor Maximilian, the king of Spain, and later, the king of England, against the French. Charles then abandons Naples, crosses the Apennines, and takes shelter in the allied territory of Piedmont. In July Ferrandino returns in triumph to Naples. The threat of Spanish and English intervention convinces Charles to make a peace with Sforza that restores Novara to the latter in exchange for recognition of French control of Genoa. In October Charles returns to France. In a diet at Worms, as part of the project for restructuring the empire, an imperial tribunal is established that is permanent and has its seat first in

Cardinal Francisco Ximenez Cisneros becomes primate of Spain.

Jerome Savonarola preaches on Job and writes in Latin his *Compendium of Revelation,* which is translated into the vernacular in the following year, his *Libro della vita viduale,* and his *De simplicitate christianae vitae.* Death of Gabriel Biel, who had become provost of the house of the Brothers of the Common Life in Einsiedel, near Tübingen. His *Collectorium super quattuor libros Sententiarum,* which he left incomplete, is finished by his disciple, Wendelin Steinbach. Leonardo da Vinci paints the fresco *The Last Supper* in the refectory of Santa Maria delle Grazie (1495–97).

Frankfurt and then in
Speyer.
At the death of John II,
his cousin, Manuel of
Aviz, known as the
Lucky, is the new king of
Portugal; he renews the
contest over the division
of colonial lands.

1496	Death of Ferrandino while still fighting French partisans with the help of the Venetians. The crown of Naples passes to his uncle, Frederick I, who completes the liberation. Approach of the Republic of Florence to democracy under the spiritual leadership of Savonarola, who strongly attacks the pope and the Roman Curia from his pulpit.	Alexander VI bestows the title of Catholic Majesty on the king of Spain.	Savonarola preaches on Amos, Ruth, and Micah. Ficino publishes his *Commentaria in Platonem* and his translation of Pseudo-Dionysius. Thomas de Vio comments on the *De ente et essentia.* Anthony de Ferraris publishes his *Dialogus de heremita.* Philip Buonaccorsi dies in Cracow. Il Perugino paints the *Crucifixion* in the church of Santa Maria Maddalena de'Pazzi in Florence.
1497	In the Republic of Florence the opposition of the oligarchic republicans (the Arrabbiati) and of the Medicis (the Bigi or Palleschi) catches fire, aided by Alexander VI. Maximilian I celebrates the marriage of his son, Philip the Handsome, to Joanna of Castile, daughter of the sovereigns of Spain. Manuel of Portugal again offers incentives for the travels begun by John II with Diaz' undertakings. Vasco da Gama sails in July and rounds the Cape (which he renames the Cape of Good Hope). First voyage to the Indies of John Cabot and his	Alexander VI excommunicates Savonarola and threatens Florence with an interdict. Expulsion of Jews and Muslims from Portugal.	Savonarola preaches on Ezekiel and writes his *Trattato contro li astrologi* (in which he takes over and popularizes the views of Pico) and his *Triumphus crucis.* He also publishes his *Apologeticum fratrum Sancti Marci,* in which he justifies the refusal of the brothers of San Marco to join the Tuscan-Romagnolan Congregation as demanded by Alexander VI, and his *Lamentum sponsae Christi.* Florentine Dominican John Caroli, his stubborn adversary, answers with a refutation of the *Apologeticum* and

son Sebastian under com-
mission from the king of
England; sailing north-
west he reaches
Newfoundland in June.

his *Contra la lamen-
tazione della falsa sposa
di Cristo e lamentazione
dello sposo*. In Ragusa
Salviati writes a defense
of Savonarola, his
Propheticae solutiones.
John Nesi writes his
*Oraculum de novo sae-
culo* in praise of
Savonarola, lauding him,
along with Ficino and
Pico, as a prophet of spiritual and cultural renewal.
Anthony Trombetta
writes his *De animarum
humanarum
purificatione*. Death of
Pomponius Laetus.
At Oxford John Colet
gives a series of lectures
on St. Paul and publishes
his commentaries on the
letters to the Romans and
the Corinthians and on
the two *Hierarchies* of
Pseudo-Dionysius.
During these years he
also writes his *De sacramento Ecclesiae* and *De
compositione sancti cor-
poris Christi mystici*, in
which he combines
Pseudo-Dionysian mysti-
cal theology with criti-
cism of the corrupt
clergy.
Conrad Celtis becomes
poet and teacher of
rhetoric at the court of
Vienna.

1498   After entering into an
agreement with Spain
(Agreement of Alcalà de
Henares) and Austria for
a real partition of Italy,
Charles VIII is ready to
implement again his plans
for conquest when he dies
suddenly (April 8).

Savonarola draws a
strong final reaction from
his enemies when he pub-
lishes his *Trattato circa il
reggimento e governo
della città di Firenze* and
his sermons on Exodus,
in which he violently at-
tacks the corruption

The duke of Orleans ascends the throne of France as Louis XII; in December he obtains a divorce from his first wife, Jeanne, and marries widowed Queen Anne of Brittany. The divorce promotes the renewal of cordial relations between the French crown and the Church, for in exchange Cesare Borgia is elected duke of the Valentinois (whence his name, Valentino). Louis XII then confirms the Peace of Étaples with the English and renews his agreements with the Spanish but without referring to the partitioning of Italy.

In Florence, on the day of Charles' death, the signoria orders the arrest of Savonarola; he is condemned as a heretic and dies at the stake the next month.

In August Vasco da Gama reaches the Indian port of Calcutta. Third voyage of Columbus, who reaches the southern continent (mouths of the Orinoco and Panama). A revolt of colonists in Haiti leads to the intervention of a royal commissioner, Francisco de Bobadilla, who arrests Columbus and sends him back to Spain. Second voyage of Cabot (begun in June), which reaches Labrador.

of the Roman Curia. Marsilius Ficino writes an *Apologia* against the accusations being accepted by the Piagnoni. Death of Christopher Landino.

Sebastian Brant publishes a collection of spiritual poems, *Varia carmina,* and brings out a richly commented (the *glossa ordinaria,* Nicholas of Lyra, patristic exegeses) edition of the Latin Bible. Preacher John Geiler, moral leader of the humanist group in Strasbourg, delivers a Lenten series inspired by Brant's *Ship of Fools.* Tilmann Riemenschneider sculpts the *Tomb of Rudolf of Scheremberg* and the *Altar of the Virgin* in Creglingen.

| 1499 | Louis XII of France enters into agreements with the Swiss and Venice and wins the support of | In Spain the repressive measures already used against the Jews are applied to the Moors (still | Death of Marsilius Ficino at his villa in Careggi. Death of Nicholas of Vernia a few months |

the pope. Then, in August, a French army, led by Lombard exile Gian Giacomo Trivulzio easily invade Milanese territory. The Moor takes refuge with his "royal nephew," Maximilian. With the support of the French, Borgia begins the destruction of the seignories cropping up in papal territory in the Romagna and establishing themselves as personal duchies. As head of a league organized with the agreement of the pope, Venice begins a crusade against Bayazid II.

In England the last resistance of the York party is overcome for good.

In the treaty of Basel, Maximilian I recognizes the independence of the Swiss, who are opposed to his reform of the empire.

numerous in the province of Granada); their goods are confiscated.

after completing his *Quaestiones adversus falsam Averroys opinionem de pluralitate intellectus et de animae felicitate,* in which, in obedience to Barozzi's warning, he abandons Averroist teaching on the soul. Salviati has his *De natura angelica* published in Florence. Michelangelo Buonarroti sculpts the Vatican *Pietà*. Peter Dorland publishes his *Viola animae,* an abridgment of Raymond Sibiuda's *Liber creaturarum*.

First journey of Erasmus to England, where he follows Colet's courses and becomes a good friend of him as well as of Grocyn and Linacre.

1500   The Moor attempts to take back Milanese territory with the help of the Swiss, who, however, sell out to the French; the Moor is defeated at Novara, captured, and deported to France, where he will die in prison in 1508. To right the imbalance thus created, the Spanish invoke the agreements of Alcalà in the partition of southern Italy: the treaty of Granada (November) sanctions the partition of Neapolitan territory between France and Spain. A diet at Augsburg

Bramante builds the cloister of Santa Maria della Pace (1500–4). Rafaello Sanzio paints *The Knight's Dream* in Urbino. Il Perugino does the frescoes in the audience chamber of the Collegio del Cambio in Perugia.

establishes the permanent
government of the empire
(the Council of State).
Charles of Habsburg (the
future Charles V) is born
of Philip the Handsome
and Joanna of Castile.
Beatrice of Aragon is re-
pudiated by Ladislaus of
Bohemia-Hungary and
returns to Naples. While
trying to round Cape
Verde, Portuguese
mariner Pedro Alvarez is
driven by a storm to the
coast of Brazil, and he
takes possession of the
country in the name of
the king of Portugal.

1501	The French army moves on Naples from Milan. Accusing Frederick I of Naples of secret agreements with the Ottomans, the pope authorizes Valentino to combine with the invading army. Naples surrenders on August 2, while the Spanish occupy Calabria and Apulia in the south. Frederick surrenders to the French and is taken to France, where he will live, with a lifetime pension, as duke of Anjou until his death (1504). Alexander I succeeds his brother, John Albert, as king of Poland. The governor of Haiti asks the king of Spain for permission to import black slaves from Africa, due to the slaughter of native workers, which has reached tragic proportions.	At the request of Alexander VI, Henry VII of England convokes a provincial council of London to have the clergy deliberate on a sum to be paid for the defense of the faith against the Mohammedans.	Michelangelo is in Florence, where he completes some important commissions, among them the *Taddei, Pitti,* and *Doni tondi,* and the *David* (1501–4). Leonardo da Vinci paints his *Gioconda* (between 1501 and 1503). Deaths of Scotist theologian Stephen (Pillet) Brûlefer, author of *Formalitates in doctrinam Scoti,* and humanist Robert Gaguin. Giles of Delft publishes a metric translation of the seven penitential psalms and, two years later, a verse paraphrase of the letter to the Romans.

1502 Definitive conquest of southern Italy with the capitulation of Tarano (March), followed by disputes between the French and the Spanish over the division of the occupied territories. Coastal explorations by Florentine Amerigo Vespucci (1499–1502) strengthen the view that the New World is not the Indies. The reports of his voyage make it clear beyond a doubt that a new continent has been discovered. Fourth and final voyage of Columbus (1502–4): sailing the coast of central America he reaches the country that will take its name, Colombia, from him.

Expulsion from Spain of all Muslims who refuse baptism.

In his *De rerum praenotione,* John Francis Pico renews Pico's condemnation of divinatory astrology. Pinturicchio paints his *Incidents in the Life of Pius II* in the Piccolomini Library of the Cathedral of Siena. Foundation of the University of Wittenberg. Having completed his philosophical studies, Martin Luther is a bachelor at the University of Erfurt and, in 1505, a master of arts.

1503 The defeat of the French at Cerignola opens the way to Naples for the Spanish. The new pope, Julius II, has Cesare Borgia arrested and does away with his duchy; Valentino manages to flee and finds shelter in Naples and then in Spain. Success of the Venetian crusade, which stops the Ottoman advance. By the treaty of Arona, the Swiss, in exchange for help given in the conquest of Milan, obtain the Ticino region from Louis XII. Vasily III succeeds Ivan III as grand duke of Moscow and begins a policy of annexing territories still independent of Russia, making himself

Death of Alexander VI. Election of Pius III (Francesco Todeschini Piccolomini of Siena), whose intentions of reforming the Church are nullified by his death after less than a month of reign. Election of Julius II (Giuliano delle Rovere of Savona, 1503–15), nephew of Sixtus IV, and an energetic pope and reorganizer of the Papal States.

Death of John Caroli. Benedictine humanist Guy Jouennau writes *Reformationis monasticae vindiciae seu defensio.* In Basel, Ulrich Surgant publishes a successful homiletic handbook for the training of preachers: *Manuale curatorum.* Humanist James Locher writes a short book to defend the value of poetry and its independence from theology. Erasmus publishes his *Enchiridion militis christiani.* Flemish painter Hieronymus Bosch paints his *Garden of Delights* (1503–4?). German painter and engraver Lukas Cranach the Elder paints his *Crucifixion.*

"Lord of All the Russias,"
with the title "Czar"
("Caesar").

1504	Surrender of the French at Gaeta on January 1. In February France and Spain sign a three-year truce in Lyons. Then, in the treaty of Blois, Louis XII acknowledges Spain's dominion over Naples in exchange for Maximilian's recognition of France's dominion over Milan. Death of Isabella of Castile; her nominal heiress is her daughter Joanna. Trade crisis in the Mediterranean and Venice's gradual loss of control over the traditional route of the spice trade.	Paul Cortese writes his *In quattuor libros Sententiarum disputationes,* in which he seeks to reconcile the Scholastic method with humanist eloquence. Anthony de Ferraris writes *De educatione.* Raffaello Sanzio paints *The Marriage of the Virgin* in Urbino. John Fisher is appointed chancellor of the University of Cambridge and bishop of Rochester. John Reuchlin writes his *Liber de arte praedicandi.* In the library of the Couvent du Parc, Erasmus comes upon Valla's *Annotationes* on the New Testament, which show him the theological fruitfulness of biblical philology. Albrecht Dürer paints *The Adoration of the Magi.* Cranach paints *The Flight into Egypt.*
1505	Creation of the Portuguese viceregal territory of the Indies. First viceroy is Francisco de Almeida.	Foundation of the University of Valencia. James Wimpfeling writes his *Apologia pro republica Christiana.* Martin Luther abandons his newly begun study of law and enters the Augustinian convent in Erfurt. Michelangelo is called to Rome to create the tomb of Julius II, a work that will torment the artist for over thirty years; part of

the project is his *Prisons*
and *Moses*. In Venice
Giovanni Bellini paints
the altarpiece for the
church of Sac Zaccaria.
Bramante plans the basil-
ica of St. Peter. German
sculptor Peter Vischer the
Elder, with the help of his
son Peter the Younger,
creates the reliquary of
St. Sebald in Nuremberg.

1506	Joanna of Castile goes mad with grief after the death of Philip the Handsome; henceforth she lives in isolation in the castile of Tordesillas. Castile is governed in her name by her father, Ferdinand of Aragon, who marries (second marriage) Germaine de Foix, niece of Louis XII. This marriage sanctions the definitive cession to Spain of Naples, which had been formally given by the king of France to his wife. Death of Berthold of Herrenberg, archbishop of Mainz, main supporter of the German party fighting for the adminis-trative reform of the em-pire; the pro-Habsburg party is strengthened, for the further reason that the death of Philip the Handsome removes the threat that the imperial title will be hereditary. Maximilian is able to re-duce the powers of the Council of State and the Chamber Tribunal. Death of Alexander of	Franciscan Cardinal Francisco Ximenez Cisneros, grand inquisitor of Spain (1506–9), in-creases persecution of the Jews, who emigrate mainly to Italy.	Giles of Viterbo is gen-eral of the Augustinians. Giorgio da Castelfrancos, known as Giorgione, paints his *Laura* and in the following years, his most representative works: *The Tempest,* the *Three Philosophers,* and the *Venus* "of Dresden." Death of Christopher Columbus at Valladolid.

Poland, who is succeeded
by his brother Sigismund
II the Elder.

1507   At a diet in Constance
Maximilian discusses the
men and money needed
in order to descend into
Italy, have himself
crowned emperor, and re-
duce French power.
Venice refuses passage to
the imperial army.

Julius II grants a plenary
indulgences to givers of
alms for the completion
of St. Peter's Basilica.

Adrian Castellesi writes
his *De vera philosophia
ex quatuor doctoribus ec-
clesiae.*
William Briçonnet com-
pletes a mission at the
papal court and during
his travels in Italy makes
acquaintance with hu-
manist and reform-
minded circles. On his
return to France he is appointed abbot of Saint-
Germain-des-Prés, where
the library becomes,
under his rule, a meeting
place for young human-
ists and reform-minded
people. Charles of
Bouelles (Bovillus) like-
wise returns from a jour-
ney to Italy and other
European countries and
dedicates his *Dialogi de
Trinitate* to Lefèvre.
Martin Luther is ordained
a priest and begins the
study of theology, guided
by Biel's commentary on
the *Sentences.* German
scholar and geographer
Marinus Waldseemüller
shows the New World on
one of his maps for the
first time, naming it
America in honor of
Vespucci.
Nicholas Copernicus de-
velops his heliocentric
hypothesis and circulates
it in a manuscript work
entitled *De hypothesibus
motuum coelestium a se
constitutis commentario-
lus.*

1508   In a battle with the Habsburg army the Venetians wrest Friuli and Istria from the imperial forces. This unleashes against Venice the animosity of all the other interested powers of Italy. In Cambrai the French, the Habsburgs, and the Spanish sign treaties of peace and friendship and form a league with the pope for the purpose of breaking Venice and dividing up its possessions. In Rome Maximilian I is given the title of emperor elect.

Tiberius Bacilieri, a master in Padua, publishes a *Lectura in tres libros de anima* in which he comes close to the Sigerian Averroism of Achillini. Anthony de Ferraris writes his *Esposizione del Pater Noster*. Michelangelo begins the frescoes on the ceiling of the Sistine Chapel in the Vatican (completed in 1512). Raffaello begins the *Stanze della Segnatura* (completed in 1511). At the suggestion of John Staupitz, vicar of the Augustinians, Martin Luther is called to lecture on ethics and exegesis at the new University of Wittenberg.

1509   War of the Cambrai League against Venice, in which Ladislaus of Bohemia-Hungary, Charles III the Good, duke of Savoy, the Estes of Ferrara, and the Gonzagas of Mantua join. On April 13 Julius pronounces an interdict on Venice, and the French enter the Veneto from Milanese territory. Venice is defeated at Agnadello (May 14), and of its territories some are invaded by enemies, others rebel. Venice then turns to diplomacy in order to divide the allies and enters into separate negotiations with the pope and the French while concentrating its military efforts

At the urging of Cardinal Ximenes de Cisneros, the king of Spain sends a crusading army against the Muslims of Oran on the African coast.

Bramante builds the church of San Pietro in Montorio. Dominican painter Bartolomeo della Porta, known as Fra Bartolomeo, a follower of Savonarola, paints *Enthroned Madonna and Saints* in the Cathedral of Lucca. James Lefèvre, who has followed Briçonnet to Saint-Germain, publishes his *Quincuplex Psalterium*. Second stay of Erasmus in England; while guest of Thomas More he writes his *Encomium Morias seu Laus stultitiae*.

against the emperor and
his vassals.
At Diu (in the Gujarat)
Francisco de Almeida in-
flicts a naval defeat on
the Egyptian fleet and on
the Venetians who are al-
lied with Egypt against
Portugal. He thus estab-
lishes the political bases
for the Portuguese colo-
nial empire, but he is recalled and replaced by
the more energetic gover-
nor, Alfonso of
Albuquerque.
Death of Henry VII of
England. He is succeeded
by Henry VIII, who mar-
ries his brother Arthur's
widow, Catherine of
Aragon, daughter of
Ferdinand and Isabella of
Spain.

1510   The pope is reconciled
with Venice (February),
lifts the interdict, and
withdraws from the
League. Louis XII, who
succeeds in drawing
Henry VIII of England
into the League, per-
suades the French
prelates to call a council
to be held in Pisa for the
purpose of judging and
suspending the pope as a
simoniac. In response,
Julius II besieges
Mirandola, annuls the
treaty of Blois, and allies
himself with the
Venetians to drive the
French from Italy.
The introduction of black
slaves into the New
World begins.

Maximilian I commis-
sions James Wimpfeling
to draft a new collection
of the *Gravamina natio-
nis Germaniae* that will
be several times updated
and brandished by the
Reformers in the coming
years. Journey of Martin
Luther to Rome on inter-
nal business of the
Augustinian Order.

Death of mystic
Catherine (Fieschi) of
Genoa. Death of Paul
Cortese shortly after pub-
lishing his *De cardi-
nalatu*. Anthony de
Ferraris debates with
Valla in his *De donatione
Constantini Magni facta
Ecclesiae*. Death of
Sandro Botticelli and of
Giorgione. In London
John Colet opens a
school dedicated to
"Jesus among the
Doctors."
Ulrich Zwingli, parish
priest of Glarona (eastern
Switzerland) writes
Favola poetica del bue,
an allegory against the
use of mercenaries in the
Swiss armies and against
the papal politics that
promote the practice.
Later, after becoming

vicar at Einsiedeln, he writes *Il labirinto* on the same subject.
In his *Contra turpem libellum Philomusi defensio theologiae scholasticae et neotericorum* James Wimpfeling roughly attacks the classicism defended by James Locher. With the publication of his *Augenspiegel,* John Reuchlin begins a controversy with Jewish convert John Pfefferkorn (author of a *Judenspiegel*) and with the Dominican theologians of Cologne who support him, among them the inquisitor James Hoogstraten, who urges the indiscriminate destruction of all Jewish books. Albrecht Dürer publishes his illustrations for the Apocalypse.

1511   Julius II becomes convinced that the real problem is the presence of foreigners in Italy, and in October he starts a new league, the Holy League, with Spain (as ruler in Naples), Rome, and Venice, in order to free Italy from foreigners ("Barbarians out!"). With the resultant alienation of Austria and then England from the League of Cambrai, the war against Venice changes into a war against the French, who are defeated by the Spaniards and the pope at Ravenna but at the cost of serious losses for the latter. Maximilian I formally joins the Holy League in November. The

The schismatic Council of Pisa, promoted by Louis XII, begins (1511–12). Philofrench cardinals Bernardine of Carvajal, Francis Borgia, William Briçonnet (the elder), Renato de Prie, Frederick Sanseverino, and Hypolytus d'Este take part. When transferred to Milan, the council declares the pope deposed and tries to restore the conciliarist decrees of Constance and Basel. Among the most energetic and active opponents of the schismatic council is Thomas de Vio (Cajetan), general of the Dominicans.

Thomas de Vio writes his *Auctoritas papae et concilii sive Ecclesiae comparata* against the Pisan council. George Benignus Salviati, a resident in Rome for some years, writes an *Apologeticum sey defensorium* to defend Francesco Maria Della Rovere, duke of Urbino, against the charge of having assassinated Cardinal Alidosi, a favorite of Julius II. Anthony Trombetta, appointed bishop of Urbino, goes to Rome to take part in the work of the council and intervenes in the commission that condemns supporters of the unicity or mortality of the soul. Raffaello paints the

French are hunted from
Milanese territory and the
duchy is restored, with
Maximilian Sforza, son
of the Moor, as duke.
Spanish occupation of
Cuba.

Stanze di Eliodoro
(1511–14). Tiziano
Vecellio (Titian) paints
*Incidents in the Life of St.
Anthony* in the Santo
school of Padua.
Agrippa of Nettesheim,
physician and astrologer
in Cologne, goes to Italy
to take part, as a theologian, in the Council of
Pisa and comes in contact
with Italian humanist
circles. Reuchlin pub-
lishes *Epistolae clarorum
virorum* in which he as-
sembles testimonies of
his contemporaries in
favor of a tolerant distinction between useful and
harmful Jewish books.
This work is followed by
the *Epistolae obscurorum
virorum,* from the human-
ist circle in Erfurt, with
Mutius Rufus, Eoban
Hessus, and John Crotus
Rubianus taking part in
the writing. With this successful work the discus-
sion changes to one on
the opposition between
the Scholastic and the humanist cultures. Martin
Luther is appointed prior
of the Augustinian con-
vent in Wittenberg.
Erasmus, at John Fisher's
invitation, begins a three-
year course of lectures in
Cambridge.

1512   With the support of the
king of Spain the Medici
return to Florence, with
the sons of Lorenzo—Gi-
uliano, Duke of Nemours,
and Cardinal Giovanni—
sharing the government.
With the occupation of

In response to the schis-
matic aims of the Council
of Pisa and yielding to
the insistence of de Vio,
Julius II convokes the
Fifth Lateran Council
(1512–17, the eighteenth
ecumenical), the principal

Peter Pomponazzi teaches
in Bologna. Thomas de
Vio comments on the *De
anima.* Giles of Viterbo
composes his *Sententiae
ad mentem Platonis.*
Benedictine Charles
Ferrand of Bruges, who

Upper Navarre (beyond the Pyrenees) Ferdinand the Catholic definitively unites all of Spain. In a diet in Triers and then in Cologne control over the Council of State is given to the imperial diet, over which the emperor presides. In order further to strengthen the central authorities of the empire, Maximilian obtains from the diet a division of Germany into ten circles or circumscriptions, subject to imperial administration and jurisdiction.

Bayazid II is forced to abdicate. He is succeeded by his son Selim I, who has great ambitions for conquests in the East.

purpose of which is to begin the reform of the Church. From the outset this council proclaims papal absolutism and the superiority of the pope over the national churches and over councils. Giles of Viterbo, who inaugurates the work (May 3), and Bernardine Zeno and Thomas de Vio, who open the first and second sessions (May 11 and 17), urge the council fathers to reform and to a crusade against the Turks. When the third session begins (December 3), Emperor Maximilian dissociates himself from French separatism and accepts the council. Archbishop William Wahram convokes a provincial council at Canterbury to deal with a revival of Lollard preaching: John Colet gives the opening address, but is harshly criticized for his reformist attitude.

attends humanist gatherings in Paris, publishes his *De animi tranquillitate* and other writings on monastic spirituality. James Lefèvre publishes a synoptic version of the Pauline letters, with commentary. Theologian and jurist James Almain, at the request of Louis XII, argues against the anticonciliarism of de Vio in his *Libellus de auctoritate Ecclesiae*. De Vio answers with an *Apologia*.

Luther, with a doctorate in theology from Erfurt, replaces Staupitz in the chair of biblical sciences, explaining the Psalms and Pauline letters in the following years.

1513   A few days before the election of a new pope, the French and Venetians agree in a new treaty of Blois on reconquering and dividing up the territory of Milan. In response Leo X promotes the Malines League, of which the king of England and the emperor become members. Louis XII stirs up Scotland against England, but the Scottish army is routed by Henry VII at the battle of Flodden. The French are defeated by the

Death of Julius II. Election of Leo X (Giovanni de'Medici, son of Lorenzo, 1513–21). The work of the council in Rome continues with the decree annulling the schismatic council and with a condemnation of all doctrines that deny the immortality of the soul (session VIII, December 9). Cajetan, convinced of the distinction between the domains of theology and philosophy, dissociates himself from the decree obliging teachers of

Anthony Trombetta dedicates to Leo X his *Quaestio de efficientia primi principii*, in which he defends the Scotist thesis on the volitional causality (and not just final, as Thomism said) of the divine principle of the movements of the heavens. The Venetian Camaldolese (Thomas Giustiniani, Vincent Quirini, Sebastian Zorzi, etc.) compose an open denunciation of ecclesiastical corruption in their *Libellus ad Leonem X*.

Italians and the imperial forces at Novara and must move out of Milanese lands (June), then by the English at Guinegatte in France (August); they sign a treaty imposing harsh conditions (September). The Venetians, now abandoned, are attacked by the coalition and defeated at the battle known as that of the "Madonna dell'Olmo" (October). Death of John of Sweden, Norway, and Denmark; he is succeeded by his son, Christian II the Wicked.

Vasco Nuñez de Balboa, a Spaniard, crosses the Isthmus of Panama and is the first to see the Pacific Ocean, which he names the Southern Sea. On the western coast he discovers many silver mines, which feed the myth of Eldorado and thereby the ambitions of the conquistadors in Central America.

philosophy to justify the conclusions of faith. A crusade against the Bohemians is proclaimed.

Niccolò Machiavelli, formerly chancellor of the extinct Florentine republic, now in retirement at San Casciano, writes his *Discorsi sopra la prima deca di Tito Livio,* a meditation on the origin, changes, and decay of the republican state, and his famous treatise *Il principe,* in which he lays the foundations of political realism. Leonardo da Vinci lives in isolation at the papal court in Rome: during this period he completes his theoretical treatise *De ludo geometrico.* Giovanni Antonio Bazzi, known as Il Sodoma, paints *The Marriage of Alexander and Roxana* at the Villa Farnesina in Rome. Josse Clichtove, disciple and collaborator of Lefèvre, publishes his *De mystica numerorum significatione.*

German painter Mathis Neithard Gothard, known as Mattias Grünewald, paints the great triptych over the altar in Isenheim (1513–16).

1514   Leo X occupies Parma and Piacenza. In August England and France sign the Peace of London, chiefly as a result of the work of Thomas Wolsey, archbishop of York. The Peace is sealed by the marriage of Louis XII (whose wife, Anne of Brittany, had died in January) with Mary of

Louis XII disavows the schismatic council and recognizes the decrees already passed by Lateran V (January). The council tackles the problem of disagreements over competence between bishops and religious orders. Leo X grants a new plenary indulgence for the building of St. Peter's basilica. In the following

In Bologna, Peter Pomponazzi publishes *Quaestio de intensione et remissione formarum* in a dispute with the Scholastic world. Giles of Viterbo dedicates his *Historia viginti saeculorum* to Leo X. Death of Bramante. Raffaello paints the *Stanze dell'Incendio di Borgo.* Titian paints his

England, sister of Henry VIII (October), but Louis dies unexpectedly on December 31. War of Bayazid II against the shah of Persia, and Turkish conquest of that country as far as lower Mesopotamia.

year, he sends young Albert of Hohenheim, Prince of Hohenzollern, recently made archbishop of Magdeburg and Mainz, to Germany as administrator of the indulgence: the revenues gained from the indulgence are to go half to the work on St. Peter's and half to the archbishop, to repay a debt contracted with the Fugger bank to pay for the confirmation of his own election. Albert puts Dominican John Tetzel in charge of preaching the indulgence; John does his job in a crude way and not without abuses.

Sacred and Profane Love. Erasmus settles in Basel and works on the publication, two years later, of his *Novum Instrumentum,* the revised Greek text of the New Testament; it is dedicated to Leo X and accompanied by a *Paraclesis,* a *Methodus,* and an *Apologia.* The inquiry into Reuchlin which the Inquisition had begun in Mainz ends in his favor, and Ulrich Hutten writes his *Trionfo di Reuchlin.*

1515   The new king of France, Francis I of Angoulême, recently married to Claudia, daughter of Louis and Anne of Brittany, pursues his father-in-law's foreign policy and readies a new campaign for the conquest of Milanese territory; the preparation is preceded by feverish diplomatic efforts to obtain the neutrality of the English and, unsuccessfully, that of the Swiss. Invasion of Lombardy (August) via the Piedmont to avoid the Swiss. Cardinal Matthäus Schiner spurs the response of the Swiss, who face the French and Venetians at Marignano (today Melegnano) on

The Lateran Council issues decrees on printing books, credit banks (Monti di pietà), and the reform of the calender.

Agrippa of Nettesheim comments on Hermes Trismegistus at the University of Paris. Death of French humanist Giles of Delft. Luther completes his commentary on the letter to the Romans and sees to the printed edition of the *Theologia deutsch.* Hieronymus Bosch paints his *Ascent of Calvary.*

September 14. The vic-
tory enables the French to
enter Milan and recon-
quer the duchy:
Maximilian Sforza yields
his ducal rights to the
king of France.
Switzerland renounces its
own expansionist ambi-
tions in Milanese territory
and from this point on
pursues a policy of strict
neutrality. The still-
existing Holy League
helps without inter-
vening.

1516   Giuliano de'Medici is
called to Rome by his
brother and leaves the
government of Florence
to Lorenzo II, son of
Piero II, who is invested
by Leo X with the duchy
of Urbino, from which he
had been driven by the
Della Roveres. The pope
begins negotiations with
the French for maintain-
ing papal possession of
Parma and Piacenza, of
the Medicean signoria in
Florence and Urbino, and
regarding the decrees of
the Lateran Council.
Permanent Peace of
Fribourg (November) be-
tween the Swiss and the
king of France, who
grants them an annual
payment and the retention
of Ticino canton, pro-
vided they never again
provide anyp enemy of
France with soldiery.
Death of Ferdinand the
Catholic; Charles of

The council takes up the
problems of ecclesiastical
discipline and the need of
reform.
Conference and agree-
ment of Bologna
(December) between the
pope and the king of
France which provides
for the abolition of the
Pragmatic Sanction in ex-
change for recognition of
the autonomy of the
Gallican church, but
under the control of both
the king and the papal authority. By this agree-
ment, it is for the king to
appoint to the more im-
portant benefices
(archiepiscopal and epis-
copal sees, abbacies,
etc.), while the lesser
benefices (curacies,
prebends, etc.) are left to
the pope. This change
significantly reduces the
autonomy of prelates,
which until now was one
of the major impulses to

Death of Baptist
Spagnoli. In Bologna
Peter Pomponazzi pub-
lishes his *De immortali-
tate animae*. First edition
of Ludovico Ariosto's
Orlando Furioso (later
editions: 1521 and 1532).
William Briçonnet be-
comes bishop of Meaux,
succeeding Ludovico
Pinelle (author of *Quinze
fontaines vitales*), who
had taught William theol-
ogy. Thus the humanist
circle of Saint-Germain
shifts to Meaux, where it
engages in intense theo-
logical and exegetical
study marked by serious
reformist tendencies.
Lefèvre is especially ac-
tive, revising the New
Testament.
Thomas More writes his
*Libellus de optimo
reipublicae statu deque
nova insula Utopia,* in
which he attacks the eco-
nomic and social

Habsburg is now king of Spain. To ensure the friendship of the king of France in support of his succession, Charles signs the treaty of Noyons, which renews the division of Italian territories: acknowledgment that Milanese territory belongs to the king of France and the Neapolitan to the king of Spain. Unrest among the Spanish nobility against Charles of Habsburg, who is regarded as a foreign ruler.
Franz von Sickingen, one of the main representatives of the movement of the German knights, goes to France and offers Francis I the support of the German nobility for his possible candidacy as emperor, since he is the only alternative to the young king of Spain. Popular protests in England against the enclosures, the fencing in of private lands at the expense of sheep herding and of the rural economy. Death of Ladislaus of Bohemia-Hungary. He is succeeded by his son Louis II, who marries Mary of Austria, sister of Charles of Habsburg.

conciliarism. The king of France commits himself, by the imposition of successive tithes on the clergy, to contribute to the crusade against the Turks.

consequences of the policy of enclosures and royal absolutism and contemplates an ideal state that is based on the principles of brotherhood, philanthropy, and the sharing of wealth. German painter and engraver Hans Holbein the Younger (son of Hans the Elder) publishes an illustrated edition of Erasmus' *Praise of Folly*. Death of Hieronymus Bosch.

1517   In March, at Cambrai, an agreement between France, Spain, and the empire confirms the agreement of Noyon. Disturbances among peasants and workers in England, while a royal commission investigates

Leo X asks the council to declare war on the Turks. An exhortation of John Francis Pico that the council pursue the assembly's reform purposes does not keep it from closing on March 6. On July 1 Leo X solemnly

Death of Anthony Trombetta. Francis Silvestri of Ferrara finishes his commentary on the *Summa contra Gentes*. Giles of Viterbo writes his *Libellus de litteris hebraicis*. Gaspar Contarini writes his *De* the enclosures. Popular disturbances in Habsburg lands against the feudal powers and the concentration of capital in the hands of powerful bankers (such as the Fuggers). Turkish conquest of Syria and Egypt, now governed by the Mamelukes. Selim I becomes caliph.

creates thirty-one cardinals, de Vio among them. A provincial council meets in Florence, with Archbishop Giulio de'Medici (the future pope Clement VII) presiding, to reform Church discipline. The bull *Ite vos in vineam* of Leo X confirms the division of the Franciscan Order into two independent orders: the Observants and the Conventuals. Luther launches his attack on the preaching of indulgences: on October 31 he attaches his ninety-five theses to the door of the Cathedral of Wittenberg in which he criticizes the practice of indulgences, vows, pilgrimages, and fasting, works which he considers inadequate to make up for the lack of faith.

officio boni ac probi episcopi. Leonardo da Vinci moves to the court of Francis I: during this period he completes his *St. John the Baptist.* The introduction of a required course in Greek at Corpus Christi College, Oxford, and the requirement of lectures on the Fathers but not on the Scholastic authors elicit a reaction from the traditionalist masters, who in the controversy don the robes of Trojan heroes besieged by the new Greeks. John Reuchlin writes his *De arte cabalistica.*

1518   Peace of London and umpteenth renewal of the agreements of Noyon.

Thomas de Vio is sent to Germany as cardinal legate to organize the crusade against the Turks. The rector of the University of Frankfurt on the Oder, a secular priest named Conrad (Kock) of Wimpen, composes theses opposed to those of Luther. These *Antitheses* are defended and published by Tetzel, who supplements them with fifty of his own that deal directly with the subject of ecclesiastical authority and the papal magisterium, which is clearly identified as the heart of the controversy.

Gaspar Contarini criticizes the teachings of Pomponazzi (whose pupil he had been) on the soul in his *De immortalitate animae,* which Pomponazzi publishes together with his own *Apologia* in response to Contarini and other opponents. Augustine Nifo takes part in the discussion with his *De immortalitate animae libellus contra Petrum Pomponacium.* Dominican Bartholomew of Spina publishes three works in defense of Thomism, maintaining against de Vio and

In April Luther defends himself in the Augustinian chapter of Heidelberg, and then writes a commentary on his theses, the *Resolutiones de virtute indulgentiarum,* which he sends to the Holy See. The pope entrusts the inquiry to Sominican Sylvester Mazzolini, who in a treatise *De potestate papae,* repeats Tetzel's theses, but in a less aggressive manner. In June at the court, Mazzolini begins the ecclesiastical trial of Luther on suspicion of heresy; Luther is summoned to appear in person in Rome within sixty days. At the intervention of Frederick the Wise, prince elector of Saxony, the trial in Rome is replaced by an examination at the imperial diet in Augsburg (October 12–14) by legate Thomas de Vio. Luther refuses to retract and, fearing arrest, flees secretly from Augsburg. A bull on indulgences, written by de Vio, is issued in Rome to explain the authoritative character of magisterial teaching on the subject. In Wittenberg, Luther appeals to a general council. Frederick the Wise refuses to hand Luther over to de Vio, since he has not yet been officially condemned as a heretic.

Pomponazzi the demonstrability by reason of the soul's immortality. Titian paints his *Feast of Venus* and his *Assumption.* Spanish sculptor Bartolomeo Ordonez, who introduces the styles of the Italian Renaissance into Spain, executes his *Monument to Cardinal Ximenes de Cisneros* in the Cathedral of Alcalá de Henares. James Lefèvre publishes *De una ex tribus Maria* and *De Maria Magdalena disceptatio,* thereby giving rise to a debate over the norms for interpreting the sacred text. Josse Clichtove intervenes in Lefèvre's defense with his *Disceptationis de Magdalena defensio.* Thomas More defends the study of the Fathers at Oxford. Zwingli is vicar in Zurich and renews his attack on the use of mercenaries and on the papacy in order to win the emancipation of the Swiss Confederation from outside forces. John Eck, a master at Ingolstadt, writes privately, at the request of the bishop of Eichstätt, some *Adnotationes* on Luther's theses showing their affinity with the teachings of Huss. Luther responds to these observations, which he calls *Obelisci,* in a polemical work entitled *Asterisci.* In Rome, Thomist Sylvester Prierias publishes a

*Dialogus in praesumptu-
osas Martini Lutheri con-
clusiones de potestate
papae,* a severe critique
of Luther's views.
Veit Stoss sculpts his
Annunciation for the
church of St. Lawrence in
Nuremberg.

1519   At the death of Lorenzo
II di Piero, Cardinal
Archbishop Giulio, natu-
ral son of Giuliano I (and
future pope Clement VII),
becomes governor of
Florence on behalf of the
pope. Death of
Maximilian at Wels. With
the financial help of the
Fuggers, Charles of
Habsburg, king of Spain,
succeeds in buying the
goodwill of the electors,
who in any case are sen-
sitive to public opinion,
which looks favorably on
the election of a German
ruler: the electoral diet of
Frankfurt unanimously
makes him king of the
Romans under the name
of Charles V. The new
emperor combines in a
single vast dominion the
crown of Spain and its
overseas colonies,
Franche-Comté, Flanders,
and the hereditary
Habsburg estates.
An expedition led by
Francisco Cortez leaves
Cuba for the conquest of
the Yucatan and Mexico,
and reaches Tenochtitlan,
capital of the Aztec kingdom, which is ruled by
Montezuma II. Ferdinand
Magellan of Portugal sets
sail, in the service of the
Spanish crown, to reach

Thomas de Vio, still in
Germany, is elected arch-
bishop of Palermo and
then, after refusing the
post, bishop of Gaeta.
Karl Miltitz, apostolic
chamberlain and notary,
is sent to Wittenberg to
win the handing over of
Luther to the ecclesiastical tribunal. He succeeds
only in negotiating with
Luther personally in
Altenberg in January and
obtaining a promise of silence, provided the si-
lence is reciprocal. The
tension is eased by the
death of Maximilian,
since Leo X wants
Frederick the Wise as
candidate for the imperial
office and does not want
to endanger relations with
him. In July a debate on
grace and free will,
planned by the Diet of
Ausburg, is held in
Leipzig between John
Eck and Carlstadt
(Andreas Rudolf
Bodenstein), a supporter
of Luther; the latter then
claims he is no longer
bound to silence and de-
bates publicly with Eck
on papal primacy. On this
occasion he denies the
primacy of the pope and
the infallibility of councils, and, for the first

In Bologna Pomponazzi
publishes a *Defensorium*
against Nifo. In the
Bologna edition the text
is followed by two series
of *Solutiones rationum* by
Chrysostom Javelli.
Thomas de Vio comments
on the letter to the
Romans. Death of
Leonardo da Vinci in
France. Raffaello paints
his *Transfiguration*
(1519–20) and Titian his
Pesaro Altarpiece for the
church of the Frari in
Venice.
In Lyons, first edition of
the French translation of
Raymond Sibiuda's *Liber
creaturarum.*
Claudio De Seyssel, arch-
bishop of Turin, dedicates
to Francis I his book *La
Grand'Monarchie de
France,* in which he of-
fers a theory of the reduction of royal absolutism
through consultation with
the representatives of the
Estates General.
Death of English human-
ist William Grocyn, mas-
ter of theology and of
Greek languages and lit-
erature at Oxford. This
fervent Aristotelean and
accurate philologist had
commented on Pseudo-
Dionysius, whose histori-
cal identity he had

the Moluccas (the Spice Islands).

time, states the formal principle of *sola scriptura*. Philip Melanchthon (Schwarzerd), a nephew of Reuchlin, follows Luther's teaching in his explanation of the letter to the Romans at Wittenberg. On August 10 Luther is condemned by the Faculty of Theology of Cologne; on November 7, by that of Louvain.
Christian II of Denmark promotes Protestant propaganda in order to weaken the authority of the clergy and invites a Wittenberg theologian to Copenhagen to preach the Reformation. He then abolishes the privileges of various convents and places them under the jurisdiction of Danish bishops, who are already dependent on the crown.

challenged. Death of John Colet in London. James Hoogstraten publishes a *Destructio Cabale* against Reuchlin, whose condemnation he wins from Rome. Louvain master of theology James Latomus (Jacques Masson) attacks Erasmus for his proposed revision of the biblical text. Erasmus publishes the second edition of his *Novum Instrumentum,* accompanied by an important theoretical justification entitled *Ratio seu compendium verae theologiae*. Hans Holbein the Younger paints his portrait of *Boniface Amerbach*. Tilmann Riemenschneider sculpts the *Tomb of Lawrence of Bibra* in the Cathedral of Würzburg.

1520 Charles V is crowned emperor at Aix-la-Chapelle (revival of the myth of Charlemagne). First results of the introduction of American gold into the European market and of the connected price revolution. Social revolts in Spain: of the brotherhoods *(hermanías)* in Valencia and the Balearic Islands (1519–22) and of the *comuneros* in Castile (1520–21).
At a meeting near Guines (Piccardy) Francis I wins the neutrality of Henry VIII of England in a possible conflict with Charles V.

On June 15, yielding to pressure from de Vio, Eck, and the Roman Dominicans, Leo X condemns Luther in the bull *Exsurge Domine*, threatening him with excommunication if he does not repent within two months. The publication of the bull in Germany is entrusted to legates Eck and Jerome Aleandro. On December 10 Luther burns the bull and the books of the *Corpus Iuris Canonici* in the square of Wittenberg.
Popular resistance in Switzerland to the policy of using mercenaries and to papal interference: the

At Mirandola, John Francis Pico publishes the six books of his *Examen vanitatis doctrinae gentium et veritatis disciplinae christianae*. Peter Pomponazzi writes his *De naturalium effectuum admirandorum causis sive de incantationius* and his *De fato, libero arbitrio et praedestinatione,* in which he opposes Pico's condemnation of astrology. Death of Francis Lichitto, adversary of Augustine Nifo and supporter of the impossibility of rationally demonstrating the immortality of the soul. Death at Barletta of

Sweden rebels against Danish rule but the revolt is put down with bloodshed: Christian II is crowned king of Sweden at Stockholm. Death of Selim I. The new sultan is Suleiman II "the Magnificent" (+ 1566), who conquers Belgrade (1521) and Rhodes, which is taken from the Knights of St. John (1522). After having Montezuma imprisoned and killed, Cortez takes possession of Mexico in the name of the king of Spain and besieges the capital, Tenochtitlan. Magellan crosses the Straits of Vittoria (now of Magellan), north of Tierra del Fuego, that lead to the Pacific Ocean.

Diet of Basel takes steps against the cornering of ecclesiastical offices and benefices by the Roman court.

George Benignus Salviati. Niccolò Machiavelli publishes his dialogues *Dell'arte della guerra* and his *Vita di Castruccio Castracani* and is commissioned by the Medici to write *Istorie fiorentine.* Dominican Ambrose Catarino Polito writes an *Apologia pro veritate catholicae doctrinae adversus Martini Lutheri dogmata.* Michelangelo is in Florence, where Cardinal Giulio de'Medici (the future Clement VII) commissions him to construct the Medici Chapel in San Lorenzo and the adjoining Biblioteca Laurenziana. Publication of the Biblia Poliglotta Complutense, with Hebrew, Greek, and Latin texts, begun with the backing of Francisco Ximenes de Cisneros. Ulrich Hutten accepts the preaching of Luther and publishes *Vadiscus seu Trias Romana,* a fiercely anti-Roman work. Between June and September Luther publishes his *To the Christian Nobility of the German Nation on the Improvement of the Christian State,* his *De captivitate Babylonicae ecclesiae preaeludium,* and *De libertate christiana;* in October he writes, in both Latin and German, *Against the Bull of the Antichrist.* In these writings he proclaims a universal priesthood, exalts the moral responsibility of the individual and the priority of faith over works as a means of salvation, limits the sacraments to baptism and the Eucharist, and urges the German princes to convoke a national reform council.

1521

After obtaining an alliance with Venice and, after lengthy negotiations with the Swiss, Francis I begins hostilities against the Habsburgs, attacking simultaneously but unsuccessfully Luxembourg and Navarre. The imperial troops occupy lower Lorraine. Charles V obtains the backing of the pope (in exchange for the restitution of Ferrara and a promise of Parma and Piacenza) and of England. He then responds to the French hostilities by occupying Lombardy.
Death of Manuel, king of Portugal, who is succeeded by his son John III.
In Sweden Gustave (Eriksson) Vasa leads a rebellion against the Danes and proclaims independence.
The Berber Arabs of North Africa, led by Keireddin (the "Barbarossa" of Christian tradition), establish a state on the coast of Algeria and begin a pirate war against Spanish ports.
Cortez conquers Tenochtitlan and massacres the inhabitants

The bull *Decet Romanum Pontificem* makes formal the excommunication of Luther, who replies with a defense in which he associates himself with the inheritance of Huss, whom he describes as a true interpreter of the Gospel. Aleandro asks Charles V to take strong action against the heretic, who is asked to attend the Diet of Worms with an imperial safe-conduct. There Luther defends himself by appealing to Scripture but is banished by the emperor. Aided by emissaries of Frederick the Wise, he takes refuge in the castle of Wartburg, where he works on his German translation of the Bible.
The Sorbonne in Paris condemns 104 propositions taken from the works of Luther. The infiltration of Lutheranism into France and the remarkable similarities that can be seen in the evangelical movement of Briçonnet, bishop of Meaux, and Lefèvre d'Étaples lead to the convocation of various provincial councils until 1526, which can be

Death of Adrian Castellesi. Francesco Guicciardini writes his *Dialoghi sul reggimento di Firenze* (1521–25). Henry VIII, king of England, writes an *Assertio septem sacramentorum* against Luther (perhaps inspired, if not directly written, by John Fisher), and the pope rewards him with the title "Defender of the Faith." First Carlstadt and then Luther (in his *De votis monasticis*) condemn priestly celibacy and the cloistered life. Carlstadt likewise anticipates Luther in defending Communion under two species, condemning private Masses, and condemning images. Philip Melanchthon espouses Luther's Paulinism in its entirety in his *Loci communes rerum theologicarum.*

without mercy.
Magellan loses his life in
the Philippines.

regarded as forming a
single Gallican council
that condemns the teach-
ings of Luther and pro-
hibits the printing of
unauthorized books on
religious subjects.
Death of Leo X in
December.

1522

Battle of La Bicocca; the
French, defeated by the
allies, abandon all
Lombard territories.
Rebellion of the knights
in Germany in the name
of the Lutheran reform
but with the political purpose of improving their
position within the imperial system and profiting
by the secularization of
ecclesiastical properties.
The movement is led by
Ulrich of Hutten and
Franz von Sickingen,
who after wresting Trier
from the archbishop, is
elected president of the
league of the knights of
the upper and middle
kingdom.
Rhodes falls to the
Ottomans.
Only one of Magellan's
five ships reaches the
Moluccas and returns to
Lisbon laden with spices
after completing the first
circumnavigation of the
world.

Election of Pope Hadrian
VI (Adrian Florent of
Utrecht, who had been
tutor of Charles V and
would be, until 1978, the
last non-Italian pope). At
a first diet-council in
Nuremberg legate Francis
Chieregati, bishop of
Teramo, seeks to imple-
ment the banishment of
Luther as provided in the
condemnation (or edict)
of Worms, and to orga-
nize the defense against
the Turkish peril. For the
first time the proposal is
officially voiced to settle
the situation by means of
a free Christian council to
be held in German terri-
tory. The Holy See does
not favor the plan, fearing
the rebirth of conciliar
and nationalistic ideas. In
Zurich Ulrich Zwingli
joins the Lutheran re-
form. Thomas de Vio is
sent to Hungary,
Bohemia, and Poland to
organize the crusade
against the Turks.

Thomas de Vio completes
his monumental commen-
tary on the *Summa theo-
logica,* on which he had
worked for about twenty
years. In Venice,
Augustinian Silvester
Meucci publishes a col-
lection of Joachimite
prophecies that would in-
fluence Giles of Viterbo.
In Paris William Budé is
director of the Royal
Library.
Death of John Reuchlin
at Stuttgart. During his
stay in the Wartburg
Luther translates the New
Testament from Greek
and then the Old
Testament.

1523

Francis I sends a new
army to Italy after enlist-
ing strong financial sup-
port. In order to have
Habsburg support against
the Turkish threat, Venice
joins the anti-French
coalition, and many other

Death of Hadrian VI in
December. Election of
Clement VII (Giulio
de'Medici, archbishop
and governor of Florence,
1523–34).
Luther approves the radi-
cal changes in worship

Thomas de Vio composes
his *Ientacula*. Giles of
Viterbo dedicates to
Hadrian VI his
*Promemoria de depra-
vato statu romanae eccle-
siae et quomodo
reformari possit et*

independent Italian states, Florence among them, follow its example. After the election of Giulio de'Medici to the papacy, Florence is governed in his name by Cardinal Silvio Passerini of Cortona and Cardinal Hippolytus de'Medici, son of Giuliano II. Sickingen dies defending Trier from siege by the great feudal lords loyal to the empire. His death weakens the movement of the knights, many of whom die in the repression, while the remaining abandon their political aims. Von Hutten leaves Germany and takes refuge in Switzerland near Zurich.

Gustave Vasa is king of Sweden. The revolt against Christian II extends even to Denmark, forcing his abdication in favor of his son, Frederick the Peaceful. Giovanni da Verrazzano, in the service of France, explores the coast of North America and discovers New York Bay and the mouth of the Hudson River.

brought about by Carlstadt and announces the reduction of the sacraments to two, baptism and the Eucharist. The senate of Zurich accepts Zwingli's program of reform that bars all forms of Catholic worship, processions, relics, and images. Meeting in Zurich of Zwingli and Carlstadt, who establish many points of agreement. Württemberg Lutheran John Oecolampadius (Hussgen) preaches at Basel in the presence of Erasmus. Martin Bucer (Butzer) spreads Lutheran teaching in Strasbourg.

debeat. Anthony Pigafetta of Vicenza tells the adventures of Magellan's ships in *Relazione del primo viaggio intorno al mondo*. Titian paints his *Bacchus and Arianna* for Alfonso d'Este. Between 1520 and 1523 painter Antonio Allegri, known as Correggio, paints the *Vision of St. John on Patmos* in the dome of S. Giovanni Evangelista in Parma.

The Meaux group publishes its French translation of the New Testament and continues work on the translation of other biblical texts. Ulrich Zwingli supports the Erasmian and Lutheran principle of *sola scriptura* in his *Una breve introduzione cristiana*.

Hans Holbein the Younger paints his portrait of *Erasmus of Rotterdam*.

1524   Francis I invades Milan, which is devastated by a plague, and besieges Pavia. He then sends an expeditionary force, led by the duke of Albani, to attack Neapolitan territory.

Seville monopolizes Spanish trade with the colonies and becomes the headquarters of the

John Peter Carafa and St. Gaetano of Thiene (+ 1547) found the Order of the Theatines, named from Chieti, ancient Teate, Carafa's diocese. Break between Luther and Carlstadt, because the latter denies the Real Presence. Second diet-council of Nuremberg, with cardinal legate

Josse Clichtove publishes his little book, *Antilutherus,* which is followed in subsequent years by other anti-Protestant polemical works.

Death of English humanist Thomas Linacre. Erasmus publishes his *Inquisitio de fide* and, a

Council for the Indies. The threat of Muslim piracy extends from Algeria to Morocco and harms the commercial interests of the Spanish and the Portuguese.

Lorenzo Campeggi presiding; the princes are urged to struggle energetically against Lutheranism. The diet in turn presents the legate with the demand for a conciliar assembly of the German nation, but Clement VII is still opposed. At a later meeting of ecclesiastical and lay dignitaries called in Ratisbon by Campeggi for the purpose of getting as many as possible of the German princes to accept the edict of Worms, a plan of reform of the Catholic clergy is drawn up and confessional "Separate Leagues" are formed to organize the fight against heresy. The Reformers, led by Bucer, prevail in Strasbourg. Willian Farel, a disciple of Lefèvre, holds a disputation in Basel against the Catholics and subsequently attacks Erasmus; he is then expelled by the Confederation and takes refuge in France.

few months later, his *De libero arbitrio diatribé sive collatio,* in which, alongside points of agreement, his unbridgeable theologico-moral difference from Luther's thought emerge. Zwingli publishes his *Commentarius de vera et false religione,* inspired by Carlstadt's ideas.

1525

Battle of Pavia: the army of Francis I that is besieging the city is badly defeated by Ferrante d'Avalos, Marquis of Pescara. Francis I is imprisoned with his two sons and taken to Madrid. The Italian states now fear the excessive power of the Habsburgs. Louise of Savoy, mother of Francis I and ruling in his place during his imprisonment, enters

William Tyndale leads the rebirth of Lollardism in England, inspired by the preaching of Luther; in Cologne he publishes a New Testament in English. At the request of Cuthbert Tunstall, bishop of London, Thomas More intervenes several times in the following years to stem the spread of Tyndale's teachings. Luther marries Katarina von Bora, a former nun.

Death of Peter Pomponazzi. Francis Silvestri writes his *Apologia de convenientia institutorum Romanae Ecclesiae cum evangelica libertate* against Luther. Francis Zorzi (Francesco Giorgio Veneto) publishes *De harmonia mundi cantica tria.* After the defeat of Francis I the Meaux group loses its royal protection; as a result of negotiations with Venice, the pope, Florence, and Francesco II Sforza (brother of Maximilian, who has been given the duchy of Milan by Charles V), and then makes an alliance with Henry VIII of England in the Treaty of Moore. The Peace of Madrid releases Francis I, but he renounces all claims to Italian territories and to Burgundy and leaves his sons in Habsburg hands. To the two cardinals governing Florence the pope adds Alessandro, duke of Città di Penne and natural son of Lorenzo II. The German feudal lords who have gone over to the Reformation—Philip of Assia and John Frederick the Prudent, elector of Saxony—respond to the steps taken at Ratisbon by joining the Protestant League of Torgau. A sizable revolt of peasants in Germany, due to the grievous economic and social conditions in which the farming class lives, subject to fiscal burdens and demands for service in the form of labor. Lutheran teachings, often misunderstood, feed the revolt, which spreads to Thuringia and Upper Austria. Preacher Thomas Münzer calls for a mystical communism, but the desire for social justice takes the form of looting and violence. Luther disowns and condemns the peasant revolt, urging

censures by the Sorbonne and of growing suspicions of Lutheran sympathies, the group finally disbands on its own. William Farel has his *Summaire et briefve déclaration d'aucuns lieux fort nécessaires à ung chascun chrestien* printed in Basel.

Martin Luther condemns the peasant movement in his *Esortazione alla pace a proposito dei dodici articoli dei contadini della Svevia* and in his little work *Contro le bande dei contadini assassini e saccheggiatori,* maintaining that social equality is a fruit of the future life. Toward the end of the year Luther writes a polemical answer to Erasmus, his *De servo arbitrio,* to which Erasmus replies in turn, the following year, in his *Hyperaspistes.*

Albrecht Dürer produces his etchings *Frederick the Wise* and *Erasmus of Rotterdam.*

princes to wipe out the rebels: the revolt is put down by the League's army, using fearful repressive measures. The Reform is introduced into Prussia: Grand Master Albert of Hohenzollern is converted to Lutheranism, secularizes the Teutonic Order, and transforms the state into a lay duchy.

1526   Charles V marries Isabella, daughter of Manuel, king of Portugal. Francis I of France enters an alliance with the Italian states (the pope, the Medici, Milan, Venice, Siena, and Lucca) and forms the League of Cognac (May 22) for the purpose of freeing Italy from the Spanish yoke. A plot of Girolamo Morone, chancellor of the duchy of Milan, against Charles V is discovered and Morone is imprisoned. Charles himself takes the title of duke, and Milan rebels against Spanish levies. The League's army begins hostilities against Charles, but Francis I delays French participation. In agreement with Charles V, Pompeo Colonna, one of the cardinals hostile to the pope, enters Rome at the head of an army of three thousand peasants gathered from the Roman countryside; they sack and ravage the outskirts of the Vatican as Clement VII takes shelter in Castel

In the convent of Montefalco Matthew of Bascio founds a new Franciscan congregation that restores the rule to its primitive severity; its members, led by Ludovic of Fossombrone, will later be called the Capuchins. Clement VII approves the Order of the Theatines. During his withdrawal in Castel Sant'Angelo, he calls a consistory of cardinals and excommunicates Colonna. The first French Protestant heretic, named Pavonas, is condemned and burned at the stake. Luther composes his "German Mass." Debate between Catholics and Lutherans in Baden. Strasbourg accepts the teachings of Zwingli. Farel spreads the Reform in Alsace.

James Sannazzaro publishes his *De partu Virginis*. Sodoma paints *Incidents from the Life of St. Catherine* in the church of San Domenico in Siena. Between 1526 and 1530 Correggio paints the *Assumption of the Virgin* in the dome of the Cathedral of Parma. Dominican Francis of Vitoria obtains the major chair of theology at the University of Salamanca. While still studying theology in Salamanca, Ignatius of Loyola (Inigo Yañez de Oñaz y Loyola) writes the *Spiritual Exercises*. Foundation of the University of Santiago. German humanist Willibald Pirckheimer publishes a debate with Oecolampadius, *De vera Christi carne et vero eius sanguine*.

Sant'Angelo. The pope
negotiates with the
Spanish viceroy of
Naples, committing him-
self to withdraw from the
League.
The Turks attack
Hungary; in the battle of
Mohacs Suleiman II de-
feats Louis II, king of
Bohemia-Hungary, who
loses his life on the field;
Hungary is partially oc-
cupied. Bohemia returns
to Habsburg rule. The
crown of Hungary goes
to John Szapolay (son of
Stephen, voivode of
Transylvania), who gov-
erns the eastern part of
the country as a vassal of
the Ottomans.

| 1527 | The pope again suspends negotiations with the emperor and tries to attack the territory of Naples. To punish the pope Charles V sends an army of Lutheran lansquenets, led by George of Frundsberg, who cross Italy laying waste to cities and countryside. In Florence a popular movement against Medici rule arises. The allied army covers the city to prevent invasion, but by doing so leaves the Germans an open route to Rome. Sack of Rome; the pope is besieged in Castel Sant'Angelo, then flees to Orvieto (where he remains until 1531), while the horde of German soldiers occupies the city for about a year and spreads out to other residential places in Latium. In | Henry VIII of England, infatuated with young Anne Boleyn, asks the pope for permission to divorce Catherine of Aragon, mother of Princess Mary but not of any male children. At the Diet of Vasteras, Gustave Vasa introduces the Protestant Reform into Sweden in order to expropriate Church lands, despite popular objections. At the Diet of Odense, Frederick I of Denmark, who has for some time allowed Protestant preaching in Schleswig, guarantees religious toleration to the Lutherans. A new provincial council at Leszyca is worried about the spread of the Lutheran heresy in Poland and promotes the | Death of Niccolò Machiavelli. Giulio Romano (Giulio Lippi), pupil and collaborator of Raffaello, works for the Gonzagas in Mantua (until his death in 1546) as architect and decorator of the ducal palace and the Palazzo del Te. In Venice, Jacopo Tatti, known as Sansovino, decorates the Loggetta of the Campanile and restores the Palazzo Corner and the Biblioteca Marciana. Foundation of the first Evangelical university, in Marburg. |

Florence an anti-Medicean oligarchic republic is established.

moral and disciplinary reform of the clergy.

1528   In Rome a cruel plague follows the sack of the city. A French army, led by Lautrec, marches on Neapolitan territory and besieges Naples on land, while the city is also threatened by the Genoese fleet captained by Andrea Doria. In exchange for a promise of Genoese independence, Doria comes to an agreement with the Spanish, and Naples is freed on its maritime side. The spread of the plague among the French troops makes the reconquest of Naples impossible.

Jerome Emiliani founds a new Order of Clerics Regular in Somasco modeled on the Theatines. Ignatius Loyola, barred from teaching in Spain, moves to France, where he gathers his first disciples.
A provincial council meets in Lyons at the behest of Francis I to study ways of rescuing his sons imprisoned in Spain, stemming the spread of the Lutheran heresy, and reforming the morals of the clergy. At almost the same time, another provincial council, meeting in Bourges, takes up the same subjects and forbids the acquisition and retention of Lutheran books. A provincial council meets in Paris, with the theologians of the Sorbonne in attendance, to oppose the spread of errors and formulate a condemnation of the Lutherans.
Thomas Wolsey, archbishop of York, is charged by Henry VIII to take up the divorce case with the pope. But Wolsey prefers instead a postponement of the decision in order to avoid strengthening the anticlerical party in England, led by Anne Boleyn's father.
Victory of the Protestant faction in Bern.
At an imperial diet in

Death of Francis Silvestri of Ferrara. Baldesar Castiglione publishes *Il libro del cortegiano*. Death of James Wimpfeling in Strasbourg. Erasmus publishes his *Ciceronianus,* in which he distances himself from the exaggerated classicism of the humanists.

Ratisbon, Campeggi con-
vokes a national German
council to meet in the following year for the pur-
pose of implementing
the edict of Worms.

1529   A new French army sent
into Italy is defeated at
Landriano near Pavia. In
the Treaty of Barcelona
(June 29), Charles V
comes to a definitive
agreement with the pope
that grants him control of
Naples and promises a
papal coronation of the
emperor in exchange for
help in restoring the
Medici in Florence. With
the League thus dis-
solved, Francis I is forced
into the Peace of Cambrai
(August 8), known as the
Peace of the Two Ladies,
because based on agree-
ments between his
mother, Louise of Savoy,
and Marguerite of
Austria, regent of the
Lowlands and aunt of
Charles V. The king re-
nounces his claim to
Naples, Flanders, and the
Artois but is able to re-
gain Burgundy and win
the freedom of his sons.
Francesco II Sforza re-
turns to Milan.
Berbers led by Kair-eddin
occupy Algiers.
The Turks of Suleiman
the Great, called in by
Szapolay against the
Habsburgs, attack
Hungary and even be-
siege Vienna, which is,
however, liberated after a
few months.

A provincial council con-
voked in London to deal
with the reform of the
clergy condemns high
living and simony and
solemnly confirms the
liberties of the Church.
Charles V again exercises
to the full his influence
on the pope and opposes
the divorce of the king of
England from his
(Charles') aunt Catherine.
The pope reserves the de-
cision to himself and
Henry VIII vents his
anger on Wolsey, who is
accused of high treason
and exiled to the diocese
of York. His place as
privileged adviser to the
king is taken by Thomas
Cromwell. At a diet-
council in Speyer, after
lively discussion, Charles
V succeeds in decreeing
the full validity of the
edict of Worms and a
solemn prohibition
against civil wars among
the German states with
religious reasons as pre-
texts.
Colloquy of Marburg:
Luther, aided by
Melanchthon, debates
with Zwingli,
Oecolampadius, and
Bucer. Their theological
differences, especially regarding the Eucharist,
prove insuperable. In the
following years only
Bucer is reconciled again

Augustine Steuco pub-
lishes his *Recognitio
Veteris Testamenti.*
Francesco Guicciardini
writes his *Ricordi*
(1528–30) and his
*Considerazioni sui
Discorsi di Machiavelli.*
Thomas More is named
Chancellor of the Realm
by Henry VIII.
Following the coming of
the Reformation to Basel,
Erasmus chooses to move
to Freiburg. In his
German catechism Luther
establishes the principles
of the Evangelical divine
service (Communion, ser-
mon, communal singing)
and of the Reformed
liturgy. Melanchthon and
Bugenhagen produce
manuals for parish
priests.
German painter and en-
graver Albrecht Altdorfer
paints the *Battle of
Alexander the Great.*

to Luther's views.
Oecolampadius imposes
the Reformation on
Basel. Luther and his followers make a series of
visits to churches and
schools in Saxony; their
ecclesiastical organiza-
tion becomes a model for
a Lutheran territorial
church.

1530   Congress of Bologna: in
the church of San
Petronio, the pope crowns
Charles V as king of
Lombardy and emperor
of the Romans. Charles
then reorganizes his
Italian domains and sends
the troops of Philibert of
Orange to besiege
Florence, which is de-
fended by Malatesta
Baglioni, and to restore
the Medici. In the coun-
tryside Florentine com-
missioner Francesco
Ferrucci gathers forces
loyal to the republic but
is defeated and loses his
life in the battle of
Gavinana near Pistoia.
Betrayal by the Baglioni
hands the city over to the
enemy: an imperial de-
cree appoints Alessandro
de'Medici lord of
Florence for life with
right of inheritance for
his sons.

In Milan Antonio Maria
Zaccaria founds the
Order of Barnabites at the
church of San Barnaba.
Needing a provisional
systematization of rela-
tions with the Lutherans
while waiting for a gen-
eral council to be con-
voked, Charles V
announces a diet in
Augsburg for April 18
and invites the heads of
the Reformed churches.
Prince elector John of
Saxony invites the spiritual heads of the evangelical movement—Luther,
Melanchthon,
Bugenhagen, and Jonas—
to meet in Torgau to pre-
pare a list of essentials to
be defended on that occa-
sion. The result is the fifteen Articles of Torgau,
on the basis of which
Melanchthon is commis-
sioned to work up the
final document to be pre-
sented to the emperor.
The result is the
Confessio Augustana,
which is presented at the
diet by seven princes and
two imperial cities as a
common expression of
evangelical faith. The
Catholic theologians
reply with a *Confutatio*

Giles of Viterbo begins
his *Schechina.* Augustine
Steuco publishes his *Pro
religione christiana ad-
versus Lutheranos.* James
Sadoleto writes his *De
liberis recte instituendis.*
Gaspar Contarini criti-
cizes the *Confessio
Augustana* in his
*Confutatio articulorum
seu quaestionum luthera-
norum.*
At the suggestion of
William Budé, Francis I
founds the Collège de
France. The *Saincte Bible
en Francoys* is published
in Antwerp; it is the re-
sult of the translation
work done by the schol-
ars of the Meaux group.
Giovanni Battista di
Jacopo, known as Rosso
Fiorentino, settles at the
court of Francis I, where,
together with Francesco
Primaticcio (a student of
Giulio Romano), who
joins him in 1532, he be-
comes the leader of the
school of Fontainebleau,
a center for the spread of
Renaissance Mannerism
in Europe.
Death of Willibald
Pirckheimer in
Nuremberg. Nicholas
Copernicus writes his *De*

pontificia, which in turn elicits a harsh answer from Melanchthon. Charles V orders a strict implementation of the edict of Worms in all of his territories. Wolsey, accused of dealing with the pope, is arrested by Henry VIII for treason and dies at Leicester on his way to London. Clement VII resists granting the divorce to Henry, who invokes a sixteenth-century law, the *Statute of Praeminire,* which said that no foreign power, even the papacy, could exercise jurisdiction in England. English cardinal Reginald Pole, in Paris for study, is obliged to ask the Sorbonne to declare null the king's marriage to Catherine of Aragon, even though he himself is openly opposed.

revolutionibus orbium coelestium, which he would not publish, however, until 1543.

1531   Intense French diplomatic activity to reach agreements with the German Protestant princes and with the pope, one of whose nieces, Catherine de'Medici, marries Henry, duke of Orleans (the future Henry II). Ferdinand of Habsburg, governor, on behalf of his brother, Charles V, of the hereditary Habsburg domains, is elected king of Germany. The Protestant princes react to the decisions of the Diet of Augsburg by forming the Smalkaldic League, with a federal army and joint treasury.

Introduction of the Inquisition into Portugal. Persecution of the Reformed in France, even while for political reasons the sovereign joins the Smalkaldic League. After Zwingli's death his successor, Bullinger, rejects reconciliation with the Lutherans. At a convocation in Canterbury Henry VIII forces the English clergy to recognize him as head of the Church of England.

Gaspar Contarini writes a commentary on the *Homocentrica,* a treatise of astronomy by Jerome Fracastoro. Domenico Beccafumi paints *Christ in Limbo* and the *Nativity of the Virgin.* Foundation of the University of Granada. In Basel, Michael Servetus, Spanish Anabaptist and Antitrinitarian physician, publishes *De Trinitatis erroribus* and then *Dialogi de Trinitate,* which raise serious concerns for Oecolampadius, Zwingli, and Bucer.

In Switzerland, after repeated violations by the Protestant cantons of earlier agreements on coexistence, the Catholics attack and defeat Zurich in the battle of Kappel, in which Zwingli loses his life.

| 1532 | Francis I enters an alliance with the sultan in preparation for a new attack on the Habsburgs. With France mediating, the Swiss Catholic and Protestant cantons reach an agreement that is summed up, for the time, in the formula *Cujus regio eius religio* (the king determines the religion). | John Peter Carafa, who has taken refuge in Venice with some Theatines after the sack of Rome, sends Clement VII a letter on Catholic renewal; it is known as *Memoriale per la Controriforma.* Religious peace of Nuremberg: at a diet-council that brings together bishops, princes, and electors, Charles V imposes the maintenance of peace at any cost between the Protestant and Catholic states; it includes a ban on armed conflicts, the suspension of all trials based on religion, and a prohibition against innovations. On the basis of this treaty the Protestant states join in the war against the Turks. Clement VII does not approve the peace treaty. Pole, who has made public his dissent from the divorce of Henry VIII, leaves the English court. | Death of Giles of Viterbo. Chrysostom Javelli writes his *Quaestiones subtilissimae* on the immortality of the soul, taking a position against Pomponazzi but also against Cajetan. François Rabelais (+ 1553) begins publication of *Gargantua and Pantagruel,* which will be completed with the posthumous appearance of Book V in 1564. |
| 1533 | Death of Frederick I of Denmark. While the deposed Christian II is still alive and fighting to regain his throne, the candidate of the Danish aristocracy, Christian III, son of Frederick, is | John Calvin, an admirer of Erasmus, composes, in a Lutheran manner, the discourse which Nicholas Cop, rector of the University of Paris, has commissioned him to write and which is read in | John Valdés, a Spanish Erasmian, settles in Naples where he creates a center for the spread of reformist ideas that make their way among the intellectuals of the Late Renaissance. Among |

hostile to the clergy because they are suspect of Lutheranism. At the death of Basil III, Ivan IV "the Terrible" (+ 1484), son of Basil's second marriage, becomes czar of Russia; he begins a political and social reform of the state.

the presence of the faculties in the church of the Trinitarians. Henry VIII assembles a court at Dunstable that annuls his marriage to Catherine and makes official his secret marriage to Anne, who is pregnant with Elizabeth. He then forces Parliament to cancel appeals to Rome in all civil and religious cases. Thomas More refuses to adopt the anti-Roman views of the king and resigns as chancellor. John Louis Vives, an Erasmian from Valencia who has been actively spreading humanism at Oxford for almost ten years, is forced to leave England.

those drawn by his preaching: Florentine Augustinian Peter Martyr Vermigli, Bernardine Ochino, Capuchin preacher, poet Mark Anthony Faminio, Peter Carnesecchi, protonotary apostolic, Giulia Gonzaga, and Vittoria Colonna. Benedict of Mantua, a disciple of Valdés, spreads his ideas in a successful book entitled *Beneficio della morte di Cristo*. Scipio Capece writes *De vate maximo*. Death of Ludovic Ariosto in Ferrara, and of John Francis Pico, assassinated in Mirandola by his nephew Galeotto. In Cologne, Agrippa of Nettesheim publishes *De occulta philosophia*.

1534

Death of Clement VII. Election of Paul III (Alessandro Farnese, a Roman, 1534–49). In Montmartre Ignatius Loyola and his followers (Francis Xavier, Pierre Lefèvre, Diego Laínez, and Alphonsus Salmeron of Toledo) take a solemn vow to devote themselves to the salvation of souls by offering their services to the pope. The English Parliament approves the *Act of Supremacy,* in which the king is proclaimed supreme head of the Church of England. The still-rebellious clergy gather in a national council in London and acknowledge the full force only of those

Death of Thomas de Vio. In his last biblical commentary, on Ecclesiastes, he says that no philosopher has been able correctly to prove the immortality of the soul. Chrysostom Javelli writes *De christiana religione,* in which he offers a synthesis of Thomism and Renaissance Platonism. In Rome Michelangelo begins to paint the *Final Judgment* in the Sistine Chapel (it will be finished in 1541). During these years he sculpts the *Pietà* in the Cathedral of Florence. Mannerist painter and engraver Francesco Mazzolo, known as Il Parmigianino, paints the *Madonna with the Long Neck.*

ecclesiastical laws that
are not at odds with the
rights of the crown, but
they demand that from
now on dispensations, fa-
vors, and indulgences be
granted only by the arch-
bishop of Canterbury.
For their resistance to the
actions of the sovereign,
John Fisher, recently ap-
pointed a cardinal, and
Thomas More are con-
demned and executed.
John Calvin breaks with
the Roman Church and
accepts the teachings of
the Swiss Reformers.
Forced to flee from Paris,
he takes refuge in
Strasbourg and then, after
various journeys, in
Basel.
Communities based on
polygamy and sharing of
possessions are founded
by the Anabaptists and
Melchiorites (followers
of Melchior Hoffmann)
in Münster, under the
leadership of Dutchmen
Jan Mathissen and Jan
Bakelzoon (or
Beukelson) and in
Lübeck under the leader-
ship of Jürgen
Wüllenwever.

1535	At the death of Francesco II Sforza Charles V takes possession of the duchy of Milan. To rein in attacks by Barbary pirates he occupies Tunis. Francisco Pizarro subjects the Inca Empire in Peru and founds the city of Lima.	In the bull *Sublimis Deus* Paul III officially approves the establishment of a commission on reform, headed by Piccolomini, who draws up a detailed decree of reform for the clergy of Rome that is published by the pope at a consistory in the next year. Gaspar Contarini and Reginald Pole are named	In Paris Dominican Ambrose Catarino Polito publishes his polemical *Annotationes* on the commentaries of Cajetan. Augustine Steuco publishes his *Cosmopoeia*. James Sadoleto publishes a commentary *In Pauli Epistolam ad Romanos* that elicits a censure from Thomas Badia, Master of the Sacred Palace.

cardinals: another important sign of the success of the Reform party.
In Geneva William Farel establishes a Reformed church, the views of which are adopted by the Great Council.
Violent restoration of episcopal authority in Münster and bloody repression of rebels.

Reginald Pole writes his *Pro ecclesiasticae unitatis defensione* against Henry VIII.
In Basel Calvin publishes his *Institutio religionis christianae*. Erasmus returns to Basel to publish his last great work of moral theology, *Ecclesiastes*.
Agrippa of Nettesheim publishes his *De incertitudine et vanitate scientiarum*. Hans Holbein the Younger paints his portrait of Henry VIII.

1536

The direct annexation of the duchy of Milan by the Spanish crown leads to a third conflict between France and the empire. French troops invade Savoy. Charles V, who is popular among Catholics because of his action in Tunis, is formally supported by the pope and attempts without success to invade Provence and Picardy.
Henry VIII repudiates Anne Boleyn, having her tried and then executed for adultery, and then marries Jane Seymour, who finally gives him a male heir, Edward.
Christian III is accepted as king of Denmark by the aristocracy and clergy, after three years of war.

In the bull *Ad Dominum gregis curam* Paul III, having reached agreement with the emperor, convokes an ecumenical council that is to meet in Mantua in May, 1537.
The consistory appoints a commission, with Contarini as president, that is to establish the dogmatic lines to be followed by the council. Its members include Carafa, Sadoleto, and Pole, among others.
In England Henry VIII orders the suppression of lesser monasteries.
Calvin arrives in Geneva and is appointed by Farel to organize the new church. Peter Caroli, pastor in Lausanne, disputes with both men over the efficacy of prayers for the dead and, following Calvin's reply, is expelled from the city.
On reaching power, Christian III of Denmark declares himself a Lutheran and, with the support of Parliament,

Chrysostom Javelli publishes his *Tractatus de animae humanae indeficientia in quadruplici via scilicet Peripatetica, Academica, Naturali et Christiana,* and, against Luther, his *Quaestio de Dei praedestinatione et reprobatione,* which is accused of Semipelagianism. Francis Zorzi publishes his *In Sacram Scripturam problemata.* Posthumous publication of the Latin translation of Aristotle's *Poetica,* the work of Alessandro de'Pazzi (1530), nephew of Lorenzo the Magnificent and author also of Italian translations of Sophocles and Euripides. Peter Aretino publishes his *Ragionamenti.*
Death of William Briçonnet in Nérac while a guest of Margueruite of Navarre.
Death of Erasmus in Basel shortly after publishing his *De puritate Ecclesiae christianae.*

expropriates the incomes
of the clergy. The
Regulations for the new
Danish Church, drawn up
by Bugenhagen, are ex-
tended to Norway as
well.

1537   While the peace party
gains the upper hand in
France, the Turkish peril
appears again in the
Balkans, and Charles V,
with the pope's support,
accepts the timeliness
of negotiating with
Francis I.

The renewal of conflict
between France and the
empire leads to a post-
ponement of the opening
of the council, as Paul III
decides to move it from
Venetian territory to
Vicenza. The reform
commission presents its
results to the pope in its
*Consilium de emendanda
ecclesia.* The reform
party turns the pope to-
ward the rapid implemen-
tation of practical steps
such as the reform of the
datary and the
Penitenzieria, but grow-
ing disagreement between
Contarini and the more
conservative members of
the commission, among
whom Carafa stands out,
prevents a quick ending
to its work.
Paul III excommunicates
Henry VIII, who then
suppresses the major
English monasteries
(1537–40) and publishes,
in English, a *Litany,* a
Book of Hours, and a
Creed.
The memorandum which
William Farel presents to
the Council of Geneva on
*Government of the
Church of Geneva* for-
malizes the removal of
the city from the rule of
the duke of Savoy. The
text shows the strong in-
fluence of Calvin's

Contarini writes a letter
De praedestinatione to
Lactantius Tolomei that
gives rise to lively de-
bates in curial circles.
Francis Guicciardini
writes his *Storia d'Italia*
(1537–40).
The Portuguese univer-
sity, which had moved
back and forth between
Lisbon and Coimbra,
settles for good in
Coimbra.

ideas on the subordina-
tion of lay society and all
civil authority to the religious society. A few days
later, the council requires
all citizens to take an
oath of fidelity to the
teaching in a *Little
Catechism* drawn up by
Calvin.

1538   Treaty of Nice: France
annexes two-thirds of the
Piedmont region at the
expense of Charles III of
Savoy, while the Spanish
occupy the remainder.
The Turkish threat leads
the emperor to religious
peace with the Protestants
at Nuremberg.
Agreement of Szapolay
with the Habsburgs, guar-
anteeing him the crown
until his death (in 1540),
when it will pass for
good to Ferdinand.
At Previsa, Suleiman II
defeats the imperial fleet
under Andrea Doria.
Turkish control of the
eastern Mediterranean is
now complete.

Papal legates arrive in
Vicenza in May but find
only a few prelates there.
The opening of the coun-
cil is therefore postponed
to April of the next year.
Ignatius Loyola and his
followers move to Rome;
he chooses the name
"Company of Jesus" for
the group.
Reginald Pole works to
promote an uprising in
England, urge Scotland to
war, and plan a league of
Catholic rulers against
Henry VIII, who takes re-
venge by having the car-
dinal's mother and
brothers executed.
Farel and Calvin meet
with representatives of
the urban councils of
Geneva on eucharistic
matters; the two men are
banished. Farel returns to
Neuchâtel; Calvin is
given hospitality by
Bucer in Strasbourg.
In Bohemia, Reformed
theologian Jan Augusta
composes the confession
of the Bohemian
Brethren, which is rati-
fied by Luther; in the following years, despite
persecution by the
Habsburgs, its teaching is
imposed on the Utraquist
Church, which is now
dying out.

James Sadoleto publishes
his *Hortensius seu de
laudibus philosophiae*.
Reginald Pole writes his
Apologia, an indictment
of Henry VIII and of the
Machiavellianism that in-
spired his errors.
Stephen Dolet, classicist
of Lyons, publishes
*Commentarii linguae
latinae*.

| 1539 | | Paul III gives oral approval to the five articles, submitted by Ignatius Loyola to Contarini, that create the Society of Jesus. Henry VIII has the English Parliament approve the *Law of the Six Articles,* by which, at the dogmatic level, the Church of England aligns itself in substance with Catholic views. Calvin's intervention, from Strasbourg, succeeds in checking an attempt by Sadoleto to bring Geneva back to obedience to the Holy See. The Reformed members of the Confederation agree on the formulation of the *Confessio helvetica.* Introduction of the Reform into the duchy of Saxony, the Brandenburg Electorate, and Iceland, and its spread in the territories of the Teutonic Order. | Jerome Seripando is prior general of the Augustinians. Death of Chrysostom Javelli. Francis de Vitoria speaks out on the consequences of colonization in the New World in his *De Indis recenter inventis* and *De Indis posterior seu De iure belli.* In Strasbourg Calvin publishes his commentary on the letter to the Romans. |
| 1540 | Charles V protests the colonial undertakings of France; Francis I answers by asking ironically to see "the testament of our father Adam" that guarantees the Spanish and Portuguese sole right to be masters of the world. | In the bull *Regiminis militantis Ecclesiae* Paul III approves the establishment of the Society of Jesus. The emperor convokes a diet of Catholic rulers in Speyer in May. Instead, the body meets in Hagenau and then, after a postponement until October, in Worms. Contarini, appointed as papal plenipotentiary, is then replaced by John Morone, bishop of Modena. | In his *Epistola de iustificatione,* addressed to Cardinal Ercole Gonzaga, Contarini maintains his own idea of "double justification," but it gives rise to much criticism, since it seems closer to Luther than to orthodoxy. Among these critics is Sadoleto, who writes his *De iustitia nobis inhaerente et de iustitia Christi imputata.* Contarini also publishes *De sacramentis christianae legis et catholicae ecclesiae* for the instruction of the |

After the death of Jane Seymour, third wife of Henry VIII, Thomas Cromwell arranges his marriage to Anne of Cleves, but the new wife does not please the king, who accuses Cromwell of high treason and has him executed in the Tower of London.

In Geneva the Evangelical party again wins a majority in the council, and there is a call from many sides for Calvin's return.

Preacher John Laski defends Calvinism in Poland and Lithuania. Poland is a mixed confessional state, due to the presence of Orthodox and Jews along with Catholics, and this situation favors the inroads of the Protestant confessions.

clergy. Augustine Steuco dedicates his *De perenni philosophia* to Paul III. Death of Francis Zorzi. Death of William Budé.

| 1541 | The Turks of Suleiman II occupy Buda. | The diet is moved to Ratisbon, with joint participation of Catholics and Protestants, to reach an agreement on convoking the council. The Holy See then sends Contarini, whose abilities as mediator it trusts for reaching a reconciliation. Hopes are based principally on an improvement of a work of John Gropper entitled *Book of Ratisbon* by a commission made up of Reformers (Melanchthon, Bucer, and Pistorius) and Catholics (Eck, Gropper, and Julius Pflug). The document is revised by Morone, Badia, and Contarini, but it is | At the death of John Valdés some of his followers, such as Julia Gonzaga, Vermigli, and Ochino, go over to Lutheranism. Reginald Pole, as legate in charge of the Patrimony of Peter, stays in Viterbo where he meets Vittoria Colonna and gathers around him a group of intellectuals who cherish ideals of a reform in union with Rome; the group is called the "Church of Viterbo." Contarini publishes his *Instructio pro praedicatoribus.* Michael Servetus settles in the Delphinate in |

impossible to reach a definitive agreement on sacramental doctrine and especially on the Eucharist. The overly conciliatory attitude of Contarini in doctrinal matters, and especially on the sacraments and justification puzzles conservative Catholics and, on the other hand, is dissatisfactory to the Protestants. The attempt at conciliation fails and Contarini is recalled to Rome.
At the insistence of Farel, Calvin returns to Geneva where a Protestant republic is established through the approval of his *Ecclesiastical Regulations* by the two urban councils.

Vienna and writes his most important work, *Christianismi restitutio,* in which he denies the Trinity and proposes a return to a Neoplatonic pantheistic monism.

1542   James V Stuart of Scotland has married Marie of Lorraine, of the powerful Guise family, and now gives his foreign policy a philofrench direction. But he is defeated by England at Solway Moss. A few months later, James dies, leaving his infant daughter, Mary Stuart, as his heir. The regent, Marie of Guise, strengthens the alliance with France. Henry VIII then makes an alliance with Charles V to oppose the power of France and plans a joint invasion. Francis I activates his alliance with the Ottomans; Suleiman again enters Hungary, while Keir-eddin, together with the French fleet, sacks Spanish

The bull of Paul III, *Initio nostri huius pontificatus* (May), appoints November 1 as the date for the beginning of the council at Trent. Morone, recently made a cardinal, is to preside. But no bishop shows up in Trent on that date.
The bull *Licet ab initio* (July) approves the establishment of the Roman Inquisition, which Carafa had already organized in preceding years.

Gaspar Contarini, papal legate in Bologna, gets into a controversy with the conservatism of Ambrose Catarino Polito and composes his *Formulario di fede,* which is signed by a number of Modenans who are suspected of heresy. As a result of new criticisms of his religious ideas, he defends himself in a *De poenitentia* and, shortly before his death, has a meeting with Bernardino Ochino, who has been summoned to Rome by the Inquisition. A few days later, Ochino flees Italy.
Dominican missionary Bartolomé de Las Casas attacks the Council of the Indies, in the presence of Charles V, for the violent

territories in Italy and takes Nice from Savoy. In exchange, the king of France must cede Toulon as a naval base for the Barbary ships.

actions of the Spanish colonists in the New World, and he writes his *Brevissima relación de la destruyción de las Indias.* Death of English poet Thomas Wyatt, an imitator of Petrarch and active at the court of Henry VIII.

1543

The emperor and the pope meet at Busseto, but although gracious, Charles V will not force the Spanish bishops in his entourage to remain in Trent. The pope again suspends the council. In the bull *Iniunctum nobis* Paul III removes the stipulation in the charter of the Society of Jesus that limits the number of its members to sixty.

Jerome Seripando writes his *De iustificatione.* Jacques Peletier, translator of Horace's *Ars poetica* into verse and an imitator of Petrarch, gives lessons on poetry to young Jacques Ronsard, thus laying the basis for the future Pléïade movement. Death of Nicholas Copernicus.

1544

The renewal of the war between France and Spain leads to the French victory at Ceresole in the Piedmont. The English are engaged in the siege of Boulogne, the Germans in that of Saint-Didier on the Marne. Francis I has time to fortify Paris and reorganize the army; as a result, Charles V realizes that it is time to negotiate peace. The Peace of Crépy in September confirms the earlier accords of Nice: France surrenders Flanders, the Artois, Naples, and Milan, and Spain gives up Burgundy. But meanwhile the English have taken Boulogne, where fighting continues for two more years.

Only after the Peace of Crépy does Charles V feel in a position to second the plan for a council, and he accepts the pope's proposal to hold it in Trent. A bull dated November 30 announces the first session for March 14, 1545.

The Sorbonne censures Cajetan's writings. Foundation of the Evangelical University of Königsberg.

1545   Paul III erects the duchy of Parma and Piacenza, recognizing as its lord Pier Luigi Farnese, duke of Castro, and his natural son.

New delays by Charles V, who again asks for a transfer of the council to Germany, thus delaying the beginning of the work at Trent until December 13. At a diet in Worms the Protestants voice their resolute refusal to take part in the council. Only the bishop of Trent represents the empire. The papal legates emphasize the dogmatic aspect of the council, while the Spaniards, who do not hide their conciliarist views, want it to concentrate on the reform of the clergy. A compromise proposed by Thomas Campeggio, bishop of Feltre, makes it possible to settle the disagreement by establishing two commissions, one for each type of problem.

Titian paints his portraits of Paul III and the pope's nephews, Alessandro and Ottavio Farnese.
In his *Défense et illustration de la langue française,* Jacques du Bellay, leader of the Pléïade, claims the right to establish a national French literature.

1546   After vain efforts to carry the war onto English soil, Francis I accepts the Peace of Arras with England, committing himself to pay a very high sum within eight years to have Boulogne back.
The separatism of the Reformed princes, who, after withdrawing from the council, also desert a regular imperial diet in Ratisbon, leads to the Smalkaldic War between the Protestants and Charles V. The first imperial victory at Ingolstadt is followed by the passage of some important

The work of the commission for dogma begins on April 8 with an analysis of the *Confessio augustana* and an organized set of opposed orthodox theses. Despite the reservations of the Erasmians, the decree *De canonicis Scripturis* asserts the authenticity of the entire Bible and the authority of the Vulgate. The debate on the doctrine of justification, which is led by the Jesuits toward the Thomist position (no salvation without good works) is dissatisfying to the Catholic reformers, among them Seripando,

Death of Augustine Nifo. Scipio Capece finishes his *De principiis rerum.* Jerome Seripando writes his *Pro confirmanda sententia de duplici iustitia catholicorum quorundam doctrina* and his *De peccato originali.*
Death of Francis de Vitoria at Salamanca. French architect Pierre Lescot builds the facade overlooking the Cour Carrée of the Louvre. Luther dies during the night of February 17–18.

members of the Protestant party to the Catholic camp, among them Maurice of Saxony, who is driven by dynastic ambitions.
In Lucca, an anti-Spanish uprising led by Francesco Burlamacchi leads to the establishment of a republican state; but Burlamacchi, who is opposed by the Milanese government, is betrayed, arrested, and executed.

Morone, and Pole. The last-named, alleging reasons of health, leaves the council and withdraws near Padua as a guest of Alvise Priuli. In Venice, trial of Peter Paul Vergerio the Younger for heresy; he is acquitted, but following on new inquiries into his activity as a Reformer, he decides to leave Italy; continuing his own work in German Switzerland and Germany, he is definitively converted to Lutheranism.

| 1547 | Anti-Spanish rebellion in Genoa; Gian Luigi Fieschi plots against the dictatorship of Andrea Doria but dies during an attempt to board Spanish ships. In Parma, a proimperial plot gets rid of Pier Luigi Farnese with the support of Ferrante Gonzaga, governor of Milan, who wants to take over the duchy. The attempt is blocked by Farnese's sons, Cardinal Alessandro and the new duke, Ottavio. Death of Francis I of France. His son, Henry II, does not hide his own intentions of not accepting his father's surrender of Flanders and the duchy of Milan. Death of Henry VIII of England. His heir, Edward VI, is aged nine. The second important imperial victory over the Lutheran princes at Mühlberg forestalls the danger of an alliance be- | The council issues its decrees on justification (January 3) and the sacraments (March 3). The pope uses the spread of an epidemic as an occasion (he distrusts Charles V's conciliatory attitude after Mühlberg) to move the council to Bologna, where its eighth session is held. Charles V strongly protests and forbids any move of the Spanish delegates, demanding a return to Trent. Charles convokes a new diet in Augsburg, where he issues laws of toleration and allows the Protestants to have Communion under both species and married priests. The diet declares the work of the council in Bologna to be illegitimate. In Rome, Spanish heretic Juan del Enzina is burned at the stake. In Venice, ecclesiastical courts obtain the right to | Death of James Sadoleto. Death in Rome of Peter Bembo, author of *Ascolani,* three dialogues on love, inspired by Plato and Ficino. Bartolomé de Las Casas continues his attack on the immoral behavior of the colonists and begins his *Historia de las Indias.* Juan de Sepúlveda, author of a chronicle of the deeds of Charles V, responds in his dialogue *Democrates secundus seu de justis causis belli,* in which he argues the legitimacy of the conquest of the New World on the basis of Aristotelean anthropology. Marguerite of Angoulême, queen of Navarre (sister of Francis I), who favors the rebirth of classicism and supports reformist ideals in France, publishes (at Lyons) a complete collection of her poetry *Les Marguerites de la* |

tween German and Bohemian Protestants. Almost all the enemies are broken; only the city of Magdeburg resists. The emperor, convinced that the religious problem must be solved by force, begins a campaign of pacification, still with the intention of getting the Protestants to the council. After a period of minority and subjection to the Boyars, Ivan IV the Terrible is crowned by Metropolitan Macarius.

use torture and to pronounce death sentences without authorization from the republic.

Marguerite des princesses. During these same years she composes the stories that will make up the *Hèptameron.*

1548   The government of Paris succeeds in having little Mary Stuart brought to France in order to betroth her to the dauphin (the future Francis II) and prevent a possible marriage to Edward VI. The result is a new conflict between France and England. Death of Sigismund I of Poland, who is succeeded by his son Sigismund II Augustus, the last national Polish monarch.

Paul III orders the temporary suspension of the council's work (February 15).
In Augsburg Charles V commissions German Catholics Julius Pflug and Michael Helding and dissident John Agricola to draw up an agreement between Protestants and Catholics that, in light of delays in the council, will lead to internal peace in Germany. The result is the *Interim* of Augsburg (May 15), which is accepted by Charles V at the diet but disapproved by Catholics and regarded as inadequate by Protestants, to whom it grants only Communion in both kinds and a married clergy. The *Interim* is opposed in almost all of southern Germany, and Magdeburg issues a direct refusal, thereby incurring an imperial ban.

Death of Augustine Steuco. Foundation of the University of Messina. Titian paints his portrait of Charles V on horseback.

Maurice of Saxony, re-
cently rewarded with an
appointment as elector
and seeking agreement
with the emperor, favors
the drawing up of a sec-
ond *Interim,* to be valid
only for Saxony, com-
posed by Melanchthon
and the bishops of
Saxony at Pegau and ap-
proved by a regional diet
at Leipzig. But this sec-
ond document also elicits
energetic reactions from
the more radical of the
Reformed.

1549

On September 17 Paul III
suspends, *sine die,* the
discussions in Bologna.
Then, in the bull *Licet
debitum* he confirms the
organization and privi-
leges of the Society of
Jesus (October) and dies
on November 10.
Protestant influences are
allowed into England
under Edward VIII and
advanced by Thomas
Cranmer, archbishop of
Canterbury and primate
of England, and by the
active presence of many
European Reformers at
the court and in the uni-
versities, among them
Vermigli, Ochino, and
Bucer, who have fled
German territory because
they had rejected the
Interim.
The Lutheran liturgy is
introduced in a *Prayer
Book* imposed by an *Act
of Uniformity.*
The *Consensus Tigurinus*
marks the formal union

In Magdeburg, Lutheran
humanist Mathias Vlacich
(Flavius Illyricus) pub-
lishes his *Catalogus
testium veritatis,* a celebration of the opponents
of the Catholic Church
down through history.

of the Reformed
Christians of Zurich with
the Genevan church of
Calvin.

| 1550 | The war between France and England ends with a mutual agreement that reduces by half the price paid for the return of Boulogne. Meanwhile Henry II enters into negotiations with the Smalkaldic League and renews hostilities with Spain. | Election in February of Julius III (Giovanni Maria de'Ciocchi dal Monte, from Monte San Savino, 1550–55). The new pope, more compliant than Paul III, yields to pressure from Charles V and reconvokes the Council of Trent for November 14. | Michelangelo sculpts his *Pietà Rondanini* (1550–55) and works on the planning of important architectural projects in Rome, among them the Piazza del Campidoglio, the Farnese Palace, and St. Peter's. Titian paints his *Martyrdom of St. Lawrence* (1550–55). Giovanni Pierluigi da Palestrina takes charge of music in San Pietro in Vaticano. Giorgio Vasari prints his *Vite dei piu eccelenti architetti, pittori e scultori italiani da Cimabue insino ai tempi nostri.* Lukas Cranach the Elder paints a self-portrait. |
| 1551 | | The council's real activity begins again on March 1, with parallel work on dogmatic definition and disciplinary reform. Once again the intransigents prevail, due mainly to the support of the Spanish prelates and the Jesuits. On October 11 a dogmatic definition on the Eucharist is adopted affirming the Real Presence, transubstantiation, and adoration of the host. At the request of Charles V the council sends German theologians a safe-conduct for coming to Trent. The king of France, intending to break the Peace of Crépy, calls a | Giovanni della Casa writes his *Galateo.* Pierre de la Ramée publishes his *Animadversiones aristotelicae.* In Basel, Flemish physician Andreas Vesalius publishes his *De humani corporis fabrica.* |

French national council
that rejects the Council of
Trent; he breaks diplo-
matic relations with the
Holy See. France is
thrown into turmoil for
some months by the re-
formist and schismatic attitudes of the sovereign.
In England, given the re-
strictions on religious
freedom, the Royal
Council conducts an in-
quiry into Princess Mary,
daughter of Henry VIII
and Catherine of Aragon,
who has become the
champion of the
Catholics. After being
compelled no longer to
celebrate the Catholic
rite, she secretly begins to
do so again a few months
later.
Commissioned by a
Polish council at
Piotrkow to reform the
morals of the clergy (as a
way of hindering the
spread of Lutheranism),
Hosjuzs, bishop of
Warmia, draws up a
*Confessio fidei chris-
tianae* that is clearly
marked by a reforming
spirit and expounds, sim-
ply and clearly, the fun-
damental truth of the
faith in response to
heresy; in the following
years it becomes a mani-
festo of Catholic faith for
the entire Polish church.

| 1552 | Agreement of Chambord between Henry II and the Protestant princes, now led once again by Maurice of Saxony, who, in a new about-face, has abandoned the Catholic | In January, delegates from Württemberg and Saxony arrive in Trent. From the outset the im- possibility of any align- ment becomes clear. In addition, the agreements | Foundation of the Gregorian University in Rome, to be run by the Jesuits. Death of Protestant theo- logian Andrew Osiander; he wrote the preface for |

cause and abrogated the *Interim* for Saxony. France occupies Toul, Metz, and Verdun and will keep them in the years to come, but not Strasbourg, which is defended by imperial troops and resists. The new conflict, which involves the empire on two fronts, with the Protestants and the French, is soon broken off by agreements reached at the Diet of Passau between Charles V and the League: the emperor recognizes the status quo in Germany, guarantees the Protestants freedom of worship and abrogation of the *Interim,* and promises to convoke a national council in order to settle the religious question.

of Passau have disowned the council. The new crisis forces Julius to suspend the council once again for two years (April 26).
The improvement in relations between France and the Holy See causes Henry II's schismatic thoughts to disappear.
The English Parliament approves a second *Act of Uniformity* and the imposition of a second and more inflexible *Prayer Book.*
The first provincial Council of Peru is held in Lima for the purpose of establishing a firm ecclesiastical discipline and especially of spreading the faith among the Indians and improving their morals.

Copernicus' *De revolutionibus,* which presented the theories as simple hypotheses, and in his *De justificatione,* he criticized the Lutheran doctrine of *sola fide* as a cause of moral indifferentism.

| 1553 | The war between France and Spain continues in a disordered and listless fashion in Italy and Germany. Death of Edward VI of England after having appointed to the throne Lady Jane Grey, daughter of his adviser, the duke of Suffolk. After Jane has ruled for 13 days, the Catholic reaction leads to Mary "the Catholic" being acclaimed queen, to the anger of the people. Death of Maurice of Saxony during a brief battle with the Marquis of Brandenburg. | Edward VI approves a combined Lutheran-Calvinist confession of forty-two articles: the English church remains a state church (of a Lutheran kind), but in doctrine and liturgy it conforms to the church of Geneva. But the death of Edward and succession of Mary introduces a radical change, with the liberation of the persecuted Catholic bishops and subsequent repression of the Reformed element. | Jacques Ronsard publishes his *Amours,* a collection of lyrics inspired by Petrarch. In Vienna, Michael Servetus publishes his *Christianismi restitutio.* The work is denounced by Calvin, through an intermediary, to the Inquisition in Vienne, but Servetus manages to escape from prison. But when he incautiously enters Genevan territory, he is arrested and accused by Calvin before the Grand Council, and then executed on the pyre on October 2. A month later, Calvin writes his *Defense of the Orthodox Faith against the Errors of Michael Servetus,* in |

which he claims for his church the right to inflict corporal punishment on heretics.
In Transylvania, Italian heretic Francesco Stancaro spreads his theories on the one divine person and the role of Christ, thus beginning the spread of Unitarianism. Death of Hans Holbein the Younger and of Lukas Cranach.

1554   Charles V abdicates as king of Naples and duke of Milan in favor of his son Philip. A few months later Philip marries Mary the Catholic.

Reginald Pole returns to England as papal legate and becomes Mary's confidential adviser. He convinces the pope not to call for the restitution of the clergy's possessions and in return obtains from Parliament the abrogation of all the anti-Roman laws passed since the time of Henry VIII.

Death of Simon Porzio (Porta) in Naples, after completing his *De rerum principiis* and the *Disputatio de humana mente,* the last document in the Renaissance debates on the immortality of the soul. Pieriluigi da Palestrina publishes his *Primo libro di Messe* and, the next year, the *Primo libro di Madrigali.* In a dispute with Calvin, Italian Reformer Celius Secundus Curione publishes *De amplitudine regni Dei,* in which he maintains that the number of the elect will be greater than the number of the damned. In Basel, Castellione publishes *De haereticis an sint persequendi.* Calvinist Theodore Beza replies with *De haereticis a civili magistratu puniendis.*

1555   Definitive end of the struggle between Charles V and the Protestant princes with the Peace of the Diet of Augsburg (August-September), which recognizes the

Death of Julius III. Election of Marcellus II (Marcello Cervini or Corvini from Montepulciano, who had been a promotor of the council), but he dies impossibility of overcoming the religious divisions and promotes the end of conflict by taking steps similar to those that proved beneficial in Switzerland: the peace holds only for the Catholic and Lutheran confessions (the latter based on the *Confessio augustana* of 1530); subjects must follow the confession of their princes or are granted the right to leave the territory *(cuius regio eius religio),* while only the imperial cities may exercise religious tolerance; the expropriation of ecclesiastical estates is convalidated until 1552 (year of the Treaty of Passau, defined as the "normative year"). From that date on, the principle of the *reservatum ecclesiasticum* holds, by which a Catholic prince of the Church who goes over to Protestantism must resign from any office and renounce his domains.

In favor, again, of his son Philip, Charles V gives up the government of Flanders and the Low Countries (October).

twenty days after his election. In May, election of Paul IV (Gian Pietro Carafa of Naples, 1555–59), who had for a long time been engaged in the struggle against heresy and the moral improvement of ecclesiastical life. In one of the first acts of his pontificate, he takes very strong measures against heretics in his bull *Cum quorundam hominum.* He then sends Luigi Lippomano, bishop of Verona, as apostolic legate to Poland with the commission to protect the faith against inroads of Protestant heresy. Cardinal-legate Reginald Pole is consecrated archbishop of Canterbury and convokes an interprovincial council at Westminster, in which questions of Church discipline (e.g., the first establishment of seminaries) are discussed and it is decided to translate the New Testament into English. In a few months' time, the return of the Catholics to power unleashes a reaction against Protestants, the violence of which Pole had not foreseen: the old laws against heresy are again in force, and many death sentences are passed that alienate the populace from the new regime. Many English Protestants flee to Scotland, among them Calvinist preacher John Knox.

1556	Truce of Vaucelles between the empire and France, which keeps the Piedmont, Toul, Metz, and Verdun. Charles V cedes the title of emperor to his brother Ferdinand and Milan, Naples, and Spain to his son Philip, and retires to the monastery of San Geronimo de Yuste in Estremadura.	Knox is exiled by Mary of Guise and returns to Geneva. Lippomano convokes a national Polish council at Lovietz, which approves a formula of faith inspired by a similar one already promulgated by the University of Louvain: a simple summary of the faith, easily circulated and maintained among the Polish people.	Foundation of the University of Sassari. Architect Andrea di Pietro della Gondola, known as Palladius, publishes his *Commento ai dieci libri dell'architettura* of Vitruvius, in which he sets forth his ideas on architectural classicism. Peter Paul Vergerio the Younger writes the *Confessio Württembergica*.
1557		Cardinal Morone, a partisan of the emperor, is accused by Paul IV of leanings to heresy because he favors justification by faith alone, and he is imprisoned in Castel Sant'Angelo. In France an edict published in Compiègne establishes the death penalty for heresy, but this does not stem the spread of Calvinism or the organization of churches on the Genevan model. Political considerations offer Paul IV an occasion for questioning Pole on his ideas on justification; Pole is removed as legate and called to Rome for trial. He justifies himself in an *Apologia,* but the trial is continued in his absence. Some Scotch Protestant nobles demand freedom of worship from Mary of Guise; they adopt the *Prayer Book* and ask John Knox to return.	

1558   A Diet of Augsburg for-
malizes Charles V's re-
nunciation of the imperial
title and acknowledges
Ferdinand I as emperor.
Two weeks later, Charles
V dies in retirement
(September 21).
Death of Portuguese king
John III, who is suc-
ceeded by his grandson,
Sebastian of Aviz, under
the regency of his grand-
mother Catherine.
Death in England of
Mary the Catholic, who
is succeeded by Elizabeth
I, daughter of Anne
Boleyn and supporter of
the Protestant party.
Philip II agrees with this
succession to avoid hav-
ing Mary Stuart, wife of
the dauphin of France,
become queen of
England.

Beginning of a harsh per-
secution of heretics in
Spain, with public con-
demnations to the pyre
("autodafé").
Two successive provin-
cial councils are held in
Edinburgh to prevent the
spread of heresy and
check acts of violent re-
bellion by Calvinists in
Scotland.

Italian Reformer James
Aconcio publishes his *De
methodo* in Basel.
Death of Reginald Pole.
Foundation of the
Evangelical University of
Jena.

1559   The Peace of Cateau-
Cambrésis ends the wars
between France and
Spain. France gives back
to Savoy the territories it
had occupied, among
them the marquisate of
Saluzzo, while Spain has
control in Italy.
Death of Henry II of
France in a tourney. His
heir, his first-born son
Francis II, is controlled
by the Guises, the rela-
tives of Mary Stuart.

Paul IV publishes the
*Index librorum prohibito-
rum.*
Death of Paul IV.
Election of Pius IV
(Giovanni Angelo
Medici), who begins the
reform of his Curia with
help of his nephew,
Cardinal Charles
Borromeo. Liberation and
rehabilitation of Cardinal
Morone.
First synod of French
Protestantism in Paris,
with Pastor Morel presid-
ing.
Elizabeth of England ap-
proves a bill that restores
supremacy to the Church;
then the Chambers vote
the *Act of Supremacy,*
which makes the queen
"supreme ruler" of the

Architect Jacopo Barozzi,
known as Vignola, builds
the Farnese Palace in
Caprarola.
Death of English theolo-
gian and humanist
Cuthbert Tunstall, author
of a *De veritate corporis
and sanguinis Domini
Nostri Jesu Christi in
Eucarestia;* he was persecuted during the reign of
Edward VI, rehabilitated
by Mary, and finally fell
into disgrace under
Elizabeth.
Flacius Illyricus begins
publication of a history of
the Church from a
Protestant standpoint; it is
known as the *Centuries
of Magdeburg.*

Church, and a new *Act of
Uniformity,* by which the
Prayer Book of 1552 is
again imposed.

| 1560 | Death of Francis II of France. He is succeeded by his ten-year-old brother, Charles IV, with the boy's mother, Catherine de'Medici, as regent. | Jerome Seripando meets with Pius IV to ask for a reopening of the council. The death of Mary of Guise leaves Scotland in the hands of the Calvinist preachers: the situation calls for the quick return of Mary Stuart, widow of Francis II of France. | Bernardo Tasso, father of Torquato, publishes *Rime* and *Amadigi,* a poem of chivalry. Death of Melanchthon. |

Abbreviations

AFP	*Archivum Fratrum Praedicatorum*
AHDLMA	*Archives d'histoire doctrinale et littéraire du Moyen Age*
AHF	*Archivum Historicum Franciscanum*
AnthAn	*Anthologica Annua*
ArchFil	*Archivio di filosofia*
ArchGeschPhil	*Archivum dür die Geschichte der Philosophie*
ArchHistPont	*Archivum Historiae Pontificiae*
ArchKult	*Archiv für Kulturgeschichte*
ArchRefGesch	*Archiv für Reformationsgeschichte*
ArchLitKirchMA	*Archiv für Literatur- und Kirchengeschichte des Mittelalters*
ArxTextCatAnt	*Arxiu de textos catalans antics*
BGPM	Beiträge zur Geschichte der Philosophie des Mittelalters
BGPTM	Beiträge zur Geschichte der Philosophie und Theologie des Mittelalters
BibHumRen	*Bibliothèque d'humanisme et renaissance*
BibSanct	*Bibliotheca Sanctorum*
BLE	*Bulletin de littérature ecclésiastique*
BIstStorArchMur	*Bullettino dell'Istituto Storico Italiano per il Medio Evo e Archivio Muratoriano*
DBI	*Dizionario Biografico degli Italiani*
DHGE	*Dictionnaire d'histoire et de géographie ecclésiastique*
DSp	*Dictionnaire de spiritualité*
DTC	*Dictionnaire de théologie catholique*
EstEcl	*Estudios Eclesiásticos*
FZTP	*Freiburger Zeitschrift für Philosophie und Theologie*

GCFI	*Giornale critico della filosofia italiana*
GCLI	*Giornale critico della letteratura italiana*
GSFI	*Giornale storico della filosofia italiana*
GSLI	*Giornale storico della letteratura italiana*
JHistPhil	*Journal of the History of Philosophy*
JWarCourt	*Journal of the Warburg and Courtauld Institutes*
MemDom	*Memorie domenicane*
MFCG	*Mitteilungen und Forschungsbeiträge der Cusanus-Gesellschaft*
OCP	*Orientalia Christiana Periodica*
RCSF	*Rivista critica della storia di filosofia*
RevEspDerCan	*Revista Española de Derecho Canónico*
RevFilNeo	*Revista di filosofia neoscolastica*
RHE	*Revue d'histoire ecclésiastique*
RHPR	*Revue d'histoire et de philosophie religieuse*
RSCI	*Rivista di Storia della Chiesa in Italia*
RSLR	*Revista di storia e letterature religiosa*
RömQ	*Römische Quartalschrift*
RTAM	*Revue de théologie ancienne et médiévale*
TheolJb	*Theologisches Jahrbuch*
TijdFil	*Tijdschrift voor Filosofie*
TRE	*Theologische Realenzyklopädie*
UmanRin	*Umanesimo e Rinascimento*

Notes

Introduction

1. See M. Winner, "Disputa und Schule von Athen," *Raffaello a Roma. Il convegno del 1983* (Rome, 1986) 29–45; H. Pfeiffer, *Zur Ikonographie von Raffaels Disputa: Egidio da Viterbo und die christlich-platonische Konzeption der Stanza della Segnatura* (Rome, 1975).

2. For a comprehensive introduction to the problems of Renaissance theological thought, a review of the most important historiographical positions, and an up-to-date bibliography, see L. W. Spitz, "Humanismus/Humanismusforschung," *TRE* 15 (Berlin–New York, 1986) 639–61, as well as the following contributions to *Renaissance Humanism: Foundations, Forms, and Legacy,* ed. A. Rabil, Jr. (Philadelphia, 1988), III. *Humanism and the Disciplines*: Ch. Trinkaus, "Italian Humanism and Scholastic Theology" (327–48); J. F. D'Amico, "Humanism and Pre-Reformation Theology" (350–79); L. W. Spitz, "Humanism and the Protestant Reformation" (380–411).

3. Francis Petrarch, *Epistolae variae* 3, in Francesci Petrarcae *Epistolae de rebus familiaribus et variae,* ed. G. Fracassetti, 3 (Florence, 1863) 311–14.

4. On these themes see J. Pelikan, *The Christian Tradition. A History of the Development of Doctrine* 4. *Reformation of Church and Dogma (1300–1700)* (Chicago-London, 1984), especially chapters 1 ("Doctrinal Pluralism in the Later Middle Ages," 10–68) and 2 ("One, Holy, Catholic, and Apostolic?" 69–126).

5. See E. De Negri, *La teologia di Lutero. Rivelazione e dialettica* (Florence, 1967), especially 59–76.

6. This is the classical judgment, which takes account chiefly of the polemical arguments of the early humanists who dissociated themselves from the Scholastic tradition; it was shared by the Petrarch of *De sui ipsius et multorum ignorantia* and the Bruni of *Libellus de disputationum usu* and has been formulated by M.-J. Congar in his exposition of Renaissance theology in his article "Théologie," *DTC* 15 (Paris, 1946) cols. 407–10; ET: *A History of Theology,* trans. and ed. H. Guthrie (Garden City, N.Y., 1968) 144–47.

7. See Congar, ibid., cols. 411–14 (ET: 147–50).

8. On the subject see A. Humbert, *Les origines de la théologie moderne* I. *La renaissance de l'antiquité chrétienne (1450–1521)* (Paris, 1911). Also, and more recently: Ch. L. Stinger, *Humanism and the Church Fathers: Ambrogio Traversari and Christian Antiquity* (Albany, 1977); E. F. Rice, Jr., "The Renaissance Idea of Christian Antiquity: Humanist

597

Patristic Scholarship," *Renaissance Humanism* (note 2, above), I. *Humanism in Italy,* 17–28.

9. See G. d'Onofrio, "Il pensiero 'convertito': il giovane Agostino," *ArchFil* 49/1–3 (1991) 323–37.

10. See A. Funkenstein, "Scholasticism and Secular Theology," in *Scepticism from the Renaissance to the Enlightenment* (Proceedings of a conference held at the Herzog-August-Bibliothek, February 22–23, 1984), ed. R. H. Popkin and Ch. B. Schmitt (Wolfenbüttler Forschungen 35; Wiesbaden, 1987) 45–54; E. Garin, *Il ritorno del filosofi antichi* (Lezioni della Scuola di Studi Superiori in Napoli 1; Naples, 1983) 101–2.

11. See J. Copin, *Montaigne traducteur de Raymond Sebon* (Mémoires et travaux des Facultés catholiques de Lille 3; Lille, 1925), especially 28–30. See below, chapter 5, section III/10.

12. Thomas More, *The confutyacyon of Tyndales answere* III (London, 1532), p. D₁, in *The Complete Works of St. Thomas More* VIII/1, ed. A. Schuster and others. (New Haven–London, 1973) 248. It is worth noting that Ps 67:7 (in the Vulgate: "qui inhabitare facit *unius moris* in domo") is here cited as "qui facit *unanimes* in domo," with an explicit reference to the *unanimitas* invoked by the theologians of the High Middle Ages. On Thomas More and the patristic sources see R. C. Marius, "Thomas More and the Early Church Fathers," *Traditio* 24 (1968) 379–407.

13. In *De revolutionibus orbium coelestium libri sex* (Warsaw, 1854) 1–2: "Ad lectorem de hypothesibus hujus operis." The Nuremberg edition of 1543 (reprinted: New York, 1965) was edited by George Joachim Retico, John Schöner, and Osiander himself.

14. See H. Baron, *The Crisis of the Early Italian Renaissance: Civic Humanism and Republican Liberty in an Age of Classicism and Tyranny* (Princeton, 1955; rev. ed. 1966) 295–300. Also, more recently, L. Panizza, "Italian Humanists and Boethius: Was Philosophy for or Against Poetry?" *New Perspectives on Renaissance Thought: Essays in the History of Science, Education, and Philosophy in Memory of Ch. B. Schmitt,* ed. J. Henry and S. Hutton (London, 1990) 48–67.

15. See F. Purnell, "The Theme of Philosophic Concord and the Sources of Ficino's Platonism," in *Marsilio Ficino e il ritorno di Platone, Studi e documenti,* ed. G. C. Garfagnini (2 vols.; Istituto Nazionale di Studi sul Rinascimento, Studi e Testi 15; Florence, 1986) II, 397–415.

16. As Augustine suggested in his *Contra Academicos* 3, 17, 37–19, 41 (PL 32:954–56), this was the chief reason that led the late Platonists of the New Academy to the moderately skeptical position, which, while not denying the existence of truth, refused to accept that human beings are able to reach it by their own powers. The question of the link between the probabilistic speculation of the New Academy and the original Platonic tradition comes up on several occasions in the philosophico-theological writings of the Renaissance; one example that may represent all is Sadoleto, who attributes to the philosophy of the Academy, both the ancient Platonic Academy and the new, probabilistic Academy the doctrine that "nothing can be perceived with certainty, nor should assent be given to anything at all," a principle that found its best application in theological discourse. See James Sadoleto, *De laudibus philosophiae* I (Lyons, 1538) 50–51 (g^v-g^{2r]}): "For what I have set down, namely, that the hidden causes of things and the knowledge of things heavenly cannot be perceived, he not only undertook to defend but even expanded, and indeed somewhat further than I like."

17. John Gerson, *De consolatione theologiae,* in *Oeuvres Complètes* IX. *L'oeuvre doctrinale,* introd., text, and notes by Msgr. Glorieux (Paris, 1973), no. 449, pp. 184–245. The

suggestion that the *De consolatione theologiae* should be regarded as symbolic of the end of medieval speculation comes from E. Gilson, *History of Christian Philosophy in the Middle Ages* (New York, 1955) 533.

18. See Gerson, *De consolatione theologiae* I, pr. 2 (pp. 188–89), especially 189: "If either the philosophers or the poets attempted to do this, they became empty-minded and, disagreeing among themselves, could hardly come up with anything except incredible errors."

19. Ibid., II, pr. 3 (p. 209).

20. See ibid. (p. 210): this is an idea which Gerson formulates in express opposition to the Avicennian doctrine attributing to prophets the possibility of communicating truths that are the object of intuition without necessarily having to accept the mediation of rationality.

21. Ibid., pr. 4 (p. 211).

22. See E. Cassirer, *Individuum und Kosmos in der Philosophie der Renaissance* (Leipzig, 1927). For a comprehensive explanation of Cusa's theological speculation see below, chapter 3. On the change of speculative parameters in the Renaissance by comparison with the Middle Ages see also H. B. Gerl, "Abstraktion und Gemeinsinn: zur Frage der Paradigmenwechsel von der Scholastik zum Humanismus in der Argumentationstheorie Lorenzo Vallas," *TijdFil* 44 (1982) 269–89; C. Knox, *Changing Christian Paradigms and Their Implications for Modern Thought* (Leiden, 1993).

23. See Nicholas of Cusa, *De Concordantia catholica* I, cap. 1, 6, ed. G. Kallen in *Opera omnia,* iussu et auctoritate Academiae Litterarum Heidelbergensis ad codicum fidem edita, XIV (Hamburg, 1963) 31–32.

24. Nicholas of Cusa, *De pace fidei,* ed. R. Klibansky and H. Bascour, in *Opera* VII (Hamburg, 1959).

25. See ibid., XIX, 68 (62): "The harmony of the religions is therefore established in the heaven of reason."

26. On the cultural and theological consequences of the fall of Constantinople and the enthusiasm of Pius II in preaching a crusade see G. Reynaud, "Observations sur l'idée de croisade au XVe siècle. De la chute de Byzance (29 mai 1493) à la mort de Pie II (16 août 1464)," *BLE* 89 (1988) 274–90; see also A. Pertusi, *La caduta di Costantinopoli* (2 vols.; Milan, 1976) (on Piccolomini see especially I, 276–77).

27. Pius II (Aeneas Silvius Piccolomini), *Lettera a Maometto II (Epistola ad Maumethem),* ed. G. Toffanin (Naples, 1953) 109–117 (text edited by A. Altamura and G. Vallese). A first and partly different version of this letter, which was included in the *Opera omnia* of Pius II (Basel, 1571) 872–904, has been published by F. Gaeta, "Sulla 'Lettera a Maometto' di Pio II," *BIstStorArchMur* 77 (1965) 127–227; this study is an excellent historico-cultural introduction to the text (the text itself occupies 195–227).

28. Pius II (Aeneas Silvius Piccolomini), *De liberorum educatione,* ed. J. St. Nelson (Studies in Medieval and Renaissance Latin Language and Literature 12; Washington, D.C., 1940) 174.

29. On the philosophical and theological importance of Pius II's ecumenical ideals see G. Radetti, "Profilo di Enea Silvio Piccolomini," *La Cultura* 9 (1971) 289–313.

30. See the index in D. Cantimori, *Eretici italiani del Cinquecento. Ricerche storiche* (Florence, 1939, 1983³); and the following studies by G. Radetti: "Francesco Pucci riformatore fiorentino e il sistema della religione naturale," *GCFI* 12 (1931) 219–31; "Il teismo universalistico di Guglielmo Postel," *Annali della R. Scuola Normale Superiore di Pisa* (Classe di Lettere, Storia e Filosofia, Ser. 2) 5 (1936) 179–95; "Riformatori ed eretici ital-

iani del secolo XVI," *GCFI* 21 (1940) 13–24, 71–97, 240–67; "Umanesimo e riforma nella prima metà del secolo XVI," ibid., 36 (1956) 301–16. Radetti has also edited, with introduction and notes, a translation of selected passages from S. Castellione under the title of *Fede, dubio, e tolleranza* (Florence, 1960); for the *De arte dubitandi* see 97–164.

31. See A. Marranzini and others, "I colloqui di Ratisbona: l'azione e le idee di Gaspare Contarini (Tavola Rotonda)," in *Gaspare Contarini e il suo tempo* (Atti del convegno, Venezia, 1–3 marzo 1985), ed. F. Cavazzana Romanelli (Venice, 1988) 167–254. On Contarini see below, chapter 8, section 9.

32. G. D. Mansi, *Sacrorum conciliorum nova et amplissima collectio* 32:842CD (reprinted: Paris, 1902); *Decrees of the Ecumenical Councils*, ed. N. P. Tanner (2 vols.; London: Sheed & Ward; Washington, D.C.: Georgetown University Press, 1990) I, 605. On the fifth Lateran Council see L. von Pastor, *History of the Popes from the Close of the Middle Ages* 8 (St. Louis, 1923) 384–413. On the participation of John Francis Pico see Ch. B. Schmitt, "Gianfrancesco Pico della Mirandola and the Fifth Lateran Council," *ArchRef* 61 (1970) 161–78. See also below, chapter 8, section 4.

33. For example, the entire second book of Sadoleto's *De laudibus philosophiae* (see note 17, above) is inspired by the idea that the limits imposed on philosophy by the probabilist position can become a real value inasmuch as, by directing the mind toward its real possibilities in knowing the truth, the limitation of the capacities of human knowledge also urges theological wisdom to adopt a fruitful orientation that is practical and moral.

Chapter 1

1. In connection with these discussions and the still-unresolved problems of the concepts "renaissance" and "humanism," I refer the reader to the texts and bibliographical data gathered in C. Vasoli, *Umanesimo e Rinascimento* (Palermo, 1969, 1976^2).

2. I am obviously referring to J. Huizinga, *Herfstijd der Middelleeuwen. Studie over Levens- en Gedachtenvormen de veertiende en vijtiende eeuw in Frankrijk en de Nederlanden* (Harlem, 1919). ET: *The Waning of the Middle Ages* (1924).

3. Still fundamental for Petrarch's activity as a philologist is G. Billanovich, *Petrarca letterato. Lo scrittoio del Petrarca* (Rome, 1947).

4. See *Briefwechsel des Cola di Rienza*, ed. K. Burdach and P. Piur (Berlin, 1912) 74–75.

5. Francis Petrarch, *Rerum memorandarum libri*, ed. G. Billanovich (Florence, 1941–42) 19.

6. Francis Petrarch, *Rerum senilium libri*, in *Opera* (Basel, 1554) ff. 879–81; Italian translation by G. Fracassetti in Francis Petrarch, *Lettere senili* I (Florence, 1869) 278–82.

7. Cited by E. Carrara, editor of the *Secretum*, in F. Petrarch, *Prose* (Naples-Milan, 1955) 58 (entire work = 21–215).

8. For the text I follow these editions: F. Petrarch, *Sui ipsius et aliorum ignorantia*, ed. P. G. Ricci, in *Prose*, 710–67; F. Petrarch, *Invectivarum contra medicum quendam libri IV*, ed. P. G. Ricci (Rome, 1950; enl. ed., 1978). On Petrarch's anti-Averroist polemics see also this *History of Theology* II, part VI, chapter 9, section 4.

9. Petrarch, *De sui ipsius et multorum ignorantia*, 712.

10. John Boccaccio, *Genealogia deorum gentilium libri*, ed. V. Romano (2 vols.; Bari, 1951).

11. For relations between Marsili and John of Celle see J. of Celle - L. Marsili, *Lettere,* ed. F. Giambonini (2 vols.; Florence, 1921).

12. For the text of this poem I refer the reader to C. Vasoli, *Studi sulla cultura della Rinascimento* (Manduria, 1968) 35–39.

13. The *Invectiva,* of which there remains only the adaptation "di grammatica in volgare" (from Latin into the vernacular), was edited by A. Wesselofski, in his edition of G. Gherardi, *Il Paradiso degli Alberti* (Bologna, 1867), vol. I, pt. II, 303–16.

14. For Dominici see ch. 2, pp. 87–98. The text of Salutati's response is in his *Epistolario,* ed. F. Novati, IV, pt. I (Rome, 1905) 205–40.

15. For this work I follow Giovanni Gherardi, *Il paradiso degli Alberti,* ed. A. Lanza (Rome, 1975), especially 126–29.

16. See I. Hijmans-Tromp, *Vita e opere di Agnolo Torini* (Leiden, 1957).

17. Coluccio Salutati, *Epistolario,* ed. F. Novati, I (Rome, 1893) 178–79.

18. Idem, *De saeculo et religione,* ed. B. L. Ullman (Florence, 1957).

19. *Epistolario* III (Rome, 1896) 285–308.

20. E. Garin, *Storia della filosofia italiana* I (Turin, 1978³) 270.

21. In Coluccio Salutati, *De nobilitate legum et medicinae. De verecundia,* ed. E. Garin (Florence, 1947) 334.

22. Idem, *De fato et fortuna,* ed. G. Bianca (Florence, 1985).

23. Ibid., 74.

24. See above, note 21.

25. Salutati, *De nobilitate legum,* 254.

26. Idem, *Epistolario* II (Rome, 1893) 289–302.

27. See above, note 14.

28. Coluccio Salutati, *De laboribus Herculis,* ed. B. L. Ullman (2 vols.; Zurich, 1951).

29. See E. Garin, *Il ritorno dei filosofi antichi* (Naples, 1983) 35–38.

30. In Leonard Bruni Aretino, *Humanistisch-philosophische Schriften,* ed. H. Baron (Leipzig-Berlin, 1928; reprinted: Wiesbaden, 1969) 81–96.

31. Leonard Bruni, *Ad Petrum Istrum dialogi,* ed. E. Garin in *Prosatori latini del Quattrocento* (Milan-Naples, 1952) 36–99.

32. In *Humanistische-philosophische Schriften* (note 30, above), 50–69.

33. Ibid., 5–19.

34. Ibid., 20–40.

35. For all the works of Bracciolini that are cited, I refer to P. Bracciolini, *Opera omnia,* ed. R. Fubini (Turin, 1964–69), who reprints texts from earlier editions and adds introductions and critical notes.

36. Lawrence Valla, *De voluptate ac vero bono declamationes ac disputationes in libros tres contractae* (Paris, 1512).

37. I follow the most recent edition, even though it is not truly critical: Lawrence Valla, *De vero falsoque bono,* ed. M. De Panizza Lorch (Bari, 1970).

38. Idem, *De libero arbitrio,* ed. M. Anfossi (Florence, 1934).

39. For the *Elegantiae linguae latinae* I refer to the Rome edition of 1471; but while waiting for a critical edition, the reader may also consult the *Praefationes* to the entire work and to the individual books in Garin, *Prosatori* (note 31, above) 594–631.

40. Lawrence Valla, *Repastinatio dialectice et philosophie,* ed. G. Zippel (2 vols.; Padua, 1982).

41. On this point see Zippel's introduction (note 40, above).

42. Ibid., II, 404.

43. Ibid., II, 405–6.

44. See below, chapter 4, section 1.

45. *Repastinatio,* 405.

46. In *Opera* (Basel, 1543) 795–801.

47. Lawrence Valla, *Collatio Novi Testamenti,* critical ed. by A. Perosa (Florence, 1970).

48. S. I. Camporeale, *Lorenzo Valla. Umanesimo e teologia* (Florence, 1972) 282.

49. I am following the edition of W. Schwan (Leipzig, 1928).

50. On Laetus see V. Zabughin, *Giulio Pomponio Leto* I (Rome, 1909); II (Grottaferrata, 1910–12).

51. *Callimaco Esperiente poeta e politico del '400. Convegno internazionale di studi* (San Gemignano, 18–20 ottobre 1985) (Florence, 1987).

52. See *Ambrogio Traversari nel VI Centenario della nascita* (Camaldoli-Florence, 15–18 ottobre 1986) (Florence, 1988).

53. Ambrose Traversari, *Epistolae,* ed. L. Mehus (Florence, 1749).

54. I am following the edition provided by A. Dini Traversari in his *Ambrogio Traversari e i suoi tempi* (Florence, 1912) 11–139, but also the Italian translation by V. Ramburini, in A. Traversari, *Hodoeporicon,* introduced by E. Garin (Florence, 1985).

55. Peter Paul Vergerio, *De ingenuis moribus et liberalibus adolescentiae studiis,* ed. A. Gnesotto in *Atti e memorie dell'Academia di Scienze, Lettere e Arti di Padova* 34 (1918) 75–156.

56. See, above all, R. Sabbadini, *La scuola e gli studi di Guarino Guarini Veronese* (Catania, 1896); idem, *Il metodo degli umanisti* (Florence, 1920); and his edition of the *Epistolario* (3 vols.; Venice, 1915–19).

57. For the documents concerning the school of Vittorino di Feltre, see E. Garin, *I classici della pedagogia italiana. L'Umanesimo* (Florence, 1958) 504–718.

Chapter 2

1. See especially C. Dionisotti, "Ermolao Barbaro e la fortuna di Suiseth," *Medioevo e Rinascimento. Studi in onore di Bruno Nardi* (Florence, 1955) I, 218–53; but see also P. O. Kristeller, "Humanism and Scholasticism in the Italian Renaissance," in his *Studies in Renaissance Thought and Letters* (Rome, 1969[2]) 553–83.

2. For clarification of the biography of Paul of Venice see A. R. Perreiah, "Bibliographical Introduction to Paul of Venice," *Augustiniana* 17 (1967) 450–61. On the theological implications of Paul's thinking on logic see also volume II of the present series, part VI, chapter 6, section 10.

3. See J. M. Bochenski, *Formale Logik* (Freiburg i. B.–Munich, 1956), but also the index in A. Maierù, *Terminologia logica della tarda scolastica* (Rome, 1972).

4. For the *Summa naturalium* I use the Venice edition of 1502 (reprinted: Hildesheim, 1970); for the *Super librum de anima,* the Venice edition of 1481.

5. See Z. Kuksewicz, "Paul de Venise et sa théorie de l'âme," *Aristotelismo veneto e scienza moderna. Atti del 25° Anno Accademico del Centro per la storia della tradizione aristotelica nel Veneto* (Padua, 1983) 297–324.

6. See ibid., 300–3. On the "Averroism" of Paul of Venice see F. Ruello, "Paul de Venise, théologien 'averroiste'?" *Multiple Averroès* (Paris, 1978) 257–72.

7. Kuksewicz, "Paul de Venise," 311–13 and 321–24.

8. See A. Poppi, *Causalità e infinità nella scuola padovana dal 1480 al 1513* (Padua, 1966) 124–28.

9. For the life and activity of Gaetano of Thiene see P. Silvestro da Valsanzibio, *Vita e dottrina di Gaetano da Thiene filosofo nell Studio de Padova* (Padua, 1949). On his teachings in logic see the index in Maierù, *Terminologia logica* (note 3, above).

10. The *Commentaria in tres libros Aristotelis de anima* were published in Padua in 1475.

11. See G. Di Napoli, *Immortalità dell'anima nel Rinascimento* (Turin, 1963) 97–105.

12. *Recollecte super octo libros Physicorum Aristotelis* (Vicenza, 1487).

13. See Poppi, *Causalità e infinità*, 128–29.

14. For his life, the works (still for the most part unpublished), and the codices in which they are preserved, see G. Ciolini, *Agostino da Roma (Favaroni, + 1443) e la sua cristologia* (Florence, 1944); D. S. Friemel, *Die theologische Prinzipienlehre des Augustinus Favaroni vom Rom OESA (+ 1443)* (Würzburg, 1950).

15. See Henry Kalteisen, *Propositiones in condemnatione libelli Augustini de Roma*, ed. W. Eckermann (Rome, 1978).

16. [The translation of Favaroni's propositions, except for the last, are taken from *Decrees of the Ecumenical Councils*, ed. N. P. Tanner (London–Washington, D.C., 1990) I, 493.—Tr.]

17. See G. Diaz, "Tratado inedito *De principatu Papae* de Augustín Favaroni OSA (+ 1443)," *Analecta Augustiniana* 53 (1990) 95–192.

18. See A. Vallone, "Favarone de'Favaroni et il suo inedito trattato *De principatu Papae*," *Studi storici in onore di Gabriele Pepe* (Bari, 1969) 499–507; idem, *Di alcuni aspetti del pensiero politico del XIV secolo* (Manduria, 1973) 177–86; idem, *Antidantismo politico del XIV secolo* (Naples, 1973) 107–20.

19. For (not always exhaustive) biographical and bibliographical information see *MemDom*, N.S. 1 (1970); the entire volume is devoted to Dominici.

20. I follow the edition of A. Ceruti (Bologna, 1889).

21. I follow the edition of A. Levasti (Florence, 1947).

22. I follow the edition of E. Hunt (Notre Dame, 1940, 1960²).

23. I follow the edition of P. Bargellini (Florence, 1927).

24. I follow the edition of M. T. Casella and G. Pozzi (Fribourg, 1969).

25. For a summary but shrewd description of Dominici's personality see G. Cracco, "Banchini, Giovanni (Giovanni Dominici, Banchelli Giovanni)," *DBI* 5 (Rome, 1963) 657–64.

26. See ch. 1, pp. 32–40.

27. See R.-L. Oechslin, "Jean Dominici (bienheureux)," *DSp* 8 (Paris, 1972) 473–80.

28. For a biography see A. D'Addario, "Antonino Pierozzi, santo," *DBI* 3 (Rome, 1961) 524–32, and G. Di Agresti, "Antonino Pierozzi," *BibSanct* 2 (Rome, 1962) 88–104. Important data is provided by C. C. Calzolai, *Bibliografia antoniniana* (Vatican City, 1961).

29. For the *Summa* I follow the Florence edition of 1741.

30. For Antoninus' teaching on the economic life see E. de Roover, *San Bernardino da Siena and Sant'Antonino of Florence: The Two Great Economic Thinkers of the Middle Ages* (Boston, 1967).

31. For the *Chronicon* I follow the Lyons edition of 1527.

32. See, mainly, G. G. Meersseman, "Ergänzung zu den Schriften des Antonius de

Carlenis von Neapel," *AFP* 5 (1935) 357–63; Th. Käppeli, *Scriptores ordinis praedicatorum Medii Aevi* 1 (Rome, 1970) 109.

33. See D. Di Agresti, "Carleni, Antonio," *DBI* 20 (Rome, 1977) 135–36.

34. See especially the index in L. Mohler, *Kardinal Bessarion als Theologe, Humanist und Staatsmann* 1 (Paderborn, 1923); G. Mercati, *Per la cronologia della vita et degli scritti di Niccolò Perotti arcivescovo di Siponte* (Rome, 1925).

35. On the *In calumniatorem Platonis*, see ch. 4, pp. 212–14.

36. See especially I. Colosio, "La *Tabula aurea* di Pietro da Bergamo," *Divus Thomas* (Piacenza) 64 (1961) 119–32; Th. Käppeli, *Scriptores ordinis praedicatorum Medii Aevi* 3 (Rome, 1980) 219.

37. See especially M. Grabmann, *Mittelalterliches Geistesleben* 3 (Munich, 1956) 390–400.

38. I am using the Lyons edition of 1580.

39. The *Opuscula* were published at Milan in 1488.

40. Ferrer's *Sermones de sanctis* were also published at Milan.

41. The *Tabula* was published at Venice in 1498.

42. G. G. Meersseman, "Een Vlaamsch Wijsger: Dominicus van Vlaanderen," *Thomistisch Tijdschrift voor katholiek Kulturleven* 1 (1930) 385–400; idem, "Het geestelijk en wijsgeerig midden van Dominicus van Vlaanderen," ibid., 590–92.

43. U. Schikowski, "Dominicus de Flandria: sein Leben, seine Schriften, seine Bedeutung," *AFP* 10 (1940) 169–221.

44. L. Mahieu, *Dominique de Flandres et sa métaphysique* (Paris, 1942); but see also A. Verde, "Domenico di Fiandra, intransigente tomista non gradito nello Studio fiorentino," *MemDom*, N.S. 7 (1976) 304–21, and Th Käppeli, *Scriptores ordinis praedicatorum Medii Aevi* 1 (Rome, 1970) 315–18.

45. I am using the Venice edition of 1565 (reprinted: New York and Frankfurt a. M., 1967).

46. See A. Ferrua, "Bandello, Vincenzo," *DBI* 5 (Rome, 1963) 666–67.

47. See X. Le Bachelet and M. Jugie, "Immaculée Conception," *DTC* 7 (Paris, 1922) cols. 845–1218, especially 1120–94.

48. See V. Marchetti, "Caroli, Giovanni," *DBI* 20 (Rome, 1977) 523–26; S. I. Camporeale, "Giovanni Caroli OP and the *Liber dierum lucensium* (Humanism and the Religious Crisis of the Late Quattrocento)," *Christianity and the Renaissance: Image and Religious Imagination in the Quattrocento* (Syracuse, 1990) 445–66.

49. On Jerome Savonarola and the events connected with his preaching see section 13 of this chapter. On John Nesi, see below, p. 232.

50. See especially B. Sewell, *Blessed Baptist of Mantua, Carmelite and Humanist (1447–1516)* (Rome, 1960); E. Coccia, *Le edizioni delle opere del Mantovano* (Rome, 1960).

51. I follow the edition in the *Opera omnia* of Spagnoli (Antwerp, 1576)

52. See below, p. 106.

53. For James of the Marches, too, see below, p. 115.

54. See, in particular, the various contributions in *Storia e cultura al Santo di Padovva fra il XIII e il XX secolo* (Vicenza, 1976).

55. See D. Cortese, "Sisto IV Papa antoniano," *Il Santo* 12 (1972) 211–71; idem, "I teologi del Santo nel secolo XV," *Storia e cultura al Santo* (note 52, above), 153–67; L. Pusci, "Profil di Francesco della Rovere, poi Sisto IV," ibid., 279–88; A. Poppi, "La teologia nell'università e nelle scuole," *Storia dell cultura veneta. Dal primo Quattrocento al*

Concilio di Trento III*** (Vicenza, 1981) 1–33, especially 28–29; C. Bianca, "Francesco della Rovere, un franscescano tra teologia e potere," *Un pontificato e una città. Sisto IV (1471–1484)* (Atti del Convegno–Roma, 3–7 dicembre 1984; Rome, 1986) 19–55; C. Vasoli, "Sisto IV professore di teologia e teologo," *Atti e Memorie della Società Savonese di Storia patria,* N.S. 24 (1988) 177–207, and now published in Vasoli, *Tre "maestri" umanisti e teologi. Studi quattrocenteschi* (Florence, 1991) 173–211.

56. *De sanguine Christi. De potentia Dei* (Rome, 1471).

57. See M.-D. Chenu, "Sang du Christ," *DTC* 14 (Paris, 1939) cols. 1094–97.

58. On the traditional links between medical studies and theology in the schools of northern Italy and especially at Padua see also volume II, part VI, chapter 9.

59. See above, note 56.

60. See below, pp. 118, 297–98. But mention must be made here at least of L. Baudry, *La querelle des futurs contingents (Louvain 1465–1475). Textes inédits* (Paris, 1950).

61. See *De futuris contingentibus* (Rome, 1473). Baudry (note 60, above) publishes a report on this sent by Della Rovere to Bessarion (113–25); it is almost identical with the text of the *incunabulum.*

62. See C. Vasoli, *Profezia e ragione. Studi sulla cultura del Cinquecento e del Seicento* (Naples, 1974) 15–127 (see 21–22 for earlier bibliography); idem, *I miti e gli astri* (Naples, 1977) 70–72; idem, *Immagini umanistiche* (Naples, 1983) 231–36; idem, *Filosofia e religione nella cultura del Rinascimento* (Naples, 1988) (see the index); idem, "Giorgio Benigno Salviati e la tensione profetica di fine Quattrocento," *Rinascimento,* N.S. 29 (1989) 53–78, reprinted in *Tre "maestri"* (note 55, above) 212–47.

63. See A. Morisi, *"Apocalypsis nova." Ricerche sull'origine e sulla formazione del testo dello pseudo Amadeo* (Rome, 1970).

64. The *De libertate et immutabilitate Dei sententiae* is preserved among the codices of the Apostolic Vatican Library, Vat. lat. 1056.

65. See P. Zvonimir Cornelius Sojat, *De voluntate hominis eiusque praeminentia et dominatione in anima secundum Georgium Dragisic (c. 1448–1520)* (Rome, 1972).

66. George Benignus Salviati, *Ad Magnanimum Laurentium Medicen* (Florence, 1489).

67. The *Opus septem quaestionum* is no. 317 of the codices in the Biblioteca Riccardiana in Florence; Florence, Biblioteca Laurenziana, Pluteo LXXXIII, 18.

68. For an explanation of the text see Vasoli, *Filosofia e religione* (note 62, above), 139–82.

69. The *In opus de natura angelica* is to be found in cod. Florence, Biblioteca Laurenziana, Pluteo XVIII, 16.

70. The *Propheticae solutiones* were published at Florence by Lorenzo the Magnificent in April 1497. But see the edition of G. C. Garfagnini, in *Rinascimento,* N.S. 29 (1989) 94–123.

71. *Opus de natura angelica* (Florence, 1499).

72. See the bibliography for the codices containing these writings.

73. *Defensio praestantissimi viri Joannis Reuchlin* (Cologne, 1917).

74. *Opus toti christinae veritati utile de arcanis catholicae veritatis . . .* (Ortona a Mare, 1518).

75. See mainly B. Nardi, *Saggi sull'aristotelismo padovano dal secolo XIV al XVI* (Florence, 1958) (see the index); A. Poppi, "Lo scotista Antonio Trombetta," *Il Santo* 2 (1962) 349–67; E. P. Mahoney, "Antonio Trombetta and Agostino Nifo on Averroes and Intelligible Species: A Philosophical Dispute at the University of Padua," in *Storia e cultura al Santo fra il XIII e il XX secolo* (Vicenza, 1976) 485–538.

76. His *Opus doctrinae scotisticae* was also published at Venice.

77. The *De animarum humanarum plurificatione* was published at Venice in 1498.

78. The *Quaestio super articulos impositos domino Gabrieli Sacerdoti* was published at Venice in 1502 as an appendix to the second edition of the *Opus in Metaphysicam Aristotelis Paduae discussum.*

79. See below, p. 393.

80. On Vernia see below, pp. 377–78.

81. See Poppi, *Causalità e infinità* (note 8, above) 281–348.

82. See E. d'Alençon, "Lychet, François," *DTC* 9 (Paris, 1926) cols. 1357–59; H. Rulang, "Unterwegs an Bañez und Molina. Lychetus und seine Diskussion mit Cajetanus über das göttliche Vorherwissen und Mitwirken," *TheolJb* 8 (1965) 364–89.

83. For the *Commentaria super libros Sententiarum et quaestiones quodlibetales* I use the Paris edition of 1519–20.

84. See G. Di Napoli, *L'immortalità dell'anima nel Rinascimento* (Turin, 1963) 194–266.

85. Of particular importance for Bernardine's life, preaching activity, and theological teachings is the summary but exhaustive treatment of R. Manselli, "Bernardino da Siena," *DBI* 9 (Rome, 1967) 215–26.

86. On these aspects of Bernardine's preaching see especially *S. Bernardino da Siena. Saggi e ricerche pubblicate nel quinto centenario della morte* (Milan, 1945); and *Bernardino predicatore nella società del suo tempo.* Atti del XVI Convegno del Centro di studi sulla spiritualità medioevale, Todi, 9–12 ottobre 1975 (Todi, 1976).

87. See especially A. E. Trutenberger, *S. Bernardino da Siena. Considerazioni sullo sviluppo dell'etica cristiana nel primo Rinascimento* (Bern, 1951); G. Rinaldi, *L'attività commerciale nel pensiero de Bernardino da Siena* (Rome, 1959); de Roover, *San Bernardino da Siena* (note 30, above).

88. See especially E. Cerulli, "Berdini, Alberto (Alberto da Sarteano)," *DBI* 8 (Rome, 1866) 800–4.

89. See F. Biccellari, "Missioni del beato Alberto da Sarteano in Oriente per l'unione della Chiesa greca e il ristabilimento dell'Osservanza dell'Ordine francescano." *Studi francescani* 11 (1939) 159–73; G. Hoffmann, "Copten und Aethiopen auf den Konzil von Florenze," *OCP* 8 (1942) 5–39.

90. See above, pp. 103, 105, 113.

91. See R. Lioi, "Giacomo della Marca," *BibSanct* 6 (Rome, 1965) 388–96 and the bibliography given there.

92. See G. Hofer, *Johannes von Capistrano* (Innsbruck, 1936).

93. See A. Chiappini, "Giovanni da Capistrano," *BibSanct* 6 (Rome, 1965) 646–56.

94. See Guarino Guarini da Verona, *Epistolario,* ed. R. Sabbadini; see above, pp. 59–60.

95. The bibliography on Savonarola is vast; I shall mention here only R. Ridolfi, *Vita di Girolamo Savonarola* (Rome, 1952; Florence, 1981[6]); D. Weinstein, *Savonarola and Florence: Prophecy and Patriotism in the Renaissance* (Princeton, 1968).

96. For the prophecies concerning Charles VIII and his descent into Italy see A. Denis, *Charles VIII et les Italiens: Histoire et Mythe* (Geneva, 1979).

97. For these writings, I use Jerome Savonarola, *Scritti filosofici,* ed. G. C. Garfagnini and E. Garin, vol. II (Rome, 1988).

98. Jerome Savonarola, *Prediche sopra Aggeo. Con il Trattato circa il reggimento e governo della città di Firenze,* ed. L. Firpo (Rome, 1965).

99. In *Scritti filosofici* I (Rome, 1982) 1–208.

100. This work is Book XI of the *Compendium logicae*.

101. See Jerome Savonarola, *Triumphus crucis. Testo latino e volgare*, ed. A. Crucitti (Rome, 1974).

102. The *Apologeticus* is published in the *Scritti filosofici* I, 208–72.

103. The *Trattato* is to be found in *Scritti filosofici* I, 273–370.

104. For an introduction to the personality and work of Roderick Sánchez de Arévalo see S. López Santidrián, "Sánchez de Arévalo (Rodrigo)," *DSp* 14 (Paris, 1989) cols. 301–3. See also below, pp. 121–22, 261.

105. For the text see H. Keniston, "A Fifteenth-Century Treatise on Education," *Bulletin Hispanique* 32 (1930) 193–217 text on 204–17.

106. For the *Vergel* I refer to the edition by F. de Uhagón (Madrid, 1900).

107. See T. Toni, *Don Rodrigo Sánchez de Arévalo. Su personalidad y actividades. El tratado "De pace et bello"* (Madrid, 1935).

108. The *Speculum* was published in Rome in 1468 and reprinted several times as well as translated into Spanish, German, and French.

109. See R. H. Trame, *Rodrigo Sánchez de Arévalo: Spanish Diplomat and Champion of the Papacy* (Washington, D.C., 1958).

110. T. Toni has published a partial edition of the *De paupertate* in *Estudios Eclesiásticos* 13 (1934) 369–98.

111. For a recent general presentation of Torquemada and his work see T. M. Izbicki, *Protector of the Faith: Cardinal Johannes de Turrecremata and the Defense of the Institutional Church* (Washington, D.C., 1981). See also below, pp. 192, 260.

112. For his statements at this council see below, p. 192.

113. See the bibliography for editions of this work.

114. For the *Summa de Ecclesia* I use the Venice edition of 1561.

Chapter 3

1. For a reconstruction of the history of theology and philosophy in the fifteenth century see now S. Swiezawski, *Histoire de la philosophie européenne au XV siècle*, adapted by M. Prokopowicz, French trans. H. Rollet and M. Prokopowicz (Paris, 1990); A. De Muralt, *L'enjeu de la philosophie médiévale. Études thomistes, scotistes, occamiennes et grégoriennes* (Leiden, 1991).

2. Nicholas of Cusa, *De filiatione Dei*, translated by W. F. Wertz as *On the Filiation of God*, in idem, *Toward a New Council of Florence: "On the Peace of Faith" and Other Works by Nicolaus of Cusa* (Washington, D.C., 1993), section V, p. 187 [henceforth translations from this book will be identified by Wertz, with page number]. The reference is to the idea of "the consonant theology of various groups," of which Eimeric of Kampen also speaks in his *Centheologicum, tractatus continens centum theologias*, codex Bruxellensis 11571–75, ff. 1r–74r. See R. Haubst, "Albertus, wie Cusanus ihn sah," in *Albertus Magnus, doctor universalis 1280–1980*, ed. G. Meyer and A. Zimmermann (Mainz, 1980) 167ff.; idem, "Zum Fortleben Alberts des Grosses, bei Heymeric von Kamp und Nikolaus von Kues," in *Studia Albertina*, Festschrift ed. B. Geyer (BGPTM, Supplbd. 4; Münster in W., 1952) 420–77; idem, *Das Bild des Einen und Dreieinen Gottes in der Welt bei Nikolaus von*

Kues (Trier, 1952); Z. Kalusa, "Das *Centheologicon* des Heymericus de Campo und die darin enthaltene Cusanus-Reminiszenzen: Hinweise und Materialen," *Traditio* 39 (1983) 457–77; R. Imbach, "Einheit des Glaubens, Spuren des Cusanischen Dialogs *De pace fidei* bei Heymericus de Campo," *FZTP* 27 (1980) 5–15.

[For works not translated in Wertz, I translate from the Italian version provided by the author. This is her own translation of Nicholas' writings, published in Turin, 1972. For *Learned Ignorance* she uses her revised translation, Rome, 1991. Page references in parentheses after Italian titles are to these versions of the author. —Tr.]

3. See especially G. Alberigo, *Chiesa conciliare. Identità e significato del conciliarismo* (Brescia, 1981). On Nicholas see 266–70 and 293–354.

4. See the analysis by T. Gregory, "Forma di conoscenza e ideali del sapere nella cultura medievale," in idem, *Sapientia mundana* (Rome, 1992) 1–59.

5. There is a vast literature on this subject. John Wenck was in Paris in 1426 and studied there in the school of John of Neuhausen. He then went to Heidelberg and in 1442–43 wrote his *De ignota litteratura* against Nicholas, who in 1449 responded with his *Defense of Learned Ignorance*. Eimeric of Kampen, Nicholas' teacher of theology, had likewise been a student of John of Neuhausen in Paris. See R. Haubst, "Johannes Wenck als Albertist," *RTAM* 18 (1951) 303–23; G. Meersseman, *Geschichte des Albertismus* (2 vols.; Paris, 1933, and Rome, 1935); H. Jedin, *Die mittelalterliche Kirche* (3 vols.; Freiburg im Br., 1968). There is an edition of the *De ignota litteratura* by E. Vansteenberghe in his *Autour de la docte ignorance. Une controverse sur la théologie mystique* (BGPM 14/2–4; Münster in W., 1915) 19–41; see also R. Haubst, "Studien zu Nikolaus von Kues und Johannes Wenck. Neue Erörterung und Nachträge," *RömQ* 53 (1958) 81–88.

6. See *On the Filiation of God* V (Wertz, 188).

7. See also G. Penzo, *Meister Eckhart, una mistica della ragione* (Padua, 1922), who discusses the problem once again. On the possible connections with the Free Spirit movement see *Il movimento del libero spirito. Testi e documenti,* ed. Romana Guarnieri (Rome, 1965); for Eckhart see 399 and passim. Nicholas wrote as follows about Eckhart in his *Apologia della dotta ignoranza* (pp. 423–24): "He [that is, Nicholas, who speaks of himself in the third person] said that in libraries here and there he had seen numerous works of Eckhart, mostly commentaries on some books of the Bible, many sermons and doctrinal discussions, and that he had also read some statements, extracted from Eckhart's writings, on the text of John, which others had annotated and refuted. . . . The master [= Nicholas] said, however, that he had never read that Eckhart thought creatures to be the Creator; and he praised Eckhart's intelligence and the study of him. But he expressed the wish that Eckhart's books be withdrawn from public circulation, because ordinary people are not up to grasping things which Eckhart often intermingles and which are not customary in other scholars, although those able to understand them find them penetrating and useful."

8. See *Liber XXIV philosophorum,* ed. B. Baeumker (BGPTM 25/1; Münster, 1928) 207–14 at 208 (and see now the edition by F. Hudry [Millon-Grenoble, 1989]). On the influence of the images of this work on Nicholas' thinking see my analysis, "Temi ermetico-neoplatonici della Dotta ignoranza," in *Il neoplatonismo nel Rinascimento,* Atti del Convegno internazionale, ed. P. Prini (Rome, 1993) 117–32.

9. See U. Eco, *Arte e bellezza nell'estetica medievale* (Milan, 1987) 158ff.

10. On the use of Albert's concept of participation, with Nicholas' references to Albert's works, see Haubst, "Albertus wie Cusanus ihn sah" (note 2, above) 167ff. Nicholas explicitly criticizes the Neoplatonic vision of the generation of the many from the one through di-

rect emanation, as well as the concept of participation that flows from this vision. In the *Dialogue on Genesis* II, he writes: "The consideration of the Platonics, however subtle it may be, that the First is unparticipably superexalted, should not disturb you. Understand indeed, that the absolute One is participated in identically in the identity, of which they say that it is after the first absolute One" (Wertz, 211). Cusanus, however, understands participation, as Albert did, "according to the dispositions of the recipient." In his view, it is even possible to admit "the Origin from the Origin" (*On the Origin,* Wertz, 344), an idea that is inconceivable for Platonists but not for Christians, and the truth of which is grounded in the trinitarian concept of God as Father, Son, and Spirit. "The ineffable Origin is therefore called neither Origin, nor many, nor not-many, nor the One, nor has it any other name, but rather before all that it exists unnameably. . . . If I see the Origin by means of contradictions, then I see everything in it. For being and not-being embrace everything, since everything that can be thought or said, either is or is not. Therefore the Origin, which is before contradiction, enfolds everything which contradiction embraces. The Origin appears in the equality of opposites" (*On the Origin,* Wertz, 356–57). In another work, *On the Hunt for Wisdom* VIII, Nicholas stresses the superiority of the "hunt" *(venatio)* conducted by "our divine theologians," who were enlightened by revelation that comes from on high and is trinitarian, over that of Plato and Aristotle (Wertz, 473–75).

11. For the concept of the "aptitude of matter" and the "aptitude of possibility," see especially *Learned Ignorance* II, 8. For the concept of "the disposition of the material" see *On Beryllus* XX (Wertz, 315).

12. See the *Dialogue on Genesis* (Wertz, 212–13).

13. See *L'idiota (The Layman)* III. *La mente:* "*Layman:* . . . our mind is a power *(vis)* of understanding; it is a virtual whole comprising all the powers of understanding. . . . The mind consists virtually of the power to signify, reason, imagine, and sense; thus it is called, as a whole, the power to signify, reason, imagine, and sense. . . . *Philosopher:* If the mind is one, whence does it have these powers of understanding? *Layman:* It has them from the unity."

14. See especially *La dotta ignoranza* I, 11 (p. 75); *On Beryllus* 1 (Wertz, 301–2). Albert the Great, too, spoke in enigmas; see *On Beryllus* 19 (Wertz, 314–15); *La mente* 6. This theme runs through Nicholas' writings; an important enigmatic figure is the infinite sphere; others are those of infinite rectitude, of the center, of the *tetrakys*. On this point see also R. Guénon, *Simboli della scienze sacra* (Paris, 1962; Ital. tr.: Milan, 1975); K. Harries, "The Infinite Sphere: Comments on the History of a Metaphor," *Journal of the History of Philosophy* 13 (1975) 5–15. On the theology of John, which is the expression of perfect theology and which Nicholas uses in contrasting the metaphysics of Aristotle with the theology of the Word, that is, the trinitarian theology that explains the Trinity as the principle of the identity of contradictories and contraries in God, see especially *On Beryllus* 25 (Wertz, 321–23); *On the Origin* (Wertz, 355–56); *On Equality* (Wertz, 362). See also W. Lentzen, *Den Glauben Christi teilen. Theologie und Verkündigung bei Nikolaus von Kues* (Stuttgart-Berlin-Cologne, 1991).

15. God is "the absolute identity of opposites," "the absolute identity of origins," "the absolute identity of attributes," that is, identity without mediation of beings, without opposition of opposites; he is beyond them; he is the nothing of negations. See especially *La dotta ignoranza* II, 4 (p. 121); I, 4 (p. 66); I, 5 (p. 67). The theme is then explained especially in *De visione Dei* and the *Apologia*.

16. See K. Jaspers, *Nikolaus Cusanus* (Munich, 1964); but he does not seem to share the idea of Christ as the privileged code of transcendence in the economy of the universe.

17. See *Compendium* 2 (Wertz, 538–39).

18. On the gift of free will and the possibility of salvation see *On the Gift of the Father of Lights,* passim (Wertz, 191–205); *On the Peace of Faith,* 1–2 (Wertz, 231–35); and, in general, the *Sermones.*

19. See especially the *Dialogue on Genesis* (Wertz, 217–20). In *On the Origin* Nicholas speaks of "the assimilating intellect" (e.g., Wertz, 349). See also *La mente,* ch. 8.

20. The idea that the world is made according to a harmonious proportion, which is the source of its beauty, is a recurring theme in Nicholas' works; see, especially, *Dialogue on Genesis; Idiota* I–II: *De sapientia.*

21. See *La mente,* chs. 7–9.

22. *Compendium* 8 (Wertz, 549).

23. *Dialogue on Genesis:* "A written book, whose language and characters are un-known—just as if one would place some Greek book of Plato's before a German, in which Plato has described the powers of his intellect—appears to me to be an appropriate enough comparison for the world. Namely, if the German occupies himself attentively with the signs, then he could conjecture some elements from the difference and concordance of the characters and sounds from the various combinations, but in no case the quiddity itself in whole or in part, except if the same were revealed to him. Hence I conjecture the world as something in which the divine power is latent configuratively. . . . This alone this book re-veals to us, that He is great and exalted above everything which can be named, whose fin-ger has written this book. . . . It is therefore manifest that neither in part nor in toto can anything of quiddity be attained by man. If human meditation inquires into this, then it de-spises its syllogistic hunting and converts itself obediently to the revealed prophetic illumi-nations, and thus advances through despising itself as if inwardly impotent to cognition and to that which it seeks" (Wertz, 223–25).

24. See *On the Truth of Faith,* e.g., ch. 19 (Wertz, 271–72).

25. *L'idiota* IV: *Gli esperimenti di statica* (521–39).

26. See *Dialogo di un Gentile e di un Cristiano su Dio nascosto* (305–31).

27. See *On the Not-Other* 20 (Wertz, 443–45) and 24 (452ff.). Dionysius is here called "the greatest theologian" (443).

28. See Margherita Porete, *Le miroir des simples âmes anienties et qui seulement de-mourent en vouloir et désir d'amour,* ed. Romana Guarnieri, in *Il movimento del libero spir-ito* (note 7, above) 513–632.

29. *On Beryllus* 36 (Wertz, 336–37).

30. See, e.g., the passage from the *Dialogue on Genesis* that is cited above in note 23.

31. See *La dotta ignoranza* I, 25 (p. 106): "Idolatry is taking the explanation of the di-vinity in images of the truth as though it were the truth itself," or, as Nicholas says else-where, idolatry is "to mistake the image for the exemplar."

32. See ibid., I, 16 (p. 85).

33. See *L'apologia della dotta ignoranza,* p. 414.

34. Ibid., p. 415.

35. For these concepts see *La dotta ignoranza, L'apologia della dotta ignoranza, On Beryllus,* and *La visione di Dio;* almost all of Nicholas' works are a clarification of this teaching. For a partial summary see E. Zellinger, *Cusanus-Konkordanz* (Munich, 1960) 90–106.

36. See *On the Not-Other* 24 (Wertz, 452–59).

37. See ibid., 459.

38. *Liber XXIV philosophorum* (note 8, above) 211. I have not followed the new edition by Hudry, whose philological reconstruction of this rule seems to be somewhat improbable historically, and, to say the least, does not match Nicholas' citation of it.

39. See *Dialogue on Genesis* (Wertz, 216–17).

40. See *La visione di Dio* 6 (pp. 552–54). On God as both eye and mirror, pp. 560 and 568; on our freedom as given to us by God, pp. 556–60. On the gift of grace and participation in it see *On the Gift of the Father of Lights* (Wertz, 194–97). In *Beryllus* Nicholas writes: "In the Father is the sufficiency of all things, but not their necessity." He repeats over and over that the greatest error of the philosophers was to think of God as necessitated; he does so especially in the works of his later years, such as *Compendium* and *The Summit of Vision,* in which he develops the idea of God as omnipotence. In this work he even writes: "All precision in this speculation is to be assigned only to the potential-itself and its appearance" (Wertz, 568). He also removes from the idea of God as potential-itself *(posse)* that of being *(possest),* because being adds nothing to the omnipotence of God, but, if anything, takes from it and limits it (570).

41. *La visione di Dio,* p. 571. Our vision is a *theôsis,* which is also defined as "filiation of God," which is, in turn, an assimilation to the vision of Christ, a grasping of the One-all, beyond the barrier of the coincidence of opposites. See also the little work, *On the Filiation of God,* which is devoted to the subject of *theôsis* (Wertz, 174–205).

42. See *On the Filiation of God* (Wertz, 174); see also U. Opfermann, *Christus-Wahrheit des Denkens* (BGPTM 33).

43. See *On the Filiation of God* (Wertz, 179, 181, 184); *Dialogue on Genesis* (Wertz, 210); *On the Origin,* passim (Wertz, 341–60). See also the introduction to F. Bertin's translation, *Trois traités sur la docte ignorance et la coincidence des opposés* (Paris, 1991).

44. Haubst, "Albertus, wie Cusanus ihn sah" (note 2, above) 167ff. See also note 10 above.

45. See *On Conjectures,* passim (Wertz, 57–147), and above, section 3.

46. See above, note 40.

47. See *On the Filiation of God* (Wertz, 186).

48. Ibid.

49. This theme is developed especially in the *Dialogue on Genesis.*

50. See *On the Filiation of God* (Wertz, 185ff.).

51. In *La visione di Dio* 11 (p. 566) Nicholas compares the world to the succession of time as measured by a clock, the concept of which is in the mind of God, which we are ignorant of and which represents the quiddity of the world; this is the image of God as the watchmaker, which was to have such success in modern philosophy.

52. See the *Apologia della dotta ignoranza,* p. 427.

53. *Dialogue on Genesis* (Wertz, 213).

54. *L'idiota* III: *La mente,* p. 473.

55. *The Theological Complement* (Wertz, 289).

56. *On the Gift of the Father of Lights* (Wertz, 194–98).

57. *L'Idiota* III: *La mente,* p. 501.

58. *L'apologia della dotta ignoranza,* p. 406.

59. See *On Searching for God,* passim (Wertz, 155–71).

60. *On the Filiation of God* (Wertz, 186–87).

61. See *Il complemento teologico,* p. 609: "If we look closely, we possess no other certitude in our knowledge except the certitude of mathematics, and this offers itself as an

enigma for our investigation of the works of God. If the wise say something important, they base it on the images of mathematics. If we desire to see obscurely the theological truth maintained by Christians, namely, that God is One and Three, we can always have recourse to the principles of mathematics" [passage not found in Wertz' translation. —Tr.]. See also *Il potere-è,* pp. 770–71.

62. See *La dotta ignoranza* 11–12 (pp. 72–75); *On Equality* (Wertz, 380–85); *Compendium* (Wertz, 548–54).

63. See *Il potere-è,* pp. 771–72.

64. See *On Beryllus* (Wertz, 301–3).

65. See *The Theological Complement* 13 (Wertz, 298).

66. See ibid., sections 3ff. (Wertz, 276ff.).

67. The infinite circulation is the coincidence of opposites. See ibid., no. 13: "In everything this side of the infinite, the measure and the measured differ according to more or less. In God, however, they coincide. The coincidence of opposites is therefore like the periphery of the infinite circle. The distance of opposites is as the periphery of the finite polygon. Therefore, in theological figures the complement of that which can be known is to know this, namely, that in the infinite the difference of the measure and the measured is in God equality or coincidence. . . . Complement in theology is therefore to behold the origin, in which what are opposites in the finite are coincidence. . . . Therefore, the opposition is the coincidence of the opposites and equality. We say that God, who is everything in everything, is the opposition of opposites. And that is nothing other than to say of Him, that He is the origin enfolding the absolute coincidence or the infinite equality" (Wertz, 298).

68. See *La dotta ignoranza* I, 21 (p. 92); *La vision di Dio* 3.

69. See *The Theological Complement* 24.

70. See *La dotta ignoranza* II, 7 (p. 127).

71. See the *Apologia della dotta ignoranza,* p. 422.

72. Nicholas' philosophy of mathematics deserves separate treatment.

73. *Apologia della dotta ignoranza,* p. 403.

74. *Le congetture* I, 9 (p. 223). [Not found in Wertz. —Tr.].

75. See K. Kremer, "Nikolaus Cusanus, 'Jede Frage über Gott, setzt das gefragte voraus' *(omnis quaestio de Deo praesupponit quaesitum),"* in *Concordia discors. Studi su Niccolò Cusano e l'umanesimo europeo offerti a G. Santinello,* ed. G. Piaia (Padua, 1993) 145–80.

76. See also *The Theological Complement* 4 (Wertz, 279–81).

77. See *L'idiota* I: *La sapienza* I, pp. 438–39.

78. *L'idiota* III: *La mente,* p. 445.

79. Ibid. The theme of the presupposition that gives theological sufficiency is taken up again by Nicholas in his dialogue *On the Peace of Faith (De pace fidei),* where it is used to maintain that all religions presuppose a single God.

Chapter 4

1. For the course of the work and debates of the Council of Ferrara-Florence I rely chiefly on J. Gill, *The Council of Florence* (Cambridge, 1950).

2. Gill, *The Council of Florence,* 349.

3. On this subject I refer to these recent collective works: *Christian Unity: The Council of Florence (1438/39–1989),* ed. G. Alberigo (Leuven, 1991); *Firenze e il Concilio del 1439,* Convegno di studi (Firenze, 29 novembre–2 dicembre 1989), ed. P. Viti (Florence, 1994).

4. For the life of Cesarini and for bibliography, see A. A. Strnad and K. Walsh, "Cesarini, Giuliano," *DBI* 24 (Rome, 1980) 188–95.

5. On Bessarion, metropolitan of Nicaea and later a cardinal of the Roman Church, see below, pp. 191–213 passim. On the Byzantine theologians of the first half of the fifteenth century (especially Plethon and Scholarius) see also vol. II of this *History,* part six.

6. On Torquemada, see above, pp. 121–23, and below, pp. 260, 282–83.

7. V. L. Perot, "Marc Eugenicos," *DTC* 9 (Paris, 1927) cols. 1968–86; and see the index in Gill, *The Council of Florence.*

8. On Andrew Chrysoberges and his brothers see G. Mercati, *Notizie di Procoro e Demetrio Cidone, Manuele Caleca e Teodoro Melitoneta e altri appunti per la storia della letteratura e della teologia bizantina del secolo XV* (Vatican City, 1931); P. R. Loernertz, "Théodore et André Chrysobergès," *AFP* 9 (1939) 1–61; M. H. Laurent, "L'activité d'André Chrysobergès," *Echos d'Orient* 1935, 414–43. But see also P. R. Loernertz, "Les Missions dominicaines en Orient," *AFP* 2 (1932) 13–14; G. Cammelli, *I dotti bizantini e le origini dell'umanesimo. I. Manuele Crisolora* (Florence, 1941) 37; and see the index in Gill, *The Council of Florence.*

9. See J. G. Sbaraglia, *Supplementum et castigatio ad scriptores trium ordinum S. Francisci* II (Rome, 1921) 192–93; C. Cenci, "Ludovico da Pirano et la sua attività letteraria," in *Arte e cultura al Santo di Padova fra il XIII e il XX secolo* (Vicenza, 1976) 265–78; C. Vasoli, "Arte della memoria e predicazione," *Medioevo e Rinascimento* 3 (1989) 310–21 at 316–38.

10. For the works of John of Montenero and the relevant bibliography see Th. Käppeli, *Scriptores Ordinis Praedicatorum Medii Aevi* II (Rome, 1975) 484–87; but see also the index in Gill, *The Council of Florence.*

11. See Sbaraglia, *Supplementum* II, 357.

12. See G. Mercati, *Scritti d'Isidoro il cardinale ruteno* (Rome, 1926).

13. On George Gemistus Plethon see also section 3 of this chapter.

14. See L. Pettit, X. A. Sidéridés, and M. Jugie, "Scholarios (Georges)," *DTC* 14 (Paris, 1941) cols. 1521–70; and see the index in Gill, *The Council of Florence.*

15. See above, chapter 1, section 9.

16. See M. H. Laurent, "Dositée de Monembasie," *DHGE* 14 (Paris, 1960) cols. 700–1.

17. On Syropoulos, his activity at the council, and his work as "chronicler," see the index in Gill, *The Council of Florence.*

18. On this subject see Volume II, part VI, chapter 12.

19. For Manetti I shall cite only works dealing more strictly with his religious ideas: S. Garofalo, "Gli umanisti italiani del secolo XV e la Bibbia," *Biblica* 27 (1946) 338–75; A. De Petris, "L'*Adversus Judaeos et Gentes* di Giannozzo Manetti," *Rinascimento,* Ser. 2, 16 (1976) 193–205; idem, "Giannozzo Manetti and his 'consolatoria,'" *BibHumRen* 41 (1979) 259–71; L. Onofri, "Sacralità, immaginazione e proposte politiche: la vita de Niccolò V di Giannozzo Manetti," *Humanistica lovaniensia* 27 (1979) 27–77; G. Fioravanti, "L'apologetica anti-giudaica di Giannozzo Manetti," *Rinascimento,* Ser. 2, 23 (1983) 3–32; R. Fubini, "L'ebraismo nei riflessi della cultural umanistica," *Medioevo e Rinascimento* 2 (1988) 283–324; M. Martelli, "Profilo ideologico di Giannozzo Manetti," *Studi italiani* 1 (1989) 3–41.

20. Vespasian of Bisticci, "Giannozzo Manetti," in his *Le vite,* ed. A. Greco, I (Florence, 1970) 485–538.

21. See Fioravanti, "L'apologetica anti-giudaica," 8.

22. Giannozzo Manetti, *De dignitate et excellentia hominis,* ed. E. R. Leonard (Padua, 1975). But see also idem, *Apologeticus,* ed. A. De Petris (Rome, 1962).

23. *De dignitate et excellentia hominis,* 77–78.

24. For Palmieri, too, I shall cite only G. Boffito, "L'eresia di Matteo Palmieri," *GSLI* 37 (1901) 1–69; F. Sarri, "La religione di Matteo Palmieri," *La Città di vita* 1 (1946) 301–23; A. Buck, "Matteo Palmieri (1406–1475) als Repräsentant des Florentiner Bürger-Humanismus," *ArchKult* 47 (1965) 77–95; C. Finzi, *Matteo Palmieri dalla "Vita civile" alla "Città di vita"* (Milan, 1984); G. M. Carpetto, *The Humanism of Matteo Palmieri* (Rome, 1984); M. Martelli, "Palmeriana," *Interpres* 5 (1983–84) 277–301.

25. Matthew Palmieri, *La "Vita civile,"* ed. crit. G. Belloni (Florence, 1982).

26. Ibid., 200–8.

27. For the *Citta di vita* it is still necessary to use the not very good edition of M. Rooke of Northampton, Mass. (2 vols.; Paris, 1927).

28. Ibid., I, ch. 5, tercets 43–45 (p. 24).

29. Ibid., I, ch. 2, tercets 39–42 (p. 9).

30. See especially R. Masai, and F. Masai, "L'oeuvre de Georges Gémiste Pléthon," *Bulletin de l'Académie Royale de Belgique, Cl. de lettres* 101 (1954) 536–55; F. Masai, *Pléthon et le platonisme de Mistra* (Paris, 1956); E. Garin, *Studi sul platonismo medioevale* (Florence, 1958) 155–90; C. M. Woodhouse, *George Gemistos Plethon: The Last of the Hellenes* (Oxford, 1986).

31. In George Gemistus Plethon, *Traité des Lois ou recueil des fragments, en partie inédits de cet ouvrage* (Paris, 1958; reprinted: Paris, 1982).

32. Ibid., 26–36.

33. See George of Trebizond, *Comparationes philosophorum Aristotelis et Platonis* (Venice, 1523; reprinted: Frankfurt, 1965) f. V 6v.

34. The work was widely circulated in manuscript; a Latin paraphrase of it was published in Venice in 1540 and immediately reprinted in Paris; then the Greek text and a Latin translation were published together at Basel in 1574. I am following the text in PG 160:881–934.

35. See George Scholarius, *Sul dubbi di Pletone dinanzi a Aristotele,* in *Oeuvres complètes de Gennade Scholarios,* ed. L. Petit and others (Paris, 1928–36) IV, 1–116.

36. See J. Monfasani, *George of Trebizond: A Biography and a Study of His Rhetoric and Logic* (Leiden, 1976); idem, *Collectanea Trapezuntiana: Texts, Documents, and Bibliographies of George of Trebizond* (Binghamton, N.Y., 1984).

37. See above, note 33.

38. On Bessarion (and for a critical edition of the Greek and Latin texts of the *In calumniatorem Platonis*) see L. Mohler, *Kardinal Bessarion als Theologe, Humanist und Staatsman* (Paderborn, 1923–42; the edition is in vol. II). But see also L. Labovsky, "Bessarione, Giovanni Basilio," *DBI* 9 (Rome, 1967) 686–96 (also published separately: Rome, 1968); idem, *Bessarion's Library and the Biblioteca Marciana* (Rome, 1979); and the collective work *Miscellanea marciana di studi bessarionei* (Padua, 1976).

39. A very extensive bibliography on Ficino is provided in P. O. Kristeller, *Marsilio Ficino and His Work After Five Hundred Years* (Florence, 1987), updated in idem, *Il pensiero filosofico de Marsilio Ficino* (Florence, 1988²) 471–76. But Kristeller's *Supplemento ficiniano* (2 vols.; Florence, 1937; reprinted: Florence, 1973) must still be consulted.

40. See I. Klutstein, *Marsilio Ficino et la théologie ancienne. Oracles Chaldaïques, Hymnes Orphiques, Hymnes de Proclus* (Florence, 1987).

41. See ibid., 3–18.

42. Mercurius Trismegistus, *Pimander* (Treviso, 1471). See Kristeller, *Marsilio Ficino and His Work,* 112–13.

43. On this subject I refer the reader to what I have written in *Filosofia e religione nella cultura del Rinascimento* (Naples, 1988) 19–73.

44. Marsilius Ficino, *Opera* (Basel, 1576; reprinted: Turin, 1983²) ff. 1–77. For the various editions see Kristeller, *Marsilio Ficino and His Work,* 113, with details.

45. See C. Vasoli, "Per le fonti del *De christiana religione* di Marsilio Ficino," *Rinascimento,* Ser. 2, 28 (1988) 135–233.

46. *Opera,* f. 4.

47. See ibid., f. 1.

48. Ibid., f. 1836.

49. Ibid., f. 25. For the Italian text I use the translation made by Ficino himself, *Libro di Marsilio Ficino della Cristiana religione* (Florence, 1475).

50. *Opera,* f. 899.

51. Ibid., ff. 78–414.

52. Ibid., ff. 1537–38.

53. I cite Ficino's own vernacular translation of the *De amore: El Libro dell'Amore,* crit. ed. S. Niccoli (Florence, 1987) 67–68.

54. For the *Libri de vita* (of which *De vita coelitus comparanda* is the third) see now the edition by C. V. Kaske and J. R. Clark (Binghamton, N.Y., 1989).

55. On the historical importance of Ficino's teachings see E. Garin, *Umanisti, artisti, scienziati. Studi sul Rinacimento italiano* (Rome, 1989) 115–24.

56. On Landino see especially R. Cardini, *La critica del Landino* (Florence, 1973); and Christopher Landino, *Scritti critici e teorici,* ed. R. Cadino (2 vols.; Rome, 1974).

57. For the *De anima* I use the edition by A. Paoli and G. Gentile in *Annali delle Università toscane* 34 (1915) 1–50; new series, 1 (1916) fasc. 2 and 3.

58. Christopher Landino, *Disputationes Camaldulenses,* ed. P. Lohe (Florence, 1980).

59. See E. Garin, *Giovanni Pico della Morandola* (Mirandola-Parma, 1963), and the collective work, *L'opera e il pensiero di Giovanni Pico della Mirandola nella storia dell'Umanesimo* (2 vols.; Florence, 1965).

60. I am following the edition by E. Garin in his *Prosatori latini del Quattrocento* (Naples-Milan, 1952) 793–863 (along with Barbarus' reply).

61. For information on the composition and publication of this work see John Pico della Mirandola, *De hominis dignitate. Heptaplus. De Ente et Uno,* ed. E. Garin (Florence, 1942) 10–13. The work itself is on pp. 459–581.

62. *De hominis dignitate,* ed. Garin, 101–65.

63. Ibid., 106.

64. Ibid., 102.

65. Ibid., 167–83.

66. Ibid., 385–441.

67. *De ente et uno,* ed. Garin, 408–10.

68. See John Pico della Mirandola, *Disputationes adversus astrologiam divinatricem,* ed. E. Garin (2 vols.; Florence, 1946–52).

69. See E. Garin, *Lo zodiaco della vita* (Rome-Bari, 1976) 95–125.

70. For the *Oraculum de novo saeculo,* see the text in the incunabulum printed in Florence on May 8, 1497, by Lorenzo de'Morgiani; and see C. Vasoli, *I miti e gli astri* (Naples, 1977) 51–72.

Chapter 5

1. M. Menéndez Pelayo, *Antología de poetas líricos castellanos* II (Madrid, 1944) 8–12.

2. See A. García y García and I. Vázquez Janeiro, "La biblioteca del arzobispo de Santiago de Compostela, Bernardo II (+ 1240)," *Antonianum* 61 (1986) 540–68.

3. See I. Vázquez Janeiro, "I tabù della storia dello scotismo," *Antonianum* 59 (1984) 337–92.

4. See J. Goñi Gaztambide, "Fray Juan de Monzón OP: su vida y sus obras (c. 1340–c. 1412)," *BolSocCastellCult* 56 (1980) 506–23.

5. See K. Reinhardt and H. Santiago Otero, *Biblioteca bíblica ibérica medieval* (Mediaevalia et humanistica 1; Madrid, 1986) 181–85.

6. See the *Cancionero de Juan Alfonso de Baena,* critical ed. J. M. Azáceta (Madrid, 1966); see the indexes under "Muxena" and "Valencia." See also W.-D. Lange, *El fraile trovador. Zeit, Leben und Werk des Diego de Valencia de León (1350?–1412?)* (Frankfurt a. M., 1971); I. Vázquez Janeiro, *Tratados castellanos sobre la predestinación y sobre la Trinidad u la Encarnación del maestro fray Diego de Valencia OFM (siglo XV). Identificación de su autoría y edición crítica* (Madrid, 1984).

7. Ed. J. M. Azáceta (note 6, above).

8. See I. Vázquez Janeiro, "Una colección de documentos del concilio de Constanza," *RevEspDerCan* 46 (1989) 115–26.

9. Ed. in Dietrich von Niem, *Dialog über Union und Reform der Kirche 1410 . . . mit einer zweiten Fassung aus dem Jahre 1415,* ed. H. Heimpel (Leipzig-Berlin, 1933) 1–86.

10. Ed. in Vázquez Janeiro, *Tratados castellanos* (note 6, above) 101–57.

11. Ed. ibid., 159–73.

12. Ed. in P. Alva y Astorga, *Monumenta antiqua seraphica pro Immaculata Conceptione Virginis Mariae* (Louvain, 1665) 441–63.

13. Ed. (as anonymous) in J. Perarnau Espelt, "Dos tratados 'espirituales' de Arnau de Vilanova en traducción castellana antigua," *AnthAn* 22–23 (1975–76) 512–29.

14. Ed. (as anonymous) in idem, "Politica, lul.lisme i Cisma d'Occident," *ArxTextCatAnt* 3 (1984) 101–46.

15. Ed. (as anonymous) J. J. Satorre, *La novela moral de Gracián (Un texto inédito del siglo XV)* (Palma de Mallorca, 1986). On the author, see I. Vázquez Janeiro, "'Gracián.' Un 'Felix' castigliano del secolo XV. Una ricerca sull'innominato autore," *Annali dell'Istituto Universitario Orientale. Sezione Romana* 34 (1992) 293–337.

16. See Reinhardt and Santiago Otero, *Biblioteca* (note 5, above) 303–12.

17. See ibid., 101–3.

18. See F. Ehrle, "Die kirchenrechtlichen Schriften Peters von Luna (Benedikt XIII)," *ArchLitKirchMA* 7 (1900) 515–75; J. Perarnau i Espelt, "Els inventaris de la Biblioteca papal de Peníscola a la mort de Benet XIII," *ArxTextCatAnt* 6 (1987) 7–295.

19. See J. D. Madurell i Marimón, "Mestre Felip de Malla," *Boletín de la Real Academia de Buenas Letras de Barcelona* 30 (1963–64) 499–626.

20. See L. Serrano, *Los conversos D. Pablo de Santa María y D. Alonso de Cartagena* (Madrid, 1942); Reinhardt and Santiago Otero, *Biblioteca* (note 5, above) 240–49.

21. See I. M. Isbicki, "A Collection of Ecclesiological Manuscripts in the Vatican Library: Vat. lat. 4106–4193," *MiscBib ApVat* 4 (1990) 100.

22. Raymond Sibiuda, *Theologia naturalis sey liber creaturarum. Faksimile Nachdruck*

der Ausgabe Sulzbach 1852. Mit literargeschichtlicher Einführung und kritischer Edition des Prologs und des Titulus I von Friedrich Stegmüller (Stuttgart–Bad Cannstatt, 1966). For the manuscript tradition see J. de Puig i Oliver, "Els manscrits del *Liber creaturarum* de Ramon Subiuda: Un inventari tothora obert," *ArxTextCatAnt* 10 (1991) 303–19. For a survey of studies of Sibiuda see idem, "Deu anys d'estudis sobre Ramon Sibiuda," ibid., 1 (1982) 277–89; idem, "Valoració crítica del pensament de Sibiuda al llarg del temps," ibid., 9 (1990) 277–368; idem, "Complements . . . ," ibid., 10 (1991) 358–90.

23. For the most complete list of his *opera omnia* see H. Zamora "Un opúsculo bíblico del Tostado desconicido," *Verdad y Vida* 31 (1973) 269–315; for the manuscripts of works on biblical exegesis see Reinhardt and Santiago Otero, *Biblioteca* (note 5, above) 64–79.

24. See Beltrán de Heredia, *Cartulario* I, 318–33; Reinhardt and Santiago Otero, *Biblioteca,* 59–62.

25. See B. Hernández Montes, "Obras de Juan de Segovia," *Repertorio de Historia de las Ciencias eclesiásticas en España* 6 (1977) 267–347; idem, *Biblioteca de Juan de Segovia. Edición y comentario de su escritura de donación* (Madrid, 1984); I. Vázquez Janeiro, "En torno a la Biblioteca de Juan de Segovia," *Antonianum* 60 (1985) 670–88.

26. See Th. Käppeli, *Scriptores Ordinis Praedicatorum Medii Aevi* III (Rome, 1980) 24–42.

27. See L. Gómez Canedo, *Don Juan de Carbajal* (Madrid, 1947).

28. See J. M. Laboa, *Rodrigo Sánchez de Arevalo, alcaide de Sant'Angelo* (Madrid, 1973). On Sánchez' political theology see above, pp. 120–23.

29. See K. Reinhardt and H. Santiago Otero, *Biblioteca* (note 5, above) 224–25.

30. See R. Hernández, *La confesión y las indulgencias. Prereforma y tradición* (Salamanca, 1978).

31. See K. Reinhardt, *Pedro de Osma y su Comentario al Símbolo "Quicumque"* (Madrid, 1977); H. Santiago Otero and K. Reinhardt, *Pedro Martínez de Osma y el método teológico. Edición de algunos escritos inéditos* (Madrid-Soria, 1987). See below, p. 274.

32. See K. Reinhardt and H. Santiago Otero, *Biblioteca* (note 5, above) 172–79.

33. See ibid., 63–64.

34. See J. Vicens Vives, *Aproximación a la Historia de España* (Barcelona, 1952); A. Castro, *La realidad histórica de España* (Mexico City, 1954); J. A. Maravall, *El concepto de España en la Edad Media* (Madrid, 1954); C. Sánchez Albornoz, *España, un enigma histórico* (Barcelona, 1956); J. Orlandis, "Sobre el origen de España y de la cultura cristiana española," in *Iglesia española y evangelización* (Toledo, 1993) 95–107.

35. Published in Perarnau Espelt, "Dos tratados" (note 13, above) 554–602.

36. A. Amore, "La predicazione del B. Matteo d'Agrigento a Barcellona e Valenza," *AFP* 49 (1956) 255–335; B. Matthaei Agrigentini, OFM, *Sermones varii,* ed. A. Amore (Rome, 1960).

37. The petition, still unpublished, is dated August 8, 1489; see Archivio Segreto Vaticano, Reg. Suppl. 907, f. 55v.

38. See I. Vázquez Janeiro, *San Bernardino de Sena y España, Notas para una historia de la predicación en la Castilla del signo XV* (Madrid, 1980).

39. See M. de Epalza, *La Tuhfa, autobiografía y polémica islamica contra el Cristianismo de Abdallah al-Taryuman (Fray Anselmo de Turmeda)* (Rome, 1971).

40. See J. Goñi Gatzambide, "Durango, Herejes de," *Diccionario de Historia eclesiástica de España,* Suplemento I (Madrid, 1987) cols. 264–67, with bibliography.

41. Archivio Segreto Vaticano, Reg. Lat. 470, f. 144rv.

42. See J. Goñi Gaztambide, *Los españoles en el concilio de Constanza. Notas biográficas* (Madrid, 1966).

43. See I. Vázquez Janeiro, "San Ildefonso y los concilios visigóticos vistos desde el siglo, XV," *EstMar* 55 (1990) 309–48.

44. [The translation of the errors of Huss and Wyclif, and the passages from the *Tomus Leonis* and the Three Chapters (below) are taken from *Decrees of the Ecumenical Councils,* ed. N. P. Tanner (London and Washington, D.C., 1990), vol. 1. —Tr.]

45. See I. Vázquez Janeiro, "*Nominetur ille doctor.* El último deseo incumplido de Juan Hus en Constanza," *Antonianum* 66 (1991) 265–300.

46. See G. Hofmann, *Papato, conciliarismo, patriarcato (1438–39)* (Rome, 1940); G. Vera-Fajardo, *La eclesiología de Juan de Segovia en la crisis conciliar* (Vitoria, 1968). On Torquemada's political theology see above, pp. 120–23.

47. See H. Ameri, *Doctrina theologorum de Immaculata B. V. Mariae Conceptione tempore concilii Basiliensis* (Rome, 1954); C. Pozo, "Culto mariano y 'definición' de la Inmaculada en el concilio de Basilea," *Scripta de Maria* 3 (1980) 609–31.

48. See I. Vázquez Janeiro, "El encomio mariano *Cunctas haereses sola interemisti.* Origen de su sentido inmaculista," *Antonianum* 66 (1991) 497–531.

49. The petitions, accompanied at times by doctrinal treatises, were sent to Emperor Sigismund; the last dates from January 1432. All the texts, preserved as anonymous, were recently published by Perarnau Espelt, "Politica, lul.isme . . ." (above, note 14) 94–191.

Chapter 6

1. Nicholas of Clamanges, *Expositio super Ysayam,* in A. Coville, *Le Traité de la ruine de l'église de Nicolas de Clamanges et la traduction française de 1564* (Paris, 1936) 103.

2. Ibid., 101.

3. See below, pp. 333–34.

4. Texts in C. Du Plessis D'Argentré, *Collectio judiciorum de novis erroribus, qui ab initio duodecimi saeculi usque ad annum 1713 in Ecclesia proscripti sunt et notati* I/2 (Paris, 1724) 258–84.

5. See ibid., 308–18.

6. See ibid., 323–24.

7. Francis Petrarch, *Rerum Senilium libri* IX, in *Opera* (Basel, 1554) f. 937.

8. John of Montreuil, *Epistola* 60, in E. Martène, *Veterum Scriptorum et Monumentorum . . . Amplissima Collectio* II (Paris, 1724) cols. 1428–29.

9. John Gerson, letter of September 29, 1392, in E. Ornato, *Jean Muret et ses amis Nicolas de Clamanges et Jean de Montreuil* (Geneva, 1969) 149.

10. John Gerson, *De sensu litterali Sacrae Scripturae,* in *Oeuvres Complètes,* ed. P. Glorieux, III (Paris, 1962) 334.

11. John Gerson, *[Contre le Roman de la Rose],* in *Oeuvres Complètes* VII/1 (Paris, 1966) 301–16.

12. John of Montreuil, *Epistole* 54 and 56, in Martène (note 8, above) cols. 1419–22.

13. See E. Langlois, "Le traité de Gerson contre le Roman de la Rose," *Romania* 45 (1918–19) 223–48. On Wimpfeling, see below, pp. 34–47.

14. There he wrote a *De laude et fructu vitae solitariae.*

15. Nicholas of Clamanges, *Liber de studio theologico ad Johannem de Pedemontio Baccalarium in Theologia, eruditum ac discretum virum,* in L. D'Achery, *Spicilegium sive Collectio veterum aliquot scriptorum* I (Paris, 1723) 473–80.

16. John Gerson, *Epistola* 3 (April 1, 1400), in *Oeuvres Complètes* II (Paris, 1960) 23–28.

17. E. Gilson, *The Spirit of Mediaeval Philosophy,* trans. A. H. C. Downs (New York, 1940) 213.

18. See A. Combes, *Essai sur la critique de Ruysbroeck par Gerson* (4 vols.; Paris, 1945–72).

19. *Imitatio Christi. Le livre de l'Internelle Consolacion. Première version française de l'Imitation de Jésus-Christ,* ed. L. Moland and Ch. d'Héricault (Paris, 1856).

20. *Épître adressée à Robert Gaguin le 1ᵉʳ Janvier 1472 par Guillaume Fichet sur l'introduction de l'imprimerie à Paris* (Paris, 1889); the letter served as an introduction to the Basel edition of the *Orthographia.*

21. Edited by P. O. Kristeller, "An Unknown Humanist Sermon on St. Stephen by Guillaume Fichet," in *Mélanges Eugène Tisserant* IV (Studi e Testi 236; Vatican City, 1964) 459–97.

22. He saw to the publication of the *Ethica Nicomachea* in Argiropulo's translation (Paris, 1493) and collaborated with Thomas Bricot on the publication of Buridan's commentaries.

23. *Septem Psalmi poenitentiales metrice compilati;* after a first "pirated" edition, the author saw to its publication at Antwerp in 1501 and at Paris in 1505 and 1510.

24. *Epistolae Beati Pauli apostoli, et Beatissimorum Jacobi, Petri, Joannis et Judae Epistolae canonicae; cum argumentis delphicis et scholiis seu postillis ascensianis* (Paris, 1503).

25. The work, which was published at the end of 1488 and the beginning of 1489, went through many printings.

26. *De mundissima virginis Mariae conceptione. . . . Cum commentario Caroli Fernandi viri eloquentis* [Paris, 1489?].

27. Robert Gaguin, *Tractatus de puritate conceptionis* ([Paris], 1505) f. a iiiʳ.

28. Ibid., f. a vᵛ.

29. Giles of Delft tested himself on the work of Peter Lombard (*Conclusiones in Sententias magistri,* Louvain, 1519), studied Buridan, and saw to the publication of the *Quaestiones morales* of Martin Lemaistre.

30. John Pico della Mirandola, letter to Ermalaus Barbarus, in his *Omnia Opera* (Paris, 1517) f. V iiiᵛ.

31. Robert Gaguin to Erasmus, letter of October, 1495, in *Opus Epistolarum,* ed. P. S. Allen, I (1906), no. 46, p. 153, lines 1–4. On Erasmus see below, pp. 351–62.

32. See William Briçonnet and Marguerite of Angoulême, *Correspondance,* ed. C. Martineau, M. Veissière, and H. Heller (2 vols.; Travaux d'humanisme et renaissance 141 and 173; Geneva, 1975–79).

33. Documents in A. L. Herminjard, *Correspondance des réformateurs* I (Geneva, 1866) no. 77, pp. 153–55, and no. 78, pp. 156–58.

34. Ibid., no. 81, pp. 171–72.

35. Jacques Lefèvre, letter to Farel, July 6, 1524, in Herminjard, *Correspondance* I, no. 103, pp. 220–21.

36. E. Amann, "Lefèvre d'Étaples, Jacques," *DTC* 9 (Paris, 1926) col. 137.

37. In the first edition the book has no title; it contains the fourteen canonical letters, the letter to the Laodiceans, the letters to Seneca, fourteen books of commentaries, and ends with the *Passio Petri* and the *Passio Pauli* of Linus. The dedication to Briçonnet is followed by an *Apologia* in which Lefèvre explains why he thinks that the Vulgate is not a work of St. Jerome.

38. Again, the work has no title. It was printed in June 1522, by Simon de Collines, and the preface was dated 1521. Each chapter of the gospels is followed by brief notes "about the letter," notes a good deal shorter than those on the Pauline letters, and by a commentary.

39. Published at Basel in 1527.

40. James Lefèvre, dedication to John of Selve of the *Psalterium David, argumentis adjectis* (1524), in G. Bedouelle, *Lefèvre d'Étaples et l'intelligence des Écritures* (Geneva, 1976) 213.

41. James Lefèvre, dedication to Briçonnet of the *Commentarii in Pauli Epistolas,* f. a iᵛ.

42. Ibid. To the lines cited he added: "I would like to urge warmly all who will read the letters of Paul contained in this volume to pay attention not so much to Paul as to the grace of Paul and to the one who bestowed this grace. All the less, then, when they read commentaries, should they focus on the authors, who are human beings, assuming that they realize the presence of spiritual life and a true nourishment for the soul. They should rather understand the fruitfulness, the power that comes from on high; they should acknowledge the real author of these [letters] and then follow him with all the purity and devotion of which they are capable. Only by acting in this way can they draw near to him who does all in all."

43. Ibid.

44. James Lefèvre, dedication to Briçonnet of the *Quincuplex Psalterium* (ed. 1513) f. a. iiʳ.

45. James Lefèvre, *Commentarius Lucae,* 24, 202, f. 256ᵛ.

46. Ibid., 204, f. 258ᵛ.

47. James Lefèvre, dedication to John of Selve of the *Psalterium David,* in Bedouelle, *Lefèvre d'Étaples* (note 40, above) 215.

48. See H. De Lubac, *Exégèse médiévale. Les quatre sens de l'écriture,* II/2 (Paris, 1964) 413.

49. Preface to *Accurata recognitio trium voluminum operum clarissimi Patris Nicolai Cusae* ([Paris], 1514) f. aa. iiᵛ.

50. The concept is borrowed from Pseudo-Dionysius; see Bedouelle, *Lefèvre d'Étaples,* 227–30.

51. These are the main counts to be read in the solemn condemnation by the Sorbonne on November 6, 1525; see the preface by M. A. Screech to *Epistres et évangiles pour les cinquante et deux semaines de l'an* (Geneva, 1964) 41–51.

52. James Lefèvre, *Commentarius in Evangelium Matthaei* 11, 103, f. 43ʳ.

53. Idem, *Commentarius in Evangelium Ioannis* 1, 12, f. 263ᵛ.

54. Idem, *Commentarius in Epistolam ad Romanos* 3, f. 72ʳ.

55. Erasmus of Rotterdam, *Apologia in Fabrum,* in *Opera,* ed. J. Le Clerc (Leiden, 1703–5) IX, 32BC–37E.

56. James Lefèvre, *De Maria Magdalena disceptatio* (Paris, 1518).

57. Idem, *De una ex tribus Maria* (Paris, 1518).

58. Josse Clichtove, *Disceptationis de Magdalena defensio* (Paris, 1519).

59. Idem, *De puritate conceptionis beatae Mariae Virginis libri duo. De dolore eiusdem sacrae Virginis in passione filii sui statione homilia. De assumptione ipsius gloriosae Virginis*

liber unus (Paris, 1513); *De laudibus sancti Ludovici regis Franciae. De laudibus sanctissimae virginis & martyris Ceciliae* (Paris, 1516); *De necessitate peccati Adae et de foelicitate culpae eiusdem apologetica disceptatio* (Paris, 1519); *De doctrina moriendi* (Paris, 1520); *De dignitate et excellentia annunciationis beatae Mariae Virginis. De benignitate et gratia visitationis eiusdem gloriosae Virginis* (Paris, 1520); *De laudibus trium antiquorum patrum, Joseph patriarchae, David regis, et Tobiae, trifidum opusculum* (Paris, 1533).

60. Idem, *De vita et moribus sacerdotum* (Paris, 1520).

61. Idem, *De veneratione sanctorum* (Paris, 1523).

Chapter 7

1. Thomas Netter, *Doctrinale antiquitatum*, Prologus (Venice: B. Blanciotti, 1757) I, col. 5.

2. Ibid., *De sacramentis* 109 (II [1758] col. 634).

3. Ibid., Prologus (I, 6): "I shall not, like Wyclif, found this teaching on empty philosophy and human wisdom, but on the word of God. I shall not, like Wyclif, erect a structure of novel concepts, but an instruction based on the teaching of the Church and of the holy Fathers of the very early tradition. My teaching is not my own but that of the one who sent me (John 7:16)."

4. Reginald Pecock, *Repressor* Iv, 8, ed. C. Babington (London, 1921) 323ff. On Valla see earlier, pp. 45–54.

5. Poggio Bracciolini, letter to Nicholas Niccoli, February 12, 1421, in *Lettere* I, ed. H. Harth (Florence, 1984) 34–35.

6. Bracciolini to the same, March 5, 1420; ibid., 8.

7. See A. Renaudet, *Erasme et l'Italie* (Geneva, 1954) 24–31.

8. Aldo Manutius, letter to Albert Pius of Carpi, which comes at the beginning of his edition of the ancient astronomers in 1499 (Hain, 1559), f. T i^v.

9. William Grocyn, letter to Aldo Manutius (August 27, 1499), which accompanies Linacre's Latin translation of the *Sphaera* of Proclus; ibid., T ii^r.

10. Thomas More, letter of March 29, 1518, to the University of Oxford, in St. Thomas More, *Selected Letters*, ed. E. F. Rogers (New Haven, 1961) 99.

11. Erasmus of Rotterdam, *Opus epistolarum*, ed. P. S. Allen (Oxford, 1906–58) I, 118, line 21.

12. Ibid., IV, 1211, lines 425–41.

13. John Colet, *Enarr. I Cor.*, ed. J. H. Lupton (London, 1874) 238–39: "But if they say, as they usually do, that the reading of pagan books helps to the understanding of the sacred writings, let them consider whether in fact they are not a very great obstacle to the purpose for which they are used; for when you act thus, you do not trust that you can understand the sacred writings with the aid of grace alone and prayer and with the help of Christ and faith; you think, instead, that you can do it by reason and the help of the pagans."

14. Ibid., 239: "Only those books are to be read which give the salutary taste of Christ, and in which Christ is set before us to be eaten. Those in which Christ is not present are a table of the demons. Do not become readers of the philosophers, companions of the demons. All truth is present on the pure and abundant table of the sacred writings."

15. John Colet, *In Eccl. Hier.,* ed. J. H. Lupton (London, 1867) 240.

16. John Colet, *Epistolae B. Pauli ad Romanos expositio litteralis,* ed. J. H. Lupton (London, 1876) 209.

17. Ibid., 251: "A wage is due those who do bodily work, but justification is given freely to those who believe. For it is through grace that human beings believe and through grace that believers are justified. But, apart from the justice that faith gives, the work of the flesh and the body is worthless in the spirit."

18. Ibid., 248.

19. John Colet, *In Eccl. Hier.,* 264–65.

20. The *Assertio* was published along with the works of Fisher at Würzburg in 1597; it is now available in a new edition by P. Fraenkel (Corpus Catholicorum 43; Münster, 1992).

21. That is how Luther described the city.

22. John Eck, *Chrysopassus praedestinationis* (1514), cited by M. Grabmann, *L'influsso di Alberto Magno sulla vita intellettuale del Medio Evo* (2nd Italian ed.; Rome, 1931) 118.

23. John Reuchlin, *De verbo mirifico* (Basel, 1494) f. a iii^r.

24. Thus Erasmus in a short biographical profile in his *Adagia* I, 4, 39, in *Opera,* ed. J. Le Clerc (Leiden [= Lugduni Batavorum; henceforth: LB] 1703–05) II, cols. 166–67.

25. Rudolf Agricola, *De formando studio* (Basel, 1553) 5–6.

26. Sebastian Brant collaborated on the edition of Petrarch that was published by Amerbach at Basel in 1496; he also translated the *De remediis,* with a preface of his own in verse: *Von der Artzney bayder Glück, des guten und widerwertigen* (Augsburg, 1532).

27. Baptist Spagnoli of Mantua (1448–1516) was more renowned beyond the Alps, especially among the followers of the *Devotio moderna,* than in Italy. James Wimpfeling saw to three editions of Baptist's *Bucolica* (1510, 1511, and 1517) and one of the *Fastorum libri* (1518). Brant published Baptist's *Opera* in three volumes at Paris in 1513. See E. Cotta, *Le edizioni delle opere del Mantovano* (Rome, 1960).

28. Wimpfeling wrote a preface for the edition of Pico's works that was published in Strasbourg in 1504.

29. See H. Kraume, *Die Gerson Übersetzung des Geiler von Kayserberg. Studien zum deutschsprachigen Gerson Rezeption* (Munich, 1980). Wimpfeling wrote a *De vita et miraculis Joannis Gerson* (Strasbourg, 1506).

30. John Geiler of Kaisersberg, *Navicula sive speculum fatuorum* (Strasbourg, 1511). See below, note 36.

31. This remark is by Wimpfeling, his biographer. James Wimpfeling and Beatus Rhenanus, *Das Leben des Johannes Geyler von Kayserberg,* ed. D. Martens and O. Herding (Munich, 1970) 58.

32. Ibid., 66–67.

33. It was perhaps no accident that the first edition of Baptist Mantovano's *Carmen contra poetas impudice loquentes* was published in Strasbourg in 1501.

34. In Erasmus, *Opus epistolarum* (note 11, above) I, 224.

35. *Sermones, partes VII* (Basel, 1494–95).

36. Sebastian Brant, *Das narren schyeff* (Nuremberg, 1494); Latin version, *Stultifera navis* (Basel, 1497), with the collaboration of James Locher.

37. *Der text des passions, oder lidens Christi* (Strasbourg, 1506).

38. *Concordantiae maiores Biblie* (Basel, 1496).

39. Of the books published during the fifteenth century about half were produced in Germany, but editions of the Bible were especially notable: we know of no less than fifty-

eight incunabula of the complete Latin Bible published in the German-speaking area (forty-one in Germany and seventeen in Basel alone); there was a further increase in these numbers in the next century.

40. James Hoogstraten (or Hochstraten) published a *Destructio Cabale seu cabalistica perfidia ab. J. Reuchlin jampridem in lucem edita* (Cologne, 1519), in which he points out the danger that lurks in any heed paid by Christians to Jewish culture.

41. *Correspondence de Martin Bucer* I (Leiden, 1979) 84–86, 100.

42. Willibald Pirckheimer, preface to his translation of Lucian's dialogue *Piscator* (Nuremberg, 1517) f. B iv^r: "If a theologian lacks rhetoric, I do not understand how he is able to proclaim the words of truth to the Christian people."

43. See his dispute with Oecolampadius on the doctrine of the Last Supper: *De vera Christi carne et vero eius sanguine, ad Joan. Oecolampadium responsio* (Nuremberg, 1526).

44. When the Poor Clares of Nuremberg, among whom his own sister Caritas, herself a woman of letters and faith, was living, saw themselves denied a choice of confessors, Pirckheimer wrote to Melanchthon professing his acceptance of the doctrine of justification by grace through faith, provided this faith be translated into a consistent behavior springing from freedom that acknowledges even the option for monastic life to be the result of a free choice: see Willibald Pirckheimer, *Opera politica, philologica et epistolica* (Frankfurt, 1610) 374–75.

45. Ibid., 372–74.

46. Erasmus, *Opus epistolarum* (note 11, above) IV, 1006, lines 142–43.

47. Ibid., III, 798, lines 20–23.

48. Ibid., III, 701, lines 35–36.

49. Erasmus, *Apotheosis Capnionis. De incomparabili heroe Joanne Reuchlin in divorum numerum relato,* in the *Colloquia,* ed. in *Opera omnia* (Amsterdam-Oxford [henceforth: AO], 1969ff.) 1/3. 267–73.

50. Erasmus, *Opus epistolarum,* I, 108.

51. The discussion is to be found in several letters (I, 109–11); Erasmus later revised and developed it and published it separately (LB V, cols. 1263–94).

52. For example, the *Salterio* (1512) of Felix of Prato, an Augustinian, and those of Dominicans Augustine Giustiniani (1516) and Santi Pagnini (1521).

53. Erasmus, *Apologia de In principio erat Sermo* in LB IX, cols. 111–22.

54. See LB IX, partially republished in the corresponding section of the AO edition.

55. Erasmus, *Opus epistolarum,* III, 694, lines 17–19.

56. Erasmus, *Ratio seu methodus compendio perveniendi ad veram theologiam,* in LB V, cols. 75–138.

57. Ibid., col. 80F: "The profession of theology consists in affections more than in sophistries."

58. Ibid., col. 77B: "Let this be your first and only goal, let this be your desire, strive for this one thing: to be changed, to be exalted, to be inspired, to be transformed into what you are learning."

59. Ibid., col. 138B: "The theologian derives his name from the divine oracles, not from human opinions. And a large part of theology is inspiration, which is not given except to those of very pure morals."

60. Ibid., col. 76C.

61. Erasmus, *Apologia ad Latomum,* LB IX, col. 106B: "It makes no difference to me whether they [the other sciences] depend on theology or theology on them, provided it be admitted that without them it is impossible to know or discuss theology."

62. Erasmus, *Ratio seu methodus,* col. 118BC.

63. Ibid., col. 124E: "But special attention is to be given to allegories . . . for of these is made up the whole of the divine scriptures, through which eternal wisdom speaks obscurely to us."

64. Erasmus, *Opus epistolarum* II, 501.

65. LB IX, cols. 1215–48.

66. Erasmus, *Ratio seu methodus,* col. 103E.

67. AO I/3, 363–74.

68. Erasmus, *De libero arbitrio,* col. 1216C.

69. Martin Luther, *Assertio omnium articulorum per bullam Leonis X novissimam damnatorum* (1529), in *Werke* VIII (Weimar, 1897), especially no. XXXVI, pp. 142–49.

70. Luther, *Werke* XVIII (Weimar, 1908) 600–787.

71. Erasmus, *Hyperaspistes diatribae adversus Servum arbitrium,* LB X, cols. 1249–1536.

72. Erasmus, *De libero arbitrio,* col. 1246B.

73. Luther, *Dictata super Psalterium,* in *Werke* IV (Weimar, 1886) 153.

74. Erasmus, *Convivium religiosum,* in AO I/3, 251.

Chapter 8

1. I refer the reader chiefly to the now classic works of D. Cantimori: *Eretici italiani del Cinquecento* (Florence, 1939), especially 1–23; *Prospettive di storia ereticale italiana del Cinquecento* (Bari, 1960), especially 27–35; and *Umanesimo e religione del Rinascimento* (Turin, 1975).

2. See C. Vasoli, *Studi sulla cultura del Rinascimento* (Manduria, 1968) 180–240; O. Niccoli, *Profeti e popolo nell'Italia del Rinascimento* (Rome-Bari, 1987).

3. See E. Garin, *Il ritorno dei filosofi antichi* (Naples, 1983) 101–3.

4. See B. Nardi, *Saggi sull'aristotelismo padovano dal secolo XIV al XVI* (Florence, 1958); A. Poppi, *Introduzione all'aristotelismo padovano* (Padua, 1970); idem, "Il problema della filosofia morale nella scuola padovana del Rinascimento," in *Platon et Aristote à la Renaissance. XVIe Colloque international de Tours* (Paris, 1976) 105–46.

5. See above, chapter 1, section 10, on the Roman Academy.

6. See P. Paschini, "Tre illustri prelati del Rinascimento, Ermolao Barbaro, Andriano Castellesi, Giovanni Grimani," *Lateranum,* N.S. 23 (1957) 43–130; idem, "Una famiglia di curiali di Roma nel Quattrocento: i Cortesi," *RSCI* 11 (1957) 1–48; R. Ricciardi, "Cortesi (Cortesius, de Cortesiis), Paolo," *DBI* 29 (Rome, 1983) 766–70.

7. The *De cardinalatu* was published by S. Gimignano, probably in 1510.

8. Published at Rome in 1504.

9. See above, p. 224.

10. See Paschini, "Tre illustri prelati" (note 6, above); G. Fragnito, "Castellesi, Adriano," *DBI* 21 (Rome, 1978) 665–71.

11. The *De vera philosophia* was published at Bologna in 1507, but I am using the Roman edition of 1775.

12. See Ch. B. Schmitt, *Gianffrancesco Pico della Mirandola (1469–1533) and His Critique of Aristotle* (L'Aja, 1967).

13. I am following the edition in Ioannis Francisci Pici *Opera omnia* (Basel, 1557; reprinted: Hildesheim, 1969) 366–709.

14. In ibid., 710–1264.

15. See Vasoli, *Studi sulla cultura* (note 2, above) 206–14; idem, *Immagini umanistiche* (Naples, 1983) 380–82.

16. See Schmitt, *Gianfrancesco Pico della Mirandola* (note 12, above).

17. See the index in Nardi, *Saggo sull'aristotelismo* (note 4, above); the index in G. di Napoli, *L'immortalità dell'anima nel Rinascimento* (Turin, 1963); the index in A. Poppi, *Causalità e infinità nella scuola padovana dal 1480 al 1513* (Padua, 1964); E. P. Mahoney, "Niccoletto Vernia on the Soul and Immortality," in *Philosophy and Humanism: Renaissance Essays in Honor of Paul Oskar Kristeller* (Leiden, 1976) 144–63. On the University of Padua and its philosophical culture see *Aristotelismo veneto e scienza moderna* (Atti del 25° anno accademico del Centro di Studi per la storia della tradizione aristotelica nel Veneto), ed. L. Olivieri (2 vols.; Padua, 1983).

18. Nardi, *Saggi sull'aristotelismo,* 95–114.

19. The *Quaestiones de pluralitate intellectus* were published in Venice in 1499.

20. See above, p. 111.

21. See the index in Nardi, *Saggi sull'aristotelismo*; Di Napoli, *L'immortalità dell'anima* (note 17, above) 203–14; E. P. Mahoney, "Agostino Nifo's Early Views on Immortality," *Journal of the History of Philosophy* 7 (1970) 451–60, and "Agostino Nifo and St. Thomas Aquinas," *MemDom,* N.S. 7 (1976) 195–225.

22. Augustine Nifo, *De intellectu et daemonibus* (Padua, 1492).

23. See below, pp. 383–84.

24. See P. O. Kristeller, *Studies in Renaissance Thought and Letters* I (Rome, 1956, 1969²) 279–86; see the index in Nardi, *Saggo sull'aristotelismo;* P.O. Kristeller, *Eight Philosophers of the Italian Renaissance* (Stanford, 1964) 72–90; B. Nardi, *Studi su Pietro Pomponazzi* (Florence, 1965); A. Poppi, *Saggi sul pensiero inedito di Pietro Pomponazzi* (Padua, 1970); M. L. Pine, *Pietro Pomponazzi, Radical Philosopher of the Renaissance* (Padua, 1986).

25. The *Quaestio* was published in Bologna in 1514.

26. I am using the Bologna edition (1516) of the *De immortalitate,* but I also have before me the edition by G. Gentile (Messina, 1925).

27. For his activity in the Catholic reform movement and for his theological views see section 9, below, of this chapter.

28. The first of Contarini's *De immortalitate animae libri* appeared anonymously, along with the *Apologia magistri Petri Pomponatii* (Bologna, 1518). It was published separately and under the author's name at Venice in 1525. But I am following the complete text of the work as given in the *Opera* of Contarini (Venice, 1578).

29. On Ambrose Fiandino see E. Garin, *Storia della filosofia italiana* II (Turin, 1973³) 525–27.

30. Augustine Nifo, *De immortalitate animae libellus adversus Petrum Pomponacium* (Venice, 1518).

31. The *Defensorium magistri Petri Pomponatii* was published in Bologna in 1519.

32. For the *De naturalium effectuum admirandorum causis, sive de incantationibus* I am using the Basel edition of 1556.

33. For the *De fato, libero arbitrio et praedestinatione* I am following the critical edition of R. Lemay (Lugano, 1957).

34. See M. Pine, "Pietro Pomponazzi and the Scholastic Doctrine of Free Will," *RCSF* 28 (1973) 3–27.

35. Pomponazzi, *De fato . . .* (Lemay, 451–54).

36. See especially Nardi, *Saggio sull'aristotelismo* (note 4, above) 112, 323, 324, 424; idem, *Studi su Pietro Pomponazzi* (note 24, above) 113, 117, 280.

37. See J. F. Groner, *Kardinal Cajetanus. Eine Gestalt aus der Reformationszeit* (Fribourg-Louvain, 1951) (with bibliography). But see also *Rationalisme analogique et humanisme théologique. La culture de Thomas de Vio "Il Gaetano"* (Actes du Colloque de Naples [1–3 novembre 1990], ed. B. Pinchard and S. Ricci; Naples, 1993).

38. For this work I follow the Rome edition of 1513.

39. I am following the Cologne edition of 1514.

40. See below, section 4.

41. I am following the edition by M. H. Laurent (Turin, 1934).

42. See A. Goergen, *Die Lehre von der Analogie nach Kardinal Cajetanus und ihre Verhältnis zu Thomas von Aquin* (Speyer, 1938). But see also E. Gilson, "Cajétan et l'existence," *TijdFil* 15 (1953) 78–85.

43. For the *Commentaria in De anima Aristotelis* I am using the edition by M. H. Laurent (Rome, 1938).

44. See Di Napoli, *L'immortalità dell'anima* (note 17, above) 214–26.

45. The biblical commentaries of de Vio are contained in the *Opera omnia quotquot in Sacrae Scripturae expositiones reperiuntur* (5 vols.; Lyons, 1639).

46. I am reading these three in *Opuscula edita per fr. Bartholomaeum de Spina* (Venice, 1517).

47. The commentary accompanies the Leonine edition of the *Summa theologica* (Rome, 1888ff.).

48. For the *Annotataiones* I am using the Lyons edition of 1544.

49. See J. Vosté, *Thomas de Vio Cardinalis Cajetanus Sacrae Paginae Magister* (Rome, 1935).

50. See M. M. Gorce, "Silvestri, François," *DTC* 14 (Paris, 1941) cols. 2085–87.

51. For the *Commentaria* on the *Summa contra Gentiles* I am using the text that accompanies the Leonine edition (vols. 13–15) of this work of St. Thomas (Rome, 1918–30).

52. See the index in Di Napoli, *L'immortalità dell'anima* (note 17, above). But see also the index in C. Giacon, *La seconda Scolastica* I (Milan, 1944).

53. For this work I am using the Venice edition of 1525; but the work was also published at Rome in that same year.

54. The *Solutiones* (commonly known as *Solutiones rationum animae immortalitatem probantium*) were published together with the *Defensorium* of Pomponazzi; see also note 31, above.

55. The work was published at Venice in 1536.

56. The *Quaestiones subtilissimae* were likewise published in Venice in 1552. But see also the *Opera omnia* (I have before me the Lyons edition of 1574).

57. See Di Napoli, *L'immortalità dell'anima,* 325–38; E. Gilson, "Autour de Pomponazzi: Problématique de l'immortalité de l'âme en Italie au début du xvie siècle," *AHDLMA* 28 (1961) 163–279 at 259–77; and see the index in P. O. Kristeller, *Le thomisme et la pensée italienne de la Renaissance* (Paris, 1967).

58. For these writings and the other works of Javelli see M.-D. Chenu, "Javelli, en religion Chrysostome de Casale," *DTC* 8 (Paris, 1924) cols. 535–37; E. Garin, *Storia della filosofia italiana* II (Turin, 1978³) 566–67. See also C. H. Lohr, "Medieval Latin Aristotle Commentaries: Authors G-k," *Renaissance Quarterly* 30 (177) 681–741, especially 730–33.

59. For a rather full description of the events at the Lateran Council see L. von Pastor, *History of the Popes from the End of the Middle Ages* 8 (St. Louis, 1923) 384–413.

60. On Giles of Viterbo see below, section 6.

61. See Ch. B. Schmitt, "Gianfrancesco Pico della Mirandola and the Fifth Lateran Council," *ArchRef* 61 (1970) 161–78.

62. See F. Secret, *Les kabbalistes chrétiens de la Renaissance* (Paris, 1964); C. Vasoli, *Profezia e ragione. Studi sulla cultura del Cinquecento e del Seicento* (Naples, 1974) 129–403; and see the index in idem, *Filosofia e religione nella cultura del Rinascimento* (Naples, 1988).

63. I am following the Venice edition of 1525.

64. For the *Problemata* I am following the Venice edition of 1536. For *L'elegante poema* and the *Commento sopra il Poema* see the recent critical edition by J.-F. Maillard (Milan, 1991).

65. See Gregory Cortese, *Opera omnia* (Padua, 1774) I, 116. For Contarini's reaction see F. Drittich, *Regesten und Briefe des Cardinals Contarini* (Braunsberg, 1881) 271–77.

66. See A. Rotondò, "La censure ecclesiastica e la cultura," in *Storia d'Italia* V. *I documenti* (Turin, 1973) 1397–1492, especially 1436–40. On the intervention of Thomas Badia as censor, see Vasoli, *Profezia e ragione* (note 62, above) 224–25.

67. See especially J. W. O'Malley, *Giles of Viterbo on Church and Reform: A Study in Renaissance Thought* (Leiden, 1968); and *Egidio da Viterbo O.S.A. e il suo tempo*. Atti del V. Convegno dell'Istituto storico agostiniano (Roma-Viterbo, 20–23 ottobre 1982) (Rome, 1983).

68. On this subject see F. Secret, "Le symbolisme de la Kabbale chrétienne dans la *Schechinah* de Egidio da Viterbo," in *Umanesimo e simbolismo* (= *ArchFil*, 1958) 131–54; see also the index in idem, *Les kabbalistes chrétiens* (note 62, above).

69. The address is printed in J. D. Mansi, *Sacrorum conciliorum nova et amplissima collectio* 32 (Paris, 1902) cols. 669–76. But see also *Oratio habita post tertiam sacri Lateranensis concilii sessionem,* ed. C. O'Reilly, *Augustiniana* 22 (1972) 80–117.

70. See Giles of Viterbo, *De aurea aetate,* ed. J. W. O'Malley, *Traditio* 25 (1969) 265–338.

71. See the index in M. Reeves, *The Influence of Prophecy in the Later Middle Ages* (Oxford, 1969).

72. Some "excerpts" from the *Sententiae* are published in E. Massa, *I fondamenti metafisici della "dignitas hominis" e testi inediti di Egidio da Viterbo* (Turin, 1954) 54–110. I refer the reader to this work for the list of codices as well.

73. See Giles of Viterbo, *Scechina e Libellus de litteris hebraicis,* ed. F. Secret (2 vols.; Rome, 1969).

74. See *Libellus de litteris hebraicis* I, 35.

75. See *Scechina* I, 68–69.

76. See ibid., I, 223–24.

77. See ibid., I, 122–23, but also 96, 195, 207, and II, 273.

78. See ibid., II, 113: "Sacred history is a mirror in which you see the shadow of things divine; if you penetrate deeply into it, it is an enigma under the veil of which you may contemplate hidden mysteries." For the text of the *Historia viginti saeculorum,* see, in particular, cod. IX. B. 14 of the Biblioteca Nazionale of Naples. And see L. G. Pelissier, *De opere historico Aegidii Cardinalis Viterbiensis* (Montpellier, 1896).

79. See T. Freundenberger, *Augustinus Steuchus aus Gubbio, Augustinerchorherr und päpstlicher Bibliothekar (1497–1548) und sein literarisches Lebenswerk* (Münster, 1935).

Ch. B. Schmitt, "Perennial Philosophy: Steuco to Leibniz," *Journal of the History of Ideas* 27 (1966) 505–32; idem, introduction to the lithographic reprint of the *De perenni philosophia* (New York–London, 1972) V–XVII; idem, *Studies in Renaissance Philosophy and Science* (London, 1981) chapters I and II; C. Vasoli, "A proposito di Agostino Steuco e della *Perennis Philosophia,*" *Atti e memorie dell'Accademia Petrarca di Lettere, Arti e Scienze,* N.S. 46 (1983–84; Arezzo, 1986) 263–92; M. Muccillo, "La *prisca theologia* nel *De perenni philosophia* di Agostino Steuco," *Rinascimento,* Ser. 2, 28 (1988) 41–111.

80. The *Recognitio Veteris Testamenti* was published in Venice in 1529, the *Pro religione christiana adversus Luteranos* in Bologna in 1530.

81. See Erasmus of Rotterdam, *Opus epistolarum,* ed. P. S. Allen (Oxford, 1906–58) IX, 204–24, 286–307.

82. The *De perenni philosophia,* after being published in Lyons in 1540 (reprinted: New York–London, 1972), was reprinted in the *Opera omnia* (Lyons, 1590) III, the text which I am following.

83. See *Opera omnia* III, f. 3ʳ.

84. See ibid., f. 105ʳ.

85. See ibid., ff. 3ᵛ, 13ʳ.

86. See ibid., ff. 20ᵛ, 41ᵛ.

87. See ibid., f. 42ᵛ.

88. S. Seidel Menchi, *Erasmo in Italia. 1520–1580* (Turin, 1987).

89. See H. Jedin, *Girolama Seripando. Sein Leben und Denken im Geisteskampf des 16. Jahrhunderts* (2 vols.; Würzburg, 1937, 1984²); R. M. Abbondanza, *Girolamo Seripando tra evangelismo e riforma cattolica* (Naples, 1971).

90. For the editions see the bibliography.

91. See R. M. Douglas, *Jacopo Sadoleto, 1477–1547, Humanist and Reformer* (Cambridge, Mass., 1959).

92. For the works of Sadoleto I follow, unless otherwise noted, the *Opera omnia* (4 vols.; Verona, 1737; reprinted: London-Ridgewood, 1964).

93. The *De liberis recte instituendis* was published in Venice in 1533.

94. For the *Hortensius* I follow the edition of A. Altamura (Naples, 1950).

95. For relations between Erasmus and Sadoleto, and for their correspondence, I refer, of course, to the *Opus epistolarum* of Erasmus (see note 81, above), beginning especially in volume 7. But see also Sadoleto, *Epistolae quotquot extant,* ed. V. Costanzi (Rome, 1760–64). Especially important are the letters of Sadoleto to Erasmus that are collected in *Opus epistolarum* I, 251–52 and 337–38.

96. A fine summary presentation of Contarini is given in G. Fragnito, "Contarini, Gasparo," *DBI* 28 (Rome, 1983) 172–92; but see also the same scholar's *Gasparo Contarini. Un magistrato veneziano al servizio della cristianità* (Florence, 1988).

97. See G. Mittarelli and A. Costadoni, *Annales Camaldulenses* 9 (Venice, 1773) 544.

98. On this subject see H. Jedin, "Vincenzo Quirini und Pietro Bembo," *Miscellanea Mercati* IV (Vatican City) 407–24, now in idem, *Kirche des Glaubens Kirche der Geschichte* (2 vols.; Freiburg i. B.-Basel-Vienna, 1972).

99. See H. Jedin, "Contarini und Camaldoli," *Archivio italiana per la storia della pietà* 2 (1953) 59–118.

100. H. Jedin, "Ein Turmerlebnis des jungen Contarini," *HistJb* 70 (1951) 115–30; reprinted in *Kirche des Glaubens. . . .*

101. See Jedin, "Contarini und Camaldoli," 100–2.

102. See F. Gilbert, "Contarini on Savonarola: An Unknown Document of 1516," *ArchRef* 59 (1968) 145–50.

103. See above, pp. 382–83.

104. For Contarini's writings I usually refer to the *Opera* (Venice, 1578). On the *De officio*, see H. Jedin, *Il tipo ideale di vescovo secondo la Riforma cattolica* (Brescia, 1950) 32–37.

105. See above, p. 378.

106. In *Annales camaldulenses* (note 97, above) 9:612–719.

107. See above, pp. 400–401.

108. Published in Drittich, *Regesten und Briefe des Cardinals Contarini* (note 65, above) 305–9.

109. See below, pp. 422–26.

110. See H. Jedin, "Gasparo Contarini e il contributo veneziano alla Riforma cattolica," *La civiltà veneziana del Rinascimento* (Florence, 1958) 103–24; reprinted in *Kirche des Glaubens.* . . .

111. Published in *Concilium Tridentinum* XII (Freiburg i. B., 1966) 151–53.

112. I follow the critical edition by H. Hünermann in Gaspar Contarini, *Gegenreformatorische Schriften (ca. 1530–1542)* (Münster, 1923) 44–67.

113. I am again following Hünermann's critical edition, 23–34. But see also *Concilium Tridentinum* XII, 314–22.

114. See, mainly, D. Fenlon, *Heresy and Obedience in Tridentine Italy: Cardinal Pole and the Counter Reformation* (Cambridge, 1972); P. Simoncelli, *Il caso Reginald Pole. Eresia e santità nelle polemiche religiose del Cinquecento* (Rome, 1977).

115. The *Pro ecclesiasticae unitatis defensione* was published in Rome in 1537 (reprinted: Farnborough, 1965); also ed. and trans. J. G. Dwyer (Westminster, Md., 1965).

116. See P. S. Donaldson, *Macchiavelli and the Mystery of the State* (New York–New Rochelle, 1988), passim.

117. See especially T. Bozza, *Nuovi studi sulla Riforma in Italia. I. Il "Beneficio di Cristo"* (Rome, 1876); Simoncelli, *Il caso Reginald Pole* (note 114, above). For Carnesecchi see O. Orolani, *Pietro Carnesecchi* (Florence, 1963). For Flaminio, see A. Pastore, *Marcantonio Flaminio. Fortune e sfortune di un chierico nell'Italia del Cinquecento* (Milan, 1981).

118. I shall refer the reader only to C. Ginzburg and A. Prosperi, *Giochi di pazienza. Un seminario sul "Beneficio di Cristo"* (Turin, 1975); P. Simoncelli, "Nuovi ipotesi sul *Beneficio di Cristo*," *Critica storica* 12 (1975) 320–88.

119. H. Jedin, *A History of the Council of Trent* II, trans. E. Graf (St. Louis: B. Herder, 1962) 279. For Pole's attitude to the council, see his *De concilio liber,* published posthumously in Rome and Venice in 1562.

120. The *De summo pontifice* was published in Louvain in 1569.

121. See especially Simoncelli, *Il caso Reginald Pole* (note 114, above) 77ff.

122. See J. J. Tellechea Idigoras, "Pole y Paoli IV. Una célebre Apologia inedita del Cardinal Inglés (1557)," *Archivum Historiae Pontificiae* 6 (1966) 133–54. But see also idem, *Fray Bartolomé Carranza y el Cardinal Pole. Un navarro en la restauración católica de Inghilterra (1554–1558)* (Pamplona, 1977).

123. There is no convincing comprehensive study of Carafa, but the following may be consulted while bearing in mind that they are now rather outdated: G. Duruy, *Il cardinal Carlo Carafa (1519–1561). Étude sur le pontificat de Paul IV* (Paris, 1982); L. Riess, *Die*

Politik Paulus IV. und seine Nepoten, Eine weltgeschichtliche Krisis des. 16. Jahrhunderts (Berlin, 1909); P. Paschini, *S. Gaetano Thiene, Gian Pietro Carafa e le origini dei chierici regolari teatini* (Rome, 1926); G. M. Monti, *Ricerche su Papa Paolo IV Carafa* (Benevento, 1923); and, of course, L. von Pastor, *History of the Popes from the Close of the Middle Ages* 14 (St. Louis, 1924) 56–494. The work of M. Firpo and D. Marcatto, *Il processo inquisitoriale del cardinal Giovanni Morone* (5 vols.; Rome, 1981–89) is fairly important.

124. For the text of the *Consilium* see *Concilium Tridentinum* XII, 131–45.

125. For bibliography on Sannazzaro see M. Corti, "Sannazzaro, Jacopo," *Dizionario critico della letterature italiana* 4 (Turin, 1986²) 82–88.

126. For the *De partu Virginis* I am using the edition by A. Altamura (Naples, 1948).

127. For general bibliographical information see C. Griggio, "De Ferraris, Antoni, detto Galateo." *Dizionario critico della letteratura italiana* 2 (Turin, 1986²) 116–22. For greater detail see A. Corsano, "Note sul pensiero religioso del Galateo," *Atti del Congress internazionale di studi dull'età aragonese* (Bari, 1972); and see the index in F. Tateo, *L'umanesimo meridionale* (Bari, 1972).

128. See C. Vecce, "Antonio Galateo e la difesa della Donazione di Costantino," *Aevum* 59 (1985) 353–60.

129. For the *De heremita* I am following the edition in E. Garin, *Prosatori latini del Quattrocento* (Milan-Naples, 1952) 1065–125.

130. See A. Jurilli, "Coordinate cronologiche dell'*Esposizione del Pater Noster* di Antonio Galateo," *GSLI* 159 (1982) 536–50.

131. See G. Parenti, "Capece, Scipione," *DBI* 18 (Rome, 1975) 425–28.

132. The most complete treatment of Porzio is still F. Fiorentino, "Simone Porzio," in his *Studi e ritratti della Rinascenza* (Bari, 1911) 81–153; but see also G. Saitta, "L'aristotelico Simone Porzio," *GCFI* 28 (1949) 279–306, and the index in Di Napoli, *L'immortalità dell'anima* (note 17, above).

133. See Di Napoli again. But see also A. L. De Gaetano, "Gelli's Eclecticism on the Question of Immortality and the Italian Version of Porzio's *De humana mente*," *Philological Quarterly* 47 (1968) 532–46.

Index of Names

Topical Index